WITHDRAWN

HARVARD LIBRARY

WITHDRAWN

RELIGION AS A HUMAN CAPACITY

NUMEN BOOK SERIES

STUDIES IN THE HISTORY OF RELIGIONS

EDITED BY

W.J. HANEGRAAFF

ADVISORY BOARD

P. Antes, M. Despland, RI.J. Hackett, M. Abumalham Mas, A.W. Geertz,
G. ter Haar, G.L. Lease, M.N. Getui, I.S. Gilhus, P. Morris, J.K. Olupona,
E. Thomassen, A. Tsukimoto, A.T. Wasim

VOLUME XCIX

RELIGION AS A HUMAN CAPACITY

A FESTSCHRIFT IN HONOR OF E. THOMAS LAWSON

EDITED BY

TIMOTHY LIGHT AND BRIAN C. WILSON

BRILL
LEIDEN · BOSTON
2004

This book is printed on acid-free paper.

Library of Congress Cataloging-in-Publication Data

Religion as a human sacrifice : a festschrift in honor of E. Thomas Lawson / edited by Timothy Light and Brian C. Wilson.
  p. cm. — (Numen book series. Studies in the history of religions: v. 99)
  Includes bibliographical references and index.
  ISBN 90-04-12676-7 (alk. paper)
  1. Religion. I. Lawson, E. Thomas. II. Light, Timothy. III. Wilson, Brian C. IV. Studies in the history of religions ; 99

BL50.R426365 2003
200—dc21

2003056284

ISSN 0169-8834
ISBN 90 04 12676 7

© *Copyright 2004 by Koninklijke Brill NV, Leiden, The Netherlands*

All rights reserved. No part of this publication may be reproduced, translated, stored in a retrieval system, or transmitted in any form or by any means, electronic, mechanical, photocopying, recording or otherwise, without prior written permission from the publisher.

*Authorization to photocopy items for internal or personal use is granted by Brill provided that the appropriate fees are paid directly to The Copyright Clearance Center, 222 Rosewood Drive, Suite 910 Danvers, MA 01923, USA.
Fees are subject to change.*

PRINTED IN THE NETHERLANDS

CONTENTS

Dedicatory Preface ix

List of Contributors xi

INTRODUCTIONS

A Brief Intellectual Biography of E. Thomas Lawson 3
  BRIAN C. WILSON

Religion as a Human Capacity 15
  TIMOTHY LIGHT

PART ONE
THEORETICAL STUDIES

1. Out Of Africa: Lessons From a By-product of Evolution   27
   PASCAL BOYER

2. Is Religion a Rube Goldberg Device?
   Or Oh, What a Difference a Theory Makes! 45
   ROBERT N. MCCAULEY

3. Why Do We Need Cognitive Theories of Religion? 65
   HARVEY WHITEHOUSE

4. Can Science Fabricate Meaning? On Ritual,
   Religion, and the Academic Study of Religion 89
   DONALD WIEBE

5. Pathways to Knowledge in Comparative Religion:
   Clearing Ground for New Conceptual Resources 105
   VEIKKO ANTTONEN

6. Comparative Religion in the State of Nature 121
   WILLIAM E. PADEN

7. Toward a Discourse Between Cognitive and Critical Theoreticians of Religion: Open Dialectic Between the Religious and the Secular 135
RUDOLF J. SIEBERT

8. Dispatches from the "Religion" Wars 161
RUSSELL T. MCCUTCHEON

PART TWO

STUDIES IN RELIGIOUS BEHAVIOR

9. Exploring Theories of Religious Violence: Nigeria's "Maitatsine" Phenomenon 193
ROSALIND I. J. HACKETT

10. What Does Jerusalem Have to Do with Amecameca? A Case Study of Colonial Mexican Sacred Space 207
BRIAN C. WILSON

11. Different Vibes: Rethinking Religion, Yet Again 221
FRANCIS L. GROSS, JR.

12. Ritual Competence and Mithraic Ritual 245
LUTHER H. MARTIN

13. Bringing Data to Mind: Empirical Claims of Lawson and McCauley's Theory of Religious Ritual 265
JUSTIN L. BARRETT

14. Communities, Ritual Violence, and Cognition: On Hopi Indian Initiations 289
ARMIN W. GEERTZ

15. On Credulity 315
BENSON SALER

16. What is the "Bible"? (Analysis of a Text Concept) 331
BRIAN MALLEY

17. Luck Beliefs: A Case of Theological Incorrectness 375
JASON SLONE

18. Cognition and Credence 395
    TIMOTHY LIGHT

Bibliography 421
Index of Names 445
Index of Subjects 452

DEDICATORY PREFACE

This book is a gift from his admirers to a greatly treasured friend and colleague. In his forty-plus year career, Tom Lawson has been a major presence in the field of religious studies. Always optimistic and cheerful, Tom has been an encouraging voice enticing others into the fascinating study of the endless variety of human ritual practices and the beliefs that inspired them. Always an enquiring mind, Tom has been a continuous gadfly constantly asking *how* and *why*—even after others thought that the end of a train of enquiry had been reached. Charismatic as a teacher and a leader, Tom has drawn students of great ability into the field and launched them on their own careers, and as chair of his home department for a record-breaking thirty-seven years, he led his immediate colleagues into the development of a modern religious studies program the structure of which has become the pattern for many others. Gentle, good-humored, a gracious listener, he has drawn the best out of immediate colleagues through suggestion and ultimately through allowing them a degree of freedom in choosing what to teach and what to study that is rarely found in organized higher education. In all of this, he has insisted upon and exemplified in his person the highest intellectual and academic standards. Tom has indeed been a model for all of us, and, as Frank Gross says in his essay in this volume, Tom is a truly lovely man. In presenting this collective gift, we ask Tom to accept it as a symbol of the affection and respect with which he is regarded by all of the authors.

The Editors

CONTRIBUTORS

Veikko Anttonen	Department of Cultural Studies, University of Turku, Turku, Finland
Justin L. Barrett	Institute for Social Research, University of Michigan, Ann Arbor, Michigan, USA
Pascal Boyer	Henry Luce Professor of Individual and Collective Memory, Washington University, St. Louis, Missouri, USA
Armin W. Geertz	Department of the Study of Religion, Aarhus University, Aarhus, Denmark
Francis L. Gross, Jr.	Department of Comparative Religion, Western Michigan University, Kalamazoo, Michigan, USA
Rosalind I. J. Hackett	Department of Religious Studies, University of Tennessee, Knoxville, Tennessee, USA
Timothy Light	Department of Comparative Religion, Western Michigan University, Kalamazoo, Michigan, USA
Luther H. Martin	Department of Religion, University of Vermont, Burlington, Vermont, USA
Robert N. McCauley	Department of Philosophy, Emory University, Atlanta, Georgia, USA
Russell T. McCutcheon	Department of Religious Studies, University of Alabama, Tuscaloosa, Alabama, USA
Brian Malley	Department of Anthropology, University of Michigan, Ann Arbor, Michigan, USA
William E. Paden	Department of Religion, University of Vermont, Burlington, Vermont, USA
Benson Saler	Department of Anthropology, Brandeis University, Waltham, Massachusetts, USA
Rudolf J. Siebert	Department of Comparative Religion, Western Michigan University, Kalamazoo, Michigan, USA
Jason Slone	Department of Religious Studies, The University of Findlay, Findlay, Ohio, USA
Harvey Whitehouse	School of Anthropological Science, Queen's University, Belfast, Northern Ireland

Donald Wiebe	Department for the Study of Religion, University of Toronto, Ontario, Canada
Brian C. Wilson	Department of Comparative Religion, Western Michigan University, Kalamazoo, Michigan, USA

INTRODUCTIONS

A BRIEF INTELLECTUAL BIOGRAPHY OF E. THOMAS LAWSON

Brian C. Wilson

Ernest Thomas Lawson was born in Cape Town, South Africa, November 27, 1931, the youngest of nine children in a working-class family of Dutch (Afrikaans) and Scottish descent.[1] Lawson grew up primarily in Mafeking, a small, dusty town in the northern Cape near the border of what was then Rhodesia. Here, his father and most of his siblings spent their lives working for the South African railroad. Lawson himself avoided this fate by insisting that he be allowed to go to high school—the first in his family to do so. He graduated from Kimberley Boy's High School in December 1949. His taste for higher education whetted, Lawson next wished to go to college, but his family didn't have the resources to send him. He therefore spent the next year clerking for the railroad and completing his military service as a bagpiper in the South African Army.

Early in 1950, the principal of the Kimberly Boy's High School, knowing of Lawson's desire for a college education, introduced him to a local department store magnate, Wilfred John Orr. Orr offered to underwrite Lawson's education with a loan. The problem now was, where to go? A Baptist missionary in Kimberley suggested that Lawson attend the Northern Baptist Theological College in Chicago, Illinois. The College, founded in 1913 by those who wished to moderate the growing liberalism within the old Northern Baptist Convention, would eventually spin off its undergraduate program as the better-known Judson College in the 1960s. Lawson applied and was quickly accepted. Booking passage on a converted troop ship out of Cape Town, he made his way to Chicago via Amsterdam, London, Montreal, and, fatefully as it turns out, Kalamazoo, Michigan.

---

[1] I'm indebted to Ruth and Jennifer Lawson for much of the information on Lawson's early life and his subsequent career at Western Michigan University (personal communication, 2/25/2003); I would also like to thank Robert N. McCauley for his insights into his collaboration with Lawson (personal communication, 1/24/2003). Thanks to Cybelle Shattuck, Timothy Light, Robert N. McCauley, and Brian Malley for reading drafts of this biography.

From 1951 to 1955, Lawson studied at Northern Baptist, although an excess of demerits for missing chapel precluded his ever graduating from that institution. Instead, Lawson applied to the Divinity School at the University of Chicago where he was admitted through examination. Over the next several years, he earned a B.D. (1958), an M.A. (1961), and a Ph.D. (1963) at the Divinity School. Here at Chicago, Lawson met and married June Lanum in 1957. It was during this time as well that Lawson became involved with Chicago Democratic politics, the nascent anti-Apartheid movement (a cause with which he was long identified), and served as a youth minister for an African American Baptist church on Chicago's South Side. In his spare time, he worked at an insurance company and as a tour guide, painted professionally, and studied piano at the Chicago Conservatory.

In 1960, the Reverend T. Thomas Wiley asked Lawson to become the youth pastor for the First Baptist Church in Kalamazoo. Perhaps still entertaining the possibility of a career of the ministry, Lawson accepted. Another Kalamazoo resident, however, would soon change his plans. Cornelius Loew, a student of Reinhold Neibuhr and Paul Tillich, was hired in 1957 to chair Western Michigan University's new department of Philosophy and Religion. Loew had already met Lawson at an academic conference, and when he arrived in Kalamazoo, he offered him a position as Instructor teaching courses in the philosophy of religion. Lawson jumped at the opportunity, offering his first classes in 1961. Promoted to Assistant Professor on completion of his dissertation in 1963, Lawson was subsequently made acting department chair after Loew was named Dean of the College of Arts and Sciences. Lawson was then confirmed as permanent head of the department after achieving the rank of Associate Professor in 1965. The following year, two years after the tragic death of his first wife, he married Ruth Jones, with whom he would have two daughters, Sonya (b. 1968) and Jennifer (b. 1971). Lawson now settled into what would become a long and exceptionally productive life in Kalamazoo.

Lawson's arrival at Western began a slow process that would radically change his intellectual interests and that of the department he now chaired. At this time, having just completed for his dissertation a work entitled "Tillich and Hartshorne: An Essay on the Sovereignty of God," Lawson continued to focus on philosophical theology. However, even before leaving the University of Chicago, he began thinking about the relationship between theology and the other disciplines of the university (although he was still wary of any inquiry which did not "take seriously enough the theological dimension in every discipline..." [Lawson 1960: 24]). Moreover, Lawson also began exploring comparatively the relationships between Christianity and other religions, ultimately concluding that one might legitimately grant "significance and value to all religious expressions including non-Christian religions" (Lawson 1961: 11). To a great degree, Lawson's subsequent intellectual development would revolve around working out the implications of interdisciplinarity and comparativism for the academic study of religion.

At the University of Chicago, Lawson had been exposed for the first time to the literature and exponents of the History of Religions School. He read avidly the works of Rudolf Otto, Joachim Wach, Mircea Eliade, C. G. Jung, and Charles Long (Lawson 1964: 294). In a review of Long's *Alpha: The Myths of Creation* (1963), Lawson wrote that "[a]ll kinds of surprises occur here. Similarities between myths which are geographically and historically worlds apart shock one into asking questions about the pervasive character of religious structures" (Lawson 1964: 294–95). In addition to Long's comparativism, Lawson also applauded his cautious interdisciplinarity: "Long makes it clear that, while the student of the history of religions is dependent upon the insights of psychology, ethnology, anthropology, philosophy and theology, he is nevertheless fundamentally concerned with the elucidation of the peculiarly *religious* structures of myth, and in a non-reductive manner" (Lawson 1964: 294). Later, Lawson would make the History of Religion's call for autonomy a cornerstone in "A Rationale for a Department of Religion in a Public University" (Lawson 1967c).

Lawson's shift away from philosophy and theology to the History of Religions was paralleled by a wholesale reorientation of the way the study of religion was pursued at Western Michigan University.[2]

---

[2] Lawson has always been anxious that each division within the university have a clear theoretical justification: "... if our university is not to degenerate into a medley of *ad hoc* departments, schools, institutes, programmes, and courses without any unity, we need to make explicit those principles and ideas which are the reason for being a university, and those long range goals toward which we may justly move with determination and integrity.... In other words, we need to ask questions of theory in the midst of our practice" (Lawson 1963a: 2).

In part this reflected Lawson's new intellectual interests, not to mention those of two Chicago graduates newly arrived in the department, H. Byron Earhart and Nancy Auer Falk; it also reflected the growing debate on the proper role of the study of religion at a public university (Lawson 1967a, 1967b, 1967c, 1967d). In June of 1967, the year Lawson was promoted to Full Professor, Religion and Philosophy became separate departments at Western. This occasioned a thorough rethinking of the department's direction and curriculum. Through a series of special meetings, the faculty decided that the goals of liberal education would be better achieved through the study of all religions on the same terms, and not by privileging Christianity as other religion departments were doing at that time—and as WMU had done at first. The program was redesigned with four components: Historical studies, Morphological and Phenomenological studies (later changed to Comparative Studies), Methodological Studies, and Constructive Studies. In so doing, Western's was the first religion department in the United States to build a program that paid as much attention to Non-Western religions as it did to those of the West. Moreover, it was also one of the first to emphasize that faculty should be chosen not for their faith commitments, but because of their academic training in the study of religion. As Lawson subsequently traveled around the country promoting Western's model, he contrasted it to the Christian-centered "seminary model" then in use in most undergraduate religion programs. Lawson called this the "zoo approach," that is, "capturing" Protestant, Catholic, and Jewish clergy "as teachers, placing them in cages and parading students before the cages telling them to take their pick" (Lawson 1967d: 48). Although the even-handed and rigorously academic treatment of all religions in Western's program was too radical for most schools to follow, Lawson's arguments and the example of the department were instrumental in gaining acceptance for the "religious studies" curricular model that soon became standard at most state universities.[3] In an effort to escape the zoo himself, Lawson turned from Christian theology to the study of African religions, a shift that would culminate in his well-known book, *Religions of Africa: Traditions in Transformation* (1985a).

---

[3] See, for example, Hayes and Welch 1973: 151–65. For a more extensive history of Comparative Religion at WMU, see www.wmich.edu/religion.

The widespread adoption of the History of Religions approach resulted in a field that was comparative, interdisciplinary, and global in outlook. In this sense, it was a boon to liberal education and a needed step away from the seminary model. And yet, despite the high hopes for the History of Religions School, it quickly became obvious to Lawson that it would never bring the kind of theoretical clarity to the field that its practitioners had promised and desired. Lawson's growing frustration at this state of affairs is plain in his review of an anthology of papers entitled, *The Study of Religion at Colleges and Universities* (1972):

> What never gets asked in this melee of virtuosity is the fundamental question of what precisely the study of religion is and what new method might be defended (sufficiently distinct from what already is being achieved in other disciplines) to justify its separate inclusion in the university. I do not think the view that the department of religion is a kind of club for people of merely similar interests, passions, or vague commitments provides sufficient rationale for either the introduction or the retention of the study of religion in the university in any other way than it already is (Lawson 1973b: 299).

The insistence of Historians of Religions on the "autonomy of the sacred" meant that the key theoretical question, the origins of religion, had either been solved (i.e., religion is an encounter with the transcendent) or, if one didn't want to adopt this theological position preferring an agnostic one instead, speculation on the origins of religion was off-limits in order to preserve the putative integrity of religious experience from reductionism. In both cases, the result was the same: the Historian of Religions abandoned theorizing in favor of more and more in-depth descriptions of the religious traditions through which the sacred was said to express itself; this in turn led to the self-fulfilling prophecy that religion was ultimately refractory to explanatory theorizing because of its complexity (Lawson 1973b). For Lawson, this was a dead end: pursuing a purely descriptive approach (usually dignified as "phenomenology") would render a department of religion into "nothing more than a cosmic garbage can of arcane probings" (Lawson 1973b: 299). Libraries were already filled with a "vast amount of literary, historical, anthropological, and sociological data," Lawson wrote, adding somewhat hyperbolically, "We don't need any more data, we need more theories about data!" (Lawson 1973a: 66–67).

In an article from 1969, Lawson had written that the failure of the History of Religions left those with a theoretical bent with a stark choice when it came to the academic study of religion: one could either openly acknowledge that their work was theological or embrace the social sciences (Lawson 1969: 437). Lawson at this time was leaning towards the latter, although the dilemma was that the social sciences were then in the grip of a theoretical paradigm almost as unproductive as the History of Religions: functionalism (and this despite the trenchant metatheoretical critiques of the functionalist paradigm emanating from within the social sciences themselves [Lawson 1973b: 300; see also Penner 1971]).[4] What is more, the dominance of functionalism within the social scientific study of religion had led to the dominance of functionalist, non-substantive definitions of religion—definitions the very vagueness of which only further muddied the field (Lawson 1973a: 65). It was clear to Lawson that not only did the field need new bold theories, but that these theories had to be constructed with clear definitions and have strong metatheoretical foundations if a productive research tradition were finally to emerge within academic study of religion. For most of the 1970s, therefore, Lawson published little, preferring to spend his time reading widely in the philosophy of science. Instead of Eliade, Long, and Wach, his seminars now began to feature Popper, Hempel, and Suppe, as well as B. R. Wilson and E. O. Wilson.

A breakthrough for Lawson came in 1977 when he was invited to participate in an eight-week NEH seminar held at Colorado College in Denver. Entitled "Biological and Social Perspectives on Human Nature," the seminar brought together the likes of such thinkers as Alan Donagan, Steven Jay Gould, Stuart Kauffman, Richard Lewontin, and Alisdair Macintyre. The goal of the seminar was to debate the notion of the "unity of science" and the appropriateness of the methods of natural science for the social sciences. Lawson came away from the seminar convinced that, far from being the bane of the academic study of religion, scientific reductionism offered the clearest and most intellectually defensible route towards the generation of powerful explanatory theories. Armed with this notion, Lawson entered the 1980s with a persistent inkling of just how such a theory might be constructed.[5]

---

[4] However, see McCauley and Lawson 1984 for a later, more appreciative appraisal of the heuristic potential of functionalist theorizing.

[5] Along these lines, Lawson joined with Donald Wiebe and Luther Martin in

Lawson had long maintained an interest in the theoretical tradition in anthropology known as Intellectualism. Intellectualism had originated in the late nineteenth century with E. B. Tylor, but was eclipsed by functionalism through most of the first half of the twentieth century, only to be revived again by such scholars as Goody, Spiro and Horton in the 1960s. For Lawson, the Intellectualist position held several advantages for the study of religion. First, it offered a clear definition of religion (e.g., "religion as belief in superhuman beings" [Spiro 1966]), and as such, it stressed the cognitive dimension of religion. Second, and perhaps just as importantly, Intellectualists were not afraid of theorizing. As Lawson wrote regarding theories of myth,

> One thing is certain. The answer to the question "What are myths, what do they mean (if they mean anything) . . . ?" will not wait for a collection and collation of all the myths in the world. . . . In fact, as the intellectualist tradition has realized, the problem is not of the inductive sort . . . It is a time for bold theories about the formal properties of religious systems, and the ingenuity to devise ways to find application for them to the welter of data which religionists have already gathered (Lawson 1978b: 521).

During much of the late 1960s and early 1970s, Intellectualists were consumed by what would come to be called the "religion and rationality" debate (for a summary, see Penner 1989). Intellectualists took as axiomatic that religious systems consisted of descriptions and interpretations of reality that were meant to be taken literally (Ross 1971). The debate, in a nutshell, centered on whether religion should therefore be considered simply science manqué or whether it was some other kind of discourse. Although hard fought with cogent arguments presented on both sides, the debate was ultimately inconclusive. To attack this question afresh, Lawson suggested looking not at the contents of science and religion, but at how the two are acquired. Here, Lawson suggested, clear differences were evident:

1985 to found the North American Association for the Study of Religion (NAASR). In the words of Martin, the three felt there was a need for a professional organization that advanced "a truly academic (non confessional) study of religion" (personal communication, 2/26/2003). More on NAASR can be found at www.as.ua.edu/naasr/. For Lawson, such an organization was necessary to combat the interpretive turn that has dominated most of the study of religion (and anthropology generally) since the late 1970s. This is a theme on which Lawson has written extensively; see Lawson 1990b, 1991a, 1996; Lawson and McCauley 1993; McCauley and Lawson 1996.

> I would conjecture that most people acquire a religion very much like they acquire their language, namely, by growing up in it. This, if it were true, would indicate that corroborated theories of the nature of religion might be more satisfactory if they were developed as theories meant to explain the acquisition of religion. It is precisely in this context of questions that the work done in linguistics and structural anthropology becomes relevant and suggestive for the theory of religion. The same question which we are asking about religion, Chomsky (1975) asked about language, and Lévi-Strauss has asked about myths, kinship systems, etc. (Lawson 1976a: 206).

From this point of view, "myths are capable of being explained and understood, apart from self-conscious adoption by believers, only when the rule-governed and cognitive operations that are concealed within them have been theoretically specified and formalized" (Lawson 1976a: 207). If such unconscious cognitive operations could be identified, then this would offer a solution to why religion continues to be acquired in the face of the successes of science. At first, Lévi-Strauss' structuralism struck Lawson as the theory to pursue, and he even produced a complex structuralist analysis of infant baptism as it is practiced in the Episcopalian Church (Lawson 1976d: 130). However, after Sperber's devastating critique of the semantic assumptions of Levi-Strauss' structuralism in *Rethinking Symbolism* (1975), it became clear to Lawson that a new cognitive theory was called for:

> Sperber has shown how the identification of myth as a system of homologies is significant in that it shows that myth is more like a system of knowledge than like a system of language. So even though using the linguistic model has been useful in making the discovery of mythic structures possible (by identifying the rule-governed nature of myth), Lévi-Strauss has in fact discovered a genuinely cognitive structure distinct from linguistic structures. Rather than identifying myth as a species of language having special properties of a semantic system, we now have the means for identifying myth as a species of knowledge, i.e. having the special properties of a cognitive system (Lawson 1978b: 520).

But what, exactly, do these cognitive systems consist of? Although myth and ritual are not literally languages, Lawson realized that they could nevertheless still be studied using some of the same theoretical models developed in linguistics, especially Chomsky's notion of "competence." Over against linguistic *performance*, Chomsky theorized that human beings possess linguistic *competence*, a largely unconscious system of knowledge that allows them not only to master a language with relatively minimal exposure, but to use and understand language creatively as well. Given this, Lawson suggested that human beings might also exhibit analogous competences with respect to other sorts of sociocultural systems. Such a competence approach to theorizing about religious ritual would proceed first by hypothesizing a set of formal properties of ritual, followed by testing these hypotheses against the intuitive judgments of actual ritual participants. To collaborate on the former, Lawson in 1979 recruited Robert N. McCauley, a former student who had gone on to become a professor of philosophy with an expertise in cognitive psychology. The result was *Rethinking Religion: Connecting Cognition and Culture* (1990), a book that would come to be cited as one of the three defining works in the emerging cognitive study of religion (Cunningham 1999: 96–101).

As Lawson would later write of *Rethinking Religion*, the premise of the book is simply that "our garden-variety cognitive equipment is largely sufficient for the generation of religious representations, especially representations of religious ritual actions" (2000a: 81). Starting with a slightly modified Intellectualist definition of religion as a belief in "culturally postulated superhuman agents" (1990: 5), Lawson and McCauley posited that religious ritual occurs when our ordinary cognitive representations of action (generated by an action-representation scheme) feature the presence of superhuman agents (generated by a religious conceptual scheme) (1990: 84ff). By identifying where an entry for a superhuman agent is inserted into the representation of a (ritual) action (i.e., as agent, object, or patient), one can then deduce a structural typology of all possible religious rituals.

Of course, not all possible religious rituals appear with the same frequency (or at all) in most religious traditions; to account for this fact, Lawson and McCauley postulated two cognitive constraints: the principle of superhuman agency (1990: 124–5) and the principle of superhuman immediacy (1990: 125–26). According to the first principle, where the superhuman agent appears in the ritual (i.e., as agent, object or patient) affects whether or not that ritual is seen as more or less fundamental to a religious tradition, and whether the ritual is perceived to be repeatable on the same object. Moreover, according to the second principle, how close the superhuman agent is to the action (i.e., as actually present or present only through the presence of a consecrated proxy, e.g., a priest, holy water, etc.), will also affect the perceived centrality of the ritual. Ultimately, the importance of these "universal principles of religious ritual structure" lies in the fact that they fulfill the second part of Lawson's cognitive project: they are hypotheses that can be tested against the intuitive judgments of actual ritual participants. In 2001, for example, Lawson successfully teamed with psychologist Justin L. Barrett to design experimental tests of some of the predictions of *Rethinking Religion* (Barrett and Lawson 2001). Further results of such testing can be found in Malley and Barrett 2003, Barrett and Malley forthcoming, and in Barrett's contribution to this volume, "Bringing Data to Mind: Empirical Claims of Lawson and McCauley's Theory of Religious Ritual."

From simply a desire to identify a productive research tradition for the academic study of religion, Lawson found himself in the forefront of the creation of a new one. As the citation of Barrett's work indicates, Lawson and McCauley had the good fortune to be working at a time when the receptiveness of anthropologists and others to the cognitive approach to the study of religion was growing. Shortly after the appearance of Lawson and McCauley's book, Pascal Boyer published his seminal *The Naturalness of Religious Ideas* (1994). From this point on, research and publication in religion and cognition expanded greatly, as did the international community of scholars engaged in the field. Such works as Guthrie's *Faces in the Clouds* (1993), Whitehouse's *Arguments and Icons: Divergent Modes of Religiosity* (2000), and Pyysiäinen's *How Religion Works: Towards a Cognitive Science of Religion* (2001) are a representative sampling of the quality and scope of the work being generated by this community. Throughout the 1990s, Lawson and McCauley themselves kept up a steady stream of publications promoting the cognitive science of religion,[6] culminating in their recently-published *Bringing Ritual to Mind: Psychological Foundations of Cultural Forms* (McCauley and Lawson 2003). Finally, Lawson joined with Boyer in 2001 to found *The Journal of Cognition and Culture* (Brill). The journal is designed to serve as an outlet for the burgeoning research being done more broadly in the cognitive science of culture.

E. Thomas Lawson's intellectual journey from theology to cognitive science has been a long one, but it's far from over. His contributions to the field continue to be widely recognized. Interest in his

---

[6] See Lawson 1993a, 1993b, 1994a, 1998, 1999, 2000a, 2000b, 2001, 2002 and Lawson and McCauley 2002.

work led to his appointment in 1991 as co-editor of *Numen* (Brill), a post he held for nearly a decade. The American Society for the Study of Religion elected Lawson to its membership in 1996, and he now serves on its Executive Board. Lawson has also received the highest honors given to faculty at Western Michigan University: the Distinguished Scholar Award (1991) and Teaching Excellence Award (1998). Finally, in 2001, Lawson completed his fortieth year at WMU, and, after nearly 37 years of service, he stepped down as chair of the department of comparative religion. However, he has no thought of retiring. His scholarly output continues unabated, he continues to organize and participate in international conferences on cognitive science, and, perhaps most importantly, he continues to inspire students and colleagues in the field.[7] I, for one, have been inspired: although few scholars are actually vouchsafed careers as rich and full as Tom's, I find in it a model of what the scholarly life can and should be. It is with great pleasure, then, that I can join with his colleagues in offering him this festschrift.

---

[7] In 2002, Lawson graduated his first doctoral student from Western's Comparative Religion program, Jason Slone. A portion of Slone's dissertation, revised as *Theological Incorrectness: Why Religious People Believe What They Shouldn't* (Oxford: Oxford University Press, forthcoming), is included as an essay in this volume.

RELIGION AS A HUMAN CAPACITY

Timothy Light

The essays prepared to honor Tom Lawson in this volume represent diverse points of view. The cognitivist theoretical explorations of Part I "Theoretical Studies" and the substantial number of applied cognitivist pieces in Part II "Studies in Religious Behavior" are certainly congruent with Lawson's major focus over the past fifteen to twenty years. However, as Wilson's biographical essay demonstrates, Tom Lawson's journey towards cognitive science began as a journey of faith and then became a relentless intellectual quest that took him through specific studies of African religion (including the excellent film strip on the Zulu creation myth), various theoretical claims and finally to the newly developing field of cognitive science. Those authors included here who do not write from a cognitivist stance certainly recall those earlier stages in Lawson's spiritual and intellectual life.

The significance of this happy coincidence extends beyond a nice congruence between admirers and the object of their admiration. An intellectual and/or faith quest is far from unusual amongst scholars of religion. Lawson's own journey is emblematic of his time in that sociologically, psychologically, and economically based accounts of human religious behavior offered as exclusive analyses had already lost much of their explanatory power by the 1970s, when Lawson's academic career hit its stride. During the same period, brain research was beginning to reveal topographical and biochemical sources for increasingly large segments of human mental and physical behavioral patterns. Responding to both trends, small subsets of widely dispersed philosophers, psychologists, sociologists, biologists, and linguists began to explore the notion that human cognition might be most productively studied as a set of processes which emanate from our natural "hard-wiring" as developed through evolution. Critical to this set of developments, of course, was Chomsky's proposal that human language behavior could be attributed to inborn universal capacities whose operations were best described in formal ways derived initially from mathematics. Many fields (including even music, as evidenced in Leonard Bernstein's famous Harvard lectures) experimented with applications of Chomsky's insights. While Lawson and McCauley's work remains the only attempt to express religious behavior in Chomsky-like generative formulaic derivations, the assumptions, concepts, and even some of the vocabulary of early generative linguistics became part of the infrastructure of much theorizing on human endowments and their manifestations.

By no means did the majority of religion scholars of the last third of the twentieth century end up with the same conclusions as did Lawson. But all of them have had to deal with the same major currents and discoveries. With each passing year, Lawson's work in particular becomes more deeply embedded into the common shared wisdom amongst scholars of religion, whatever their theoretical orientation. Whether or not one is convinced by cognitivist claims, it is not unfair to suggest that the cognitive turn has become the most dramatically challenging theory of its time.

The title of this book, *Religion as a Human Capacity*, has been chosen both to symbolize the importance of Lawson's work and to reflect a common motif which runs throughout the essays gathered here. For cognitive scientists, the primary faculties with which we are "hard-wired" (particularly our given ability to recognize cause and agency and to have intuition about what is normal in the physical world) make it entirely natural that most humans would develop conceptions like those found in extant religions. For the others whose work is included here, the *human* character of religion is what is worth attending to. This book is intended to celebrate Tom's critical contributions to cognitive studies of religion and to celebrate the degree to which his ultimate goal of scholarship as a search for truth is matched by those who have been his friends and been influenced by him, even though their own theoretical persuasions may differ from his.

Part One: Theoretical Studies

Part I "Theoretical Studies" begins with five cognitive explorations followed by two very different views which nevertheless refer extensively to cognitivist claims, and is concluded with a defense of the study of theory.

The theoretical essays begin with Boyer's most concise statement of his strong version of a cognitive approach to religion. As a "byproduct of evolution," Boyer contends, religion arose from capacities which were developed by humans and their ancestors to adapt to their changing environments. There is no physiological locus for religious sensibilities, no "God-Spot." Rather, capacities with which we are otherwise endowed—for example, the recognition of movement, direction, quantity, size, cause, effect, agency, and an expectation that events will occur along the lines which intuitions based on these capacities would imply, and a very strong ability to infer from what we already know—set us up with a high probability that we will interpret many phenomena in ways that that turn out to be what we call religions when our intuitions appear to have been violated by our perceptions.

Boyer's rigorous reductionism is continued in McCauley's examination of the notion and validity of theories of religion. To be scientific, he reminds us, we must value theories only to the degree to which they prove empirically predictive. In applying to religion the colloquial American metaphor "Rube Goldberg Device," McCauley argues that religions collect together disparate human psychological features which are otherwise unlinked. Recognizing the difficulty in identifying an abstract property or set of properties which remain characteristic of all religions, McCauley nonetheless resists seeing religion as only a loose class of family resemblances. Instead, he agrees with Boyer that the best candidate for the common distinctive feature of religions is the counter-intuitiveness of representations. Yet, granting the weakness of this desideratum because it also obtains in many other spheres of human activity, he concludes with a call for continuing theoretical development in tandem with rigorous experimentation.

In discussing why we need cognitive theories of religion, Whitehouse continues the concern of Boyer and McCauley. Because our thoughts and feelings emanate from our natural physiology, accounts of religion which do not begin with biological materialism end up producing faulty ontologies. Briefly examining and then dismissing the major theories of religion offered in the second half of the nineteenth century and first half of the twentieth century, Whitehouse argues that the most hopeful strategy for identifying a new theory of religion lies in following the cognitive sciences in seeking to distinguish and understand universal mechanisms of human cognition, and he concludes his essay with a subtly ironic analysis of the social and cultic behavior of academic guilds, for whom reductionism is incorrectly rejected as an insult rather than simply a factual description.

Wiebe's discussion continues the insistence on science qua science and the need to rigorously distinguish what can be empirically demonstrated from what is meaningful. Analyzing in considerable detail Rappaport's *Ritual and Religion in the Making of Humanity* (1999), Wiebe expresses appreciation for Rapport's positive evaluation of religion in its role as creator of meaning, and specifically praises Rapport's argument that religion "operates in a digital, rather than an analogical, fashion and 'separates the before from the after with absolute clarity . . . [thereby making itself] admirably suited to impose upon the continua of nature, generally, distinctions much sharper than nature's own.'" However, Wiebe insists, Rappaport then extends this insight into "a mystical statement about the world as a whole thinking about itself," to which Wiebe replies, "Science . . . cannot fabricate meaning without distortion of its fundamentally epistemic objective." That blunt definition of the division of work between scientific statements and all other statements underscores the presupposition of the preceding essays as well.

Anttonen's essay speaks to the impasse for cognitive science implicit in McCauley's acknowledgement of the insufficiency in defining religion through its reliance on counter-intuitive concepts through arguing for the centrality of *both* Lawson and McCauley's Culturally Postulated Superhuman Agent (CPS-Agent) *and* reviving the category *sacred* within a cognitive framework. A methodology which lacks either cognitive or social factors will end up missing the actual distinctiveness of religion. Sacred spaces, times, persons, actions form the social correlate to counter-intuitiveness, and those phenomena are clearly observable and always identified with what is analyzed as *religion* in a society.

Paden continues the significant caution introduced by Anttonen. Standard cognitive science, he holds, neglects the critical importance to human makeup of social patterning and merely treats this "sociality in individualistic terms." But, he argues, social behavior is fundamental to adaptation, both in the sense that groups adapt as groups, and individuals in the sense that individuals carry group imprints (or basic hard-wiring) which significantly enhance and render more efficient their individually oriented adaptive capacities. Stated in standard cognitive science diction, "Inferential activity will involve not only Pleistocene push buttons, but complex social, personal and emotional associations (many of them unconscious)." The gauntlet thrown down with this sentence may well characterize an important topic for discussion (and perhaps debate) among cognitive scientists in the coming years. If we are to talk of inborn human capacity, how much of that capacity is inherent in individuals and how much is inherent in or activated only by membership in social groups?

Siebert's analysis of cognitive approaches to religion from the viewpoint of Critical Theory of the Frankfort School introduces a dramatically different note. Systematizing the ongoing dialogue which he and Tom Lawson have conducted during their nearly four decades as colleagues in the same department, he notes first that the highest compliment one scholar can offer another is serious criticism. Siebert urges that the level of abstraction on which cognitive science operates misses a great deal of what religion is actually about, which can be found only in concrete particularities. Siebert contends that "mind/brain" where cognitive scientists locate basic human abilities is a very ill defined concept. And he contrasts the direct relation between Critical Theory and moral statement with the positivist attempt at values-exclusion inherent in cognitivist methods. Ultimately, these and many other problems which Siebert notes in the cognitivist stance seem both to blind the researcher in ritual to something so basic as the function of music and to miss the power of transcendence.

Part I concludes with McCutcheon's account of the trials faced by an individual who specializes in theories of religion rather than in any specific religious tradition. Coming to religion with a socio-political predilection, McCutcheon argues that even the evolution and current usages of the term *religion* symbolize political realities. During the period when the European notion of nation-state was spreading, *religion* migrated from denoting principally a corporate enterprise to an interior and individualistic concern, and with that redefinition, *religion* and its associated rhetoric became a useful tool in social engineering. Reminding us that all scholarship is provincial in background and orientation, he notes that, "There is a real difference in tone between the work of critics acknowledging their situatedness, on the one hand, and the wok of equally provincial guardians of the self-appointed center who tirelessly portray their own interests as definitive of all possible interests." Without critics whose fieldwork conducted amongst theory and theoreticians, the importance of this difference is easily lost.

Part Two: Studies in Religious Behavior

Part II "Studies in Religious Behavior" begins with four interestingly diverse essays and concludes with six written from a cognitive standpoint.

Irrespective of their theoretical tilt, all of the essays in this section seem to reflect the concern shared by Anttonen and Paden in that they deal both with the individual and his or her social context. Whether they spotlight individual psyches or corporately shared concepts and behavior may in these instances depend more on the precise phenomenon being studied at the moment (e.g., the Bible, political insurrection for a millennialist purpose, the creation of pilgrimage sites, etc.) than on any long held theoretical disposition by the author of the study. In any case, each essay and the collection taken together illustrate persuasively how much of human behavior is religious and why this critical human capacity can be ignored in social studies only at the risk of neglecting critical elements of human motivation and mode of behavior.

Hackett's penetrating examination of religious violence in Nigeria recounts in detail the emergence in 1980 of *Maitatsine* ('one who damns,' *nom de guerre* of Muhammadu Marwa, a dissident religious teacher) in the city of Kano, Nigeria. Maitatsine and his followers held Kano under siege for three weeks before being subdued. Subsequent official inquiries heard witnesses blaming Zionists, Qaddafi, or the CIA for fomenting the civil conflict. Hackett shows that multiple factors were at play, including poverty, political impotence, and being marginalized by modernization. Tracing Maitatsine's roots back to *mahdism* 'millennialism,' Hackett concludes that "the original Maitatsine incident... has become the metonym or paradigm for religious violence among Nigerians, despite the fact that it was primarily a local phenomenon and an intrareligious rather than an interreligious conflict."

Wilson recounts a significant chapter in the layered mixture which became Mexican Catholicism. At Amecameca, Franciscan missionaries established as a pilgrimage site a grotto dedicated to an earlier deceased comrade, Fray Martin de Valencia, which was sanctified by a vision of St. Francis himself. Subsequently, the cave was taken over by Dominicans, though eventually the Martinist cult re-emerged to become co-equal with a Dominican crucifix shrine that had replaced it. Unbeknownst to the original designers of this Catholic sacred space, the mountain where the cave was located had been one of the most important landmarks before the Conquest, and, similar to actual practice at Guadalupe, indigenous people joined pilgrimages to the site with their own religious orientations largely intact. Wilson summarizes this fascinating tale of interreligious and intrareligious syncretism with the telling observation that the Franciscans seem ironically to have "created not only an archetypal Franciscan pilgrimage shrine at Amecameca, but a kind of Nahua temple as well."

Writing colloquially and largely directed towards a second-person reader, Gross examines three areas of religious experience which often trouble practitioners in the modern world: the absence of an experientially verifiable dual world, the true nature of scripture as myth, and that nature of religious organizations as simply human bureaucracies with the same structures and features as all other bureaucracies. Gross's viewpoint here is that of a comparativist-practitioner, and his aim is to show that the realism which develops in one's faith through maturation is reinforced and explicated by looking at one's own tradition in the light of others.

Leading off for the cognitively oriented studies, Martin analyzes a Mythraic initiation ritual in terms of the competence/performance dichotomy which Lawson and McCauley have applied so fruitfully to ritual (Lawson and McCauley 1990; McCauley and Lawson 2002). He further demonstrates that the available archaeological and textual data describing now long-extinct group behavior confirm Lawson and McCauley's distinction between special agent and special patient rituals, with the once-occurring initiation ritual pertaining to the former, and the quite variable and frequent ritual meal to the latter.

Barrett also examines the predictions of Lawson and McCauley's theory of ritual. Segmenting the claims into one general and six specific hypotheses, Barrett finds that experimental data support the lion's share of Lawson and McCauley's proposals. That support is weak for the Sensory Pageantry Hypothesis, and the data do not support the Centrality Hypothesis. Barrett undertakes these experiments because the precise explicitness of the Lawson-McCauley hypotheses allows empirical tests, something that is frequently not true of proposals regarding religion. He concludes with the suggestion that others join him forwarding the field through serious experimental testing of genuinely falsifiable hypotheses.

In his eclectically synthetic treatment of Hopi initiation rituals, Geertz shows that the crisis of identity and belongingness attendant upon pubescent boys learning that the numinous Katsina Dancers are none other than their own older male relatives can be understood as a dialectic between society and the self. Drawing both on Dennett's "Multiple Drafts Model" in which the brain's parallel processing capacity establishes "virtual selves" and on Berger and Luckmann's expansion of Schutz's "sedimentation," he concludes that "communities are active causal factors in the construction of virtual selves," which are "cognitively embodied but develop through the dialectics of external and internal techniques for imparting communal values, sentiments, and worldviews."

Early in Saler's provocative essay on credulity comes the pregnant statement: "*The individual, in short, is cognitively or informationally dependent on others*" (italics in the original). Credulity—confidence in the expected normalcy of entities and events—is an evolutionarily developed skill that is necessary for functioning, as it makes possible the flow and learning of information. Because we cannot transmit the contents of our brains to each other, we must be endowed with what Wallace terms "mutually facilitating equivalence structures" that give us complementary expectations and hence encourage acceptance of the information we receive. Acceptance, that is, unless other credible data contradicts what we are being told, for evolutionary adaptation has also endowed us with analytical and skeptical abilities that help us sort out helpful perceptions from those which may be harmful.

Malley's fascinating essay outlines what "the Bible" signifies to the members of a particular Evangelical Protestant congregation in the American Midwest. After determining that when these conservative members of a Bible-based church mention the Bible, they are not referring to a specific physical book, a particular translation, or a particular original text, he concludes that "the Bible" is a shared concept which includes its name, a typical recognizable appearance, an expected text, and the assumption of a common meaning. This, he concludes, suggests that the concept "the Bible" serves cognitively to link a given set of artifacts to the cultural meaning-system of Evangelical culture, and culturally to signify patterns of behavior with the Bible in that subsection of society.

Slone examines human luck behavior as an example of the inference-drawing capacity which cognitive scientists posit as humans' principal engine for explaining and extending perceptions. While systemically distinguishing luck behavior from religion, Slone demonstrates that the contrast between formal reasoning and actual human use of probability parallels Barrett's distinction between systematic theology and the "theologically incorrect" ideas of how the gods function that we normally function with in the midst of "on-line" situations. After reminding readers that, while large sets of reiterated events tend to pattern symmetrically, each event or series of events occurs independently so that betting on "the law of averages" is a wager on a chimera. Nevertheless, the gambler's very abductive reasoning reflected in jumping to a conclusion which seems to solve a current problem rather than following a long path of verifiable logic is a critical survival skill, as its speed, efficiency, and continuing flexibility in responding to environments fosters repeated adaptability.

Finally among the cognitivists, Light discusses an encounter between Tom Lawson and a young Zulu man performing and exegeting a ritual, Light argues that while religious credence (whether stated formally in an *I believe . . .* formula or implicitly in explicating rituals) statements may not carry the same force of conviction as do ordinary *belief* statements, they do reflect the most ordinary patterns of thought and are as natural as any form of cognition. Employing compartmentalization to embrace contradictions, building up meaning and meaningfulness through the development of multiple contextual linkages, and expanding through redefining newly encountered information as familiar, both the most formal creedal statements and nonce formulations of conviction shaped to fit the moment mirror the rest of human thought. He concludes proposing that, among cognitivist analytical tools, a Mental-Space analysis is best suited to account for such behavior.

* * *

These essays, a collective gift to Tom Lawson, are also presented to the field of religious studies not only as diverse reflections of the interests which have engaged Lawson's powerful mind over four decades, but as record of the engagement of an important swath of field-wide concerns as the twenty-first century gets underway. There is little knowing how religion will be viewed in 2050 and even less in 2100. But right now, even amongst scholars who also happen to be religious participants, the phenomena of human beings connecting with what they perceive to be the numinous is systematically examined as a human and humane matter. And it is in that spirit that we offer this collection.

PART ONE

THEORETICAL STUDIES

1. OUT OF AFRICA:
LESSONS FROM A BY-PRODUCT OF EVOLUTION

Pascal Boyer

Dr Faust: *Habe nun, ach! Philosophie,*
Juristerei und Medizin,
Und leider auch Theologie
Durchaus studiert, mit heißem Bemühn.
Da steh ich nun, ich armer Tor!

Faust, I, 1

What happens in religion can be explained in terms of human propensities that would be there, religion or not. The study of religion is like that of politics, poetry, gardening or mass murder. Such a study simultaneously *deflates* and *reduces* those cultural phenomena. It shows that they are only particular illustrations of more general processes of human behavior and also shows that they are explained by these processes. Indeed, one great merit of cognitive approaches is to show how the human notions and norms and behaviors we usually call "religion" can be explained in terms of mental processes and social dynamics that are potentially present in all human beings and present in a variety of other cultural domains. This is also why the dull business of demarcating what is "religion" from what is not is better left to lexicographers; it should not unduly trouble scholars. Whether accounts of religion are of interest depends, not on where they place its boundaries but on how they account for the observed behavior they purport to explain. Cognitive studies of religion, inaugurated by such works as *Rethinking Religion*, offer such causal accounts. My aim here is to recapitulate some of the achievements of this novel enterprise and to point to some possibly important, though as yet unexplored consequences.

Organized and Traditional

We commonly call "religions" two rather disparate sets of objects. There is a set of so-called "world religions" or doctrines of great diffusion, such as Judaism, Buddhism or Islam. There is also what anthropologists, when they are in the mood for categorization, call "traditional" religions: systems of beliefs and practices that are firmly rooted in some local social relations, with little explicit theology and no corporation or guild of religious officers. For many understandable reasons, scholars of religion have generally established their base-camp in a thorough knowledge of "world religions." From this starting point they then tried to climb all the way up to a general understanding of religion in human kind. This however was not always very successful, despite the many new and fascinating vistas opened to scholarly exploration. This was probably unavoidable. Studying doctrinal religions is all too likely to lead one onto a false trail, as far as religion in general is concerned. This is because doctrinal, so-called "world" religions are a secondary, derivative development of a much more general and deeply human tendency to imagine important supernatural agents and to entertain precise descriptions of their powers. Without an understanding of this general mental disposition one does not understand much of the special case of "religions" armed with an official personnel, some theologians, an important economic role and an affinity for political power. So bongo drums (as a metonym for religion in general) are very likely to explain a lot that we need to know about crucifixes (standing for corporate, doctrinal religion) rather than the other way around.

The focus on what we are familiar with—those highly doctrinal phenomena people call "world religions"—is the source of many a confused view about religion. For instance, it is in my experience exceedingly difficult to convince most people of straight facts that are familiar to any anthropologist: that most religion is not about the creation of the world, that it is rarely about God, that it is very seldom about the salvation of the soul. More important and even more difficult to impress upon most people: most religion has no doctrine, no set catalogue of beliefs that most members should adhere to, no overall and integrated statements about supernatural agents. Most religion is piecemeal, mostly implicit, often less than perfectly consistent and, most importantly, *focused on concrete circumstances*. People use their religious concepts to account for their uncle's death or their child's illness or their neighbor's good fortune, not to explain the persistence of evil or the existence of the universe. So most religion in the world has nothing to do with what our common explanations of religion would assume.

Another error is just as common and even more damaging. It consists in thinking that some societies or groups happen to have "world" or "organized religion" and others have what would be generally called "traditional religion," in the same way as some people are nomadic and others sedentary. In this view, the Kwaio people in the Solomon Islands for instance have a religion that happens to be of the "traditional" type (no set doctrine, no interest in cosmic conundrums, no explicit discourse about transcendence), while that of Christian Americans is of the "organized" type. This way of seeing the contrast between those two genres of religious activity may seem plausible enough. It seems to be accepted, if tacitly, in most general presentations of the subject, student textbooks and scholarly reflections. It is in fact terribly misguided and the origin of many confusions in the study of religious thought.

The contrast is misguided because so-called "organized" religion, with explicit doctrine and specialized personnel, never *displaces* the other kind; it *supplements* it. It is an add-on, an extra layer, an additional growth. What anthropologists usually describe as "traditional" religion is based on ways of thinking—about supernatural agents, about their interest in moral action, about their responsibility in human misfortune, etc.—that we find in all human groups. True, in some societies (including the ones most readers of this book belong to) there is *also* a totally different, integrated, explicitly argued version of religion, produced and fostered by specialists gathered in corporate associations. But this, the evidence suggests, does not really change most people's intuitive adherence to the more common ways of thinking. Many Christians probably think that, as far as religion is concerned, their minds are filled with Christian doctrine, or at least with notions and norms derived from Christian teachings. Most professionals of religion, as it were, priests and ministers and theologians, maintain a similar belief. Many students of religion also believe that. But nothing could be further from the truth. Doctrinal religion is a veneer that certainly covers, often conceals non-doctrinal concepts but which would not hold without the underlying material.

Indeed, people's adherence to the doctrine actually requires intuitive, generally unconscious ways of thinking that stray far from the doctrine and in some cases contradict it.

Out of Africa: Religious Thinking in Generic Human Beings

To understand why this is so, it may be of help to recapitulate the key conclusions of cognitive studies of religious thought and behavior. Though the research program is still developing, it already provides us with a broad sketch of general features of religious concepts and ritual, as well as detailed studies of few—too few—empirical cases. Here are the essential points in my view:

- The way we acquire, store, organize religious concepts is to a large extent inaccessible to conscious inspection.

This is not so surprising, since the mechanics of concept acquisition and maintenance *in general,* just like other cognitive mechanics, are outside conscious access. We do not know or experience how our visual cortices translate retinal images into the illusions of 3–D scenes. We do not know or experience how other cortical networks produce grammatical sentences. In the same way, we do not know or experience the processes whereby we attribute agency to unobserved agents, or moral judgments to those same imagined agents. The way to reveal how this takes place is not, or not just, to ask people what their "beliefs" are—for people do not believe what they believe they believe. The only way is to run experiments, test models of cognitive structure, measure how well these models account for observed religious behavior.

- Most religious concepts are parasitic upon mental systems that would be there, religion or not.

Cognitive studies reach a similar conclusion in several distinct domains of religious thought. It turns out that having religious concepts does not require specific mechanisms in the mind, dedicated to religion. Compare with vision for instance, or language comprehension, or the understanding of other people's emotions, which all require specific functional structures. Religion seems to be *parasitic* in the sense that all the systems involved in its acquisition and its mental effects would be there, religion or not. Naturally, there is nothing especially derogatory in saying that religion is parasitic in this precise sense, since aesthetic pleasure for instance is parasitic in that way too. Let me recall some of the domains in which this parasitic nature of religion is best illustrated:

- Religious ritual is parasitic upon action representations.

The pattern for cognitive explanations of religious behavior was set by *Rethinking Religion*. That volume demonstrated that the processes whereby human beings represent actions *in general* (any action from the humble to the sublime, from the quotidian to the heroic) are sufficient to account for the structure of religious ritual. But *Religion Explained* also pointed to two features that were found in many other domains. First, what explained the apparently specific features of the religious domain was a minor modification or "tweaking" of the more common processes. Second, these common processes are spontaneously activated in people, they do not require cultural transmission; only the specific features that "tweak" them are socially transmitted. Beyond ritual action, one can observe similar features in other domains of religion:

- Religious agency (gods, spirits, ancestors, etc.) belongs to a larger repertoire of supernatural agents defined as violations of intuitions about agents.

This is the clearest example of the tweaking process. The material of religion does not in this respect differ from that of folklore. There is a small repertoire of possible types of supernatural characters, most of whom are found in folktales and other minor cultural domains, though some of them are the important gods or spirits or ancestors of "religion." Most of these agents are explicitly defined as having counter-intuitive properties that violate general expectations about agents. They are sometimes undetectable, or prescient, or eternal. The way people represent such agents activates the enormous but inaccessible machinery of "theory of mind" and other mental systems that provide us with a representation of agents, their intentions and their beliefs. All this is inaccessible to conscious inspection and requires no social transmission. On the other hand, what is socially transmitted are the counter-intuitive features: this one is omniscient, that one can go through walls, another one was born of a virgin, etc.

- Interaction with religious agents is parasitic upon cognitive systems for social interaction.

Social interaction requires the operation of complex mental systems: to represent not just other people's beliefs and their intentions, but also the extent to which they can be trusted, the extent to which they find us trustworthy, how social exchange works, how to detect cheaters, how to build alliances, and so on. Again, these mental systems are largely inaccessible, only their output is consciously represented. Now interaction with supernatural agents, through sacrifice, ritual, prayer, etc., is framed by those systems. Although the agents are said to be very special, the way people think about interaction with them is directly mapped from their interaction with other people.

• Religious morality is parasitic upon non-religious moral intuitions.

Developmental research shows the early appearance and systematic organization of moral intuitions: a set of precise feelings evoked by the consideration of actual and possible courses of action. Although people often state that their moral rules are a consequence of the existence or of the decrees of supernatural agents, it is quite clear that such intuitions are present, independent of religious concepts. Moral intuitions appear long before children represent the powers of supernatural agents, they appear in the same way in cultures where no one is much interested in supernatural agents, and in similar ways regardless of what kind of supernatural agents are locally important. Indeed, it is difficult to find evidence that religious teachings have any effect on people's moral intuitions.[1] Religious concepts do not change people's moral intuitions but frame these intuitions in terms that make them easier to think about. For instance, in most human groups supernatural agents are thought to be interested parties in people's interactions. Given this assumption, having the intuition that an action is wrong becomes having the expectation that a personalized agent disapproves of it. The social consequences of the latter way of representing the situation are much clearer to the agent, as they are handled by specialized mental systems for social interaction. This notion of gods and spirits as interested parties is

---

[1] Most students of religion take for granted that religiously coded morality *must* have an effect on people's moral intuitions. I have yet to come across any actual *evidence* for this effect. True, people's explicit discourse, whereby they justify the intuitions, is certainly affected by local religious concepts. But that kind of discourse is *a posteriori*. We have no evidence that it modifies the intuitions themselves. On the contrary, cross-cultural evidence shows a great convergence in moral intuitions despite great differences both in explicit moral codes and in supernatural beliefs.

far more salient in people's moral inferences than the notion of these agents as moral legislators or moral exemplars.

- Notions of ritual specialists are based on non-religious notions of causal essence.

In most human groups some people are thought to be in a privileged position to interact with supernatural agents. A clan's patriarch is evidently the best interlocutor for the ancestors, a local shaman has what it takes to negotiate with wayward spirits. People think of such ritual specialists as having some internal, vaguely defined quality that sets them apart from the common folk. Learning to perform the rites, or acquiring the secret anti-witchcraft recipes, are secondary; what matters most is possession of that internal capacity, construed in quasi-biological terms. This is where, once again, what may have seemed a specifically religious phenomenon is derived from common cognition. The notion of a hidden causal essence that cannot be observed yet explains outward form and behavior, is a crucial feature of our spontaneous, intuitive way of thinking about living species. Here it is transferred upon a pseudo-natural kind, as it were: a subkind of human agents with different essential characteristics.

Note that, so far, we have considered the most important domains of religious thought and behavior—supernatural agency, ritual action, morality, misfortune, ritual specialists—without mentioning what would be to some people the *sine qua non* of religion. There has been no mention of transcendence, of infinite power, of cosmology, of how souls get saved or why evil exists. This is because such questions are blithely ignored by most people in most places in the world, and have been so for most of human history, as far as evidence can tell. Religion does not exist because of the need to answer such questions, far from it. Such questions are a special, local development that arose in societies where religion had become the affair of a guild of specialists. If by religion we understand the thoughts and actions of actual people in actual human groups, these doctrinal questions seem to be a late, minor, derivative phenomenon.[2]

---

[2] That religious guilds and their doctrines then have enormous political and social effects should not make us forget that essential point. Too often in the study of religion, what is said to count is an abstract model of the doctrine itself, rather than the thoughts or actions of the people who embrace it. But if we want to explain actual historical development, the latter is what matters.

Most religious thought has no doctrine for any of these questions, because it has no doctrine at all. If we understand by doctrine a minimally integrated set of coherent assumptions about supernatural agents, their powers, the justification for rituals, the reasons why some people interact with the gods rather than others, etc., it is quite clear that in most groups in the world one can find no such thing. This has in some quarters fuelled a long-lasting misunderstanding between scholars of religion and anthropologists. The former assumed that people outside organized religion must have some doctrine, only a rather esoteric one, or a mytho-poetic one, or an enacted one; anthropologists tried hard to show that in most human groups coherent religious behavior is combined with vague, fragmentary, idiosyncratic and often less than perfectly coherent accounts of supernatural agents.

Indeed, one must remember that, as far as anthropological and cognitive evidence can guide us, the situation is quite similar in groups where there is some official religious doctrine. Again, this is one of those anthropological findings that some students of religion do not seem to register, or whose import they fail to see. In places where a doctrine is available (indeed where people are taught that doctrine), and believe themselves to hold the beliefs typical of the doctrine, there is large and converging evidence that their actual thoughts and intuitions are similar to what I described so far, rather than to the doctrine itself. People may well be taught and repeat that religious agents are transcendent, yet they see their gods as very close interlocutors; they are taught and repeat that gods are omniscient and in fact assume that the gods have cognitive limitations, for instance, cannot attend to many things at the same time, like any human being. They are taught and repeat that a statue is just a symbol of the god, yet assume that the actual artifact is endowed with special powers.

To sum up, most religious thinking seems to proceed in a way that requires no special doctrine: only an explicit mention of the few "tweaks" to add to ordinary cognition. Indeed, religious systems of most societies throughout history have worked in that way. This is going on even when there *is* a doctrine, and more surprisingly even when people themselves believe they believe in the doctrine.

Out of the Fertile Crescent: Religious Thinking by Professionals

As I said above, doctrinal religion does not displace the general, intuitive kind, but it adds to it an extra layer of explicit concepts and norms. This new layer is characterized by explicit and coherent links between the various concepts, a definition of a domain of "religion" as specific, *sui generis* (something that is missing in most human groups), the presence of an organized group of religious scholars or specialists.

Why and how does that happen? Why is it the case that some human societies have that extra accretion of concepts and social relations centered on supernatural concepts? Why is there organized religion at all? The way this process is described by religious groups themselves is in terms of a myth of origin or an epic. The narrative says that a new doctrine appeared, that it gradually convinced more and more people, that the doctrine stemmed from a set of important texts or from a revelation, that proper transmission and maintenance of the doctrine and rites required an organized group of scholars or priests. So the tenets of doctrine were there first and their social effects were among the many consequences of people's adherence to those articles of faith.

Obviously, such a narrative belongs to the register of fairly tales rather than serious scholarship. What the historical evidence says is both more complex and more plausible. Complex polities originated in a few regions of the world, a few millennia ago and became states, small kingdoms empires or city-states. Their complex economies and embryonic markets meant that many activities became the province of specialized groups, craftsmen in particular. These groups or guilds worked as cartels, often maintaining an exclusive grip on the delivery of particular goods or services. They organized training, often kept a *numerus clausus* of new practitioners, sometimes arranged uniform prices and generally guaranteed a certain quality of service. This happened in most trades and crafts, for the intensification of agriculture meant that most people were far too busy to practice these activities and that enough surplus was generated to feed specialists.

The provision of religious services is no exception to this trend. Together with guilds of merchants or blacksmiths or butchers there appear groups of ritual officers and other specialists of the supernatural. They generally operate a monopoly, with an exclusive right to perform particular rites. They form centralized organizations that maintain a strict a strict control over new candidates. They try to bind as closely as possible with sources of political power. They, naturally, work on the assumption that they do provide something and that what they provide could not be obtained elsewhere.

However, the special nature of the commodity they provide means that religious guilds cannot operate entirely in the same way as craftsmen's associations. First, there is of course no objective way to determine whether any religion is better than any other, whereas people can always observe that the trained and experienced cobbler makes better shoes than they themselves would. So, however strongly the guild may claim that its rites are the only way of obtaining particular results, people are fickle and may at any moment decide that some cheaper, home-made recipe is just as good. Second, precisely because of that elusive quality of supernatural services, *there is always some competition*. In most complex polities, there is an organized guild of religious practitioners *as well as* a whole variety of informal providers, local shamans, wizards, healers, inspired idiots and ominous dreamers. Some of these competitors are the shamans and other local specialists found in most human groups. Their claim to efficacy is based on local reputation, on apprenticeship with a famed specialist, on supposed connections to local supernatural agents, in general on their own individual characteristics.

In most cases, the guild uses whatever political clout it can garner to dissolve this competition, demote it, relegate it to unimportant or local rituals, hinder its operation or the transmission of its recipes. This is bound to fail in the long run, for the strength of informal practice is precisely that it is informal and can therefore be started anew at very low cost. As all religious specialists know, the war against what they tend to call superstition is never-ending.

Religious guilds, being cartels of specialists, tend to unify the provision of services: that is, they try to promote the notion that, to some extent, the same service will be provided by any member of the guild. They also try to promote the complementary notion, that no one outside the guild could provide this service. This has consequences for the presentation of religious specialists. Local specialists like shamans and diviners are authoritative only in a particular place; the guild potentially covers any territory. Local specialists are supposed to be different by internal nature from other people; the guild describes its members as specially trained. A religious guild promises to deliver a stable, uniform kind of service that only it can provide, but also a service that any member of the guild will provide in the same way. Proper service depends not on the personal qualities of the specialists but on their being similar to any other member of the guild. Naturally, a group like that will claim connection, not to local spirits and ancestors but to larger-scale supernatural agents with whom the guild proposes to interact with in the same way, regardless of the particular place and customers.

The differences also extend to the concepts put forward in the guilds. It is quite natural for a shaman to construe his locally recognized powers as a link to *local* supernatural agents. By contrast, specialists who endeavor to operate on a large market, indeed on any market that is available, naturally think of themselves as interacting with highly abstract, delocalized, cosmic gods. A local shaman tends to interact with social groups: a family, a lineage. His interventions are said to protect the bones of the lineage or restore a family's defiled honor. By contrast, guilds generally tend to garner help from central political power and consequently address not local groups but the individual. Hence their insistence on such notions as the individual soul, one's personal merit, one's salvation.

It is quite natural for a local specialist to use flexible, highly variable ritual recipes, using his personal knowledge of situations and customers. A guild by contrast, trying to make most of its members' interchangeability, is bound to insist on highly codified, inflexible ritual recipes. Because of all these trends, members of religious guilds generally use literate codes and other texts to maintain uniform provision of religious services. Given that such guilds only appeared in complex polities and that these very often had some writing system, it is not surprising that the guilds also used writing. A great advantage of writing is that it facilitates the uniformity of service and practice that is the main selling point of such professional groups. So religious guilds that set great store by literate sources, written transmission and the kind of systematic argument made easier by writing, are more likely to subsist than groups that ignored the technology of writing. Conversely, given that uniformity and substitutability are important assets of the guild, any appeal to personal charismatic features or shamanistic revelation are actively discouraged.[3]

---

[3] Incidentally, to say that guilds act against the competition, exert some coherent political influence, or maintain their predominance through the use of particular concepts does not mean that these social groups are *agents*. All it means is that most members of such groups tend to adopt a strategy of coalitional solidarity with the guild; social and political effects stem from these aggregated strategies.

These common social factors—the constitution of a cartel of religious specialists, its requirements in terms of uniformity and stability—explain the convergent features of many such religious groups: their insistence on cosmic questions rather than particular misfortune as the foundation of religious behavior, their notions of personal salvation as opposed to collective security, and more generally, the idea that religion requires a doctrine, that it is based on a doctrine, that its outward manifestations are consequences of the doctrine: all statements that make sense as the self-serving discourse of professionals, but should not bamboozle students of religion, whose job it is to explain religious thought and behavior as they occur, not as the guild wishes.

A Darwinian By-Product

All these historical facts show how quite a few theories of religion have got things diametrically wrong. If you assume that the source of religion lies in metaphysical questions for which human kind needs answers—like the destiny of the soul or the creation of the universe or the origin of evil—you mistake a recent and regional development, itself limited to professional associations, for a general feature of human minds. Religion certainly is old, but it is not about that at all. It is about daily occurrences and interaction with imagined agents of a counter-intuitive nature.

That religion in this sense is "old" is not disputed, although what is old by historical standards is quite recent in the archaeological record. It is very likely that by the time modern humans came out of Africa, they had the kind of supernatural imagination that founds religious concepts. It is quite certain that this imagination was active by the time of what is generally called the "cultural revolution," the sudden explosion of cultural artifacts that show both great innovations and the beginnings of cultural style. It is also clear that dead bodies were the object of much special preparation by that time, being left adorned, accompanied with various artifacts or laid down to rest in special positions. We do not know whether those people also associated dead bodies with concepts of supernatural agents, a frequent feature of modern religion. To sum up, the kind of concepts and practices that we find the world over seem to appear right at the same time as all the mental capacities that are typical of the modern human mind.

However, the appearance of religion is not an important evolutionary event, because it is only a fairly predictable by-product of mental capacities that would have appeared, religion or not. As I said above, most features of religion seem to be fairly simple "tweakings" of ordinary conceptual and inferential capacities that we find in all human minds. Now *those* capacities are an outcome of evolution and their appearance was a major event. For instance, the capacity to represent non-actual states of affairs and to draw consequences for such representations grounds people's perception of their past as well as their deliberation about future action. Developing such a capacity is a major evolutionary event; as a minor consequence, it also allows one to imagine supernatural agents. In a similar way, the extraordinary complexity of human "theory of mind" (one's intuitive explanation of others and own behavior in terms of intentions and beliefs) was a major development that resulted in uniquely complex social interaction; it also allowed people to entertain complex thoughts about interaction with imagined agents. Modern humans also have an instinctive fear of invisible contaminants (like the pathogens of rotting bodies, blood, feces, etc.) and an intuitive notion of invisible contagion; such a cognitive adaptation is of great value. It also allows, as a by-product, the development of notions of invisible power ("the sacred," "taboo," "pollution," etc.) that we find in religious imagination.

Obviously, the fact that people entertain religious thoughts at all can have important consequences, that we sometimes mistake for the explanation of religion. Once people find their imagined agents plausible, they can use them at times to allay anxiety like more pliable versions of real agents; once the versions of imagined agents differ from one culture to another, they can be used as convenient ethnic markers; once rituals are organized, a willingness to undergo gruesome ordeals can work a signal of commitment to the group. All this is familiar to all students of religion. It would be a mistake, however, to mistake any of these social or personal effects of religion for a plausible evolutionary scenario. People did not create religion to allay their fears, first because it does not and second because people cannot create just any convenient fantasy and find it plausible. People did not create religion to foster good morality and group solidarity, because such a strategy would be vulnerable to defectors and quickly unravel.

We are left with a conclusion that many evolutionary biologists would find unsurprising—and most students of religion unpalatable: that religion is like dancing, music, ethnocentrism or body-ornaments:

something that most humans are very good at learning and almost incapable of resisting, may sometimes have important consequences, yet has no other explanation than the quirks of the way evolution made our brains. What may make all this unpleasant or unacceptable to some people is the belief that important phenomena should have important causes, or at least their own, special causes. But cognitive models suggest that religion is not really special and requires no special mental process, no exceptional evolutionary event.

No Reason for Religion

Cognitive accounts of religion even suggest that there is no good *reason* for the existence of religious thoughts and behaviors. There is not even a single *cause* for them. Rather, the most plausible scenario we have makes it a by-product of a whole variety of cognitive adaptations, of mental systems that we have for a good reason. This causal account clashes with most people's expectations, particularly with those of religious adherents. We generally tend to think that people for instance perform a particular ritual for some reason: indeed, the first thing we always do is ask them what the reason is. But cognitive models seem to suggest that this is not the most profitable strategy, that the explanation for religious notions lies in processes that people cannot be aware of, so that the explicit reasons ("we sacrifice to the ancestors because they protect us") is at best a rationalization of thoughts and behaviors that would occur anyway.

This is an unavoidable consequence of scientific reduction, but it is important to understand what it really means. At this point, it may be of help to return to Lawson and McCauley's model of ritual action in *Rethinking Religion*. Some commentators have complained—and many a student will have concurred—that the core theory of ritual, the system of rules and principles that generate well-formed descriptions of ritual actions, was "too formal." It explains what is often a matter of great emotion and interest, goats beheaded and chickens disemboweled, commandments recited and sacred texts committed to memory, in terms of a list of abstract formulae and terms such as "agent-slot" or "object-filter." In my view, if there was a small defect in the model, and any scope for improvement, it was that the model was not formal enough, perhaps included too many commonsense intuitions about supernatural agents and their role. For instance, the model assumed that supernatural agents were thought to have "super-permanent" effects. That is to say, if people for instance assume that the ancestors really were present during the ritual and turned the neophyte into a proper member of the group, then this effect cannot be undone, unless another ritual with the appropriate structural reversal is performed. Now it would seem to most anthropologists that the attribution of such "super-permanent" effects to imagined agents is generally not an assumption, but rather a conjecture that is strengthened by ritual performance. It is therefore important to elucidate why rituals have such consequences: why they make people think that supernatural agents were really involved. (This crucial point is addressed in *Bringing Ritual to Mind*, where contrasted ways of enhancing transmission—thought sensory pageantry or doctrinal elaboration—also strengthen people's intuitions about the imagined agents' real participation).

This complaint (that the Action Representation model was overly formal) points to a very general characteristic of cognitive models, in this as in any other domain. They explain the occurrence of thoughts in terms that demote the usually central role of reasons. That is, what explains why we have this or that concept is *not* what we would ourselves come up with if asked to explain it. So far, people are used to this kind of explanation, for instance from popular Freudian accounts of emotion and behavior. Freudian and other fantasies of that kind tell people that, beneath what they think are the reasons for their behavior, lies an entirely inaccessible domain of other reasons. In contrast to this, scientific studies of mental phenomena say something far more disturbing: that beneath our reasons for having particular thoughts there is an inaccessible domain of processes that do not consist in reasons at all. That is, each of our thoughts is caused by processes that do not consist in "thoughts" in the sense of explicit combinations of the concepts we can name. We think we see an elephant for a good reason, namely that there is one in front of us; but the study of visual perception tells us that all this is achieved in the cortex by extremely complex neural processes, none of which resembles the "elephant" concept. To take an example from higher processes, the reasons why we remember particular stories and forget others are not really "reasons." We may well think we recall a story because it makes a lot of sense or answers a lot of questions we had. But these are only consequences of the fact that we recall it in the first place, and this is caused by memory processes that do not consist in "reasons."

So religious concepts function in that way too. A believer may well think she has such concepts because they explain a lot, or because they are awesome and beautiful stories, or because life would make no sense if they were false, or because it makes her happy, or because most other people seem to accept them. All these are real consequences of having the concepts, but non-starters as explanations for why one acquired them in the first place and why they appeared in human cultures at all. The poorest such explanation, incidentally, is that people spontaneously and intuitively adhere to religious concepts because religious concepts are *true*. (One comes across this argument surprisingly often in debates about religion). Besides solving the delicate problem of deciding *which* religious concepts are true, between all the incompatible, mutually refuting versions available, proponents of this simple explanation also have to ignore two major facts of human history: there is no limit to the range of false concepts people can sincerely and intuitively find plausible; conversely, there is a vast domain of true concepts that our minds find it exceedingly difficult to acquire, as science shows every day. Given the colossal evidence for both tendencies, the fact that most humans find a particular representation is certainly no guarantee of validity, far from it.

Whither the Study of Religion?

Like fish, innovative scholars form schools. *Rethinking Religion* spawned a whole series of related works, showing that the cognitive study of religion was a coherent and valuable research program. Indeed, the various features summarized in the previous pages were taken for the work from at least five different scholars, which I suppose counts as a school if not quite a swarm. The program is bound to expand, as more scholars find inspiration in the early models, detect their many flaws and provide us with better accounts of varieties of religious thought and behavior. Inasmuch as it is successful, this research program will certainly escape the narrow confines of the study of religion. It is one of the inevitable, indeed desirable consequences of cognitive models that "religion" is shown to be no more special than other cultural domains.

Another predictable development is that our accounts of particular features of religion will be grounded in much more precise accounts of mental functioning, in particular in finer-grained accounts of brain function. There is no need to postulate any religious organ in the brain, no more than there is a literature organ or a social life center in cortical structures. But uncovering the underpinnings of ordinary concept-acquisition and inference, in terms of neural circuitry, is bound to tell us a lot about the processes whereby the most baroque imaginings acquire inherent plausibility. Obviously, all this goes in the direction of further reduction and deflation, which may shock many people who joined the study of religion to find precisely the opposite, an antidote to a perceived excess of reduction. But such a move towards explanation in terms of fine-grained brain processes is both possible and inevitable. Sensitive souls who find reduction shocking, indeed faint at the merest whiff of a causal explanation, should not just steer clear of the cognitive study of religion; they should avoid study altogether.

It is both a privilege and an achievement to show science that a particular domain of reality can indeed be reduced, that is explained, where people thought it was either impossible or undesirable. The study of religious ritual in terms of action representation and of the latter as a cognitive process was one of those inaugural events. Whatever the difficulties and uncertainties of a first model, it made it possible to think of many other domains of religious behavior, indeed of many other domains of culture, as similarly constrained by the operation of human cognitive machinery.

2. IS RELIGION A RUBE GOLDBERG DEVICE? OR OH, WHAT A DIFFERENCE A THEORY MAKES!

Robert N. McCauley

Introduction

Prudence, if not sheer logical necessity, dictates that when discussing something, it helps to have some idea of what you are talking about. This is why even the most experienced scholars periodically discuss their terms. Those discussions rarely, if ever, settle anything more than discussants' (sometimes differing) words for a few readily recognizable regions in the relevant semantic sea, but, even so, obtaining clarity is no small accomplishment and often a valuable preliminary to achieving substantive progress within a field.

Scholarly shorthand for such exchanges holds that they concern "definitions,"[1] but, at best, that is misleading—at least if it presumes that "definitions" are capable of ever doing anything *definitive*, i.e., once and for all. *Up front*, with empirical matters at least, clarifying the (provisional) meanings of terms is simply a useful tool for either initiating or renewing inquiry. *In media res*, it is one means for delineating some of the points of conflict between competing accounts of things. The best we get—when a few such competitions actually result in a clear course—are some semantic buoys. Comparatively fixed points (after all, buoys still bob around on the waves), they mark a few safe channels for our communicative comings and goings. But from the surface (where all of us are simultaneously repairing and bailing the *S. S. Neurath*), not even those familiar with the locale know *for sure* whether the cables anchoring those buoys continue to

---

[1] I shall throughout this paper employ the punctuation used in most contemporary American philosophy. Standard quotation marks (" ") will serve two purposes: (1) as designating text produced by someone else specifically or as scare quotes indicating broader, accepted but questionable usage or (2) to indicate a term (as opposed to the corresponding concept). Single quotation marks (' ') will indicate concepts (as opposed to their corresponding terms). Both uses of standard quotation marks in the sentence at hand are scare quotes.

hold. Moreover, such buoys are always close to shore, and the definitive pretenses of dictionaries of both the common and scholarly varieties notwithstanding, sailing beyond the horizon to catch big fish, let alone to explore new worlds, requires crossing vast buoyless stretches of that semantic sea. Because definitions are far more limited markers than they are usually cracked up to be, Tom Lawson and I have not hesitated to discuss them or propose them *tentatively* in the process of theorizing about religious ritual. Their value turns primarily on the value of the waterways they mark and our resulting ability to find our way around.

Scrupulous conceptual analysis of the sort analytic philosophers undertake will enable inquirers to sail further from shore, but it still requires keeping landmarks or, at least, some of those buoys within sight. By contrast, the most interesting semantic conflicts in science arise further out to sea. They are the latent consequences of the competition of theories following different courses as they sail throughout the world. Such theories are the things wherein we catch those big fish, including such scientific trophy fish as novel predictions, penetrating explanations, and solutions to our practical problems. In science many of the concepts deployed are, finally, only as good as the empirical success of the theories in which they figure. Because empirical theories are conjectural, they are tentative. Their fates are always subject to the next new set of empirical findings. But if the theories are tentative, then so are at least some of their most central concepts' contents. Thus, talk of "definitions" in empirical domains is *never* the final word, because wherever empirical science is introduced, there are no *final* words.

If—within the framework of semantic analysis—the activity of empirical science is to be metaphorically associated with traversing the oceans, then the cognitive accounts of religiosity that Lawson and I and others have advanced over the past decade have sailed through some rough waters (see, for example, Lawson and McCauley 1990 and McCauley and Lawson 2002; Whitehouse 1992 and 2000; Guthrie 1993; Boyer 1994 and 2001b; Hinde, 1999; Pyysiäinen 2001 and Atran 2002). These proposals vary in their ambition (since my and Lawson's theory focuses on religious ritual only, it is probably the least ambitious in this group), but each aims to explain familiar features of religion on the basis of various proclivities of the human mind.

Why have the waters been rough, i.e., why should such cognitive proposals prove *semantically* disruptive? So imbalanced are inquiries about religion that the pursuit of *any* explanatory theory induces disorientation in most traditional scholars in that field. Confronting cognitive theories in particular can be downright vertiginous. Cognitive proposals about religion are theoretically novel,[2] and nothing matches the potential of novel scientific theories to disrupt accepted categories.

The conceptual explosiveness of such an account may not be instantly obvious. These cognitive theories' novelty begins with a broad fundamental commitment they all share, viz., that *from a cognitive standpoint* religious thought and action involve nothing out of the ordinary. That assumption runs thoroughly contrary to the predilections of conventional scholars of religion (and, *not coincidentally*, of the religious as well), who forestall even the possibility of empirically disconfirming their views by insisting that religious phenomena pose unique epistemic challenges that can never be solved by the standard methods of rational inquiry. By contrast, cognitive theorists maintain that what makes religion what it is turns on perfectly *ordinary* variations arising and persisting in the course of the operations of comparably *ordinary* mental machinery. Thus, accounting for religious belief and conduct requires neither employing special methods nor even postulating distinctively religious faculties. Lawson and I, for example, have steadfastly argued that participants' representations and knowledge of their religious rituals relies on garden variety cognitive capacities (concerning the representation of agents and their actions), which develop quite naturally in every normal human being.

Endangering the standard picture of *homo religiosus* as the manifestation of the extraordinary and the corresponding pleas of scholars of religion for special methods for its study are only the first two of at least three important conceptual challenges these cognitive theories pose for conventional approaches in the study of religion. Lawson and I have explicated these first two in earlier papers (Lawson and McCauley 1993 and McCauley and Lawson 1996, respectively). Closely connected to these two is a third that turns on specific empirical implications of these cognitive theories that simultaneously threaten the coherence of religion (and religions) as *socio-cultural* phenomena yet support a conception of these phenomena in which their comparatively

---

[2] Such accounts have been around for nearly three decades, though. Dan Sperber began to outline this approach to symbolism generally in the 1970s, e.g., Sperber 1975.

simple-minded counter-intuitiveness is one of their *necessary* features. It is this third challenge to many standard approaches to religion that this paper explicates.

Religion as a Rube Goldberg Device[3]

Cognitive theories of religion hold that the various attitudes, values, beliefs, and behaviors associated with religion emerge from routine variations in the functioning of common components of our mental equipment. The mind does not contain a specific department of religion. Instead, religion exploits a diverse collection of emotional and cognitive inclinations in human beings that enjoy neither logical nor psychological unity. The upshot of this analysis is that *cognitively speaking* religion is a Rube Goldberg device, which is to say that it is an exceedingly complicated contraption calling on all sorts of psychological propensities that are, otherwise, usually unlinked. The standard features of religious mentality and conduct are cobbled together from the susceptibilities of a disparate compilation of psychological dispositions[4] that typically develop in normal human minds for very different reasons—both from one another and from anything having to do with religion.

Those dispositions develop typically, because the resulting mental reflexes they undergird served our ancestors well in dealing with a host of problems their physical and social environments presented, just as they continue most of the time to serve us well when we deal with the same problems. These various mental capacities and their instantaneous operations conferred adaptive advantages on the organisms who possessed them. The abilities to do such things as detect agents, recognize individual conspecifics, and read their minds from their faces (and their behaviors) are just the sorts of capacities that not only increase organisms' inclusive fitness but make life a lot more interesting overall. Whether these abilities begin as dedicated, task

---

[3] Named after the humorous imaginary machines created by the Pultizer-Prize winning American cartoonist, Rube Goldberg (1883–1970), a "Rube Goldberg device" is any device that is "unnecessarily complicated, impractical or ingenious" (Oxford English Dictionary). (eds.)

[4] For a discussion of the relation between adaptive cognitive dispositions and their various latent susceptibilities, see Sperber 1996a: 66–67.

specific systems, many end up seeming to operate that way as a result of standard cognitive development. Since, comparatively early in human development, the mind responds to some stimuli (facial, social, linguistic, etc.) instantly, automatically, and unreflectively, the resulting knowledge is overwhelmingly intuitive and any underlying principles that might be guiding such behavior—if such principles are psychologically real—are tacit. (Elman et al. 1996 suggests that the psychological reality of such "principles" need not entail the possession of either symbolic representations or the rules that allegedly govern them.)

Sometimes quite specific stimuli seem sufficient to trigger these systems. Often the cuing of such mental reflexes engenders powerful feelings in human beings as well as characteristic intuitions and behaviors (Boyer 2001b). The effects are often transparent not just to observers but sometimes even to the subject. Consider, for example, the feelings and behaviors associated with the perception of contaminated food or of the inability of an informant to make eye contact or of unfairness in assessments or of the influence of social hierarchies in the distribution of opportunities and resources. All other things being equal, the human beings in each of these scenarios typically experience distinctive feelings that can instantly propel them into characteristic behaviors—here, acts and attitudes of avoidance, suspicion, complaint, and obsequiousness, respectively.

But how do such dispositions outfit human beings for *religion*? The crucial point is that such features of modern human minds have rendered them susceptible to generating and retaining a variety of representations, beliefs, and practices that presume *counter-intuitive* arrangements, i.e., representations that do not conform to our instant, automatic, unreflective expectations. These include *representations* of Yogi Bear, talking wolves that can plausibly be mistaken for grandmothers, and Superman, *beliefs* in everything from Lassie, Santa Claus, fairies, and leprechauns to ghosts, ancestors, angels, and gods, and *practices* such as theater and ritual. Precisely what form these representations, beliefs, and practices take is mostly a function of what is in the air locally and, needless to say, not all of them are religious (a point to which I shall return later in this paper). So, this is only part of the story, but it is a very important part.

Cognitive theorists offer at least three (mutually consistent) accounts of how counter-intuitive representations that we regard as religious come about. The first two concentrate on their origins, the first and third on their persistence. Inspired, in part, by a long tradition of intellectualist theorizing in anthropology that holds that humans entertain religious beliefs because they explain things, the first account maintains that when humans confront anomalous phenomena, i.e., phenomena that violate their intuitive expectations, they naturally generate *counter*-intuitive representations in order to make sense of these states of affairs. Surprising, unexpected counter-intuitive experiences inspire the construction of otherwise unexpected, counter-intuitive representations to make sense of them. Note, such experiences are just as capable of stimulating what we may come to deem scientific speculations as religious ones. Science, however, inevitably advances proposals that are far less modestly counter-intuitive than those religion recruits. Science invariably traffics in representations that arise from *genuinely extraordinary* variations on our standard mental contents. So, for example, sooner or later, it abandons appeals to agent causality. One firm correlate of scientific progress has been its steadily increasing restriction of the domains in which teleological explanations are licit (Churchland 1989). Religions, by contrast, rely overwhelmingly on the states of mind and actions of counter-intuitive agents to explain things (McCauley 2000).

The second account (Guthrie 1993—but also see Burkert 1996) is that these counter-intuitive representations arise, in effect, as the results of cognitive false alarms. Although plenty of theorists, at least since Tylor, have made much of dreams, they are not the central issue here. The range of conditions capable of activating the mental reflexes I have been discussing do not infallibly correlate with the objective variables that led to their development. Consequently, they err on the side of liberality. They are not perfect detectors. So, for example, even when we have compelling evidence to the contrary, our default hypothesis for explaining unexpected sounds (especially in the dark) is that they have resulted from some agent's actions (and we begin searching for the agent responsible). The force of the associated emotions and intuitions is such that it is a very short step to explanations of the unsuccessful searches in terms of hypothesizing empirically undetectable agents. Because every normal human being is susceptible to such emotionally compelling, cognitive misfires (in a variety of domains), every culture has emerged with a panoply of ancestors, angels, brownies, cherubim, demons, devils, elves, genies, ghosts, ghouls, gnomes, goblins, gods, gremlins, fairies, fiends, imps, leprechauns, mermaids, nymphs, phantoms, pixies, poltergeists, saints, seraphim, sirens, sorcerers, specters, spirits, sprites, vampires, warlocks, witches, and wizards, let alone golems, sylphs, or zombies or representations of animals, plants, objects, and places possessing counter-intuitive properties. Cultures the world over take forms that manipulate such dispositions. They have developed all sorts of ways of stimulating these false positive responses by activating the relevant perceptual systems—from fashioning simple human-like objects that visually cue the presence of additional agents to producing motion pictures that visually cue the presence of additional worlds. The questions remain, though, why only some of the representations that these false alarms create persist and why some, but not others, among those that persist count as religious.

The third account (e.g., Sperber 1975 and 1996a) focuses on the first of these two questions. On this account how such counter-intuitive representations originate is not the critical issue. They may just occur randomly. The more pressing question is why they persist and get transmitted to others. The answer, broadly speaking, is that the persisting representations are the ones that survive the culling wrought by processes of selection. Just as humans find some foods particularly good to eat, they find some symbols—as Lévi-Strauss suggested—representations that are particularly good to think. What makes representations psychologically appealing constitutes most of the operative selection forces here. We tend to transmit representations when they have enough of the following properties. First, they are not only readily *recognizable* but often *attention grabbing*. Physical structures that manifest a symmetry along a vertical axis are rare in nature (outside of the animal kingdom) but abundant in culture. Structures of this sort with two spots resembling eyes commandeer humans' attention particularly effectively. Second, they are *easily remembered*. Persisting representations, especially in non-literate settings, provide important insights about the character of human memory (McCauley 1999). So, for example, people tend to remember verbal representations that rhythmically rhyme. Third, like diseases, they are *communicable*. Frequently, the features that make a representation memorable will also make it easier to transmit. Usually, tunes are unforgettable precisely because they are so easy to sing, hum, or whistle. By contrast, representations that possess none of these features, like scientific theories, are far less likely to get transmitted spontaneously (McCauley 2000). Finally, these representations *motivate* people to spend their time and energies transmitting these representations to other people.

If we believe God is the secret to happiness and human fulfillment and we want those whom we care about to have happy, fulfilled lives, then we will tend to transmit representations of God to those whom we care about. Or if part of some idea is that rewards will accrue to those who propagate that idea, this will increase the probability that it gets propagated. On this third account religions should mostly be understood in terms of distributions of similar representations, attitudes, and beliefs about counter-intuitive agents in human populations, where those mental representations are causally related to one another and to a set of public representations (such as statements, practices, clothing, icons, statues, buildings, etc.).

Each of the various cognitive theorists subscribes to some or all of these accounts. The crucial point, though, is that all three presume that the eruption of religious representations in human populations relies neither on a uniquely religious set nor even on any integrated set of sensibilities or cognitive capacities. Instead, religion (along with such things as civil ceremonies and superstition, folk tales and fantasy, and magic and music) largely results from *the latent consequences of normal variation* in the operations of fallible perceptual and cognitive heuristics enshrined in human minds that otherwise aid us in managing problems from a wide array of domains.[5] (Had he thought of it, portraying religion for what it is at the cognitive level might have won Goldberg another Pulitzer.)

Whither 'Religion'?

But the second question remains. Why do some but not all of those persisting counter-intuitive representations count as *religious* representations?

Perhaps, one of these cognitive theories' most interesting implications for the study of religion is the suggestion that this query already begs a critical question itself, viz., whether there is, any longer, a

---

[5] Consider, for example, Burkert's observation (1996: 22–23) that: "There is probably a cluster of factors in evolution and a cluster of functions served by new avenues of communication; functions may also be lost or altered. Nonetheless certain persistent and permanent patterns emerge and even seem to control interactions, since all these events occur within a unique landscape to which they are adapted. What we discern are the tracks of biology followed by cultural choice."

principled basis for delimiting a subset of our representations as the "religious" ones. If, cognitively speaking, human religiosity is a Rube Goldberg device, what, then, are the scientific grounds for identifying specific socio-cultural phenomena as religious? Because human religiosity is a hodgepodge at the psychological level, are religions—construed at the socio-cultural level—comparable miscellanies? Is 'religion' (whether the term is preceded by an article or not) a viable, analytical category for social science? These cognitive analyses suggest some grounds for skepticism about the conceptual glue that purportedly holds these outcomes (of our diverse dispositions' susceptibilities) together as distinct, socio-cultural systems that the term "religion" denotes. It appears that theorists in the social sciences must bear the burden of demonstrating the respects in which 'religion' is an explanatorily useful category in order to stave off the suspicion that, like the concept 'constellation,' it only delineates superficial (indeed, accidental!) patterns that reveal little or nothing about the phenomena it designates but only something about the perspective humans are inclined to take on these things prior to self-consciously reflecting on them theoretically.

Psychological analyses are not the only source of these skeptical worries. Straightforward observations about religion at the socio-cultural level also introduce problems. At least two additional considerations contribute to pessimism about the explanatory probity of the concept 'religion.' On the one hand, religion turns out to be too many things, while on the other, too many *other* things that are clearly *not* religion turn out to share some of the most prominent features of religion. Consequently, many suggest that 'religion' seems likely to be a family resemblance concept *at best* (Saler 1993).

First, no one has come up with a property that all and only religions possess. From High Church Anglicanism to Theravada Buddhism, from the Ghost Dancers of the Sioux to worshipers of the Japanese Emperor, from the religions of the Nuer, the Zande, and the Zulu to resurgent Islamic fundamentalism, from Hinduism to the Quakers and Shakers, pondering the diversity of phenomena that constitute even the paradigmatic examples of what we call "religions" quickly hints at the challenge that formulating jointly necessary and sufficient conditions for the concept's application poses (see Boyer 2001b: 6–10). Pyysiäinen (2001: 4) holds that "... it is doubtful whether a scientific category of religion can be constructed, because the category includes so many different kinds of phenomena that the cohesiveness of the category cannot be accounted for by any one theory." Boyer (2001b) explains some of this diversity by stressing the differences in the subsets of the cognitive dispositions and their susceptibilities—from one case to the next—that get exploited. Ultimately, both are suggesting, though, that the things that we call "religions" pre-theoretically include too sprawling a range of phenomena to render 'religion' a very penetrating explanatory concept.

Nor is establishing sufficient conditions for religion easy. It seems every bit as challenging to identify a property that *only* religions have as it is to identify one that all and only religions do. Sampling the assortment of counter-intuitive representations that humans are capable of entertaining prefigured this second basis for pessimism. The problem is that religions piece together patterns of emotion, thinking, and conduct that occur in many other settings that certainly fail to square with our pre-theoretic views of the "religious."

As the list I supplied earlier revealed, religion has not cornered the market on agents with counter-intuitive properties. They abound in folk tales and fiction as well as in cartoons, comic books, and commercials. They are also sometimes one of the marks of lunacy. However normal it may seem, it is striking that humans have *no* problem with Mickey, Minnie, Donald, and Goofy talking, having pets, and going on picnics. These short steps to the counter-intuitive are not confined to proliferating non-standard agents. Not only could Mighty Mouse fly, he produced contrails, which could function like ropes to bind up bad guys (who, incidentally, were almost always cats who wore clothes and drove cars).

The same is true with ritual. All religions include rituals, but many other forms of human activity and association employ ritual as well. Whether loosely characterized as nothing more than the repetition of specific actions (reading the same bedtime story night after night) or more technically portrayed in terms of those repeated actions' absence of instrumentality and (in many cases) their provocation of human emotions, rituals thrive in many other areas of human endeavor. From commencement exercises, to the opening and closing ceremonies of the Olympics, to the initiations of fraternal organizations, repeated, non-instrumental actions are utilized for marking events, which sometimes have no trace of the religious about them.

Accompanying the invention of agriculture, centralized governments employed both religion and the mechanisms it exploits for their own preservation (Diamond 1998). These regimes enlisted many of the most standard religious gimmicks. They apotheosized rulers. They created civil ceremonies. Some of the most venerated sites in the world pervaded by some of the most rigidly ritualized forms of human conduct are those associated with national and political identities, such as tombs of unknown soldiers. So, it seems that appeals to counter-intuitive representations or to ritual or to sacred spaces will not suffice to differentiate the religious.

Any number of interested parties to debates about the definition of "religion" over the past few decades will see vindication for their views, first, in these failures to supply even sufficient criteria for religion (let alone necessary and sufficient criteria) and, second, in the consensus among the new cognitive theories that religion relies on a psychological infrastructure that only Rube Goldberg would have designed. For additional reasons having to do with the status of their discipline, cultural anthropologists have typically regarded religion overall as well as its characteristic accouterments—myths, rituals, and sacred spaces—as instances of *general* cultural patterns in which humans find meanings. Religion is (only) one among many cultural systems; religious myths shade indistinguishably into secular myths, fables, and folk tales; religious ritual operates no differently than ritual operates anywhere else. Whether they hoped to delineate general theories of the cultural patterns or, eschewing such goals, they aimed to explicate the webs of implied meaning, cultural anthropologists have largely resisted the notion that the religious constitutes a unique domain worthy of specialized theories. Since the 1950s the interpreters of symbolic meanings (and the subsequent post-modern elaborations of their stance) have dominated this discipline.[6]

These trends are similar to ones in the academic study of religion over the same time period. Scholars of religion have also generally preferred to be interpreters of meanings rather than theorists about patterns. If they wish to avoid even the appearance of an interest in explanatory theorizing and if meanings are wherever they can be found, then formulating precise criteria for what should count as religion in order to test scientific proposals holds no attractions. It only restricts their purview.[7] Prominent religious thinkers of the time

---

[6] Clifford Geertz's *The Interpretation of Cultures* (1973) has emerged as a *locus classicus* of this approach to religion (however, see Pyysiäinen 2001, chapter 3).

[7] Because civic ceremonies or, for that matter, football games, occasion the sorts of passion, ritual, and group solidarity that we find in many religious communities,

gave these scholars added support for advocating a wide-open account of what might count as religion.[8] Wilfrid Cantwell Smith (1964) noted how various ancient cultures did not even possess the concept 'religion,' and Paul Tillich maintained that the religious included any object or expression of "ultimate" human concern. The possibilities are endless (see Lawson 1999).

The notion of religion as a thoroughly open concept presents no problems for the newest manifestations of interest in religion—either scholarly or devotional. With regard to the former, whatever objections and qualifications recent post-modern thinkers may have advanced in response to the broadly hermeneutic agenda of interpretive anthropologists and scholars of religion, the former do not substantially differ from the latter on the questions at hand. If anything, post-modern thinkers are even less sympathetic with proposing definitions, let alone ones linked to the theoretical projects of social or psychological science. On the views of most post-modernists, even the attempt to advance testable theories about human thought and action that employ comparatively precise definitions of key concepts does nothing more than perpetuate restrictive "essentializing" activities that result in repressive formulations restricting human freedom. On the devotional front, the newest forms of popular religiosity are (in)famous precisely for blurring traditional religious conceptions with considerably less elaborated ideas that emphasize the primacy of religious feeling and experience. On these views meditation, aroma therapy, or listening to the latest New Age musicians can just as authentically instantiate human religiosity as reading the Qur'an, saying the Rosary, or attending services on the High Holy Days.

---

it does not follow that either nationalism or football are religions or that civic celebrations or football games are best understood as religious events. Without the formulation, testing, and corroboration of explicit explanatory theories that treat all of these phenomena on a par, assertions of this sort remain suggestive metaphors at best.

[8] Pyysiäinen (2001: 152–54) identifies a further contributing factor. In effect, he argues that those who insisted that all religions are worldviews also ended up diluting the concepts in question by eventually confusing this claim with its converse, viz., all worldviews are religions. The conversion of a universal affirmative proposition is, of course, an invalid inference.

Oh, What a Difference a Theory Makes!

Up to this point, I have mostly been sailing with the wind, but I must now begin to tack. That is because far too often scholars of religion have—from our inability to establish either necessary and sufficient conditions or even just sufficient conditions for religion—drawn the stronger conclusion that we, therefore, cannot make sense of any *necessary* conditions for religion either, i.e., that there is no property that all religions share. This conclusion is stronger, because the standard of stating some necessary condition is so weak. Although this conclusion may be true, I tack here for three reasons.[9] First, not only is this negative conclusion *much* stronger, but, second, the inference is fallacious. Third and more important, in cases like this, the best way to ascertain whether this conclusion is true is to press ahead *theoretically* and, therefore, *empirically*—at least in any inquiry that aims to be counted among the empirical sciences. To repeat, it is usually a theory's explanatory and predictive success that is the principal variable determining the fate of the concepts (and their "definitions") that it presumes (see footnote 6 above).

Rather than advance this stronger conclusion directly, though, most of its advocates highlight one of its consequences. If we will forever remain unable to establish any necessary conditions for religion, then it follows that trafficking in counter-intuitive representations, in particular, cannot be a necessary condition for something to count as religious.[10] Religions, on this view, need not be about the gods (or ancestors or angels or saints or miraculous events, etc.). This is a conclusion that various sociologists, anthropologists, and scholars of religion have pressed over the past few decades, and they will be inclined, no doubt, to take solace from the general drift of the cognitive analyses I have sketched above.

Parallels between the study of language and the study of religion that Lawson and I have highlighted before (e.g., 1990, chapters 3,

---

[9] I am not the only one to tack. Pyysiäinen, 2002 proposes, as will I, that the possession and use of counter-intuitive representations is a plausible necessary condition for productive theorizing about the religious. As Pyysiäinen and I (below) acknowledge, it is Boyer (1994 and 2001) who proposed the 'counter-intuitive' as the central analytical category and who has worked through the principal difficulties that its explication requires.

[10] See, for example, Levine 1998, but by all means be sure to consult McCauley and Lawson 1998 as well!

4, and 6) may only reinforce that inclination. We have underscored how, since the nineteenth century, progress in the study of language has inspired new approaches in the study of other facets of culture and in the study of religion in particular. Our earliest conception of our own project was precisely that we were updating the study of religion in the light of new developments in language study to which scholars of religion had yet to attend.[11] However controversial his views otherwise, Noam Chomsky was the first major proponent of construing linguistics as a sub-discipline of cognitive psychology. Yet the cognitive turn in language study, at least in Chomsky's hands, led to a similar sort of dissatisfaction with the notions of language and languages that many scholars of religion have expressed about their putative object(s) of study.

Further scrutiny of Chomsky's views here, though, will disclose how limited are the consolations of cognitivism for the semantic pessimism of interpreters of religion(s) and of many of their postmodern critics. Chomsky (1986: 20) attacks what he calls "externalized language," i.e., a notion of language as "a collection (or system) of actions and behaviors." He denies that penetrating explanatory theories in this domain will have much, if anything, to do with either externalized language or a commonsense conception of language, and he correctly insists that this failure of our best theories to square with commonsense is not unusual in science (1980: 90 and 1986: 15).

"So far," semantic pessimists might comment to themselves, "so good." But only "so far," for here is the rub. Chomsky certainly does *not* propose to abandon the concept "language" altogether. He (1986: 27) argues, instead, for what he calls "internalized language," which is "a structure in the mind." He advocates this conception of language (basically what he has generally referred to before as a speaker's "linguistic competence"), because of the role it plays in what aims to be successful scientific theorizing about this area of human mentality and action. He defends a notion of internalized language because of how it functions in a larger linguistic theory that has fruitful explanatory and predictive consequences. The gen-

---

[11] We cannot claim much success on this front, if a major invited address at the most recent meeting of the International Association for the History of Religions in Durban, South Africa (2000) that focused on comparisons between the contemporary study of religion and the work of Ferdinand de Saussure (who, after all, died in 1913) is any indication of the current state of the field's engagement with theorizing and research on language!

eral point Chomsky is making here that I want to emphasize is that a penetrating account of the cognitive mechanisms and processes (whatever their character) that are responsible for shaping and generating our linguistic output would constitute a solid foundation for beginning to make sense of concepts like 'language' and 'languages.'

Clearly, the *principal* worries of cognitive theorists (about whether the everyday use of the term "religion" will square with their accounts of the psychological underpinnings of the relevant patterns of thought and action) differ from the worries with that term (and the concept for which it stands) that trouble interpreters of religion, their postmodern critics, and religious devotees. However, the differences do *not* stop there. This is not a matter of people of different orientations coming to the same conclusion on grounds that only partially overlap, because *the conclusions on which they settle are not, in fact, the same*. Whether cognitive theorists are thoroughgoing semantic and explanatory reductionists, as Boyer (2001b) appears to be, or semantic holists and explanatory pluralists, like Lawson and myself (1990: 1–2 and chapter 6 and McCauley 1996), not only are they not out to discard the notion of religion altogether, they are also united on at least two additional fronts. First, they all insist that the success of explanatory theories in science should guide our semantic commitments, but, second and more important for my immediate purpose, their preoccupation with rendering their proposals testable requires that they elucidate as clearly as possible the *recurrent patterns* of individual and collective behavior their theories are out to address (Boyer 1994). As Pyysiäinen claims, "... it is possible to study the various recurrent similarities that go under the general name of 'religion,' without committing oneself to any a priori assumptions about the cohesiveness of the category of religion" (2001: 5). That we may be currently agnostic about the usefulness of 'religion' as a socio-cultural category does not preclude advancing suggestions about features that the socio-cultural patterns to be explained share.

It is, then, from healthy preoccupations with their theories' testability that cognitivists' interests in specifying necessary properties of those recurrent patterns spring. For reasons I outlined in the introductory section, attempts at characterizing these patterns, i.e., what—in the scholarly shorthand—we call "defining" them, are always tentative. Those definitions' improvement (or replacement) results from a never-ending negotiation between theoretical reflection and empirical research. Diligence at this process insures ongoing concern with these theories' testability, which, in turn, warrants further diligence. The two enterprises, viz., testing hypotheses empirically and improving our accounts of the semantics of the theoretically central terms, are mutually reinforcing. Neglect of these matters renders theories immune to an increasing range of potential empirical objections. Raising empirical objections in science presupposes theories that use terms precisely enough that we can ascertain those theories' empirical consequences. Concluding that we cannot even specify necessary conditions for religion and, therefore, abandoning any attempt to do so has not convinced anyone, including the semantically pessimistic interpreters of religion who have adopted this line of argument, to abstain from using the term "religion" and its cognates. Semantic pessimists may get to have and eat their cake, but it comes at what cognitivists regard as an unacceptable cost, viz., our ability to formulate empirically testable theories in this domain.

The antecedents of current cognitive proposals are not too difficult to sketch. At the turn of the last century, scholars were content to talk about *gods* as an earmark of religion. Ethnographers' findings about the diverse kinds of counter-intuitive agents to be found in the world's cultures and modern theologians' growing wariness about gods as persons encouraged scholars to employ less specific proposals about the necessary conditions for religion in terms of notions like the *holy*, the *sacred*, and the *supernatural*. Neither the vagueness of these notions nor the transparent theological agendas that motivated them recommended them to scientifically minded theorists. In part as a remedy for these liabilities, Melford Spiro (1966) proposed that all religions deal with *culturally postulated superhuman beings*. As we began to explore the cognitive foundations of ritual and the central role of agents in the representation of action, Lawson and I proposed amending Spiro's formulation, speaking, instead, about culturally postulated superhuman *agents*. Looking at how two different cognitive mechanisms, viz., an action representation system and a conceptual scheme containing religious representations, interacted to produce specific forms of ritual knowledge that religious participants typically possess was the principal inspiration for this modification (1990: 103).

All of these were improvements and at least the last two were directly motivated by a concern with developing empirically responsible theories, but Boyer provided what was, by far, the most important breakthrough. (After all, short of some metaphysical sleight of hand, cultures are not the sorts of things that are capable of postulating anything, as Lawson and I should have recognized.) Boyer advanced (e.g., 1994) the notion of the *counter-intuitiveness* of representations for characterizing what all religious ontologies have in common. And although the most arresting features of religion circulate around peculiar agents, their states of mind, and their actions, counter-intuitiveness constitutes a much more well designed analytical tool than these earlier formulations, since not only can it handle such agents, it can also account for the other oddities at the fringes of many religious ontologies that may not involve agency (such as plants that live forever).

Boyer has argued that religious ontologies are populated by entities that involve minimal variations on robust intuitive knowledge about ontological matters in a specific triple of domains (viz., physics, biology, and psychology) (Boyer 2001b and Boyer and Walker 2000). Religious representations remain only modestly counter-intuitive, because that enables them to approximate a cognitive optimum. Since they are *counter-intuitive* they grab our attention and are easy to recall. Since they are only *modestly* so, they leave the overwhelming majority of our intuitive knowledge about the relevant ontological categories intact, from which we are entitled to draw a vast array of inferences for free.[12] Consequently, we know how the ancestors think, because we know how agents think generally.

Of course, as I noted earlier, not all modestly counter-intuitive representations are religious representations. (Recall the Big Bad Wolf and Mighty Mouse's contrails.) But since the current semantic task is less ambitious, the fact that the notion of modest counter-intuitiveness can make sense of more than just religious representations is not a problem here. The goal is simply to supply some feature that all of the relevant patterns exhibit. The emerging operative hypothesis is that some involvement of modestly counter-intuitive representations is a necessary feature of religious phenomena. The crucial point is that this is not mere semantic legislation. Not only does it capture all of the paradigmatic cases, it captures them on the basis of systematic theory:

- that explains and predicts a wide array of their salient features,
- that seeks and possesses a good deal of consilience with the closely related sciences (as opposed to insulating itself from criticism via

---

[12] This is just what the far more radically counter-intuitive representations that science usually generates do not permit (McCauley 2000).

claims for disciplinary autonomy or for a subject matter that is *sui generis*), and
- that, thereby, promises to generate new insights about the phenomena in question, which constitute bases for formulating new empirical and experimental tests.

The excellence of counter-intuitiveness as an analytical tool, then, resides in its scientific motivation and, more specifically, in its impeccable cognitive credentials. Boyer has neatly articulated an account of the underlying mechanisms of the human mind that are reliably implicated in the patterns of thought and action that constitute the targeted recurring phenomena, whatever the fate of religion and religions as socio-cultural phenomena (see Pyysiäinen 2001: ix). As a result of these mechanisms, all of the patterns cognitive theories are out to address inevitably involve counter-intuitive representations. That those theories provide a strategically unified set of explanations for these patterns, that the phenomena which these patterns encompass constitute virtually all uncontroversial cases of religious phenomena, and that those uncontroversial cases stretch across both cultures and times redounds not only to their benefit but to the benefit of the characterization they offer of religion.

The final premise of this last argument points to another pivotal advantage of this account. If all normal human beings do, in fact, find themselves equipped early on with the mental dispositions on which cognitive theories focus, then both the testimony of ethnographers and historians about the pervasiveness of religion and what we know about the ease with which these mechanisms can be exploited suggest that all humans will inevitably generate counter-intuitive representations. This enables us to gain a glimpse, at least, of the *possibility* of formulating a (psychologically motivated) concept of religion that is *comparatively* uncontaminated by either ethnocentrism or anachronism.

Are Rube Goldberg Mechanisms Really Mechanisms?

Merely glimpsed or fully formulated, does such a psychologically motivated concept of religion entitle us to reintroduce talk into *social* science (as opposed to psychological science) about religion and religions as socio-cultural realities? Boyer and Pyysiäinen seem to think not. For example, Pyysiäinen (2001: 2) argues: "A general theory of religion would require that there exists a separate class of religious phenomena that can be explained by a set of distinct laws. This is not the case if religious representations are actually produced by cognitive mechanisms that also produce non-religious representations." He draws his negative conclusion from two premises. The first is that to establish the credentials of 'religion' and 'religions' within social science requires developing a theory that is useful and testable and that employs these concepts essentially. However, the second is that we should not expect the development of such a theory. He argues for that premise on the ground that the assumption cognitive theories share, viz., that religion, from a cognitive standpoint, is a collection of beliefs and behaviors that arise from a hodgepodge of psychological dispositions responsible for many other kinds of counter-intuitive representations, suggests that such a theory is unlikely.

These observations may suggest it, but it does not guarantee it. Three considerations come to mind. First, thoroughgoing explanatory and semantic reductionism offers a misleading picture of science. The viability of inquiries at higher levels of analysis in science does not depend upon their theories mapping neatly on to those that dominate research at lower levels. Consilience is one of the most important of the scientific virtues. But it, nonetheless, constitutes but one constraint in what is certainly a *multiple* constraint satisfaction problem, viz., finding the best configuration among a host of virtues (and vices) for the purpose of deciding among available, competing theories. If social scientists can formulate theories by virtue of which we are able to identify, explain, and predict systematic patterns among socio-cultural phenomena, then nothing about the disunity of their underlying psychological infrastructures is likely to dislodge them. Theories about the behaviors of markets and mobs probably qualify. The power of our pre-theoretic intuitions to the contrary notwithstanding, current social scientific proposals about languages and religions, admittedly, do present much closer calls.

Second, this story about cross-scientific relations also has a straightforwardly positive side. Instead of imposing rigid constraints on upper level theories, research at lower levels of analysis (e.g., the psychological) provides opportunities and resources for inquiries at higher levels (e.g., the socio-cultural) (McCauley and Bechtel 2001). As I outlined in the previous section, cognitive theories have already made good headway in supporting the counter-intuitiveness of representations as a necessary condition for religious phenomena. This provides social scientists interested in theorizing about religion direction about which patterns probably deserve the greatest attention. Prima facie, events centered around groups of individuals' willingness to call themselves "Free Methodists" or "Roman Catholics" or "Kivung" probably do, whereas these social scientists should probably devote less attention to Fourth of July celebrations, Republican conventions, Teamsters' strikes, and Steeler games.

Finally, I have, in effect, argued that testing scientific theories empirically is critical to the process of ascertaining plausible necessary conditions for the phenomena the theories are out to explain. By itself, though, the counter-intuitiveness of representations is an extremely weak condition on the "religious," since so many other sorts of representations—from those in cartoons to those in science— also fit the bill. But noting *that* fact need not stymie subsequent theorizing. Rather it is a provocation to formulate proposals about additional necessary conditions for something to count as religious,[13] which, in turn, will stimulate further empirical research. To repeat, these moments in scientific inquiry are mutually reinforcing.[14]

For nearly three decades, no one has done more than Tom Lawson to foster this process within the study of religion. Nor has anyone had a clearer view of its pivotal importance for making progress in that field.[15]

---

[13] By the end of his book, Pyysiäinen has, admirably, done just that, conjecturing that religious representations can be distinguished from other counter-intuitive representations by virtue of the fact that they also are simultaneously organized around agent-representations in particular, taken to be literally true (the cavils of theologians, notwithstanding), and employed similarly across populations in issues of "life management" (Pyysiäinen 2001: 71, 227–28, and 235–36).

[14] Contrast Pyysiäinen's comment at the opening of *How Religion Works*: "There is no scientific theory of religion as a whole ... 'religion' is not a scientific, explanatory category, but merely a heuristic device, used by scholars to lump together phenomena that seem to have some kind of family-resemblance" (2001: 1). I think that trying to draw any strong distinction between "scientific, explanatory" categories and heuristic devices (in this sense) is forlorn. I strongly prefer the philosophy of science Pyysiäinen lays out in the final pages of his book (see especially, 233–34) and in his subsequent paper (Pyysiäinen, 2002: 112) to that with which he opens *How Religion Works*.

[15] For this, and so much else, we are all indebted to Tom. Of course, the list of my debts to him stretch much further. In short, I am profoundly grateful to him as my teacher, as my collaborator, but, most of all, as my friend.

3. WHY DO WE NEED COGNITIVE THEORIES OF RELIGION?

Harvey Whitehouse

Scores of different schools of thought have claimed to explain religion. And thousands of scholars have contributed to the ensuing debates using evidence from such diverse sources as history, archaeology, theology, sociology, ethnography, philosophy, and even astronomy and mathematics. E. Thomas Lawson, whom this volume honors, is widely and justly credited with being among the first to recognize the importance of developing a cognitive approach to the understanding of religion. But what reasons do we have for supposing that yet another set of theories will really help?

The short answer is that a great many existing theories of religion are ontologically flawed or untestable (and, in some cases, both). During the second half of the twentieth century, a drift towards hermeneutic and phenomenological approaches to the study of culture has led to declining interest in explaining religion at all. In overcoming many of these problems, the cognitive sciences offer a radically new way forward. I will argue that social/cultural anthropology, as a branch of these new sciences, is uniquely positioned to supply crucial sources of data for the development of explanatory theories of religion and could make crucial contributions to cross-disciplinary collaboration. But first, certain problems need to be overcome.

The Problem of Faulty Ontology

Thoughts and feelings consist of processes occurring in people's nervous systems, whether or not these are influenced by events in their immediate environments. Attention, perception, language, memory, dreaming, introspection, inference, empathy—in fact, every aspect of human experience and mentation is reducible in principle to organic processes and the developmental histories that shape them. The extraordinarily complex neural computations through which these effects are generated did not appear mysteriously overnight. They came into being through processes of evolution, shaped in part by principles of natural selection. Although we are very far from having the full story of how these processes unfolded, it is now possible to grasp many of the general mechanisms involved and to piece together some of the chronology. In all likelihood, we will know a lot more about neural evolution through future scientific advances. But even now it is reasonable to assume that all the complex things that go on inside human beings and in the world around them have material causes, and that ideas about cultural "forces" are part of what needs to be explained, not part of the explanation.

Because of our evolved cognitive architecture, humans everywhere are inclined to *reify* patterns of culture and social interaction, turning them into objects or even agentive forces with causal efficacy. It seems perfectly sensible to say, for instance, that most English children know the story of Goldilocks—as if "the story" has some kind of existence that is external to the children who come to know it. It is a small step from this to thinking of cultural phenomena as agent-like—imagining, for instance, that trade unions sometimes try to "bring down" governments or that terrorism can "threaten" national security. Such ideas are undoubtedly useful as a way of schematizing the complexity of the world around us, the better to determine our own responses to it, but the ontology they imply imposes heavy costs on a scientific understanding of culture and society. As Plotkin succinctly puts it (2001: 94):

> Because culture ... is some kind of complex interlocking organization of many minds, it is the most complicated thing in the known universe. Nonetheless, culture ... is not some kind of untouchable nonphysical essence that fills the spaces between people making up a society. Culture is what happens in people's minds when they interact in certain ways with other minds and with the artifacts that are often central to those interactions.

It follows that a story is not a "thing" even when it is written down and stored in a book (which *is*, of course, a thing). Rather, a well-known story consists of numerous recognizably similar narratives "stored" in the minds of those who know it. Even if a story is based upon a single written text, faithfully reproduced in millions of copies distributed around the world, the story itself does not exist in the patterns of ink on the pages of such books but only in the minds of readers capable of interpreting these patterns. As such, the story has no single instantiation but literally millions (all recognizably similar but almost never identical).[1] By the same token, national security is not really something that can be "threatened." True, terrorists can pose a very real threat to human life, and *people* can *feel* threatened (whether the perceived dangers are actually present or not), but as soon as we try to think about the distributed effects of terrorist actions, we run the risk of conflating the metaphorical and the literal. It is not just "ordinary" people who typically find this point rather hard to grasp, it has also proved a stumbling block for many professional social theorists.

Few would dispute that Emile Durkheim had a great and enduring impact on the sociology (and anthropology) of religion, and on the study of society and culture more generally. Durkheim was a highly original thinker. He was also a skilful teacher, blessed with a coterie of brilliant students, many of whom became great scholars in their own right. But Durkheim's work (e.g., 1933 [1893], 1964a [1896], 1964b [1915]) was tarnished by his deliberate reification of society. Although there is much to be salvaged from Durkheim's scholarship, the most unproductive thread running though the entire corpus was his insistence on the presence of an order of reality (a set of "social facts") somehow hovering above the heads of individuals. Rather than supposing that this "reality" was only a fiction, upon which the additional fictions of religion were at least partially constructed, Durkheim was preoccupied with showing that the fictions of religion were really a kind of highly coded discourse about something real (a society, greater than the sum of its parts). Unfortunately, this unnecessary, and fundamentally misleading, aspect of Durkheim's sociology of religion proved to be one of the most influential.

Nowhere has Durkheim's faulty ontology been more faithfully reproduced and extended than in the tradition of social thought known as "structural functionalism," which dominated social anthropology for several decades.[2] The central thesis of structural functionalism was that every social institution had the function of reinforcing

---

[1] Dan Sperber has done more than perhaps any other scholar in exposing both the problems of and solutions to sociocultural reification (e.g. see Sperber 1996a).

[2] The development and proliferation of Durkheim's faulty ontology was not an entirely straightforward matter, however. Malinowski, for instance, was an arch empiricist, whose theory of "primary functions" (1944) was explicitly driven by the desire to link cultural abstractions to concrete biological needs. Malinowski sensed the ontological confusion behind Durkheim's rhetoric and repeatedly opposed himself

certain other social institutions, thereby ensuring the stable reproduction of the society over time. This functionalist reasoning pervaded the work of some of the discipline's most brilliant practitioners: Gregory Bateson (1936), Evans-Pritchard (1940), Raymond Firth (1964), Meyer Fortes (1945), Mary Douglas (1970 [1966]), Victor Turner (1957), Max Gluckman (1963), Fredrik Barth (1964)—to name but a few. Most of these scholars also lived long enough to get caught up in the tide of anti-functionalist rhetoric that engulfed social and cultural anthropology from the early 1970s, and tried to reformulate their perspectives. The fact that institutions sometimes seemed to conflict with the conditions of reproduction of many others, and that societies seldom achieved conditions of stasis, presented a problem for functionalism. The problem was not a crippling one, however, and cannot account adequately for the more or less unanimous abandonment of functionalist reasoning. A more important factor was probably the shift from explanatory to hermeneutic models of culture. Unfortunately, these "new" perspectives often retained vestiges of the faulty ontology that had plagued structural functionalism from the outset.

An obvious example would be the interpretivist approach, championed by Clifford Geertz, which re-cast Durkheim's "social facts" as "public meanings." According to Strauss and Quinn (1997: Chapter Two), Geertz used the word "meaning" in at least three different senses and he likewise alluded to the "publicness" of meaning in a

---

to it. Nevertheless, according to Leach (1957: 136): "despite his advocacy of empiricism, Malinowski was really searching all the time for concepts of the middle range of generality... Culture is too abstract; the individual is too concrete." In the end, Malinowski's concept of primary functions proved to be a failed compromise. What Malinowski called "the principles of social organisation, of legal constitution, of economics and religion" (1935: 317) were no more readily observable or "concrete" by virtue of being linked to the satisfaction of physiological requirements. Moreover, the theory now became enmeshed in tautology: if social institutions persist, they must be satisfying biological needs and, therefore, all enduring cultural arrangements are functional (in virtue of satisfying biological needs). Partly for these reasons, the notion of primary functions had limited influence in the development of social/cultural anthropology. By contrast, Malinowski's concept of "secondary functions," which held that the function of institutions was the role they played in the reproduction of other institutions, had a much more enduring impact. This kind of functionalism, notwithstanding various attempts to "concretize" its claims in the thoughts and actions of individuals (e.g. Firth's 1964 distinction between "social organization" and "social structure"), harbored and at times exacerbated the faulty ontology pervading Durkheim's work.

number of different ways. Geertz's rhetoric against psychological views of culture, in which meanings are understood to be outcomes of interior processing, slipped between these varied concepts of meaning-as-public in ways that were often far from transparent. Nevertheless, there are several passages in Geertz's work, some of them very well known, where it is easy to pin him down. Consider, for instance, the following lines from his celebrated article on "thick description" (1973: 10):

> Culture, this acted document, thus is public, like a burlesqued wink or a mock sheep raid. Though ideational, it does not exist in someone's head; though unphysical, it is not an occult entity... The thing to ask about the burlesqued wink or a mock sheep raid is not what their ontological status is. It is the same as that of rocks on the one hand and dreams on the other—they are things of this world.

Here, Geertz's faulty ontology could not be clearer. For him, culture is an abstract, non-physical structure that exists *outside of people's heads*. Where it exists, however, must be a mystery, however strongly Geertz protests. As Strauss and Quinn rightly ask: "If culture (a pattern of meaning) is 'unphysical,' how can it have the same ontological status as a rock or a mock sheep raid?" (1997: 19).

Thus, the decline of structural functionalism was not necessarily accompanied by an accurate and widely accepted diagnosis of its ills, less still by appropriate methods of treatment. The real problem with functionalist theories was neither that some institutions were dysfunctional (or functionally neutral), nor that societies change. No theory should be expected to account for everything—and if only some patterns of functional integration could be identified in a given society that would have been an important insight, well worth preserving. The real defect of structural functionalism was its inability to explain how functional integration came about, and this was largely due to the poor ontological foundations of the approach. A religious dogma cannot help to bolster a system of inheritance in any meaningful sense, because dogmas and relations of descent are not exterior to mentation, but rather they are more or less convergent constructs that somehow manage to be recalled or (re-)constructed by human minds. Even this is a loose way of talking but it is a better starting point. Unless we accept that religious dogmas and relations based on common descent are located *in minds*, not in the spaces around or above them, we cannot hope to explain how relations of functional integration (or social conflict and transformation) could come into being, for instance via processes of distributed cognition. But if we are to succeed, we require some very precise, logically tenable, and reliably testable models of mind. Psychological theories of religion have at least as illustrious a history as functionalist ones and, what is more, they get their basic ontology right. Unfortunately, many of them have been untestable and, in some cases, substantially tautological.

The Problem of Untestability

The second half of the nineteenth century saw a proliferation of highly ingenious theories of religion, establishing trajectories rather different from Durkheim's (although one can readily identify areas of common ground as well). One of these trajectories came to be known as the "intellectualist" perspective on religion, championed in particular by Max Müller (1889), Herbert Spencer (1876), Edward Tylor (1871), and James Frazer (1922). In different ways, all four of these scholars envisaged religion as a response to what they saw as a basic human need for an intellectual framework capable of resolving the great existential mysteries of life. For Müller, religion addressed the mystery of infinity, for Spencer and Tylor it responded to the mysteries of dreaming, intangibility, and duality, and for Frazer religion was a rather cunning response to the failure of magic. It is not necessary to devote space to a detailed summary of this scholarship (many excellent ones have already been published),[3] but only to note some of its main strengths and weaknesses. The greatest strength of the intellectualist approach was its insistence on the right kind of ontology—religion, it asserted, could be explained in terms of properties of the human psyche. The main drawback was that none of these scholars had a sound model of what the human psyche might be like. The strategy of nineteenth-century intellectualists was to try to imagine themselves in the position of ancient populations, as religious thinking first began to emerge. What, they asked themselves, would have struck *them* as puzzling about the world, as it presented itself through the mechanisms of a newly evolved self-consciousness? Malinowski later used the weaknesses of speculative historical recon-

---

[3] See, for instance, Morris 1987.

struction as a way of justifying his brand of functionalism. In a later and rather more devastating critique of the intellectualist project, Evans-Pritchard described its psychological method as roughly equivalent to asking the question "if I were a horse . . .?" (1965: Chapter Two). As well as poor standards of substantiation, however, there were problems of circularity in this nineteenth-century scholarship. Religions often do supply answers to certain aspects of human experience that might otherwise seem puzzling. But the presence of answers to existential questions in the form of religious theories does not necessarily imply some pre-existing need for them.

So fundamental and obvious did these flaws appear to subsequent generations of anthropologists that the most valuable aspect of this early scholarship was overlooked—namely, the realization that the right place to look for the origins and causes of religion must be in the minds that create (and continually recreate) it. Having missed this crucial point, social anthropology became preoccupied elsewhere. But another, potentially more promising line of reasoning lurked on the peripheries of the discipline. Its instigator was the founder of psychoanalytic psychology, Sigmund Freud.

Freud's (1938 [1913]) theory of religion turned on a rather startling hypothesis about the origins of the incest taboo. Freud argued that all male children experience a deep intra-psychic conflict between desire for exclusive possession of the mother and fear that this desire will be punished by the father. The normal outcome of this dilemma, he maintained, is complete repression of the sexual drives from around age five to adolescence. According to the hypothesis, repressed incestuous desires for the mother and patricidal fantasies towards the father, amount to a fundamental syndrome in male psychological development, which Freud labeled the "Oedipus Complex." The next step was to argue that this complex was the principal *cause* of religions everywhere.

In *Totem and Taboo*, Freud speculated that all human populations were originally organized into patriarchal families, from which boys were driven out by their fathers upon reaching maturity (each son thus being required to set up his own family independently). One day, however, a group of sons joined together in a successful plot to kill their father, whose corpse they then consumed. Later, the sons were racked with guilt, which they sought to assuage by establishing an incest prohibition. By proscribing incestuous desire for the mother, the sons hoped to prevent further acts of patricide.

Nevertheless, a sense of guilt at their heinous crime was passed down through the generations and came to form the foundation of all religious thought. According to Freud, all religions were (and are) founded on the guilt occasioned by this original Oedipal conflict. Using examples from a range of religious traditions, Freud pointed to evidence of symbolic expressions, both in ritual and religious narratives, of the primordial crimes of patricide, cannibalism, and incest. What is the consumption of the Eucharistic Host, Freud asked, other than the act of killing and eating God (i.e. the father figure)? Was not Adam's crime in the myth of Genesis a cannibalistic attack on the Almighty Father (symbolized by the forbidden fruit of the Tree of Life)? That this original sin involved the taking of a life seems to be confirmed by the fact that Christian redemption required the giving of a life on the part of the son, Jesus Christ.

Taken at one level, Freud's argument is as absurdly speculative as the historical reconstructions of the origins of religion advanced by nineteenth-century intellectuals. But Freud's argument does not have to be taken that way. It is not necessary to postulate an *actual* historical act of patricide (as did Freud)[4] but merely to suppose that each new generation of male children commits this terrible crime, not in reality but in fantasy.

Freud's general theory achieved some influence among anthropologists of religion, particularly after disillusionment with functionalism had set in. Meyer Fortes, originally one of the most talented exponents of structural functionalism, was drawn increasingly to psychoanalytic interpretations of religion in later life (e.g. 1980). Barth (1987), LaBarre (1970), Leach (1958), Obeyesekere (1981), Spiro (1965), Turner (1967), and many other luminaries likewise borrowed from Freud in their attempts to explain a diversity of religious practices and beliefs. This was laudable, insofar as it was at least partly motivated by a desire to adopt the right kind of ontological stance. All these scholars had come to appreciate, at least for the purposes of certain problems of explanation, that the organization of minds played a role in the shaping of mental outputs (of which culture is constituted). Unfortunately, however, psychoanalytic psychology, even in its most advanced and recent incarnations, typically exhibits major problems of circularity and untestability.

---

[4] This is made clear in Freud's corresponence with Kroeber, to which the latter alluded in his review of *Totem and Taboo*.

In essence, Freud's claim was that people are driven by mostly dark and dangerous fantasies, of which they are not aware. There is nothing exceptional or even implausible about this claim, in principle: it is obvious that much of what goes on in people's minds is not conscious. The problem is how to determine whether this unconscious content is as Freud imagined it. But most Freudians do not try to *test* their beliefs about the unconscious. On the contrary, they assume that these beliefs are correct and interpret everything they see accordingly. When patients challenge the interpretations of their Freudian analysts, this is seen as repression; when they *agree* with their analysts, this is upheld as evidence that the theory is *correct*, because they have now obtained some conscious awareness of content that *used to be unconscious*. An insightful investigation into the circularity and untestability of this strategy is presented by Ernest Gellner in his erudite treatise *The Psychoanalytic Movement*. As Gellner puts it (1985: 156–7):

> The idea that certain types of infancy experiences lead to certain types of adult personality, is testable if either of the two domains (early experiences or adult personalities) is subdivided, with some reasonable degree of precision and above all of *independence*, into sub-categories. Then, *and only then*, can one say that there is some kind of functional relation, as specified in the theory, linking members of the one domain to those of the other. In fact, of course, the sub-categorization in either domain is (1) extremely loose and wooly, and (2) entirely under the control of that very theory which is to be tested, i.e. imposed on the material by it and by the privileged practitioners/operators of the theory and of its therapeutic associated practices.

When structural functionalism fell into decline, anthropologists of religion were inclined to try out all kinds of alternative perspectives. Psychoanalysis only turned the heads of a minority of scholars, and at least in part because of the drawbacks I have indicated. Marxism, however, also won some influential converts.

Marx's theories of technological and economic determinism[5] had some obvious appeals for those with a taste for scientific explanations of human history. As a student I fell under its spell, like many others. Social formations and transformations, it seemed, could be

---

[5] A particularly succinct summary of these theories is provided by McMurtry 1978: Chapters 7 and 8.

explained in terms of material causes (forces and relations of production) which determined the content of religion, political organization, ideology, legal institutions—indeed, the whole of culture—on principles of selection. The independent variable driving selection appeared to be levels of technological advancement and the stage of development of the production relations. Everything hinged, of course, on being able to distinguish forces and relations of production and, then, to separate both (as causes) from the legal/political/religious/ideological superstructure (as effects). This is where, for me, the theory turned out to be disappointing. Once again, the problem was one of circularity.

What are "relations of production" if not relations of ownership? And what are relations of ownership if not legal/political/religious/ideological constructs? How can the one be said to cause the other if they are really just one and the same set of representations? The longer I struggled with dense and jargon-ridden Marxist literature, the less confident I became that there might be plausible answers to these fundamental questions. To argue that production relations concern distributions of powers whereas legal relations concern distributions of rights, seemed to me the ultimate tautology, since in all practical circumstances the latter were merely a (substantial) subset of the former. Moreover, the central argument of Marxism, that the plough (economic infrastructure) is mightier than the sword (political superstructure) seemed to founder on the fact that both ploughs and swords are items of technology and that the different relations of persons to these forces of production and coercion are quintessentially political/jural relations. In order for patterns of exploitation to be reproduced, clearly certain kinds of ideas (including religious ideas) had to be selected, in preference to ones that would be non-compliant with those production relations. But historical materialism could not explain *how* these compliant forms were selected—beyond tautological claims about economic determinism and vague murmurings about the supervisory prominence of the ruling class in the organs of cultural dissemination. Conspiracy theory at least had the merit of allowing individual agency into the picture—but only at the cost of obvious and gross oversimplification of processes of cultural transmission.

In some revealing autobiographical passages, Karl Popper has described a similar experience of disappointment with psychoanalytic and Marxian movements (except that, with regard to the former, it was Alfred Adler rather than Sigmund Freud who directly impinged upon Popper's formative milieu). He wrote:

> My friends who were admirers of Marx, Freud, and Adler, were impressed by a number of points common to all their theories, and especially by their apparent *explanatory* power. These theories ... seemed to have an effect of intellectual conversion or revelation, opening your eyes to a new truth hidden from those not yet initiated. Once your eyes were thus opened you saw confirming instances everywhere: the world was full of *verifications* of the theory. Whatever happened always confirmed it ... It was precisely this fact—that they always fitted, that they were always confirmed—which in the eyes of their admirers constituted the strongest argument in favour of these theories. It began to dawn on me that this apparent strength was in fact their weakness (1963: 34–5, emphases in original).

The Problem of the Hermeneutic Vortex

The decline of structural functionalism was accompanied by the resurrection or invention of a wide range of 'isms.' Some of these, as suggested above, were ontologically flawed and/or untestable, but those that really gained a lasting grip (and remain in the ascendant today) exhibited an even more sinister trait, in the form of an avowed antipathy towards explanation in general, and the principles and methods of the natural sciences in particular. Why was this?

In a penetrating assessment of much contemporary academic research on religion, Lawson and McCauley (1993) attribute the growth of anti-scientific prejudices in anthropology to a crisis of conscience. Over the last two decades in particular, anthropologists have paid increasingly close attention to evidence of collusion between ethnographic research, at least in its early stages of development, and colonial imperialist projects. In the guise of scientific enquiry, anthropologists had (often unwittingly) sharpened the tools of colonial oppression, by providing valuable intelligence on subject populations and on the likely effectiveness or otherwise of alternative methods of imposing external control. From the 1970s onwards, scholars increasingly favored a new "hermeneutic" approach, emphasizing core values of humanism and relativism, directed towards the "understanding" (translation and interpretation) of culture, rather than the production of generalizing and falsifiable theories that might (in the wrong hands) be used to strengthen hegemonic control of relatively deprived or disempowered populations. In short, many anthropologists have sought redemption for the sins of their ancestors by sacrificing science on the altar of hermeneutics.

According to Lawson and McCauley, this hermeneutic turn has now established itself as a kind of "vortex," sucking in all those whose consciences are (rightly) pricked by the historical contributions of early anthropology to processes of political domination and economic exploitation. But they are at pains to point out that the anti-scientific rhetoric of this new generation of scholars[6] was, and is, entirely unnecessary. We all agree that precise, well-substantiated theories can be used immorally. And we probably also share a common understanding of what constitutes an immoral use of such knowledge. What seems utterly baffling is that argument that, in order to avoid the misuse of high quality information, we should instead produce information of a lower quality. Or (as is more typically proposed, if only implicitly, by the hermeneutic camp), we should produce information of *indeterminate* quality (see Lawson and McCauley 1993: 205–6).

The situation, however, is both worse and better than Lawson and McCauley suggest, at least in the case of anthropology. It is worse insofar as the hermeneutic vortex probably derives much of its current appeal from sources rather less noble than a crisis of conscience with regard to colonial oppression. It is better in that the vortex in question may be more a matter of rhetoric than a reliable guide to anthropological practice. The latter issue is discussed in the next section. The former, however, requires some swift clarification.

Why is a sense of guilt insufficient to account for the widespread anti-scientific rhetoric in anthropology? The answer is implicit in Lawson and McCauley's observation that "the connection between scientific aspirations for anthropological research and collusion with imperialism is not a necessary one" (1993: 204). Are we really to believe that our hermeneutic friends could have failed to spot this? To have exercised so much ingenuity in the propagation of such an implausible position suggests the presence of other motivations. In pondering why so many contemporary anthropologists reject the "science" label, David Shankland (2001) identifies a number of possible factors, among which the "crisis-of-conscience rationale" is not even mentioned:

---

[6] They mention in particular Geertz (1973) and Clifford and Marcus (1986).

I have not conducted a systematic survey, but it seems that most friends and colleagues object to various aspects of the epithet ["anthropology as science"]: that it implies a dedication to numerical analysis; that it is based on the inherently implausible premise that the world can be analysed from a value-free viewpoint; that is encroaches upon the personal freedom to explore a sense of self in interaction with other human beings, a freedom that lies at the heart of the discipline; that it implies a sense of certainty that can never be assured, given the tools at our disposal.

Noting that these misgivings are seldom informed by an understanding of what real-world sciences are all about, Shankland proceeds to argue that such attitudes are not really reflected either in the principal concerns and activities of most anthropologists. So we are forced back to the question: why does this anti-scientific rhetoric exist at all? Part of the answer may lie in general principles of coalition-formation.

Anthropologists, like the members of many other academic disciplines, are organized into corporate groups, recruitment to which is based on a combination of successful initiation (culminating in the award to PhD degrees) and notionally open competition among initiated applicants for somewhat scarce university posts. These corporate groups are usually called "departments" (sometimes also "schools" or "institutes"). Cognate subjects, divided into departments at the same organizational level, together form larger units, usually known in the UK as "faculties," directly managed by "deans." These corporate groups are in competition for scarce financial resources. Faculties compete with other faculties for central university funds. Departments in the same faculty compete with each other for students (of graded value) and shares of other resources controlled (at least to some extent) by deans. Departments have other sources of income, however, including government research grants and (at present in the UK) special rewards based on points scored in a government-sponsored competition known as the "RAE" (Research Assessment Exercise). Although competition in the RAE is among departments in the same subject area, it is more generally the case that anthropologists are in competition with non-anthropologists, either at the level of departments or at the national level. The reason is that the most valuable resources of all (in monetary terms) are students, followed by forms of research income for which competition is encouraged across disciplines. Anthropologists formulate strategies, at the level of departments and also nationally though professional organizations, to advance their interests *as a subject area* in this competitive setting. My impression is that, although the UK system has many peculiar features of its own, this general pattern is much the same all around the world.

In such a political climate, loyalty to one's own discipline is a matter of considerable importance. Cheating or defection, on the part of colleagues, can have serious material consequences for the group, which are on the whole explicitly recognized. But even if that were not the case, the very fact of being organized into professional guilds (academic departments and professional associations), meeting at the same conferences, reading and contributing to the same journals, ostensibly sharing the same creed (e.g. Relativism Is Right, Ethnocentricism Is Wrong, etc.), and tracing descent from the same intellectual ancestors, is more than enough to engender a sense of in-group versus out-group. In short, members of the in-group (social and cultural anthropologists) implicitly (and sometimes explicitly) are concerned to protect the integrity of their discipline against corruption or invasion/colonization by out-groups (including the cognitive sciences). What evidence is there of such a concern and how is it expressed?

Among social and cultural anthropologists, whether in informal conversations, seminars, or published work, it is quite common for the term "reductionism" to be used as an insult (or at least to indicate a negative evaluation of the argument advanced). On the face of it, this is rather odd because reductionist strategies hold out considerably more promise in explaining sociocultural phenomena than do non-reductive strategies. A negative attitude towards reductionism is, of course, consistent with the sort of faulty ontology discussed earlier. According to this ontology, social and cultural phenomena have nothing to do with individual mentation, and are irreducible to it. But the crucial question still remains: why would anybody believe that?

One possible answer is that at least some anthropologists, with varying degrees of conscious awareness, are concerned that the reduction of cultural phenomena to psychological processes would threaten the integrity of their discipline—in the worst possible scenario perhaps relegating it to a rather insignificant and under-funded branch of psychology. At professional lectures and seminars I have witnessed scenes in which anthropologists who employ arguments developed in evolutionary psychology have been accused of being agents of an imperialistic cognitive science. Judging by the murmurings of assent to this view, particularly in post-conference chit-chat, such accusations are quite widely and readily endorsed.

Cross-disciplinary discussions about "human nature" provide an excellent opportunity to observe the fears and biases of anthropologists on this score. The question "what is human nature?" tends to draw a neat line between social/cultural anthropologists and the rest of the world. The former camp will usually tell you, often in ways that are hard to decipher or pin down (more about that shortly), that human nature is culturally constructed. Even those who allow some nativist assumptions to creep in, will still insist that what makes us human is mostly fashioned in radically different ways at different times and places, and thus is culturally relative. Non-anthropologists (e.g. various types of biologists, archaeologists, psychologists, and so on) will typically argue that the nature-nurture debate is now defunct and that, although there are many recurrent features of human cognitive architecture, these are outcomes of a complex combination of genetic and developmental/environmental conditions. The two camps will talk past each other and most participants will go away in a state of bewilderment and frustration. Many of the anthropologists will be reassured that they have done their bit to repel the invaders. The "invaders" will not understand that they are seen as invaders, will wonder how they managed to cause offence, and will probably make a mental note to avoid debates with anthropologists in the future.

As well as struggling to preserve a distinctive subject matter, anthropologists often display proprietary attachments to their research methodology, and many resist contamination or borrowing from other research areas. Quantitative (especially advanced statistical) methods are still quite sparingly used in the discipline, and the emphasis is on long-term, qualitative research using participant observation and interviews as the primary techniques of data-collection. A significant consequence of this approach is that the ethnographer's vision is saturated by the complexity and muddle of social life. To tackle *any* topic without some lengthy pontification on issues of gender, colonization, globalization, alterity, nationalism, and so on would be a serious *faux pas*. But the urge to cover all these different topics in the same breath, without attempting to discriminate (based on transparent evidence) the relative importance of each, is of dubious value. There are many occasions where this process of discrimination may be served in obvious ways by the use of quantitative data. Often, such data are not collected at all. At least part of the reason, I suggest, boils down once again to protectionist urges within the professional guild.

Consider first the fact that, although anthropologists proclaim the superiority of their research methods over those of quantitative social research, very few would seem to relish the opportunity to teach courses on participant observation or interview techniques (although many do so with varying degrees of reluctance). Many anthropologists avow that ethnographic research is mainly a matter of common sense and does not warrant the sort of close scrutiny demanded by the unenlightened bureaucrats who fund our fieldwork projects and the training of our doctoral students. This lack of interest in methods cannot be because we believe them to have been perfected, beyond improvement. The problem of how to gather information about the mental processes of other people, in terms consistent with the vast corpus of knowledge available from related "real world sciences," has been grossly under-investigated. If anthropologists really prized their research methods for other-than-rhetorical reasons, their efforts in both teaching and research would, I think, be allocated very differently.

Anthropological suspicions with regard to experimental methods are rationalized slightly differently. Such methods, it is often supposed, are potentially demeaning to participants (e.g. "tricking" them into delivering information that is not of their own choosing, or treating them as mere objects rather than as equals and collaborators). Many anthropologists are also inclined to assume that experimental approaches could not possibly identify all the relevant confounds and/or find ways of overcoming their effects. My impression, however, is that although such attitudes and assumptions can be widely and readily triggered among anthropologists they are seldom based on knowledge or experience of the methods in question. Again, we have to ask why and at least part of the answer might be the urge to preserve a distinctively anthropological methodology and to compete for research funding against disciplines that lack the techniques we claim as our own.

Consider now a second nexus of factors. In addition to a range of attitudes that seem to be aimed at defending the integrity and identity of the discipline, there are some rather distinctive aesthetics in social and cultural anthropology, which conflict with the methods and objectives of the natural sciences. Something needs to be said about that too, if we are to obtain a fuller understanding of anti-cognitivist prejudices. By the 'aesthetics' of the discipline, I really mean the principles (at times implicit, at others explicitly formulated) by which we judge scholarship to be "good" (e.g., richly-textured, nuanced, sophisticated, etc.) or "bad" (e.g., "naïve," "reductionist," "simplistic," etc.).

Among the principles that seem to be quite widely operative is a preference for literary flourish over clarity and precision. Non-anthropologists have often asked me why anthropologists seem to use such extravagant language and complex metaphors to convey what might be considered rather simple points. In small workshops, why do we insist on reading out (often rather pompous) prose when we could instead use overheads and informal illustrations? Why do many of us put so much store by jargon, and yet seem to resist defining it? The answer is partly that we value erudition and the arts of scholarly writing. Geertz's impact on us surely owes more to his exceptional eloquence, wit, and wide-ranging education than his theoretical and methodological ideas, which were at turns quite obscure, trivial, or simply mistaken. Much the same could be said of other heroes and luminaries. Above all, however, we like to be interpreters of what we read and hear. Opportunities to do that vary in inverse proportion to the clarity and precision of the work. The more ambiguous and uncertain the author's meaning, the less easy it is to dismiss and the more fertile it becomes as a trigger for one's own ideas. Taken to extremes in some postmodernist scholarship, this principle is the ally rather than the enemy of that most prized attribute of all in contemporary social and cultural anthropology: critical originality. To the extent that you can give the impression of saying something important and new, while saying as little as possible that could be directly tested, maximizing the possibility for others to cite (usually on principles of thematic association) what you may have said, your work is likely to be widely appreciated. More than once I have been offered the following genuinely friendly advice from internationally respected colleagues: "Harvey, the story you are trying to tell would be so much more interesting, to a wider range of your colleagues, if you could only manage to 'vague it up'." The term "vague it up" was only used once—in fact that is the only time I heard it uttered.

But the gist of this advice has been conveyed to me on several occasions. If I have applied that advice, however well meant, it has not been my intention to do so.

Another conspicuous symptom of the great store placed on literary flourish is that the anthropologists' texts are often treated as vastly more interesting than the concepts and practices of the people to whom these texts ostensibly refer. For instance, improbable comparisons are commonly made between concepts attributed to non-academic (and often non-literate) populations, on the one hand, and those adopted in essayist traditions of Western philosophy and literary criticism, on the other. Indeed, the more improbable such tropes, the more "original" and thus "interesting" they are likely to be considered. A good example of this attitude may be seen in the preoccupation of many anthropologists with the discovery (or more mystical "apprehension") of the meanings of their own terminology—as if this is likely to provide indispensable insights into the far-flung cultural representations they claim to be investigating. As Francisco Gil-White astutely observes (2001: 238):

> In anthropology it is customary to spill much ink trying to wrest control of the meaning of its terms of art from other anthropologists, as if defining a word were equivalent to providing an explanation or making an intellectual contribution. Many proceed as if the meaning of a word—itself apparently of profound importance—was something to be discovered through careful application of quasi-philosophical reflection, and the anthropologist was the professional whose task was to discover it.

I have suggested that anti-scientific prejudices among anthropologists are at least partly driven by protectionist urges within the professional coalition but that these prejudices are also consonant with a dominant aesthetic that values erudition, creative interpretation, and critical originality over precise empirical evidence and explanation. But, even if that is true, it still leaves important questions unanswered. Academic disciplines closely allied to anthropology also exhibit coalitional thinking and for much the same reasons, but not all of them reject the science label; on the whole, social/cultural anthropologists were at one time eager to portray themselves as scientists, but no longer. So what put anthropologists on a different trajectory from many of their neighbors and ancestors?

The "crisis of conscience" theory could well contain a lot of truth but it has its limitations. Archaeologists have ample reason to feel guilty over past collusions with colonial projects for the purposes of appropriating valuable artifacts. Their work also proceeds in circumstances of political contestation, often more acute than those faced by anthropologists. After all, the claims of several great religions and numerous political ideologies are potentially testable on the basis of archaeological data. Why, then, should a substantial sector of the archaeological coalition have sought to retain its identity as a science, rather than to adopt the same evasive tactics as its anthropological neighbors? The answer, perhaps, is that pricked consciences and the fear of generating potentially dangerous intelligence are not the main causes of hermeneutic escapism. The real core of the matter is this: the coalition of social/cultural anthropologists has had to face a much more serious threat than almost any other academic discipline in the post-colonial era, namely *the loss of its defining subject matter*.

Ethnography began as the study of "savages," rapidly re-described as "tribal" or "uncentralized" peoples and, later still, as "nonliterate" or "traditional" societies. But, when all is said and done, anthropology was definitively the study of *colonized peoples*. With hindsight, one might think it was foolish to build the identity of a discipline on such an historically transitory subject matter. But there it is. The *extraordinary defensiveness* of the coalition arises directly from *that extraordinary dilemma*. We are dealing with a coalition that really *has* had cause to fear dissolution, to fear being taken over by neighboring disciplines. And the greatest threat of all originally came from the real-world sciences. Why? Because disciplines like archaeology and psychology shared our most fundamental origins and aims, and provided the most relevant and commensurate principles of investigation. Anthropologists could no longer afford to identify themselves with that sector of the academy. As overwhelmingly middle class scholars, steeped in the aesthetics of the Western art cult, hermeneutics and its offshoots provided the obvious place to look for new identities. Now that the field of "cultural studies" has established itself as a major threat from *within* the place of sanctuary, it is of course hard for members of the anthropology coalition to decide where to turn next.

Much more could be said about all these problems and I readily concede that the above observations are anecdotal and impressionistic.[7] The extent to which they contain some truth may be judged

---

[7] Through informal discussions of this topic with anthropologist colleagues, I have

by others in the profession who have conducted participant observation among anthropologists for longer than I and, collectively, in a vastly greater range of circumstances. Moreover, two points should be added. First, even if my assessment is roughly accurate, anthropology is certainly not the only discipline to be constrained in its work by professional prejudices that both respond and contribute to the political contexts in which they operate. An honest appraisal of other fields (including the various branches of cognitive science) would undoubtedly discover comparable processes, unfolding in different ways. But it would be mistaken to infer from this that all knowledge gained through academic research is merely an expression of politically motivated maneuvers and the prevailing aesthetics of the profession. Research can certainly be of scientific importance, regardless of the political context that happened to spawn it. Second, and following from this, the research achievements of anthropology are very considerable. Although I have been focusing on shortcomings, I propose now to highlight what I see as the major contributions of the discipline, at least as far as the study of religion is concerned. In the process, I hope to show that the distinctive identity and long-term survival of the discipline (although a subsidiary concern here) is not only consistent with inter-disciplinary dialogue and collaboration, but can actually be served by that.

---

come across a number of alternative (though potentially compatible) diagnoses of the current penchant for obscurity in much contemporary scholarship within the discipline. Among the more pessimistic appraisals gathered was the view that anthropological institutions recruit self-selectively: "one could say that by all sorts of subtle cues, anthropology departments indicate that you have to like a certain vague, aesthetically-driven, associative style of thinking in order to join. Having recently gone through the files of more than 160 applicants for anthropology posts at my university, I can say that about five of them described their research as addressing questions that could be answered by considering relevant evidence according to a specific methodology. All the others said that they had studied x in the context of y (e.g. 'clubbing in Martinique in the context of global images of black masculinity') without saying why on earth one should consider that rather than anything else. The way my colleagues discussed the applications . . . never raised that question. What people discussed was whether the resulting associations were original (e.g. 'clubbing and black masculinity had been done before by someone else in Jamaica [that's bad] but this candidate did it by focusing on gay males with children [original = good] but I found the dissertation ponderous [bad] although he did have a lucid discussion of Foucault [good],' etc.)." As this informant went on to suggest (in keeping with the ethical requirements of such research his/her views are here anonymized): any critique of obscurity in contemporary anthropological thinking may prove pointless since people are seldom "reasoned out of" ideas they were never "reasoned into" in the first place.

Where Should We Look for a New Theory of Religion?

Of all the places we should look for tools, information, and guidance in explaining religion, social/cultural anthropology is probably one of the most important. In light of the foregoing criticisms of that area of research, how is such a claim to be justified? The first point to make is that, as noted earlier, the hermeneutic vortex is rather less powerful than one might suppose. Shankland (2001) suggests that those anthropologists who, at least until the middle of the last century, were quite comfortable with the science label, were actually doing much the same kind of field research as contemporary anthropologists:

> It is commonplace to claim to reject this earlier research as a paradigm for today's activity. However, what in fact has changed? Much less then might be supposed from the apparently sweeping rejection of the past. If Malinowski were to return and make a brisk tour around today's departments, he would be astonished, not at the differences, but at the substantial similarities with the research and fieldwork model that he proposed.

Thus, even if the rise of hermeneutics has made scientific theory building somewhat unfashionable, and to that extent has genuinely obstructed it, little has changed with regard to the empirically oriented methodologies of anthropologists. Shankland rightly points out some the disadvantages of this lack of fundamental change in approaches to field research (in particular the failure to develop more collaborative approaches to data-gathering) but the fact remains that no other discipline rivals anthropology's breadth of information on religious variation. Even if some of that information has been obscured by poor strategies of presentation and lack of theoretical substance, a huge volume of ethnographic data remains and will continue to grow, as the bedrock of anthropological knowledge. What is special about that knowledge is not only that it encompasses many populations on the margins of, and even entirely outside, the so-called world religions, but also that it is based on first-hand, intricately detailed experience.

Linked to this, my second point concerns the unique value of long-term qualitative research based on participant observation. Conducted in a systematic way, this kind of research is capable of generating a much richer picture of religious discourse and practice than even the most advanced techniques of archaeology and historiography, which after all have only physical remains and surviving documents as sources of information. But ethnographic research cannot tell us everything. We still need to know how the situations we observe came to be as they are, and so we need to work in partnership with historians and archaeologists. We also cannot rely exclusively on what people say to us, or even to each other, about their religious ideas and actions. If we are to learn about various forms of implicit learning and cognitive organization some openness to experimental techniques is indispensable. If we want to know how religious knowledge is remembered and transmitted, we should be free to borrow designs from psychological studies of recall in real-world (i.e., non-laboratory) settings. Our methodologies can be as eclectic as we like, without running the risk of polluting or replacing those upon which are discipline was originally founded.

Just as the knowledge obtained from participant observation can be enriched and extended by other sorts of data, so our capacity for obtaining and understanding those other data may depend on adequate qualitative research. Imagine what would happen if a cognitive psychologist, whose only experience of experimental research had been with American undergraduate participants, was then sent to run the same experiments in inner New Guinea. Unless this psychologist had first conducted a long period of something very like participant observation, it is almost certain that the experiments would be a disaster. Anthropological knowledge may be vital for the gathering or cultural/psychological data in all situations with which researchers are profoundly unfamiliar.

My third reason for stressing the importance of anthropological knowledge is simply that the discipline has recently spawned more than it fair share of instructive perspectives on religion. Important contributions have also undoubtedly come from archaeology (e.g., Steven Mithen 1996), comparative religion (e.g., Ilkka Pyysiäinen 2001), biology (e.g., Robert Hinde 1999), and philosophy (e.g., R.N. McCauley 2001). In some cases, collaboration between these disciplines has proven especially productive (e.g., Lawson and McCauley 1990, McCauley and Lawson 2002). But the list of scientific theories of religion advanced by social/cultural anthropologists is unrivalled by any other discipline. The works of Astuti (2001), Atran (2002), Bloch (1988), Boyer (1990, 2001a), D'Andrade (1995), Guthrie (1993), Sperber (1985, 1996a; Sperber and Wilson 1986), and Strauss and Quinn (1997), for instance, owe a profound debt to the cognitive sciences (of which they have come to form part) but the anthropological contributions *remain* distinctively anthropological. How is this to be squared with my earlier claim that the hermeneutic turn in anthropology has obstructed explanatory theories of religion?

The answer, I think, has to do with the dominant aesthetics of social and cultural anthropology. The preoccupation with critical originality has turned the discipline into a sort of intellectual red light district in which almost anything goes. To me, the squalid and depressing side to this is an overly permissive attitude towards obscurity and muddled argument. The more positive aspect to it is that anthropology seminars and conferences provide fairly safe places in which to test out really wild and imaginative ideas. Professional anthropologists seldom run the risk of destroying their reputations simply because they say a few mad things in public. When compared with the restrictive demands of more scientifically oriented neighboring disciplines, such as archaeology or psychology, one can readily see certain benefits of this. There are very few principles (apart from ordinary humanistic and liberal ones) that anthropological audiences insist upon, and no theories too sacred to challenge. The creed of relativism can be violated and even the crime of ethnocentricism (whether real or imagined) will be tolerated up to a point. Thus, to adopt a cognitivist stance may lead to unpopularity (I hope this will change), but anthropology is such a broad and tolerant church that it really does have space for everybody. This is not such a bad breeding ground for new theories, even scientific ones, as long as their creators are prepared to look for wider audiences. My point, then, is really that anthropology could have done much more (and can do more in the future) to encourage explanatory theories, by abandoning certain prejudices, out-growing its passion for obscurity, and still retaining its underlying culture of tolerance.

The other main place I think we should look in our quest for a new theory of religion is to the cognitive sciences. By that, I mean a loose conglomeration of research areas that includes cognitive anthropology (there *is* such a sub-field which, though quite small has a distinguished history), neuroscience, artificial intelligence, certain fields of linguistics, and cognitive psychology. The reason we should look there is simple. Culture (including religion) is an effect of mental activity, which arises through the interaction of people with their environments. There are, of course, aspects of the way our minds work that appear to be very much the same everywhere. Understanding these universal mechanisms holds out the promise of explaining how their activation might constrain and shape patterns of culture and social organization all around the world. The challenge is to bring together the knowledge of several disciplines. We need to understand the psychic unity of our species, but we also need to know as much as possible about the diversity of human culture and social morphology. This should be a process, not of academic invasion and colonization, but of alliance and collaboration.

4. CAN SCIENCE FABRICATE MEANING?
ON RITUAL, RELIGION, AND THE ACADEMIC
STUDY OF RELIGION[1]

DONALD WIEBE

Rappaport's recent *Ritual and Religion in the Making of Humanity* (1999; henceforth *Ritual and Religion*), in my judgment, is a book of special significance to those scholars in the field of Religious Studies engaged in the longstanding methodological dispute over the role of *theology*[2] in the *academic study of religion*.[3] An outsider to Religious Studies, and not, therefore, directly engaged in this dispute, Rappaport's project here nevertheless provides support for those who champion a role for *theology* in the field, and helps ground their claim that the discipline of Religious Studies is both scientific—and therefore academically legitimate and respectable—and a source of knowledge beyond that which can ever be provided by science alone. Rappaport's primary concern in *Ritual and Religion*, it is clear, is to provide a scientific

---

[1] It is a pleasure to have been invited to contribute to this festschrift in honor of Tom Lawson. Given Lawson's interests in the persistent methodological wrangling over the role of theology in the academic study of religion, and his critical interests in religious thought and ritual practice, Rappaport's work is of peculiar relevance to his overall project in the study of religion.
I wish to thank Ulla Lehtonen for her critical comments on an early draft of this paper presented, at her invitation, to a session on the work of Rappaport at the XVIIIth International Congress of the International Association for the History of Religions in Durban, South Africa (August, 2000), and for introducing me to Keith Hart by way of the discussion paper discussed there. I wish also to thank Keith Hart for his critical response to that early draft of this paper. Although he is still likely to disagree with the position I espouse here, and with the assumptions on which my critique of Rappaport stands, his comments have helped me clarify the argument in several places, and I am grateful to him for the time he devoted to that end.

[2] By "theology" here I do not refer merely to the discipline so named in seminaries and divinity schools but rather more broadly to a general religious or confessional orientation.

[3] By "academic study of religion" I mean to refer to that kind of study appropriate in the context of the modern Western research university which concedes the boundaries set by the ideal of scientific knowledge in that context (See Wiebe, 2000 and 2002).

account of religion—a self-consciously anthropological account that proceeds exclusively on the basis of naturalistic assumptions. And it appears from his unsystematic methodological remarks that for him science alone can provide us with *knowledge* about the world (in contrast to the truth or meaning of the world) and he consequently adopts an explanatory and theoretical approach, rather than an interpretive (hermeneutical) one, in his attempt to gain an understanding of how religion functions in nature. Such an approach, according to Rappaport, will reveal that the major conceptual and experiential constituents of religion—the sacred, the numinous, the occult, the divine, and the Holy—are the creations of ritual, and the task of the scientist (*qua* scientist), he insists, is to render an analysis of ritual's internal logic and its impact or relationship to an independently existing world.[4] As he puts it, his book can be read simply "as a treatise on the logical entailments, social consequences, and subjective effects of ritual participation" (407) in society. However, as the advertisement Rappaport provides on the first page of the book suggests,[5] his argument here can be "construed as in some degree religious as well as about religion" because he aims to show "that religion can and must be reconciled with science" (i). And even though Rappaport does not spend a great deal of time elaborating the religious character of his argument, it is implicit throughout the book and, in my judgment, dominates it, subordinating the import of his scientific work to his religious agenda.

Keith Hart's foreword to the book focuses attention on Rappaport's religious agenda in this work and appears to constitute a special kind of "preparation" of readers to assist them in understanding Rappaport's broader project in *Ritual and Religion*. According to Hart, Rappaport's

---

[4] Although Rappaport for the most part limits himself in this book to analyzing ritual's internal logic, it is clear that he does not think anthropology irrelevant to our functioning in the world, for his concerns go far beyond merely the search for knowledge. As he pointed out elsewhere, anthropology not only provides explanations of ritual and religion, but also of their impact upon or relationship to an independently existing world. Thus, as he argues in his "Epilogue, 1984" (1984) to *Pigs for the Ancestors* (1968), anthropology by its very existence contains or offers a critique of society. Insisting that criticism requires a theory of correction, he writes: "I believe that anthropology does have something to offer to the development of a theory or theories of correction. If this seems presumptuous or dangerous we should keep in mind that social policy is at present informed by views of the world, its ills, and ways to cure its ills provided by other disciplines no better founded and considerably less humane than our own" (431).

[5] Rappaport, it has been reported to me by Keith Hart, was responsible for the blurb that appeared on the very first page of the book.

underlying motivation in this work is to respond to the spiritual malaise of modern humanity created by science. Hart suggests that for Rappaport, as for Durkheim before him, "[s]cience appeared to have driven religion from the field as a serious intellectual ground for the organization of society..." (xiv) and that Rappaport recognizes that science can not in some substitute fashion perform the functions for society originally rendered by religion. Hart also claims that whereas Durkheim left this problem unaddressed, Rappaport does not. According to Hart, that is, Rappaport makes a contribution in this book to "future attempts to construct a religion compatible with the scientific laws ruling in a world for which humanity is ultimately responsible, as that part of life on this planet which is able to think" (xiv-xv). And he praises Rappaport's naturalistic account of ritual and religion both because it is science *and* because it attempts "to lay the groundwork for the development of a new religion adequate to the circumstances humanity will encounter in the twenty-first century" (xiv). For Rappaport, claims Hart, religion not only furnishes a connection between the self and an external force, but is also tied to science in its desire to know the world objectively, and to the arts in its desire for self-expression, and is, therefore, able to provide humankind both knowledge and meaning—or, better, meaningful knowledge—of the world (xv). An analysis of *Ritual and Religion*, I will show here, proves Hart's assessment of the import of Rappaport's work to be essentially correct. And if Rappaport's hybrid religio-scientific enterprise is also "academically credible" (i.e., intellectually justifiable), it is clear that a resolution to the methodological debate over the role of *theology* in Religious Studies will have been achieved in favor of those calling for a plurality of approaches to understanding religion that includes the *theological*. I shall argue here, however, that the proposed hybrid anthropological enterprise is not intellectually justifiable because it requires a "science" that, like religion, can, and ought to, fabricate meaning, and that "the meaning of the universe," although fabricated (both by religion and, apparently, by science), is not merely an illusion (fabrication) but something that can be known. In light of Rappaport's own scientific account of the role of "religion and ritual in the making of humanity," I will show that his hybrid enterprise is either incoherent or indistinguishable from religion itself.[6] Little by way of counter-argument,

---

[6] My account of Rappaport's work here will, I think, show that this major claim

I think, will be required for this because an account of Rappaport's claims—not only in *Ritual and Religion* but also in his other publications—about science and our general knowledge of the world, and an understanding of the views he holds about our scientific knowledge of ritual and religion will, I think, reveal irresolvable tensions that undermine the force of his implicit—religiously inspired—"religious argument" that he suggests justifies important to human adaptation and evolution in the world because the world, subject only to causal laws, is utterly devoid of intrinsic meaning. As he puts it, only the human species lives—and can only live—"in terms of meanings it must *construct* in a world devoid of intrinsic meaning but subject to physical law" (1, emphasis added). It is ritual, Rappaport further claims, that is central to the construction of meaning, and fundamental to the development of ritual is the human capacity for linguistic communication. "It is a major thesis of this book," he writes, "that it is in the nature of religion to fabricate the Word, the True Word upon which the truth of symbols and the convictions that they establish stand" (2). Not only is the world devoid of meaning, Rappaport points out, but the ability of members of human communities to lie poses a threat to social interaction by undermining the orderliness that depends upon reliable communication. "All social orders," he argues, "protect themselves, and must protect themselves in some degree, against the disordering power of the linguistically liberated imagination, and tolerance of alternatives is therefore limited in even the most liberal societies" (417). And it is in this regard that Rappaport maintains that religion has adaptive evolutionary significance for the human species (that is, with what he calls "sanctity" becoming a functional replacement for genetic determination of behavior [418]). "Religion," he writes, "has been the ground upon which human life has stood since humans first became humans, that is, since they first spoke words and sentences" because it was able, he repeats, to fabricate meanings "in a world devoid of intrinsic meaning" (406).[7] As I shall point out below, ritual and religion over-

---

is really a religious knowledge claim that lies beyond adjudication by the sciences and therefore undermines science. I draw that conclusion because transcending the boundaries of a particular discourse is in essence to abrogate those boundaries, which in turn, subordinates that discourse to a form of control by the meta-discourse by means of which the boundaries were transcended.

[7] In "Epilogue, 1984" Rappaport claims that trying to understand a species that

come the possibility of the lie by sanctifying a particular discourse which in turn creates a set of "convictions" that ground an invariant order of human community. Rappaport is aware that this characterization of his project sets up a "contradiction between the epistemology of discovery defining science and the ontology of meaning underlying the symbolic [ritual] aspect of the world..." (22), but nevertheless thinks their reconciliation is possible.

After providing a definition of ritual (as the social act that is basic to humanity because it is an enriched means of communication), Rappaport produces an ingenious and persuasive argument to show how the ritual event operates in a digital, rather than an analogical, fashion and "separates the before from the after with absolute clarity ... [thereby making itself] admirably suited to *impose* upon the continua of nature, generally, distinctions much sharper than nature's own" (96, emphasis added). Thus rituals, he argues, impose structures on their participants that obligate them to a particular form of life; rituals, that is, create conventions and invests them with a morality that constrains their lives. He asserts: "To perform a liturgy is at one and the same time to conform to its order and to realize it or make it substantial. *Liturgical performance not only recognizes the authority of the connections it represents, it gives them their very existence*" (125). "To summarize," he continues, "the existence of a conventional order is contingent upon its acceptance; in fact, a rule or understanding cannot be said to be a convention unless it is accepted. In ritual, however, acceptance and existence entail each other, for a liturgical order is perforce accepted in its realization, in, that is to say, the performance which gives it substance" (137). In subsequent elaboration on the claim that ritual acts communicate in a digital rather than analogical mode, Rappaport shows that this "naturalization" of convention actually happens "supernaturally": "It is entertaining to note," he writes, "that convention becomes part of nature by being accounted for supernaturally" (166). Establishing this claim begins

---

lives in terms of meanings in a universe devoid of meaning but constituted by natural law is the essential problematic of ecological anthropology "which not only describes the human condition but provides a set of supracultural criteria in terms of which human actions can be assessed" (402). His suggestion that "ecological anthropology" is therefore necessarily ideological, however, is not persuasive, for the reflective enterprise of assessing the adaptiveness of particular cultural understandings, conventions, and actions, as he puts it (402), is clearly distinguishable from the political enterprise of addressing contemporary problems.

with his discussion of "Time, Eternity, and Liturgical Order" (chapter 6) where he demonstrates how liturgical orders construct the temporal orders of mundane society by overriding the idiosyncratic and unreliable nature of the human sense of the passage of time, which, he maintains, "provide[s] a well-marked road along which each individual's temporal experience can travel" (177). Continuing this line of thought Rappaport then demonstrates how community is a ritually-generated state of mind that in turn creates *a mode of thought* vastly different from that which prevails in ordinary time. "Participation in ritual," he demonstrates, "encourages *alteration* of consciousness from the rationality which presumably prevails during daily life and which presumably guides ordinary affairs, towards states which ... may be called numinous" (219, emphasis added). And it is that alteration of consciousness that creates the hierarchical dimension of ritual, enabling rituals to construct meanings that are ineffable. This forces consciousness out of its mundane patterns of thought (257) and allows it to create what he calls Ultimate Sacred Postulates (regarding the power of spirits, etc. [263]) which stand beyond fact and logic and even serve as grounds for them (275).[8]

The primary significance of such Ultimate Sacred Postulates, as Rappaport explains, is that they make possible what he calls sanctified discourse—that is, they make possible a set of fabricated truths that are true only by virtue of the fact that they are known ritually and are, therefore, beyond empirical testability or falsifiability. They are, that is, unquestionable, and therefore, sanctified and sacred. Yet, strangely, by virtue of that fact these "convictions," are also—although, as I shall point out below, problematically so—factual knowledge about the world. "When that which is performatively established is a concept or understanding," writes Rappaport,

> the performative is immediately transformed into a constative. That is, a performative expression which in its liturgical utterance establishes some cosmic entity, quality, or power as a social or cultural fact makes it subsequently possible to construe that self-same expression as a statement. To establish God's existence as a social fact through the ritual recitation of, say, the *Shema*, makes it immediately possible to interpret

---

[8] I agree entirely with Rappaport in this judgment. Rappaport in my opinion, however, fails to recognize the full import of that claim. I have provided an elaboration of my views on "modes of thought" in *The Irony of Theology and the Nature of Religious Thought* (1991).

the sentence "The Lord Our God the Lord is One" *as a report or description of a state of affairs existing independently of the sentence or, at least, any instance of its uttering* (279, emphasis added).

(Rappaport nevertheless also acknowledges that if no one ever uttered the *Shema*, the Ultimate Sacred Postulate would cease to be a social fact, and therefore would also cease to exist. In being ignored, so to speak, that Ultimate Sacred Postulate would be invalidated, but he insists that it would not—and cannot be—falsified [280]). Even though these "truths of sanctity" constitute knowledge for the participant in ritual—in that they are taken by them to be descriptions of states of affairs—Rappaport nevertheless insists (inconsistently) that they "do not violate the correspondence theory of truth . . . [but] merely stand it on its head" (297), a matter to which I will return below.[9]

In a discussion of "Truth and Order" (chapter 11) and "The Numinous, the Holy, and the Divine" (chapter 12) Rappaport elaborates further the notion of sanctification and provides persuasive arguments in support of the claim that "[t]he truth of divine orders as well as divine beings is established in ritual" (345) because religious experience is created by ritual and involves a learning very different from that of ordinary everyday reason (388). Rappaport here seems

---

[9] This tension is even more visible in Rappaport's "Epilogue, 1984" in his discussion of "Objective and Subjective Principles in Anthropology." Rappaport agrees here that science requires obedience to a principle of objectivity, but he also insists that this does not hold for all knowledge claims (433). If it did, he claims, it would be impossible to investigate the relationship of "the conventionally constructed and the naturally constituted" (434). I fail to see, however, why that follows, unless, of course, one presumes that "the conventionally constructed" can only be compared to "the naturally constituted" as an alternative science. But Rappaport makes no such assumption in his analysis of "cognized models" of the world ("On Cognized Models" [1979]) which he clearly distinguishes from "operational models" that accord with the assumptions and methods of the natural sciences. As he points out there, "[t]he criterion of adequacy for a cognized model is not its accuracy but its adaptive effectiveness" (98); truth or falsity applies to operational models only. Indeed, Rappaport is quite aware that the destruction of meaning in the cognized models may well be *intrinsic* to the "developments" represented by operational models of the world. He writes: "The coherence, orderliness, and meaningfulness of the conceptual structures liturgy organizes stand in striking contrast to those of modern society, for it would seem that the order of knowledge has been inverted in the course of history. Ultimate knowledge has become knowledge of fact" (129). The reason characteristic of cognized models, therefore, is what in pre-modern European thought was known as "right reason" which is radically different from the reasoning or scientific reason of the modern, scientific West, and it hardly seems appropriate for Rappaport to insist that the two must be cognitively comparable. (On "right reason" see also Wiebe, 2000.)

to be deliberately differentiating "truth" from "knowledge" in the same fashion that he has earlier distinguished "meaning" from "knowledge." But he then goes on to claim, without the benefit of argument and at odds with that earlier demarcation, that the learning that derives from religious experience constitutes a cognitive achievement that complements our scientific knowledge of the world. Thus, he claims that "the mode of understanding encouraged by liturgy may make up for some of ... [reason's] deficiencies" (402) and he concludes: "In sum, ritual in general, and religious experience in particular, do not always hide the world from conscious reason behind a veil of supernatural illusion. Rather, they may pierce the veil of illusions behind which unaided reason hides the world from *comprehensive human understanding*" (404, emphasis added); and "comprehensive human understanding," it must be understood, is different from scientific understanding in that, for Rappaport, comprehension, unlike science, "is not merely intellectual" (459), yet produces knowledge.[10]

In the final chapter of his book—"The Breaking of the Holy and Its Salvation"—Rappaport's main concern is with what he calls the pathologies of religion. But it is his discussion here of the costs of the liberation of science and secular thought from the sacred that is of particular importance to my critique of his "religious argument" about knowledge. He clearly acknowledges that the liberation of science from religion occurred, and admits that science, and secular thought in general, counteracts ritual and undermines the sacred; that it subverts the "understandings" (convictions [2]) on which human ways of life are founded. "With the Enlightenment, and more particularly with the emergence of modern science," he writes, "*an order of knowledge* very different from Egypt's Ma'at, the Zoroastrian Asha

---

[10] Rappaport's notion of "comprehensive human understanding" that produces a knowledge that is not merely intellectual is, it seems to me, a locution for the notion of "right reason" referred to in note 9 above. Rappaport elaborates on this in "Truth and Order" (chapter 11 of *Ritual and Religion*) and, more succinctly, in his discussion of "Economism, Ecologism, and Logos" in his "Epilogue, 1984," in which he identifies reason with Heraclitus's notion of *logos* as order (308). Such a *logos* possesses *aletheia* in the sense Rappaport uses the notion of "truth" in *Ritual and Religion*; that is, as manufactured meaning that orders the universe. The *logos* (reason) in human beings is the counterpart to the principle "through which the cosmos is generated, ordered, unified, and maintained" (309); it is a part of the general *logos* that "achieves awareness" in human consciousness and is something to be lived and not merely grasped intellectually and theoretically (310). It is, therefore, a moral imperative more than a cognitive act; something to be followed and not merely thought.

or Maring *nomane* comes to prevail. Indeed, the new order of knowledge invests the structure of *Logoi* generally" (449, emphasis added). Thus, as with the truths of sanctity "standing the correspondence theory on its head," so here "[w]hen, in the course of evolution, secular thought in general and scientific thought in particular, is liberated from religion this structure of knowledge is stood on its head" (450). Not surprisingly, this tension between scientific and religious claims to knowledge of the world has not—at least not entirely—escaped Rappaport's attention as the following lengthy quotation makes clear:

> The reordering of knowledge that has *finally* liberated humanity to explore the physical world and to discover its laws is, *in its very nature*, not only hostile to "superstition" and "magic" but also to the sacred and sanctified conceptions on which the distinctively human components of the world are founded, and the sacred and sanctified processes through which human institutions are constructed. The epistemologies that have been spectacularly successful in illuminating the ways in which physical aspects of the world work, when shone on humanity's conventional foundations, show them to be fabrications and thus, in a world in which objectivity and fact *seem to own truth*, delusory (451, emphasis added).[11]

But it is surprising, I think, that having recognized the tension between these two modes of thought, and the apparent incommensurability between scientific and religious claims to knowledge, he dismisses the problem as illusory, on the ground that the everyday world of common sense and science *only seems to be one of objectivity and fact*. But this stance clearly contradicts his earlier position regarding the nature

---

[11] As Rappaport puts it in "On Cognized Models" (1979): "For a report or description to be a report or description, and not a lie, myth, or fiction, the state of affairs to which it supposedly corresponds must exist independently of and prior to the report or description" (138). But the "knowledge" provided by ritual and religion—that is, by cognized models of the world—seems to flout that rule because it establishes its truths (conventions, fictions) performatively (which he dubs a mystified creation [138]). Nevertheless, Rappaport claims that a cognized model is true *if* it corresponds to natural laws (wittingly or otherwise) *and* "provides an order of understanding that leads those for whom it is meaningful to act in ways that are in harmony with natural processes..." (141). But there is no justification here for the further claim that a description of the *truth content* of the cognized model corresponds to a state of affairs that exists independently of and prior to the performative emergence of that truth, and it cannot, therefore, be understood as constituting knowledge of the (meta-physical) world that is in any fashion comparable to the scientific knowledge of operational models of the world.

of scientific thought in relation to ritual and religion; indeed, this stance contradicts the epistemic position implicit in the approach he takes to understanding the nature of ritual and religion. Rappaport claims, however, that even though we can analytically distinguish "the physically constituted from the culturally constructed, the two cannot be separated in nature and the world is increasingly an outcome of their interaction" (456). I do not disagree with this assessment, but this fact does not justify his further claim regarding the commensurability or compatibility of the scientific and religious modes of thought. But Rappaport seems convinced that because humankind is in need of a mode of thought that is both scientific and yet moves beyond mere observation of the world to its transformation (459), scientific and religious modes of thought can be incommensurable yet complementary.[12] Other than stating that the future of the human species depends upon the ultimate coherence of scientific and religious modes of thought, however, Rappaport provides no argument to show that where such a harmony exists, we are intellectually compelled to accept the fabricated truths of the cognized model concerned as genuinely adding to our knowledge about the world.[13] Indeed, as I have already indicated, his own approach to understanding the nature of ritual and religion undermines that claim and

---

[12] This, of course, is an ideal Rappaport hopes will be achieved. He is quite clear that "understandings" may be flawed by incompleteness and self-serving errors; human communities are, he points out, "only loosely constrained by their nature from constructing self-destructive or even world-destroying follies" (1999, 370).

[13] In "Adaptive Structure and Its Disorders" (1979) Rappaport is no doubt right to claim that the concept of adaptation when applied to human society requires the anthropologist to "take account of meaning as well as cause, and of the complex dynamic of their relationship" (158) but this does not imply that the "knowledge claims" of the cognized models are of a comparable order to those in the operational model of the world. Indeed, this has been the essential discovery of his own scientific theory of ritual which has led him to distinguish the "truth" of myth and ritual as "adequacy" from the knowledge of the sciences (see note 10 above). When this is properly understood, one can agree entirely with Rappaport's following claim about the nature of the anthropological enterprise: "Two enterprises have proceeded in anthropology since its earliest days. One, objective in its aspirations and inspired by biological disciplines, seeks explanation and is concerned to discover laws and causes. The other, subjective in its orientation and influenced by philosophy, linguistics, and the humanities, attempts interpretation of the two and seeks to elucidate meanings. I take any radical separation of the two to be misguided, for the relationship between them, with all of its difficulty, ambiguity, and tension, is a reflection of, or metaphor for, the condition of a species that lives in terms of meanings in a physical world devoid of intrinsic meaning but subject to causal law" (1979, 158). (On the problem of objectivity and subjectivity, see also note 9 above.)

shows that it is itself a bit of sanctified discourse. Confirmation of reading Rappaport's argument in this way, moreover, can be found in his response to the charge of incoherence against such a claim; such a charge should not disturb us, he claims, because "the twentieth century has taught us that the faith of the nineteenth in reason may have been too sanguine" (400); because "[c]onscious reason... is often narrowly self-serving" (401); and "because reason alone [cannot] provide a secure and sound basis for social life even if it could be freed from the nonrational" (401).

In light of Rappaport's implicit critique of scientific reasoning and support for a return to "right reason," (i.e., to the notion that the truth or adequacy of ritual must, because it is true in this sense, provide us with knowledge), it is not surprising to see that Rappaport sets out on a quest for a science that is simultaneously a religion, or that the science he seeks must be a postmodern science, or that he accepts Stephen Toulmin's suggestion that ecology is such a postmodern science that not only concerns itself with a search for "an explanation of nature but [is also] a reflection upon nature and a guide for acting in nature" (459). But even in the very brief account he provides of the religious nature of the science of ecology it appears to me that what we have here is not science but rather a new form of nature religion. And although Rappaport may be right in his argument that if evolution is to continue humans will have to do more than think about the world, this does not justify his claims about postmodern science, ecology, or religious knowledge, nor does it underwrite his somewhat mystical claim that the human species "is that part of the world through which the world as a whole can think about itself" (461). Toulmin's own account of the value of ecology, however, raises doubt about the kind of use to which Rappaport seems to be putting the notion here. Toulmin notes, for example, that one must recognize that ecology exists, so to speak, both as a natural science and as a philosophical outlook (1982, 265). Although he insists that postmodern science (of the kind encouraged by Gregory Bateson) has undermined the older view of value-free natural science, and that "the expansion of scientific enquiry into the human realm is compelling us to abandon the Cartesian dichotomies and look for ways of 'reinserting' humanity into the world of nature" (255), he nevertheless also insists that ecology "should not be a field for doctrinal or denominational disagreements" (273). "Preachers who exhort good Christians to let their Christianity permeate all their thinking, so that they may even end up with (say) a 'Christian arithmetic'," he writes, "invite Leibnitz's objection that arithmetic is just not like that—even God himself cannot alter, or contravene, the truths of mathematics. And, if we were told that good Christians must subscribe to a different science of ecology from other people, a parallel objection might well be pressed" (274). Rappaport could justifiably claim that Toulmin's view of the emergence of a postmodern conception of science underwrites his own mystical view of ecology in that, according to Toulmin, ecology's quest to reinsert humanity into the world of nature draws the scientist towards religious and philosophical ideas (262) and that from "this combined [scientific and religio-philosophical] point of view, it is once again possible to reunite the worlds of humanity and nature into a true 'cosmos'" (264). However, Rappaport would also be obliged to recognize Toulmin's own earlier critiques of cosmologists like Arthur Koestler, Pierre Teilhard de Chardin, Jacques Monod, Francois Jacob, Carl Sagan as visionary romantics, or boxed-in structuralists and dichotomist Cartesians, or reckless theologians. Writing of Koestler, for example, Toulmin points out that it is only if "we insist on the distinction between Science as a theoretical hypothesis and Science as the material for *Weltanshauungen*, [that] it becomes possible to disentangle Koestler's message from its theoretical wrappings" (137) and make its theological character explicit. Yet Toulmin appears to ignore his own advice to others to prevent us from projecting our ambitions onto our cosmologies. He writes: "[N]one but the most naive Marxian and Christian historiographers still see the Hand of God, or the Dialectic, in the detailed sequence of temporal events. The same lesson will eventually get through to our twentieth-century natural theologians also. For there is no reason to see the history of Nature, either, as pregnant with a message; and it is human vanity, equally, to claim a basis in science for an unquenchable evolutionary optimism like Teilhard's or Huxley's, or for a dark and romantic irrationalism" (138), or, we might add, for Rappaport's mystical ecology.

Toulmin seems to transform the postmodern scientists (like Gregory Bateson) into priests despite his counsel in part one of *The Return to Cosmology* not to indulge in such a process (81). Of such "Thinking About the Universe" (Part I) he writes: "The Creation, the Apocalypse, the foundations of Morality, the Justification of Virtue: these are problems of perennial interest, and our contemporary scientific myths are only one installment in the series of attempted solutions" (84–85). Yet his own account of ecology in his discussion of "Postmodern

Science and Natural Religion" is no less mythic despite the conclusion he draws about "the death of the spectator" and "the abandonment of Cartesian dichotomies" in earlier sections of the book. Furthermore, Toulmin simply ignores the scientific concern for consistency; despite his claim that "[o]nly a broader, more coordinated view of the world of this [ecological] kind can pick up once again the legitimate tasks undertaken by the traditional cosmology before the "'new philosophers' of the seventeenth century led to its dismantlement" (256), that is, he also insists that "[o]n the primary and fundamental level, disciplinary abstraction and specialization became, and still remain, the first rule of effective scientific analysis" (229).

Given Rappaport's mystical statement about the world as a whole thinking about itself (461), it is quite understandable that Hart in the foreword to *Ritual and Religion* claims Rappaport's real, though unstated, aim to be the creation of a new religion, and the creation of the possibility for us to get in touch with the wholeness of things (xvi–xvii) so that we may be able to "answer the world's crisis" (xvi) and "explore new regions of human possibility" (xix). Also understandable is Hart's claim that Rappaport's vision "invites us to rethink the modernist movement which launched our century and has sustained the universities as a privileged enclave within it" (xix). I find these judgments deeply troubling, however, and especially so the last, for it implies the rejection of modern science and the recreation of the research university into a sacred venue for the forging of a new religion (with a common human agenda) (xviii). The implications of such a development for Religious Studies as an academic and scientific undertaking are clear. Even though Hart claims that science was "the means towards formulating fresh approaches to religion on the basis of sound knowledge of the human condition" (xviii) it now appears that it will be subverted and replaced by religion. And subversion it would have to be for Rappaport's argument for the difference of kind between scientific and religious modes of thought is every bit as cogent as is his scientific account of the nature and role of ritual and religion in the making and sustaining of humanity. Knowledge and meaning for him are not co-extensive, as the summary statement on this issue in the final chapter of his book clearly indicates:

> If physical laws and the states of affairs they constitute are to be known they must be discovered and explained. In contrast, the meanings by which humanity lives must be constructed and accepted. Laws and facts and the scientific procedures for discovering them may provide

> some of the materials out of which meanings are made, but they do not themselves constitute meaning nor can they do meaning's work of organizing human action. Conversely, although constructed meanings are often represented as discovered law, they do not constitute nature. Laws of the sort discovered by physics, chemistry, and biology, and the states of affairs contingent upon them are the case whether or not they are known. The lawful emergence, in the course of evolution, of the ability to construct meanings more or less independent of the characteristics of the physical world [see 416] did not exempt humans from physical law but did increase by magnitudes their capacities not only to conceive the social world but to misunderstand the physical world as well (453).

Science, it is clear then, cannot fabricate meaning without distortion of its fundamentally epistemic objective, and Rappaport's interest in the postmodern science of ecology is not a scientific interest but an attempt to create a new religion. The notion of postmodern science he invokes here seems simply to involve the rejection of modern science altogether rather than its reconstruction, for despite his claims that religion does not violate the correspondence theory of truth (297) and that science "stands religious epistemology on its head" (450) he also insists that neither ritual in general nor religious experience in particular always mask the world from science but rather that they can get at some aspect of reality which unaided reason cannot touch. The fact that Ultimate Sacred Postulates are unfalsifiable and numinous religious experiences are both unfalsifiable and undeniable creates logical problems for the scientific mode of thought (unaided reason), he maintains, should not trouble us because we gain more than we lose. He writes:

> *The unfalsifiable supported by the undeniable yields the unquestionable, which transforms the dubious, the arbitrary, and the conventional into the correct, the necessary, and the natural.* This structure is the foundation upon which the human way of life stands, and it is realized in ritual (405).

But this structure is not the structure of science; indeed, it ultimately undermines science by pressing it to adopt methods foreign to its own nature in order to complete its cognitive understanding of the world in light of extra-cognitive goals. Rappaport's attempt to reconcile religion with science in this manner must, therefore, be judged a failure, although the scientific account he provides of ritual and religion is, I think, a significant scientific contribution to our understanding of the evolutionary development of humankind. The fact that science and religion have been or still are both fundamental and necessary elements of our civilization, as I have already pointed out, does not itself justify acceptance of Rappaport's extra-scientific beliefs. Beliefs in science function in an essentially cognitive capacity [providing knowledge] whereas ritual and religious beliefs function primarily in a catechetical fashion[14]—that is, socially rather than epistemically—making the two modes of thought essentially incommensurable. However, because ritual and religion presume their fabrications to mirror the world yet remain untestable in principle, science and religion are also incompatible. And Rappaport's quest to reconcile them seems to suggest a somewhat hidden antipathy to modern science. It is also, in my judgment, ultimately futile, and patching the hole in the spiritual existence of modern humanity cannot, therefore, be achieved by this route. However, and more importantly, science can be damaged in the attempt to use it in this way.

---

[14] This notion is borrowed from Peter Munz, *Knowledge of Our Growth of Knowledge* (1985).

5. PATHWAYS TO KNOWLEDGE IN COMPARATIVE RELIGION: CLEARING GROUND FOR NEW CONCEPTUAL RESOURCES

Veikko Anttonen

The Issue of a Second-Order Tradition

Since the formative years of the discipline, scholars of comparative religion have constructed their conceptual frameworks in order to delineate the underlying structures of knowledge that justify the cross-cultural use of the notion "religion" and that provide, for the purposes of scientific redescription, grounds to theorize and analyze its variegated forms of representation. Since the subject area of comparative religion does not comprise only the most prototypical members in the category of religion, such as Judaism, Christianity and Islam, but also its non-prototypical, aberrant, anomalous and marginal members (attributed as primitive, archaic, primal, magical, cultic, etc.), the diversity of theoretical and methodological approaches, designated as polymethodism, has become a distinctive mark that characterizes the intellectual climate in the field. Nevertheless, ever since the master builders of the discipline there has persisted a strong undercurrent among the successors to overcome polymethodism and achieve a wider consensus over the fundamental issues on the basis of which both the object of the study and the identity of the discipline can be constituted.

At the IAHR conference on methodology that was organized by the late Lauri Honko in Turku, Finland in 1973, Walter H. Capps raised the issue concerning the conceptual foundation on which the science of religion rests. He argued that the field does not have a center that all practitioners can agree upon. As a remedy for the conceptual disparateness, Capps introduced a solution offered by the English philosopher John Locke. Scholars of religion need to become conscious of the corporate intelligence of their collectivity. Religion scholars need to clear ground and remove some of the rubbish that lies in the way to knowledge. Capps held the view that the science of religion as a subject-field has no clear, direct, self-sustaining second-order tradition (Capps 1979: 179). By the notion of second-order tradition Capps refers to the succession of knowledge within the community of scholars that materializes in actual research practice and in its metaphysics. It is the passing down—nurturing—of "systematic thought patterns of the prominent master builders" (Capps 1979: 178) on the basis of which representatives of the field can discuss ways of understanding and explaining religion as well as ways of organizing their first-hand descriptions of research data. Sociologically speaking, second-order tradition is an explicit recognition of the intellectual heritage of the discipline that practitioners share with each other and on the basis of which membership in the thought-collectivity[1] of scholars takes place.

According to Capps, the science of comparative religion lacks a specific narrative form that would help its practitioners relate to the past and to construe their conception of the field and make operational definitions of religion. Without a second order tradition it is difficult for practitioners to find orientation and establish identity (Capps 1979: 180). However, it is extremely important to emphasize that practitioners cannot take an ideological position according to which knowledge is attained only by "apostolic" succession. In the main, such a position is argued by Eric J. Sharpe in his narrative *Comparative Religion: A History* (1975). The author fails to provide a problem-centered treatment of the theoretical and methodological issues needed to take into consideration in exploring the vast array of sociocultural and mental factors—philosophical, psychological, sociological, ethnological, cognitive, political—that play a decisive role in the formation of our comprehension of religion as a conceptual entity.

At the Turku conference, the primary goal was to map out theoretical and methodological requirements that could bring text-oriented historians of religions and those interested in the quantitative and qualitative approaches in the social sciences into a closer connection with each other. This goal was not, however, achieved (see Geertz and McCutcheon 2000: 18). The rubbish still lingers on.

---

[1] The term *Denkkollektiv* in German was coined by Ludvig Fleck, an Austrian historian of science in his book *Die Entstehung und Entwicklung einer wissenschaftliche Tatsache* (1935).

In the context of postmodernism, the academic field of Religious Studies has become—as Willi Braun writes—"a bewildering jungle" (Braun 2000: 5). There are theorists in the present-day scholarship who on the one hand are eager to posit theological properties to culture (see Taylor 1999) and on the other hand those who eschew theology in all of its forms and dimensions. A good example of the latter is Timothy Fitzgerald's book *The Ideology of Religious Studies* (2000). Fitzgerald suggests that the problem of religion would be solved if we abandon the notion of religion from our scholarly toolkit. He argues that Religious Studies departments should be transformed into Cultural Studies departments.[2] According to Fitzgerald, phenomenologists of religion disguise their theological agenda as an objective human science akin to sociology, although distinct from sociology. Instead of engaging in this cloak work, he suggests that what we are studying under rubric of religion should be based on the study of institutionalized values and their relation to power (See Fitzgerald 2000: 10).

My personal conviction is that our scholarly task would not be altered if theology were eliminated, along with the concept of religion, and replaced by culture. We would still have to map the same territory. While promoting the view according to which religion as a subject is based on fantasy, Fitzgerald seems to be worried about something else than the lack of clarity in using scholarly concepts. Although "religion" is culturally biased towards Christianity as a folk-theoretical notion in Western popular discourse, it has become an established designative label in lexical systems of both Western and non-Western languages and cultures. As a noun, religion is nevertheless an arbitrary linguistic invention that appeared on the scene quite late in history.[3] In a manner similar to other designative labels

---

[2] This has already taken place in my university in Turku in 1974 when the Department of Cultural Studies was founded comprising four independent fields of study: comparative religion, folklore, ethnology and archaeology. The discipline of comparative religion, however, was already established in 1963.

[3] In my native language, which is Finnish, the noun *uskonto* denoting "religion" was literally invented by one of the founders of the first newspaper in Finland in 1848. The noun is derived from the verb "to believe," *uskoa* in Finnish. It was only the non-confessional, public, plural discourse on various faiths that generated the need for this distinct category. Ideological background for the change was, of course, the Protestant Reformation, the Enlightenment and the National Romanticism; the spread of a noun "religion" in German and Swedish; and the emergence of various migrant groups with differing worldviews (viz., Jews, Muslims and Gypsies).

in our lexicon—such as art, history, arithmetic, literature, sexuality, poetry, politics that mostly originate from the 19th century, "religion" is an apt category to employ even for members who may not show much resemblance with other offspring of the family (see Saler 2000). As it is the case with any words and concepts, the semantic content of religion can vary according to the context of discourse. This should not be a problem for the language user. In academic discourse based on the scholarly traditions of humanities and social sciences, religion can be used as a cross-cultural rubric under which to carry out research. The only fundamental requirement is that scholarly discourses need to be linked inseparably with the specifically designed theories of religion to meet the problem area that is being elaborated. As Jonathan Z. Smith has argued, it is a shared interest in theory that unites the fragmented field (or non-field) of Religious Studies (cited from Taylor 1999: 52). By those characteristic features and levels of analysis on the basis of which we pick out cultural materials for our analytical purposes with specific theoretical tools in mind, we are able to illuminate "religion" in that very analytical sense of the term in which we are employing the notion in order to achieve our scholarly goals.

In the study of religion we need theories that do not concern only those cultural concepts and categories on the basis of which adherents of various religio-cultural traditions, whether Western or non-Western, construe their comprehension of themselves, their membership communities, or other units of reality in their religious ontology. A provocative author, Russell McCutcheon, is worth remembering in this context. He presents a strong ideological argument for promoting social theory of religion by maneuvering his major thrust against theological notion of religion as it is represented in the study of religion in general and in the phenomenology of religion in particular. However highly we may esteem the Enlightenment heritage that set the science of comparative religion apart from theology, it is the institutional status of a religious tradition as official and legitimate—especially in the context of the nation-states in 19th-century Europe—that forms the basis on which public discourse on religion is carried out. For this specific reason, the scientific notion of "religion," i.e. religion as a category, does not come naturally. It is fueled by an additional intellectual interest in the subject area before the category and subsequent classificatory questions (see Smith 2000: 39–43) become established as a model for thought. Folk theory of religion comes naturally and can be taken as "a self-evidently meaningful, apolitical, unique phenomenon that causes other things to happen but is itself uncaused since it is an indescribable impulse and personal conviction" (McCutcheon 2001: 17). In his books *Manufacturing Religion* (1997) and *Critics not Caretakers. Redescribing the Public Study of Religion* (2001) McCutcheon aims to disentangle the study of religion from the social practices—whether they take place in the field of science or in elsewhere in the public discourse—in which the subjectivist position is dominant. In the short run, scholars of religion can do very little, if nothing, to change the public view at large. There is a causal link between the folk theory of religion and the questionable academic status of comparative religion. In order to draw a bolder line between theology and the academic study of religion, and perhaps to improve its public appeal, McCutcheon suggests a shift in methodology towards a redescription rather than description. Redescribing religion means awareness of "how we carry out scholarship and teaching in a public context where we are accountable to widely operating scholarly standards of evidence, argumentation, and refutation" (2001: 17). This kind of shift has actually taken place already in the 1960s when the notion of the human body became a major analytic focus for sociology and cultural anthropology. Gradually religion scholars also came adopt the body-theoretical approach to cultural materials and to acknowledge the fact that corporeality plays an important role in religious practices. Distinctions between the ideal and the real, the symbolic and the imaginative, the mental and the material, which characterize not only cultural, but also religious thought, is in the last analysis constrained by the very corporeality of human beings. Since religion is both a natural and non-natural creation of corporeal human beings, corporeality needs to be taken into consideration in analyzing religion.

Although McCutcheon's program is sound and highly recommendable, it does not suffice to clear ground for new conceptual resources. The social theory of religion needs to be complemented by cognitive factors. The notion of embodied knowledge means that religious representations are not only constrained by sociocultural factors, but also cognitive—in the connectionist sense of the term. The discipline of comparative religion—qua scientific discipline—needs scientific theories to pick out new objects and phenomena for study. Requirements of scientific progress and compatibility of findings with other academic fields in all walks of science, humanities, social and natural, is of utmost importance in creating corporate intelligence for the field. The cognitive science of religion does not, however, comprise a single, unified theoretical framework and research methodology. As Stewart Guthrie has pointed out, "although we approach religion cognitively, we do so from quite different directions" (Guthrie 2002: 40). In spite of the differences in approaches, scholars of cognition, however, share the conviction that the new field provides a set of powerful tools for explaining underlying structures of knowledge that become operative every time people organize various kinds of religious knowledge that is available to them in their cultural environment. Although cognitive approaches to religion have not been developed to solve theoretical problems that scholars of religion encounter in the face of drastic economic, political and sociocultural changes taking place in the globalized world, they can help us to explain the complex interplay between the material and the mental, and to contribute to our understanding of the role that religion plays in the ways people acquire, represent and transmit cultural information. Approaching religion scientifically entails critical attitudes towards religious typologies that anthropologists and phenomenologists of religion have produced. Typologies and classifications do not have much explanatory value unless further questions are raised on the biologically and evolutionary evolved capacities that provide the natural foundation on which the human capacity for culture and religion rests.

Cognitive approaches to religious materials alter significantly the view that we have of religion as a human universal. Cognitive scientists wrestle with the explanatory role of external reality on the mind/brain system. As the human mind and brain has co-evolved together with "external" reality, scholars claim that we should take neither external reality nor the mind/brain as a fixed given. Neither has objective existence: the boundary between them is in some sense a negotiable one. Cognitive processes are not dependent on either internal or external mechanisms, but the continuous interaction between them. It is thus not necessary to think that there are neat dividing lines between perception, cognition and action; nor is the brain just a problem-solving central unit, but rather, an interface of embodied action (See Clark 1999; Pyysiäinen 2001: 39).

Incorporating the Durkheimian Legacy into Theorizing Ritual Mastery

By connecting the cognitive and the cultural, E. Thomas Lawson and Robert N. McCauley (1990: 219–220) have come up with the theory to explain peoples' competence for religion in general and religious ritual in particular. Lawson and McCauley postulate that agent causality is an invariant constituent on which the ritual form is generated and is the key factor in distinguishing ritual from other actions (see Lawson and McCauley 1990; 2002). According to their view, the pivotal element that qualifies an action as ritual and constrains its form, is the participants' presumptions about culturally postulated superhuman agents (CPS). In respect to explanations on cross-cultural regularities in ritual actions, they emphasize that the representation of a CPS-agent in some specific sequence in the overall structure of ritual action, plays a far more conclusive role in the representation of religious action than do the meanings that people assign to their actions (Lawson and McCauley 1990 and 2002).

Jonathan Z. Smith has emphasized that a person becomes a religious expert by the ability to think with and to manipulate structures of knowledge such as dualistic oppositional classes such as the sacred and the profane (see Smith 2000: 38–39). Although the explanatory value of the notion of the sacred has been contested in present-day social scientific and cognitive approach to religion (see McCutcheon 2001: 64, 181; Guthrie 1996), scholars of comparative religion who engage themselves in rediscriptive scholarship should not throw out the baby with the bathwater without giving a second thought to the role of this category in explanatory methodology. McCutcheon is correct in pointing out that the notion is a free-floating signifier to religious persons in various religio-cultural traditions and contexts (McCutcheon 2001: 181), but it is not the meaning of the notion in the various contexts of its use that matters, but the logic of thinking on which its cultural use is based. Religion scholars need to use inductive reasoning and explore the characteristics of its various attributions.

Anthropological evidence shows that to set apart and mark off something for ritual purposes is a recurrent feature in human cultural thought. People are universally engaged in sacred-making activities by employing such instruments as water, a candle, smoke, or events such as chanting, reading, singing, making a fire or killing an animal. For their "set-apartness" it suffices that they are treated with distinct behavioral rules, prescriptions and signs of respect. Usually these ritual actions are performed in specific places and times with specific persons performing the actions with reference to specific gods as receivers of actions. Depending on the community, people have been engaged in actions such as blessing and sacrificing by employing water and blood as ritual instruments for transmitting culturally meaningful information.

These actions are comparable to any other actions in the normal course of everyday social life. People run water from a spigot into a jug everyday, just as pigs are slaughtered in barns. Everyday actions are not seen as ritual and they do not require a specific form of action representation. But once water is run from a spigot into a jug and presented to a specific person, e.g., a priest, for blessing, or once blood is extracted from the body of a person by a healer in order to purify the body and restore the vital energy, or once household animals such as lambs, rams, pigs or geese are slaughtered at a specific place, on a specific spot and accompanied with specific formal liturgical acts and phrases, we are confronted with ritual form and with the specific form of rule-governed behavior designated by the term "sacred." The presence of a CPS-agent in a specific sequence in the structure of ritual is not a necessary constituent to qualify an action as religious ritual. Features that are displayed in linguistic and ethnographic sources in which the attribute "sacred" appears, can be taken as functional alternatives that determine the form and the organization of religious ritual.

As the scholarly literature on the subject indicates (see Anttonen 1996a, 1996b, 1999, 2000; 2002; Benveniste 1973; Colpe 1987; Comstock 1981; Guthrie 1996; Paden 1991, 1992, 1994, 1996, 1999, 2000; Penner 1989; Smith 1987), there are multiple and controversial ways of assessing the analytical significance of the notion of the "sacred" in comparative religion. Sigmund Freud theorized that man is in the main a rule-following animal. He held that vernacular terms denoting "sacred" in various languages are so-called primal words, in the sense that these terms have antithetical meanings. In Latin, for example, *sacer* means both holy and accursed. Antithetical signification implies that humans, according to Freud, not only follow rules, but are also inclined to act in diametrical opposition to them (Freud 1957; see also Szasz 1984: 162). Within the intellectual legacy of Emile Durkheim, scholars of religion use the notion of "sacred" to refer to that gray area between opposing category positions in which conceptual contents of the presence of non- or super-human agents become activated. In the Durkheimian approach, the emphasis does not lie on the unconscious mental contents of an individual, but on the social collectivity. Durkheim treated expressions of sacrality as collective representations which form a common ground for cognition and which bind members of a social group together and unites them into a single whole (see Durkheim 1995). Mary Douglas developed the Durkheimian notion of the sacred into a theory of risks and dangers that lie at the margins—both at the margins of the human body and at the margins of a society. According to Douglas, the idea of the sacred is based on the precariousness of the cultural categories guiding human thinking and behavior. Douglas holds that the sacred is the universe in its dynamic aspect. Its boundaries are inexplicable "because the reasons for any particular way of defining the sacred are embedded in the social consensus which it protects" (Douglas 1978: xv). Even though Douglas did not aim to creating an anthropological theory of the sacred, the positive and negative aspects of sacrality are combined in her analysis. She treats the sacred as order, unity and integrity, while the negative aspect of the sacred, taboo and the contagious, consists of elements that threaten the maintenance of that order (see Douglas 1989). Douglas also relies on the work of Claude Lévi-Strauss who postulated the notion of sacrality as closely connected with the maintenance of order in the universe. By occupying places that are allocated to sacred objects, people sustain their sense of control over the balance of their world structure. They also become obsessed by beliefs and omens concerning substances and specific properties they perceive to be polluting and thus putting their systems of categories in danger (Lévi-Strauss 1966: 10; cf. Smith 1978: 147–151). Roy A. Rappaport held that the key element in the idea of sacrality is its role in ritual communication. Rappaport places the issue of sacrality in an evolutionary framework and examines how human language, ritual acts and increased conceptual capacities contribute to adaptive flexibility. Rappaport treats the unquestionableness of ultimate sacred postulates as invariant canons on which the foundation of ritual systems rest. Rappaport posits that "(i)nsofar as the quality of the unquestionableness is the essence of the sacred, the sacred in itself is a product of the very form which is ritual, or rather, of the incorporation of language into ritual form" (Rappaport 1999, 286).

In my own study (1996a), I have investigated diverse linguistic, folkloristic and ethnographic materials with an aim to explaining why the notion of the sacred exists in the first place and to disclose the system of logic that governs the formation of its conceptual content over time. I have concentrated on folkloric materials from Finland and other North-Eurasian cultures. I have sought to explore such questions as why specific topographically exceptional places, especially along waterways or along paths in the wilderness, such as springs, rapids, marshes, lakes and mountains, are chosen as "sacred" and invested with ideas of agency and power. I have also looked at the systems of thinking and behavior on the basis of which specific members in ontological categories, both living and non-living kinds, artifacts and events, have been classified as sacred. I have sought for the cognitive origins of the temporal systems, still valid today, in which there are sacred days are set in opposition to non-sacred days. I have taken a closer look at the conceptual systems prevalent in the Mediterranean culture area dominated by Judaic, Christian and Islamic religious traditions and explored the normative foundation on the basis of which the relationships between Jews and Muslims, as well as a certain class of animals are organized. In order to understand the cognitive origins of dietary rules among the Jews and the Muslims, I have traced the logic of their thinking behind the system of categorization in which "pig" is assigned the status of defiled (forbidden, tabooed, and thus sacred) animal.

Finding answers to these fundamental questions is a concern not only of only ethnographers, anthropologists, sociologists and phenomenologists of religion, but also for scholars of human cognition. Even though the semantic contents of words and concepts denoting "sacred" in various languages vary according to time and place, there are, however, common characteristics in representations that do not vary from culture to culture. Mental representations of human beings are inseparably linked with systems of categorization in which certain cross-cultural regularities can be discerned over cultural variance. In order to track down the recurrent features in the ways people of different cultural traditions set apart times, persons, animals, places and locations and attach specific behavioral rules and norms to them in order to protect their value, scholars of religion can create a general and empirically tractable theory.

In construing the theory of "sacred" as a cognitive category, I have put aside the phenomenological approach and its fundamental notion of manifestation. For something to manifest presupposes an assertion that there exists an ontologically distinct, numinous source for diffuse elements of life (see Otto 1924; Eliade 1959; Ricoeur 1995: 48–55; Ryba 2000). I have followed George Lakoff and Mark Johnson who have suggested a shift from the fictive nature of phenomenological approach to more systematic knowledge on the operations of the human mind. "The phenomenological person," Lakoff and Johnson write, "who through phenomenological introspection alone can discover everything there is to know about the mind and nature of experience, is a fiction. Although we can have a theory of a vast, rapidly and automatically operating cognitive unconscious, we have no direct conscious access to its operation and therefore to most of our thought. Phenomenological reflection, though valuable in revealing the structure of experience, must be supplemented by empirical research into the cognitive unconscious" (Lakoff and Johnson, 1999: 5). In the academic study of religion, Gavin Flood, although departing from the theoretical and methodological stand that I entertain in my work, has pointed his critical finger at such Husserlian assumptions as the "transcendental ego," an overarching rationality, and the adequacy of the phenomenological method to increase our knowledge of religions and traditions embedded within their cultural and historical context (see Flood 1999: 91–116). In addition to issues of representation, language, subjectivity and intersubjectivity that Flood cites (see also Giddens 1987), the fatal inadequacy of the phenomenological method concerns the operations of human mind.

In my cognitive framing of the issue of sacrality I have set out to explore the human mind and its capacity to generate specific types of public representations in which anomalous identity is expressed in respect to established systems of categories in specific social contexts. A class of fantastic animals is a case in point that displays the logic behind sacred-naming activity. As Dan Sperber points out, animals, objects and phenomena that are perceived as hybrid, aberrant, marginal, paradoxical, different, exceptional and whose position within specific taxa is comprehended as ambiguous, are more likely to draw symbolic content (see Sperber 1996b). The same holds true with respect to persons, social and ethnic groups perceived to be defiled or deviant social positions. Emotions, which play an important role in the religious arena, is an excellent test-case about which we can attempt to create a water-tight theory of principles that underlie categorization. While prototype-effect (see Saler 2000) may provide the cognitive foundation which determines the criteria by which entities in the categories of living kinds and non-living kinds are classified, an exclusive taxonomy of sentiments is much more problematic to come by: an emotion can at the same time be an instance of love, hatred, tenderness and esteem (Sperber 1996b: 151). There are no clear category boundaries for inclusion of a sentiment in specific category. Rudolf Otto's famous characterization of the numinous (the sacred) as a category the members of which show modalities of two distinct modes of being: "shaking" (*tremendum*) and "fascinating" (*fascinans*), is actually a case in point. Otto's conceptualization does not contradict the category-theoretical thesis in which is posits that the sacred is generated in the gray area between opposing category positions. The fact that in human languages and cultures there have evolved over thousands of years both folk-theoretical and more elaborate theological, i.e. doctrinally codified, notions of the "sacred" indicates that human beings have some specific form of mental imagery, a pattern of thought, a cultural logic—or perhaps, as Pascal Boyer sees the issue, an obsession (Boyer 2001b: 237), on the basis of which emotionally loaded events, objects, places and times, persons and animals are set apart and marked off as instances of a specific category. According to Sperber, in religious imagination there are two metarepresentational options (second-order representations) that stand out as most common: things with exceptional qualities, showing intuition-violating properties, and things with perfect and ideal qualities (see Sperber 1996b).

Categorization of space is a major cognitive property on which the notion of sacrality as well as various forms of religious representations and ritual behavior rests. Ethnographically speaking, one of the most salient features in the ways people conceptualize territories and spaces is to distinguish inhabited from uninhabited areas. An ethnographer of religion occupies the driver's seat in explaining why spiritual entities, gods and spirits, are created in the very same process in which distinctions and oppositions are marked between habited and inhabited areas, and between the human and the animal world. In myths and epic narratives, the supernatural world of gods and spirits is regularly located "beyond" or "beneath" the spaces and territories of human habitation (see Tarkka 1994: 292–296). Human beings set apart and mark off places in order to create points of contact between the human and the non-human realms of life. In the ethnographic literature on sacred sites and sacred places (see e.g.

Carmichael et al. 1994) we find that there are certain topographical characteristics linked to the attribution of sacrality to a site and to determine its social function. Features such as caves, holes and openings in the ground, cracks between rocks are documented ritualized spaces which, for instance, shamans employ to exit and then re-enter the world in ordinary reality. These points are not necessarily permanently established as permanent locations for ritual purposes; they can just as well be casual or event-specific and thus based on both semantic and episodic memory (see Whitehouse 2002: 138).

On the basis of findings in cognitive psychology, Harvey Whitehouse shows that the nature of the human memory system is a two-way street. The contents of memory can be divided into implicit and explicit, short- and long-term domains, but it is the latter that plays central role in religion. Long-term memory is sub-divided into episodic and semantic memory. Episodic memory deals with autobiographical events and experiences in our lives while semantic memory consists of general knowledge about things in the world. It is used to distill and encode implicit, unconscious knowledge into an explicit exegesis of their meanings (see Whitehouse 2002: 142–145). The theory that Whitehouse has put forth concerns the distinction or rather a spectrum between two modes of religiosity, i.e. imagistic and doctrinal modes. According to him, various domains of memory systems are activated differently in doctrinal and imagistic modes of religiosity (Whitehouse, forthcoming). In the imagistic mode of religiosity there are specific autobiographical moments and emotionally loaded experiences that are associated on specific sites as contexts of ritual activity. These sites do not need to be set apart from the space of everyday social life by visible markers such as walls, fences, pillars, statues or stones; ritual sites can be both constructed or non-constructed. Locations that are selected for small or large, repeated or non-repeated rituals can be based both on episodic and semantic memory and serve the purposes of both imagistic and doctrinal modes of religiosity. Ritual sites can be accidental spots in an uninhabited region of wilderness or, for that matter, in the context of modern urban environment, randomly situated in the midst of a metropolitan setting. Notwithstanding the location, in the imagistic mode of religiosity, a site set apart as "sacred" is selected by "revelation," i.e., by a process of disclosure as Whitehouse (2000: 19) defines the concept. In the doctrinal mode of religiosity, ritual spaces are inseparably linked with the religious teachings and with the institution of rites, which, as Whitehouse posits, need to be activated frequently since "doctrines and narratives would be impossible to learn and remember if they were rarely transmitted" (Whitehouse, forthcoming).

Epilogue

In clearing ground for pathways to new knowledge in comparative religion, I strongly advocate the line of research based on explanatory methodology in which both cognitive and social factors are combined. Such a category-theoretical approach to cultural materials (see Anttonen 2002) is designed to explain both folk religion and organized religion. The theory that I have put forward on the "sacred" as a category-boundary is a strategic tool in this paradigm. The versatile attributions of the notion both as a linguistic term in vernacular and as a religious concept are important sources of information for religion scholars—as categories are in general for cognitive linguists. Both reveal the operation of the human mind and identify mechanisms that generate "the religious" in the context of language use and in ritual behavior. It is not the notion that matters, but the underlying patterns of thinking that lie behind the versatile use of the notion. The focal point in comparative scholarship on this notion should be the relation between language and attributes by which an element or a form of behavior is perceived as "different" or attention-grabbing and set apart for ritual purposes. On the basis of evidence of its use, it can be argued that human beings have a disposition to invest a special referential value and inferential potential to categorical boundary-points. Anomalies and counter-intuitive representations in religious literature and folklore testify to the significance of boundary-points in information processing. This disposition is activated both in reference to physical and as well as non-physical entities (consider, for example, locations with non-negotiable value for individuals and social collectives). Attribution of specific rules, interdictions and prohibitions to specific natural or man-made items, or spaces such as churches, cemeteries and other sanctuaries and sacrificial groves, as well as emotions such as love, fear and fascination are causally connected with the liminal space which can be created in any place in any system of categories. As Ray Jackendoff argues, memory would be virtually useless without categorization. According to Jackendoff the ability to categorize is perhaps the essential aspect of cognition. "It is not just a matter of the semantics of predicative sentences: it is central to all cognitive psychology" (Jackendoff 1987: 135). The importance of categorization does not only concern the truth-value of the membership-inclusion of a specific item in a specific category, but the internal representations that we have of the item and that category. "Categorization judgement," as Jackendoff writes, "is the outcome of the juxtaposition and comparison of two information structures" (Jackendoff 1987: 135). The theory of conceptual structure that Jackendoff has put forth places special emphasis on conceptually "lingua franca" areas within the overall organization of the computational mind and its sets of correspondence rules (see Jackendoff 1987: 124–125). As a category-boundary, that which is set apart as "sacred" points to such "lingua franca" areas of the computational mind.

6. COMPARATIVE RELIGION IN THE STATE OF NATURE

William E. Paden

Against the influences of postmodernism, the turn toward panhuman universals and linkages with evolutionary and cognitive science is surely one of the important new movements in the study of religion. It remains to be seen just how complementary the partnership will be. Certainly the early returns in research, such as that of E. Thomas Lawson and Robert McCauley (1990, 2002) and Pascal Boyer (1994, 2001b) are productive and promising. As an historian of religion and longtime student of patterns that ground cultural variation, I welcome the opportunity to discuss here some models for juxtaposing and bridging cognitivist and comparativist perspectives.

As for my premises, I do see human cultures—and hence, religious cultures—to be continuous with biological evolution, and read the ontological "universes" and behavioral systems acted out in religious theatres as remarkable illustrations of what nature "does." And this same nature so engages herself not only in showing such ingenuity in habitat formations, but also in submitting to the mind's selective structurings. The contributions of Walter Burkert (1996), Roy Rappaport (1999), and David Sloan Wilson (2002), along with that of the cognitivists, seem to me important steps along the way toward including the study of religion in our scientific knowledge of the world while restoring comparative perspective in a new context.

On the surface, at least, cognitivists seem to have a goal that should interest comparative religion scholars, namely, looking behind cultural diversity to find species-level design mechanisms, and showing how those psychologically adaptive features select for certain kinds of behaviors and environmental arrangements. As Lawson and McCauley put it, "We maintain that *common* structures of human cognitive systems impose constraints on cultural forms" (1995: 355); and they add, "Eschewing general, explanatory theories that identify . . . stable patterns underlying the appearances condemns scholars to lives of contemplating nothing but a parade of details" (354). Stated that way, the identification of metacultural functions (Tooby and Cosmides

1992: 88–92) could be seen as potentially consistent with or complementary to the cross-cultural study of patternings in religious history.

In this study I would like to examine those and related issues. The first part proposes ways that comparative religion can find linkages between historical material and evolutionary perspectives, particularly in the notion of infrastructural behavioral universals. The second part focuses entirely on the notion of group-level behaviors, which I take to be a way of expanding the cognitivist program and consequently forming a bridge between the analytical vocabularies of historians of religion and scientific thought; and the last part looks at some examples of group behavior that are especially constitutive in religious environments.

Panhuman Behavioral Functions

In a recent publication I outlined a case for analyzing religion as environmentally constrained improvisations on and canalizations of universal behavioral dispositions (Paden 2001b). I understood these behavioral functions as infrastructural to the kinds of particular actions that are played out and given inflection in cultural settings, much the way the capacity for language acquisition underlies actual language performance. A behavioral phonetics approach also allows us to deconstruct the notion of religion into its undercurrent phenotypic patterns, each with its adaptive function, each with some kind of relation to evolved capacities. In that sense, it is a model that partly redresses the issue of underspecified descriptions of religion and the related problem of single explanations for multiple dispositions (cf. Boyer 2001b: 50; Paden 1998: 91–93).

My previous focus was on the opportunities that this schematization afforded for restoring comparative perspective in a time otherwise dominated by postmodern rejections of cross-cultural categories. I argued that a transcultural, panhuman behavioral grammar does not squelch inner-cultural significations, that it allows specific variations to be highlighted, and that the content differences of the cultural variations then become rich and historically/locally revealing, thus redeeming the universal categories from the charge of vacuousness. I had summarized, "The *ways* religious cultures 'do' these behaviors directs attention to difference; *that* they all do them forms a point of comparability and invites theoretic interest" (2001b: 281).

I use "universal" here not as a Platonic noun, but with an adverbial sense, as in "certain kinds of behaviors are found universally." This links the notions of generality and universality, implying that the formation of general concepts about universally recurring behaviors is both a human construction and also a construction *about* something that exists in some aspect. It does not mean that all universal behaviors are always present all the time.

The universals I refer to here are not particular actions, but generic actions. They are the behavioral functions that are present in sets of actions. Relevant to the study of religion, and cast in their verbal, gerundial form, a few salient examples of general social behaviors include:

- Forming bonds with one's group
- Defending group order and punishing infractions of it
- Distinguishing kin and nonkin
- Socializing the young
- Exercising cooperative behaviors
- Recognizing authority and its symbolic objects
- Honoring ancestors

Enormously complex religious forms build on these elementary, intuitive proclivities. These functions can be instantiated in numerous kinds of particular actions, such as chanting, writing, monitoring one's thoughts, dancing—essentially limitless forms of surface behaviors.

Insofar as sociality includes the formation of cultural environments, other kinds of behavioral patterns appear:

- Replicating and rehearsing group histories
- Recalling exemplary "historical" (or ancestral) figures or models as prototypes for imitation
- Regenerating/remembering sacred prototypes by periodic performances
- Marking important occasions and roles with ritual behaviors
- Endowing certain objects or persons with superhuman status, authority, charisma
- Interacting with postulated superhuman beings
- Classifying/mapping time and space
- Coordinating a world to inhabit

These etic reductions have a high level of generality, representing the adaptive functions of kinds of behaviors. It is hard to imagine religion or culture without these dispositions. Such "X-ray" functions map, and in a sense, translate, what goes on behind the cultural surface of what people think they are doing. I would attribute to such patterns what Tooby and Cosmides say of the "tools of evolutionary functional analysis," namely, that they "function as an organ of perception, bringing the blurry world of human psychological and behavioral phenomena into sharp focus and allowing one to discern the formerly obscured level of our richly organized species-typical functional architecture" (1992: 67).

The above list is simple and of course could be expanded. Thus there are conceptual behaviors, e.g., "attributing causality to events and objects," or "attributing meaning to objects"; and there are self-modification behaviors, such as "experimenting with alternative forms of consciousness," "disciplining mind and body to effect certain kinds of fitness," or "using ideas to guide behavior and sort out behavioral options." Such genera suggest any number of further etic formulations, simple or complex. These aptitudes count among the streets and highways that have been grooved in our minds for ages.

The question of the relation of this "human ethosystems" approach (Fox: 1989: 20ff, 116ff)—to "information-processing" universals then becomes pertinent, possibly productive, and at the least might lead to clarifying differences.

Whatever the unconscious origins of human motivation, there remains the wide phenotypic world of behavior—presumably the environmental outcome or expression of all that is unconscious and hardwired. Behavior analysis, in my terminology, is not just a redescription of cultural actions, and not just an assortment of any or all particular actions (the usual approach in studies of human ethology), but an identification of the generic aspect of behavior sets relative to recurrent ways humans construct environments. This answers, I believe, the concern of Tooby and Cosmides that behavior is "too kaleidoscopic" and variable a category to capture meaningful species-typical uniformities (1992: 64).

Generic behaviors here are more like infrastructural, bottom-up dispositions than top-down thematizations; more like a set of architectural tools than instances of mere taxonomic recurrence or topical organization. Accordingly, the model is not the Standard Social Science Model, which cognitivism opposes and which is construed as the notion that the individual mind is a blank slate or at best a generalized learning capacity on which cultures write themselves (Tooby and Cosmides 1992: 24–49).

In most forms of cognitivist research, "social culture" is mere abstract background. According to Boyer, though, this methodological displacement does not mean that culture is a trivial matter, but only "that variations in those [cultural] conditions do not bring about corresponding variations in the aspects we want to explain" (1994: 295). In my schema, however, there is a linkage of the behavioral dispositions that *underlie* cultural variation (all societies transmit pasts/histories, mark important occasions, display authority, etc.) and the selective functions of the evolved panhuman social mind. We are therefore interested not just in the variations, but in the default settings that make the variation a variation on a common chord. The chords, I would claim, are common because they resonate with our evolved nature as life forms.

Thus, the behaviors listed above in some ways seem to represent manifestations *of* design programs (defense, imitation, cooperation, etc.) or combinations thereof. As universal behaviors, how could they not? And ultimately, what is the difference between calling something a mental disposition and calling it a behavioral disposition? What is the difference between an adaptive mental skill and its expressions in the world of behavior?

In the broadest sense, mental behaviors can also qualify as behaviors, unconscious or not. The brain is always "determining meaning." "Sorting out costs and risks in coalitional affiliations" could count as behavior, or "accessing one's mental files on other individuals." Indeed, "information processing" itself could be construed as a kind of mother of all behaviors. In short, behavior is not just a matter of a particular jump or yell. It is also the function that it is effecting.

Again, the points made by evolutionary psychology about mental functions seem to me to apply here as well: "understanding function makes an important and sometimes pivotal contribution to understanding design in systems that are otherwise bewildering in their complexity;" and, "guidance as to function vastly simplifies the problem of organizing the data in a way that illuminates the structure of the mind" (Barkow et al. 1992: 11).

Understandably, behavior and cognition are conceptual lenses that determine different genres of research. But the parallelism seems to me potentially complementary and collaborative rather than remote or oppositional.

In one sense, the process of abstracting from and thus mapping the cultural/religious surface in terms of explanatory or translative models is what comparative religion scholars have been doing for years (Smith 1998), but the interpretation of this tradition and its future is disputed. Many tend to see it as hopelessly biased by theological interests or naively bound to classificatory rather than explanatory schemas. In my view, however, the pursuit of structuring forces that underlie the history of religions has not been an entirely lost cause and I have argued that some opportunities for an analytical comparativism that goes beyond theology and the simple encyclopedic mode are available in the literature (Paden 2000a, 2000b, 2001a). In short, I find comparativist/evolutionary capital in the behavioral, habitative aspects of the History of Religions approach (mythicization, ritualization, making and inhabiting worlds, etc.), especially when connected with patterns of social formation linked to kinship-maintenance, and political authorization.

The Issue of Group-Level Constraints and Behaviors

As these social behaviors may not on the surface seem to be in any way commensurate with "adaptive, information-processing mechanisms," I need to review a few points that position the above discussion with regard to the notion of "objective" group constraints.

Cognitivism, in establishing itself as a scientific alternative to the Standard Social Science Model, has a built-in bias that undervalues the constraining power of group-level forces. Certainly it does affirm that we are a social species fully geared for social interaction—empirical studies of cooperative patterns are impressively rich (cf. Tooby and Cosmides 1992) and hold much promise for scholars of religious behavior—but it conceives this sociality in individualistic terms. In D.S. Wilson's phrasing, cognitivists tend to regard individuals as "self-contained cognitive units" (32). For scholars like Boyer, "society" is simply a concept, a folk notion, as are ideas about "essential" membership in a group, and such notions about solidarity ultimately rest on psychological mechanisms, namely coalitional intuitions. Such computations involve unconscious-level mental processing of the costs and benefits of coalition making, including the costs of defections from coalitions (Boyer 2001b: 288). Affiliations are selected by such choices, and this is why we submit to our "own" groups and are suspicious about those of others.

At the same time, this intuitionism does not seem to dispense with the point that groups function as organisms in their own right and have constraining force on individual minds. Boyer allows that the social processes "are real and their consequences are real too," even though people do not understand the hidden forces (2001b: 252), and, because of our heavy investment in concepts about collective identity, he even concedes that the group comes to have "a life of its own," indeed, a kind of "magic" (253). This begins to sound like an invitation to *The Elementary Forms of Religious Life*.

Whether as an incidental, make-believe, byproduct of our coalitional computations, or as an "objective" reality, groups (a more concrete category than "society") do have their constraining power to create conformity and punish defection. Individual minds will calculate the risks and benefits of heeding any particular taboo, but one could argue that it is the social nature of the mind that makes these calculations germane in the first place. At the least, we have a standoff here on which came causally first (individual or group). Group identity and its moral, coercive functions are surely part of our adaptive psychic inheritance and should not be shortchanged, depotentiated or underdeveloped just because one is focusing on microprocesses of mental transmission. Social roles and pressures are more than input cues or concepts. Hence, we can note here Henry Plotkin's urgings that, "Social constructions are powerful causal forces in cultures, and explaining them is not some optional extra to a science of culture. Understanding and explaining social constructions is absolutely essential" (105). He proposes that cognitivists need to find the psychological mechanisms that predispose humans to the function of "social force," which "takes in many phenomena described variously by social psychologists as conformity, cohesiveness, and obedience" (105).

David Sloan Wilson has recently made a renewed, evidential case for considering groups as adaptive organisms, particularly as they generate "moral orders" as constraining, functional mechanisms (2002). No enemy of cognitivist work, Wilson presents extensive documentation for the need to recognize group psychologies along with other design forms, giving new scientific currency to the old analogy of groups and hives. In a comparativist model one could show that it is groups that form worlds (hives) of time and space, genealogy, commemorative displays, moral norms, and which solicit self-sacrifice, modes of sharing, and so forth. It is just because the mind is socially constructed, in this organic sense, that it constructs the world socially.

The mind's equipments are always contextualized in the midst of social practice and value, so that its evolutionary constraints are themselves constrained by additional environmental and psychological complexities. The mind, then, does not come innocent and empty to the house of its own evolved capacities. Inferential activity will involve not only Pleistocene push buttons, but complex social, personal and emotional associations (many of them unconscious).

Granted the foundational importance of the microprocessing model, there remains a kind of de facto autonomy (the aforementioned magic) to group dynamics. The hive may be conceptual in the mind of the bee, and thus not a "natural" reality, but it functions as one. It is the conceptual field in which individual lives and deaths transpire. So even if group culture is but the perpetually reconstructed output transmission of individual minds, even if it is always a *selection*, it still, then, assumes a weighted objectivity, a life of its own, as Boyer had to allow (2001b: 253). Ironically, and Boyer notes the coincidence, too (1994: 37 n. 4), Durkheim (presumably the arch representative of the Standard Social Science Model) clearly traced that social weight to individual representations *of* it, repeatedly stressing that society exists and lives only in and through individual minds (1995: 351).[1] In this sense, one could use the model that the mind not only transmits/reconstructs that weight as a conceptual representation, but also accepts it, internalizes it, applies it, imitates it, is motivated by it, or engages in forms of mental and physical self-modification in terms of it. Thus, the Durkheimian valence of the coerciveness of social life through mythic and ritual performances, whatever its period-piece rhetoric and exaggerations, does not vanish by positing psychological mechanisms as the cause of its [social life's] own transmission. Nor do the analyses of sociologies of knowledge, affirming as they do, that "worlds" are contingent on the selections of individual minds, or indeed, can hang on "the thin thread of conversation" (Berger 1969: 17).

---

[1] There are number of parallels between Durkheim and cognitivism. In both, one could say that psychological transmission is what bears the reality of society. In both, that reality is "represented" in terms of ideas about individuals being "of the same essence" as the group's totemic symbol, and yet that representation is passed on only because of the unconscious, intuitive principle it expresses. In both, cultural representations provoke "public behaviors that cause others to hold them too" (cf. Sperber 1996a: 100); in both, a function of rituals is to enhance the participant's motivation to transmit them (Lawson and McCauley 2002: passim).

Thus, for purposes of the study of religion, the fact that the social patterns are picked and transmitted by the mind does not change the influence of the patterns. In terms of patterns of behavioral effect or output, what is the difference between saying that religion "activates... *inference systems*... that govern our most intense emotions, shape our interaction with other people, give us moral feelings, and organize social groups" (Boyer 2001b: 135, my emphasis), and saying directly, "*religion* (or 'the group') activates intense emotions, shapes interaction with others, etc.?" One should be careful about replacing the "mind-blindness" of social science with a new social blindness.

I conclude that constraints, their selectivities, and their phenotypic patternings, form a multi-level repertoire: molecular life, brain physiology, mental and social design functions (including overrides), and finally, in the light of day, cultural and subcultural programs (rules of chess, Benedictine monasticism, Parisian fashion world).

Macro-Patterns: Encompassing Design Functions

I here expand but briefly upon three of the schemata mentioned above in the outline of basic behavioral functions. These have functionality in every human society and play key roles in determining the many religious formations that build on them. My hypothesis is (1) that these are behaviors that link religion with nature and hence explanatory levels "all the way down" (biologically) and thus are not merely unmoored abstract ideas about society or culture, and (2) that they also describe organizational, descriptive features of religious world adaptations, including the concept of the sacred (albeit "naturalized"), and thus constitute central areas of research in religious studies. Broad as they are, I submit that they are active ways groups form environments.

Worldmaking

Boyer likens the mind to a manor-house estate, where a variety of workers "downstairs" carry out very different functions to maintain the whole operation (2001b: 93). But comparison of estates *with each other* also shows another level of differentiation. Estate-making is a social, habitative behavior that is itself an adaptive group function:

Organisms and their colonies select, form and inhabit collective environmental worlds. Religious formations are often egregious examples of this generic, self-determining process. The notion of worldmaking, construed as a social behavior, links the world of cognition and the world of mythmaking. Myth and ritual, which configure time and space in relation to culturally postulated sacralities, then become understood as forms of life-world organization.

Religious estates are filled out, grounded, and transmitted through canalized behaviors that mark out world territories via collective forms of history-making, renewal rites, schemata of order and authority, displays, exchange and cooperation, and integrative applications to sociopolitical environments. This seems to me consistent with the cognitivist points that, "Anthropological orthodoxy to the contrary, human life is full of structure that recurs from culture to culture . . ."; and, it is the existence of "a common metacultural structure, which includes universal mechanisms specialized to mesh with the social world, that makes the transmission of variable cultural forms possible" (Tooby and Cosmides 1992: 88, 91). The way syncretic parts and institutions in religious movements are selected or constrained by the factor of "rules" of sacred identity is a promising area for study in relation to cognitivist research (Light 2000). F. J. Odling-Smee's model of "Niche-Constructing Phenotypes" (1988) may also bear relevance here, as well as Brian Malley's suggestive models about the application of complexity theory to religious "order" (1995: 16–21).

I am not suggesting that all religions are homogeneous estates. Religious people are connected with many kinds of collective networks and segments of different estates, and always act locally. Worldmaking follows unpredictable opportunities. I am assuming, though, that human environment production and habitative structuring is a process that can be studied by evolutionary models, and that has an integrative dynamic by which it selects or incorporates workable cultural materials according to regulative cultural prototypes. World is a product, even a byproduct, always in motion, of choices in an environment. At the same time, the product becomes the producer; the representations, given objectivized weight, become the constraints. Where culturally constructed kin (or "species" identity) factors play roles in world definition, and where superhuman endowments reinforce those factors, the inviolability of the (estate) system, is ratcheted up.

Sacred Order and Systemic Identity

It follows that a world is a kind of floating order in the midst of chaos. World stability, or perceived stability, is always at stake. Most organisms have defensive systems, and humans, as social beings, conceive of the estate maintenance in terms of certain rules and guidelines to be observed. Roy Rappaport's model has tried to link this with notions of sacrality-as-inviolability and place its function in evolutionary contexts:

> Sanctity in the absence of genetic specification of behavior stabilizes the conventions of particular societies by certifying directives, authorities who may issue directives, and all of the mythic discourse that connects the present to the beginning, establishing as correct particular meanings from among the great range of meanings available to the genetically unbounded human imagination. (321)

It is not clear to me, though, why such sacrality needs to be understood only in the absence of a genetic base. Life-forms depend on boundaries at every level of territory and order, so that inviolability, and hence sacredness, are ultimately expressions of life-maintaining mechanisms (Paden 2000c). In this sense, behaviors that succeed in selecting effective forms of system maintenance could be understood as forms of adaptive fitness based on intuitive mental designs. For humans, the external cues where mental decisions take place are in the culturally patterned versions of moral and ritual expectations, rules of purity and honor, authority and territory maintenance, doctrinal orthodoxy, grid and group markers (à la Mary Douglas) and loyalty-display occasions.

Group order always connects with complicated political and social variables and thus other nested "orders." But conformity to the rules of right conduct and resolving transgressions will always be a group trait that can be identified.

Reciprocity with Sacred Objects

A major schema of religious behavior is displaying and serving culturally postulated sacred objects. The objects themselves are entirely the creation of the group, and they "go with" the group's identity as a collectivity. They are not sacred to those outside the group. They take the form of patron gods, relics of saints, ancestral sites, living gurus, divine monarchs, holy scriptures, medicine bundles, and so forth. Looking behind the thousands of historical examples of this and observing that these concrete "objects" empower members of the group in return for their devotion and are pretexts for individuals to perform special acts of loyalty, is already to begin to offer an explanation.

At one level, behavioral modularity and heterogeneity seem to rule here, for relations to these objects take place in quite variable genres and functions. The objects draw occasion for celebrations, political legitimations, social stability, submission to authority, artistic expression, paranoia, dissociation, obsession, ascetic restraint, sensual abandon (including orgiastic hysteria), atonement for perceived offenses, communal sharing, psychological redirection, and so forth. Each of these behaviors links with a different psychological capacity and design, and is therefore subject matter for different kinds of explanatory theories, depending on exactly which aspect is in question, and the social context of that aspect.

But in spite of the plural, individualistically particularized factors of "relations to sacred objects," and granting the microprocessing at the inferential, transmissive level, there is also a broad, social "macro" function to sacred objects. It is a *social* behavior to form authorizing sacred objects as stabilizing identifiers and reinforcers for the group and as a public means for individual members to express their needs *in the context of a stable group symbol*. This is evident from a wide-angled, or aerial, comparative perspective. The sacra of societies then begin to appear, in sociobiological terms, like species-identity vehicles: The sacred objects are in some respects "like" the queen bee, who, with her royal offspring, are given pride of place and served the special royal foods. The excessive status displays of the object (mythicizations, royal residences, holy scripture representing the blueprint of all creation), and the nonordinary, self-sacrificing and devotional performances and repertoires that are activated by the submissive, dependent relationship, all suggest a strong group (or kin) identity-enhancing function. "Sacred symbols," in D. S. Wilson's terms, "provide a mechanism for representing a moral system and putting it into action" (227). At one potential theoretic level, at least, this links the Durkheimian analysis of socially constructed sacred objects with the genetically grounded kin-selection theories of William Hamilton, a relationship noted by Luther H. Martin (2001). We submit to the requirements and reciprocities of the object that represents the group, to the extent that it is believed to mark and embody one's identity in the group. Long live the queen.

Concluding Points

The study of religion has always included the pursuit of patterns. Many of these have been construed as ways that the mind structures the world. Religion has thus been conceived as formed according to kinds of language (e.g. Cassirer), ego-unconscious dynamics (e.g. Freudian/Jungian theory), patterns of social cohesion (Durkheimian tradition), modes of thought (Tylor, Horton, structuralism) or mythic and ritual behavior (Eliade). In each case, the patterning mind "selects for" some rather than other external representations; in each case, scholars look for the real patterns that lie behind the chaotic surface, and for increasing levels of specification relative to the genre of behavior in question. Studying the way subjects respond to objects—the mind being layered with so many social, cultural, emotional, psychopathological, gendered and environmental constraints—becomes the work of many fields and levels of abstraction. All of the above were attempts, in their time, to divide religion at the real joints. Religious representations, as Boyer points out, "instantiate indefinitely many generalizations, and therefore could be seen from different angles" (1994: 294).

At the same time that comparative religion is seeking to recover a sense of pattern behind cultural difference, cognitive science now presents itself as the new angle on religion. Finding complementary aspects of these programs would seem to augur well for the future of each.

7. TOWARD A DISCOURSE BETWEEN COGNITIVE AND CRITICAL THEORETICIANS OF RELIGION: OPEN DIALECTIC BETWEEN THE RELIGIOUS AND THE SECULAR

Rudolf J. Siebert

E. Thomas Lawson and I have been colleagues and have cooperated with each other in the WMU Department of Comparative Religion almost daily since he hired me 37 years ago. I am still grateful to Tom for his positive decision at that time, and also for persuading me two years later not to accept the Chair in the Religion Department of the University of Peoria, Illinois, but to continue my work on the critical theory of religion in Kalamazoo and later on in Dubrovnik, Croatia, and in Yalta, Ukraine, which he supported most graciously through the years.

A Passion for Theory

What has bound Tom and me together most as colleagues and friends throughout all these years was our deep interest not only in diverse religious traditions and phenomena, but also in the formation of a comprehensive theory about religion. For over three decades I have admired Tom's passion for theory in an academic environment which has been more inclined toward data. I witnessed how Tom moved in search of an adequate theory of religion through the philosophy of science and then, when its aporetical tendencies became visible, into the theory of action, and then specifically into cognitivism as it had been developed since the 1960s. Tom and I shared this passion for theory: he for cognitivism and I for the praxis philosophy, or more specifically for the critical theory of society of the Frankfurt School.[1] We never fell for the theories of neo-conservatism

---

[1] For more on the critical theory of religion and on the Frankfurt School in general, see references to Siebert, Adorno, Habermas, and Horkheimer in the bibliography.

or deconstructionism. It is the purpose of this essay to honor Tom and his work in cognitivism from the standpoint of the critical theory of society. If this essay contains any criticism then this is because I am of the opinion that no greater honor can be given to a scholar and his work than that it is found worthy of constructive critique.

I still remember step by step, how Tom developed a cognitive theory of religion. Tom concentrated particularly on ritual actions and systems understood as subsystems of total religious systems. Here Tom focused wisely not only on the world religions, which came into existence in the Axial Age, such as Buddhism and Christianity, but also smaller-scale religions, particularly the religion of the Zulus. South Africa was Tom's original homeland. There he became aware of and familiar with the Zulus and their religion. Tom himself grew up in the Reformation paradigm of Christianity and even went through the ritual of ordination. Thus, Tom is as knowledgeable of the Zulu religion as of the different paradigms of Christianity and likes to compare them. While Tom came to his cognitive theory of religion from his experiences in the Reformation paradigm, I came to the critical theory of religion from my experiences in the Roman Catholic paradigm. In discourse, it is always important for scholars to remember where they are coming from.

As Tom's cognitive theory of religion, or more specifically his cognitive psychology of ritual actions and subsystems, developed, he incorporated into it elements from a variety of cognitive sciences. Thus, Tom participated fully in the linguistic turn, which in the 1970s took place both inside and outside the cognitive sciences. Tom's cognitive theory of ritual was so strongly influenced by the analytical methods, the vocabulary, the grammar, and the logic of linguistics, particularly Chomsky's model of linguistic competence, that today his work cannot be understood without knowing this discipline very well. Tom outlined a structure for religious rituals analogous to that which Chomsky developed for linguistics. At the same time, however, it seems that Tom and his colleagues have a hard time offering a plausible account of the constraints that might explain this structure. Tom offers the structure as an explanation of religious rituals, but it seems that this structure, if it is descriptively accurate, must itself be explained. In any case, reading Tom's articles and books, one often has the impression that he constructed his cognitive psychology of religion more or less parallel to the development and structure of linguistics: there is a natural language and thus there is a natural religion.

While the methodological form of Tom's cognitive theory of ritual actions and systems comes mainly from linguistics, the rich empirical materials are derived no longer from missionaries or from their colleagues, the diplomats of the colonial powers, but from a more objective structural or cognitive anthropology. The many elaborate diagrams through which Tom describes the internal functional and legitimating interrelationships among the structural elements remind me again and again of similar diagrams in chemistry or physics books or also in psychology or anthropology texts (in so far as they belong to the positivistic tradition and as such imitate the so successful natural sciences). As Tom developed his cognitive theory of religion more and more in analogy to linguistics, he stressed more the human potential of language and memory than the evolutionary universals of work and tool, sexuality and eroticism, the struggle for recognition and nationhood. In the perspective of the critical theory of religion, of course all five could throw new and interesting light on religion in general and its myths and ritual activities in particular. There is a price to be paid for limiting oneself to one human potential: this is evident in Marx's theory of religion which is rooted in the evolutionary universal of work and tool; or Freud's theory of religion, which is based on the human potential of sexuality; or Nietzsche's theory of religion which has its foundation in the evolutionary potential of the struggle for recognition; or Hitler's folkish theory of religion which feeds upon the source of racially determined nationhood. My point is that religion and its myths and rituals have not only linguistic, but also economic, erotic, political and national aspects which are worthy of interpretation and explanation.

Universal Principles

Tom's cognitive theory of religion provides a detailed, lucid review of the dogmatics of the modern positivistic study of religion. Tom draws particularly on the insights of three cognitive approaches to the study of religion: intellectualism, symbolism and structuralism. He prefers intellectualism. Tom's thorough discussion of the dogmatics of the positivistic study of religion in general and of the cognitive approaches in particular bring out important points of great value and also serious criticism. It is against this dogmatic background that Tom uses analogies between language and religious ritual. Tom presents a formal system for the representation of actions. He couples this system with a religious conceptual scheme, e.g., myth and history, theology, and sacred texts such as revelations, poetry and hagiography. Tom hopes to yield universal principles for all religious ritual systems. As a specific feature of his cognitive theory of religion, he developed a set of universal principles which determines a limited amount of fundamental ontologies. The principles regulate religious as well as secular acts and systems, particularly sacred as well as profane ritual actions, structures and systems. The principles even seem to determine the plurality of human cultures which postulate the superhuman agents. Even after they had been banned from scientific discourse by positivists, these superhuman agents reappear again in Tom's cognitive theory of rituals as the most important factor, differentiating religious actions and systems from secular ones.

From the perspective of the dialectical theory of religion, the cognitive theory of religion is in danger of falling victim to the general trend in the positivistic social sciences: namely, that theories of action turn only too fast into system theories. Most of the time, Tom and his colleagues do not speak about concrete ritual actions but rather about more or less abstract ritual structures and systems as integral parts of broader religious systems. To the contrary, the critical theory of religion stresses concreteness. Only the concrete is true! Social and cultural and particularly religious systems and the principles and ontologies which guide them, are true only if they are present in and mediated through the concrete actions and interactions of the experiencing subjects who continually reproduce them and are, of course, also determined by them. In fascist Germany, the Gestapo discovered and caught hidden socialists through counting how many times they used in their speeches the word "concrete," because for the latter the right or true society, which had not yet come to pass, was necessarily to be concrete, while the wrong or untrue system, in which they actually lived and acted and fought, was abstract. The dialectical theory of religion aims at alternative Future III—a society in which people are not only mere functional agents but are in possession of their non-arbitrary autonomy and sovereignty, and in which they are no longer alienated from each other, but enjoy concreteness, i.e., solidarity, a friendly and helpful living together in the mutual recognition of their human dignity, human rights and equality. That precisely would be the concrete or true society, which unfortunately is not yet the case in advanced capitalist or socialist societies. Whether religion could possibly make a contribution to the arrival of alternative Future III—is one of the fundamental pragmatic questions of the critical theory of religion.

The principles of the cognitive theory of religion, which Tom and his friends have discovered, seem to be constant and not subject to historical variations. The critical theorist of religion is reminded by the limited set of invariant principles or categories in the cognitive theory of religion of Plato's heaven of constant, ahistorical ideas. The cognitive theory of religion seems to internalize Plato's objective ideas into the human subject. The limited and fixed set of principles which informs and steers religious as well as secular acts, structures and systems, also recalls, for the dialectical theorist of religion, Kant's subjective idealism or transcendentalism, his "Copernican turn," his research into the fundamental, constant, and ahistorical categories in the human subject which make all experience possible in the first place. Contrary to Plato and Kant and the cognitive theory of religion, the critical theory of religion stresses the historical mediation of everything between heaven and earth. The dialectical theory of religion tries to emancipate itself from Platonism as well as from Kantian transcendentalism: it seeks to de-Platonize and de-transcendentalize itself. The reason for this is its opposition to all philosophies of domination, particularly folkish and nationalistic ones which stress "eternal" ideas in order to give hold and security to the ruling classes in different nations and civilizations. Already in the Greek Religion of Beauty and Fate, the God of time, Chronos, who gave birth to his children, but also soon swallowed them up again, had to be castrated in order to give stability to the city state of Athens with its 4000 free citizens ruling 100,000 slaves.

The fundamental principles of the cognitive theory of religion makes the critical theorist of religion ask the question concerning their location. As with Eliade we are never sure where his constant, ahistorical archetypes were really located. We could only deduce from his position on the far Hegelian and folkish Right, that his archetypes were perhaps rooted in the spirit of the nation or of the race. Jung likewise placed his constant, historically invariable archetypes of *anima, animus,* self and their shadows, into what he called the collective unconscious. Tom and his friends seem to posit their set of eternal principles into what they call the mind/brain. The principles seem to be a function of the mind/brain. If this is so, then the constant character of the cognitive set of principles presupposes, of course, the invariable character of the mind/brain itself. That poses a problem, since the brain adapts itself and evolves ever so slowly as does the whole human body and nature in its totality. That creates a particular problem when man himself takes over his own evolution, including that of his brain and mind, in the form of the bio-sciences and technologies, the psychological manipulation of memory, stem cell research, cloning—all on the way to alternative Future I: the totally administered society in which humanity could possibly accelerate the speed of the evolutionary process.

In spite of the fact that in the evolutionary process the cognitive principles must necessarily lose their apparently constant character and turn into historical variables like everything else, they do nevertheless contain in themselves—since they regulate religious as well as secular actions, structures and systems—the most ambitious promise to bridge the modern dichotomy between the sacred and the profane. Since the cognitive theory of religion is nevertheless an entirely secular enterprise, it seeks to reconcile the sacred and the profane from a secular perspective. The promise of such reconciliation has, of course, great significance for the other antagonisms in advanced capitalist society: between man and nature, between the genders, among the races, among the nations, between the classes, etc. This promise must not therefore be taken lightly.

Theory Formation

Tom and his friends have engaged in a most exciting theory formation: the creation of a cognitive theory of religion. The claims of the dialectical theory of religion concerning the formation of a theory which would be adequate at this point in history after Hegel, Marx, Schopenhauer, Nietzsche and Freud, as well as the critical theorists Horkheimer, Benjamin, Adorno, Fromm, Marcuse, Habermas, etc. are threefold. First, such a theory must try to comprehend its object in its constitution. Secondly, such a theory must make evident the interdependence between the mode of the constitution of the object and that of the subject. Thirdly, such a theory must make understandable these objective and subjective processes of constitution out of the over-arching process of natural, social and cultural evolution. Since Hegel, the fundamental problem of theory formation, including the construction of a theory of religion, has been under debate. Neither the critical nor the cognitive theory of religion can avoid this historical presupposition. It seems to me that, so far, the cognitive theory is stronger in meeting the first claim than the second and third. Here a psychology and sociology of cognitivism may be as necessary and helpful as a cognitive psychology and sociology. Perhaps they could explain to us why particularly scholars who came from the Reformation Paradigm of Christianity (which reduced drastically the rituals of the Orthodox and Roman Catholic Paradigms because they were not Biblical) and who came from the capitalist world (which diminished rituals even further because they got in the way of profitable work), are so very much interested in rituals. Is it a matter of compensation? Of course, the study of religious rituals does not lead the cognitivist necessarily back to more intensive and extensive actual performance of rituals: to the contrary. Certainly the secular cognitive theory of religion is not intended to bring secular people and societies back to the religion which they left behind long ago.

The danger for the cognitive as well as for the critical theorists of religion is that they do not differentiate and keep apart sufficiently the constitution of their object, e.g. myth and rituals, on one hand, and their own subjective constitution as human beings and scholars on the other. Through the centuries, Christians had to learn to sharply differentiate between the objective constitution of the historical, itinerant rabbi, Jesus of Nazareth and his life, teaching and communicative actions on one hand, and on the other hand, the subjective constitution of the believers who made of him the Jesus of faith, the mythological and ritual Christ, the Pantocrator. Today, Buddhists have to do the same concerning the historical Gautama, and the Muslims concerning the historical Muhammad. Already the early comparative religionist, Creuzer, a contemporary of Hegel, was reproached for not having distinguished clearly enough between his own personal constitution as a romantic scholar and the constitution of the myths and rituals which he studied. Like the Neo-Platonists in Antiquity, Creuzer was criticized for having projected thoughts, categories, principles, interpretations and explanations into the objective constitution of the myths and rituals. He was also criticized for having searched in the myth and rituals for structures and systems, for which there was historical evidence or justification. The critics of Creuzer argued that the people, the poets, and the priests, no matter how great their wisdom otherwise, nevertheless knew nothing of such principles and ontologies which were completely inappropriate to their time. This latter point was, of course, correct. Those people, poets, and priests were not traditional Neo-Platonists or modern cognitivists or critical theorists. The nations and their poets, magicians, priests, from the Zulus to the Christians, indeed did not conceive of this universality which they then intentionally wrapped into symbolic form. Creuzer, of course, never asserted this. If, however, premodern peoples, poets or priests did not see in their myths and rituals what modern cognitivists or critical theorists see in them, it does not follow that their representations and ritual actions were not nevertheless symbols. Premodern peoples lived not in prosaic conditions, as we do in advanced capitalist society, but rather in somewhat poetical circumstances. Therefore, these premodern nations did not bring to their consciousness what was for them the innermost and deepest being in the form of thoughts, but rather in the shapes of their imagination. Doing so, these premodern peoples did not—as the cognitivists and critical theorists do today—separate the general abstract concepts from the concrete images present in their myths and rituals. That this is really the case, cognitivists and critical theorists of religion have to accept if they want to continue their work productively.

Interpretation and Explanation

In his cognitive theory of religion, Tom makes the attempt to reconcile the methodological antagonism between interpretation, which was usually practiced in the humanities, and explanation, which was usually done in the natural sciences and in the positivistic and naturalistic social sciences. Tom challenges the view that rejects explanatory theories of religion in favor of solely interpretative approaches. He proposes and defends a cognitive approach that recognizes the interaction of interpretation and explanation against the subordination of one to the other. For Tom, the interpretative and the explanatory approaches are no longer competitive but rather complementary. Both approaches seem to be equally vital not only for the study of religion but for other symbolic-cultural systems as well. Still, Tom seems somewhat more inclined toward explanation and to launch the reconciliation with the interpretative approach from the explanatory side. Thus, as Tom borrows analytical methods from linguistics and other cognitive sciences, he makes a strong plea for combining interpretation with a structural explanation of religion, particularly religious rituals. Of course, such structural explanation is far from unproblematic. Nevertheless, like the Kabbalist scholar Scholem, so also has Chomsky used extremely positivistic means in order to reach completely unpositivistic goals. The cognitive theory of religion could do the same. The structural functionalist Luhmann always knew (at least from the experience of his wife, who died from cancer), that religion means much more than what any positivistic theory, including his own, could possibly say about it. Will the cognitive theory of religion come to the same insight some day? I hope so.

Particularly in recent years, I have observed that Tom's cognitive theory of religion turned more and more into a specific, detailed cognitive explanation of religious rituals. Tom began more and more to explore the psychological foundations of religious ritual actions, structures and systems. He discovered that participants recall religious rituals to ensure a sense of continuity across performances. Those religious rituals motivate the participants to transmit and re-perform them. According to Tom and his friends, most religious rituals are supposed to exploit either high performance frequency or extraordinary emotional stimulation to enhance their recollection. Tom asserts that the participants' cognitive representations of ritual forms explain much about the ritual systems.

On the basis of a wide range of evidence, Tom tries to explain the evolution of the religions. Tom remains fascinated by the emerging cognitive science of religion, which he hopes will be able to develop general profiles of religious ritual systems and connect them with larger religious systems, possibly even with macro-economic and political subsystems in different types of societies. I have, of course, always been amazed about Tom's confidence in participants' ability to know, to have cognitive representations of the ritual activities, structures and systems, in which they participate. Eliade had been much more skeptical. Eliade believed that he knew much more of the meanings of e.g., angels, sacrifices, priesthood, etc., in each religion than did the participating believers. I must always think of the Catholic parishioner whom Tom likes to take for an example, when he speaks about participants in religious rituals. This parishioner blesses himself with the sign of the cross after dipping his hand into the holy water whenever he enters a church building. He is accustomed to do so from childhood. The ritual has long become a habit. For the parishioner, there is less awareness, knowledge, consciousness involved, the more he practices the ritual.

I know from over sixty years of participation and observation—which should count for something—that the parishioner puts his hand also into the font and blesses himself on Good Friday when there is no holy water at all because it has to be newly consecrated during the Easter Vigil. The parishioner as habitual performer of the ritual is obviously not aware of the presence or absence of the holy water and even less of the ritual principles involved and even less of the culturally postulated superhuman agents, in this case the Trinity. I am quite sure that the Catholic parishioner who puts his hand into the font, no matter if there is holy water in it or not, has not much of a clear representation or notion in his mind/brain concerning the legitimating ritual connections—which Tom tries to trace—between the present or absent holy water and its consecration by the priest, between the consecration of the water and the priest's ordination, between the priest's ordination and the apostolic succession of the Pope, and between the apostolic succession and the foundation of the church by Jesus (leaving aside the problematic nature of all of this). Strangely enough, while on the one hand the parishioner may not be fully aware of the cognitive elements in the rituals he participates in, the priest who prepares two parishioners for the sacrament of marriage may tell them, that a mere cognitive familiarity with the ritual may not be sufficient for performing it. Nothing is simple in religion.

In any case, Tom likes the parishioners, the untheological little people, the common folks, who enjoy the rituals surrounding the saints and their relics, rather than the great theologians like Origen, Augustine, Aquinas, Luther, Zwingli, Calvin or the great thinkers on religion like Schelling, Hegel, Whitehead, or Habermas, the builders of great systems of thought. Tom is very democratic as citizen and as scholar, and rightly so. Luther criticized those rituals and relics of the little people in the name of the purity of faith, but his father confessor, Staupitz, protected them. I also like the Catholic parishioners who faithfully perform their rituals with or without relics, week after week. There are so many of them, over a billion, and I am one of them. Of course, best of all I love believers like Münzer.

Münzer stressed the normative elements in the myths and rituals and in 1525 started an ill-fated revolution against Charles V and the feudal lords in the name of the Sermon on the Mount. I love Münzer's present-day successors, the liberation theologians and their Base Christian Communities fighting against their modern capitalist exploiters and oppressors and predators. When shortly before the fall of the Berlin Wall I saw for the last time Münzer's picture on the 10 Mark bill of the German Democratic Republic, I said to myself: poor Thomas, you have lost another revolution! However, the little people will prevail! In general the critical theorist of religion loves and embraces them both: the little people and their myths and rituals *and* the great theologians and philosophers and their thoughts. He prefers religious or secular communities who make room for both the intellectuals and the masses. He hopes that the former will become more sensuous and the latter will become more thoughtful, and thus they shall move closer to each other. Anti-intellectualism will not solve the problem, particularly not the anti-intellectualism of intellectuals. The very fact that all people share supposedly the same mind/brain does as such not yet resolve this or any other of the many antagonisms of civil society, nor do the finite culturally postulated and produced superhuman agents. The evolving mind/brain and its limited God-hypostasies may even be responsible in the first place for the social and intellectual dichotomies the cognitivists want to resolve. Who else should be responsible? In any case, de-differentiation means regression in evolutionary terms. Of course, we don't want that!

Ontic, Normative and Expressive Elements

In the perspective of the critical theory of religion, rituals like the mass consist of ontic, normative, and expressive elements. While the cognitive theory of religion is very strong concerning the ontic aspects of rituals, it is somewhat weaker in relation to its expressive aspects and neglects particularly the normative, i.e. moral and ethical aspects. Of course, from the positivistic standpoint no morality or ethics can be deduced. Considered purely scientifically, to hate is not worse than to love. There is for the positivist no logically cogent justification why I should not hate if I shall thereby avoid disadvantages in social life. The positivist can say in the sense of Orwell's description of alternative Future I, that war—e.g., against Iraq—is as good or bad as peace; that freedom is as good or bad as slavery, serfdom or wage labor. That is so, because the positivist cannot justify that one ought not to hate. Positivism does not find any instance which would transcend human beings, societies and their projections, and which would differentiate between helpfulness and greed for profit, goodness and cruelty, avarice and self-devotion. That is true also for a cognitivism which merely knows of culturally postulated and socially produced superhuman beings, but not of a real unreified Transcendence. Simply to talk about human instincts and the evolution of virtue and cooperation is not good enough: the ought cannot be deduced from being.

Positivistic logic also remains mute. It does not recognize any position of preeminence concerning the moral cast of mind, or the ethical way of thinking, outlook, attitude or conviction. All modern attempts from Kant's critique of practical reason to Apel's linguistic formal pragmatic, which seeks to justify morality and ethics through reference to a Beyond rather than through earthly prudence, has been based on harmonistic illusions. In known history, morality and ethics ultimately trace back to and are grounded in and justified by religion and its myths and rituals. Precisely for this reason, it is so important for cognitive and critical theorists of religion to pay attention to the normative semantic potential in myths and rituals and to allow at least some of it to migrate into the discourse of the expert cultures and through it into the communicative actions of the life of the modern world, which are in great need of it for their survival. Such secularization of the normative semantic potential in myth and ritual does not mean, of course, its profanization in the negative, blasphemous sense in which the Jewish, Christian and Islamic prophets understood it. Secularization must rather be understood in the context of Jewish universalism. The Rabbis developed such universalism out of the conviction expressed in the Torah, that even the heathen nations paid tribute to a Supreme Being and in this way honored the name of Yahweh. Their offerings were thus presented indirectly to Yahweh, and their other morally and ethically good actions were animated by a pure spirit. Because Tom as chair of the department was aware of the importance of the normative potential in myth or rituals, he let me—perhaps in spite of his cognitive theory of religion which does not contain a cognitive ethics—teach a course on religion and social ethics for over three decades. For that I am very grateful to him.

The critical theorist of religion is impressed by the insight of Kant, Schelling, Hölderlin and Hegel that in the future the whole of religion and metaphysics was to be concretely superseded by morality and ethics. Such ethics were to contain nothing less than a complete system of all ideas or, what was the same, of all practical postulates, including Kant's postulates of God—what the cognitivists now call the superhuman agents—and that of freedom and immortality. According to Habermas, neither the propositional use of language or science, nor the expressive use of language in art, can possibly inherit the mantle of religion in a postmodern age. Only the normative use of language or morality, set communicatively aflow and developed into a discourse ethics, can possibly replace the authority of the sacred, if indeed it needs replacement. Certainly, Tom and I always agreed in our preference for liberation theology and its emphasis on morality and ethics over the "God-is-Dead" theology. The liberation theologian Ernesto Cardenal and his base Christian community, the farmers of Solentiname in Nicaragua, celebrated continually the traditional ritual of the mass and read the Gospels. However, most importantly, Cardenal and his farmers then adapted and applied the Gospels' ethical values and moral norms to their political situation in Nicaragua, and were motivated by these values to continue their revolutionary struggle against the oppressive and exploitative Samosa regime.

For critical theorists of religion, even the churches seem to have a preference for the ontic aspects of their liturgies over the normative ones. Most amazing is the immunity of believers to the deep contradictions between the ontic and normative elements in their rituals. Thus, in the Orthodox and Roman Catholic Paradigms of Christianity, there is a deep dichotomy between the ontic aspect—the Creator God—and the normative one—the Redeemer God—and the connected theodicy problem in the ritual of the mass: why do bad things continually happen to good people. A good creation does not need redemption. A creation which needs redemption cannot be good. It seems that it is the expressive element, the Holy Spirit, that bridges the abyss between the Father and the Son, the Creator and Redeemer God, and thus forces the antagonistic ontic and normative aspects together in the ritual system, and also holds them together in the dogmatic system, thus solving the theodicy problem. It seems to me that the cognitive theory of religion shows a similar indifference toward dissonances and contradictions in the structure of ritual systems as do some of the world religions. The critical theory of religion, however, is highly sensitive to those ritual antagonisms and focuses on them in order to resolve and reconcile them. Such reconciliation cannot happen through the mere deemphasis or neglect of the normative element in myths and rituals and the connected theodicy problem. While the critical theory of religion does in no way neglect the ontic and expressive elements in religious rituals, it nevertheless stresses most emphatically their normative elements, not of domination, but rather of liberation.

In the perspective of the critical theory, to the extent that religious worldviews, including their myths and rituals, are impoverished in the process of cultural modernization, their normative content is formalized and detached from substantive religious interpretations. Practical reason can no longer be founded in the transcendental subject as Kant had done. The communicative ethics intrinsic to the critical theory of society now, after the linguistic turn, appeals only to fundamental norms of rational speech, an ultimate fact of reason. Of course, if this is taken to be a simple fact, capable of no further explanation, it is not possible to see why there should still issue from it a normative force that organizes the self-understanding of people and orients their actions. Nevertheless, critical theorists have worked within a framework of a communicative or discourse ethics which consist of five linguistically rooted validity claims: truth in relation to nature, honesty in relation to man's inner world, rightfulness in relation to the social world, tastefulness in relation to the cultural world and understandability in relation to the world of language—all in terms of a law of universalization which aims at an unlimited communication community. Here is a broad field of discourse and cooperation between cognitivists and critical theorists aimed at a new secular ethics on a linguistic basis.

According to the perspective of the dialectical theory of religion, as soon as the participants in any religious ritual must carry a big book of commentaries in order to interpret, for example, the ritual actions of a priest celebrating the Orthodox or Roman Catholic mass, we must assume that the *homo symbolicus* is not entirely well any longer in modernity. There was a time when the participants could "see" or intuit immediately the meanings of the rituals they performed. That is no longer the case in the modern age. Many Americans still have a hard time "seeing" and "reading" and comprehending the very precise and, for traditional Muslims, obvious symbolism of the *talion* ritual of the 9/11 attack against the World Trade Center in New York and the Pentagon in Washington D.C.— representations of the "Great Satan" of bourgeois modernity. The same symbolic blindness happens in relation to the mutual, almost symmetrical *talion* rituals between Palestinians and Israelis in the process of the recent Intifada, including human sacrifices on both sides. As modern people, we Americans take everything literally. Symbolism inside or outside religious rituals seems no longer to be our thing. It is something for historians.

Often one meets older religious people in the West who still believe in Providence and still pray for providential interventions into their and other peoples' lives, but who have become rather alienated from religious rituals because they experience them as unnecessary, primitive, archaic, mechanical, petrified, or meaningless reifications of their real, living faith. These believers take seriously Jesus' words to the Samaritan woman, who took everything literally, that the hour would come when she and her people would worship the Father neither on the mountain nor in the temple in Jerusalem. God is Spirit and thus, whoever worships him must do so in spirit and truth, and not in rituals on certain sacred mountains or in certain sacred buildings, which may neither be sufficiently spiritual nor true. Maybe a more advanced religious consciousness will make this hour true and will aim at a religion with few or no myths or rituals. Certainly religion and rituals are not identical, nor are religion and myths. A de-ritualized and de-mythologized religion is thinkable and may become real in alternative Future III—a free and communicatively rational society.

Of course, the cognitive theorist of religion correctly does not consider it to be his task to revive old rituals, or to re-ritualize the modernized and secularized life world, or even merely to make them more understandable and comprehensible for believers so that they can perform them more meaningfully. That remains the task of the faith communities themselves: e.g., the liturgical reform at the occasion of the Second Vatican Council in the Roman Catholic Church. The cognitivist collects, studies and analyzes the rituals from different religions in their evolutionary sequence, but he does not necessarily practice them nor does he necessarily want to improve their praxis. A cognitivist is just a cognitivist. The cognitive theory of religion is as sharply separated from religious praxis, as positivistic economics is from the actual economic subsystem of civil society, which is characterized by instrumental action and rationality and steered through the medium of money; or positivistic political science is from the actual political subsystem, which is also characterized by functional action and rationality, but steered through the medium of power. There exists no cognitive program to re-ritualize the increasingly disenchanted life world in advanced capitalist societies, which is still characterized somewhat by communicative action and rationality and steered through the medium of moral norms and ethical values. On the other hand, one of the tasks of the critical theory of religion is to engage in the theory/praxis dialectic, and thus to allow some semantic potentials to migrate from the depth of myths and rituals, rescuing them through inversion or translation into the secular discourse among the expert cultures, including cognitivism. In this way, they can be introduced into communicative and even economic and political action in order to stem new waves of re-barbarization.

The Positivistic Approach

During the past 37 years I have not missed an opportunity to tell Tom that he was teaching and doing research and developing his cognitive psychology of religious rituals in the context of the great traditions of positivism and naturalism. Comte founded the philosophical system called positivism, which was based on the assumption that truth was completely represented by observable phenomena and scientifically verified facts and data. Of course, positivism was much older than Comte. There had been earlier religious and secular forms of positivism, before modern positivism appeared in French rationalistic and British empiricistic forms. Tom has always been more on the rationalistic than the empiricistic side. Twentieth-century positivism reached its climax in the Vienna School. In the 1930s the Vienna School became so popular in American universities that it was no longer considered to be "Continental." The Frankfurt School, however, has always been considered "Continental," no matter how much it became globalized. Soon modern positivism gained its ultimate victory in American universities in the form of the "scientific philosophy." It continues to be dominant up to the present. Cognitivism constitutes a new wave in the long history of positivism, which like all previous forms considers all earlier types as still too "theological" or "metaphysical" and asserts that it alone has reached most fully and once and for all, the post-religious and post-metaphysical age.

With Adorno, I define positivism as the anti-metaphysical metaphysics of what is the case. The positivist studies everything simply because it is there, at hand, the case, a fact, a datum. The critical theorist looks at what is the case, but always in terms of its relevance to man as individual and species-being on his long march from animality to alternative Future III—a society in which personal autonomy and universal, i.e. anamnestic, present and proleptic solidarity, will be reconciled. The critical theory is certainly not value-free in Weber's sense. It continually struggles for the truth as the negation of the untruth (understood as false consciousness) and the masking of race, national and class interests. While the cognitivist explores, explains and interprets religious or secular rituals simply because they are the case, the dialectician looks at them in reference to what they contribute not to domination but rather to the liberation-elements present in a particular religion, its myths and rituals, and thus to the emancipation of its believers. The positivist in general and the cognitivist in particular conforms to what is the case in advanced capitalist society. The critical theorist looks for the potential in what is the case. That, of course, makes him easily a nonconformist and outsider who threatens the *status quo* which will only change in order to avoid any kind of transformation toward alternative Future III. Contrary to the positivist, the critical theorist is engaged in a theory/praxis dialectic: he breaks up theory at a certain point in order to practice it; he then returns again to theory in order to enrich it with the newly gained practical experience; and then with it, he re-enters praxis again until alternative Future III is achieved. Since religion is mainly concerned with hope, i.e., what is not, or better still what is not yet the case, a genuine believer cannot be a positivist and a honest positivist cannot be a believer. The greatest mistake a religious believer can make is to present what is not yet the case as being already the case and thus to turn into a positivist. The greatest mistake the positivist can make is to overstep his scientific competence and to deny the possibility that what is not yet the case will never be the case, e.g. the appearance of the Jewish, Christian or Islamic Messiah.

For a long time, I have had the suspicion—and I have informed Tom about it—that positivism in general and cognitivism in particular (and even the cognitive theory of religion) supports, consciously or unconsciously, the already powerful trend in civil society toward alternative Future I—the totally administered, mechanized, computerized and robotized society. None of my friends knows better than Tom the trend in civil society (and even in the university) toward alternative Future I. Again and again, Tom has directed my attention to it through the years. The nanotechnologists are already designing technically assisted life processes of the human organism fusing man and the machine. According to this "nano-vision," self-replicating tiny robots circle through the human body and connect themselves with the organic material in order to, for example, halt the aging process or to increase the functions of the cerebrum. Moreover, computer engineers are designing robots of the future, which will be autonomous, and which will condemn the concrete human being of flesh and blood as an obsolete, run-down model which has come to a standstill and its end. According to such computer scientists and engineers, the bottlenecks of the human hardware can be overcome. They promise to make software, abstracted from the human brain, that is not only immortal, but also perfect.

Today gene research and technology are being used to design a genetic communitarianism, according to which different subcultures push for the eugenic self-improvement and optimization of the human species in different directions. In this way, the unity of the reference of all human beings who could understand and mutually recognize each other as members of the same moral community is put into question. Today we can no longer assume that there will be in alternative Future I a single successor to what has been regarded as human nature. We must consider the possibility that at some point in Future I, different groups of human beings may follow divergent paths of development through the use of genetic science and technology. If this occurs, there will be different groups of beings, each with its own nature, related to one another only through a common ancestor, the former human race, just as there are now different species of animals who evolved from common ancestors through random mutation and natural selection.

According to the critical theory of religion, such an altered human body is a fantastic image of the fast arriving alternative Future I— a scientifically and technocratically ritualized society. It seems to me that so far the cognitive science of religion does not propose ways in which religion or religious myth and rituals could possibly help to correct the trend toward alternative Future I. It seems, rather, that human agents which for centuries have been conditioned in different cultures to follow the more or less conscious script of religious rituals may be the best candidates for a smooth adaptation to the profane scientistic and technocratic rituals of alternative Future I.

Theodicy

The critical theorist of religion remembers that Freud once said that Christians were poorly Christened. Under the thin veneer of Christianity, Christians have remained what their ancestors were: barbarically polytheistic. According to Freud, the Christians were badly christened insofar as they accepted and obeyed the liberating Gospel only in a highly sublimated form, which left the social reality as unfree and irrational as it had been before. Certainly, cognitive psychology, which believes to have progressed far beyond Freud, has done enormous work to explore the structures of ritual systems. It also sees the particular ritual system in the context of the wider religious systems. But it does not go further and does not concern itself with the broader antagonistic social and historical systems, in which the particular religions and their rituals are imbedded. Therefore it cannot, as Freud did before, differentiate between a good and bad performance of a ritual or between its manifest, superficial, conscious and its deeper latent unconscious aspects, which may stand in utter contradiction to the former. Since cognitive psychology ignores, like all positivism, the time core in the religions and their myths and rituals, it cannot see where they may have come from, thus it cannot know where they may go, and thus it also cannot confront them in their actuality with their potentiality in order to correct them.

According to the critical theorists, repression in the technical Freudian sense played only a minor role in the institutionalization of Christianity. However, there took place in Christianity a transformation of the original revolutionary content: instead of the deritualized kingdom of the spirit came the highly ritualized power of the church. This deflection from the original objective of Christianity took place in broad daylight, consciously and with public argumentation and justification. Equally open was the armed struggle of institutionalized Christianity against the heretics, who tried to rescue the unsublimated, not yet ritualized revolutionary content of Christianity.

There were plausible instrumental motives behind the bloody counter-revolutionary religious wars which filled the Christian era. However, the cruel and organized slaughter of Cathari, Albigensians, Anabaptists, Brothers of the Free Spirit, Edomites, as well of slaves, peasants and paupers who revolted under the sign of the cross, the burning of witches—this sadistic extermination of the weak—suggested that unconscious instinctual forces broke through all communicative rationality and rationalization. The executioners and their bands fought the specter of a liberation which they desired, but which they were compelled to reject. In the twentieth century, these radical religious tendencies have come to life in the priests and ministers who have joined the struggle against fascism in all its forms. Most recently, these radical religious tendencies have been realized in bishops, priests and nuns who have made common cause with the liberation movements in the Third World, especially in Latin America. Many of them have been sadistically murdered by members of the School of the Americas in Fort Benning, Georgia. Critical and cognitive theorists must learn to differentiate between this revolutionary church abroad and the bourgeois church at home and judge them both in terms of their own Gospel values.

In the view of the dialectical theory of religion, what Freud had called the crime against the Son, had to be forgotten by the killing of those whose practices recalled the crime. It took centuries of progress and domestication before the repressed was mastered by the power of bourgeois-capitalist civilization. But at its late stage, its instrumental rationality seemed to explode in another return of the repressed. In the twentieth century, the image of liberation, which had become increasingly realistic, was suppressed the world over. Concentration and labor camps, the trials and tribulations of non-conformists, released a hatred and fury which indicates the total mobilization against the return of the repressed. Cognitivism seems to have a hard time differentiating clearly within the religions between tendencies toward liberation and domination, between radical and conservative or reactionary religion, between humanistic and authoritarian religion. The critical theory of religion understands "radical" in the sense of Marx's statement in his "Critique of Hegel's Philosophy of Right": "To be radical is to grasp things by the root. But for man the root is man himself."

Cognitive psychology seems to be, like the conservative content of Hegel's philosophy of law or religion, but unlike Marx's historical materialism and Freud's psychoanalytical philosophy, not radical enough. Critical and cognitive theorists must learn to differentiate between the radical and the bourgeois religion and judge them both in terms of their own ethical values and moral norms and by their own humanistic potential.

In the perspective of the critical theory of religion, the historical development of religion, its myths and rituals, contains a basic ambivalence between the image of domination and the image of liberation. Freud stressed the role of religion in the historical deflection of energy from real improvement of the human condition to an imaginary world of eternal salvation. Freud thought that the disappearance of this illusion would greatly accelerate the material and intellectual progress of mankind. Freud praised science and scientific reason as the great liberating force against religion. Perhaps no other idea shows Freud closer to the great tradition of the Enlightenment, but also, no other statement demonstrates Freud more clearly succumbing to what Horkheimer and Adorno have called the dialectic of enlightenment. In the present period of civilization, the progressive ideas of rationalism can be recaptured only when they are reformulated. The function of science and of religion has changed, as has their interrelation. To this also the new cognitive theory of religion gives witness. Within the total mobilization of man and nature which marks the present period, science is one of the most destructive instruments against that freedom from fear which it once promised. The scientific attitude has long since ceased to be the militant antagonist of religion, which has equally effectively discarded its explosive radical and revolutionary elements and has often provided people with a clear conscience in the face of suffering and guilt. Certainly, cognitivism has made its peace with religion. It is this development which has opened up for cognitive science the way to reintroduce again into the scientific discourse not only natural religions and their myth and rituals, but also even superhuman agents, from which generations of Enlightenment thinkers have tried to emancipate humankind. Thus it seems to help extinguish all the hope that religion could provide.

In the perspective of the dialectical theory of religion, in the household of culture, the functions of science, particularly cognitive science, and religion tend to become complementary. Through their present usage, both science and religion deny the hopes which they once aroused, and teach people to appreciate the facts and data in a world of alienation: the metaphysics of what is the case in advanced capitalist society. In this sense, religion is no longer an illusion. Its academic promotion often falls in line with the predominant positivist trend, of which cognitive science is the most recent expression. Where religion still preserves the uncompromised eschatological aspirations for peace and happiness, its illusions still have a higher truth value than a science which works for their elimination. The repressed and transfigured radical and revolutionary content of religion cannot be liberated by surrendering it to the scientific attitude in its positivistic form such as the cognitive sciences. In contrast to it, the critical theory of religion explores the not yet fully actualized potential of religion to conquer alienation, to transcend mere facticity, to revive hope, to promote peace, to make happiness possible, to diminish suffering.

Several years ago I asked Tom and his cognitivist friends what good their cognitive theory of religion could possibly do me when I traveled to Dubrovnik, Croatia, then in the grip of a terrible civil war. Tom and his colleagues told me that it would do no good to pack the cognitivist theory into my suitcase and take it with me into the civil war or into any other crisis situation. It seemed to me that cognitivism had been constructed for normal times and not for contingency situations, and thus it has no genuine ethics nor theodicy. To the contrary, the critical theory of society was as much a materialistic theodicy as Hegel's dialectical philosophy had been an idealistic one. The critical theory is a theodicy not only in Weber's sense. Weber understood as theodicy every theoretical effort to explain the suffering in this world. In its original sense, theodicy meant the justification of God or the gods in the face of injustice and evil in their world. Thus, in Weber's sense, the teachings of Marx and Freud could also be seen as theodicies. The critical theory is a theodicy in the sense that without thoughts of the truth, no knowledge is possible of its opposite. Therefore, true philosophy and science must be critical and pessimistic. Thus, the critical theory does not abstractly negate the totally Other, the absolute truth: the wholly Other is rather the determinate or concrete negation of the world of the slaughterhouse and Golgotha; of all that on earth that is called injustice, human abandonment and alienation. For the critical theorist, without thoughts of an unthinkable infinite happiness, there is no consciousness of the earthly transitory happiness, which in view of its transitoriness cannot be overcome and can never be without sorrow. This is what differentiates critical theory from the cognitive theory of religion.

It seems to the critical theorist, that religions had reached their climax when they were able to answer the theodicy problem at a certain level of human evolution, and that they moved into crisis and possibly became obsolete when they were no longer able to do so. As there are dead languages, so there are dead religions as well: Zoroastrianism, the Religion of Light and Darkness or Good and Evil; the Syrian Religion of Pain; the Egyptian Religion of Riddle; the Greek Religion of Beauty and Fate; the Roman Religion of Utility, etc. Admittedly, the word theodicy is modern. We owe it to Leibnitz and Voltaire. But the issue is very old, reaching down even to the evolutionary stage of magic and fetishistic consciousness and its rituals. On the evolutionary level of Judaism, more precisely in 450 B.C., the second temple had been rebuilt in Jerusalem and all its rituals had been restored again, but the high hopes of the exiles returned from Babylon had not been fulfilled. The lamp of religious enthusiasm burned but dimly in that moment of Israel's history and both priests and people treated myths and rituals with weary indifference. Israel began to doubt whether there was a righteous Governor of the universe. That precisely was one of Israel's many experiences with theodicy. In the 1940s, during the Shoah, in Auschwitz, the rabbis even put God on trial and found him guilty, and some of them afterwards stopped all prayers and rituals. Today, ninety percent of the Israelis have lost their faith in consequence of the Shoah and have stopped participating in religious rituals. Israel had a *talion* theodicy and a test theodicy. Both types of theodicies became meaningless through the Shoah and meaningless, too, became their myths and rituals.

In the perspective of the critical theory of religion, the very fact that the religious myths and rituals of persecuted believers in direst need are of no avail is the most monstrous expression of the theodicy problem. Without God, eternal truth has just as little a foothold as infinite love. Indeed, they become unthinkable notions. Of course, the monstrosity is never a cogent argument against the assertion or denial of a state of affairs. Neither the positivistic nor the dialectical logic contains a law to the effect that a judgment is false when its consequence would be despair. From the perspective of the critical theory of religion, however, there cannot be any universal solidarity with the victims of the merciless historical process, when past crimes and the sufferings and the humiliations and the misery of past generations appear irreversible in the secular gaze and beyond redress. This old theodicy problem is one which faces all modern societies in a very new form since the religious traditions, the myths and rituals, the superhuman agents, have largely lost their former authority. The critical theorist of religion observes in civil society palpable regressions into new forms of polytheistic paganism similar to those which appeared 70 years ago in Germany in the name of the folkish philosophy of life. In the view of the dialectical theory of religion, the present magical, or fetishistic, or polytheist pagan regressions undercut the ego-identity that had once been achieved by means of the major world religions. If that is the case, then the cognitive and the critical theorists of religion must not try to escape from the monstrous theodicy problem present in the myths and rituals which they explore. Rather they have to find ways to salvage, if not the substance, then at any rate the humanizing power and the legacy of religious traditions, the semantic potential in myths and rituals, for secular society. Such semantic potential might be rescued not as a religious but rather as a secular, humanistic legacy.

In the view of the dialectical theory of religion, at the primitive and archaic stages of social evolution, the problem of survival—and thus people's experiences of contingencies in dealing with outer nature—were so drastic and dramatic, that they had to be counterbalanced by the narrative production of an illusion of order. With increased control over outer nature, secular knowledge became independent from religious worldviews and their myths and rituals. The religions were increasingly restricted to functions of social integration, particularly rituals. The sciences eventually established a monopoly on the explanation and interpretation of outer nature and finally also of internal nature in the form of modern psychology. The sciences devalued inherited religious and metaphysical global interpretations, and transformed the mode of religious faith into a scientistic attitude that permits only a secular faith in the objectivizing sciences, including the cognitive sciences. In this domain of science contingencies are recognized and to a large extent technically mastered and their consequences made at least bearable. Natural catastrophes are defined as worldwide social events. Their effects are blunted by large-scale administrative operations. Interestingly enough, the consequences of war belong in this category of administered humanity.

In the perspective of the dialectical theory of religion, however, with growing complexity in areas of social co-existence, a number of new contingencies have been produced, without a proportionate growth in the ability to master them. Hence, the need for interpretations that overcome contingency and divest not-yet-controlled accidents of their accidental character, no longer arises in relation to outer nature. However, it is regenerated in an intensified form by suffering from uncontrolled societal processes. Today in 2003, the positivistic social sciences, including the cognitive social sciences, can no longer take on the functions of religious or metaphysical world views. Instead, at the same time that they dissolve the religious and metaphysical illusion of order last produced by Schelling's and Hegel's objectivistic philosophy of history, the positivistic social sciences contribute to an increase in avoidable contingencies. This is so because in their present state the social sciences, including the cognitive social sciences, do not produce technical knowledge that civil society could use for mastering contingency. The positivistic social sciences, including the cognitive sciences, also do not have the confidence in the ability of strong theoretical strategies to penetrate the multiplicity of apparent, nominalistically produced contingencies and make the objective context of social evolution accessible. Considering the risks to individual life that exist de facto, a theory that could interpret away the facticities of loneliness and guilt, sickness and death—as myths and rituals once did—is not even conceivable. Contingencies that are irremovably attached to the bodily and moral constitution of the individual can be raised to consciousness only as contingency. Thus cognitivists must, like all scientists and indeed all modern people, live in principle disconsolately with the contingencies, i.e. with the unresolved theodicy problem.

In the view of the critical theory of religion, philosophical and scientific theories, like cognitivism, have lost their extra-everyday status. That precisely is the reason why today in civil society post-religious and post-metaphysical thinking, e.g. cognitivism, coexists side by side with a religious praxis, even ritual praxis. As long as religious language carries with it inspiring, even necessary semantic content, which still avoids the expressive energy of a philosophical or scientific language, and which still awaits the translation into justifying discourse, philosophical and scientific theory, including cognitivism, will also, in their post-religious and post-metaphysical form, not be able to replace or repress religion. Tom's cognitive theory of religion affirms precisely that fact.

Conclusion

In the face of the new polytheistic mythologies that are spreading in civil society today as they did seven decades ago in fascist Europe, the critical theorist of religion emphasizes what connects radical enlightenment with the monotheistic religions, namely, the element of Transcendence which grants to the ego, held captive in its environment, the distance from the world in its totality and from himself or herself which truly opens up a perspective without which neither personal autonomy nor universal solidarity can be acquired, a perspective based on linguistically mediated, mutual, symmetrical recognition. This common element between monotheism and radical enlightenment, Transcendence, does in no way touch upon the conviction that nothing of the semantic material and potential in the depth of religious myths and rituals will continue unchanged. The semantic content of every religion will have to expose itself to the test of whether it can migrate into secular discourse. But this secularizing integration of religious mythical or ritual contents into secular discourse is the very opposite of a neo-pagan regression behind that self-understanding, individual autonomy and anamnestic, present and proleptic solidarity, which entered world history the first time with the teachings of the Jewish, Christian and Islamic prophets. Obviously, the weak, merely linguistic, transcendence of universal validity claims beyond all individual speakers, cannot possibly replace the strong unreified religious Transcendence of the monotheistic religions, the imageless and nameless Wholly Other, the Infinite, the radically Non-Identical, the absolutely New, as the negation of the slaughterhouse of nature and history and the source of unconditional meaning and ethical validity claims. I hope very much that cognitive and critical theorists of religion will fully participate in the discourse among expert cultures, and will engage themselves in the inversion or translation of religious mythical and ritual semantic material and potential into secular modern society so that it may help to promote the trend toward alternative Future III—a society in which personal sovereignty and universal solidarity will be truly reconciled.

8. DISPATCHES FROM THE "RELIGION" WARS

Russell T. McCutcheon

Two memories, both influential of my later thinking, come to mind when I think of Tom Lawson's contributions to the study of religion.

First, it is sometime in the early 1990s at the University of Toronto and I have just come across a review essay published in the journal *Numen* written by Lawson entitled, "Dispatches from the Methodological Wars" (1991a). There, he reviews two works, Pascal Boyer's *Tradition as Truth and Communication* (1990) and Hans Penner's *Impasse and Resolution* (1989). For Lawson, what is commendable about these two books is that they depart from the usual phenomenological approach to the study of religion and, instead, are driven by naturalistic theories (cognitive science-based theory in the case of the former and structuralist in the case of the latter). As the subtitle of his own co-written book had already made clear (Lawson and McCauley 1990), Lawson's attraction to these two authors' works had much to do with the manner in which they help to make possible an explanatory connection between the cultural and the cognitive level of analysis, a connection prevented by what he characterized in that review essay as the personalistic and hermeneutical studies of many who populate what, quoting Penner, he aptly termed "the academic battlefield."

I was a doctoral student when I first read this essay, and the image of the disciplinary arena as a site of battle was slowly dawning on me; during the coming few years, as I was increasingly exposed to the intellectual and political stakes within the academy (made all too apparent in my schooling at the University of Toronto, under the guidance of Neil McMullin and Donald Wiebe), I kept coming back to Lawson's and Penner's notion of the academic battlefield and the importance of having seasoned veterans send periodic communiqués back from the front. Often these reports are encrypted, as in those that go by the seemingly neutral names of "state of the art" or essays assessing the "retrospect and prospect" of the field. However, despite these euphemisms (i.e., a rose by any other name....), I came to recognize in them tactical dispatches indicative of a shifting and permeable front; if everything was well and smoothly working, there would be no need to assess where we have been and where we ought to be going, and thus no need to judge the current condition of our collective enterprise. After all, we only make maps when we either don't know where we're going or are trying to legitimize where we happen to have found ourselves.

By entitling his essay "Dispatches," and by describing academia as a battlefield, Lawson was among a small group who seemed to me to be calling things by their real names by leaving far behind the myth of academia as a disembodied life of the mind. Instead, they understood disputes over ways of demarcating an object of study, the appropriate ways of study it, and the types of institutions that sprang up around both data and methods, as being contests with considerable stakes. Most recently, I think of Gary Lease's essay, "Fighting over Religion (Notes from the Front)" as another example in this genre, since it is an essay that makes plain that "the rock over which the contestants [in the war over religion] was the issue of definition" (1999: 478). Influenced by writers such as Lawson, I have used the image of a dispatch in print on a couple of occasions, for despite the common, liberal humanist penchant to act as if everyone somehow naturally gets along with each other, the notion of a dispatch nicely conveys that social formations—academic disciplines included—are comprised of competing interests, contradictions, and countless skirmishes—some epic, some forgettable. In that specific social group we know as our academic home, they are taking place in the pages of journals, in conversations between panelists and their conference audiences, around a conference table in the midst of a faculty meeting, during job interviews, in lectures and seminars, even in decisions regarding not only who deserves the honor of having their career celebrated in a festschrift but who deserves the honor of contributing to such a celebration.

The idea of writing a dispatch appeals to me not only because I consider it to be an accurate assessment of the tactical nature of our reports from the front lines; it is also appealing because it takes seriously that all we as scholars have is a thoroughly historical perspective. Despite our hopes and best rhetorical flourishes, we lack a god's eye viewpoint and therefore lack access to the big picture or the epic sweep of the unfolding drama that, in the study of religion at least, our informants generally claim to possess. Reflecting on the spot in which we happen to find ourselves, knowing only a small piece of the map, using the tools available to us, and asking how we got to where we happen to be and where we might go from there, we therefore have no choice but to offer open-ended, fallible, and thus strategic communiqués, bulletins, progress reports, and brief updates. Historically-based scholarship, I have come to conclude, is thus an act of *ad hocery*. Dispatches on works-in-progress are all we have.

Seeing scholarship as a series of tactical dispatches, as a temporary and thus never-ending work-in-progress, has something to do with my second memory of Lawson's influence on my work. It is now sometime late in 1994, I think, and I have started my career by working as an Instructor on a yearly contract at the University of Tennessee, Knoxville. In the intervening years I had met Tom in person at a couple of American Academy of Religion (AAR) meetings and had begun interacting with him in his role as a member of the editorial advisory board to the North American Association for the Study of Religion's (NAASR) journal, *Method and Theory in the Study of Religion*. I had purchased a copy of *Rethinking Religion* at the University of Tennessee bookstore and, while reading it, I developed a rather uneasy sense that those in the human sciences whose work is in some way biologically or psychologically based were in the position to offer what could be considered a final, definitive explanation, thus trumping all other approaches. Given that my own developing interests had much to do with what I would now term the politics of classification, I was concerned at the time with the possibility that some geneticist or maybe even a cognitivist would come along and, in explaining not only my data but both me and my work on the data as well, all in one fell swoop, would effectively pull the rug out from under my own intellectual curiosities. "It's all in the genes" or "That's just how cognition works," would, then, be the ultimate metaphysical reduction. It was not that I feared becoming someone else's data, but that such a definitive, ultimate explanation might curtail my own work. Since he was quickly emerging as one of a small group of people recognized as experts in the application of cognitive sciences to the study of ritual, I emailed this concern to Lawson.

Although I no longer have a copy of his reply (though I recall printing it out and keeping it for some time), I still recall his response: intellectual curiosities are a function of one's theories—change the theory and something new in the data comes to light. Simply put, there are no final explanations. In hindsight, I'd like to think that I already knew this, for at Donald Wiebe's insistence back in Toronto I had read some Karl Popper and had been persuaded that scholarship was driven by bold deductive theories. But, given the concern that motivated my email to Lawson, I can't help but think that I was still laboring under the assumption (shared by theologians, natural scientists, and vulgar Marxists alike) that some aspect of the world is more basic, foundational, or real than all others. For some, "genes," "the brain," and "the principles that govern cognition"—much like "class consciousness" and "experiences of the sacred"—all seemed like a good candidate for such a foundation. But in a few brief emailed lines, Lawson disabused me of this assumption. What's more, I saw that, despite our different theories and the different data these theories made available for scrutiny, our work was part of the same historically-based, tactical, explanatory pursuit we call the human sciences (something far from the humanities, I would say). We both presumed that our scholarship—like the human beliefs, practices, and institutions we each studied—was a strategic work in progress driven by specific interests, assumptions, commitments, and theories, rather than a quest for the enduring human spirit.

Battlefields, dispatches, and the open-ended, problem-oriented nature of scholarship: these are some of the things that I have taken away with me from Tom Lawson's work. Given the likelihood of some contributors to this volume exploring complex topics in the cognitive study of religion, I fear that naming these specific items as being what I have gained from him may strike some as inconsequential. Given that I work in a rather different content area from Lawson, I instead choose to see these as gifts across theoretical settings, suggesting just how rich his work actually is. After all, it is hardly a challenge to influence those who share your theoretical interests, data, and attend the same professional meetings. To have an impact on those who do not share your curiosities and the data with which you satisfy these curiosities is, to my way of thinking, the mark of a scholar who has truly impacted a wider disciplinary pursuit.

All this is to say that I began learning from Lawson just over a decade ago, when he sent back to the rest of us his brief dispatch from the muddy trenches; putting to good use the insights that I have gained from him, as my contribution to a festschrift in his honor I would like to update his dispatch with a few of my own.

Before offering this report from the edge, however, I should caution the overly optimistic reader by prefacing it by saying that some things at the front have not changed all that much—the rations are not any better, socks still get just as wet in the mud, and the dominance of what Lawson correctly identified as the personalistic and hermeneutical approaches is still firmly in place. For instance, in his report on some recent works on religion in the U.S., Alan Wolfe has rightly observed that "[m]any recent books want to know *what faith means to the faithful*" (2002: B8; emphasis added). While this continued hermeneutical, personalistic bias—one that limits the study of religion to reproducing uninterrogated self-disclosure—will no doubt strike some readers as lamentable, it will strike others as evidence of the utter failure of the explanatory turn in the study of religion. I can hear someone asking, "If explanatory studies are as powerful as some of their users claim them to be, why have they not won the day?"[1] I do not see it this way, however; for, over the past few decades, a new generation of scholars have been able to bypass the traditional rites of passage and trials of initiation through which our intellectual predecessors had to pass. Because a small number of these scholars—most of whom, like Lawson, were initially trained to describe features of one or another world religion, set of myths and rituals, or ancient period and text—eventually came to understand theories, and not self-evidently interesting religious data, as the driving force of our intellectual labor and the institutions in which we toil, writers such as myself no longer have to specialize first in the nuanced, empathetic description of this or that world religion, region, cultural setting, or historical period. Simply put, thanks to these scholars the brute facts are not as brutish as they were once thought to be and, because of this, the academic battlefield has slowly become as legitimate a place as any to do one's fieldwork.

With this slow but steady progress in mind, a prefatory dispatch from the "religion" wars originates from the rather highly charged setting of a curtained job interview booth at the annual meeting of the American Academy of Religion/Society of Biblical Literature. In the early 1990s, I was shortlisted for one of the first advertised positions in a religious studies department for a scholar of method and

---

[1] In writing this line I realize that this question is eerily similar to the proverbial anti-evolutionist query: "If evolution exists, then why are there still monkeys?"

theory, and several of the faculty were conducting brief, initial interviews. Although I do not remember all that much from the brief interview, I do have a vivid memory of one of the interviewers asking me where I got my hands dirty (for earlier comments on this sort of question, see McCutcheon 1997: 6–7). I recall answering something about studying methods and theories used by scholars of religion. This answer was obviously unsatisfactory for, as I recall it, the questioner rephrased the query, observing that if he got his hands dirty studying Japanese religions, and, if, for example, another got his hands dirty studying African religions, then where did I dirty my scholarly hands. At that moment it was apparent that the old hermeneutical, descriptivist bias was hovering over the interview booth. He might just as well have come out and said: "Theories are fine and dandy, but what real things do you actually study?"[2]

Thinking back on this episode, I cannot help but juxtapose it to the case of my former M.A. student—Matthew Waggoner—who, as I write this essay, has recently passed his qualifying doctoral examination at the University of California, Santa Cruz, in the cross-disciplinary History of Consciousness program. Working with Gary Lease, Angela Davis and Jim Clifford, he has been encouraged to dive headlong into a thoroughly theoretical dissertation. His supervisory committee had no difficulty understanding Matt to "get his hands dirty" studying theories; after all, doing theory is a form of practice, not idle navel-gazing awaiting practical application. This, however, was not an understanding that I experienced in that small curtained interview booth. Instead, as a professor had once argued, theory was likened more to a snowblower that was useful in moving around the pre-existent brute facts. Seeing theories more like snow-making machines, in answer to that rephrased interview question I said that I understood the job ad to be looking for a scholar

---

[2] This naive realist position is significantly different from that which has recently been put forward by William Arnal (2001a). Arnal argues that the immaturity of our field is evident from the fact that when we engage in theory we generally leave behind specific data and talk only in abstractions. "[W]hen confronted with the theoretical vacuity of our field, when faced with the imperative to be self-conscious about what we are doing, we take recourse in abstraction" (210), he writes in a review essay on the collection of essays, *Secular Theories on Religion* (Jensen and Rothstein [eds.] 2000). For Arnal, theory is "a way of shaping our approach to data in a way that is in turn informed by data" (214). This dialectical relationship is something lost on those with a phenomenological bent who pose the "dirty hands" question.

of methods and theories of religion. Seeing myself to be at least one example of just such a scholar, I looked around the room and said I did my fieldwork at academic conferences such as the one we were all attending at that moment. Needless to say, informing one's interviewers that they are candidates for the status of data does not go over well.

I draw on this minor, personal memory in order to make the point that, as a direct result of the efforts of an earlier generation working in theoretically unfriendly situations—one such laborer would be Lawson himself—a small number of scholars now legitimately study not just myths but contests over what gets to count as "myth" (e.g., Lincoln 1999), not only rituals but the impact of "ritual" (e.g., Bell 1992), not only religious experiences but the rhetoric of "experience" (e.g., Sharf 1998), and, in some cases, not simply religions but the battles over the effects of the very category "religion" itself (most recently, see Smith 1998, Molnár 2002). Although lagging significantly behind a number of other human sciences, such openly theoretical work has now become a legitimate (though, admittedly, still marginal) enterprise in the academic study of religion. For example, tenure-track positions in "theory and method" are now being advertised in our field. Despite such openings, however, an interesting study could focus on the sort of scholars who are hired into these recently advertised positions, followed by the types of undergraduate and graduate courses that go by this name. My suspicion is that the increasing integration of "theory and method" into our field could very well represent a domestication of what was once seen as the dangers of theory. To state the case far too simply, some scholars whose work fall under this designation may simply use Paul Ricoeur's work to offer a "close reading" or this or that text.

This suspicion is based on the manner in which the dominant discourse has already successfully appropriated "theory talk," as evidenced in the AAR's book series, "Reflection and Theory in the Study of Religion." As described by the Academy, this series publishes works

> that contribute to theoretical reflection in theology, ethics, philosophy, hermeneutics, methodologies, comparative religion, and the like. The series is particularly interested in contemporary approaches that employ gender, class, sexuality, and race philosophies in constructive analyses" (see *Religious Studies News* 17/2 [2002]: 5 for the description of the series).

Among the mainly philosophically-oriented volumes published so far in this series[3] is *Converging on Culture: Theologians in Dialogue with Cultural Analysis and Criticism* (Brown et al. 2001), a volume described at its publisher's web site as follows:

> Theologians are increasingly looking to cultural analysis and criticism, rather than philosophy, as a dialogue partner for cross-disciplinary studies. This book explores the importance of this shift by bringing together scholars from a variety of theological perspectives to analyze different contemporary theories of culture and cultural movements. The essays here examine the theoretical relationship between theology and cultural studies and then discuss a series of controversial topics that cry out for theological reflection.

Keeping in mind the presumed relationship between theory and issues "crying out" for theological reflection, we can say that in some regards the battle lines at the front have not changed all that much. However, even if a bad case of trenchfoot still awaits anyone interested in theory who stays in the mud too long, the very fact that an increasing number of people are intent on charting our field's intellectual and institutional skirmishes—both past and present—is a significant development. As my contribution to this volume I'd therefore like to do a little charting of my own. So, with a tip of my dented helmet to Lawson, I offer the following dispatches from the wars of "religion." My hope is that they help to illustrate some of what is at stake in our use of "religion" in naming a seemingly distinct subset of otherwise mundane cultural practices.

Choosing the title that I have for this chapter, I hope, makes explicit that, in the case of the early modern conflicts we commonly call the European "wars of religion," something political was and continues to be at stake in seeing these historical contests as somehow driven by conflicting doctrines on the afterlife and disagreements over interior beliefs in invisible beings, instead of seeing such theological conflicts as part of the rhetorical means by which competing groups contested such practical issues as access to resources and wealth as well as the limits of social space and identity. Making the shift from thinking of religions as self-contained belief systems to

---

[3] Keeping in mind the long-disputed place philosophical method has held in such organizations as the IAHR, this series' emphasis on philosophy of religion warrants attention.

seeing "religion" as a socio-rhetorical tool useful in the always messy business of social formation requires that one do an archeology of the term itself. After a bit of digging it becomes apparent that beginning somewhere around sixteenth-century in Europe, there was a significant shift in the manner in which the term "religion" was used. As argued by Jonathan Z. Smith (1998: 270–1), between the sixteenth and eighteenth centuries a change occurred, such that a concept/word that was once reserved for naming behaviors and membership within institutions (e.g., denoting one's membership within a monastic community) came to be universalized, interiorized, and thus privatized. A suitable early example would be the onetime Greek professor and Martin Luther's Wittenberg spokesman, Philip Melanchton (d. 1560), who, in 1549, gave assent to the partial restoration of Roman Catholic liturgy. "He did so," writes Tracy, "because he believed that outer forms of worship were 'indifferent things' [Greek: *adiaphora*] that could be accepted if essential doctrine was not compromised" (1999: 93). Obviously connected with the practical successes of various sixteenth-century Reformers' rhetorics (e.g., the subversion of an established institution by privileging the lone reader, nicely accomplished by Martin Luther's quest for original meaning [the doctrine of *sola scriptura*] or, as Smith suggests, Huldrych Zwingli's and John Calvin's association of religion with personal piety), Smith describes how, by the eighteenth century, the one-time ritual and institutional contexts of such commonly found terms as "reverence", "service", "adoration", and "worship" "have been all but evacuated of ritual connotations, and seem more to denote *a state of mind*" (271; italics added). As he then goes on to observe,

> [t]his shift to belief as the defining characteristic of religion (stressed in the German preference for the term *Glaube* over *Religion*, used in the increasingly English usage of 'faiths' as a synonym for 'religions') raised a host of interrelated questions of credibility and truth.

By shifting the ground from ritual to belief—from observable practice and institutions to private feeling and sentiment—a whole new set of criteria were needed to adjudicate not the propriety of following the prescribed ritual behaviors but the supposed authenticity, meaning, and depth of one's inner experience. And of course, along with these new criteria came new institutions in which these criteria were debated, canonized, and applied, along with new collections of authenticity experts who interpreted and implemented the rules, as well as new forms of prescribed behaviors incumbent on all those who professed (i.e., wished to provide compelling evidence of) true belief. We have here an early instance of the manner in which the very public and obviously political rhetoric of privatized faith and experience proved to be a highly effective means by which to institute and organize an emergent, oppositional group intent on unseating long established institutions, centers of political power, and systems of social rank and entitlement.

This shift on the part of those marginal to, and thus disenfranchised from, the centers of traditional authority—a typically Protestant shift that demoted uniform exterior practice (e.g., ritual, institution, social rank, etc.) to the status of mere "indifferent things" by means of a rhetoric of interiorized faith and privacy (as is also found not only in William James's first Gifford Lecture, where he criticized "conventional observances" as being mere secondhand, dull habits, but also in the old phenomenological distinction between essence and manifestation)—was a useful rhetorical and thus political move for negotiating competing senses of credibility, rank, legitimacy, and value. It provided an escape from a dominant environment while also providing an alternative basis for authorizing oppositional meaning and for contesting identities. Given that during this time the slow shift to the European nation-state was also taking place—a shift that entailed a dramatic reorganization of peoples, boundaries, ideas of self-identity—efficient tools were required for re-classifying and managing ever more diverse and widely scattered populations; the universalization and privatization provided by the discourse on faith proved an effective technique of social engineering.

With all this in mind, the wars over the rhetoric of "religion" can be understood as a specific site where groups compete, by means of dueling classification techniques, over scarce resources. Foreign/domestic, unclean/clean, intolerant/tolerant, superstitious/religious are among some of these techniques; most recently, discourses on cults/religions and, post-September 11, 2001, U.S., European, and Israeli domestic discourses on terrorists/freedom fighter (as well as Muslim discourses on "the infidels"), have been added to the arsenal of those wishing to reinvent themselves by delegitimizing the political goals of competing social groups. For instance, as made plain by the British Prime Minister, Tony Blair, in his televised October 7, 2001, speech to the British people, calling those who carried out the September 11th attacks "Islamic terrorists" is, in his words, an insult to Islam.

For those such as Blair who use "religion" to denote a politically ineffectual system of spiritual beliefs, it is more than an insult, for it is actually a contradiction in terms insomuch as "religion" is a classification only extended to "peaceful" and therefore "civil" social movements that do not conflict with dominant groups' practical interests. In fact, we now seem to have new classifications that reflect this: whereas a "Muslim" remains a peaceful, rational, politically neutral, and thus tolerant person, an "Islamisist" is an irrational person who puts into practice dangerous politics (as phrased by Rushdie 2001).

As I hope is by now clear, quite apart from an interest in theorizing religious behaviors, I believe that an under-studied technique for accomplishing the never-ending work of engineering a social group's continued existence involves studying the means by which groups classify certain sorts of acts, institutions, and people as religious/secular. Like the "dirty hands" episode at a job interview, scrimmages over "religion" and "civility" take place not simply in heated political speeches, such as Blair's or George W. Bush's, but also in the various discursive sites that comprise the academy: in the classroom; in professional periodicals; at scholarly conferences; and in monographs. It is to these assorted sites that I now wish to turn.

Several years ago, I had the good fortune to be invited to visit an undergraduate class of religious studies majors at the University of Vermont. The professor, a good friend of Lawson's—and, along with Wiebe, the third member of NAASR's founding trinity—Luther Martin, was using a book of mine (1997) in his class as a springboard into a variety of theoretical issues in the contemporary field. His students tackled one chapter per week and, each week, he invited different colleagues to attend the class, to provide their own input and take the discussion wherever they wished. With funding from their department's undergraduate religious studies student association, he kindly arranged for me to attend the class near the conclusion of the course. His students had a number of questions, comments, and insightful criticisms, and so I was suitably—and quite enjoyably— grilled by them.

What stands out most in my mind from that wonderful visit—and what comprises my second dispatch—was learning that the pleasant city of Burlington, Vermont, complete with its cobblestone downtown street open only to strollers and shoppers looking for a good deal on fresh maple syrup, could be a tactical site in the war over "religion" and how to study "it." For a number of colleagues found the critique of the discourse on sui generis religion, or what could also be termed the religion *qua* private affair tradition in the study of religion, to be an attack on a straw man. In other words, during their visits to the class some of them informed the students that, although scholars such as Mircea Eliade (d. 1986), along with his many University of Chicago graduates, did indeed have an impact on the field in the 1960s and 1970s, few people read his work anymore or studied religion in that manner. Simply put, Martin's students were informed that a critique of the politics of the so-called "Chicago school" and its presumption that religion, religious impulses, and religious experiences were free of the kinds of social causes and psychological preconditions that affect all other forms of human production was a rather misguided witch hunt that mis-portrayed the discipline into which these undergraduate students were being initiated.

Taking seriously this criticism—a criticism that went to the very heart of my book, and one which some of the students repeated to me in person—I replied by asking how many of these colleagues would, then, agree that those practices we generally call religious are utterly ordinary human events wholly explicable by appeal to any one of the epistemological tools used throughout such human sciences as sociology or psychology or anthropology. The answer: few. For many, I learned, "things religious" were somehow distinct and set apart from the hurly-burly world of mundane human comings and goings—an apartness signaled (or, as I would say, established) by appeals to various rhetorics, e.g., deep meaning, close reading, origins, profound truths, authenticity, uniquely personal experiences, and aesthetic sensibilities.

Hearing this answer to my question, I realized that I had a paradox on my hands: on the one hand the critique was said to be an attack on a straw man, yet on the other, the people maintaining this position held—to my way of thinking, at least—the very views targeted by the critique. I found it fascinating that, for some reason, some of my readers were not able to see themselves in the mirror that I thought I was holding up to them. Perhaps they misread this critique as being concerned only with Eliade's work, I thought, rather than being a critique of the techniques in use throughout an entire academic discipline—the critique just happened to use Eliade's work (along with the work of such influential scholars as the late Wilfred Cantwell Smith, Huston Smith, and many others of the current generation of scholars) as a convenient entry point, treating him as one scholar, among others, whose work represented wider trends. Although they may not have been ardent readers of, say, Eliade's work, they nonetheless appeared to me to share a viewpoint basic to his work. But attributing a misreading to my friend's colleagues struck me as hardly fair; after all, they are more than likely very intelligent people and astute readers skilled in the nuances of searching for the deep meaning of a text. What's more, attributing a misreading would rest on a troublesome notion, my supposedly privileged authorial intention, thus lodging the matter within problems of hermeneutics. Along with Lawson, I place myself within a tradition of scholarship that problematizes the field's enduring preoccupation with issues of correct interpretation, personal meaning, and personal choice; whereas his interests involve the cognitive constraints that make meaningful existence possible, mine revolve around the political constraints that do the same work. It therefore seemed hardly appropriate to invoke the privilege of "right meaning" in my own defense. Surely there had to be something more to it than this.

Because there are few things worse than for a young scholar to be told his new book is *passé* even before the shine has worn off of the dust jacket, this memory stuck with me. I continued to mull over how academic disciplines develop, how scholars develop a sense of themselves as inhabiting these disciplines, how disciplines rise to dominance, how they are interconnected to larger economic and political forces, how those who oppose such developments can effectively make tactical interventions that have some consequence, and what all this had to do with that slippery collection of things that some of us call religion. During the next few years I explored these topics in discrete essays, each of which was prompted by some specific question or, more than likely, some irritation that resulted from reading work published in our field's primary journals or in the popular media. In hindsight I have come to see that they all explore a common issue made apparent in that University of Vermont classroom: how to apply a social theory to an academic discipline in order to explain the role played by various rhetorics in creating and sustaining seemingly coherent and lasting social identities. These identities, like all social identities, come with issues of turf and privilege and the never-ending threat of fracture and dissolution. What's more, the apparent homogeneity of these social identities is a continual, hindsight concoction.

In connecting up the dots in just this fashion, I had in mind an aside made by Gary Lease concerning the need to write a natural history of institutions, such as the institution of using "religion" to name part of the otherwise contingent, social world. As I have quoted him before, writing such a history would require assembling a "catalog of strategies for *maintaining* paradoxes, *fighting* over dissonances, and *surviving* breakdowns" (Lease 1994: 475). As I went on to say elsewhere, "[s]uch a catalog would amount to a map of the many social sites where myths and rituals are developed and deployed for one of the primary ways in which social formations are constructed, maintained, contested, and rebuilt is through the active process of mythmaking" (2001: 31). Just as with all social formations, this mythmaking activity takes place all across culture, within academic disciplines no less, by means of certain rhetorical techniques that comprise "the play of forces at work in a field of power and knowledge" (Ransom 1997: 24), forces that can be mapped across the various stages in the discipline's natural history.

Tackling such a natural history was likely impossible not long ago since many in the field then—and, as my experience with colleagues and students today suggests, many today as well—took religion to be such a fundamental component of human minds and societies that they could not historicize the very category and were thus incapable of working outside the operating system established by several hundred years of thinking inside the "religion" box. Because entertaining a thoroughly naturalistic explanation for things that some argued to be irreducibly religious was the first step toward writing a natural history of "religion," those of us who now study the category itself stand in the shadow of previous generations bold enough to entertain that religion might not necessarily be religious. Or, as Susan Sontag asked in 1961 in a *New York Review of Books* essay on Walter Kaufmann's *Religion from Tolstoy to Camus*, entitled, "Piety without Content": "Does the notion 'religion' have any serious *religious* meaning at all?" (2001: 252). Her answer?

> My own view is that one cannot be religious in general any more than one can speak language in general; at any given moment one speaks French or English or Swahili or Japanese, but not "language." Similarly one is not "a religionist," but a believing Catholic, Jew, Presbyterian, Shintoist, or Tallensi.... [F]or a believer, the concept of "religion" (and of deciding to become religious) makes no sense as a category. (For a rationalist critic, from Lucretius to Voltaire to Freud, the term

does have a certain polemical sense when, typically, he opposes "religion" on the one hand to "science" or "reason" on the other.) Neither does it make sense as a concept of objective sociological and historical inquiry. To be religious is always to be in some sense an adherent (even as a heretic) to a specific symbolism and a specific historic community.... It is to be involved in specific beliefs and practices, not just to give assent to the philosophical assertions that a being whom we may call God exists, that life has meaning, etc. Religion is not equivalent to the theistic proposition. (253)

Although not often cited, or more than likely read, by scholars of religion, her forty year old essay is surprisingly prescient, for it stakes out some of the crucial skirmishes that came to comprise the war on "religion." From the often-used religion/language analogy (an analogy easily datable to nineteenth-century philologically-influenced scholarship on religion), to the claim that generalized scholarship operates on a level far different from any specific group's so-called lived experience and self-understanding, and finally to her insight that "religion" is in fact a polemical (or, I would say, rhetorical) tool, Sontag's brief essay sets the stage for much of what is today happening in the academy. Her displeasure with the manner in which "soft-headed" and "intellectually pompous" (253) liberal writers universalize the notion of religion is a sentiment likely shared by at least some contemporary combatants in this battle.

However, after acknowledging this debt to those who first demythologized religion, we must recognize that the object of study in, say, David Hume's classic natural history of religion is rather different from that which we can study by means of Lease's recommendation. The key difference? Scholars such as Hume himself, like all those who deploy this category to name certain sorts of human practices, comprise but one instance of our data. To rephrase, this new natural history is curious as to how scholars such as Hume so easily selected this and not that set of human behaviors (the so-called brute facts that some say beg to be taken into account [see Strenski (2001: 694) for a recent defense of brute facts]) to place under the category "religion."

Now, by writing a "natural history" I mean something significantly less ambitious than our eighteenth- and nineteenth-century predecessors once did; I mean simply that it is a history which, to borrow from the late British Marxist literary critic Raymond Williams (1990: 121–127), presumes social groups to go through at least three stages that are analytically distinguishable: emergent, dominant, and residual (see also McCutcheon 2001: ch. 2). In writing such a history, several presumptions are key: (1) nothing springs from the ground fully formed; (2) there exists no narrative necessity to social change (a.k.a. Destiny); (3) all social movements are fractured systems, always in flux, from which (4) alienated and discarded residue forms the raw materials that, under some new, previously unforeseen circumstance, *might* lead to the emergence of new social groups intent on establishing through narrative their own exclusive rights to exist and patrol a specific turf by claims of uniqueness and exceptionality.[4] These presumptions are applicable to all social groups, from the nation-state, ethnic groups, and the family, to collections of scholars working within what we call academic disciplines. For example, the claim to autonomy, turf, and privilege that we commonly refer to as the nationalist doctrine of "American exceptionalism," has much the same effect as the claim that religion is sui generis has among those who call themselves Historians of Religions. Whereas the former was widely used (and still in use) to assist in the production of the U.S. nation-state, the latter was a popular technique for establishing and policing an intellectual and institutional space in which to work, both in the "late nineteenth and early twentieth centuries [among] ... the newly emergent social sciences" (Smith 2001: 136; e.g., see Durkheim [1995: 15]) as well as in the re-establishment of the study of religion in the U.S. in the mid-twentieth century. A natural history must be applicable to all of these instances.

The basis of this approach to writing a natural history of a scholarly pursuit and its tools of classification—if we drop the nineteenth-century overtones of "naturalness" and add a heaping tablespoon of irony, we might simply call it a genealogy—can be summed up in two related comments made by Foucault: "What is found at the historical beginning of things is not the inviolable identity of their origin; it is the dissension of other things. It is disparity"; and "[t]he forces operating in history are not controlled by destiny or regulative mechanisms, but respond to haphazard conflicts" (1977: 142, 154). Moving beyond explanatory studies of religion to an explanatory

---

[4] As Jim Clifford phrased it: "'Post-' is always shadowed by 'neo-'" (1997: 277). Or, as sung by the Minneapolis rock trio, Semisonic, in their hit song from 1998, "Closing Time": "Every new beginning comes from some other beginning's end."

study of "religion," and those who use it in their professional lives, requires us to examine the role this classification plays as a regulative mechanism, drawing up an inventory of the ad hoc rhetorical and narrative techniques—what Willi Braun once called slippery abstractions—employed in those onetime chance conflicts and opportunities that, now in hindsight, we see as comprising one coherent academic discipline.

With this developing social theory in mind—notably the presumed role played by polemics and rhetorics for, to repeat Lease, "*maintaining* paradoxes, *fighting* over dissonances, and *surviving* breakdowns"— I offer a third dispatch, concerning a skirmish that took place in the pages of our field's main professional newspapers, *Religious Studies News*. It was a October 2000 interview with the well known Princeton scholar, David Carrasco (2000), an interview I had not read when it first came out but one that my friend and former colleague, Jack Llewellyn, later told me that I must read. (As graduates of the University of Chicago, both Lawson and Llewellyn enable me to say, with all honesty: "Some of my best friends are Chicago grads.") Because Carrasco made a point in the interview to champion what he called "real critical dialogue" among colleagues, rather than a "critical put down of various positions," I wrote him a letter in late March 2001, pursuing topics that I found problematic in his interview. In my letter I focused on the fact that the topic of the "Chicago school" comes up early in the interview, when Carrasco commented:

> I'm impressed by how often some critics reduce the methods and approaches we learned in the '70s and '80s to their own provincial views of what Eliade, Long, Smith, Kitagawa, Wheatley and others were and in some cases still are doing. The comparative approach, the ensemble of texts, the critical respect for various expressions of the sacred continue to be valuable tools for me. (2000: 16)

Later in the interview he elaborated by saying that he therefore maintains in his work a "respect for religious symbols as religious: vehicles for various modes of sacrality."

With the paradox presented by my colleagues in Vermont in my mind, I was curious about, on the one had, Carrasco's dismissal of so-called provincial critics of the "Chicago school" and, on the other, with how close his choice of words were to those themes that are easily found throughout Eliade's body of work (though not in J. Z. Smith's or Bruce Lincoln's work, of course, suggesting that Carrasco ought to be more careful in how he uses "the Chicago school"; for this reason, it is likely more useful to talk about the discourse on sui generis religion or the private affair tradition in our field). For example, we see in both Carrasco's and Eliade's work references to the "provincial" nature of scholarship with which they disagree, and they both refer to such things as "expressions of the sacred," "modalities of the sacred," "religious experience," "religious imagination," "depth of genius," etc. Ironically, in criticizing those who have misrepresented the complexity of Chicago school, Carrasco's brief interview presents a nicely distilled example of the very things that some writers have critiqued for their lack of theoretical specificity and their undisclosed politics. Much like analyzing a news conference from the Pentagon, I found in his text imperialist rhetorics of center and periphery, home and abroad, *en vogue* and *passé*, domestic and foreign, city and country, relevant and irrelevant coupled with rhetorics of depth and shallowness being used amidst denials of their use.

In fact, it is hard not to hear echoes of previous battles in Carrasco's words; as Johannes Wolfart pointed out to me, we find the strategic rhetoric of provincialization in use at least as far back as Imperial Rome's efforts to manage the lands they conquered outside of Italy. For instance, as Peter Brown observes, in documents dating from the late Roman Empire,

> [p]easants ... and ... pagans treated as no better than countryfolk, were consistently presented as passive and congenitally simple minded, so that they could be expected to follow the gentle, because orderly, lead of their natural superiors into the true faith. Among the upper classes, a combination of browbeating and cajolery was the stuff of late Roman politics. (1997: 45)

Although use of the term "provincial"—like writing a "state of the art"—seems to have an almost cultured ring to it—it is not difficult to hear in it the same "browbeating and cajolery" that, to many contemporary ears, cannot help but be heard in any group's effort to legitimize their own social world by claiming that their competitors are unlearned and thus unenlightened "heathens" (originally referring to those who inhabited the heath, that wide, flat, uncultivated waste area outside the limits of the town), "pagans" (derived from the Latin *paganus* and referring to those who inhabited the *pagus* or the country district), or perhaps "gentiles" (from the pre-pejorative Greek. γενος and then the Latin *genus*, specifying identity based on birth, kind, or stock, easily then used for defining those of other, lesser birthrights). Hearing this condescending rhetoric of centers and peripheries, towns and peasants, cultured and unlettered, proper and improper, meant that, much like the professors who labeled criticisms of sui generis religion a straw man argument, Carrasco's interview stuck me as a classic example of "having one's cake and eating it too"—amidst earnest calls for serious exchange we find an unquestioned orthodoxy artfully reproducing its self-declared territorial prerogative by means of paternalistic dismissals of alternative viewpoints. Amazingly, those who brandish such heavy-handed rhetorics to banish competitors to the hinterlands are all too often seen as great liberal pluralists and inclusivists forging a bold, new collective will. More recently, Carol Zaleski's endearing "Letter to William James" comes to mind as but another example of this rhetorical technique. "Why does the *Varieties* endure when other academic studies of religion become so quickly dated?," she asks. "[Y]our work endures while others lose currency as soon as they wear thin enough to reveal their ideological slant" (2002: 32). Apparently those with whom we agree are seamless and float far above the fray, free of ideology, influence, and point of view; whereas the merely fashionable, those whose stitching is easily visible, are of obviously lesser quality. Could it not be that James's work endures not because it is timeless but because of the utility of his interiorist rhetorics? Linked only to the special private center of the seemingly lone individual, it can be all things to all people and thus useful in countless changing social exchanges and negotiations. Scholarship that presumes an essential, interior subject retains its currency because it sponsors the illusion of permanence and endurance.

In the spirit of real, critical dialogue, my letter's question to Carrasco was two-fold. First, given the quintessential "Chicago" manner in which he spoke of the field, its data, the scholar of religion's respectful task, etc., precisely how have critics misread Eliade and others? After all, his interview struck me as a case in point for the Chicago school's shortcomings, for when I finished reading it I was no clearer on precisely what the scholar of religion in this tradition actually studies. Religion, it seems, is deep and meaningful and deserving of respect, but what, precisely is it and how does the scholar know this about it? This led directly to my second question: To what, I asked, in the observable world of human practices does the taxon "the sacred" actually refer? Surely, *its* supposed expressions are observable (hence scholars' enduring preoccupation with the categories of myth, ritual, and symbol), but what is the antecedent to the possessive pronoun "its"? Is it merely a necessary theoretical/disciplinary postulate, as Dan Pals maintained more than a decade ago in a spirited exchange with Robert Segal and Donald Wiebe? Is it an intentional being, as in when Eliade talks about "the sacred manifesting itself"? Or, still further, is it an irreducible, Kantian component of human consciousness, much as Rudolf Otto and even F. Max Müller once held and, more recently, as some argue, as Eliade himself actually meant? In other words, apart from rhetorics of genius, so-called depth experiences, and the circular, terribly uninformative, and unargued assertion that we ought to treat "religious symbols as religious," Carrasco's interview left me unilluminated as to what it is that we as scholars of religion are actually doing when we say we are studying religion. But what is most fascinating was that such circular comments have taken on the role of truisms—they routinely appear in the literature in our field and seem to be persuasive to most (or at least many) of the field's practitioners and certainly to many, if not most, of its students. Instead of meeting with frowns and head scratching, using this rhetoric in a scholarly article or in a conference presentation usually prompts a lot of silent head nodding in agreement, much like the Zen Buddhist tale concerning the Venerable Mahakasyapa who alone smiled in silent recognition when the Buddha once held up a flower. Because the blossom of "treating religious symbols as religion" is utterly without scent or substance, it is all the more curious how it could smell so sweet to others.

Now, of course the people whom we study employ such rhetorics all the time; given the sort of social theory with which some critics work, such rhetorics are thought to play an important role in reproducing various groups' social identities, authorities, etc. Insomuch as our students are largely drawn from these very communities, it should come as no surprise that, when used in our classes, these rhetorics strike them as very comfortable and familiar. In fact, strong teaching evaluations in our field may be more an indication of the instructor's ability to placate his or her students by parading out a few therapeutically useful rhetorical phrases than of their ability to provoke people to have a novel thought. But playing to the audience in the hope for strong teaching evaluations cannot fully explain the continued use of these rhetorics in our classrooms and in our scholarship. So just why is it that we continue to find so many scholars of religion reproducing these very rhetorics in their purely descriptivist scholarship, rather than, as Durkheim did a hundred years ago, redescribing them in a new, explanatory vocabulary? "If one isn't content with description," Foucault wrote, "if one wants to try and explain a victory or a defeat, then one does have to pose the problems in terms of strategies and ask, 'Why did that work? How did that hold up?'" (1980: 209). Developing a social theory of "religion," then, is an effort to document further, and attempt to account for, the victory of a certain sort of institution by means of its specific, strategic rhetoric.

To be sure, the North American study of religion as practiced over the past forty years has gained considerable institutional turf by drawing on these useful rhetorical techniques—attesting to the social impact of these devices. However, as observed by Jonathan Z. Smith some time ago, coming out of our mouths and our pens, these rhetorics are a rather unoriginal and unimaginative repetition of what the people under study (at least those on the politically liberal end of things) are already saying about themselves, prompting me to wonder what scholarship-as-repetition has to gain? As should be clear, I tend to think that we're in the business of doing something other than simply rewording indigenous reports; the scholar of religion is not a prophet (lit. a mouth-piece). Now, "the sacred" is, of course, part of a second order, reductive language, making it much more than a mere paraphrase—after all, I'm not sure anyone thinks they are experiencing "the sacred" when they, say, eat a wafer and drink wine while hearing the words, "Take, eat, in remembrance of me" or while they circumambulate the Ka'bah. "The sacred" reduces, organizes, and thus productively homogenizes various potentially competing local taxonomies into one grand discourse, thus allowing novel comparison and juxtaposition to take place. (Question: without "the sacred" as an organizing concept, how would Eliade have written his *Patterns in Comparative Religion*?) Should one already believe that there is something enduring and deeply human(e) that escapes the grasp of observation, then I suppose the reduction inevitably involved in talk of "the sacred," "creativity," and "depth," and "genius" passes unnoticed. But, as I have argued elsewhere, such a study is more akin to a liberal practice of religious pluralism than a species of the human sciences as practiced in the public university. For those of us who study religion, and the naming of cultural practices as religion, as a fascinating yet all too human socio-cognitive activity, a means whereby historical agents accomplish this or that practical activity—one of which is social formation—utilizing the language of "the sacred," and the motives that drive such utilization, are insufficient for attaining our goals.

It is precisely the hope to do something other than merely paraphrase the participant taxonomies under study that drives those who Carrasco and many others unfairly (but, given their social interests, understandably) deride as the misinformed, provincial critics of the Chicago school. Despite the obviously pejorative sense of this characterization, it is, ironically, an accurate description; given that Foucault understood the role of critique to be "the art of not being governed so much" (1996: 384), such criticism indeed arises from the unruly margins. But, if—as I suggested at the outset of this essay—*all* scholarship is constituted by tactical, provincial communiqués, then there is a very real difference in tone between the work of critics acknowledging their situatedness, on the one hand, and the work of equally provincial guardians of the self-appointed center who tirelessly portray their own interests as definitive of all possible interests. For example, take Eliade's own early series of Romanian articles newspaper entitled "Letters to a Provincial" in which he addressed what he took to be the so-called young generation of interwar Romanians. In this series of articles he wrote to an idealized

> "provincial" or parochial type.... To this "provincial" I gave lessons in manliness and heroism, I summoned him to shake off clichés, indolence, and mediocrity.... I was obsessed by the fear that our generation, the only *free* generation in the history of the Romanian people, would not have time to accomplish its "mission" (Eliade 1990: 135).

Rather than offering such wise counsel to those on the regional margins of the authoritative center, bulletins from the wars over "religion" revel in their own edginess; they are an intentional reaction against the pomposity of the self-appointed center and its gatekeepers. Like all dispatches, then, this one is a report *from* a provincial to his peers who are, inevitably, but other provincials—because, at the end of the day, all we've got is a "dispersion of centers" (Foucault 1990: 34) where members of differing groups work tirelessly to authorize their specific local as the universal.

Since critics of "religion" are hardly above the fray, I therefore admit to having an interest in what one possible future might hold; my work is therefore not innocent navel-gazing since it works to authorize but a new local perspective. The catalog I have in mind is therefore the first step toward establishing an alternative object of study, constitutive of an alternative "we." The "we" that I have in mind is a group interested in examining those devices whereby our colleagues establish what Peter Brown, in his studies of early Christianity, has nicely termed an "imaginative room for manœuvre" (1997: 14). By this I mean the techniques and devices—the rites of passage, if you will—whereby people understand and portray themselves self-evidently *as* colleagues—or maybe I should say how they think and act themselves *into* colleagues, *into* scholars, *into* members of a guild, *into* sharing common values, *into* pursuing common disciplinary goals, and, in fact, *into* individuals with stable subjectivities and even *into* citizens possessing such intangible things as "inalienable rights."[5] Examining these techniques attempts to answer a question posed by Foucault: "Which kind of political techniques, which technology of government, has been put into work and used and developed in the general framework of the reason of state in order to make of the individual a significant element for the state?" (1988: 153). My answer to his question is that such concepts as "religion," "faith," "spirit," "experience," "authenticity," etc.—and the organized domains of human practice entailed and curtailed by such concepts—are just such techniques. The future of this one academic field, then, may have more to do with studying the production of subjectivities, privacies, and the sorts of self/State complexes that they make possible than it does with having "respect for religious symbols as religious," whatever that may mean. The future site where scholars dirty their hands the most may turn out to be historicizing rhetorics of "religion," "spirit," and "faith," etc., studying them as "the new techniques by which the individual could be integrated into the social entity" (Foucault 1988: 153). This future field is thus occupied with examining the conceptual and practical techniques used in the process of political marginalism (Foucault 1988: 152).

Such a field would focus on the rhetorical "play of forces" that helps to provide the conceptual and practical context for disparate people to experience themselves *as* private, meaningful, and valuable selves, related in this or that manner to other equally private selves.

---

[5] The role played by a festschrift in helping to create a career by seemingly capping it off (by providing some sense of closure by means of retrospection), could itself be an object of study in the manufacture of a sense of professionalism.

Without intending to be any sort of orthodox or definitive application of Foucault's work, it aims to investigate "the way by which, through some political technology of individuals, we have been led to recognize ourselves as a society, as a part of a social entity, as part of a nation or of a state" (1988: 146). Recalling my Vermont experience, in attempting to study what Foucault termed "political technology of individuals" (146), there can be little hope that the alien image that appears to some of my readers will be easily recognizable. Although I have no interest in exploring his developmental psychoanalytic theory, it is nonetheless somewhat as Jacques Lacan argued in a 1949 conference paper, later published as, "The Mirror-state as Formative of the Function of the I" (1982); the image will more than likely appear to many as a lie, as a silly, maybe even offensive, caricature that dances briefly on the outskirts of town in a fun house mirror, distorting beyond all recognition that which they see when, in the safety of their mind's eye, they experience themselves *as* selves integrated into various groups. Shifting attention from enjoying such self-perceptions to problematizing how they are possible is therefore a tough sell. Following Foucault, I take it to be the role of the critic "to disturb people's mental habits," all in an effort to help change the circumstances in which we have ideas and build groups.

With the topic of disturbing mental habits in mind, my fourth dispatch is once again wired in from the national meeting of the American Academy of Religion and the Society of Biblical Literature, this time in Denver, Colorado, in 2001. At this meeting some of us attempted to critique one way that we maintain ourselves as "scholars" and "experts": the self-important ribbons that hang from some attendees' name badges. Instead of saying "Author," "Exhibitor," "Program Unit Chair," or "Donor," a small number of us proudly displayed colorful ribbons proclaiming "I can count to ten," "I like myself," "I try my best," "I'm a winner," and "Old Fart" (proudly worn by Luther Martin, if my memory serves me well). I elected to wear a bright yellow one with cute little red and blue stars on it, saying in gold print, "4th Place." Although some people immediately "got" the meaning of this meaningless signifier—after all, not many people draw attention to themselves by displaying a ribbon that basically says they lost so badly that they didn't even mount the podium—a surprising number of well-meaning people congratulated me and then asked what I had done to win it (i.e., what I had done so poorly as to lose so badly). The expectant looks on their faces, while they waited for my answer, were like little exclamation marks, highlighting their inability to see the structure of imposed identity and self-importance that we employ to make sense of ourselves at such mass meetings—techniques that enable a supposedly seamless "us" (after all, we are all simply "members of the academy," something communicated by the fact of our name badges and institutional affiliations) to rank and distinguish amongst ourselves, thus making the academy a meaningful, discursive space where difference and similarity can co-mingle. Instead, they could only put these rules into practice and use them to understand my—and, in relation to me, now their own—apparently new-found status. That something is lost in explaining parody—saying, "Well, you see, as with all signifiers, in itself the ribbon is meaningless and empty, and is thus a lampoon of the supposedly stable meaning and self-identity that we all seem to derive from those other ribbons some of us get to wear . . ."—goes without saying. Looking into their faces, I felt like I was trying to explain why the campfire scene in Mel Brooks's "Blazing Saddles" was funny or how a "Knock-Knock" joke is supposed to work. Such moments are awkward because they make clear that both you and your well-meaning interlocutor are part of the discourse, are implicated, and thus the joke is on—in fact, the joke *is*—us. Sometimes I simply answered by saying, "Ah, don't ask"—which, at the time, I thought was quite funny, but which I now see to have been a way of side-stepping the entire issue, making it akin to what Roland Barthes once called a feint at the right moment or what Wiebe aptly termed a failure of nerve.

This sense of a "feint at the right moment" makes clear that there is a risk that attends trying to explain such jokes. Magicians who share secrets do not win friends. Jonathan Z. Smith has written on the manner in which keeping the joke's principles close to home actually allows us to pull the wool over our students' eyes.

> In the case of the introductory courses, we produce incredibly mysterious objects because the students have not seen the legerdemain by which the object has appeared. The students sense that they are not in on the joke, that there is something that they don't get, so they reduce the experience to "Well, it's his or her opinion."

While calling on scholars to show their students what is up their sleeves, he identifies another sort of what he calls disciplinary lies, lies necessary for any productive scholarship to take place.

> On the other hand, disciplinary lying—the conventions within a discipline—enables me to get moving. You have to allow me some measure of monomania if I am to get anywhere. I can't do my work when I have to stop and entertain every other opinion under the sun. This is why such work must always be done in a corporate setting, so that the monomanias mutually abrade against, so that they relativize each other; so that the students, the initiates, are let in on the joke. (Smith n.d.)

Identifying the rhetorics and recipes and "lies" that circulate and make possible these things we call religion and the study of religion is thus not meant as a criticism of either—as if we could get on with the business of studying human behavior free of such devices. Extrapolating from Smith's comments we can say that such rhetorical devices are necessary for any sense of a group to exist and, subsequently, for any sense to be made of the group's existence. Identifying these rhetorics is simply an attempt to deflate the monomania that exists when one set of local interests are so dominant as to be effectively represented as the only interests worth pursuing, as the only game in town, and thus portraying them as altogether free of the competitive marketplace of ideas and interests.

My final dispatch concerns a step toward just such a project that appears to have been made over a decade ago by Peter Harrison, in his thorough and impressive book, *"Religion" and the Religions in the English Enlightenment*. On the opening page he writes:

> The concepts "religion" and "the religions," as we presently understand them, emerged quite late in Western thought, during the Enlightenment. Between them, these two notions provided a new framework for classifying particular aspects of human life. (1)

Harrison's book is thus an exercise in studying the practical impact of categories during a specific period of European history. However, despite his misgivings concerning Cantwell Smith's preference for "faith" over "religion" (misgivings clearly spelled out in Harrison's epilogue [174–5]), he nonetheless employs this traditional distinction, thus undermining what strikes me as the most promising and provocative part of his study. For example, soon after we find the above quoted thesis statement, Harrison elaborates by employing the very interior/exterior, private/public scheme he appears to historicize: "In the present work I shall be examining in more detail this process of *the objectification of religious faith*" (2; emphasis added). Rather than seeing the concept and institution of "religion" or "faith" as one technique whereby an interior, seemingly apolitical zone is fabricated and named, Harrison seems to presume the existence of an inner, purely subjective disposition or attitude that somehow predates (both chronologically and logically) its social setting, thus being objectified, externalized, expressed, manifested, controlled, or reified by means of the word "religion." This is nothing other than the old notion of sui generis religion by yet another name. What such critics seem to take away with one hand, they swiftly restore with the other.

A similar technique is found in an even more recent essay on the "strengths and weaknesses" of Durkheim's contributions to the study of religion. After acknowledging that "the word religion is our word," Thomas Idinopulos elaborates:

> The word, religion, is our modern word for the very good reason that the sheer differentiation of functions and roles in modern life forces us to distinguish between politics, labor, commerce, leisure, art, religion, etc. The word, religion, acquired its own distinct meaning when the forces of secularization became so dominant in western culture that religious belief and practice became distinctly human acts. For once secularity became fully evident in society it was possible to speak by contrast of the religious way of life. (2002: 9–10)

Instead of seeing the practical use of "religion" in opposition to "secularity" to have been one of the techniques that enabled the so-called process of modernist differentiation, Idinopulos argues that the brute fact of socio-political differentiation "forces us to distinguish" within what previously seems to have been a homogeneously sacred realm. Or, as Idinopulos phrases it, due to the unholy "forces of secularization . . . religious belief and practice *became* distinctly human acts" (emphasis added). Prior to secularization, and prior to religious beliefs and practices *becoming* human acts, I presume they were simply religious acts. Drawing on the proverbial example of the ancient person as one who lives in a thoroughly romantic world of uniform meaning, he goes on to say, "this interweaving of religion with everything else in life was true of archaic people" (10). But if "religion" is indeed *our* word, then how can it be used so easily to discuss just what archaic people did or did not weave together? Taking his own position seriously means that it is impossible to talk about religion prior to so-called secularization, and thus ancient people—who no doubt used classification systems of their own in an elaborate manner—must therefore have inhabited a world which was neither religious nor secular, neither sacred nor profane. Apart from pitching what he admits to be a local word backward in time as if it refers to some necessary feature of human experience (this is a technique commonly found in nationalist studies of nationalism, as in when a current sense of the nation is pitched backward in history), the trouble with his evidently Cantwell Smithian analysis is that in attempting to historicize the word "religion," Idinopulos romanticizes ancient life by presupposing that sacred and secular refer to historically distinct things (or, better put, "forces"), with one arising after the other.[6] As stated above, whereas the *word* "religion" has a history, the *concept* seems to be eternal and universal. Presuming these two discursive moments to be substantively different, and that one (i.e., religion as concept, or religion-as-matter-of-fact) historically precedes the other (i.e., the forces of secularization that invented the word "religion")— rather than seeing word/concept and religious/secular as part of the same socio-rhetorical moment, as devices for concocting meaningful worlds by means of the varying degree of tension in which they can be held—signifies that Idinopulos's work yet reproduces the strategy that this essay is seeking to historicize. In his essay we read the old, old story of a homogenous, meaningful past fractured and thus desacralized by the impersonal forces of modernity. It is a story that holds much allure for scholars knee deep in contests over the shape of their own institutions.

Although in writing the conclusion to this essay's series of progress reports I could cite the words from Harrison's own concluding chapter—"I hope that this study has highlighted the need to revise some cherished assumptions about the constructs 'religion' and 'the religions'" (175)—the future of the study of "religion" (and, as Foucault once said, the quotation marks have a certain importance) does not lie in the direction of searching for a more adequate or accurate definition of religion that accords with, protects, or recovers the interior and prior zone called faith. Neither does it share the presumption that a homogeneously sacred sphere or zone of faith lies in the historical background of the sadly limited, modernist, and disillu-

---

[6] I identify his work as influenced by Cantwell Smith because Smith's nearly forty year old book, *The Meaning and End of Religion*, is the only work on "religion" that Idinopulos cites (see 9, n. 18). This is not to say that newer works are somehow more valuable; however, I cannot see how anyone can discuss the historicity of "religion" without taking into account Jonathan Z. Smith's many contributions to this topic, contributions consistently made over the past twenty years.

sioned sacred/secular dichotomy. Instead, *it lies in the direction of thoroughly historicizing the private/public, belief/practice, Church/State, and sacred/secular binaries*, scrutinizing their historical development, their rhetorical deployment, questioning the narrative widely accepted by historians that the engine of secularization drives European history, and asking what is entailed in presuming that *any* moment of human praxis—including the praxis of discourses on privacy, intuition, feeling, piety, and faith—somehow escapes the uncharted ebb and flow of contingent and thus contestable social history. It lies in the direction of taking seriously Jonathan Z. Smith's well known but surprisingly under-utilized position that "[r]eligion is not a native category. It is not a first person term of self-categorization. It is a category imposed from the outside on some aspect of native culture" (1998: 269).

Studying the techniques of this imposition, and the specific sites where they are deployed, is accomplished through charting the wars of "religion." They are wars where assertions and *ad hominem* arguments can carry the day and where passions rise all too easily. That those who oppose such charting activities have little recourse but to fall back on name calling (I think here of Paul Griffiths' attempts to discredit the work of such scholars as Donald Wiebe) or making feeble proclamations concerning such things as the "loss of grip on reality" supposedly suffered by those with whom one disagrees (Strenski 2002: 429), should be sufficient evidence that there is indeed a war over the very notion of "religion": how to use it, where and when to use it, and who can use it. Luckily, it is ink and not blood that is being spilled in this contest. As has been suggested elsewhere (Arnal 2001b; Asad 1999; McCutcheon 2003), perhaps it is this very idea of a set apart zone of ostensibly pure and apolitical human belief and private faith that allows people to construct this thing they call "civil discourse" in the first place and which affords those in dominant groups—such as scribes and scholars—the luxury of drawing only ink and not blood with their rhetorical blows. Arguing this in greater detail must, however, await a future dispatch from the "religion" wars.[7]

---

[7] Portions of this text are derived from McCutcheon 2003.

PART TWO

STUDIES IN RELIGIOUS BEHAVIOR

9. EXPLORING THEORIES OF RELIGIOUS VIOLENCE: NIGERIA'S "MAITATSINE" PHENOMENON

Rosalind I. J. Hackett

Introduction[1]

In 1997, Bruce Lincoln, writing on "Conflict," lamented the dearth of scholarly analysis of religion by "serious students of conflict" and the parallel neglect of conflict by scholars of religion (Lincoln 1997). Likewise, in the introduction to his new volume on *Religion and Violence*, Hent de Vries regrets the fact that protagonists in current debates surrounding multiculturalism, citizenship, immigration, and democracy "seem unwilling to allow religion more than a marginal position in the constitution, definition and redefinition of the public sphere" (Vries 2001; cf also Hall 2002). He also avers, somewhat prophetically, that "[t]o address violence in relation to religion and in all the further complexity of its origins, mediations, and effects seems a topical project."

Indeed the tragic events of September 11th, 2001 served to generate a flood of publications on religiously motivated violence, notably with regard to radical or political Islam.[2] Nigeria has featured in some of these discussions because of its history of tensions and violence between Muslims and Christians. Most recently these interreligious tensions have been sparked by moves to implement full Shari'a in several northern states.[3] In the present essay I examine a particularly formative

---

[1] An earlier version of this paper was presented at the Center for Millennial Studies annual conference, November 3–5, 2001. Valuable suggestions were received from Richard Landes and David Cook. I am also grateful to Jonathan Reynolds for supplementary sources, to Matthews A. Ojo for helpful additions, and to Ibrahim Ado-Kurawa for his critical comments. Portions of this essay appear in the volume edited by Maria de Lourdes Beldi de Alcântara on the proceedings of the Seminar on Methodology and Theory in Research on Religion, Santos, Brazil, May 20–22, 2002 (forthcoming).

[2] Cf. Kingston 2001 for a critique of the oversimplified links between Islam and violence. For more nuanced texts, see Esposito 2002 and Rashid 2002.

[3] In March 2002 the Nigerian Minister of Justice and Attorney-General, Kanu Godwin Agabi, declared the application of strict Islamic or Shari'a law as unconstitutional. He emphasized the need for equality before the law and to eliminate

incident of religious conflict in Nigeria, in light of the panoply of theoretical interpretations adduced by "insiders" and "outsiders" to account for such unprecedented violence in a country previously known for its religious tolerance.

This particular case study has been teased out of my larger work on religious conflict in Nigeria (Hackett forthcoming) and on questions of religious freedom and conflict in Africa more generally (Hackett 2000, 2001). My focus here was provoked not just by the current heightened attention to geo-religious realities (Eck 2000), but also by the outbreak of religiously-related communal riots which occurred in northern Nigeria just before September 11th. As I read vivid and heart-rending narratives of the fighting and destruction in Jos my mind traveled back to the time when I had been living in southern Nigeria. One evening in 1980 the Muslim trader who used to come to our house and sell African art started recounting tales of mass killings in the north of the country. I shall always remember his throat-cutting gesture and the fear in his eyes when we asked how serious it was. Before long news of a major uprising led by a mysterious figure known as "Maitatsine" in the great northern city of Kano was flooding the front pages of our newspapers.

What is of particular interest to me in my ongoing research on the Nigerian religious scene is the way that this millennialist Islamic or Islamist movement has assumed metonymic status in the psyche of Africa's most populous nation. Notwithstanding the localized nature of the violence, and the death of the leader in 1980, subsequent sporadic uprisings of Maitatsine followers in other parts of the country, with the attendant media spotlight, have sustained the fears of Nigerians regarding the explosive potential of religious violence. The development of a "generalized concept" of Maitatsine was noted by Niels Kastefelt in an earlier piece examining the impact of rumors of "invisible magical powers" on popular political culture in the early 1980s (Kastefelt 1989; cf also Lubeck 1985: 367). Even today, when communal clashes occur, for whatever reason, the name of Maitatsine is frequently invoked as historical memory and explanation. For example, a local ethnic conflict in 1998/99 in Lagos between northerners and southerners was initially described in the press as a new outbreak of "Maitatsine" even though this explanation was later chal-

---

discriminatory punishments against Muslims. ("Justice Minister Says Sharia against Constitution." UN Integrated Regional Information Networks, March 21, 2002).

lenged by the authorities. While the non-Nigerian origins and un-Islamic orientation of the movement's leader were underlined in the aftermath of the original crisis in 1980, for many southern (Christian) Nigerians this albeit extremist movement evoked old and new concerns about Islamization. The movement's rejection of many worldly ways and modern accouterments further reinforced ideas about Islamic resistance to Western education and development so integral to the more progressive southern part of the country.

A rich body of literature is now available on millennialism and apocalypticism more generally that can offer fresh perspectives on Maitatsine as a religious movement (see, e.g. Barkun 1996; Mayer 2001; Robbins and Palmer 1997; Wessinger 2000). For example, the recent work by sociologist John R. Hall et al., which explores the link between apocalyptic movements and violence, highlights not only internal dynamics and conflict with outsiders, but also the significance of historical memory (Hall, Schuyler, and Trinh 2000). The latter idea is particularly illuminating with regard to the Maitatsine movement and its Mahdist connections, as well as its more contemporary "manifestations" or "reverberations." The role played by the modern media in exacerbating public fears by recalling events and similarly infamous "cults" around the world hardly needs emphasizing (Hackett 2003).

In this vein, the Maitatsine movement can be viewed as one element in the wider, burgeoning phenomenon of radical religious expression or religious fundamentalism. This is underscored by Michael Watts, in his insightful study of Islamic modernities and civil society in the city of Kano, and of the Maitatsine movement in particular (Watts 1996). He shows how Maitatsine's reformist, even utopian, message inscribed itself into a dynamic, discursive tradition that dated back to colonial times of debating Muslim identity and correct practice. In that respect this controversial religious leader was not, in Watts' view, an "isolated fanatic" (Watts 1996: 279). Like other critics of the status quo he was in and out of jail, and deported on occasion. This resonates with Jonathan Z. Smith's call to students of religion to treat extremist religious groups (he was using the example of Jonestown) not as "unique" or "utterly exotic" but "to reduce [them] to the category of the known and the knowable" (Smith 1982: 111–12).

One of the primary hallmarks of these more radically oriented religious movements is their location at the fringes of modernity, and their condemnation of Western liberalism and modernism (see, e.g., Lawrence 1995). Birgit Meyer's work on Ghanian pentecostalism, for example, reveals the ambivalence toward modernity which characterizes many such religious groups situated at the post-colonialist, post-missionary juncture (Meyer 1999). Watts also notes the ambiguity and contradiction in Maitatsine's critique of materialism and the West. He promoted a simple disciplined life while also advocating the political control of modern institutions (Watts 1996). In line with this, Watts argues that much of Islamism is in fact new and modern because, rather than returning to some mythical past, it "involved contesting some Islamic traditions and creating new ones by a direct engagement with capitalist modernity read through new scripturalist understandings of Islam" (Watts 1996: 283–84). He describes the Maitatsine insurrection as a "parochial sort of political Islam" and a "powerful, if counterhegemonic reading and critique of the Nigerian oil boom and of the Nigerian ruling classes" (Watts 1996: 282).

What follows is a (re)examination of the Maitatsine movement in light of the above-mentioned theories of religious violence, as well as more "local" and contextual interpretations. It is hoped that this brief excursus through this interpretive maze will not only explain the movement's paradigmatic status in the popular imagination and with regard to state power, but also lend support to John Hall's position that *a single theory linking religion and violence is inappropriate* (Hall 2002). As he appropriately states, "religious violence is embedded in moments of history and structures of culture." We turn now to the most formative moment of the Maitatsine narrative.

Tales of Horror and Heroism

In December, 1980 the city of Kano erupted virtually into civil war, as a result of violent clashes with the followers of a dissident religious teacher, Muhammadu Marwa otherwise known as "Maitatsine" ("the one who damns"). The details of Maitatsine's life, the growth of the movement, and the 1980 revolt by his followers, which led to the death of more than 4,177 people (including Maitatsine himself),[4] and the subsequent uprisings in the early 80s, and again in

---

[4] According to the Aniagolu Commission of Inquiry, which was reprinted in

1993, have been well documented by a number of authors (Nicolas 1981; Christelow 1985; Lubeck 1985; Isichei 1987; Hiskett 1987; Clarke 1987; Kastefelt 1989). Kano became the stage for an outbreak of violence on a scale not seen in Nigeria since the Civil War in 1967–70. Many see this incident as the turning point in terms of religious intolerance in Nigeria.[5]

Tales of horror and heroism abounded in the series of clashes between Maitatsine followers (or 'Yan Tatsine) and the authorities (Christelow 1985: 17f). In late November, the governor, Abubakar Rimi, responding to complaints about property expropriation and indoctrination of young boys, as well as police harassment, ordered Maitatsine and his followers to vacate the area they occupied in the city. Instead, the latter brought reinforcements from the countryside. For several months prior to that the police had claimed that it was too dangerous to enter the ward occupied by the group. There had also been failed efforts by some local government officials, legislators, and senior police officers to curb the abusive and illegal religious preaching (Falola 1998: 151). However it was the rumor that the Maitatsine planned to take over the two principal *jumaat* mosques of the city that eventually propelled the governor to send in the police and the army. The resultant turmoil, which ceased around the end of December when the army was sent in and Maitatsine was killed, was graphically depicted in the media.[6]

The reactions of the state and its security agents raise another level of discussion among scholars of new religious movements, that of the role of "perceptions" and "interpretations" of each group of the other in a crisis situation. Known as the "interpretive approach" it sees

> the orientations and behavior of problematic movements with apocalyptic worldviews as significantly influenced by the actions and perceived dispositions of groups in their environment, particularly groups

---

thirty-five installments in the *New Nigerian* from November 13, 1981–January 2, 1982. Unofficial estimates of deaths run as high as 10,000 (Kastefelt 1989: 84).

[5] In fact, the Aniagolu Report (1981: 106) reports that a total of 34 clashes between rival religious groups in the Northern states had preceded the Maitatsine episode, in most cases requiring police intervention. The Report indicated that steps had been taken from 1979 by the government in the form of an Advisory Council on Hajj Affairs and an edict (from the Sokoto State government) to regulate Islamic religious preachers.

[6] The Nigerian Television Authority produced a documentary entitled "55 Minutes of Maitatsine" which was first aired on July 21, 1984. See the favorable review of it in the *Sunday New Nigerian*, September 2, 1984.

and individuals who are perceived as distinctly *hostile* to the movement, such as state authorities, anti-movement activists, and recriminating apostates (Robbins 1997: 15; see also Kaplan 1997).

This approach seeks to challenge analyses which essentialize such movements as inherently violent, direct more attention to the "variable balance of internal and external influences underlying various episodes" (Robbins 1997: 19). In the case of Maitatsine, it would seem that the inaction rather than the over-reaction of the state is more notable, at least in the earlier stages. This is generally more the case in the Nigerian context, but as we shall see in the next section, the inefficacy of the security forces often fuels wider interpretations of conflict situations, as well as allowing local disorder to flourish. The data available on the Maitatsine incident do not provide the details of the dynamics of the escalating violence, as are available for other movements such as Aum Shinrikyo, the Peoples Temple, or the Branch Davidians (see, e.g., Hall, Schuyler, and Trinh 2000; Wessinger 2000).

Discourses of Deviancy and Conspiracy

For nearly three weeks, Muhammad Marwa and his young recruits held this ancient walled city, renowned as a center of international trade from the mid-eighteenth century, under siege. The 'Yan Tatsine outnumbered the police, and even managed to commandeer many of their weapons. They occupied some buildings and destroyed others. Many Kano inhabitants fled the city as the economy ground to a halt and the assaults and fatalities began to mount. When the devastation was assessed, and the recriminations began, the movement was, not surprisingly, roundly condemned in most quarters. Many Nigerian Muslims were concerned to disclaim the movement and its leader as Muslims.[7] Some even went as far as describing Maitatsine as satanic. Muslim leaders emphasized that their religion was one of peace, and urged the government to take the necessary action regarding the "fanatics" and "violators of the constitutional principle of religious tolerance" (see Falola 1998: 156).[8]

---

[7] See, for example, Ibrahim Sulaiman, "The Kano Uprising—A Muslim View," *Sunday New Nigerian*, June 6, 1982.

[8] On the negative reaction of the main anti-Sufi group, 'Yan Izala, to its being linked with 'Yan Maitatsine see Loimeier 1997: 220.

Arjun Appadurai has written suggestively of the growing relationship between globalizing forces and a "new order of uncertainty in social life," frequently countered by the certainty of violence, notably in relation to the body (Appadurai 1998). The presence of large numbers of West African immigrants, including Maitatsine himself who was from neighboring Cameroon, fomented a number of conspiracy theories (Isichei 1987: 205).[9] These were readily fueled by journalistic accounts which picked up on the fears and rumors generated by this violent episode (Christelow 1985: 69). For example, Zahradeen (1988: 75), a journalist who was involved with the coverage of the incident, writes about the purported "Jewish connection" of the Maitatsine movement, as publicly announced even by then Governor Abubakar Rimi. In fact, it was a university lecturer, Mallam Shehu Umar Abdullah, who informed the Aniagolu Tribunal that there was a link between Maitatsine and Zionist forces. The latter were purportedly angry at their failure to bring Nigeria under their influence, and used the "Zionist-controlled Western media to launch a campaign of calumny against Nigeria" (Zahradeen 1988: 107). This was further endorsed by then Major Haliru Akilu of Military Intelligence, who, in his testimony to the tribunal, spoke of the manipulation of movements like Maitatsine by "international intelligence firms." Similarly, theories sprung up about the role of Qaddafi, the Saudis and the CIA, or at very least, the manipulation of events by power-hungry Nigerians (see Isichei 1987: n. 76–78).

The Muslim Students Society (MSS), known for its militant activism, claimed in one of its publications that the "Maitatsine phenomenon" was being exploited by anti-Islamic forces, notably the government.[10] They described it as a *fitnah* or an extraneous movement aimed at destroying or undermining Islam, and whose destructive activities remained unchecked by the police and armed forces.[11] The MSS objected to Maitatsine followers being referred to by government

---

[9] Christelow (1985:83–84) points out that actual figures do not bear out the large numbers of foreigners in the movement, and that this popular perception was a defense mechanism.

[10] *Radiance* (Kano), [1981/2]: 36–40.

[11] "Fitna" is defined as a "burning with fire, a melting of (metals) in order to separate or distinguish the bad from the good, a means whereby the condition of a man is evinced in respect of good or evil, [also] punishment, chastisement, conflict among people, faction and sedition, discord, dissension, difference of opinions, misleading [or] causing to err, seduction, temptation" (E. Lane, *An Arabic-English Lexicon*). Information from David Cook, November 7, 2001.

officials as "Muslim religious fanatics" or "Islamic fundamentalists," as they deemed the practices of the group to be deviant, non-interactionist, and un-Islamic (praying separately, facing north, and slandering the Sunna). Facing Jerusalem rather than Mecca was in their eyes the result of the influence of "Israeli-based Baha'i Movement."[12] Furthermore, the fact that many of the analyses of the movement came down to the centrality of socio-economic factors was an indication to the MSS of the alliance between "the Zaria Marxist clique and the Jos Christian missionary establishment."

Poverty and Politics

In the efforts to comprehend the 1980 riots socio-economic considerations tended to dominate. Increased migration in the north, higher unemployment, inadaptation of Qur'anic students, an ethnic and cultural reaction of poorly integrated non-Hausas in Hausa Muslim society were all cited as destabilizing factors in the 1980 riots (see, e.g., Barkindo 1993; Hiskett 1987: 221–22; Lubeck 1985). A disaffected class, made up of both rural and urban followers, was ripe for the anti-modernist message of Maitatsine—symbolized in the ban on radios, buttons, watches, bicycles, and automobiles. For these reasons, Watts avers that Maitatsine's controversial religious teachings-syncretist, prophetic, revivalist—should receive less attention than his "anti-materialist, class-based reading of the moral superiority of the Qur'an which led him to attack decadence, profligacy, and moral decay" (Watts 1996: 282). Similarly, Lubeck concentrates on the clash between pre-capitalist and capitalist networks as reflected in the worsening social and economic status of the *gardawa* or peripatetic students of a Qur'anic mallam or teacher during the oil boom (Lubeck 1985: 371–72). He notes that Maitatsine's followers began appropriating private land prior to the main disturbances, claiming that plots of land and markets belonged to Allah and his people (Lubeck 1985: 386–87).

Religious and political analyst Matthew Hassan Kukah lays more emphasis on the contemporary political climate, pointing to the pre-

---

[12] Jerusalem's significance for Islam is very eschatological. Personal communication, Richard Landes, November 3, 2001.

existing tensions between the Kano state governor, Alhaji Abubakar Rimi, and the Emir of Kano, as well as the internal divisions within the ruling party, the People's Redemption Party (Kukah 1993: 154–56). Rimi's fraternizing with emissaries from Maitatsine—as potential political allies—meant that he could not call out the police. He saw the disturbances in Kano as a suitable irritant for his political opponents.[13] Peter Clarke notes, however, that there was nothing unusual for wealthy and powerful Muslims to ask "clerics" to pray for them on the basis of their supposed mystical powers derived from their nomadic existence (Clarke and Linden 1984: 120).

Religion scholar Muhammed Sani Umar challenges the easy attribution of the movement's momentum to a revolt of the oppressed against the oppressed, despite its creative potential as a theory.[14] The fact that the Maitatsine also attacked fellow members of the oppressed vitiates this interpretation, in his view. He also poses the trenchant question, "why is it that only the Northern part of the country shall provide [a] religious platform for revolting against the system that operates in the whole of the country?" In addition to these peculiarities, he points significantly to the lack of direct, voluntary and uncoerced information from the Maitatsine followers themselves about their beliefs and motivations.

Watts offers a more nuanced materialist analysis of this destructive religious movement by situating it within "two locally constituted global force-fields," namely Islam and capitalism (Watts 1996). He lays important emphasis on the actual *experience* of the oil boom by Kano residents. This was mediated by the state in the form of corruption and violent, undisciplined security forces (the police were popularly referred to as *daggal* or the devil), the family and associational spheres of civil society, and the return to civilian party politics of 1979. This latter development generated a political space more conducive to radical, populist critique of the Sufi brotherhoods associated with feudal elites.[15] Watts points not just to the "anarchic and chaotic growth of Kano city" but also the "changing material basis

---

[13] It should be noted that manipulationist theories of religious conflict are popular with several Nigerian scholars (see, e.g., Usman 1987).

[14] *Clarion* 1, 3 (October 1985).

[15] Talal Asad writes of the struggles for "discursive dominance" and the difficulties of securing "orthodoxy" in conditions of radical change (Asad 1992: 210–11, cited in Watts 1996: 272–73).

of commoners' life and what it implied for the brute realities of urban living" (Watts 1996: 271).

In an examination of new forms of territoriality and sovereignty in Africa, Achille Mbembe writes of the ways in which religious movements may reconfigure, even conquer, the urban space (Mbembe 1999: 7–8). Maitatsine's efforts to create a zone of both refuge and protest in Kano are apposite here. South Asian specialist and political scientist Ashutosh Varshney has shown how, in the case of India, communally integrated associational life can serve as an agent of peace by restraining those, including powerful politicians, who would polarize religious groups along communal lines (Varshney 2001). The isolationist tactics and exogenous (rural areas or neighboring countries) origins of many of the members of this Nigerian movement reinforce this idea.

Mahdism and Millennialism

Some scholars lend more focus to the religious, specifically millennialist, orientation of the movement. Central to the mahdist or messianic tradition in northern Nigeria, argues Clarke, is that "the process of 'redemption,' the onset of the millennium involves a form of defensive 'war'" (Clarke and Linden 1984: 121). There was a growing awareness of Ayatollah Khomeini's achievements in Iran, and this may have inspired more aggressive tactics in Maitatsine's movement (Clarke and Linden 1984: 121). Furthermore, it was the beginning of a new Muslim century—1400 or 1979/80 C.E. was believed to be the end of the world for millennialist Muslims after which all the world would be converted to Islam (Al-Karsani 1993).[16] Some of Kano's leading scholars indeed saw the crisis as evidence of "Signs of the Hour" which in Islamic eschatological thought is related to the idea that at the end of every century a *mujaddid* or renewer may arise to restore order (Barkindo 1993: 99). Christelow argues that there was a clear mahdist motif operating through 'Yan Tatsine (Christelow 1985: see also Clarke 1987). He attributes this in part

---

[16] Al-Karsani, in comparing Sudanese and Nigerian patterns of millennial Islam, shows that both used the images and messages to express popular discontent and grievances, but that the Nigerian form tended toward more militant action (Al-Karsani 1993: 151).

to the fact that Maitatsine came from Northern Cameroon where several mahdist movements had operated during the colonial period. The 'Yan Tatsine, in his opinion, also bore resemblance to a branch of the Tijaniyya sufi order known as the Hamaliyya, in that they were reclusive.

The fact that Maitatsine rejected the Hadith and the sunna, and arrogated to himself the role of prophet after downgrading the status of the Prophet Muhammad to "just another Arab" served to create an "intense religious fervor" and, simultaneously, "a frightening moral anarchy" (Christelow 1985: 83). It was this, suggests Christelow, that accounted for the distinctiveness of this movement and its appeal to those who, for reasons of youth and/or poverty, felt the need to be "different and defiant" (Christelow 1985: 84).[17] The controversial preacher based his pared-down reading of the Qu'ran in local, pre-Islamic conditions (Watts 1996: 260). Zahradeen also described how Maitatsine's appearance—he had a squint in one eye—contributed to the fear that he was the "Dujal," the one-eyed anti-Christ, who would fight gallantly against the true faith of Islam at the beginning of the end of the world (Watts 1996: 11).

The belief in a form of crisis before the Last Days and that the Mahdi has direct communication with Allah has a long history in Nigeria (Williams and Falola 1995: 167–70). This revolutionary ideology was deployed by the jihadists of the nineteenth century in their anti-colonialist struggles. The reformer, Uthman dan Fodio, drew on mahdist ideas in his writings prior to the jihad in northern Nigeria, but denied his perceived status as a Mahdi after the jihad ended. His son perpetuated the mahdist tradition by prophesying the appearance of the Mahdi between 1882 and 1979. It is reported that many people abandoned their homes in pursuit of the Mahdi.

Historians Lovejoy and Hogendorn argue that the wave of revolutionary mahdism that swept through the Sokoto Caliphate in 1905–6 needs to be distinguished from other forms of mahdism as it had

---

[17] Barkindo, who is a historian of the region, also suggests that this movement should be seen against the increased militancy of Christians (notably the youth) from the late 1970s onwards. The numerous publications by the Christian Association of Nigeria (CAN) caused Muslims to think more critically about their religion (Barkindo 1993: 99). He also sees the overall trend in Kano during that period to employ Islamic solutions to urban problems, with the building of mosques, schools, and the creation of government committees involving both academics and leading ʿulama, as influencing the growth of Islamism (Barkindo 1993: 100–105).

strong divisions on the basis of class (Lovejoy and Hogendorn 1990). This particular revolt attracted "disgruntled peasants, fugitive slaves and radical clerics" on a wide scale but not the local aristocracy. Had this revolutionary form of mahdism not been so weak in terms of military strategy and not relied so heavily on supernatural means, they might have "altered the course of early colonial history" (Lovejoy and Hogendorn 1990: 243). As it was, they served to entrench the relationship between the British and the indigenous rulers.

The quest for a Mahdi who could initiate a new order of peace, unity, and order took some Nigerians to Sudan where mahdist movements had challenged British colonial rule. Hayatu ibn Said, the great-great-grandson of dan Fodio, was said to be influenced by the Sudanese Mahdi 'Abd al-Rahman al-Mahdi in his efforts to establish a mahdist nucleus in the Sokoto Caliphate in the early 1920s (Ibrahim 1980). The Sudanese Mahdi wrote a letter to his would-be Khalifa in the West advising him that when "the day" comes the guns of the Christians would not go off (Ibrahim 1980: 218). Two other mahdist states were established in northern Nigeria through cooperation between Nigerians and Sudanese, but they ended in failure (Williams and Falola 1995: 167–70). That notwithstanding, militant mahdist elements persisted in battles against colonial rule in the early twentieth century. Survivors of these battles migrated to the Sudan. The mahdist tradition was also sustained and propagated by the annual pilgrimage to Mecca as many Nigerians passed through the Sudan en route to Mecca. They brought back mahdist ideas and literature.

Maitatsine as Metonym

Despite the fact that the government cremated Maitatsine's body to prevent his tomb becoming a site of martyrdom and pilgrimage, and has since symbolically built a police station on the ruins of his home, further outbreaks of violence linked to the Maitatsine occurred in subsequent years as surviving members of the group, discontented and poor, spread to other areas. Some were also released from prison in 1982—a highly unpopular decision by then President Shagari. The disturbances took place at Bullumkutu, Maiduguri (October 1982), Rigassa/Tudun-wada, Kaduna State (October 1982), Yola, Gongola State (February-March 1984), and Gombe, Bauchi State (April 1985). It was then not until 1993 that the *Citizen* magazine carried an article entitled, "The Volcano Erupts Again" or "Maitatsine—Act VI."[18] It described how, between January 19–22 in Funtua, violence erupted between a variant of the 'Yan Tatsine known as the Kalakato and the authorities. What purportedly began as a dispute between Islamic scholars turned into a rampage with reports of up to 400 deaths, as members of the movement attacked government buildings. The Sarkin Maska or district head of Funtua, Alhaji Idris Sambo, whose palace was also targeted, declared that the whole incident was politically motivated. But the report emphasizes that a body of opinion suggested that the movement was linked to an extreme form of Qur'anic recitation. Members of this movement were primarily hostile toward the police, but not toward the general populace (which was not the case with the original movement which attacked both Muslims and Christians).[19]

The Nigerian psyche was indelibly marked by the original Maitatsine incident since it marked the first real incident of religiously related violence on a large scale. In effect it has become the metonym or paradigm for religious violence among Nigerians, despite the fact that it was primarily a local phenomenon and an intrareligious, rather than an interreligious, conflict. Umar asked somewhat prophetically in the 1985 Academic Staff Union newspaper "Is Maitatsine Here to Stay?[20] In his recent account of religious violence in Nigeria, historian Toyin Falola claims that the movement proved especially paradigmatic as President Shagari's 1981 New Year's broadcast became a model of government reaction to all subsequent violent outbreaks of the 1980s and 1990s (Falola 1998: 157f). This comprised an expression of shock, an appeal for cooperation of the public, and a promise to investigate. Indeed every major outbreak of violence has resulted in a panel of inquiry, similar to the 1981 Tribunal of Inquiry headed by Justice Anthony Aniagolu, to analyze the causes of the violence. Furthermore, the government sought to absolve itself of connection to the crisis, blaming the disturbances on external forces

---

[18] See the *Citizen*, February 1, 1993.
[19] Clashes occurred in a Lagos suburb, Abule-Taylor, Agege, in August 1997 and again a year later, between police and a group of "Muslim fundamentalists" (*The Week*, 6 August 1998). Following this the religious identity of those implicated is disputed. But again in December 1998 *P.M. News* reports that "Maitatsine Fanatics Held in Lagos" (December 24, 1998) after the arrest of 18 of the "zealots" by the Special Armed Robbery Squad and the confiscation of home-made guns, knives, machetes, charms and amulets, as well as "inciting religious books and pamphlets."
[20] *Clarion*, 1, 3 (October 1985).

inimical to Nigeria's national interests. It tried to deny the interpretation of the crisis as a religious war, perhaps in order to avoid casting one religion (in this case, Islam) in a negative light, or harming interreligious relations.

As alluded to earlier, Muslim scholars themselves have been keen to dismiss Maitatsine's reformist claims, declaring him to be a heretical, self-proclaimed prophet and "at best a Muslim deviant; at worst, a charlatan who took advantage of our societal weakness."[21] His purported spiritual powers drew followers and patrons while eliciting accusations of excessive "fetishism" from others.[22] His own wife described him as a magician (Birai 1991: 197). The "riddle" of his political protests and close connections with a number of prominent politicians, businessmen, and civil servants will likely remain unsolved (Birai 1991: 197).

Because sources on Maitatsine's political and religious aspirations are indeed limited he will undoubtedly retain his enigmatic and controversial status. However, neither this nor the discursive strategies of religious leaders and politicians to deny his authenticity as a ("true") Muslim should prevent us from recognizing the religious dimensions of this conflict. As Bruce Lincoln aptly states, communities that define themselves in terms of their religion will wage their conflicts primarily around rival claims to material and non-material resources (Lincoln 1997). This is helpful in generating more relevant and nuanced interpretations, and problematizing those which tend to polarize the religious and the secular—a somewhat untenable perspective in the case of African Islam. That notwithstanding, Lincoln's argument that religious collectivities or "fractions" have often been the most effective in exploiting contradictions between nation and state in recent years also resonates strongly with the Nigerian context. He is less sanguine when it comes to religious discourse and practice providing the resources for peace. Perhaps, as South Africa did in terms of turning a country marred by racial conflict into a "rainbow nation," Nigeria could surprise everyone and generate a new model of post-colonial religious pluralism drawing on indigenous ideas of tolerance and global ideals of democracy and human rights.

---

[21] Jibril Aminu, *Observations* (Delta Publications, 1988: 64), cited in Birai 1991: 198.
[22] *New Nigerian*, Kaduna, February 21, 1982, cited in Birai 1991: 198.

10. WHAT DOES JERUSALEM HAVE TO DO WITH AMECAMECA? A CASE STUDY OF COLONIAL MEXICAN SACRED SPACE[1]

Brian C. Wilson

One of the most popular pilgrimages in New Spain during the sixteenth century centered on the image of the Virgin Mary venerated near Mexico City on the hill of Tepeyac. The origins of this pilgrimage site were ancient, as it was already a pilgrimage destination for the Nahuas (Aztecs) before the conquest. There, it was said that they venerated an image of Tonantzin, of whom the famous Franciscan ethnographer Bernadino de Sahagún wrote, "The first of these goddesses was called Cihuacóatl, which means wife of the Serpent; they also call her Tonantzin, which means 'our mother'" (quoted in Lafaye 1987: 211). The shrine at Tepeyac attracted people from points beyond the valley of Mexico and was well known before the conquest (Martinez Marin 1972: 161–78; 166–68).

The association of Tepeyac with the Virgin Mary went back to the first days of the conquest. We are told by Bernal Díaz de Castillo in his history of 1568 that during the siege of Tenochtitlan, one of Cortés' lieutenants, the infamous Gonzalo de Sandoval, made his headquarters at Tepeyac, and it is supposed that he erected a shrine to the Virgin Mary there (quoted in Lafaye 1987: 232). After the conquest was completed, a statue of the Virgin Mary, copied from the Virgin of Guadalupe in Extremadura in Spain, was installed at the site (Lafaye 1987: 232–33). Following church precedent, the Franciscans encouraged the investing of pagan sites with Christian symbols, and for a time they even seem to have encouraged the continuation of Nahua pilgrimages to what was now called the Virgin of Guadalupe at Tepeyac (Lafaye 1987: 215). Later, in the 1550s, this statue was replaced by the painting which can be seen there to this day. Late in the sixteenth century, pious legends began to grow up around the sanctuary and the painting, the earliest concerning

---

[1] Originally presented at Western Michigan University, February 12, 1996.

healing miracles, with later legends recounting an apparition of the Virgin Mary to an Nahua shepherd, identified as Juan Diego.[2] By this time though, the pilgrimage site had long since passed out of the hands of the Franciscans and into the firm grip of their archrivals, the secular clergy.

Despite their initial promotion of the Tepeyac pilgrimage, the Franciscans ultimately became its most vigorous opponents. Since veneration of indigenous images persisted in the valley of Mexico well until the second half of the sixteenth century, the Franciscans became paranoid about any practice which—however remotely—preserved pagan belief and practice. Thus Sahagún, for example, in his *Historia general* (1576), denounced the cult of the Virgin Mary of Tepeyac since the Nahua who frequented it referred to the image there as the indigenous goddess, Tonantzin (Lafaye 1987: 216).[3] Sahagún saw the pilgrimage as nothing more nor less than an insidious confusion of Christianity with paganism, or, worse, as a camouflage for purely pagan practices. Years earlier, in 1556, a prominent Franciscan preacher had denounced the Guadalupe pilgrimage from the pulpit of San Francisco in similar terms. With the civil authorities present, Father Fray Francisco de Bustamente protested against the new cult, which he considered illegitimate and impure, and he singled out the archbishop of Mexico City, Alonso de Montúfar, for especially harsh criticism for his promotion of it (Lafaye 1987: 238). Bustamente argued in this sermon that

> nothing was better calculated to keep the Indians from becoming good Christians than the cult of our Lady of Guadalupe. Ever since their conversion they have been told that they should not believe in idols, but only in God and Our Lady... To tell them now that an image painted by an Indian could work miracles will utterly confuse them and tear up the vine that has been planted (quoted in Lafaye 1987: 238).

---

[2] For a pious account of the apparitions, see Johnston, 1981: 25–48; see also Turner and Turner 1978: 82–85.

[3] Burkhardt argues the provocative thesis that "Tonantzin" was not an authentic pre-conquest goddess: "[In Tonantzin, the] Indians were not perpetuating memories of pre-Columbian goddesses but were projecting elements of their Christian worship into their pre-Christian past, conceptualizing their ancient worship in terms of Mary. Tepeyacac [sic] being holy to Mary, when questioned on ancient worship at the site they assumed that it had always been holy to a figure similar to her and named this figure Tonantzin...". For Burkhardt, the Virgin of Guadalupe at Tepeyac is a syncretic figure because she represents the assimilation of the Christian Mary with Nahua notions of "heaven," not because she was assimilated with a pre-existing Aztec goddess (Burkhardt, 1993: 208).

Jacques Lafaye cogently argues that Montúfar and the secular clergy actually tolerated a certain amount of syncretism when it came to this pilgrimage cult since the cult tended to tie the *iglesia indiana* closer to the *iglesia española* by conspicuously bringing Spaniards and Nahuas together in an exceedingly popular form of worship within sight of the capital, Mexico City (Lafaye 1987: 238–40). Thus the Franciscans, who sought desperately to retain control over the *iglesia indiana* by maintaining a policy of strict separation, lost no opportunity in attacking the pilgrimage to Tepeyac. For them, it now represented both a theological *and* a political threat.

This is not to say that the Franciscans in 16th-century Mexico ceased to encourage pilgrimage of any kind, however. While they denounced the cult of the Virgin of Guadalupe, they nevertheless energetically promoted what they considered "purer," Franciscan-controlled pilgrimages throughout the region, and to this end, they carefully created shrines where they believed none had existed before. One of the most interesting of these Franciscan-inspired pilgrimages was centered on a Nahua town to the southeast of Mexico City, Amecameca. This pilgrimage found its focus on the personality of the famous leader of the first twelve Franciscan missionaries to New Spain, Fray Martín de Valencia (c. 1473–1534).

During the last years of his life, Fray Martín used to frequent a small cave on the side of a volcanic peak on the outskirts of Amecameca, using the cave as a kind of hermitage. When Martín died, in 1534, the Franciscans seized on the potential of the cave of Amecameca as a shrine, and in order to promote interest in the Amecameca pilgrimage, the Franciscans soon developed standardized hagiographical accounts of the wonders of Fray Martín's life.[4] Common to most Franciscan hagiography, these biographies of Fray Martín were careful to highlight those incidents in Martín's life in Spain and Mexico which paralleled those in the life of St. Francis.[5]

---

[4] For primary accounts of the shrine from the sixteenth to the nineteenth centuries, see the collection of Vera 1881. For the earliest life of Fray Martín, see Fray Francisco Jiménez, edited by P. Atanasio López under the title, "Vida de Fray Martín de Valencia, escrita por su compañero Fr. Francisco Jiménez," 1926. All subsequent biographies that I know of were derived from Jiménez.

[5] Accounts of Martín de Valencia's life written in New Spain during the sixteenth and seventeenth centuries can be found in the following: Motolinía, 1971 [c. 1540]; Mendieta, 1870 [c. 1590]; Oroz, 1972 [c. 1590]; Torquemada, 1975–83 [c. 1615]; Ventancurt, 1961 [1698]. Written in Spain: Anonymous, 1971 [c. 1620].

One of Martín's colleagues, himself one of the Twelve, went farther than most in this regard. Fray Toribio de Benevente (Motolinía), in describing Martín's sojourn at Amecameca, drew parallels not only between Fray Martín and St. Francis, but also between Amecameca and La Verna, the mountain peak retreat of St. Francis in Italy (Motolinía 1971: 158). Motolinía, for example, talked about how in between "frightful austerities" and protracted meditations on Christ's Passion, Fray Martín would take time to tend to the wild birds of the place and was often seen holding conversations with them, just as St. Francis did at La Verna. Indeed, when Martín died, the birds were to be seen no more. More important in terms of connecting Amecameca with La Verna though, was Motolinía's claim that Fray Martín had actually been visited at the peak by the spirits of St. Francis and St. Anthony. For, just as St. Francis had been assured of his salvation through his experience with the Seraphic Christ at La Verna, so too was Fray Martín assured of his salvation by his vision of the stigmatized St. Francis at Amecameca (Motolinía 1971: 158).

In time, Amecameca became a popular pilgrimage destination for Nahuas and Spaniards alike, and while it could hardly compete with the popularity of the Virgin of Guadalupe at Tepeyac, the Franciscans nevertheless viewed it with pride. Not only was it a pilgrimage in honor of a local Franciscan hero, but the site seemed completely free of signs of previous pagan use and therefore the danger of "confusions," as Sahagún was to put it, was considerably lessened. It was quite a blow, then, when sometime between 1537 and 1550, the Franciscans lost control of Amecameca and its cave-shrine to the Dominicans (Jalpa Flores 1993: 147–94). For, although this seems to have been part of the continuing process of reorganization of ecclesiastical territories that was then occurring during this period throughout the Valley of Mexico, the transition from Franciscan control to Dominican control was not a smooth one. According to Chimalpahin Cuauhtlehuanitzin, a contemporary Nahua chronicler from the Amecameca area, devotion to the Franciscans continued to remain high for years after the transfer despite the Dominicans' best efforts to supplant them. Ultimately, the cave-shrine at Amecameca became the focal point of this bitter territorial rivalry (quoted in Jalpa Flores 1993: 176).

In the late 1550s, the Dominican vicar, Juan Paez, introduced into Amecameca the *Cofradía del Descendimiento y Sepulchro de Cristo Nuestro Señor*, a lay brotherhood devoted to the celebration of the burial of Christ in the Holy Sepulcher.[6] This confraternity, which the Dominicans had created in Mexico especially for the Nahuas, was routinely established in the larger towns within Dominican control. In Amecameca, the Dominicans decided that Martín de Valencia's cave would be an ideal place to install the brotherhood's devotional image, a full-size polychrome plaster image of the recumbent crucified Christ—*el Santo Entierro*. Along with this image, the Dominicans also installed an altar in the cave so that a mass could be said every Friday in perpetual celebration of Christ's Passion. In addition, and perhaps to make the Dominican control of the shrine even more explicit, every Easter Sunday the image of the *Santo Entierro* was removed from the cave and carried in procession by members of the confraternity to the Dominican monastery-church at the center of the town.

So successful was the Dominicans' promotion of this new cult that, again according to Chimalpahin, the memory of Fray Martín was gradually being erased from the place (Jalpa Flores 1993: 176). That is, until some thirty years later when an amazing discovery was to reverse Fray Martín's slide into oblivion and revive his cult at the cave-shrine. In 1584, Martín de Valencia's relics—his tunic, two cassocks, and a hair shirt—were recovered in Amecameca under rather mysterious circumstances. Fortunately for the memory of Fray Martín, the rift between the Franciscans and the Dominicans had by this time either healed or been forgotten, for after some small delay the Dominicans installed the relics in the cave at Amecameca alongside the image of the *Santo Entierro*. From then on, the cave became even more popular than ever as a combined Franciscan and Dominican shrine.

We find all these events narrated in a highly synthetic but very engaging way by Gerónimo de Mendieta in his *Historia eclesiástica indiana* (c. 1590s) (Mendieta 1870: 602–605). Since Mendieta's narrative has many interesting things to say about the shrine, it is worth quoting in full:

> The famous memory of the sainted Fr. Martín de Valencia which is maintained today in the town of Amecameca, demands that particular attention . . . be devoted to it. Thus, one must know that this town

---

[6] Fray Augustin Davila Padilla O. P., *Historia de la Fundación y discurso de la Provincia de Santiago de México* (Madrid, 1596), quoted in Vera 1881: 12–13.

of Amecameca is ten or twelve leagues from Mexico to the east, in the lap of a high, fiery volcano, which frequently sends forth from its top-most vent plumes and thick clouds of smoke and ash. This town was, according to the former government of the Indians when they were infidels, of the province of Tlalmanalco, [and] where that man of God, Martín de Valencia, had his principal lodgings while he lived, and where his body was entombed for more than thirty years after his death. And not only that place, which is no more than two short leagues from Tlalmanalco, but many others were under the control and care of our friars who lived there. And after the Indians had been converted and indoctrinated, the Domincan fathers founded a monastery in Amecameca.

Amecameca had at the southwest end of town a volcanic peak almost in the form of a pyramid, very high, graceful and somewhat covered by trees, at whose summit one could lord over and enjoy a sight of all that surrounded it, which is a very pleasant valley, situated, as I have said, at the foot of the volcano[;] and between its foothills and its summit, to one side of the peak, one having climbed about forty or fifty yards, is a natural cave formed in the living rock about 15 feet wide and a little more long and a little less high, like a hermitage, prepared like all the world to welcome to its dwelling all who have a taste for the solitary life.

And thus this place was the particular recreation of the spiritual servant of God, Martín de Valencia, and he frequented the place as much as he could; so much so that in order to enjoy that place, he liked to dwell in Tlalmanalco more than in any other convent, and very often he would come there, as much to visit and indoctrinate the Indians of that town which was in his charge, as to recollect himself and give all his attention to God in that cave, without the noise of people and without the interruptions of business. There he spent his days of rigorous fasts and days of Lent; there he truly exercised himself in his accustomed penances; there he spent days and nights in continuous prayer and meditation on the crucified Christ, mortifying his body with diverse means of affliction and punishment. There it is told that he used to go out in the morning to a forest and pray under a great tree that was there, and upon sitting there the tree would swell with birds which would sing him lovely songs, such that it appeared that they came there to help him praise God. And when he left from there, the birds left as well, and after his death the birds were never seen there again.

It is also told of his life that in that hermitage there appeared to that man of God Fathers Saint Francis and Saint Anthony, and leaving him consoled in the extreme, they certified for him from God that he was a son of salvation. The Indians, who knew well what the holy man was doing there, admired his austerity, and they were greatly edified, and were confirmed in their hearts the opinion of his sanctity that they had conceived because of the other virtues that they knew he possessed and the doctrine which he had taught them, seeing that his actions conformed exactly to the words of his evangelical preaching and not doubting that he was a saint and one chosen by God.

When this blessed one died, they put themselves on vigil and guarded what little clothes he had, having this faith and devotion, that Our Lord by his intercession and by means of his worldly goods, mercies would be done for them and they would be aided in their times of need. And they have been so perseverant in this devotion that they kept these relics hidden for a space of some fifty years, passing them from hand to hand during those great plagues that have occurred in New Spain, without giving any part of them away, not to those friars of San Francisco who had them under their care when the holy man died, nor those fathers of Saint Dominic who later came to that town, until the year 1584 when Our Lord wished to discover them and show them to all in the following way.

There was at that time acting as vicar of the monastery in Amecameca a venerable old father who had been the Provincial Vicar of the Order of Preachers in New Spain, Fr. Juan Paez by name, very devoted to Fr. Martín de Valencia, due to the fame of his sanctity which had flown through those regions always amongst the religious of all orders, and the seculars, Spanish as well as Indians. And by contemplation in that cave where he used to retreat in order to give himself wholly to God (which after then was always called the cave of the sainted Fr. Martín de Valencia), this religious had managed to maintain himself in that house for many years. And in the said year of '84, finding himself in the presence of some Indians who worked in the monastery speaking with fervor and zeal of the things of that man of God, Fr. Martín, and showing himself desirous of finding out about his corpse and his relics, one of the Indians who was present told him in secret afterwards that the town had for many years kept some relics of the saint, and he told him how and where he might see them. He made an inquiry after them, and following clues, came to find a hairshirt of horse hair and a very rough tunic which belonged to the man of God, and two poor cassocks of local linen, in which he used to say mass. Fr. Juan Paez thought himself very rich with these finds, and he could not contain his pleasure and contentment.

Later he told his Provincial about what had happened: he was commanded that he should carry [the relics] to the convent of Santo Domingo in Mexico City. He carried them off, promising that he would return them and that they would not keep them. All the friars of that convent saw them and kissed them with devotion and reverence. They were then returned to the vicar of the town of Amecameca, and they were put with much reverence in the sacristy of the convent.

> And the news of the finding of the relics coming to be common knowledge, many devout persons came to ask after them. They were given some small parts of the tunic and the hairshirt. But it being recognized that if this continued there would be nothing left, it was decided that they should be preserved, [and] the cave on the peak was readied to receive them.
>
> On one side of the cave was put an altar on which to say mass, and on the other side a great deep box which was closed and served as tomb for a very devoutly-made statue of Christ, which was laid in it, and at the foot of the Christ statue was kept a small box covered with an iron grill in which was kept the tunic and the hairshirt, in such a way that they could be seen but not removed. The cassocks were kept on the other side, loose, so that they could be shown and be seen. And even though the cave had doors and a good lock with which it could be shut, it nevertheless was continuously guarded by Indians from a small hut close by. These would sound the hours with a bell which they had high on the peak, when they were sounded below in the monastery. Every Friday a priest would ascend to the cave to celebrate mass there in memory of the Passion of the Lord, which was always venerated by the sainted Fr. Martín in that sacred place with his prayers and his tears and excruciating acts of penance.
>
> At any time Indians are frequently gathered [there], especially during the day, and no less those neighboring Spaniards and those passing through, because it is on the royal road and much frequented by those who travel from Mexico City to Puebla, and from Puebla back to Mexico City. When the relics are shown, it is with much solemnity. The Vicar ascends with those who may happen to be there, they ring the bell, and the people gather; some candles are lit, as well as a silver lamp which hangs from a boulder in the middle of the cave, although during the day there is plenty of light which enters by the door, and the singers begin to sing in *canto de órgano* some mournful motet about the Passion. Then the Vicar arrives wearing the surplice and cassock, he opens the box, and he makes a prayer over the sepulcher of the Lord, censes the statue of Christ and then the relics, and he shows them to those surrounding him. He does this with all devotion, and together with the circumstances of the place, and the roughness of those clothes, and the memory of the saint and of the penance that he did there, the hardest hearts are softened, such that scarcely anyone who enters into that cave does not leave contrite and full of tears (Mendieta 1870: 602–605; translation mine).

Several interesting things can be remarked about Mendieta's account. The point of Mendieta's narrative was, of course, to introduce a new generation to the Franciscan symbolism of Amecameca. He thus rehearses all the hagiographical elements which tied Fray Martín at Amecameca to St. Francis at La Verna. Curiously, Mendieta does not attempt to deny the presence of the cult of the *Santo Entierro*, nor does any of the rancor which must have existed between the Dominicans and the Franciscans appear in Mendieta's account. Thus, in addition to Valencia's relics, Mendieta cheerfully mentions the image of the recumbent Jesus and leaves out none of the details which marked the cave as a Dominican copy of the Holy Sepulcher. These included the reliquary, itself called *el sepulcro del Señor* in the original Spanish; the boulder and the (admittedly superfluous) silver lamp, both marking the "Golgotha" of the shrine; and lastly, the ubiquitous songs sung in that holy cave, always a "mournful motet about the Passion." Perhaps the equanimity of Mendieta's account must be seen in the context of the times in which he was writing: by the end of the sixteenth century all the regular orders in Mexico were having to pull together to collectively withstand the attack of the secular clergy on their *doctrinas* (cf. Poole 1968 and Ennis 1971). Thus, while Mendieta re-makes Fr. Juan Paez into a booster for the cult of Martín de Valencia, perhaps out of a spirit of regular solidarity Mendieta had become a promoter of the Dominicans' *Santo Entierro*.

On the other hand, perhaps Mendieta saw in his narrative an opportunity to "Franciscanize" the *Santo Entierro*. There was nothing really incompatible between the characterization of Amecameca as La Verna and its characterization as Jerusalem, at least for the Franciscans. After all, during the Middle Ages the Franciscans had legitimated their reform program by promoting typological correspondences between Francis and Christ. The correspondences were chiefly symbolized by Francis' reception of the stigmata from the Seraphic Christ at his retreat on the peak at La Verna. As the Franciscans increasingly identified St. Francis with Christ during the fifteenth century, La Verna became increasingly associated with Jerusalem and Assisi with Bethlehem. In the end, the Franciscans came to promote pilgrimage to La Verna and Assisi as a kind of surrogate pilgrimage to the Holy Land (Milhou 1983: 269, 292).[7] In the minds of the

---

[7] Bonaventure, in the Prologue to his *The Journey of the Mind to God*, makes an explicit typological comparison between St. Francis/La Verna and Christ/Jerusalem (1960: 5–7). It is interesting to note that such close identification of St. Francis with Christ and La Verna with Golgotha was seen as somewhat blasphemous by some of the earliest Franciscans: see, for example, Brother Giles' (d. 1261) satirical remarks about La Verna in the "Vita Beati Fratris Efidii" in Brooke 1970: 337–41. The identification of Jerusalem/Bethlehem with La Verna/Golgotha reached its apogee in the late sixteenth and early seventeenth centuries: see Askew 1969: 280–306.

Franciscans, therefore, Amecameca could easily absorb simultaneous homologization to La Verna *and* to Jerusalem. Taken together, such layering of mythological and geographical meanings would only deepen the essential Franciscan character of the shrine: Martín de Valencia (Amecameca) = St. Francis (La Verna) = Christ (Jerusalem).

Amecameca, however, was probably an even more complex case of layering than this, for in addition to having multiple meanings in the minds of the Franciscans, it also had symbolic resonances in the minds of the Nahuas of which the Franciscans were wholly unaware. For example, the peak of Amecameca was not free from "pagan associations" as the Franciscans seem to have thought it was, but was actually one of the most important pre-conquest landmarks in the Chalco-Amecameca area. According to Susan Schroeder, local pre-conquest legend connected the peak at Amecameca with Chalchiuhmomoztli, the sacred mountain on which the Amecameca territorial polity (*altepetl*) had been formally established centuries before (Schroeder 1991: 31, 53). Thus, the peak at Amecameca was not just a neutral feature in the local topography, but the very center of local Nahua identity before the conquest.

The sacred pre-conquest associations of the peak, however, do not explain one of the more interesting and dramatic elements in Mendieta's narrative: the Nahuas' secret preservation of Martín de Valencia's relics. Mendieta, of course, saw the Nahuas responding to Martín as a saint and explained their actions accordingly. Nevertheless, we must remember that the relics were spirited away in 1537—a scant four or five years after the area became a target for intensive Christian missionization (Schroeder 1991: 98). Had the Nahuas of Amecameca really internalized the European cult of saints so quickly? Did they really respond to Fray Martín as a saint? This is unlikely. But even if the Nahuas *did* see Fray Martín as a Christian saint, this would be more than slightly ironic since the earliest records left of Martín's life in Mexico indicate that he came to hate the Nahuas over time and thought little of their spiritual state (Jiménez 1926: 67). A year before he died, Martín de Valencia even tried to charter a ship to sail to China, in order to find people he considered more worthy of Christianity (Mendienta 1870: 594). When this failed, Martín, who never managed to learn an Indian language, retired to Amecameca to live out his life in solitude (Jiménez 1926: 79, n. 6). It is doubtful that the Indians of Amecameca had much interaction with him while he lived in Amecameca or that the friar encouraged such interaction. Considering that a virtuous Nahua life was an intensely communal one, it would seem likely that the Indians saw Martín de Valencia more as a slightly mad misanthrope than as a saint.

We can account for the Indians' behavior better, I think, if we interpret it in terms of indigenous categories. The historical anthropologist Jorge Klor de Alva, for example, suggests an indigenous framework in which Fray Martín might have fit into the Nahua cosmology. As Klor de Alva tells us,

> As was the case for most sixteenth-century Christians, Nahuas experienced their religiosity primarily as a social phenomenon. Human ("civilized") existence was possible only in the context of participation in a social whole that expanded out from the lineage to the local community and finally to the regional polity that wove the various hamlets into a single unit. Spiritually speaking the moral community was made up of those individuals who recognized as theirs the sacred bundle, *tlaquimilolli*, made up of the relics and/or belongings of the divinized founder—tutelary deity or mythical hero. The physical remains of this man-cum-god were part of the supernatural powers of the universe and therefore functioned as a channel through which flowed the sacred forces that empowered, protected, legitimated, and gave a common identity to the village or town. Logically, the *tlaquimilolli* was housed in the temple that represented the sacred center of the community. Many of these sacred bundles were hidden, and others were destroyed after the Spanish missionaries insinuated themselves into the local capitals and proceeded to destroy the ancient temples (Klor de Alva 1993: 178).

We know from indigenous records that the first Franciscans who came to Amecameca did in fact burn the local temple, and probably the sacred bundle of the local divinized founder was then lost (Schroeder 1989: 24). In a way this signaled an end to the identity of the town; and yet, the imaginative structures still existed in the minds of the Indians whereby a new divinized founder could be located, this time in the guise of a Franciscan, Martín de Valencia. The sacred power of this new "founder" was not based on any special relationship between the town and Martín de Valencia, but on the sacred power he embodied and channeled as a kind of shamanic figure to the Indians. For, although during his life Martín may not have had a very good relationship with the Indians of Amecameca, they nevertheless did understand him as the Spanish imperial representative of the sacred and therefore as some kind of a holy man. Hence, when Martín died, his relics could be used according to indigenous categories to recreate an identity for the Amecameca area. The fact that the Indians hid the sacred bundle from the Franciscans seems to indicate that their conception of it linked it to the older idea of *tlaquimilolli* and not necessarily with European ideas of saints' relics. After all, the Franciscans had destroyed the first *tlaquimilolli*, and if they knew there was a new one, they were likely to destroy that one too. When, decades later, the bundle was accidentally discovered, the Indians were exceedingly anxious to keep the bundle in Amecameca, and they were clearly relieved when they were told that the relics were to be deposited in the cave of Amecameca under a locked iron grill (Mendieta 1870: 605). And what more appropriate place than Chalchiuhmomoztli, the sacred mountain on which the Amecamecans had previously incorporated themselves?

The Franciscans underestimated both the tenacity and the imaginative resources which allowed the Indians to retain much of their belief systems in the face of forced conversion. But of course, the Franciscans had an almost absolute faith that an acknowledgment of the sacrality of a Christian symbol necessarily meant a kind of mystical acceptance of the entire religious worldview and cosmology behind it. Nevertheless, changing a culture's religious worldview and cosmology overnight is nearly impossible. As the work of the historical anthropologist Louise Burkhardt has shown, when the Spanish destroyed the indigenous system of sacred symbols in Mexico and imposed a Christian one, the Indians did not immediately abandon their religious worldview and cosmology (Burkhardt 1989). Rather, the evidence seems to suggest that they struggled to reinterpret as best they could Catholic symbols and rituals according to indigenous categories, a process facilitated when there was a formal correspondence between one culture's symbols and rituals and the other's.[8] In the correspondence between the *tlaquimilolli* and Fray Martín's relics, we can perhaps see precisely that process occurring. Thus, it is quite possible that the Franciscans had unknowingly created not only an

---

[8] Although the issue of syncreticism was not explicitly explored in *Rethinking Religion* (1990), if Lawson and McCauley are correct that the same cognitive constraints on the structure of religious ritual operate cross-culturally, then it is not suprising that such ritual syncreticism as outlined in this chapter occurs. For a discussion of a possible cognitive mechanism for conceptual syncretism, see Light's chapter in this volume.

archetypal Franciscan pilgrimage shrine at Amecameca, but a kind of Nahua temple as well. The great irony of Amecameca, then, is that in an effort to escape the "insidious syncretism" of the shrine of the Virgin of Guadalupe, the Franciscans actually managed to create instead a site that was just as complex, layered—and syncretic.

11. DIFFERENT VIBES: RETHINKING RELIGION, YET AGAIN

Francis L. Gross, Jr.

I. *One World—The Church as Evolving*

This essay is about one leg in the journey of one's religious life. The author is fully aware that this journey has as many legs as a centipede. This is but one. I do know that this bit of rethinking is in a different realm, perhaps a different universe than the rethinking of religion espoused by Dr. Thomas Lawson, in whose honor I write this piece. One gives what one can. And so I say, perhaps to a person of a different cast of mind than those who think like my lovely friend, Tom Lawson:

I want to explain first that you and I live in just one world. You might say, "That's no great insight. Everybody knows that." And I reply, "Well, almost everybody, but a lot of people formally committed to churches hear about two worlds all the time from their priests, rabbis, ministers, mullahs, and especially from their theologians."

The two worlds they so frequently speak of are the natural world and the supernatural world. The supernatural world is what you might call "the God stuff." Some people call it grace; some call it the world of heavenly things, but the idea is that superimposed upon the regular, every-day world in which you and I live is another world, the world from which come miracles and other interventions of God in the life of the universe. I can remember quite clearly an ancient and revered teacher of theology lecturing me and other young Jesuits in training on the debate of just how many seconds or minutes a person could live a sinless life without what Catholics call "actual grace." Actual grace was a divine intervention, large or small, in the life of one of God's people.

Living with your head and heart in these two different worlds can be confusing! Sometimes the churches say that the "natural" world has one set of rules, the supernatural one another set. It's very hard to reason about a set of rules given us directly by God. The preacher says, "These are God's rules; that's that! Just be quiet and do what the rules say. You don't have to think about them, just keep them."

When you were a child, there were rules like that in your family. Most of them made sense too. "Dinner is at 6:30 P.M. Don't pick your nose. Don't slurp when you're taking your soup or drinking a glass of milk." Things like that. When I was a small boy and asked my mother "Why do I hafta not slurp or pick my nose?" the answer I got from her was usually pretty direct. "It's bad manners to slurp; and it's not polite to pick your nose." Period. That was that.

I hasten to add that as I got older I made up my own mind what bad manners were. I questioned many of those things I learned from my mom when I was a kid. In this spirit, I think one should question the religious parallels to good manners. The world of the rules my mom and dad expected me to follow, slowly, as the years went by and I grew into my teens, became a part of the things I could question. I began to make up my own mind about such things.

Developmental psychologists tell us that as we mature, something like what I have just described on the home scene should also happen in other areas of one's life, including religion (Erikson 1963: 261–63). I can remember thinking to myself, questioning the idea of two worlds, one natural (and usually seen as evil), the other supernatural, invariably higher and always good. Here's how I began to think: "There really is just one world. That's all I ever see and feel. I think God and I live in it together." Slowly, in the school of hard knocks, I came to realize that I had no experience of a supernatural hot line to God. God, it seemed to me, doesn't have a phone number or a place of residence where I can look him up. And maybe he's not a him, but a her, or even an it! (Davies 2001: 2)

It seemed to me that God is in the whole world, not having any special church and without a special residence. As Alice Walker says, in a the person of her character Shug in *The Color Purple*:

> God is inside you and inside everybody else. You come into the world with God. . . . It ain't a picture show. It ain't something you can look at apart from anything else, including yourself (Walker 1982: 166–67).

How well I remember the telling retort of God, played by George Burns in the movie *Oh, God*! to the expostulation of a young man whom God-George Burns had chosen for a special mission. The young man exploded, "Why choose me? I don't even belong to a church?" God's response was, "Me neither."

Looking for divine interventions in our lives is a rather subtle way of thinking that God is quite literally in heaven and pays special attention to earthly stuff only when the divine phone rings and someone asks for something.

If you assume that God is here all the time, in the world and looking after it, it's pretty obvious that it's more mature to say, "Thy will be done" than it is to say, "God, help me pass Algebra." I might add that if you ever put God in charge of Algebra, instead of taking the time to learn it, well that's a good way to flunk Algebra. How do you know? You learn the hard way, by experience. Don't take my word for it; look into your own life experiences. Special Divine interventions don't occur much in school, not to mention the rest of our ordinary lives. As the New Testament says, "The rain falls on the just and the unjust alike." God's workings in the world are just as natural as can be. They are everywhere. Jesus said, speaking of keeping the Sabbath laws, "The Sabbath was made for humans, and not the other way round." He knew that there is no set-for-all-times-and-places formulation of supernatural laws. Divine commands fit human nature for the simple reason that God is the author of all the world, not just the churchy part. I remember a grandmother who once advised her granddaughter, "If you don't go to church, Jesus will cry."

"No he won't, Gramma," said the small one, "Church is for us, not for Jesus." And if she promptly got her mouth washed out with soap, it was mostly for impertinence rather than for lacking in theological rigor. She was a smart little girl.

There's nothing strange or mysterious or supernatural about love being the heart of the Gospel as well as the heart of the Hebrew Scriptures and the Qur'an. Put another way, if we use religion to try to avoid responsibility, asking God to do what we ourselves are too lazy to do or too selfish to do, we are not adults! (Freud 1961: 26–30) Many religious people see a divine dimension to the world, but it is part of the world and not set off from it. To imagine that my prayers have to get some sort of heavenly and supernatural zap for me to have them answered does not fit the experience of most of us. The novelist Mary Doria Russell, speaking of her own conversion to Judaism, writes,

> When you convert to Judaism in a post-Holocaust world, you know two things for sure: one is that being Jewish can get you killed; the other is that God won't rescue you (Russell 1996: 409).

And you know too, that you pass Algebra if you work at it, and not if you don't. Asking for things in prayer is a most natural thing to do, especially if it's the night before the Algebra exam; but in the heart of an adult, what underlies all prayer is trust that the divine one will give us enough daily bread. As someone wisely said, "Divine grace IS THE WORLD, penetrated with the presence of God."

Now, to another supposition. Stated simply, it says that religious traditions are living things which grow and change like other living things. To imagine your religious tradition as something which happened once and then remained frozen for all time, fixed on that one, brief time of privilege is to close your eyes to history and to be more than a little naive about solving moral and ethical questions as they occur uniquely in every age, including today, the now time in which you and I live. I don't mean to deny that there are certain privileged times in every religious tradition. Certainly the days when Jesus lived were special ones in the whole history of Christianity. Muslims believe that the lifetime of the Prophet had a uniqueness that no other moment or period in Muslim history can equal. Jews believe that the Exodus event was a unique and central time in their history. Those special times are honored, remembered, and revered. The point I am making is that religious traditions, and that includes Christianity, do not have visible blueprints given at their beginnings, which the human founders and those who have followed them have only to consult to find out what to do about this or that problem of worship or morality.

The twelve apostles did not gather together in the upper room the day after Pentecost, say Mass, and go each to his appointed corner of the world to set up shop: Thomas to India, Peter to Rome, James to Jerusalem, John to the island of Patmos: each one to get on with the divine outline of detailed instructions kept carefully in his billfold, so as to be able to check each day as to what should be done and by whom. The followers of the Buddha and the prophet Muhammad had the same situation.

There is, for example, nearly nothing in the Gospels about how the Christian community is to worship or what form of organization it should take. I can still remember my shock as a young priest when I discovered that the word "priest" is never used in the Gospels or other New Testament writings to refer to Christian clergy. It is used to describe Jesus, the body of the church as a whole; it is used with reference to priests of other religions, but never for individual Christian clergy (Kung 1967: 364). The idea of an ordained priesthood developed in some parts of Christianity; in other parts, other systems of order developed and were later discarded and still later revived (Von Campenhausen 1969). I might add that Judaism as we know it today has a variety of forms of organization, some quite democratic, some quite autocratic. There is an amazing variety within the Buddhist tradition, as we are today aware, when the Buddhism of the lamas of Tibet is often in the news. The Buddhism of Zen, for example, is quite different from Tibetan Buddhism in organization, prayer, and customs.[1] There are lots of different kinds of Buddhists, Jews, Christians and Muslims, each one of which developed slowly within the tradition of certain founding fathers and mothers.

One of the reasons that the study of comparative religion is so enlightening is that there are startling parallels between different religions and startling differences too. All of them have grown slowly after an initial spark. None of them is encased in some unchangeable and perfect form which is the model for all times. A look at the scriptures themselves from a scholarly point of view, reveals clearly that the holy books of all religions took time to assemble, almost always existing in an oral form before they were written down. Almost always the decision as to which of the early texts in a given religion were *the* holy texts had to be made years after they were written down. Those who made the decision were human beings, like you and me, who lived after that first and sacred early time. For example, Christians didn't settle on which groups of early the early Christian writings made up what we call the New Testament until more than three hundred years after Jesus himself lived and died.[2] This and other facets of Christianity took years to develop; decisions about them were made after much argument, prayer, disagreement and controversy. Sometimes it amazes me when I realize that it took more than four hundred years to arrive at a consensus within the Christian body as to whether Jesus was truly a man and truly a God.[3] Given a core truth, Christianity is a tradition that has

---

[1] "Buddhism, 1. History" in Crim 1989: 124–26.
[2] "New Testament Quotations in Patristic Authors" in Achtemeir 1985: 701–2.
[3] "Chalcedon, The Definition of" in Cross 1997: 315.

developed down though the centuries. And it is still developing.[4] I do not hesitate to use the word "evolution" for this process (Teilhard de Chardin 1964).

I say this because to say that there was only one holy time and place is also, it seems to me, to come very close to saying that God, as the Deists believe, worked hard at the beginning of the world and then went fishing, leaving the world to work things out on its own.[5] Some would say that the divinity was also present in a special way at a few other special times. A Christian example of this might be the early years of the Protestant Reformation. From this perspective, the presence of God in the world is a sometime thing, rather than a continuous thing.

My point here is to let you, the reader, know that I write from the perspective of one who perceives the world as "charged with the grandeur of God" (Gerard Manley Hopkins quoted in Pick 1953: 13). I believe that the divine presence is not restricted to certain supernatural events, to certain special moments in history, or even to special people. My perspective is that the creator is always at work in all places and in all times. Our task is to learn to recognize that divine presence and to revere the created world as the inevitable place where we will or will not be successful in searching for God (Fox 1983: 42–56). This essay is dedicated to the process of spelling out the details of that search, given this author's point of view concerning God's presence in the world in all times and in all places.

As a corollary to this idea of developing church bodies and church beliefs, I want to make a comment about the stability of the world. How well I remember asking one of my grade school teachers, call her Sister Mary, how come it was that God did all sorts of marvels in both Old and New Testament, but didn't seem to bother with such things today.[6] At the time I had a vivid recollection that I had

---

[4] Cf. John Courtney Murray's comments on the development of doctrine in the "Declaration on Religious Freedom" in Abbott 1966: 673.

[5] "Deism" in Cross 1997: 465.

[6] I know full well that American nuns have changed. I am quoting a nun who taught me in the late 1930s. Many American nuns today, more than sixty years later, would point to a long history of prayers for the advancement for their congregations, while noting as well that despite millions of prayers, there is not a single Roman Catholic nun in the world who is a first class citizen in the Roman Catholic Church. First class citizens among Catholics, despite theories to the contrary, continue to be priests and bishops. So much for nuns and prayers of petition.

prayed to get a horse for Christmas. I looked carefully around the Christmas tree in my home on Christmas morning; a horse, I reasoned would be pretty obvious around a Christmas tree. It didn't take long for me to see that there was no horse under the tree. I went outside into the snowy acres around our house to see if my horse might be tied to one of the elm trees in our front yard. No horse. I looked in the garage, but there was nothing there except two rather battered Ford sedans belonging to my mom and dad. When I went down the hill to check out if God maybe got mixed up and put my horse in the chicken house, well I mean there was no horse. I knew I had been betrayed. "Thanks a lot, God," I muttered, "See if I ever ask *You* for anything again!" In all honesty I have to confess that I kept right on asking for things, such was my hope of success, until years later when I wanted to pass the Algebra final in college without knowing much Algebra. That didn't work either.

Anyway, Sister Mary told me I didn't get the horse because God knew, maybe, that I would have got bucked off, maybe right there on Christmas Day, and perhaps would have landed on a rock, head first and would have been dead the same day I got the horse; and that God didn't give me the horse for that or some other good reason. "Yeah, right," thought I. "And," continued Sister Mary with reference to all those miracles which were answers to prayers in the Bible, like the Israelites walking right through the ocean to get away from the Egyptians, "Well, that was because Moses and the Israelites were better people than we are, and if we really had faith, we could do the same thing." I don't have to tell you that the only time I ever tried walking through water like Moses and the Israelites was an attempt to cross through a deep pool of water in the creek that ran on our property when I was a boy. I did this in order to escape from a neighborhood bully. My brave attempt took place on a winter day when the creek was frozen solid. Even then it was slippery as all get out, and I nearly broke my you-know-what when I fell down on it. The water didn't part for me nor did God arrange to make my passage less slippery despite my fervent prayers.

You may say that the writer of this chapter started blaspheming at an early age; or possibly you might say, "Something like that happened to me one time." My point is that I have come to believe that nature's laws and God's actions within those laws do not change from age to age. The laws of gravity were just as powerful in Moses' time as now. People died from disease then and now. They had to work for food and shelter too. God and nature stayed the same, but people in different times and cultures described what happened to them in different ways. I really don't know what happened when the Israelites marched through the sea to get away from the Egyptians, but my own experience leads me to bet that it was more likely that the tide came in and got the Egyptians rather than some sort of temporary repeal of the laws of nature.

Before going further, a word on asking God for this and that. One can't avoid knowing that religious people all over the world ask for things. Buddhists ask for things; Muslims ask for things; Jews ask for things; Christians of all stripes ask for things. The Lord's Prayer, so dear to most Christians, asks "Give us this day our daily bread" and "forgive us our trespasses" and "lead us not into temptation." There's no escaping religious petition in any religion. Well, then? I do note that just before the words of the Lord's Prayer in St. Matthew's Gospel are the words: "... your Father knows what you need before your ask him" (Matthew 6:8). The injunctions of the Our Father are not bargains; they are expressions of trust. And there is a world of difference between the two. Earnest requests for horses, no matter how natural, are at bottom bargains. Implicit in them is the idea that God is running a kind of divine lottery. If you buy enough tickets, your chances for getting what you want go up. Petitions to God of any kind, make sense only as expressions of trust rather than hopes for sudden divine intervention in the normal course of things.

Nature's laws, after all, are a part of divine creation. It would seem strange to me that God would have to violate God's own laws to get our attention or heed our petitions. So, when I read the sacred stories of Old and New Testament I am inclined to think that the miracles and interventions of God were within the laws of nature as I know them rather than apart from them. It makes little sense to me that God should act in an entirely different way in one era of history rather than another. God stays the same; we humans change in our ways of understanding and expressing ourselves. I really do believe that under God's providence I have been saved from countless disasters, just as the ancient Hebrews were. The difference is that I see my deliverances as coming within the laws of the world as I know it. I am not bashful about seeing my God's interventions in my life within the holy laws of nature, not outside them, and that mature requests of God are expressions of trust rather than hopes that an old guy with a beard will set the workings of the world aside in order to provide me with the jelly beans of my choice. When I ask for daily bread, I'm like a child at table asking for more bread and jelly. His mother knows his needs and will take care of them, whether or not he asks. Asking is an expression of politeness and trust in her caring.

My ancestors in faith, Abraham and Moses, Miriam and Ruth, Muhammad, and the Buddha are my brothers and sisters in faith whose deliverances were real, just as mine are. They, however, knowing little of modern science, described their experiences of divine intervention according to their cultures and understandings of nature. That these descriptions differ from my own ways of writing should come as a surprise to no one. Speaking of contemporary art forms, I find the movies of Frederico Fellini to be marvelous examples of people searching for God and the sacred in today's world. My favorites among Fellini's films are *Amarcord*, *The Nights of Cabiria*, *8 1/2*, and *La Dolce Vita*. The contemporary American novelist and anthropologist, Mary Doria Russell, has two fine novels on the search for the divine: *The Sparrow* (1996) and *Children of God* (1998). I know of no one who speaks more eloquently of the presence of God in all times and places than Pierre Teilhard de Chardin (1965). There are others, but we have a start.

So, we have looked at the universe as just one divine entity, that religions by their very nature grow and change along with the world around them. I would add that the following and last piece of this essay, which concerns itself with how to read scripture, is also basic to the search. It is continuation of this essay's theme of basic presuppositions.

II. *How to Read Scripture*

A number of years ago, my wife, our two small sons, and I spent a month in India staying with friends in an Indian household in New Delhi. Being right there in the center of a country with a religious tradition far older than my own, I was curious about the great stories of the Hindu religion. Everyone, it seemed, had a favorite one. There was a story of Ganesha, the Hindu deity with an elephant's head and human body, who is pictured in close company with a cobra and whose mode of transportation was a rat's back. He is associated with all kinds of things, among them riches, humor and paradox.

In this particular story Ganesha made a bet with another Indian god as to which of the two could travel around the world in the shortest time. The bet being made, Ganesha's rival in the bet immediately took off at great speed in the race with Ganesha to circle the globe. He swam oceans, climbed mountains, and crossed deserts in his journey. He was often hungry; his life was threatened dozens of times by the elements and by hostile strangers. He held fast to his purpose, however, arriving back in India several years later, scarred and exhausted, but joyful at having finished his encirclement of the world in what seemed to him to be record time. As he approached the appointed place where the race was to be finished, he was surprised to see Ganesha sound asleep on his pallet, fat, contented and clearly never having left home. Ganesha opened one eye and saw his rival approaching in the distance. He rose, yawned, stretched in a leisurely manner, and ambled the few steps to the house next door, where his mother lived. He called out to her and asked her to come outside for a moment. As soon as she came, his rival now being quite close to the finish line and in full view, Ganesha walked slowly around his mother's sari clad figure. As he did so, he explained his action in a loud voice that his approaching rival could hear. He stated that his mother was the center of his world, and that he, having completed his journey round the world more quickly than his rival, was the winner of the bet.

This charming story about the importance of mothers is one of the sacred tales of south Indian religion. It has reminded me that the Gospels tell a number of tales about the importance of the mother of Jesus in the Christian scriptures: stories about Mary's conceiving and birthing of the child Jesus, stories of her influence over him when he was a child, stories of her lack of influence over him in his adult and public life, stories of her presence at his crucifixion.

One of the things that really struck me about the story concerning Ganesha and his mother was the fact that no one among the listeners asked if this fanciful adventure really occurred. Furthermore, no one wanted to question how anyone, even a god, could have an elephant's head on top of a man's body or how such a creature could ride on a rat, be the close company of a cobra without being bitten, or more to the point, whether or not this contest among the gods had really, historically happened.

And yet, in my own tradition there is currently, and not for the first time, a really gargantuan scholarly attempt to find out just which events told in the Gospels really occurred and which ones did not (Crossan 1997). I'm not so much concerned with the learned diggings into the origins of the New Testament records of Jesus as I am with the possibility that such ventures can obscure the reality that the sacred stories of Christianity are not written as biography or history as most people understand these terms. I recall the words of a very wise man in another religious tradition about his own visions, experiences and prophecies. His name is Black Elk and he was a holy man among the Oglala Sioux nation of our own North American continent. In commenting on his own visions and sacred tales of the Oglala Sioux people, Black Elk said, "I don't know whether these things happened or not, but I know that they are true" (1932: 1–2).

I also recall a decade of teaching an undergraduate course at Western Michigan University entitled *The Christian Tradition*. This course is part of the offerings of the Department of Comparative Religion in that University. If there was and is one single overarching difficulty in teaching a broad university course in the Christian tradition, it is the problem of teaching students to read the Gospels as sacred myths rather than blow-by-blow biographical and historical accounts of the life of Jesus of Nazareth. A large number of the students I have taught want the Gospels either to be exact historical accounts, or if they are not, as piously fraudulent attempts to deceive the reader about the life and importance of Jesus.

What is the problem? I don't think it is so much the task of explaining that religious myths in all religions are receptacles of spiritual truth rather mere history or biography. Certainly that is a scholarly path well traveled. To ask what a Gospel story means, or whether it happened or not, is no revolutionary approach to reading the Bible. Mircea Eliade and many other respectable scholars of the recent past have taught us to look deeper into the great stories of religious traditions rather than trivializing them with arguments as to how the entire earth could have been covered by a flood or how Noah managed to assemble all the fauna of the world in one not very large boat, or how Jonah managed to live three days in a fish's stomach before emerging fresh as a daisy to preach to the Ninevites. It is certainly trivializing one of the New Testament accounts of the infancy of Jesus to argue about how a star could rest over a single dwelling without reducing the entire area to cinders. It is surely a superficial reading of the resurrection accounts of the gospels to attempt to harmonize the various descriptions of how Mary Magdalene was able to be in so many places at the same time. If one wishes to reconcile her seemingly simultaneous presence at sundry events in the various Gospel accounts of the resurrection of Jesus, that's a formidable task. Mary would have had to been at least a world class sprinter to account for her various morning ventures on Easter day. I don't think that understanding the truth and meaning of scripture stories as always to some extent symbolic demands a special intelligence on the part of students of any age, whether those in my college classrooms or those who seek on their own to investigate the meaning of these or those sacred scriptures.

I have found, sometimes to my own amazement, that presenting the Gospel story through the medium of film or theater often cuts through student paralysis of mind as regards the inerrancy and literal truth of the Christian scriptures. Such a condition of paralysis often enough invades the minds of students who realize that it is naive to read scripture as though it were a news account of a totally sacred and hence inerrant nature. Having abandoned naivety, they are often in real agony. "What do we have left?" they ask.

And I myself ask, "Is this a theological problem?" Are religious people largely mindless folk who cannot accept a more subtle form of understanding their own sacred writings? Why is this such a problem among people who regularly attend movies and read novels without notable anguish that the truth in them, although real, is fictional. How can this be a problem for people who have watched "Seinfeld" without throwing conniptions over whether or not Jerry and his friends really exist?

"There is more at stake here than there is in some TV sitcom," you say, and I grant you that. For religious people, the holy books are important in ways that no other books are. And yet it still seems strange to me that I can hear Muslim students tell me with straight faces that the entire Qur'an was dictated to Muhammad, word for word, in Arabic, just as the text is today. These are people who are engaged in university studies, students of engineering and computer science, budding historians, linguists. They are often not naive as regards other kinds of knowing and reading. Those who major in physics and chemistry know very well, for example, that the models given us for atomic and molecular structure are useful constructs. These models are not what an atom or molecule would look like if one had a microscope powerful enough to actually see an atom or molecule. They are models which are useful in harnessing and otherwise using various atoms and the compounds thereof. After all, one learns in high school that scientists use two mutually contradictory explanations of the phenomena of light, the wave theory and the particle theory. Both theories have their practical uses, and scientifically trained people do not get upset that these and other useful theories of the physical sciences often enough contradict each other. Scientists know that the real contradiction lies not in the reality of the phenomena of light, but in the incomplete nature of theories which seek to explain it.

What is going on? Why all this trouble over an obviously simplistic understanding of sacred texts? I would offer you the reader an intuition based on developmental psychology. I believe that what is going on is often a cognitional and psychological difficulty rather than a religious one. Robert Kegan of Harvard is quoted as saying in this context, "Don't ask a flea to describe what a dog is like and expect a good answer. All the flea knows about a dog is that the dog is lunch."[7]

What's the point? The flea is too close to the dog to have a good view. I might add that for a person to know herself is a most difficult enterprise for the same reason. Other people can see your virtues, peculiarities and faults more clearly than you yourself can. They have more distance.

Let's get back to film and theater. There is a wonderfully funny musical version of the Gospel story called *Cotton Patch Gospel*, music by Harry Chapin. It places the Gospel story in rural Georgia. It is a musical, using the folk-music idiom of Harry Chapin; it is a redneck version of the Gospel. My students love it. I have shown another film of the Gospel story as well, a movie entitled *Jesus of Montreal*. It has been well received also. You will know other stage and movie versions of the Gospel story, such as the musicals *Godspell* and Andrew Lloyd Weber's *Jesus Christ Superstar*. The power of these adaptations, I believe, lies in the engulfing quality of good theater. Once you are taken in you can see and feel the Gospel message without all the baggage which ties it down to one and only one meaning, and often

---

[7] Personal communication with author. For more on Kegan's understanding on "embeddedness," see Kegan 1982: 29–45.

to one and only one church. Such is the truth of theater and film, thus its power.

And again I ask myself, "What is going on here?" Perhaps what people need in matters of reading scripture is some way of either immersing themselves more deeply in the story or some other way of being able to have enough distance from it to be able to see it with more perspective. What did Black Elk mean when he said, "I don't know whether these things happened or not, but I know that they are true?"

I might add here a note on fundamentalist Christian students I have had in class. After all, it might be quite simple for a person to say, "Basically, the only real problem one has in seeing a deeper and less literal meaning in scriptures lies in whether or not one's approach to Christianity or Islam or Buddhism smacks of 'fundamentalism' or not." Fundamentalists are often described by liberals with great condescension, as people of narrow religious vision, people who are at heart bigots, not very bright intellectually, and certainly mean-spirited. There is a sort of sarcastic litany of saints used here in the liberal community... Tammy Faye, Jim Baker, Pat Robertson, Oral Roberts, Benny Hin... it's a nice list, and the clincher is of course that some of these people are in jail from having defrauded their equally simple-minded constituents of large amounts of money in the name of the Lord Jesus.

I hasten to add here, that I am aware that there are bigots in every religion, including Christianity, and that I am very aware that liberal bigots are just as simple-minded as conservative ones. I am reminded of a student in one of my university classes who blurted out these words when being skewered by another student for his literal interpretation of the creation story in the Bible's book of Genesis. He said, "I do read the Bible more literally than you do, but I'm *not* crazy!" Our literalist knew very well that the creation accounts in the book of Genesis are not scientific accounts but religious accounts. He wasn't nearly as narrow-minded as his liberal classmates hoped he would be. Their picture of his belief was clearly more narrow-minded and distorted than his own response. Literalism and narrow-mindedness are not the sole possessions of fundamentalist Christians or literalist Muslims. The religious left can be just as brittle and overly focused as those whom they criticize. They just have a different set of unassailable beliefs. No one has a corner on narrowness. I am in hopes that the third part of this essay will shed some light on the matter of rigidity in religious belief.

III. *In Over Our Heads*

I want here to talk with you about ways of knowing things. Developmental psychology's concern with how people learn began with Jean Piaget's studies concerning how children learn (Ginsburg and Opper 1969: 1–25). The contemporary post-Piaget learning theorist who interests me most is Robert Kegan (1982, 1994). What he has to say about the learning process has a lot to do with having an intelligent attitude towards churches. Let me explain briefly. Kegan, following the earlier thinking of Piaget, sees the way people think as not merely our progressing by the amassing of more and more data, but changing how we classify what we know. He has a six stage learning theory. Each stage of organizing and classifying includes the previous ones but is more complex. Teenagers, he tells us, have a complicated way of understanding their world. They often differ from children, whose thinking is characterized by a kind of basic logic, which normally does not include the understanding of other people's motivations.

The little kids are quite practical. They see their world in a good, businesslike manner. If you have the money, you can buy the groceries. If you don't, you can't buy them. If you are nice to your mother, she is likely to give you a cookie; if you are troublesome to her, chances are there will be no cookie. Your friends are people who are useful to you and generally nice to you. You don't worry about whether your mom is having a bad day except in so far as how that might affect your chances to get a cookie or watch your favorite program on TV.

Young men and women in their teens often understand the world and the people in it in a more complex way than they did as children, because they are usually more reflective and have a sharpened awareness of the feelings of other people. They discover a kind of loyalty to friends which includes the understanding that a friend might be having a bad day or a headache. Consequent to such awareness comes a kind of loyalty to friends which goes well beyond the pragmatic approach of children. If my best buddy in middle school is in a bad mood and not approachable, I can understand this and keep on being her friend. I can empathize with her situation. Maybe her dad is an alcoholic and this very morning is passed out on the floor of her house right at the front door. She had to step over his body to leave the house. No wonder she's blue and cranky today. She's my friend and I feel bad for her situation. I understand! Earlier in life I might have said, "She's mean today, so too bad for her! I don't like her anymore!" If you see this new way of knowing on the part of teenagers, you'll go a long way in seeing why middle and high school kids band together in cliques, why they often do stand by one another in a pinch.

From this new perspective, I might even take the rap for a friend who gets in trouble a lot. I'll confess to having written something vulgar on the chalkboard in English class to protect my friend who actually wrote the message, because I know my pal has been in all sorts of trouble this week and doesn't need a phone call to his home from the principal of the school about her behavior. My new-found ability to look beneath the surface is an important basis for the loyalty I show my friends and family.

The learning stage which follows this way of knowing has an even wider scope. Instead of just focusing on individuals, it includes the understanding of systems. Here's an example. A number of years ago when I had a lot of veterans of the Viet Nam war in my undergraduate college classes, I noticed that these ex-G.I.s were a very savvy bunch of people. They had learned to survive as members of the U.S. Army or Navy in Viet Nam by figuring out the system. Sometimes it was a matter of life or death. You learned to bend or disregard Army regulations in order to stay alive. I'll give you an example of how these folks used their knowledge of how the system works to get what they needed as university undergraduates. Large universities are bureaucratic organizations, as are the armed forces of our country. If you had learned how to survive in the army, then you might well see that large university structures are not all that different from those of the armed services.

At the time I'm speaking of, the early 1970s, there was a period at the beginning of each semester in most large colleges and universities called "Drops and Adds." If you wanted to get into a course late, or if you wanted to drop a course you had signed up for, you went down to the university gymnasium to remedy your class schedule. In the gym there were large numbers of tables arranged on the playing floor, each one presided over by one of the professors in a given department of study. There was a table for history, one for economics, one for sociology, in short one for every department in the university. A professor sat at each department table with a list of the numbers of students currently enrolled in each course offered by that department, every thing from English 101 to graduate courses on Chaucer, all at one table. If you wanted to drop the graduate course in Chaucer, you waited in line at the English department table until your turn came up. When your turn came, you asked that your name be scratched from the Chaucer course. This in turn left an opening for somebody else to sign up to take that same course. Believe me, the long hours that this process took were painful for both students and profs alike. Students were never sure that by the time each one got to the head of the line the course she or he wanted to enroll in had room for another student.

Now, let's go back to my veterans from the service. They had learned all sorts of survival skills operating in the huge bureaucracy that is the armed services. They had learned these skills in a deadly war. Survival depended on knowing how to manipulate the system. One of my grizzled veterans told me he never had much trouble with drops and adds. He just hung around a given table until the professor seated there had to leave the table for a few minutes to go to the john or take a smoke. As soon as a given professor left his seat vacant, my veteran friend walked up to the empty seat, sat down, and after dealing with a student or two, simply enrolled himself in the course he wanted, quietly leaving the empty chair before its regular occupant returned. He knew very well that most of the people in line had no idea who he was; they assumed for the moment that he was a professor. He used this bit of impersonation to get the class he wanted. All the other long-suffering students continued to wait in line in that roulette game called drops and adds. Often they did not get what they wanted. They didn't understand the system! I might add that my purpose in telling you this story is not to decide whether or not my crafty former soldier was morally right or wrong in his approach to adding classes. My purpose is to show you that he had learned the ins and outs of large bureaucracies and how to put his insights to use in getting into a needed class.

To survive in any large system, it helps to know how it works. You might ask, "How do you learn such things?" And I would answer, "You can learn them in college, but you won't ever have a course teaching such things." You learn them in the school of hard knocks. You learn by being desperate. You learn by getting clobbered. If you don't learn to be what I call "school-wise," there is a very good chance that you'll never graduate, or if you do, your course of studies will be a nearly endless line of frustrations. It will take you a lot longer to thread your way through school than the students who figure out the university system. We are talking here about a way of understanding. Those vets knew that the big impersonal system of the university would not take pity on them. They knew that their honored status as veterans would not change the picture when it came to getting into the classes they needed. They had learned to back off from the system, to observe it carefully, to know what it could and could not do for them. The word "savvy" is a good one to describe what these men and women knew.

Now, I want to remind you that many churches are large systems, having a number of things in common with universities and the armed services. If you want to be happy as a Catholic, as a Protestant, a Jew, a Muslim, a Buddhist, indeed in almost any religion which involves large systems, you'd better understand them. "Were religions always this complex?" you ask. I don't think so, frankly. Things are usually smaller and more personal at the beginnings of religious movements. I'll try to explain.

Robert Kegan once mentioned in a lecture that he himself had grown up in a very tight Jewish community, Hasidic in its origins, located in a suburb of New York City. Everything you needed was there in that small compact community. You were educated within it; you practiced your profession or business within it. You lived within walking distance of the synagogue. You married Jewish; you ate Jewish. You had a beautiful and very old system of worship and correct behavior which went back three thousand years in its wisdom. The Jewish community took care of you. Everything was familiar and had been familiar for a long time. There was wisdom there.

I'd like to add that I grew up in a system quite similar to Robert Kegan's. I grew up in a large Catholic clan. My cousins on my father's side, and there were fifty-eight of them, all grew up in Catholic families, went to parochial schools, Catholic high schools, and if they went to college, went to Catholic colleges, even Catholic law schools and medical schools. I remember a very early argument with my mother in which I insisted that the word friend and the word cousin meant the same thing. My family was my world. My father was the only one of the seven brothers and four sisters in his family to marry someone not a Roman Catholic. I wasn't quite the same as the other Gross cousins, but there were so many of them, not to mention their Catholic mothers and fathers, that my own immediate family's small deviation from the all-Catholic norm made little difference in my family's way of looking at things. On my mother's side there were a few cousins, a scant ten, and although my sisters and I knew them, we knew even as children that they were not like us. They were outsiders whose wisdom and morals were frankly suspect. We had a system which was venerable and wise, not quite as old and venerable as the Kegan clan's Judaism, but nonetheless a highly encompassing and very rich system. We had good resources within the Catholic ghetto, and the family up to my time stayed close to each other in worship, in work, and in love.

Then something happened to both American Jews and Catholics. I'll give you a somewhat arbitrary date for the change, the turbulent 1960s. The world got bigger. The tight groups we belonged to became more porous as the people within them became more American and less set apart and suspicious of wisdom outside our communities. Both Jews and Catholics today are a part of ordinary American life, for the most part. Our priests and rabbis are not regarded as having all the answers any more.[8] Life is more fluid and less stable, but above all, more complex. We are now a part of a pluralistic society, what Lawrence Kohlberg once called the postconventional world. Neither Kegan's rabbi nor my Jesuit teachers are the only authorities. I teach at a publicly supported university of 30,000 students instead of a small Catholic college. Kegan teaches at Harvard instead of a yeshiva. There is more than one system for both of us as well as the many thousands of other American Jews and Catholics whose roots are in enclosed communities.

The old days are gone. Decisions are more complex. Being a Hasidic Jew or a Roman Catholic is not enough nourishment any more, because I no longer live and work surrounded by a familiar wisdom which has fed and protected me. How do I learn to operate in such a bewildering pluralism? How can I trust my church when I know that it is one of many churches? If I continue to think that my people and my ways are the only ones that count, I'm headed for trouble at work, in my family, and in my church itself.

When I was a kid the faults of our elders and our priests were often covered by the system. We didn't talk about cousins who were divorced, uncles who were alcoholics, or priests who were pedophiles.

---

[8] The current uproar in this country over priest pedophiles is a clear indicator that Roman Catholics are now part of the mainstream of American life. Priests who prey on children will no longer be protected by the walls of the Catholic ghetto. They are subject to the law of the state like everyone else.

We certainly didn't share our scandals with the larger world we lived in. I didn't know that my grandfather had ended his life by suicide until I was seventeen years old, and then it wasn't my parents who told me. How did I learn to deal with my new world, my world which had few secrets, my world in which nobody was infallible any more, not even the Pope? Certainly one common way of coping was to pretend that the world had not changed, to keep on believing that my church had all the answers, and that someone benign and usually related to me would look after me and cover for me if I had trouble at work, to keep on denying that anyone in my circle could ever have a marriage that ended in divorce: "Catholics don't believe in divorce." That was the party line long after it was no longer true. What a shock then when I realized in middle age that one of my classmates in high school was indicted on seventeen counts of extortion and murder as the don of the Syrian mafia in St. Louis. What an even larger shock when priests in my own church were featured in the news media of the entire country as pedophiles, some of them being sent to prison like ordinary people. Bitterness and cynicism or a continuing naivety are often the results of people who were formerly protected by a system which is no longer the only system.

There is, however, a possibility other than naivety for dealing with a system which has been cut down to size, a system which no longer is the only way to go. This other way has to do with a wider way of knowing, a more complex way of understanding. I recall that when I was a Jesuit seminarian studying to become a priest, there was one teacher in my course of training who had a decidedly different approach from the ordinary one to the laws of the church to which all of us belonged. He mentioned to me on the occasion of the marriage of one of his nieces that it was a wise thing for young Catholics to marry in front of a judge rather than a priest. The church, we both knew, did not recognize civil marriages for Roman Catholics. "If the marriage doesn't work out," said my teacher, "Each one of the civilly married couple will be free to marry again because the church doesn't recognize civil marriages. If it all works out well, then they can always have a second ceremony after a few years, a Catholic ceremony, thus making them respectable in the church. Now," said my prof, "doesn't that make sense?"

It didn't make sense to me at all. Here was a respectable priest advising a couple to break church law, which meant committing a serious sin, for which they would both be punished in hell if they did not repent this bad action sometime later in their lifetimes. I didn't get it. I was puzzled and not a little put off by this solution for dealing with the sacred rules of my church. For years I wondered how a priest, who was also the head of the philosophy department at St. Louis University and hence no fool—how could he *say* things like that?

Today, more than forty years later, I understand his point of view more clearly. This was a man who had come to a more complex understanding of the church of which he was a loyal member, tied even more closely by his priesthood and his membership in the Jesuit Order. He knew that church laws change with the times, but that something called culture lag prevented this large, international system from changing quickly. When a here and now situation arose which jeopardized the future of young couples of good will, he advised breaking the law. His was the vision of a person who had enough breadth of vision to realize that large systems all change slowly, including churches, and that one must realize this limitation and find a practical solution.

The Jesuit system of casuistry, which sought by intellectual sleight of hand to bend the laws of a church top-heavy in legality, had a similar perspective. People whose thought processes were insightful enough learned to engage in various forms of sophistry when the rules became impossible to keep. One learns to be a sneak in large systems. My veteran of Viet Nam understood that very well when he realized he'd never get the class he wanted by being honest. I might add that should you the reader find being a sneak under certain circumstances a shameful and immoral way to act, I'd like to point out something to you which may help. Here's my point. Women, as opposed to men, have taken liberties with law throughout history. Many in the community of women, as Carol Gilligan so wisely pointed out a number of years ago, know well that often times the persons involved in moral decisions are more important than the principles at stake (1982: 64–105). My own work on Teresa of Avila, a canonized Roman Catholic saint, shows very clearly that Teresa understood the church system within which she lived and worked. As a woman, even as a nun, she had precious little authority to make the changes in religious life she brought about in the Carmelite Order. "Sometimes," said Teresa in a now famous letter to one of her prioresses, "one must dissemble a little" (quoted in Gross and Gross 1993: 175–78).

Now, back to the church, the church as system, the church as bureaucracy. Bishops, mullahs, rabbis, lamas and other church officials with middle level authority are bureaucrats just as deans of universities are, just as mayors of cities are, and CEOs in the business world. Middle level officials in systems don't get where they are by being overly imaginative, overly principled, or even overly honest. They are generally persons who are regarded as safe by the persons higher up in the ladder of authority in this or that system. If I expect church officials to somehow be entirely different from other bureaucrats, I am being naive. I am refusing to accept these persons as human and subject to the pressures that other people in similar structures have to deal with. If there is a cardinal archbishop anywhere in these United States who is not very good at dealing with large sums of money, his name is not known to me.

Now, what are we talking about here? We are not saying that church people and church organizations are bad. We are saying that they are human and the structures they work in are human as well. G. K. Chesterton once commented, speaking of churches, "Christianity hasn't failed; it's never been tried."[9] It is very difficult to have a lot of power and be holy at the same time. When one says that power tends to corrupt and that absolute power corrupts absolutely, the churches and church officials are not exempt from this truism.[10]

So, if I put my church where it belongs, if I see it as a human institution with human officers and people, then I can deal sanely with it. Then I will not expect things from it that it cannot give me. Then I can see that Mafia members are often church goers, that bishops are sometimes grasping and secretive, and that ordinary church members are often hypocritical. I can see the humanity of my church, because it and the people in it are human just like all the other people outside it. What do I have a right to expect? I have a right to expect that my church is a good organization, not

---

[9] Quoted in Bartlett 1980: 742, #2.
[10] "Lord Acton," in Partington 1981: 1. Lord Acton is also quoted in response to a question about his membership in the Catholic Church. Acton was clearly against the notion of papal infallibility, so when it was defined by the first Vatican Council, he was questioned as to whether he would leave the church. These are his words: "Because the bishops of my church made fools of themselves in Rome, it does not follow that I should leave my church."

perfect, not supernaturally different, just good. I have the right to expect the mayor of my city to be good too, as well as the dean of my college. If I expect any of these systems people to be somehow above it all, I am asking for the common run of church people to be uncommon folk indeed. I will expect them to have answers for me which I need not examine myself. I will expect them to be somehow exempt from the normal foibles of good people and good systems. I need not be cynical or bitter, just wise enough to expect the people in my church to be real people and the systems whereby they organize themselves to be very much part of the world in which other systems live.

If the reader finds these comments on bureaucracies and bureaucrats negative in tone, I should want to add here that good bureaucrats, secular and sacred, often expect their subjects to be wise enough to realize that not all laws are for all the people. I once sat in front of a county board which concerned itself with building regulations in a county just outside my home town of Kalamazoo, Michigan. I had acquired a tract of wooded land and wanted to erect a small building on it where I would be able to retreat from time to time from academic life. The five members of the board told me that they would not give me such a permit, citing a county ordinance which said that any building in the county had to be accessible to fire trucks. Such trucks would ensure the occupants of the building some safety in case of fire or medical emergency. They also told me that it would be dangerous to have such a hideaway, because illegal migrant Mexicans might use it for shelter if they were being chased by immigration officials. We do have migrant workers who come to Michigan to pick cherries and apples during the late summer, but the board's objection still struck me as bizarre. We were dealing with one small house, hardly likely to become much of a place of refuge for illegal immigrants on the lam. As far as the danger to anyone if the building burned down, that was ludicrous. I said as much to the board members. One of them looked at me quizzically and said, "You aren't very smart, are ya?" That didn't help. I left the meeting angry and confused at being refused what seemed to me to be a legitimate request. The next morning I awoke with a picture in my mind's eye of a grizzled rural board member looking fixedly at me and making that comment about my not being very smart. Then suddenly it came to me. The board, for reasons of their own, didn't want to give me permission to build, but they expected me to be smart enough to go quietly ahead with my building project. The migrants were a smoke screen; the accessability of the house to fire trucks was the law. They weren't going to say on the record that I should break the law; but they were puzzled that a university professor was not smart enough to read between the lines. I built the house; there was no trouble. It has stood now for nearly a decade, studiously ignored by the county board, a small monument to a tacit agreement between me and a quite astute group of county bureaucrats. They expected me to understand the system!

This is the end of an essay which might be entitled, "Presuppositions for Sane Living in a Church body." The basic themes of this essay, in case you have forgotten, are as follows. First, there is only one world, sacred and profane are really not separate categories. Second, when one reads holy scriptures in nearly any religious tradition it is of vital importance to know that at heart that much of their wisdom is written as sacred myth rather than objective reporting. Third, in any search for God and church in a pluralistic age, it is vital to see churches and churchly people as having the characteristics of other human systems as well as the people who are part of those systems.

I am delighted to have written this essay as part of a festschrift in honor of Professor Thomas Lawson. He has been and is, a friend, a learned colleague, and a lovely man.

Finis Libelli, non autem Viae

12. RITUAL COMPETENCE AND MITHRAIC RITUAL

Luther H. Martin

I

> There must in the nature of human institutions be a mental language common to all nations, which uniformly grasps the substance of things feasible in human social life and expresses it with as many diverse modifications as these same things may have diverse aspects.... This common mental language is proper to our Science, by whose light... scholars will be enabled to construct a mental vocabulary common to all.
>
> —Giambattista Vico

In 1741, Johann Peter Süssmilch, a Prussian clergyman and founder of the principles of modern statistics, argued that the logical perfection of grammar demonstrated its divine origin (Süssmilch 1741; Graf 1996). While Süssmilch's argument from design was opposed to contemporaneous views that language was a human invention, his trope of divinity supported Vico's conviction of its ubiquitous uniformity (Vico 1744: ¶161).[1] Warrant for Vico's conviction about a fundamentally natural and "mental" language common to humanity albeit with the potential for diverse historical expressions awaited Noam Chomsky's distinction between linguistic competence and linguistic performance, or knowledge about language in contrast to its use (Chomsky 1965), a proposal that moved linguistic theory into the emerging field of cognitive psychology.

The cognitive endeavor to write a grammar for the "common mental language" of human beings pursued by Chomsky has been

---

[1] Süssmilch was influenced by his reading of William Derham's *Physico-Theology: or, a Demonstration of Being and Attributes of God, from Works of Creation* (1713), (Süssmilch 1741: 13). The first edition of Vico's *Principi di una Scienza Nuova* was published in 1725 (Napoli: F. Mosca).

employed by E. Thomas Lawson and Robert N. McCauley to formulate a theory of religious ritual competence (Lawson and McCauley 1990; McCauley and Lawson 2002). They invite researchers, especially ethnographers, to assess their theory "to see if... [it] will stand up to further tests" (McCauley and Lawson 2002: 37; Lawson and McCauley 1990: 176–177). The issue I should like to explore here, however, is to what extent the Lawson and McCauley theory of ritual competence and the hypotheses about religious ritual form predicted by this theory are "proper" to the historiographical "science" envisioned by Vico.

Although a cognitive science of religion had been proposed in 1980 (Guthrie 1980) and Lawson and McCauley had launched such a study with their cognitive theory of ritual competence in 1990, to my knowledge, Thomas Lawson was the first to challenge historians to recognize the relevance of cognitive science for their study of religion. In 1994, Lawson observed that:

> Historians have often been only too willing to assign the problem of the persistence of... [religious] notions to psychologists, anthropologists, philosophers, theologians, or, in desperation, the therapeutically inclined.

They do so, he concluded:

> at the expense of recognizing that *if they are willing to make assumptions about the transmission of tradition, then it is their job to help in identifying the mechanisms which underwrite such a process* (Lawson 1994a: 483).

Lawson argued, in other words, that history is not an *explanans* but must be the *explanandum*; it is precisely the "emergence, development and persistence" of particularistic historical ideas and practices that beg for explanation (Lawson and McCauley 1993).

The relentless problem of all historiography is its instantiation of the logical fallacy of affirming the consequent, i.e., that the truth of the antecedent may be argued from the truth of the consequent, for all historiography proceeds, by definition, as a reconstruction of past events (and causes) on the basis of surviving historical remains. As I have argued elsewhere, the appealing feature of cognitive models is that they go behind the familiar metaphors, typologies or sets of concepts—themselves based on descriptions of historical remains—to advance theoretical explanations for historical formations that are grounded in universal features of human cognition (Martin 2002: 31).

Following Dan Sperber's contention that macro-scale phenomena must be understood as the collective outcome of processes at the micro-level (Sperber 1996a: 64), Lawson and McCauley argue that their theory of religious ritual competence identifies one of the underlying micro-processes that motivates the development of religious ritual systems and affects their historical arrangement in ways that increase the probabilities of their continued transmission (McCauley and Lawson 2002: 43, 179). Explicit instruction concerning religious rituals, they argue, "is, at least sometimes, completely absent and about which, therefore, participants must have some form of intuitive knowledge." Knowledge of those forms is revealed by the acquisition of and successful participation in rituals (2002: 4–5; 1990: 2–3), and, they presume, by the researches of the cognitive sciences. By attempting to write a cognitive grammar of religious ritual form, Lawson and McCauley propose to describe a common human structure that historians might employ to sort out surfeits of historical data where they may exist, on the one hand, and to fill in the gaps where there is a deficiency of data, on the other. By doing so, they offer probabilistic constraints on the fallacies that can be concluded from an anomic positing of historical possibility. To employ such models in historiographical reconstruction assumes, of course, their validity. The assessment of the validity of Lawson and McCauley's model of religious ritual form is currently an ongoing project by historians as by anthropologists (Vial 1999; Martin, forthcoming). Assuming a heuristic validity for the model is itself another form of assessment if employment of that model, in consideration of the greatest amount of available historical data, is able to produce a plausible account of past occurrences in the absence of credible alternatives.

II

> Mithras, God of the Morning, our trumpets waken the Wall!
> Rome is above the Nations, but Thou art over all!
>
> —Rudyard Kipling

The Roman cult of Mithraism flourished throughout the Roman Empire from the end of the first until the end of the fourth centuries A.D. when it, like all non-Christian religions, came under the interdictions of the Christian emperor Theodosius. Because of its transcultural distribution and transgenerational persistence, Mithraism can offer a significant case study for the history of religions in late antiquity. Although no texts, myths or sets of doctrine have survived from Mithraic sources,[2] a profusion of archaeological remains, architectural and iconographic, have been discovered at numerous sites throughout the expanse of the Roman Empire attesting to a rich ritual life among Mithraists. Inferences made about the exact character of Mithraic ritual from these data are, however, inconclusive and often contradictory (Beck 2000: 145). Mithraism can, therefore, also provide a relevant case study for assessing the historiographical implications of Lawson and McCauley's theory of religious ritual form.

For Lawson and McCauley, participants' cognitive representations of religious rituals utilize the same cognitive system as that employed in the representation of any action (McCauley and Lawson 2002: 115). Religious rituals, in other words, are actions like any human action and, like any human action, they require agents, both actors and those acted upon or "patients" (McCauley and Lawson 2002: 23). What differentiates religious rituals from ordinary, non-religious, actions is, in the theory of Lawson and McCauley, the "principle of superhuman agency," i.e., the commitment by participants to roles played by culturally postulated superhuman agents (CPS-agents) in their representations of religious rituals (Lawson and McCauley 1990: 61, 124–125; McCauley and Lawson 2002: 8). It is the different "roles that CPS-agents play in rituals' representations" that differentiate types of religious ritual (McCauley and Lawson 2002: 26).

CPS-agents are conceived as powerful agents that "serve as the guarantor of cosmic (as opposed to conventional) authority in religious systems" (McCauley and Lawson 2002: 22). There is no question that the central CPS-agent of Mithraism is Mithras. A depiction of Mithras slaying a bull (the tauroctony), represented on frescos or,

---

[2] I have suggested that, apart from local possibilities, no "canonical" texts, myths or sets of doctrine were ever produced by Mithraists. Rather, Mithraism belongs to what Harvey Whitehouse has termed an "imagistic" mode of religiosity (Whitehouse 2000; see Martin, forthcoming). "When non-linguistic public representations play... a central role in the transmission of culture knowledge," however, Lawson and McCauley question "the faithful replication of that knowledge" (McCauley and Lawson 2002: 38). Beck has proposed that "extensive norms reinforcing... [a Mithraic] religious identity over time and space" were transmitted through Mithraic iconography (Beck 2000: 172 and n. 123). The anthropologist Fredrik Barth has suggested that such non-linguistic knowledge is transmitted as "broad themes" which cannot be reduced to "unambiguous propositional form" (McCauley and Lawson 2002: 67, citing Barth 1975: 211, 1987: 66–67).

Mithraic tauroctony from the "Mithraeum of the Circus Maximus," Rome (*CIMRM* 434–435). (Photo by L. Martin)

more commonly, on carved reliefs, is the only imagistic feature common to all Mithraic finds.

The elements of this tauroctonous scene—a raven, a dog, a serpent, a scorpion, even the bull itself—have been identified with empyrean constellations (Corvus, Canis Minor or Major, Hydra, Scorpio, Taurus). The tauroctony is often flanked by images of the sun and the moon and/or is sometimes bordered by the twelve signs of the zodiac. Mithras' "cosmic authority" is confirmed, in other words, by the superimposition of his image in the act of slaying the bull upon a map of the heavens (Beck 1998: 125)—although the exact significance of this cosmic act remains unclear. We might venture the general observation, however, that the tauroctonous image, in the context of Graeco-Roman popular mentality, dominated as it was by astrological/ astronomical significations, was almost certainly a Mithraic representation for negotiating the terrestrial world, widely perceived among Graeco-Roman philosophies and religions as ruled by chance (Gk: *tychē, heimarmenē*; Lt: *fortuna*), in light of an alternative cosmic order personified and guaranteed by Mithras (Martin 1987, esp. 113–18). Lawson and McCauley predict that participants in a particular ritual system will consider that such (soteriological) changes in their religious world are brought about through transactions with such CPS-agents as Mithras (McCauley and Lawson 2002: 14–15), and this transformation is most clearly exemplified in the Mithraic rite of initiation.

Mithraic Initiation

For Lawson and McCauley, initiation rites generally are examples of "special agent rituals" in which either the CPS-agent or his/her surrogate is considered to serve as the actor in the ritual. A surrogate for the CPS-agent is defined by the comparative immediacy of his/her ritually mediated relationship to the CPS-agent (McCauley and Lawson 2002: 26, 33). This "principle of superhuman immediacy" refers to the number of enabling rituals, i.e., those antecedent rituals "whose successful completion is necessary for the completion of the current ritual" (McCauley and Lawson 2002: 116), required in order to connect the ritual agents with the CPS-agent (Lawson and McCauley 1990: 125; McCauley and Lawson 2002: 27). Such rituals which involve appeal to fewer enabling actions in order to implicate a superhuman agent are considered to be the more central in a religious system (Lawson 1994a: 493; Lawson and McCauley 1990: 125; McCauley and Lawson 2002: 27).

The "Father" (*Pater*) of any particular Mithraic community and the highest grade of Mithraic initiation was the ritual agent most immediately related to Mithras in the cult's ritual structure. In an apparent depiction of Mithraic initiation on a cup discovered in a mithraeum in Mainz (Horn 1994; Beck 2000), the initiating agent is portrayed as wearing a Persian cap (Beck: 2000 Pl. XIII), the symbol of the "Father" according to the symbolic representations of the seven grades of initiation depicted on the mosaic floor of the Felicissimus Mithraeum in Ostia (*CIMRM* 299) and part of the distinctive garb worn by Mithras in all of his representations. This "immediacy" of the Father to Mithras is obtained as the consequence of his ritually "ascending" the initiatory "ladder," described by Celsus (Origen, *c. Cels.* 6.22) and portrayed in the grade mosaic of the Felicissimus Mithraeum, a progressive, sevenfold series of enabling rituals themselves presided over by an antecedent Father in a chain of authority that, Lawson and McCauley predict, extends back to some founding act by Mithras himself, at least implicitly (the Mithraic genealogy of which, if explicated at all, remains unclear).

The Father, the agent ritually most-closely-connected to Mithras, clearly acts in a way that effects a change in the initiate's religious status; upon initiation, the initiate is henceforth considered to be initiated (McCauley and Lawson 2002: 13), i.e., to be a Mithraic "insider" (McCauley and Lawson 2002: 15). This change in religious status wrought by special agent rituals is, according to Lawson and McCauley, considered to be "super-permanent," as is characteristic of initiation rituals generally (Lawson and McCauley 1990: 134), and is, consequently, a ritual performed but once by any initiate (or once by any initiate per grade of initiation).

Special agent rituals, according to Lawson and McCauley, typically involve high sensory pageantry and a consequent emotional response on the part of participants which contributes to the memorability of these one-time rituals (McCauley and Lawson 2002: Ch. 2; see Martin, forthcoming). In the scene depicted on the Mainz vessel, for example, the initiating Father aims an arrow from his drawn bow directly at the initiate who is portrayed as smaller, naked and vulnerable (Beck 2000: Pl. XIII). The "terror of the scene" (Beck 2000: 150) recalls that of the scenes of initiation in the Mithraeum of Capua Vetere where the initiate, also portrayed as naked, is menaced by sword and fire (Vermaseren 1971: 24–42; on "rites of terror" and initiation, see Whitehouse 2000: 18–33).

According to Lawson and McCauley, the "high emotion" associated with initiation rituals triggers a "cognitive alarm" that "tends both to marshal and to focus cognitive resources on its apparent causes, which, if vindicated by subsequent developments, marks the events as especially memorable" and "potentially significant . . . in [the initiates'] lives," a highly desirable strategy for a central but non-repeated ritual (McCauley and Lawson 2002: 113, 188, see 77–85; for an extended discussion of this aspect of Mithraic initiation, see Martin, forthcoming).

Since special agent rituals are, in the predictions of Lawson and McCauley, central to the religious system, they are, consequently, unlikely to involve any kind of formal variation or substitutions (McCauley and Lawson 2002: 33). Not surprisingly, Mithraic initiation remains the most consistently documented of all Mithraic rituals.

Mithraeum of the "Seven Spheres," Ostia (*CIMRM* 239–245) (Photo by L. Martin)

The Mithraic Meal

In addition to initiation into membership, it is also clear that the Mithraic communities held communal meals. A meal is portrayed in extant Mithraic imagery more often than any other scene apart from the tauroctony (e.g., *CIMRM* 390, r5; 693a; 782, 1175; Stewardson and Saunders 1967: 68). And, a feature common to virtually every mithraeum was the *triclinia*, or "eating-couches," along its side walls.

In the architectural iconography of the mithraeum, the lateral "eating couches" flanked and framed the ubiquitous tauroctonous image of Mithras which was always displayed on the third or back wall, the place that in a domestic dining room would often be occupied by a third *triclinium*. Table protocol in the Hellenistic world assigned or accorded places at the table according to social position. Plutarch reports that the position at the center of the three-table configuration was reserved especially by Persians as the place of royal or highest honor (Plu. *Mor.* 619 B), precisely the position where the tauroctonous image of Mithras was situated in all mithraea. As Manfred Clauss concludes, the Persian god Mithras "himself was always the host" of the Mithraic meal (Clauss 2001: 113). In fact, several tauroctonous reliefs have been discovered which are reversible to show a scene of Mithras "hosting" the meal (e.g., *CIMRM* 397, 641, 1083, 1137, 1896) and these apparently were displayed during the meal itself. The frequency with which the meal was depicted in Mithraic imagery, the ubiquity of the *triclinia* as a dominant architectural feature of mithraea and the centrality of Mithras' iconic presence at the meal all support a conclusion that the meal was a regular feature of Mithraic life (Clauss 2001: 61).

But was this meal a ritual at all, or simply an iterated religio-social act by a group that has been characterized as primarily a "Religion der Loyalität" (Merkelbach 1984: viii, 153–188)? Were the Mithraic meals, in other words, simply occasions at which Mithraists came together in fellowship as was common to religious and social associations of the period generally (Wilson 1996: 12; Kloppenborg 1996: 25–56; Beck 1996: 182), a fraternal act celebrated in the presence of and/or with their patron deity that rendered "visible the fact that whose who take part are members of one and the same group" (Kane 1975: 348–50; Clauss 2001: 113)?

In the technical sense employed by Lawson and McCauley, religious rituals, in contrast to religious acts, "are actions in which an agent does something to a patient" (McCauley and Lawson 2002: 13). Can, in other words, the Mithraic meal be described in terms both of agents who act and of recipients of that action and, if so, who/what were they? Since the *Pater* and the *Heliodromus*, the ritual surrogates of Mithras and Helios,[3] are depicted as presiding over the meal (e.g., *CIMRM* 1896), might it have been a component of the rites of initiation as is, in other contexts, often the case (Stewardson and Saunders 1967: 68; Clauss 2001: 113)? But when participants in the Mithraic meals were portrayed, they are masked, indicating an (antecedent) grade of initiation (e.g., *CIMRM* 483, 1896). The meal could not, therefore, have been an initiation rite for which the participants in the meal were acted upon, i.e., in which they were the patients or the recipients of the ritual act, since they were already initiates. Rather, the meal was clearly an act in which the role of agent was played by initiates who consumed a meal, the patient/object of the action. For the Mithraic meal to qualify as a religious ritual in the technical sense employed by Lawson and McCauley, therefore, the elements of the meal itself must have been thought of as having some sort of ritual connection with Mithras, the CPS-agent, that would have rendered it the patient/object of the act of eating by participant/agents.

Lawson and McCauley term rituals in which "the most direct connection with the gods" is through the patient/object of the ritual, "special patient rituals" (McCauley and Lawson 2002: 26). In this type of ritual, the role of CPS-agents is "typically passive" and their "presence in the ritual less vital." By this interpretation, the presence of Mithras at the meal would have been less that of presiding host and more that of honored guest. "[S]ince it is not the ... [CPS-agents] who have acted, these rituals' effects are not super-permanent. Consequently ... they must be repeated at periodic intervals" (Lawson and McCauley 1990: 135), as the Mithraic meals seemed to be. The *triclinia* as the central architectural feature of mithraea, the portrayal of Mithras' honored presence at the communal meal and of his own participation in the meal together with Helios all argue for the conclusion that the Mithraic meal was a special patient religious ritual.

---

[3] The *Heliodromus* ("Sun-Runner") was the sixth and highest grade of Mithraic initiation after that of Father. Helios was identified in Mithraic imagery and epithet with Mithras as "Mithras Sol Invictus."

Special patient rituals "are invariably connected with other rituals" (McCauley and Lawson 15), i.e., with other "actions in which CPS-agents play a role" (McCauley and Lawson 2002: 13). What was the ritual connection of Mithras to the elements of the meal? Does, in other words, Mithras' tauroctonous presence at the meal define in some way the object of the participant's action? Were, for example, the elements of the Mithraic meal understood to have been (symbolic) sustenance of some sort provided by Mithras as suggested by some portrayals of Mithras as hunter (Merkelbach 1984: 3–6)? Or, since Mithras and Helios were themselves often depicted as sharing a meal while sitting on the hide of a bull (e.g., *CIMRM* 42.13, 49, 483, 835.2, 966.C5, 988, 1036.2, 1082.2), presumably the bull that is portrayed as being slain in the omnipresent tauroctonous scene,[4] might the meal's sustenance have been the meat of the bull—or that of some smaller, substitute animal more appropriate to the exiguous space available for the performance of ritual in most mithraea (Kane 1975: 350; on substitutions as a formally permissible characteristic of special patient rituals, see McCauley and Lawson 2002: 32)?

As I have argued elsewhere, the Mithraic tauroctonous image could only have been viewed in the larger context of Roman religiosity as a depiction of ritual sacrifice (Martin 1994: 218) and public perceptions of Mithraism, according to literary evidence from Herodotus to Pallas, did associate Mithraism with sacrifice, albeit in different ways: sacrifice *to* Mithras (Hdt. 1.131; Strab. *Geog.* 15.3), sacrifice *taught by* Mithras (Plu. *Is. et Os.* 46), and sacrifice *in the name of Mithras* (Plu. *Pom.* 24–25, Pallas, cited in Porph. *Abst.* 2.56) (Martin 1994: 218 and n. 5). Was, in other words, the Mithraic meal a sacramental act, having something to do with salvation, that in some sense was analogous to the contemporaneously developing Christian meal (Justin, *Apol.* 1.66; Tert. *De praescr.* 40; Vermaseren 1963: 103–104; Stewardson and Saunders 1967: 71; Beck 2000: 175)? Or was the sacrificial character of Mithraism an "outsider" misperception of Mithraic imagery?

Although it remains unclear exactly what the connection between Mithras and the meal or the elements of the meal might have been, participants in the meal would in all probability have concluded by

---

[4] A reciprocal relationship between Mithras' slaying of the bull and the celebration of a shared meal while sitting on the hide of the bull is suggested by the reversible reliefs.

analogy from Mithraic architecture and imagery that such a connection existed. (On the analogic encoding and transmission of knowledge in Mithraism, see Martin, forthcoming). It is nevertheless clear that any "ritually mediated connection" of Mithras to the meal (the patient/object) was "comparatively less intimate" than was the case of Mithras to the Father/actor in the Mithraic initiation. By contrast to the "super-permanent" change in status wrought by initiation, such "ritually less-well-connected" rituals as the meal carry comparatively less finality. As such, their repetition was necessary to maintain the ritual's efficacy (McCauley and Lawson 2002: 31). And since the objects of special patient rituals are comparatively more removed from the CPS-agent by enabling rituals than are special agents, they "often display greater latitude about their instruments, their patients, and even their procedures" (McCauley and Lawson 2002: 32). Consequently, the nature of the Mithraic meal might have been either sacramental or fraternal, even within the same community (Beck 1996: 182), its precise character subject to local or regional variation.[5]

The answer to such questions depends, of course, on the role(s) of Mithras (the CPS-agent) and the connection of Mithras to the possibilities of ritual agents that are postulated in the particular conceptual systems of Mithraism. Lawson and McCauley's religious ritual form hypotheses address the structure of rituals and predict, therefore, nothing of their historical, i.e., semantic and cultural, contents (McCauley and Lawson 2002: 9–10). What the Lawson and McCauley hypotheses do predict, however, is that special patient rituals are repeated, that they become, as a consequence, more routinized than special agent rituals and that they involve comparatively less pageantry—and this seems fairly to characterize the Mithraic meals. The Mithraic meals constituted, in other words, what Robert Turcan has termed the "liturgie ordinaire" of the Mithraists (Turcan 1993: 78, and cited by Beck 2000: 146).

---

[5] The variability in possible interpretations of the Mithraic meal by local Mithraic groups suggests that its fraternal character might have provided occasions for the recruitment of new members, as is the case with some modern "secret societies" which invite potential members to attend their "private rituals" along with initiate members (Bryan, 2001; Martin, forthcoming).

The Mithraic Procession of the Sun-Runner

Roger Beck, one of the foremost scholars of Mithraism, has recently described a third, processional Mithraic ritual (Beck 2000). Beck reconstructs this ritual primarily on the basis of the second scene portrayed on the Mainz Mithraic cup (Beck 2000: Pl. XIV), from a passage about Mithraic cosmology preserved in Porphyry's *De Antro Nympharum*,[6] and from the universal design of mithraea as a "likeness" (*eikona*) of the cosmos.[7] This diverse documentation suggests that the ritual—assuming the validity of Beck's reconstruction—was widely, if not universally, practiced (Beck 2000: 157). In a complex but convincing argument, Beck concludes that this ritual was an enactment of a solar drama in which the *Heliodromus* ("Sun-Runner"), escorted by two figures representing Cautes and Cautopates (see n. 5) and preceded by an initiate of the grade *Miles* (Beck 2000: 157),[8] led a processional miming the solar journey (*dromus*) around the aisle of the mithraeum,[9] itself a "scale model" of the cosmos, intimating, thereby, the genesis and soteriological apogenesis of souls (Beck 2000: 159; 163–4). Beck concludes that "[t]he enactment of this mystery ... is precisely the business of Mithraists meeting in their mithraeum" (Beck 2000: 163).

The question, of course, is to what extent Lawson and McCauley's hypotheses are helpful in determining the formal type of the Mithraic processional and, consequently, its relationship to Mithraic initiation

---

[6] "To Mithras as his proper seat, they assigned the equinoxes ... As creator and master of genesis, Mithras is set at the equator with the northern signs to his right and the southern signs to his left. They set Cautes to the south because of its heat and Cautopates to the north because of the coldness of its wind" (Porph. *De Antr. Nymph.* 24). Cautes and Cautopates are two torchbearers widely represented in Mithraic imagery, the former portrayed with a raised torch, the latter portrayed with a lowered torch.

[7] "Similarly, the Persians call the place a cave where they introduce an initiate to the mysteries, revealing to him the path by which souls descend and go back again. For Eubulus tells us that Zoroaster was the first to dedicate a natural cave in honour of Mithras, the creator and father of all ... This cave bore for him the image of the cosmos which Mithras had created, and the things which the cave contained, by their proportionate arrangement, provided him with the symbols of the elements and the climates of the cosmos" (Porph. *De Antr. Nymph.* 6).

[8] When portrayed or described, *Miles* or "Soldier" was the third grade of Mithraic initiation.

[9] A "metaphorical journey" within the confines of ritual space is similarly characteristic of modern secret societies (Buckley 2000: 166).

on the one hand and to the Mithraic meal on the other. This question again revolves around a determination of who occupied the role of agent and who that of the recipient of the action of this ritual. The answer will determine whether the processional was a didactic component of, or a soteriological complement to, Mithraic initiation.

On the one hand, Beck argues that the processional presents a "doctrinal truth" (Beck 2000: 157) and, as such, is an "integral part of the mithraeum's rites of initiation" (Beck 2000: 159). By this interpretation, the processional would be a special agent ritual, led by the *Heliodromus*, the surrogate of Helios, who acts through didactic ritual to instruct new initiates in the central cosmic presumptions of Mithraism. As such, we would expect this ritual to be performed but once per new initiate (although those already holding an initiatory grade would likely have witnessed and even participated in the ritual multiple times thus reinforcing—as in the case of initiation—its didactic import).

On the other hand, it is, also by Beck's reconstruction, the initiates who are the agents of the ritual, traveling through the "scale model" of the cosmos on a "metaphorical journey" which mimes "within their mithraeum...the [cosmic] destiny of [their] souls" (Beck 2000: 160). As this cosmic destiny leads the initiates beyond the celestial spheres of the cosmos towards the "ideal world" (Beck 2000: 168), it would seem as though it is Mithras who, as representative of this ideal world, would be the welcoming recipient of a soteriological act on the part of initiates. By this interpretation, the processional would be a special patient ritual in that the object/patient of the ritual would be the CPS-agent himself, or his surrogate, the Father, who is otherwise absent from the depiction of the procession on the Mainz cup.

The Mainz cup shows that *Miles*, or initiates of at least the third grade of initiation, were participants in the procession. But were the two grades of initiate inferior to *Miles*, the grades of Raven and *Nymphus*, also participants in the procession as actors or were they participants as patient/recipients of the ritual act? And, although the leader of the ritual, the Sun-Runner, is represented as the sixth of the seven Mithraic initiatory grades and is, therefore, "ritually less-well-connected" to the CPS-agent than is the recipient of the ritual, Mithras himself, the Sun-Runner is, as we have seen, also portrayed in Mithraic imagery as an alternate surrogate of Mithras (see n. 3).

We might conclude that the ritual form hypotheses of Lawson and

McCauley confirms Beck's contention that the Mithraic processional was an important part of Mithraic business. While not an initiation rite *per se*, the Mithraic procession would, however, seem to have been a special agent, didactic ritual complementary to Mithraic initiation—as the two complementary scenes on the Mainz cup suggest—in which a "ritually less-well-connected" leader, together with "ritually less-well-connected" agents, initiates of the grade of *Miles* or higher, might well have performed the ritual for the instructive benefit of those even less ritually well-connected, the Ravens and *Nymphae*. Although non-repeatable with respect to new initiates, initiates of the second grade, *Nymphus*, and higher would have observed this ritual repeatedly—as in the case of initiation—whereas those of the third grade, *Miles*, and higher seemed also to have been frequent participants in this ritual as well. In this way the information conveyed by these rites concerning Mithraic "salvation" would not only be introduced to new initiates but would also be reinforced among the membership of the group (Barth 1975: 101). This relationship of the roles of patient/audience characteristic of the total sequence of initiations, including its attendant processions, would have provided a certain balance between memorability and didactic reinforcement within the Mithraic ritual system.

The Mithraic Ritual System

We can conclude that the Mithraic ritual system included both special agent rituals (initiation, the procession of the Sun-Runner) and special patient rituals (the Mithraic meal).[10] The distinction between initiation and the procession of the Sun-Runner as special agent rituals, on the one hand, and the Mithraic meals as special patient rituals, on the other, is, of course, significant. According to Lawson and McCauley, the ratio of special agent to special patient rituals make up any particular ritual system's complement of rituals (McCauley and Lawson 2002: 181). An unbalanced system, in which there is a bias towards one type of ritual form over the other, will be short-lived even if

---

[10] Despite the probability of local and regional variations in Mithraic ritual form and content, it is nevertheless proper to speak of a "Mithraic ritual system" because their historical connections and borrowings (Barth 1987: 8, cited by McCauley and Lawson 2002: 72) and because of the "norms" transmitted in their performance and in Mithraic imagery.

widespread (McCauley and Lawson 2002: 198), for special agent rituals alone require increasingly greater expenditures of resources (with decreasing effect) in order to ensure the high levels of sensory pageantry associated with the cognitive and transmissive efficacy of such rites while the repetitive nature of special patient rituals tend towards habituation, tedium and, finally, irrelevance (McCauley and Lawson 2002: 185). A "balanced" ritual system, on the other hand, contributes to the stability and survival of religious systems. The felicitous balance of the Mithraic ritual system, both within the special agent rituals themselves and between special agent and special patient rituals, offers one explanation for the widely distributed, three hundred year ascendancy of Mithraism.

Nevertheless, it was the special agent rituals of (graded) initiation(s) and the complementary procession of the Sun-Runner which dominated the Mithraic ritual system and which the special patient ritual of the meal seemed to reference. Whereas initiation remains the most clearly and consistently documented feature of Mithraism and seemed to be a universal Mithraic practice, Mithraic special patient rituals apparently were variable, subject to regional variation in both form and practice. The Mithraic special agent ritual and its didactic processional complement were, in other words, the more stable and influential of the two ritual forms. Such special agent rituals are dominant in imagistic systems whereby religious knowledge is transmitted through imagery and performance whereas special patient rituals are dominant in doctrinal systems whereby religious knowledge is transmitted through well-formulated instruction (Lawson and McCauley 1990: 125).[11] It now seems clear that Mithraism was a system in which its knowledge was analogically encoded and trans-

---

[11] The distinction between "imagistic" and "doctrinal" "modes of religiosity" was first proposed by Harvey Whitehouse, on the basis of his work in Papua New Guinea, as contrasting sets of politico-religious dynamics characterized by "particular patterns of codification, transmission, cognitive processing and political association (Whitehouse 2000: 1; see 1995). Lawson and McCauley spend much of *Bringing Ritual to Mind* (2002) discussing how their own analysis of Whitehouse's ethnography "reveals larger patterns in the evolution of religious ritual systems (and of religious systems generally)" than does Whitehouse's explanation (McCauley and Lawson 2002: 7, chs. 3, 4, 5). Although there are significant differences between the theory of Whitehouse and that of Lawson and McCauley, the predictions of the two theories largely coincide with respect to non-repeatable special agent rituals and to repeatable special patient rituals (McCauley and Lawson 2002: 146–48), just those rituals that seem to be documented by Mithraic practice.

mitted through its iconic and performative imagery. On the other hand, Mithraic doctrine, belief, or even myth, seemed to be a matter of regional or even local exegesis, if they ever existed at all (Martin, forthcoming). Finally, it can be suggested that the ratio of special agent rituals to the special patient rituals in the Mithraic ritual system, and that between imagistic and doctrinal modes of transmission (Whitehouse 2000), was less balanced than was that of Christianity as it emerged from the fourth century.[12]

III

> In the signs of religion and the laws of salvation form necessarily prevails over essence...
>
> —Anatole France

When Abbot Maël, the purblind missionary of Anatole France's satire of Western civilization, *Penguin Island*, mistakenly baptized a colony of penguins, a surprised assembly of the saints met in paradise to consider the ritual's validity. Following upon their learned disputations,

---

[12] The connection of the central CPS-agent in Christianity (Christ) to baptism (initiation) and to its shared meal is made explicit in a uniformly controlled, coherent set of doctrine. According to the Roman Catholic "doctrine of the real presence," for example, when the body and blood of Jesus are consumed, these surrogate elements for the CPS-agent both serve as the patients of this ritual and "constitute the initial appearance of a CPS-agent" in its structural description (McCauley and Lawson 2002: 118). Because of this postulated immediacy of the CPS-agent, the eucharist, a repeated, special patient ritual came to be considered more important than baptism in the Catholic ritual system and central to it (McCauley and Lawson 2002: 34). This balance of repeated high participation in a comparatively high-sensory laden ritual, stabilized by the conceptual control of doctrinal formulations and transmitted through them, ensured an intuitive (cognitive) bias towards Christianity over the comparatively less-well-balanced ritual system of Mithraism (McCauley and Lawson 2002: 181–82). This cognitive appeal of Christianity, we might conclude, was one of the factors, along with its readily transmitted doctrinal modality, which influenced the rapid and widespread acceptance of early Christianity and which contributed, consequently, to one Roman emperor's acceptance of Christianity as a licit religion of Rome in the early fourth century and another's interdictions of all non-Christian religions by the end of the same century. Because of the doctrinal character of Christianity, historians have attempted, with limited success, to explain the early appeal of Christianity solely on the basis of its teachings, the general import of which are largely shared, as we might expect, with other contemporaneous philosophies and religions (see e.g., Beck 2000: 174 and n. 132).

they concluded that "the validity of a sacrament solely depends upon its form" (France 1975: 38). And so it is for Lawson and McCauley but, as we have seen, for reasons quite other from those of claims to superhuman authority. Lawson and McCauley's theory of ritual competence emphasizes that theoretical generalizations about rituals cannot be made on the basis of such culturally contingent meanings and interpretations but only upon the formal syntax of religious ritual actions which are structured by the way in which the human cognitive system represents any action generally (McCauley and Lawson 2002: 10). From our brief attempt to assess the utility of Lawson and McCauley's predictions concerning religious ritual form for historiographic research, we might suggest several conclusions about our case study, the place of ritual in the Roman cult of Mithraism.

- It comes as no surprise that Lawson and McCauley's predictions about special agent rituals are confirmed by what is known of the Mithraic rite of initiation. This is largely because common formal features of initiation/entry rituals have already been widely documented by ethnographic and historical evidence.[13] These predictions also strongly suggest that the Mithraic procession of the Sun-Runner was, as reconstructed, a special agent ritual.
- Lawson and McCauley's ritual form hypotheses do, however, allow us to differentiate special agent from special patient rituals and to conclude, thereby, that the Mithraic meals were, in the technical sense of Lawson and McCauley's hypotheses, not special agent or initiatory rituals but special patient rituals.
- The identification and differentiation of the forms of the Mithraic rituals allows us further to identify a relationship among Mithraic rituals whereby the repeated special patient rituals related to and referenced the super-permanent effects of initiation. This relative stability of the Mithraic ritual system, as defined by the comparative balance of its forms, offers a contribution to considerations

---

[13] Some seventy-five years ago, Raffaele Pettazzoni noted morphological parallels between the initiation rites of the Greek mystery cults and those of some Australian tribes (Pettazzoni 1924: 21–44; I am indebted to Professor Giovanni Casadio for this reference), and forty years ago, Maarten Vermaseren, one of the great scholars of Mithraism, suggested that certain features of Mithraism might be found among what he then termed "the primitive peoples of Australia, Africa and America today" (Vermaseren 1963: 129).

about the appeal of this movement in late antiquity that provide an alternative to conclusions about the attractiveness of Mithraism based upon questionable reconstructions of Mithraic teachings. The content of Mithraic teachings, of their significance or meaning—which all evidence indicates was a regional or even local characteristic of Mithraism—is, of course, postulated by its various conceptual systems and is beyond the pale of the formal analysis of religious ritual addressed by Lawson and McCauley.

Lawson and McCauley's cognitive theory of religious ritual competence and their hypotheses about religious ritual form highlight the formal ways in which the concept of agency and the roles attributed to agency have been represented by subjects in the conceptual systems of particular religious groups. And they have offered historians a cognitive model for differentiating the formal conditions whereby representations of certain action conditions in the historical data might be attributed to roles occupied by particular agents but not to others, and to which performative role these representations of certain actions might be attributed. As one noted historian of religion has recently concluded, "not everything that is subjective is also arbitrary" (Kippenberg 2002: 189).

13. BRINGING DATA TO MIND: EMPIRICAL CLAIMS OF LAWSON AND McCAULEY'S THEORY OF RELIGIOUS RITUAL

Justin L. Barrett

Scholars of comparative religion and cognitive scientists of religion continue to give E. Thomas Lawson's and Robert McCauley's cognitive theory of religious ritual considerable attention. Detailed in *Rethinking Religion: Connecting Cognition and Culture* (1990) and *Bringing Ritual to Mind: Psychological Foundations of Cultural Forms* (2002), the theory draws upon insights from cognitive and developmental psychology, linguistics, and the cognitive sciences more generally to make bold, *testable* empirical claims about the mechanisms that support and promote religious ritual. Lawson and McCauley argue that observers and participants in religious rituals generate the bulk of judgments and intuitions regarding religious rituals through use of ordinary, essentially universal conceptual systems. Their hypothesis runs against the grain of most anthropological theories, which regards ritual practices, because of their impressive cross-cultural variation, as wholly the result of "enculturation," unconstrained by any psychological factors. Thus, an assumption of most anthropological theories of religion is that persons not properly "enculturated" in a system would have little ability to reason about the thoughts and activities in that system. In contrast, Lawson and McCauley have adopted the position that the human mind is not a *tabula rasa* that is filled by "Culture." As cognitive scientists have repeatedly demonstrated, the human mind comes into the world with many biases that shape the sorts of information able to be processed and how that information will be processed. At least by early childhood, children of all cultures—by virtue of being members of the same species living in a common world—possess a number of specialized mental devices or systems for making sense of the world around them, a world that includes religious thought and action. These biases in perception, thought, and concept formation shape the sorts of thinking and acting that may become a part of the cultural environment, including religious traditions.

In addition to the novelty of their theoretical proposal, it is the testability and falsifiability of corollary claims that makes Lawson and McCauley's theory distinctive and worthy of even more attention. This cognitive theory produces at least one general claim and a number of specific claims about religious rituals. In this essay, I summarize existing experimental tests of these claims and suggest some directions for the research program Lawson and McCauley have initiated. But first, some theoretical detail is needed.

What is a Religious Ritual?

Lawson and McCauley circumscribe "religious rituals" as acts in which (1) someone (2) does something (3) to someone or something (4) in order to bring about some non-natural consequence (5) by virtue of appeal to superhuman agency. All five elements are necessary for an action to qualify as a religious ritual under this theoretical framework. For example, a person who shoots a special arrow into a cloud in order to solicit a god for rain would be performing a religious ritual. However, shooting a special arrow into a cloud to cause rain *without* any appeal to a superhuman agent, e.g., through magic, would not constitute a religious ritual. Likewise, a religious worship service or engaging in prayer do not *necessarily* constitute a religious ritual, and often do not. Why? Someone may be acting but not necessarily acting on any object or "patient." A typical Catholic Mass, however, may include several religious rituals such as blessings with holy water upon entry, the blessing of the Host, the Eucharist, a baptism, and so forth; as well as several non-ritual religious actions such as singing or praying.

Though the narrowness of this definition of religious ritual may dissatisfy some scholars of religion, its precision pays dividends in being able to relate religious ritual action and accompanying mental representations to known conceptual structures discussed by cognitive scientists. Patterns in religious rituals within and across religious traditions become tractable in terms of identifiable mechanisms instead of vague and ontologically dubious forces, institutions, or entities.

The General Claim

Having identified religious rituals as specific actions, Lawson and McCauley further argue that the primary conceptual tool participants and observers use to process religious rituals is an "action representation system"—a conceptual system or device posited to operate in reasoning about any action, religious or not. At some level, any person shooting any arrow into any cloud is processed similarly regardless of whether the acts are religiously motivated or not. When observing such an action, the action representation system, in conjunction with other systems responsible for reasoning about agents and their actions, automatically and often tacitly begins trying to determine the intentions of the actor, the goal of the action, the probable consequences of the action, and so forth. The action representation system drives explanations and predictions on the basis of identifying the actor, the action, and the object. Once these "slots" are filled, the device starts generating inferences. Just as in ordinary actions, rituals are not merely events that happen but actions caused and directed by the intentions of an actor or agent.

Developing Lawson and McCauley's general claim, Barrett and Lawson (2001) further theorized that since religious rituals consist of actions that evoke superhuman power to justify non-natural consequences, the sort of cognition ritual intuitions invoke is *social* cognition, cognition governing how intentional agents act in ways to motivate the action of others. The inference system identified by psychologists that is responsible for this sort of reasoning is sometimes referred to as "naïve psychology" and includes the "theory of mind" device that computes beliefs, desires, and emotional states of intentional agents. Once the action representation system identifies an event as an action, by virtue of identifying an intentional agent prompting the action, naïve psychology is activated to generate auxiliary predictions and interpretations of the action. In religious rituals, the action performed (someone doing something to something in order to get a god to do something) is understood as a *social act* and invokes roles (e.g., communicator, petitioner, audience) that are part of the cognitive-representational repertoire used by all humans on a daily basis. If these roles are part of everyday cognition rather than a special theological domain, very little additional information about the relationships between the agents should be necessary to generate relevant inferences about the potential success of the action.

This appeal to universally occurring cognitive architecture (an action representation system and naïve psychology) spawns a general claim of the theory: how religious rituals are conceptualized, and thus how they are performed, is directly shaped by ordinary conceptual structures and processes. That is, under normal developmental circumstances in *any* cultural context people acquire the necessary cognitive tools for making sense of religious rituals. Special, culture- or religion-specific tools are unnecessary. The upshot of this general claim is the prediction that "ritually naïve" observers—observers with only minimal information about the ritual action but essentially no information about the religion or ritual system—will still have predictable, converging intuitions about the probable outcome or efficacy of a given ritual.

This hypothesis may be termed the Ritual Competence Hypothesis, for this prediction is analogous to being able to identify a sentence as grammatical or not simply on the basis of identifying the subject, verb, and object as legitimate even if the semantic content of the subject, verb, and object is unknown. The Ritual Competence Hypothesis serves as an alternative to the null hypothesis that ritually naïve observers would have no converging intuitions regarding how a ritual should or should not be structured to be efficacious.

Some Specific Predictions

Primacy of Agency Hypothesis

Because of the fundamental role identifying an agent plays in distinguishing an action from a mere event, Lawson and McCauley go on to predict that ritual observers and participants will intuitively judge that having a proper agent initiating the ritual is relatively more important than performing precisely the correct action. That is, for a ritual to be successful and bring about the desired consequences, first and foremost, the ritual must be conducted by a qualified intentional agent. Otherwise, the ritual might not even qualify as an action. Thus, perhaps surprisingly, when informants consider whether a ritual is likely to succeed, Lawson and McCauley predict that informants will regard performance of the correct action to be of lesser importance than having the proper performer. I will call this the Primacy of Agency Hypothesis.

Note that this prediction runs counter to common-sense thinking about ritual. Scholars and lay-people alike commonly regard rituals as acts for which a set of actions must be followed precisely in order to bring about the desired consequences. Lawson and McCauley, in contrast, predict that even ritually naïve observers would recognize that a necessary feature of any religious ritual is the presence of an appropriate *agent* performing the ritual. Specifics of the action hold secondary importance.

Right Intentions Hypothesis

If, as argued by Barrett and Lawson (2001), social causal cognition underlies naïve observers' judgments of religious ritual efficacy, an additional prediction can be made: having an appropriate agent is not only important in religious rituals because of the need for an agent to make the event into an action, but also because an intentional agent may have appropriate *intentions* to motivate the action. As with human-human interactions, a god who detects that a ritual agent has performed a ritual with the wrong intentions might be judged to be less likely to grant the ritual request. If a child tries to please his mother by preparing her breakfast in bed, she is likely to warmly receive the gesture even if the correct procedure of preparing the meal was not carried out properly and the consequence is burned toast and eggs with shells. Her positive reaction is due to her ability to read the intentions of her son. If, however, the child was perfectly capable of preparing a fine breakfast but passive-aggressively bungled it, the mother would likely react quite differently. Critical to judgments in social causation is not merely the action performed but also the action intended. If social cognition undergirds ritual intuitions, then even ritually naïve observers should rate having the correct intentions as more important than a particular action, *provided* that the other person in the social exchange is aware of the "good intentions."

The Right Intentions Hypothesis adds texture to the Primacy of Agency Hypothesis. While the Right Intentions Hypothesis assumes a proper *intentional* agent (consistent with the Primacy of Agency Hypothesis), it suggests that in some contexts performing a correct action will be more important relative to the agent and the agent's intentions. How so? For rituals in which the god appealed to has full access to the ritual agent's intentions, actions would be expected to be less important than when the god does not have full access to intentions. A less-than-omniscient god may have to read intentions through actions, just like humans do. Consequently, proper performance of the ritual action is the primary way in which intentions are made known, and thus the action would be relatively more important.

Repeatability Hypothesis

Lawson and McCauley capture the importance of agency to the action representation system with their "principle of superhuman agency" or PSA. They claim that the action representation system does not only identify the agent initiating the ritual action. Because religious ritual actions do not have standard causal relations between the action and intended outcomes, the action representation system pays particular attention to additional agency injected at one of three "slots" in the action structure. Lawson and McCauley observe that in religious rituals, culturally postulated superhuman agency is injected into a religious ritual in any of three locations: the agent slot, as when a god or specially empowered person does the acting; the patient slot, as when a god or specially empowered person or object receives the action; or the instrument slot, as when a specially empowered instrument is used in the action.

To illustrate, take some examples. The Catholic practice of crossing oneself with holy water when entering a sanctuary injects superhuman agency into the instrument slot. The agent of the ritual is a lay-person entering the sanctuary, the action is crossing, the patient is also the lay-person, and the instrument is "holy" water—water that has been given special power through a previous ritual. Crossing with holy water is an example of what Lawson and McCauley call a "special instrument ritual" because the most direct connection to a superhuman agent lies in the instrument slot. The Lutheran baptism ritual is an example of a "special agent ritual." The agent is a minister who has been given special power through a previous ritual. The action is sprinkling. The patient is an infant and the instrument is water. Many Hindu pujas, especially those in which an offering is given to a god are examples of rituals in which the superhuman agency is injected in the patient slot, or "special patient rituals." In these rituals, a lay-person serves as the agent who gives a food or flower offering to the god. Thus, the patient is the god, a superhuman agent.

The Principle of Superhuman Agency simply notes that the action representation system treats actions in which superhuman agency has been injected in the agent slot (as opposed to the patient or instrument slots) as having special properties. For these "special agent rituals," one of these properties is that when a god (or a representative of the god) performs an act, it is intuitively regarded as having more weight, more permanence than when an ordinary human performs an act. "When the gods do things, they are done once and for all" (McCauley and Lawson 2002: 30–31). Thus, special agent rituals are not repeatable for the particular combination of agents, patients, and outcomes involved (at least without first ritually reversing the consequences). Once a Lutheran child is baptized, *that child* need never be baptized again, even though other baptisms in the same community may take place. However, special instrument and special patient rituals may be repeated. Pujas are typically performed repeatedly throughout one's life time. Crossing oneself with holy water is done prior to every Mass.

Potential Reversibility Hypothesis

A prediction related to the Repeatability Hypothesis is the Potential Reversibility Hypothesis. Because special instrument and special patient ritual do not enjoy any special permanence, their consequences wear off, and the rituals may need to be repeated again, but they need not be ritually reversed. They naturally decay, removing the necessity of reversing them ritually. However, special agent rituals may be ritually reversed, and must be ritually reversed if undoing the consequences of the ritual is desired.

For example, in many religious traditions priests or ministers are ritually ordained though a special agent ritual. In order for the person to be de-frocked or lose their special status, it must be ritually removed. Similarly, in many, if not most religions marriages require a special agent ritual that is never repeated but may be reversed in the case of divorce.

I call this the *Potential* Reversibility Hypothesis because Lawson and McCauley insist that special agent rituals are only potentially reversible but may not be actually reversed in practice, whereas special patient and special instrument rituals are simply not reversed ritually. To illustrate, it would be surprising if any religion allowed for an offering to a god to be ritually taken back.

Sensory Pageantry Hypothesis

Less intimately connected to the functioning of the action representation system, Lawson and McCauley make a prediction regarding how much "pizzazz" a ritual is likely to have in order to produce emotional arousal. Through considerations of mnemonics and motivation for conducting rituals, McCauley and Lawson (2002) argue that special agent rituals will have more sensory pageantry *relative to other rituals within the same system*. These special agent rituals arouse emotional responses that help convince participants that something profound and "superpermanent" has transpired. As noted when discussing the Repeatability Hypothesis, when superhuman agency acts through the agent slot, the consequences are non-transitory and profound. Emotional stimulation may help convince participants that such a change of affairs has occurred and subsequently motivate them to perform similar rituals on others in the future. Thus, over time, high sensory pageantry special agent rituals may enjoy a selective advantage. Such emotional investment is less important and more costly (because of frequency of performance) for repeated rituals.

System Centrality Hypothesis

As noted above, religious rituals typically gain their connection to superhuman agency through some previously performed ritual. Thus, not only may representations of ritual structures contain a description of the surface-level action (including agent, patient, instrument, and action), but also deeper descriptions of how previously performed rituals impact the surface-level. For the sake of the Centrality Hypothesis, what is needed is simply some awareness of how *immediate* superhuman agency is in the action representation. For example, in the Catholic Eucharist, the god's body (Jesus) is consumed by participants, and thus the superhuman agent is represented in the patient slot as immediately present. In an ordination ritual in the same tradition, a layperson becomes a priest by being ordained by someone who was ordained by someone who was ordained by someone who was ordained by someone, and so on. Thus, though superhuman agency (through Apostolic Succession) operates through the ordaining priest in the ritual's action structure, the superhuman agent is not immediate but deeply embedded. Lawson and McCauley predict that rituals in which the superhuman agent is relatively more immediately represented will be relatively more important or *central* to the ritual system or religion. That is, "the fewer enabling actions to which appeal must be made in order to implicate a superhuman agent, the more fundamental the ritual is to the religious system in question" (1990: 125).

Summary of Predictions

The Lawson and McCauley theory may thus be analyzed into general and a number of specific claims. The *General Hypothesis* is that religious ritual is structured by garden-variety cognition, an account resonate with the work of other cognitive scientists of religion (e.g., Barrett 2000; Boyer 1994, 2001b; Whitehouse 2000.). Thus, ritually naïve observers should have converging intuitions regarding various aspects of a given ritual's likely efficacy. The first two specific claims pertain to these judgments of efficacy. The remaining four predictions concern expected patterns across religious systems.

- The *Primacy of Agency Hypothesis* is that having the proper sort of performer—an intentional agent—is more important than having the precise action.
- The *Right Intentions Hypothesis* entails that when a god is directly aware of the agent's intentions, having the right sort of actions is more important than flawlessly performing the ritual action to the ritual's efficacy.
- The *Repeatability Hypothesis* claims that special instrument and special patient rituals practiced in actual religious systems will tend to be repeated or at least repeatable within the system but special agent rituals will not be (without having been reversed first).
- The *Potential Reversibility Hypothesis* states that special agent rituals will have the potential to be ritually reversed whereas other rituals will not be reversible.
- Sensory pageantry to evoke emotion will be greater in special agent rituals than other rituals within the same system according to the *Sensory Pageantry Hypothesis*.

- The *Centrality Hypothesis* posits that rituals requiring many previous rituals to implicate a superhuman agent will be less central than those requiring fewer previous rituals or especially those for which a superhuman agent is immediately present.

Empirical Tests of the Predictions

Testing the Primacy of Agency and General Hypotheses

Barrett and Lawson (2001, Experiment 2) tested both the General Hypothesis and the Primacy of Agency Hypothesis by asking a group of ritually naïve adults (American Protestants) to offer judgments for the likelihood of a number of fictitious "rituals" to be successful. Though fictitious, these rituals constituted a relevant test because they met the Lawson and McCauley specifications for ritual form. Their fictitiousness enabled a "cleaner" test of the hypothesis than would have been possible in a more ecologically valid context because participants were unable to draw upon any knowledge of actual rituals. The experimenter presented each participant with a set of eight fictitious rituals each followed by variations of the prototype. Participants rated the variations for likelihood of replicating the prototype rituals' success. Through random assignment, one group of participants considered rituals that were clearly religious (i.e., connected to superhuman agency), whereas another group considered the same ritual stripped of any religious reference but told they were odd actions on another world. One ritual, for example, read:

Given that a special person cleans a trumpet with a special cloth and the village is protected from an epidemic, how likely is each of the following actions to protect the village from an epidemic? Please rate each action: 1 = extremely likely the action will work, 7 = extremely unlikely.

(a) A special person cleans a trumpet with a special plant.
(b) A special beetle cleans a trumpet with a special cloth.
(c) A special person cleans a trumpet with a special paper.
(d) A special dog cleans a trumpet with a special cloth.
(e) A special person covers a trumpet with a special cloth.
(f) A special person stuffs a trumpet with a special cloth.
(g) A special person cleans a trumpet with a special cloth.

The presentation order of each type of variation was randomized for each item. In the "religious" condition, the packet of ritual ratings included an explanation of the term "special": "For the following ratings, 'special' means someone or something that has been given special properties or authority by the gods. All of the following are proposed religious actions. Try to use as much of the rating scales as is reasonable." In the "other-world" condition, the word "special" was dropped from the descriptions, and the packet included a different explanation: "All of the following are proposed actions on a world very much like ours. Try to use as much of the rating scales as is reasonable."

Consonant with the Primacy of Agency Hypothesis, Barrett and Lawson predicted that participants or observers of a religious ritual would judge having the right kind of agent as being more important than doing exactly the right kind of action, unlike in mechanistic causation.

In the religious condition, participants rated the rituals with agents different from the prototypes as significantly (at the .05-level) less likely to be successful than rituals in which the action was different than the action in the prototype, supporting the Primacy of Agency Hypothesis. Participants gave agent-changed rituals an average rating of 5.0 compared with an average of 3.99 for the action-changed rituals. In contrast, when participants rated the same rituals in the other-world condition, the agent was no longer considered important for the success of the ritual. Indeed, agent-changed rituals were rated as significantly more likely to succeed (mean = 2.96) than action-changed rituals (mean = 3.93). Figure 1 illustrates these results.

That relative judgments reversed between the two conditions, strongly supports the interpretation that participants used different intuitive theories of causation to generate inferences about the efficacy of the actions in the two different conditions. In the other-world condition, participants used ordinary mechanistic causal expectations—the action is more important to bring about a particular state of affairs than the agent. When the same actions were performed as appeals to superhuman agency, intuitions changed as they would in situations of ordinary social causation with *agency* acquiring the primary role in determining the outcome.

These participants with essentially no knowledge of the ritual system in question (because the ritual system was fictitious) did not offer mixed or arbitrary judgments about the rituals' efficacy. Rather, they

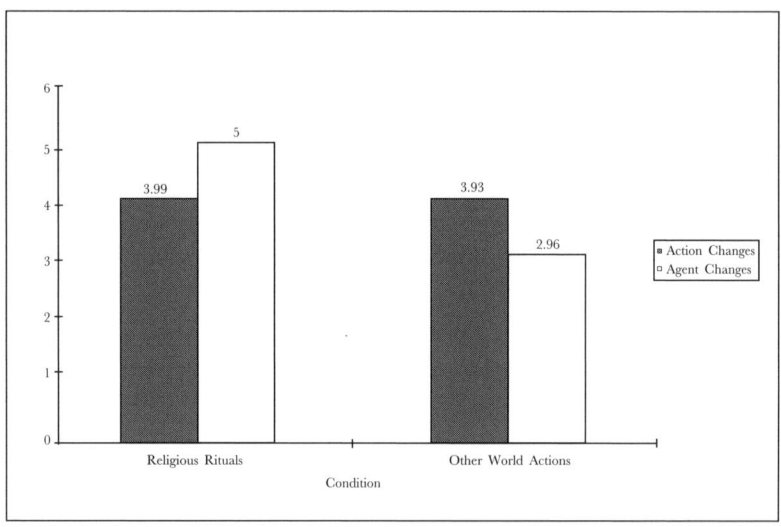

Figure 1: Adapted from Barrett and Lawson (2001). Mean ratings of rituals' likely effectiveness as a function of change type in either a religious or "other world" setting. Agent-changed sequences were rated as significantly less likely to be successful than action-changed sequences in the religious condition only. Agent-changed sequences were rated as significantly more likely to be successful than action-changed sequences in the "other-world" cognition.

converged on predicted judgments concerning the relative role of actions versus agents involved. This fact supports—but certainly does not prove—the General Hypothesis that ordinary cognition structures religious rituals.

Testing the Right Intentions and General Hypotheses

Barrett (2002) tested whether right intentions matter more than specific actions for judgments of success of rituals using fictitious rituals as in the Barrett and Lawson (2001) Experiments. American Protestant college students served as the participants.

The experimenter randomly divided the participants into two conditions. In both conditions, participants evaluated six rituals each followed by five variations on the prototypes. For example:

Given that: Intending to cause a drought, a special person knocks two special stones together and a drought occurs, how likely is each of the following actions to *cause a drought*? Please rate each action: 1 = extremely likely the action will work, 7 = extremely unlikely.

(a) Intending to cause a drought, a special person rubs two special stones together.
(b) Intending to cause an earthquake, a special person knocks to special stones together.
(c) Intending to cause a drought, a special person knocks two special shoes together.
(d) Not intending to cause a drought, a special person knocks two special stones together.
(e) Intending to cause a drought, a special person knocks two special stones together.

Of the five permutations, one differed from the original in intended consequence for the ritual, one negated the original intentions of the ritual, one described a different action, one used a different instrument, and one was a reiteration of the original. These variations appeared in random order. The negated intention variation and the changed action variation represented the contrast of interest between not having the correct intentions and not performing the correct action. The remaining items served as distracters.

In one condition, named the "Smart god" condition, participants were told that "For each situation, 'special' means someone or something given unusual properties or authority by a superhuman being who can read minds, knows all, has amazing powers, and is immortal." In the "Dumb god" condition, the description was changed to emphasize a god with fallible knowledge: "For each situation, 'special' means someone or something given unusual properties or authority by a superhuman being who *cannot* read minds, *doesn't* know everything, has amazing powers, and is immortal." Thus, the two contrasts of interest were whether intentions mattered more than actions and whether this difference changed if the god in question had to read intentions through the actions (Dumb god) as opposed to being able to read minds directly.

Consistent with the Right Intentions Hypothesis, participants in the Smart god condition rated versions of the prototype rituals with negated intentions but the same action (e.g., Not intending to cause a drought) as significantly less likely to bring about the original consequence (mean = 4.31) than versions with a changed action but maintained intentions (mean = 3.36). Apparently, when the god could know intentions, participants judged intentions as more important for ritual efficacy than the particular action, resonating with the Primacy of Agency Hypothesis.

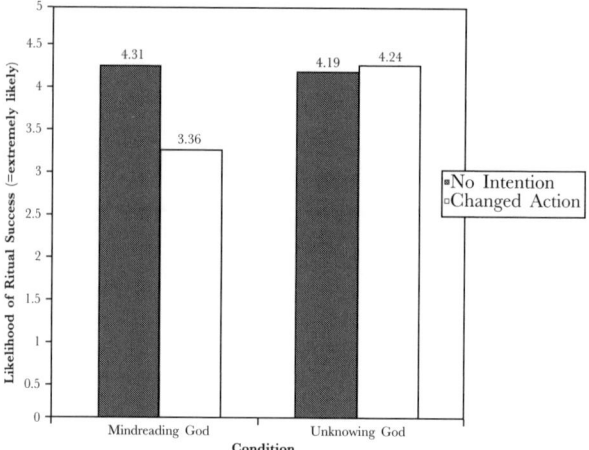

Figure 2: Adapted from Barrett (2002). Mean ratings for likelihood of ritual success. Changing the ritual action was significantly less damaging to the judged efficacy in the condition with a mind-reading god than when the god could not read minds.

In both conditions having proper intentions was regarded as comparably important for the success of the ritual, but participants in the Dumb god condition judged performing a different action as significantly more damaging to the success of the ritual (mean = 4.24) than in the Smart god condition. Participants' judgments seemed to follow predictable reasoning about interactions with people: when the intentions are known, religious rituals performed for gods with infallible knowledge need not follow the action precisely. It is the thought that counts. But fallible gods must read intentions through the actions and so performing the correct action takes on similar importance with having the correct intentions. This experiment supports the Right Intentions Hypothesis and also supports Lawson and McCauley's general claim that ritual intuitions involve regular garden-variety cognitive resources rather than specifically theological ones. Figure 2 illustrates these results.

Testing the Repeatability, Potential Reversibility, and Sensory Pageantry Hypotheses

Whereas the Primacy of Agency and Right Intentions Hypotheses may be addressed through experimentation on ritually naïve participants, the Repeatability, Potential Reversibility, and Sensory Pageantry

Hypotheses are primarily predictions about what is the case in the actual ritual practices of religious traditions. Thus, a sensible place to begin looking for empirical evidence supporting or challenging these hypotheses is participants in religious ritual systems. In a study using informants from Hindu, Jewish, and Muslim communities living in the United States, Malley and Barrett (2003) used structured interviews to elicit just this sort of data.

Rather than ask ritual experts whose perspective may not be representative of religion "on the ground," university students recruited through campus organizations served as informants. Trained students who identified themselves with the three religious communities served as interviewers. Interviewers gave informants a simplified version of the Lawson and McCauley ritual definition and asked what actions in their religions might be rituals. For each ritual that informants identified, interviewers asked for a description so as to determine how each informant understood each ritual's relation to a superhuman agent. Based on these interviews, rituals were categorized as either special agent rituals or special patient/instrument. Follow-up questions ascertained whether informants regarded the ritual as repeatable, potentially reversible, relatively emotional, and involving relatively high sensory pageantry for the patient.

Five religious acts received mention by multiple Hindu informants, eight by multiple Jewish informants, and four by multiple Muslim informants as rituals under Lawson and McCauley's definition. Thus, analyses concern 18 rituals: the Thread Ceremony, Wedding, Abhishekam, Aarthi, and Raksha Bandhan, from Hinduism; the Bris, Bar/Bat Mitzvah, Wedding, Conversion, Mikvah, Burning Chametz, Lighting Shabbat Candle, Havadalah, and Messuzzah from Judaism; and the Wedding, Divorce, Hajj, and Wuduu from Islam. The six met the criteria for special agent rituals with the other 12 being special instrument/patient rituals.

Repeatability Hypothesis Results
Fifteen of the 18 rituals, a significant majority of the rituals at the .01-level, satisfied the prediction the Repeatability Hypothesis. Informants judged none of the six special agent rituals (Thread Ceremony, Hindu Wedding, Bris, Conversion, Muslim Wedding and Divorce) to be repeatable. Conversely, informants claimed only three of the twelve special instrument/patient rituals might be repeated. Table 1 presents these results.

Potential Reversibility Hypothesis Results

For one ritual, the Jewish conversion ritual, no convergence of opinion was discernable regarding reversibility. Of the remaining 17 rituals, 13 met the Potential Reversibility Hypothesis predictions. Informants judged only one of 12 special instrument/patient rituals as potentially reversible, inconsistent with Lawson and McCauley's prediction. Three of the five special agent rituals were rated as not potentially reversible, contrary to the hypothesis: the Hindu Thread Ceremony and Wedding, and the Jewish Bris. Despite these incongruities, successfully predicting 13 out of 17 rituals along the dichotomous dimension of reversibility reaches statistical significance at the .05-level, and consequently must be counted as supporting the hypothesis. Table 1 presents these results.

Table 1: Summary of Repeatability and Reversibility Results from Malley and Barrett (2003). Bold type indicates results inconsistent with Lawson and McCauley's predictions

Rituals	**Special...**	**Repeatable?**	**Reversible?**
Hinduism			
Thread Ceremony	Agent	No	**No**
Wedding	Agent	No	**No**
Abishekam	Patient	Yes	No
Aarthi	Patient	Yes	No
Raksha Bandhan	Instr.	Yes	No
Judaism			
Bris	Agent	No	**No**
Bar/Bat Mitzvah	Instrument	**No**	No
Wedding	Instrument	**No**	No
Conversion	Agent	No	*Inconclusive*
Mikvah	Instrument	Yes	No
Burning Chametz	Instrument	Yes	No
Lighting Shabbat Candles	Instrument	Yes	No
Havadalah	Instrument	Yes	No
Messuzzah	Instrument	**No**	**Yes**
Islam			
Wedding	Agent	No	Yes
Divorce	Agent	No	Yes
Hajj	Patient	Yes	No
Wuduu	Instrument	Yes	No
Accuracy		15 of 18 p = 0.004	13 of 17 p = 0.025

Sensory Pageantry Hypothesis
Malley and Barrett used two measures relevant to sensory pageantry. One was simply a 10-point scale rating of sensory pageantry for the ritual. The other was a similar 10-point rating of the likely emotionality of the experience for the primary human participants of the ritual action. The reason for the second measure was McCauley and Lawson's (2002) insistence that the predicted presence of relatively high sensory pageantry in special agent rituals comes about through its success in arousing emotions and subsequently motivating further similar performance of the ritual. Informants rated each ritual they suggested on both dimensions and the investigators subsequently calculated mean ratings for each ritual on each dimension.

The Sensory Pageantry Hypothesis predicts that special agent rituals would receive higher sensory pageantry (and presumably emotionality) ratings than special instrument/patient rituals from the same tradition. Thus, mean ratings for each special agent ritual within each religious tradition was compared to mean ratings for the special instrument/patient rituals, resulting in 24 comparisons. For instance, the mean sensory pageantry rating for the Hindu Wedding and the Thread Ceremony (both special agent rituals) were each compared to these ratings for the Hindu Abishekam, Aarthi, and Raksha Bandhan rituals. Of these 24 comparisons using the sensory pageantry ratings, 16 met predictions, falling short of statistical significance but trending in the correct direction. Notable exceptions include the Jewish Wedding and Bar/Bat Mitzvah being rated higher in sensory pageantry than the Bris, a special agent ritual from within the same system; and the Muslim Hajj or pilgrimage, which was rated as having higher sensory pageantry than the Muslim divorce ritual. However, in their 2002 volume, McCauley and Lawson concede that "reversing" rituals such as a divorce ritual do not necessarily meet the special agent ritual predictions of the Sensory Pageantry Hypothesis, and frequently do have much lower sensory pageantry than special instrument/patient rituals.

Turning to the emotionality ratings, Lawson and McCauley's prediction fares better. Of the 24 comparisons between special agent and other rituals, 18 agreed with the hypothesis and one was inconclusive; a result statistically significant at the .01-level.

Though perhaps not as strongly supported at the Repeatability or Potential Reversibility Hypotheses, overall the Sensory Pageantry Hypothesis receives modest support from Malley and Barrett's (2003) study of three major religious systems.

Testing the Centrality Hypothesis

Inspired by McCauley and Lawson's suggestions for how to cognitively test their Centrality Hypothesis (2003: 34–35), Barrett and Malley (forthcoming) examined how well the hypothesis predicted intuitions of American Protestant Christians from Calvinist theological backgrounds. Thirty-nine young adults who identified themselves with any of a number of North American Calvinist denominations (e.g., Christian Reformed Church, the Reformed Church of America) participated. Participants completed a series of ratings regarding six rituals: Baptism, Wedding, Ordination, the Communion/Lord's Supper, Confirmation, and Child dedications. Child dedications, more common among "believer"-baptizing denominations as a substitute for infant baptism, was reported as rarely practiced in this population, and so was not included in analyses.

The experimenter asked participants to make three different ratings, two on seven-point scales and one as a ranking:

- "Please rate the following ceremonies for how important they are to your religious faith tradition, 1 = no difference, 7 = enormous difference."
- "Imagine if the following rituals were no longer practiced. Please rate how big a difference that would make to your religious faith tradition, 1 = no difference, 7 = enormous difference."
- "If you absolutely had to stop practicing one of the ceremonies in your religious tradition, which one would it be? Please rank the following ceremonies."

Though the Centrality Hypothesis' predictions are ambiguous with regard to how some of the rituals compare to each other in terms of "centrality," a few predictions are clear. As in Catholicism, even without the doctrine of transubstantiation, the Lord's Supper emphasizes the presence of Jesus as represented by the bread and wine. Thus, God is immediately present and must be the most "central" ritual in the system. As special agent rituals in that an ordained minister serves as the agent, Baptisms, Confirmations, and Weddings must not be more central than Ordination. They all require that an ordination has taken place. However, it could be argued that Ordination requires that both Baptism and Confirmation have taken place on the candidate for Ordination. Lawson and McCauley's work offers little help in disentangling this chicken-and-egg problem. None of the other rituals presuppose the wedding ritual and because no claim to the immediacy of God is in the ritual, it can be no more central than any other ritual. Consequently, a conservative theoretical ranking of centrality from most to least, based on Lawson and McCauley's theory would be: Lord's Supper; Ordination, Baptism, and Confirmation in something of a three-way tie, with Ordination perhaps more central; and finally, Wedding.

However, none of the three different measures of Centrality offer any support of actual Calvinists cognitively holding this ranking. When rating the importance of each ritual to their faith, Communion/Lord's Supper was rated as most important (mean = 6.08), Baptism and Confirmation were statistically indistinguishable as the next most important (means, 5.87 and 5.81 respectively), followed by Ordination (mean = 5.4) and Wedding (mean = 5.26) statistically indistinguishable. Using this measure, though the Lord's Supper came out on top, as predicted, and Wedding came out on the bottom, Ordination was rated as statistically significantly less important than Baptism, even though the ritual system would fold without it. The story becomes even cloudier when considering the other two measures.

When asked how big a difference it would make to the faith to stop practicing a given ritual, once again, participants rated the Lord's Supper as most "central" (mean = 5.92). However, the next most "central" ritual, based on this measure, was Wedding (mean = 5.77). Baptism (mean = 5.28), Ordination (mean = 4.82), and Confirmation (mean = 4.70) were not significantly different from each other. Contrary to the Centrality Hypothesis, participants did rate the loss of the Wedding ritual as having a significantly greater impact than losing Ordination. Finally, when participants ranked which rituals they themselves would be willing to give up if they absolutely had to, the first they would give up was Ordination, followed by Baptism, Wedding, and Confirmation in an essential tie, and Lord's Supper last.

Results from Barrett and Malley (forthcoming) offered little support for the Centrality Hypothesis among Calvinist Protestants. Perhaps in other ritual systems the predictions may fare better. However, the difficulty with which clear predictions could be made raises some concerns regarding the utility of this aspect of Lawson and McCauley's theory.

Future Directions for Empirical Explorations

Though McCauley and Lawson (2002) make further finer-grained predictions, especially regarding the relationship between ritual type (special agent, instrument, or patient), frequency, and sensory pageantry, these additional predictions presuppose the accuracy of many of those hypotheses presented above. Thus, though initially supported with only one exception, advancing and refining the cognitive study of religious ritual requires additional attempts to falsify Lawson and McCauley's hypotheses. These investigations may require further experimental data-collection, however, at least initially, carefully-gathered ethnographic and historical data may be more valuable.

The Primacy of Agency and Right Intentions Hypotheses

Perhaps Barrett and Lawson's (2001) results represent the particular, agent-centered sort of social cognition of American adults, and would not generalize to other peoples. The robustness of young children's attention to and reasoning about the mental states of intentional agents across cultures casts doubt on this criticism (Wellman, Cross and Watson 2001). Nevertheless, as in the difference between reasoning about rituals in systems with mind-reading versus non-mind-reading gods (Barrett 2002), replicating Barrett and Lawson's experiments in other cultural contexts could illuminate additional factors that bear upon judgments of ritual efficacy that remain within the domain of ordinary cognition.

More valuable still could be systematically documenting ritual observers' and participants' explanations for why actual rituals in real-world ritual systems do and do not fail. A simple prediction based on the Primacy of Agency and Right Intention Hypotheses is that when rituals fail in a system that has all-knowing gods, not having maintained proper intentions or the agent not being qualified will be a more frequent suggestion for failure than having performed the ritual incorrectly. However, in systems with fallible gods, when a ritual fails, it would be predicted that claims the ritual was performed incorrectly would be relatively more numerous. Whitehouse (1996) reported a related example. He observed that the Pomio Kivung people of East New Britain Island in Papua New Guinea take great care to have the right intentions and mental states when performing rituals directed at their spirit-ancestors who have strong knowledge of mental states. In contrast, when performing rituals for the forest spirits (sega), performing the action precisely is considered much more important than states of mind. This sort of dissociation nicely illustrates and supports the Right Intentions Hypothesis in action, but more data would garner more confidence.

The Repeatability and Potential Reversibility Hypotheses

As two sides of the same coin, the Repeatability and Reversibility Hypotheses may be further tested together, in a manner similar to Malley and Barrett's (2003). A desirable project would be to amass reports on a large number of rituals from a large number of layperson informants from a large number of religious groups. Not only could such data demonstrate whether Lawson and McCauley's hypotheses successfully predict real-world intuitions, but also provide a large enough set of cases for discerning what other factors may contribute to repeatability and reversibility. For instance, contrary to prediction, the Jewish Bris was rated as non-reversible. Might that have been because of the permanent nature of the physical change involved for the initiate? Perhaps other infant-initiations requiring physical change are judged non-reversible, and infant-initiations that require no physical change (e.g., Catholic baptism) are judged reversible (e.g., through excommunication). A large corpus of these sort of data would be particularly helpful to tease apart these dynamics.

Gauging intuitions of participants in systems would be informative but is not the only relevant data. Actually observing and tabulating ritual practices would bear upon these hypotheses. The Repeatability Hypothesis predicts that in a religious community, special agent rituals will *not* be repeated (without first being reversed) with the same participants—not just that people of that group would *judge* the rituals non-repeatable. Such a claim may be scrutinized by tabulation. For instance, in a longitudinal or historical study through church records in a Catholic town, one could count the number of weddings, baptisms, and ordinations (all special agent rituals) and how many were repeated. How many were ritually reversed? This could be compared with the number of crossing-rituals and Eucharist observances, and how many times they were repeated or reversed. Though this particular example may seem like shooting fish in a barrel, these relationships between ritual form and repeatability and reversibility have not previously been explained. But perhaps the results in a different religious setting might not be so cut-and-dried and would thus be valuable data to accumulate.

The Sensory Pageantry Hypothesis

Researchers could make the same sorts of observations, both through structured interview and observation, for the Sensory Pageantry Hypothesis as for the Repeatability and Potential Reversibility Hypotheses. Additionally, more direct measures of the emotionality (a theorized consequence of sensory pageantry) of a given ritual for various participants may be conducted. Though many measures, such as pulse, blood pressure, and neuronal activation, are intrusive, some less intrusive measures such as measuring stress hormones in saliva spit into a vial are becoming practical. Still less intrusively, and more directly aimed at sensory pageantry, some physical conditions of a ritual situation may be measured such as temperature, loudness, humidity, brightness, chemical concentrations related to olfaction, and number of persons per square meter, and so forth. One could measure ordinary, household levels on these various physical dimensions to establish a base rate and then measure them at a number of rituals. The Sensory Pageantry Hypothesis would predict that special agent rituals (such as weddings in many traditions) would be more extreme on these sorts of measures than special instrument or patient rituals in the same traditions.

The Centrality Hypothesis

Given its shaky status based on Barrett and Malley's (forthcoming) investigation of the Centrality Hypothesis, perhaps this hypothesis requires most immediate attention. Not only does circularity in ritual systems (i.e., one ritual presupposes another that presupposes it) create difficulties for making firm predictions regarding centrality, but data from American Protestants offers no support for the predictions. Indeed, the data suggest that additional factors not identified by the Centrality Hypothesis may be more powerful at determining participants' judgments regarding centrality. However, these observations do not preclude the possibility that the Centrality Hypothesis, once rendered more precise, may provide great predictive and explanatory power in other ritual systems. Hence, researchers should attempt to falsify the hypothesis in other traditions.

In addition to using a questionnaire methodology such as Barrett and Malley's, the Centrality Hypothesis is ripe for historical and ethnographic scrutiny. A number of measurable behavioral implications spring from the Centrality Hypothesis. Individual congregations of the same religion or church should not vary on practicing central rituals but only peripheral ones. Variation in practice of central rituals would be the mark of schism or differences in religious identification. Likewise, variation in *how* a ritual is performed would be less likely for central rituals than peripheral ones. Barrett and Malley found that only a minority of their Calvinist Protestant informants represented communities that practice a Child Dedication ritual. This observation is predictable from the fact that such a ritual, when practiced, does not serve as a prerequisite for any other ritual and does not evoke any immediacy of God. However, if a church decided to stop practicing the Lord's Supper, a schism would be predicted to occur. The history of many religions may be mined for this variety of precious data.

Conclusion

As described above, one general and six specific hypotheses derived from Lawson and McCauely's cognitive theory of religious ritual have been subjected to empirical testing. Research to date supports all but the Centrality Hypothesis, with the support for the Sensory Pageantry Hypothesis being weaker than for the other supported specific hypotheses. For theoretical and empirical reasons Lawson and McCauley's primary observation, that ordinary cognitive structures and processes inform and constrain religious rituals, appears well-founded. Because of the operation of these ordinary cognitive systems, well-formed and efficacious rituals will be judged to be those that have an appropriate intentional agent with appropriate intentions to complete the ritual as prescribed. When the god appealed to through the ritual has the ability to read these intentions directly, these right intentions will be judged more important for ritual efficacy than strict adherence to ritual actions. Preliminary evidence also supports the conclusions that rituals for which superhuman agency is represented as acting through the agent of the ritual (i.e., special agent rituals) will tend to be non-repeatable, potentially reversible, and relatively high in sensory pageantry and emotionality. Conversely, rituals for which superhuman agency is represented as action through the instrument or patient in the ritual (i.e., special instrument or special patient rituals), will tend to be repeatable, non-reversible, and relatively low in sensory pageantry and emotionality.

That Lawson and McCauley's theory has spawned such a broad range of empirically testable and falsifiable predictions regarding religious ritual is a strong testament to its valuable contribution to the study of religion. That the theory enjoys initial support on most points should encourage scholars to look even closer and the potential promise or pitfalls of this provocative cognitive theory.

14. COMMUNITIES, RITUAL VIOLENCE, AND COGNITION: ON HOPI INDIAN INITIATIONS

Armin W. Geertz

> Phrenology, as everyone knows, is a way of reading someone's character, aptitude and abilities by examining the bumps and hollows on their head. Therefore—according to the kind of logical thinking that characterizes the Ankh-Morpork mind—it should be possible to *mould* someone's character by *giving* them carefully graded bumps in all the right places. You can go into a shop and order an artistic temperament with a tendency to introspection and a side order of hysteria. What you actually *get* is hit on the head with a selection of different size mallets, but it creates employment and keeps the money in circulation, and that's the main thing.
>
> A clarification on the talents of Zorgo the Retrophrenologist in Terry Pratchett's novel *Men at Arms* [1998]: 155.

Preface

There is something exhilarating about periods of pioneering insights in academic work. It attracts all the right kinds of people: a little offbeat, a good sense of humor, and a willingness to try absolutely outrageous things. This has been, and indeed still is, the case in cognitive studies. We are witnessing the pioneering use of cognitive theories in the study of religion. In fact, the application of cognitive theories in any field is still a pioneering endeavor, and we are getting new reports, new discoveries, new sensations every single day. This does require some sort of humor in the face of the enormity of it all.

This is what meets the eye when confronted by Tom Lawson: a penetrating gaze, an easy laugh, and vertigo at the edge of the brink. Tom stands tall in the cognitive study of religion. For that matter, Tom stands tall wherever he happens to be.

I dedicate this small contribution to Tom's festschrift. It wasn't originally written for him, but his book on rethinking religion started the ball rolling in the phrenological hills of my mind.[1]

Introduction

Communities are wonderful things. They provide standards for human behavior and human relations. They regulate relations between individuals and groups. They decide on important issues like what constitutes a man, what constitutes a woman, and how relations between them ought to be. They create contexts for identity, meaning, morality and politics. They decide what is good and what is evil. They are, in sociologist Émile Durkheim's words, ultimate authorities, forces that raise individuals above themselves. A community is a consciousness of consciousnesses, and the highest form of human mind (Durkheim 1995: 16–17, 211–16, 445, 447–48).

Indigenous peoples are good examples to choose when exploring topics like religion and community, because they demonstrate the variety and creativity of humanity. But it should be noted here that I am not suggesting that indigenous peoples are communalistic with no individualism, as some Western social philosophers have claimed. There are enough examples of individualism and dissidence in indigenous societies to dissuade from this point of view.[2]

What is Community?

Let me attempt to formulate a few characteristics of community before moving on to my main points. In the opening encomium, I claimed that community is the source of just about everything and,

---

[1] This is a revised version of a paper read at the annual conference of the British Association for the Study of Religions (BASR) on "Religion and Community," 10–13 September 2001, in Cambridge hosted together with the European Association for the Study of Religions (EASR). The paper was entitled "Religion and Community in Indigenous Contexts" and has appeared in the BASR Occasional Papers series. Permission to publish this paper is gratefully acknowledged.

[2] There are many anthropologists who concur on this matter. A relevant example is Africanist Godfrey Lienhardt in his essay "Self: Public, Private. Some African Representations" (1991).

furthermore, that it is a wonderful thing. Well . . . I take that back. Community is only wonderful half the time. I have chosen for this paper some hairy examples of the downside of community in order to drive the point home. Community is not just a social or institutional context. It is the creator of meanings, worlds, hermeneutical strategies and a lot of other things that help individual humans to make it through existence in a fairly meaningful way.

Sociologists have been quite taken up with this and similar terms. In an article from 1955, sociologist G. A. Hillery reviewed 94 definitions of community and concluded: "beyond the concept that people are involved in community, there is no complete agreement as to the nature of community" (1955: 119). The term is often used as a synonym for society, group, social system, and social organization. There have also been a number of efforts at typology, for instance Joachim Wach's and Milton Yinger's typologies of religious communities (Wach 1962; Yinger 1965, 1970; see also Robertson 1970).

Some authors use community in a more limited context. Gideon Sjoberg suggested a modification of Talcott Parson's definition (1951: 91):

> A community is a collectivity of actors sharing a limited territorial area as the base for carrying out the greatest share of their daily activities. This definition implies that persons interact within a *local* institutional complex which provides a wide range of basic services, yet it also takes into consideration the fact that the community is not necessarily a self-sufficient unit (Sjoberg 1959: 114–15).

This definition would apply to indigenous contexts, which normally are restricted in terms of size and territoriality, but this definition is perhaps too narrow. At any rate, community today has grown exponentially so that we often speak about the global village, the global community and the international community. It is not necessarily size, or even location, that determines the convergence of individuals in communities. And thus, it might seem more appropriate to choose communication and meaning construction as defining characteristics of community. Reformulating Sjoberg we might define community as a *collectivity of actors sharing meanings and activities in the context of a common worldview*. Such a definition draws heavily on Clifford Geertz's hermeneutic and semiotic concept of culture.

This focus on meaning, on community as a moral body, neither negates nor neglects day-to-day living in the world, as will become clear later in this paper. Communities practice and produce a whole series of human universals ranging from language and communication, naming and taxonomy, notions of person, kinship, gender, and age, as well as laws, customs, etiquette, aesthetics, worldviews, and religion to the more mundane concerns of shelter, tool-making, subsistence activities and sexual reproduction (cf. Brown 1991).

Religious communities, on the other hand, are more specifically focused. In many societies, communities are both religious and secular, depending on the time and context. In this sense, communities mark entrances into (initiation), changes during (transition rituals) and exits from (funerals) the community. Ritual and pageant mark important community activities and are integral to maintaining and shaping community norms and identity. The community consists as well of differentiation in the group based on function and merit. Religious validation adorns social markings such as gender, family, and clan and integrates these in terms of the natural and sacred world. In fact, community is often conceived as a sacred or semi-sacred entity in itself (cf. Weckman 1987: 566–71).

Cognition and Community

Let us change perspective for a moment and see what community does to the individual. It may strike some listeners that approaching community through the individual is like putting the horse on the saddle. But humor me for a moment. I hope that in the end, you will see the wisdom of this strategy.

Long ago, Émile Durkheim presented significant insights on religion, community and society. I am not a Durkheimian, but I think that his insights on a number of matters are just as relevant today as they were at the turn of the twentieth century. Durkheim promoted the insight that all humans are inherently dual beings, namely, an individual being with its basis in the body and a social being representing the highest reality in the intellectual and moral realm (1995: 15). Reading Durkheim today, we are struck by how psychologized his social theory was. Society for him is the collective consciousness of individuals coming together under common aims, truths, and sensibilities. Individuals and communities presuppose each other, nurture each other, and express themselves through each other. Thus, said Durkheim: "there is something impersonal in us because there is something social in us, and since social life embraces both representations and practices, that impersonality extends quite naturally to ideas as well as to actions" (1995: 447).

These were interesting ideas at the time. They have since then become more commonplace in various guises in psychological and cognitive theory. One of Durkheim's contemporaries, the pragmatist and a founding father of social psychology in the United States, George Herbert Mead, was working along similar lines. Let us briefly dwell on a few of his main concepts and theories.

Mead was not interested in individualistic psychology but more in the role of society in the development of the mind. He focused on the dynamics of social action and postulated that both meaning and mind have their origins in the social act through reflexiveness. To Mead the self is constructed through role taking, during which the social attitudes of the "generalized other" exert influence on the conduct of the individual and on the development of the self. Thus the "I" becomes aware of the social "me," or, a telling phrase, "the mind as the individual importation of the social process" (1962: 186). As he wrote concerning the mind:

> Mind arises in the social process only when that process as a whole enters into, or is present in, the experience of any one of the given individuals involved in that process. When this occurs the individual becomes self-conscious and has a mind; he becomes aware of his relations to that process as a whole, and to the other individuals participating in it with him; he becomes aware of that process as modified by the reactions and interactions of the individuals—including himself—who are carrying it on.... It is by means of reflexiveness—the turning-back of the experience of the individual upon himself—that the whole social process is thus brought into the experience of the individuals involved in it; it is by such means, which enable the individual to take the attitude of the other toward himself, that the individual is able consciously to adjust himself to that process, and to modify the resultant of that process in any given social act in terms of his adjustment to it. Reflexiveness, then, is the essential condition, within the social process, for the development of mind (Mead 1962: 134).

The same with intelligence:

> It is generally recognized that the specifically social expressions of intelligence, or the exercise of what is often called "social intelligence," depend upon the given individual's ability to take the roles of, or "put himself in the place of," the other individuals implicated with him in given social situations; and upon his consequent sensitivity to their attitudes toward himself and toward one another. These specifically social expressions of intelligence, of course, acquire unique significance in

> terms of our view that the whole nature of intelligence is social to the very core—that this putting of one's self in the places of others, this taking by one's self of their roles or attitudes, is not merely one of the various aspects or expressions of intelligence or of intelligent behavior, but is the very essence of its character (Mead 1962: 141, n. 3).

And, even more importantly, the same with the self. It is the social process that is responsible for the appearance of the self: we are one thing to one person and another thing to another. We discuss politics with one, religion with another. We are lovers for one and enemies for another. And there are parts of the self that exist only in relationship to itself (Mead 1962: 142). The integration of these various selves into a unified whole occurs through reflexiveness:

> The reflexive character of self-consciousness enables the individual to contemplate himself as a whole; his ability to take the social attitudes of other individuals and also of the generalized other toward himself, within the given organized society of which he is a member, makes possible his bringing himself, as an objective whole, within his own experiential purview; and thus he can consciously integrate and unify the various aspects of his self, to form a single consistent and coherent and organized personality. Moreover, by the same means, he can undertake and effect intelligent reconstructions of that self or personality in terms of its relations to the given social order, whenever the exigencies of adaptation to his social environment demand such reconstructions (Mead 1962: 309, n. 19).

There is, thus, a dialectic between the individual self, the individual mind and society. Society stamps the pattern of its organized social behavior on its individual members and gives the individual a mind that allows conscious conversation with his or her self "in terms of the social attitudes which constitute the structure of his self and which embody the pattern of human society's organized behavior as reflected in that structure." On the other hand, this mind makes it possible for the individual to set the stamp of its "further developing self" upon the structure and organization of human society thus being able to reconstruct or modify the patterns of group behavior (Mead 1962: 263, n. 10).

I have dwelt at some length on Mead in order to help us understand the dynamics of community and individual. But how much of this is still scientifically viable in light of recent insights drawn from developmental psychology and cognitive psychology? Perhaps one of the most significant discoveries in cognitive science that may give us a clue to the significance and function of religion is the emerging understanding of consciousness. One of the main proponents of the so-called "Multiple Drafts Model," Daniel C. Dennett at Tufts University, explained this model in his book *Consciousness Explained* from 1991:

> According to the Multiple Drafts model, all varieties of perception—indeed, all varieties of thought or mental activity—are accomplished in the brain by parallel, multitrack processes of interpretation and elaboration of sensory inputs. Information entering the nervous system is under continuous 'editorial revision'....

These editorial processes occur in various parts of the brain. The novel feature of the Multiple Drafts model is that "feature detections or discriminations *only have to be made once*," which means that:

> ... once a particular "observation" of some feature has been made, by a specialized, localized portion of the brain, the information content thus fixed does not have to be sent somewhere else to be *re*discriminated by some "master" discriminator. In other words, discrimination does not lead to a re*presentation* of the already discriminated feature for the benefit of the audience in the Cartesian Theater—for there is no Cartesian Theater....

These various discriminations occur over the course of time as:

> ... something *rather like* a narrative stream or sequence, which can be thought of as subject to continual editing by many processes distributed around in the brain, and continuing indefinitely into the future. This stream of contents is only rather like a narrative because of its multiplicity; at any point in time there are multiple "drafts" of narrative fragments at various stages of editing in various places in the brain... (Dennett 1991: 111, 112–23).

Dennett's main hypothesis is that the conscious subject is a *virtual* subject. This virtual person is like a virtual machine. In supposing that there is a stream-of-consciousness virtual machine in the memosphere, even though there is no shared machine language between brains, methods of transmission throughout the culture must be "social, highly context-sensitive, and to some degree self-organizing and self-correcting." Furthermore, the fact that human beings can share this "software" must mean that the shared systems have a "high degree of lability and format tolerance." The methods of transfer, however, are limited to socialization. In answer to what problems this virtual machine is supposed to solve, Dennett invokes the psychologist Julian Jaynes (1976), who argued that:

> ... its capacities for self-exhortation and self-reminding are a prerequisite for the sorts of elaborated and long-term bouts of self-control without which agriculture, building projects, and other civilized and civilizing activities could not be organized (1991: 221–22).

It is my hypothesis that community and religion, in terms of Dennett's thesis, could then be conceived of as handy instruments to shape and control virtual persons and selves, and thereby to reinforce and re-construct culture and civilization from brain to brain and generation to generation (cf. Geertz 1999). The community, in Mead's terms, consists of individuals busily contributing to the process of communal generalization through the dual activity of systematizing and reformulating their multiple selves in terms of the values and attitudes of the generalized other. In Dennett's perspective, as I understand him, this process could then be understood as the communal maintenance of consciousness and identity both for itself and its constituents.

Dennett's theory is not uncontested. One of his more formidable critics, philosopher John Searle, dismisses the theory because it ignores in his words the subjective feel of experience, which he calls "qualia." Pain for instance besides being a neuro-physiological exchange of impulses is also a specific internal qualitative feeling. Consciousness does not have bodily sensation comparable to pain, but it has the quality of "ontological subjectivity." In his opinion, Dennett's theory ignores the subjective feelings that are the data that a theory of consciousness should explain (Searle 1997: 98–99). Searle believes that the brain causes conscious experiences that are inner, qualitative, and subjective states (Searle 1997: 110). Dennett dismisses Searle's criticism because it sides with the traditionalist assumption that "intuitions we all have about consciousness" are bedrock and time-tested (Dennett's response is reprinted in Searle 1997: 115). Unfortunately the two have been arguing for decades, so it is difficult for non-specialists to figure out what is going on.

Another way of approaching this crucial problem has been formulated by neuroscientists Gerald M. Edelman and Giulio Tononi at the Neurosciences Institute in La Jolla, California. They are well known, among other things, for their experiments with NOMAD (Neurally Organized Mobile Adaptive Device), the thinking robot.[3]

---

[3] Cf. their website www.nsi.edu/public/index2.asp.

Concerning qualia, they emphatically state that no theory or description can ever substitute an individual's experience of a quale, no matter how correct the theory is in describing underlying mechanisms. They posit that each quale corresponds to different states of the dynamic core:

> ... which can be differentiated from billions of other states within a neural space comprising a large number of dimensions. The relevant dimensions are given by the number of neuronal groups whose activities, integrated through reentrant interactions, constitute a dynamic core of high complexity. Qualia are therefore high-dimensional discriminations.

These discriminations are multimodel and body-centered and are carried out:

> ... by the proprioceptive, kinesthetic, and autonomic systems that are present in the embryo and infant's brain, particularly in the brain stem. All subsequent qualia can be referable to this initial set of discriminations, which constitute the basis of the most primitive self (Edelman and Tononi 2001: 157).

The key to their theory is what they call the "dynamic core." This is the subset of the neuronal groups in our brain which contribute directly to conscious experience. It is dynamic because it is an everchanging ongoing integration of neurons mostly within the thalamocortical system. The general properties of conscious experience are emitted "by linking these properties to the specific neural processes that can give rise to them" (Edelman and Tonino 2001: 140). In other words, they confirm William James' insight at the turn of the twentieth century that consciousness is a process and not a thing. It is, in the words of Edelman and Tononi, a dynamic core based on neural interactions "rather than just on a structure, a property of some neurons, or their location" (2001: 146). Conscious experience is integrated, private, coherent, differentiated, and informative. It depends on the distribution of information from many parts of our brain, and it is context-dependent. It is flexible and adaptive, thus being able to respond to and learn from unexpected associations. Even though we can differentiate among billions of different conscious states within a fraction of a second, there are limits to "how many partially independent sub-processes can be sustained within the core without interfering with its integration and coherence" (Edelman and Tonino 2001: 150). Because the dynamic core is unified and integrated, it moves from one "global state" to another and thus has a serial nature, like a series of scenes that follow one after the other. Thus consciousness is a process that is both continuous and continually changing at a rate of about 100 milliseconds. The dynamic core, then, "can maintain its unity over time even if its composition may be constantly changing" (Edelman and Tonino 2001: 152).

Now, getting back to my main point, they emphasize that consciousness "in its full range" does not arise solely in the brain, because according to their theory, the "higher brain functions require interactions both with the world and with other persons" (Edelman and Tonino 2001: xii). They summarize their findings as follows:

> we argue that neural changes that lead to language are behind the emergence of higher-order consciousness.... Once higher-order consciousness begins to emerge, a self can be constructed from social and affective relationships. This self (entailing the development of a self-conscious agent, a subject) goes far beyond the biologically based individuality of an animal with primary consciousness. The emergence of the self leads to a refinement of phenomenological experience, tying feelings to thoughts, to culture, and to beliefs. It liberates imagination and opens thought to the vast domains of metaphor. It can even lead to a temporary escape, while still remaining conscious, from the temporal shackles of the remembered present (Edelman and Tonino 2001: 193).

This insight coincides well with the whole realm of narrative theory in developmental psychology and in anthropological psychology. The basic idea, according to Edelman and Tononi, is that the child develops the "true subject" by constructing scenes via primary consciousness. These scenes rapidly develop with the help of concepts refurbished through gesture, speech, and language (Edelman and Tonino 2001: 198). This process continues throughout life and is clearly dependent on social interaction. This fascinating topic of "transactional selves," "narrative selves," etc., deserves more mention (e.g., Bruner 1968; Sarbin 1986; Goldschmidt 1990), but I must move on to the social side of community.

A cardinal point that most psychologists have noted is that humans are extraordinarily transparent to each other. The intersubjectivity regularly referred to in this paper assumes, in Jerome Bruner's words, that we have easy access into each other's minds, an access that cannot be explained simply by empathy (1986: 57). Human beings, he noted:

> ... must come equipped with the means not only to calibrate the workings of their minds against one another, but to calibrate the worlds in

which they live through the subtle means of reference. In effect, then, this is the means whereby we know Other Minds and their possible worlds (Bruner 1986: 64).

The Construction of Community

As any sensible teenager will tell you, community norms are somewhat—if not completely—arbitrary and restrictive. This is because they are consensual. Constructivist theories have been around for quite a while. Durkheim, once again, can serve as a starting point. He noted that the categories that societies provide are based on a minimal moral consensus as well as a logical consensus (1995: 16). These two elements prefigure the famous analytical categories introduced by Clifford Geertz during the 1960s, namely "ethos" and "worldview." The two confirm each other in an effective tautology. The world is made intelligible by the logic of a community's worldview, and this logic is inevitably felt to be right as sensed by the community's ethos.

The Austrian phenomenological sociologist Alfred Schutz argued that social realities organize the principles of our *Lebenswelt*, and that the meaning of the experience of living in a certain way and its interpretation are always retrospective. The two conditions in the construction of meaningful worlds are, according to Schutz, a stock of knowledge about the world organized into features and horizons, and the interpretive procedures themselves (1971).

Peter Berger and Thomas Luckmann helped revive Schutz's phenomenological sociology in their programmatic sociology of knowledge, which concerns itself with all that passes as knowledge in a society and the consequent social construction of reality (1966; see also Searle 1995). Their primary focus is on the processes of institutionalization and socialization which ensure the persistence of typificatory schemes. In their 1966 study of the social construction of reality, they developed the idea of "sedimentation," which posits that human experiences congeal in recollection as sediment. This sediment becomes social when objectivated in a sign system. They argued that its transformation into a generally available object of knowledge allows it to be incorporated into a larger body of tradition. The argument runs further that this aggregate of collective sedimentations can be acquired monothetically, that is, as cohesive wholes, "without reconstructing their original process of formation" as "knowledge" by specified "knowers" to others in the social network. All three instances—knowledge, knowers, and non-knowers—are defined in terms of what is socially defined as reality. It is especially in the realm of the definition, transmission, and maintenance of social meaning that control and legitimation procedures become paramount (1987: 134; see also Geertz 1994).

The socially objectivated meanings become systematized or at least encompassed by a community's symbolic universe. The symbolic universe is conceived, according to Berger and Luckmann, "as the matrix of *all* socially objectivated and subjectively real meanings; the entire historic society and the entire biography of the individual are seen as events taking place *within* this universe." Furthermore, a point that is relevant here is that the meaning-bestowing capacity of a symbolic universe though constructed by social objectivations "far exceeds the domain of social life, so that the individual may 'locate' himself within it even in his most solitary experiences" (1987: 114).

I will refrain from discussing the critical discussion that has been occurring inside and outside constructionist theory during the last decades, not least from realist camps, and move on to my examples instead (cf. Miller and Holstein 1993; Holstein and Miller 1993). In an earlier paper, I demonstrated how two situations recorded during fieldwork among the Hopi Indians of northeastern Arizona could be described and understood in terms of social psychology (Geertz 1990). I showed how public confession served as the reaffirmation of community values through shame, and how guilt served a similar function in private situations. In this paper, these and other examples will be taken up.

Community as Control

Communities control the maintenance of their symbolic universes and the applications of generalized identity by many means. One of the efficient means is the use of ritual and pageantry. In rituals and pageants we not only find expressions of community values and sensitivities but we also find their veritable construction and maintenance.

The Hopi Indians are well known for their colorful ceremonial pageants. In former times they could last up to 16 days at a time, sometimes more, but with the exception of one or two towns, the ceremonial calendar has become greatly reduced. About 10,000 Hopis are situated in 10 pueblo villages on or just below the southwestern mesa fingers of the Colorado Plateau near the edge of the Painted Desert of northeastern Arizona. One village lies outside the Hopi Reservation right next to Tuba City. Hopi society consists of loosely organized matriclans, each with their own religious traditions, sacred paraphernalia, housing and land holdings. The clan mother owns clan material and spiritual property, and her brother uses them on her behalf. The rights and possessions of each clan are legitimated in their oral traditions, and these rights are based on knowledge and cultic power. Hopi religion is a good example of the legitimation and maintenance of each clan's symbolic universe, and it would make sense that much time and effort is given to this legitimation and maintenance, even more so because of the simple fact that other clans are continually vying for power and legitimation in the face of conflicting claims and conflicting traditions. Thus, Hopis spend a lot of time narrating their clan traditions, or at least relevant edited and re-edited portions of those traditions, to each other. In my study of Hopi prophecies, I demonstrated to what extremes Hopis will go in maintaining their interests, even to the point of constructing new prophecies in the guise of ancient traditions (Geertz 1994). One of the most puzzling aspects of Hopi culture and religion is the initiation of young children of both genders aged 8–10 into the masked Katsina cult. Katsinas are conceived to be gods and spirits with close ties to the flora, fauna and other natural, especially meteorological, phenomena. This initiation is prerequisite for further mobility in the Hopi system of prestige and authority. Consequently, the children and their parents are put under enormous social pressure to go through with the ritual.

The initiation occurs during the great spring ceremony called Powamuya during the month of February. The themes of the ceremony are the invocation of warmth, germination, growth, the initiation of children, and the main actor is the god of fertility Muy'ingwa (cf. Geertz 1987; Geertz and Lomatuway'ma 1987; Voth 1901; Bradfield 1973). The ceremony marks the first half of the Katsina cycle when the Powamuy Fraternity turns over responsibility for the rest of the season to the other fraternity responsible for the Katsina cult, namely the Katsina Fraternity. Initiations into both fraternities occur during this ceremony but, whereas the initiates of the Powamuy Fraternity are not subjected to violence, the initiates of the Katsina Fraternity are ritually whipped with yucca under great tumult, screaming and intimidation (witnessed also by the Powamuy initiates). The Katsina Fraternity wears the masks during the Katsina dances and requires therefore a special initiation. But why the violence?

First of all, it is clear that communal values and sensitivities are imparted during the ceremony both through the pageantry, song and dance itself, but especially through the instructions given by none other than Muy'ingwa himself, as well as by the elders of the two fraternities. Muy'ingwa arrives from the center of the symbolic world. He poetically describes in an archaic and repetitive language the cosmic regions and says that the children must learn the ceremonies. Finally, he breaks the mesmeric spell and announces that the children must be whipped in order to "enlighten their hearts" (Voth 1901: 101). Suddenly several deities with frightening masks descend on the children and whip them one at a time while grunting, howling, rattling, trampling and brandishing their whips. One Hopi man, the famous Don Talayesva, never forgot his initiation. Because of disciplinary problems, he was whipped twice the normal amount of four strikes, so that blood ran down his backside (Simmons 1942: 83).

Two days later, the children are exposed to a shocking revelation during a midnight dance held in the secret ceremonial chambers. The dancing Katsinas, the gods that they have known, loved and feared all the years of their tender childhood, take off their masks and reveal that they are humans, that they are the uncles, fathers and older brothers of the initiates. The above-mentioned Don Talayesva wrote in his autobiography:

> They were not spirits, but human beings. I recognized nearly every one of them and felt very unhappy, because I had been told all my life that the Katcinas were gods. I was especially shocked and angry when I saw all my uncles, fathers, and clan brothers dancing as Katcinas. I felt the worst when I saw my own father—and whenever he glanced at me I turned my face away. When the dances were over the head man told us with a stern face that we now knew who the Katcinas really were and that if we ever talked about this to uninitiated children we would get a thrashing even worse than the one we had received the night before. "A long time ago," said he, "a child was whipped to death for telling the secret." I felt sure that I would never tell (Simmons 1942: 84).

Needless to say, Don became a responsible, model citizen, or at least he tried to anyway.

Scholars have debated on why this seemingly peaceful people apply such violent measures to young children. It is clear that in order to ensure a continual supply of dancers to don the masks, sing the songs and dance the dances, the children have to learn the truth one way or other. It is also clear that the initiation legitimizes communal values and norms and allows the neophyte to accrue further knowledge of Hopi cosmology and theology. But not only knowledge is at stake. The use and control of clan masks cannot be had without initiation. Furthermore, initiation is the doorway to all later social engagement.

Social psychologist Dorothy Eggan argued in 1956 that emotional commitment is at stake in Hopi socialization processes (Eggan 1956). In the continual process of deliberate instruction in kinship and community obligations, clan history and mythology, work and social roles, she argued, the Hopis use fear "as a means of personal and social control and for the purposes of personal and group protection." She further claimed that the children are taught: "techniques for the displacement of anxiety, as well as procedures which the adults believed would prolong life." She wrote:

> Constantly one heard during work or play, running through all activity like a connecting thread: "Listen to the old people—they are wise"; or, "Our old uncles taught us that way—it is the *right* way." Around the communal bowl, in the kiva, everywhere this instruction went on; stories, dream adventures, and actual experiences such as journeys away from the reservation were told and retold. And children, in the warmth and security of this intimate extended family and clan group, with no intruding outside experiences to modify the impact until they were forced to go to an alien school, learned what it meant to be a good Hopi from a wide variety of determined teachers who had very definite—and *mutually consistent*—ideas of what a good Hopi is (Eggan 1956: 351).

Eggan wrote that in the accounts she had collected about the initiation and subsequent revelation, it was evident that a process of reorganizing the emotions held towards the Katsinas is thereby triggered. She claimed that the disillusion is held more firmly in adult memories than the actual physical ordeal. A shock like that, she added, can operate in both negative and positive ways. It can and does, in this example, lead at first to religious disenchantment, resentment, and anger. But it can also lead to the mobilization of an individual's dormant potentialities. In Mead's terms, it would constitute the mobilization of certain values of the generalized other. In this case, Eggan claimed, it is the reinforcement of the individual's need to belong:

> He had the satisfaction of increased status along with the burden of increasing responsibility, as the adults continued to teach him "the important things and conformity gradually became a value in itself. . . . It was both the means *and* the goal. Conformity surrounded the Hopi—child or adult—with everything he could hope to have or to be; outside it there was only the feeling tone of rejection. Since there were no bewildering choices presented (as in the case in our socialization process), the "maturation drive" could only function to produce an ego-ideal in accord with the cultural ideal, however wide the discrepancy between ideal and reality on both levels (1956: 364).

Another Hopi man, Emory Sekaquaptewa, recounted how the initiation strengthened him and helped him realize the true nature of the Katsinas:

> When it is revealed to him that the kachina is just an impersonation, an impersonation which possesses a spiritual essence, the child's security is not destroyed. Instead the experience strengthens the individual in another phase of his life in the community (Sekaquaptewa 1976: 38).

Sekaquaptewa claimed that the initiation helped him to learn that his childlike fantasizing concerning the Katsinas could, in fact, be continued in adult life on another level. From now on, the adult must learn to project himself into the spirit world in order to achieve spiritual experience. For him, the Katsina dance is more than aesthetic:

> I feel that what happens to a man when he is performer is that if he understands the essence of the kachina, when he dons the mask he loses his identity and actually becomes what he is representing. . . . The spiritual fulfillment of a man depends on how he is able to project himself into the spiritual world as he performs. He really doesn't perform for the third parties who form the audience. Rather the audience becomes his personal self. He tries to express to himself his own conceptions about the spiritual ideals that he sees in the kachina. He is able to do so behind the mask because he has lost his personal identity. . . . The idea of performing to yourself is a rather difficult one for me to describe in terms of a theory. . . . But the essence of the kachina ceremony for me as a participant has to do with the ability to project oneself into the make-believe world, the world of ideas and images which sustain that particular representation (Sekaquaptewa 1976: 39).

I don't think that George Herbert Mead could have said it better! A quote from Durkheim is relevant at this point:

> The force of the collectivity is not wholly external; it does not move us entirely from outside. Indeed, because society can exist only in and by means of individual minds, it must enter into us and become organized within us. That force thus becomes an integral part of our being and, by the same stroke, uplifts it and brings it to maturity (1995: 211).

The great shock for Hopi initiates is not so much the whipping as it is the revelation. Even many years later, the revelation maintains its hold in memory. Anthropologist Harvey Whitehouse introduced a distinction that may throw some light on how this occurs. He distinguishes between two divergent modes of religiosity dubbed "doctrinal" and "imagistic." The latter mode is especially relevant in the context of Hopi initiation. Whitehouse writes:

> The imagistic mode consists of the tendency, within certain small-scale or regionally fragmented ritual traditions and cults, for revelations to be transmitted through sporadic collective action, evoking multivocal iconic imagery, encoded in memory as distinct episodes, and producing highly cohesive and particularistic social ties (2000: 1).

Whitehouse's understanding of the imagistic mode was developed among other things on the basis of Brown and Kulik's theory of "flashbulb memory" (1992), which was further developed by Wright and Gaskell (1992). The theory proposes that surprising, intense, and emotionally arousing circumstances stimulate long-term memory, so that they not only are remembered quite clearly but they become even more vivid over the years (Whitehouse 2000: 90). When confronted by circumstances that violate existing cognitive schemas, the mind evidently searches frantically for relevant schemas, and failing this, a unique schema is encoded. An important point is that the emotional excitation that accompanies the encoding process is crucial to the whole process:

> Such memories of distinct episodes may endure a lifetime, both because repetition of the surprising event is unlikely and because, even if a substantially similar event is experienced, the traces left by the first will have been so strongly reinforced by excessive emissions from the brain's emotional centres that the original set of representations will retain much of its salience, detail, and uniqueness (Whitehouse 2000: 9).

This certainly is the case with Hopi Katsina initiation. Even though it would be a misrepresentation to characterize Hopi religion as imagistic, or even that the Katsina initiation is devoid of doctrinal techniques, it is nevertheless the case that the initiation is highly emotional, physically emphatic, and the revelation is undeniably imagistic. It is not so much a matter of what Hopi initiates are told, rather it is what they see and feel emotionally and corporeally that creates a life-long impact on them.

The Communal Construction of Good and Evil

There is one more point that needs to be made before moving on to other examples. The crux of Hopi identity is in their concept of the heart. This complex issue is central to Hopi ideas of good and evil and, ultimately, of ideal society. The evidence indicates that the Hopi ritual person is the ideal person. He or she embodies all of the qualities of what it means to be Hopi. The word *hopi* means "well behaved, well mannered," and it indicates that the person is humble, hospitable, good humored, helpful, peaceful, diligent, and so on (for Hopi ethics, see Brandt 1954; Voegelin and Voegelin 1960; Geertz 1986; Geertz and Lomatuway'ma 1987). Of such a person it is said, *pam loma'unangway'ta,* "he has a good heart." A good and pure heart is essential to a proper lifestyle and is of supreme importance in ritual activity. Dorothy Eggan captured the essence of this idea in her 1956 article:

> A good heart is a positive thing, something which is never out of a Hopi's mind. It means a heart at peace with itself and one's fellows. There is no worry, unhappiness, envy, malice, nor any other disturbing emotion in a good heart. In this state, cooperation, whether in the extended household or in the fields and ceremonies, was selfless and easy. Unfortunately, such a conception of a good heart is also impossible of attainment. Yet if a Hopi did not keep a good heart he might fall ill and die, or the ceremonies—and thus the vital crops—might fail, for . . . only those with good hearts were effective in prayer. Thus we see that the Hopi concept of a good heart included conformity to all rules of Hopi good conduct, both external and internal. To the extent that it was internalized—and all Hopi biographical material known to the writer suggests strongly that it was effectively internalized—it might reasonably be called a quite universal culturally patterned and culturally consistent Hopi "super-ego" (1956: 360–61).

This super-ego is clearly evident by the continuous probing of one's heart, the constant anguish about whether the illness or death of a family member was due to one's bad heart, the constant examination of the hearts of their neighbors, and so on. A commonly heard statement, noted by Eggan, is, "It is those NN clan people who ruined this ceremony! They have bad hearts and they quarrel too much. That bad wind came up and now we will get no rain" (1956: 361).

People say about those who are well behaved that "they have followed the right path" (*puma put pöhutwat angya*). My analysis of various statements and sources has led me to postulate that this path refers to a Hopi causal chain:

> The Hopi conceive of human life as an integral part of a chain reaction. It is a logical sequence of givens: proper attitude and the careful completing of ceremonials bring the clouds, which drop their moisture and nourish their children (the corn and vegetation). The crops are harvested and human life is regenerated, the stages of life continue and the Hopi ideal is reached: to become old and die in one's sleep (Geertz 1986: 48).

The causal chain is dependent on the morals of each individual—especially the chiefs—and on the proper completion of the ceremonies. In order to complete the ceremonies properly, one must be initiated into clan knowledge and tradition. Ritual persons are spoken of as *pam qatsit aw hintsaki*, "he/she works for life," in other words, human life is equated with ritual life.

The main psychological activity during all ritual contexts (ceremonial as well as non-ceremonial) is that of nurturing the state of mind which can maintain the holistic image of reality mentioned above. It is a matter of concentration: *tunatya*, "intention." The sponsor of a ceremonial or a dance is called *tunatyay'taqa*, "he who has an intention, i.e., a sponsor." Proper intention is integral to the above-mentioned causal chain. An old Hopi maxim is: "When one carefully pays heed, and always concentrates on it, then he will be the one to have influence on these clouds, this is what they say."[4]

If a host, or anyone for that matter, breaks a link anywhere in the chain, it affects the rest of the chain. Thus, a host who is unknowledgeable or immoral or evil fails to entice the gods and spirits to participate in the ceremonial, and the rain clouds therefore stay away from the area and do not nourish the crops. Without crops, irreparable damage is done to the whole fabric of life, and the people starve,

---

[4] *Pu' pay pas antsaniiqa, pas put sutsep aw tunatyawtaqa, pam hapi pu' paasat imuy oo'omawtuy amumi tuyqawiy'taniqat pay yan pi lavayta* (Geertz and Lomatuway'ma 1987: 320).

become ill and die. Thus, this concentration is a communal matter. Everyone must concentrate and do it wholeheartedly. Not only the men, but the women as well. As one woman told me:

> We have in our hearts only to see the crops. And these women probably do not have any bad thoughts within themselves when they prepared food for the performers and took it to the kiva. Through their hard work they will earn a (good) harvest, and they have this in mind as they do it.[5]

It would be instructive to recall the words of George Herbert Mead at this juncture concerning ritual in a social psychological perspective:

> Thus, for example, the cult, in its primitive form, is merely the social embodiment of the relation between the given social group or community and its physical environment—an organized social means, adopted by the individual members of that group or community, of entering into social relations with that environment, or (in a sense) of carrying on conversations with it; and in this way that environment becomes part of the total generalized other for each of the individual members of the given social group or community (1962: 154, n. 7).

The easiest way for a witch or evil-hearted person to make life difficult for his or her fellows is to destroy that collective concentration by sowing discontent, doubt, and criticism, as well as actively fighting it with evil ritual concentration. One does not, however, have to be evil in order to ruin things. One can have egoistic intentions when sponsoring a dance or one can simply sponsor a dance carelessly. The downside of Hopi ethics is the role of witchcraft and gossip. I will attend to witchcraft in a moment. On gossip, Dorothy Eggan correctly noted:

> In this situation, where belonging was so important, and a good heart so vital to the feeling of belonging, gossip is the potential and actual "social cancer" of the Hopi tribe. It is devastating to individual security and is often senselessly false and cruel, but in a country where cooperation was the only hope of survival, it was the *servant* as well as the policeman of the tribe. Not lightly would any Hopi voluntarily acquire the title Kahopi—"*not* Hopi," and therefore not good. Throughout the Hopi life span the word kahopi . . . was heard, until it pene-

---

[5] *Pay itam putsa' natwanit aw yoyrikyaniqey, tunatyawyungwa. Pu' ima momoyam son hiita nukushiita angqe' tunatyawkyaakyang, itamungem piw pangso kivami naakwayit tumaltotangwu. Maqsoni'am piw hiita natwanit aasataniqat oovi, piw sonqe tuwat yan wuuwankyaakyangw pantotingwu* (Geertz and Lomatuway'ma 1987: 292).

trated to the very core of one's mind. It was said softly and gently at first to tiny offenders, through "Kahopi tiyo" or "Kahopi mana" to older children, still quietly but with stern intent, until the word sometimes assumed a crescendo of feeling as a whole clan or even a whole community might condemn an individual as *Kahopi* (1956: 362–63; see also my chapter on gossip and information management, Geertz 1994: 210–14).

Gossip can be seen as a social cancer, but it is important to realize its potential as one of the major expressions of social identity in traditional Hopi contexts. I have argued elsewhere that gossip defines the identity of self and redefines the roles and identities of others. It is an on-going dialogue about oneself and others and, therefore for better or for worse, it is a kind of narrated ethics. It serves as a social conscience judging everyday behavior in relation to cultural and ethical ideals (Geertz 1994: 211–12, 213). I was told by one of my consultants after a long oratory on the importance of pure thoughts and concentration on the causal chain and how people unfortunately perform ceremonials today for selfish gain or to impress others: "really, those who wish to do evil with or to the katsinas can actually do it." He also referred to the fact that some katsina dancers are not beneath practicing love magic on unresponsive girls.[6]

There are only a few studies on Hopi witchcraft and sorcery. The best are the short 1943 article by ethnographer Mischa Titiev, a chapter in linguist Ekkehart Malotki's book on Hopi ruin legends, and his recent book on witchcraft, shamanism and magic (Titev 1943; Malokti 1993; Malokti and Gary 2001). I have also collected interview material, some of which I have published (Geertz and Lomatuway'ma 1987; Geertz 1994). This material gives an intimidating impression of powerlessness and abject fear of occult attack by witches or sorcerers. Those who deliberately commit evil can come from one's own matrilineage or one's closest family members, with the result that suspicion, gossip and spite often pollute family and interpersonal relations. During my stays among the Hopis, a significant amount of time was spent listening to gossip about whether this or that person was a witch or sorcerer. My analysis of the evidence revealed a causal chain of the evil life which mirrors the above-mentioned causal chain of the good life. Whereas the latter

---

[6] Geertz and Lomatuway'ma 1987: 236: *Pay pas antsa piw pumuy katsinmuy akw nunukpanninik pay piw sonqe patsaki* (307).

is meant to ensure *suyanisqatsi*, "a harmonious and tranquil life," the former ensures *koyaanisqatsi*, "a corrupt life, a life out of balance." These two lives reveal an opposition between the good religious life and the evil magic one. Magic and sorcery are purportedly practiced by people who need to increase their own life expectancy—which is shortened because of their pact with evil—through the occult murder of close relatives. They are initiated into the sorcerers' society just like the good people are initiated into the religious fraternities, and like them they are organized along the same hierarchical lines and perform the same kinds of rituals. Their activities are motivated by evil intentions, in other words, in opposition to the host of a religious ceremonial, the sorcerer is a *nukustunatyay'taqa*, "he who has an evil intention."

Once again, Dorothy Eggan demonstrated how insidious the idea of evil is inculcated in Hopi individuals:

> It is true that we, too, are told we should keep good hearts and love our neighbors as ourselves. But we are not told that, if we do not, our babies will die, *now, this year!* Some children are told that if they do not obey the various "commandments" they learn in different churches they will eventually burn in a lake of hell fire, but they usually know that many of their world doubt this. In contrast, Hopi children constantly *saw* babies die because a parent's heart was not right; they *saw* evil winds come up and crops fail for the same reason; they *saw* adults sicken and die because of bad thoughts or witchcraft (to which bad thoughts rendered a person more vulnerable). Thus they learned to *fear* the results of a bad heart whether it belonged to themselves or to others. There were witches, bogey Kachinas, and in objective reality famine and thirst to fear. Along with these fears were taught mechanisms for the displacement of anxiety, including the services of medicine men, confession and exorcism to get rid of bad thoughts, and cooperative nonaggression with one's fellows, even those who were known to be witches. But the best technique was that which included all the values in the positive process of keeping a good heart, and of "uniting our hearts" in family, clan, and fraternal society—in short, the best protection was to be *Hopi* rather than *Kahopi* (1956: 363).

There are a whole range of topics in this quote that deserve closer attention, but for lack of space, I will restrict myself to one interesting example of this socially imposed, internalized hermeneutic that was related to me by one of my consultants (see Geertz 1994: 18ff; Geertz 1994: 63ff). He was participating in a Katsina dance when suddenly his mask began choking him. Keeping his problem hidden from the other participants, he succumbed to the mask and admitted his guilt to it. He then pleaded with the mask to forgive him:

> As we were about to go, I put my mask on. But it suddenly cut my breath short! It felt like someone had tied my throat.... I tried to pull it off, but I could not at first. Then it finally came loose and I got my mask off real fast. I waited until I was ready to step on the cornmeal path. Then I prayed to my mask, "Please don't do this to me! Please don't!" I prayed for his forgiveness. For him not to bother me so that I could enjoy myself. I wanted to perform the dance well. This is what I thought to myself, what I thought to my mask, as I put it back on (Geertz 1990: 321–22).

After that he could breathe easily, see clearly, dance all day without getting tired and sing loudly without losing his voice. As he said, "My friend had punished me for neglecting him," i.e., he had not followed the proper ritual procedure, and he had failed the causal chain of the good life.

The situation illustrates, as you may have guessed by now, the voice of the "generalized other" assuming the organized social attitudes of the group, and in this manner the community exercises control over the conduct of its members. As Mead said:

> And only through the taking by individuals of the attitude or attitudes of the generalized other toward themselves is the existence of a universe of discourse, as that system of common or social meanings which thinking presupposes as its context, rendered possible (1962: 156).

Thus, when my consultant punishes himself and has an intense internal dialogue with his leather mask, this strikes me as an example of the field of mind being co-extensive with and including all the components of "the field of the social process of experience and behavior." As Mead wrote, "If mind is socially constituted, then the field or locus of any given individual mind must extend as far as the social activity or apparatus of social relations which constitutes it extends" (1962: 223, n. 25). My consultant, on the other hand, believed that he was carrying on a true inner dialogue with both the spirit of the mask and the ancestors:

> And my grandfathers used to tell me, even though the mask is made of leather, it will become a spirit, so you can pray to it. It is spirit even though it does not look like much. It is nothing but leather, but the spirit takes over. They [the katsinas] are the ones that help you along your life path. If you really believe in it, it will help you throughout your life (Geertz 1990: 322).

But it can also be interpreted as a result of the role that human communication plays in constructing the self and internalizing the values, attitudes and sentiments of the community.

Conclusion

Much more could be said on this topic, but I think my points have been made. Briefly, communities are active causal factors in the construction of virtual selves. These selves are cognitively embodied but develop through the dialectics of external and internal techniques for imparting communal values, sentiments, and worldviews. The external techniques are socialization, instruction, affect, ritual, and other mechanisms of universe maintenance. The internal techniques consist of internalization, the continual narrative with the social other, self-exhortation by the communal super-ego, or the communal maintenance of consciousness. The community consists of individuals busily contributing to the process of communal generalization through the dual activity of systematizing and reformulating—literally narrating—their multiple selves in terms of the values and attitudes of the generalized other.

I have tried in this paper to show the continuity between early sociologists and social psychologists and recent cognitive theory, and to demonstrate their viability in interpreting evidence concerning Hopi Indian religion.

Postscript

After presenting this paper, a question was raised from the floor concerning the nature/nurture problem as well as the problem of Free Will. People are born with talents and proclivities which social psychology cannot account for. Nor can social psychology account for the individual's Free Will. I could only agree that cognitive research is based on materialist, behaviorist, and mechanical theories and that social psychology is based on behavior.

It is interesting that the question of Free Will plays little or no part in cognitive research. One can read the hesitancy in Francis Crick's account in his book *The Astonishing Hypothesis*, where several of the main cognitive scientists were still on virgin ground concerning Free Will. Crick's hypothesis about Free Will assumes that there is a part of the brain that is concerned with planning future actions. The individual is not conscious of the complicated computations that occur in this region of the brain, only of the decisions it makes. These computations as well as the decision to act on a certain plan are subject to the structure of the brain and to inputs from its various parts, but the brain will in such instances appear to itself to have Free Will. Sometimes the brain makes choices that cannot be explained. In such circumstances, the brain:

> ... can attempt to explain to itself why it made a certain choice (by using introspection). Sometimes it may reach the correct conclusion. At other times it will either not know or, more likely, will confabulate, because it has no conscious knowledge of the "reason" for the choice. This implies that there must be a mechanism for confabulation, meaning that given a certain amount of evidence, which may or may not be misleading, part of the brain will jump to the simplest conclusion (Crick 1995: 266).

Further neurological studies seem to confirm that this "Free Will" is located in a region called the *anterior cingulate sulcus*, next to Brodmann's area 24, a region that receives a large amount of inputs from the higher sensory regions and is located at or near the higher levels of the motor system (Crick 1995: 267–68). Such a notion of Free Will is so alien to what we in the human sciences associate with the term that I am at a loss about what to do with it. On the one hand, this view of Free Will fits in well with the descriptions and claims made in this paper. On the other hand, it raises fundamental challenges concerning the nature of human beings to philosophers and theologians as well as to scholars in religious studies, anthropology, sociology and psychology. It seems that the more we learn about humans, the more alien they/we become.

15. ON CREDULITY

Benson Saler

In everyday speech the word "credulity" often occurs in a perjorative context. Credulity means a readiness or willingness to believe on the basis of little or no evidence. A person deemed credulous is thus someone who, in the judgment of another, is credited with a disposition, or a realized disposition, to believe too readily or too easily. Judgment is often rendered on the basis of observing someone appear to accept belief where, in the opinion of the judger, there is dubious or insufficient evidence for acceptance.

Credulity is widespread in human life. Indeed, if we divorce it from its pejorative connotations and look at the fundamental phenomenon involved, credulity is quite important in human life. In terms of a cost-benefit analysis, its benefits greatly outweigh its costs. Further, credulity is of immense evolutionary significance. In order to argue those claims expeditiously, however, we need a less judgmental sense of credulity than that normally encountered in everyday speech. So in order to strip the phenomenon down to basics while minimizing any immediate judgmental evaluation of it, I offer this stipulative definition: Credulity is the acceptance or justification of belief largely or entirely on the basis of human testimony.

If you accept that stipulative definition, then we are all credulous to a great extent. Much that we claim to know or believe is based largely or entirely on what we have heard or read. I, for instance, believe in the germ theory of disease (at least to the extent that I understand it). But I have never attempted to justify my belief by systematic efforts to look for and evaluate evidence. All of my friends say that germs cause disease, as do my primary care physician and other authority figures. They all seem to suppose, moreover, that competent people have checked it out, and so, too, do I. Most of my other knowledge claims or beliefs depend on similar sources. I think it very likely, moreover, that that is also true of the reader.

Widespread and habitual credulity on the part of just about everyone carries both benefits and costs for the individual. On a greater plane of abstraction, moreover, credulity can be said to be both functional and dysfunctional for human societies. We can argue, furthermore, that both credulity and the development of what we may call skeptical constraints have been of importance for the evolution of humankind. Let us take each in turn.

Credulity and the Individual

An obvious benefit of credulity for the individual is that it facilitates the accessing of information stored elsewhere. Reciprocally, one of its more obvious costs is that it facilitates the acquisition of misinformation.

Throughout our lives we depend on others for much of the information that we utilize. We learn from others not only in what they say (or write), but in observing what they do and in hearing about them from third parties. In the course of benefiting cognitively from others, however, we sometimes suffer by appropriating their errors and follies. In any case, the vast amount of information that we process and utilize derives in great measure from our fellow human beings. *The individual, in short, is cognitively or informationally dependent on others.*

Dependency is the condition of looking to others for the satisfaction of one's needs and wants. As we mature we usually become less dependent on our parents or other early caretakers for subsistence, and there is likely to be an emotional weaning as well. For most of us, however, there is likely to be an *increase* rather than a decrease in informational dependency as we mature. Not only does cognitive dependency typically increase, it widens with respect to the informational sources accessed. Beginning with parents or early caretakers, the maturing individual increasingly accesses other informational sources, it being important for multiple kinds of competency to acquire and process new information of increasingly diverse kinds.

Most individuals do not simply receive information from others. They re-work what they receive in keeping with their established representations and understandings. Even if the information acquired is not distorted by noise in the initial transmission, significant alteration of the information processed may take place through enrichment or de-emphasis. Indeed, there are screening or editing mechanisms of various sorts that ordinarily come into play.

Information that strongly conflicts with our established ideas and expectations about the world may be rejected outright or accepted only provisionally or conditionally. Further, evaluations of sources may well play a role, even if the individual doing the evaluating cannot explicitly or consciously formulate all of the factors that enter into the evaluation. The channeling of purported information is very important, and appraisals of the characteristics of channels are likely to play significant roles in whether or not, or how readily, or how conditionally, information may be accepted. Account may be taken of such things as the social status and credentials of the source, beliefs about the track record of the source, whether or not the informational transmission is accompanied by reassuring body displays (eye contacts, facial expressions, and/or other valued stimuli), wide social support for the putative information, and so forth.

We humans employ a multiplicity of evaluative criteria, some of them rather subtle. At the same time, however, we sometimes readily or precipitously accept information because we have no alternative sources of information or because we are strongly disposed to do so by fervent wishes, desperation, social pressures, or a host of other possible motivating factors. And, it needs to be said, some persons may be less evaluative or more accepting of what is proffered than are others.

All of us, nevertheless, are credulous to significant extents. Two salient (and partly overlapping) expressions of credulity are suggested by the terms "trust" and "faith."

Trust, in the sense that concerns us, is reliance on another person's, or on other people's, veracity, integrity, or predictability. We may, for instance, trust a certain person to do a certain thing. Or we accept the information that someone supplies on trust. Trust, so conceived, is a positive restatement of credulity. As such, it is vital factor in the conduct of social life. We commonly trust in others to do various things, to behave in expected ways, and to supply information on which we can rely.

Trust is of great significance in science as well as in much else. Contemporary science in our society is deservedly famous for its skeptical epistemology, its celebration of the idea that claims to knowledge should be systematically tested rather than facilely accepted. In actual practice, however, skeptical epistemology is not thoroughgoing. It is impossible to monitor everything or to attempt to review all claims. In consequence, scientists are obliged to take much on trust. They do, however, make efforts to safeguard that trust. Part of their structure of safeguards can be discerned in such prophylactic measures as rigorous professional training, demanding requirements for advanced degrees, apprenticeship to senior scientists, and so on. Graduate and "post doc" training in the sciences is intended to do more than enhance the knowledge and skills of the person undergoing it; it is also intended to weed out weak candidates and to produce credentialed scientists upon whom other scientists can rely.

The importance of trust in the sciences is instructive because of the explicit importance that scientists accord to skeptical epistemology. In much else in life we are less consciously or explicitly skeptical, and we are even more dependent on implicit trust. Every time we cross a bridge without care or worry we implicitly trust the engineers and builders who designed and constructed it. Every time we drive without concern through a tunnel we implicitly trust its builders to have done their jobs properly. (I am indebted to Charles A. Ziegler for these examples.) When regulatory agencies and manufacturers establish safety standards for an electrical appliance that will be used by the public, they trust that people will use the appliance in anticipated ways, for otherwise safeguards would have to be so complex and costly that the product would be unviable, commercially and perhaps functionally. In these and in many other ways trust is implicitly, and sometimes explicitly, widespread.

Despite trust's importance in our lives, however, widespread dependence on it can have its downsides. While individuals often depend on the trust of others to engage in mutually satisfying interactions, sometimes trust is abused. Con men, hoaxers, and practical jokers, to say nothing of terrorists and serial killers, frequently depend on the trust of others for their own satisfactions. Trust can and often does facilitate the acquisition of misinformation, sometimes with unfortunate consequences, regardless of whether the misinformation is disseminated intentionally or not. Trust, even when deemed a positive expression of credulity, is thus multifaceted.

Faith implies confidence in propositions, persons, or the likely occurrence of envisioned events. The term, moreover, is often used in contemporary English to indicate a confidence that need not rest on "evidence" or "facts," at least in the most common acceptations of those terms. Faith suggests an inner certainty or confidence. It need not depend on outer validation. This does not mean, however, that it is never ascribed a source outside of the person.

In a fairly extreme example, that of certain Christian theological traditions, which assign great importance to faith, faith in the truths of Christianity is declared to come ultimately from God. Individuals, numbers of theologians assert, attain their faith by God's grace. That faith, moreover, is held to transform the individual, cognitively and in other ways. In Augustine of Hippo's admonitory expression of that tradition,

> Understanding is the reward of faith. Therefore seek not to understand so that you may believe, but believe so that you may understand. (*On the Gospel of St. John*, 29.6)

Christian theological traditions respecting faith constitute what numbers of Westerners deem to be some of the clearest or best examples of what they understand by that term. It is important to note, however, that popular parlance does not restrict faith to a religious context. Among the many uses of the term, some of the more prominent include faith in persons to whom we attribute various qualities (honesty, probity, conscientiousness, whatever), faith in "human nature" (claimed confidence, for instance, that individuals or collectivities of persons will behave in expected ways), or faith that events will transpire in some predicted sequence. These uses, moreover, do not exhaust actual and possible applications of the term. Its association with religion is nevertheless important and instructive, even if not exhaustive.

A strong argument has been made that religious ideas typically include some counter-intuitive elements (Boyer 1994, 2001b; Pyysiäinen 2001). That is, the objects posited in religious ideas—gods, ghosts, spirits, etc.—to some extent either violate expectations that we have about prototypical members of the macro category to which they pertain or they are credited with one or more features that we normally associate with some other category. Thus, for instance, in many religions the gods neither eat nor die, whereas more prototypical exemplars of the macro category *person* normally do both. And in various parts of the world witches are depicted as having, and exercising, the power to fly, although they are neither birds nor aviators. Yet while the objects posited in religious ideas typically depart in some ways from expectations grounded in our intuitive ontologies, they nevertheless conform to them in other respects. Thus, for example, gods typically are credited with will, purpose, and various other important qualities and capacities associated with the person category (Guthrie 1993, Boyer 1994). As Boyer (1994, 2001b) persuasively argues, confirmation of our ontological intuitions and expectations renders posited religious objects plausible and easy to learn, while their "attention-getting" departures from those intuitions and expectations make them memorable.

Faith in the existence and persistence of posited religious objects thus signals acceptance of the reality of the counter-intuitive. One may argue that much the same thing could be said about modern science, since it, too, often suggests the counter-intuitive. What could be more counter-intuitive than quantum mechanics? But there is a difference. The constructs of science are recognized to be constructs. They are provisional, in keeping with the skeptical epistemology discussed earlier. Ideally, they should not be taken on faith. Efforts should be made to test them and to find something better. Posited religious objects and narratives, however, even when in principle refutable, are usually not subject to systematic refutational efforts, nor is there an institutionalized imperative to find something better. If they are plausible because they accord to a significant extent with already established understandings and expectations albeit departing from them in some arresting particulars, and if they appear to answer in significant fashion to interests and desires, they may become part of one's archive of ideas.

Cognitively, faith is not extraordinary. It is a motivated and prioritized storage of ideas that have survived filtration and are marked as authoritative. Typically, moreover, those ideas are strongly affect-laden relative to desires, and their positive cathexis often serves as a barrier to subsequent refutation—albeit in the right combination of circumstances cathexis may sometimes eventually prove to be an emotional door to loss of faith. When ideas originate outside of the individual, we could choose to characterize faith in them as an intensified form of credulity. But inasmuch as all ideas are framed by a language of ideas and, if expressed, are expressed within such a framework, faith is always a matter of credulity, if only contextually.

Credulity and Society

In 1950, a committee of anthropologists and sociologists—David F. Aberle, Albert K. Cohen, Arthur K. Davis, Marion Levy, and Francis Sutton—published a paper entitled "The Functional Prerequisites of a Society." Influenced to a significant extent by the theoretical and analytical perspectives of the sociologist Talcott Parsons, Aberle et al. supply a list of supposedly necessary basic conditions for the existence, functioning, and continuation of human societies. The list includes "shared cognitive orientations" and a "shared, articulated set of goals."

At first glance, the above two "prerequisites" may seem reasonable or perhaps, in the judgment of some, even obvious. One can, however, raise questions about the meaning of "shared." Does it suggest identity in orientations and goals or only some sort of approximation? How indeed, except by citing colloquial conventions (which may be out of place in anything as solemn as an exercise in formulating "functional prerequisites"), do we justify the notion that individuals, the loci of cognitive orientations and goals, "share" them? Voicing or publicly endorsing orientations and goals that are articulated by others signals public agreement. But can two people actually *share* what we normally regard as internal mental phenomena? Even if this question is resolved, however, there is a further difficulty that inhibits our acceptance of the requirements proffered by Aberle et al.

In a masterful criticism of the idea that human society could not exist and persist unless there was a sharing of cognitive orientations and goals, the anthropologist Anthony F. C. Wallace (1961a, 1961b) demonstrates formally that individuals with different understandings and different goals may nevertheless support and sustain mutually satisfying social transactions. What is necessary, Wallace argues, is not "sharing" but, rather, what he terms "mutually facilitating equivalence structures." That is, social actors must entertain complementary expectations that if they behave in certain ways others will act in a predictable manner. If I do x, alter will do y. Such expectations, of course, must be realized more often than not lest they become extinguished. But the actors need not actually "share" cognitive orientations and goals for satisfying relations to occur and to be reinforced. Nor need they know the cognitive orientations and motives of other people. Indeed, Wallace argues, they need not even know the social identities of those with whom they interact.

One of Wallace's examples is the "tooth-fairy" scenario: a child looses a tooth, places it under its pillow at night, and awakens to find the tooth gone and money in its place. The child supposes that she has interacted with the tooth-fairy, whereas in reality, of course, it was a parent who made the switch. The parent's goal, we may suppose, was different from the child's. Further, the parent and child have different understandings of the transaction, and the child is ignorant of the identity of the actual actor who took the tooth and replaced it with money. But the expectations of child and parent, though different in cognitive content, were mutually facilitating.

Wallace (1961b: 40) goes on to argue that cognitive "*non*-uniformity" can be deemed "a functional desideratum" of human societies. All human societies, including those considered to be relatively "small-scale," typically include a considerable diversity of roles. Competent performance of those roles involves a great deal of knowledge. If we were to measure the complexity of societies in terms of the diversity of roles, then the cognitive complement of that measure would be a measure of cognitive complexity on a societal level. Contemporary American society, for example, is very complex in both. But even so-called "primitive" societies (i.e., typically and classically, small-scale societies of non-literate persons) exhibit a good deal of role diversity and a corresponding cognitive complexity.

As Wallace points out, if everyone in a human society were obliged to know everything requisite to competent discharge of social roles, the complexity of roles would be drastically constrained by the cognitive capacities of most individuals. But nowhere that I know of is that actually the case. Roles are numerous and the continuance of all societies depends on knowledge that exceeds the knowledge of any individual. As Wallace (1961b: 40) puts it, "... cognitive non-uniformity sub-serves two important functions: (1) it permits a more complex system to arise than most, or any, of its participants can comprehend; (2) it liberates the participants in a system from the heavy burden of knowing each other's motivations."

Various other social scientists had made points that support Wallace's view. Thus, for instance, in a paper on "Some Social Functions of Ignorance," Wilbert E. Moore and Melvin Tumin (1949) argue impressively that in human social orders successful role playing sometimes requires cognitive inequality between actors. Indeed, as in the case of typical physician-patient interactions in contemporary American society, the authority of one role-player rests on an assumption of special knowledge and a complementary ignorance on the part of the other. But Wallace's treatment, in my opinion, goes beyond the contributions of his predecessors both in its global perspective and in the elegance of its formal proofs.

"Evidently," Wallace writes, "groups, as well as individuals, can integrate their behaviors into reliable systems by means of equivalence structures, without extensive motivational or cognitive sharing" (1961b: 40). Allowing, then, for the likelihood of a good deal of motivational and cognitive diversity in a human society—a diversity, indeed, in personality variables as well as in cognition—Wallace suggests that the task of the social scientist is to comprehend how such diversity is organized. His major answer, as already indicated, is by the establishment of partial, mutually facilitating equivalence structures, "a system of equivalent behavioral expectancies" (1961b: 41). These constitute an "*implicit contract*," in the general sense of the term "contract," and, Wallace contends,

> society is, as Rousseau intuited, built upon a set of continually changing social contracts which are possible only because human beings have cognitive equipment adequate to their maintenance and renewal. Culture can be conceived as a set of standardized models of such contractual relationships, in which the equivalent roles are specified and available for implementation to any two parties whose motives make their adoption promising. The relationship is based not on a sharing, but on a complementarity of cognitions and motives. (1961b: 41).

Culture, in Wallace's view,

> shifts in policy from generation to generation with kaleidoscopic variety, and is characterized internally not by uniformity, but by diversity of both individuals and groups, many of whom are in continuous and overt conflict in one sub-system and in active cooperation in another. Culture, as seen from this viewpoint, becomes not so much a superorganic thing *sui generis*, but policy, tacitly and gradually concocted by groups of people for the furtherance of their interests; also contract, established by practice, between and among individuals to organize their strivings into mutually facilitating equivalence structures. (Wallace 1961: 28)

Adopting and adapting that perspective, we can characterize a human society as constituting, at any one moment, a pool of information to which social actors have differential, *and differently motivated*, access. Credulity facilitates both the flow and appropriation of information while other mechanisms (such as social proprieties conventionally related to distinctions in age, sex, and, more broadly, social identity and role playing) serve to inhibit or channel its diffusion.

A human society is characteristically strengthened by the richness of its informational pool, without the necessity of that information being equally available to everyone. Indeed, as pointed out earlier, informational complexity beyond the cognitive capacities of individuals is made possible by the differential participation of those individuals in the pool. At the same time, however, the social value of an informational pool would be compromised or subverted unless there were mechanisms to facilitate appropriation. Credulity is one such mechanism.

Evolutionary Considerations

One sometimes hears this complaint about commercials on television: the advertisers and/or stations, it is alleged, increase the sound level of commercials above the level used for ordinary program transmissions in order to get the auditor's attention. That allegation is probably false in the great majority of cases. Sound level is regulated by code, and it is in the interests of most television stations to adhere to code. If one were to measure sound level in decibels, program materials and commercials would often be found to be about the same. The impression of greater loudness in ads is an artifact of the care (and expense) that some producers of television advertisements devote to reducing background noise in their commercials. Signal to noise ratios are sometimes higher in TV ads than in TV programs, and that, indeed, may get the auditor's attention.

Now, signal to noise ratios ought to be taken into account in certain sorts of evolutionary studies. The phylogenetic scale evinces, as it were, diverse strategies for distinguishing signals from background noise in cases of locating food, finding mates, avoiding predators, and in other important activities. Signals, of course, are quite diverse and include more than sonic signals. But whether signals be auditory, visual, tactile, olfactory, kinetic, thermal, or combinations of these and others, their utility or effectiveness is often related to their experienced strength relative to the experiential capacities of living things. In brief, their adaptive significance rests not only on the signals themselves but on the discriminative powers of organisms.

On the human level, the diversity of potential signals and the diversity of potential background noises increase greatly. Complexity, moreover, is expanded by considerations relating to the *reliability* of signals. Reliability may be compromised or enhanced not only by factors directly affecting cue discriminations, stimulus generalizations, extinctions (e.g., "The Boy Who Cried Wolf"), and the like, but by subtle rhetorical, kinetic, and other ploys that may, as it were, italicize signals and messages in ways that further stimulate the receiver to productive actions or that effectively subvert her attentions and energies by deceptions. Deception, of course, is encountered elsewhere in the phylogenetic scale. The diversity of animal camouflages is one sort of example, and "playing dead" is another. But humans have—and often exercise—greater capacities to deceive than do other animals.

Deceiving by word, by deed, by body posture, by facial features, by vagueness or ambiguity, by silence, and by other means, is common among humans. Sometimes it is inadvertent. But often it is intentional, and it may be diversely motivated (as we suppose in English by employing such expressions as "white lie," "noble lie," "damn lie," and so forth). Scanning or monitoring devices for detecting deceptions in the conduct of human life can be useful if effective. Indeed, we are disposed by evolutionary endowments to make efforts to assess reliability, if only subliminally. At the same time, however, we are disposed to be credulous, and that, too, is a disposition with an evolutionary foundation. I shall take up each in turn. But before doing so, it is worth noting (based on informal observations made in my own society and in others) that some individuals may be more given to skepticism than various of their fellows, while some appear to be rather more credulous than others. Stronger or weaker dispositions in either case may relate to the personal experiences of different individuals and to a myriad of variables such as childhood socialization, education, employment, and so on. Considered more abstractly, however, variable intensities of dispositions in a population respecting skepticism and credulity hint at polymorphism, and that also suggests an evolutionary consideration.

Reliability

Human reliability assessments are rooted in genetically transmitted sensitivities and dispositions that have adaptive significance. Charles Ziegler furnishes an example that spills over to an ironic contemporary application:

> Most higher vertebrates produce specific sounds (e.g., cries that attract mates or warn of predators). Although the production of, and response to, such sounds might be considered a form of communication, there

> is no need to assume that the animals recognize it as such. It is only necessary to assume that the animal is programmed genetically to make a certain sound when, say, the mating "drive" is experienced and that conspecifics of the opposite sex are programmed to respond to that sound with mating behavior...
>
> By introspection and inference from observing others, we know that phylogenetic responses to certain sounds are still with us and that information conveyed in this way has a high "believability quotient." Those of us who have heard, say, piercing screams of fear or rage can testify that the same information sonically conveyed by speech (e.g., "I am afraid" or "I am angry") has much less impact. Why is this so?
>
> Using "reverse engineering" it is possible to describe—at least at the level of systematics—how the "instinctive" response to certain sounds occurs.... In the case of input sensed as sound, a neural "shunt" must exist that performs rudimentary signal processing wherein the incoming sound pattern is compared with phylogenetically stored patterns. If a match occurs the "shunt" bypasses the neural mechanisms that constitute the usual intervening cognitive steps and triggers the appropriate emotion (e.g., fear or anger) which is followed by "the assignment of action"...
>
> In effect, if a certain internal state prompts an animal to make a certain sound, that sound "automatically" induces an appropriate internal state in conspecifics. In humans, the response produced by the "shunt" can be ignored, but the response itself is "automatic." Indeed, this is why the most banal horror movie can "work" if it includes loud and convincing screams of fear. This sound will always induce in us a frisson of fear despite the banal plot and the knowledge that we are safely sitting in a theater. We can consciously repress "the assignment of action," (i.e., flight), and remain in our seats, but the "shunt" insures that "the assignment of affect" (i.e., fear) occurs, however momentarily, as an involuntary response. (Ziegler n.d.: 53–54)

There are various other sensitivities and excitations that negatively or positively affect the "believability quotient" and that appear to be genetically disposed. Among the more popularly recognized—as sometimes described by novelists in portrayals of character in social interactions—are eye behaviors in face-to-face contacts (e.g., pupil dilations and alterations in blinking behavior), other aspects of facial expressions (e.g., smiles, frowns, lip tremors, eyebrow arching, etc.), facial pallor or blotches or colorations, body postures and tics, vocal tremors or other vocal behaviors that affect the evaluation of messages transmitted in speech, and so forth. These are often involuntary on the part of the signaler. Further, those who "read" or "audit" them may not be consciously aware that they are taking them into account in assessing the reliability of information proffered.

While the above can be regarded as genetically disposed, there are also, of course, learned modalities of reliability assessment respecting the credentials of informational sources and the plausibility and probability of truth claims. These latter, which are culturally variable, are related in complex and subtle ways to the former, which constitute natural resemblances among human beings.

In exploring ethno-epistemological traditions in the ethnographic literature, for example, we find that different cultures, while tending to support similar evaluative sensitivities relating to face-to-face informational transmissions, also accord importance to different modalities for receiving and validating different sorts of information. Thus, for instance, seventeenth century and some later Iroquois value and make efforts to obey what they take to be imperatives delivered in certain ways in dreams (Wallace 1958), Zande maintain that the poison oracles of their princes are infallible (Evans-Pritchard 1937), and other populations are variously reported to repose a generalized confidence in seers, divinations, omens, astrological computations, and so forth, while often being prepared to explain, or to explain away, discrete failures in the truth claims and predictions entered in specific cases. Further, as Pascal Boyer (1994, 2001b) cogently argues, the entertainment, elaboration, and cultural transmission of religious ideas are crucially affected by inference systems that are supported and constrained by the panhuman architecture of the human brain and common existential experiences. This means, he points out, that not everything goes insofar as the successful transmission of religious ideas is concerned, and it helps to explain why there are broad family resemblances in various religious ideas entertained by populations who differ culturally.

Credulity

I suggested earlier that credulity, as defined in this essay, promotes the accessing and utilization of information stored outside of any given individual, that it facilitates the achievement of cognitive complexity, and that it is generally a cost-effective way of enabling persons within a social group to coordinate their cognitive resources. The possible costs include dissemination of misinformation, the narrowing or closing off of avenues of potentially useful information and ratiocination, and the diversion of energies that might be gainfully employed elsewhere. On balance, I think that the likely benefits outweigh potential costs, all the more so since dispositions to credulity are ameliorated to some extent by dispositions to skepticism and reliability assessments.

If one accepts the several components of the view expressed above, then we can go on to argue that credulity has been a phenomenon of immense evolutionary and societal importance. Indeed, human life as we know it could not have emerged or persisted without it.

Impressive arguments have been made to the effect that the architecture of the human brain evolved to its present state during the Pleistocene, and that that architecture is adapted to a Paleolithic life-style, a life-style in which humans lived in small groups that depended on hunting and gathering (Barkow, Cosmides, and Tooby 1992; Mithen 1996). Such small groups were loci of cooperation and nurturing, and that includes informational exchanges.

Means for distinguishing between insiders and outsiders were important for husbanding and distributing resources and channeling nurturing. Such means would facilitate and support social solidarity. They may have included language markers, so that even in territories where speech was mutually intelligible groups could nevertheless be distinguished by dialectical variants or perhaps very slight but recognizable variations in pronouncing some sounds. Other distinguishing devices may have included variations in dress or adornment, odors, traditions, and so forth. And, of course, the memories of group members were important for distinguishing between insiders and outsiders. Further, sensitivities and traditions that discouraged and perhaps punished freeloaders or cheats could also have had social and survival value. Another factor making for solidarity in the in-group and enhancing survival prospects may have been a willingness or readiness to accept information proffered within the group.

Just as credulity can enlarge an individual's informational resources and facilitate cognitive coordination within groups, so, too, can it be something of a condition for group membership and social solidarity. That is, an individual affirms and validates group membership by accepting—or appearing to accept—much of the information seemingly endorsed and proffered by the group. Too much overt skepticism would subvert group solidarity. Hence the realization of dispositions to credulity is not only typically accomplished within a social framework, *but such realizations and the dispositions that fund them are themselves factors making for human sociability.*

We can readily imagine how this was the case in small-scale Paleolithic societies, but we can also comprehend how it is the case in our complex contemporary world, with its increasing requirements for information. An arresting problem is how our Paleolithic mind-brain and its dispositions to credulity may cope with the dangers of our present condition. We cannot be free of credulity. Happily, however, evolution has also endowed us with critical faculties for evaluating many informational claims, faculties that, with appropriate cultivation, can be applied to the assessment of still more claims. Ultimately, it is our polymorphism that may preserve us as we increasingly face dangers of our own making.

16. WHAT IS "THE BIBLE"?
(ANALYSIS OF A TEXT CONCEPT)[1]

Brian Malley

Since the interpretive turn in the human sciences, the trope of "culture as text" has dominated cultural theory, calling attention to the multi-layered, often complex meaning structures found in cultural events (Ricoeur 1971; Geertz 1973; Schneider 1980 [1968]). Yet Michael Silverstein and Greg Urban have recently pointed out that "entextualization"—paring off a bit of a discursive event (a "text") and reperforming it during another event (a new "context")—is itself a way of making culture. *Text*, they note (1996: 2),

> is a metadiscursive notion, useful to participants in a culture as a way of creating an image of a durable, shared culture immanent in or even undifferentiated from its ensemble of realized or even potential texts. It is a metadiscursive construct—"this stretch of discourse is a text whose meaning is . . ."—that grows out of and refers to actual cultural practices, which themselves are presumably to be studied ethnographically, in addition to constituting the essence of ethnographic method itself.

On this view, the entextualization of a stretch of discourse is a tool of cultural participants and their ethnographers alike (cf. Clifford and Marcus 1986), for both of whom it is a way of *organizing* the *implications* of a verbal event, albeit for their distinctive audiences.

This, in my view, raises questions of cognition. I take *culture* to be socially transmitted *patterns* of thought and behavior, including the designation of certain stretches of discourse as "meaning"-laden "texts." I take *cognition* to be the *organization* of the brain's information-processing, the *structure* of mental activities (a la Chomsky 1957; von Neumann 1958; Bateson 1972)—including the designation of certain stretches of discourse as "meaning"-laden "texts." The problem of discursive organization is thus at once cultural and cognitive.

---

[1] Thanks to Paulo Sousa, Larry Hirschfeld, the Michigan Society of Fellows, Ilkka Pyysiäinen, Rob Williams, and especially Barbara Sarnecka and Webb Keane for their comments on earlier drafts of this essay.

The present essay is an ethnographic case study of one small part of this discourse-organizing activity, the categorization of text-artifacts. The case I shall examine is that of "the Bible," as this term is deployed by American evangelical Christians, especially those in a particular community, that of Creekside Baptist Church. Given a number of different texts that count as Bibles, what do the people of Creekside Baptist mean by "the Bible"?

Creekside Baptist is a predominantly white evangelical church of about 350–400 attendees, lying on the outskirts of Ann Arbor, Michigan. The church's proximity to the University of Michigan and its location in the relatively affluent town of Ann Arbor mean that its attendees are mostly well educated, middle-class professionals: teachers, engineers, nurses, university professors, lawyers, computer programmers, and so forth. My research there consisted of a survey, observations, and interviews between 1997 and 2001.[2]

"The Bible" occupies a prominent place at Creekside Baptist: doctrinally, the Bible is regarded as the authoritative and inspired word of God, the primary source of revelation for Christians today. (This doctrine is a defining feature of evangelical institutions, cf. Smith and Emerson 1998; Noll 2001.) Attendees bring their Bibles to church, and Sunday morning services feature the reading of one or more passages of scripture before the preacher gives an expository sermon. Sunday school classes too take for their lessons stories or moral teachings from the Bible, and young children in particular are encouraged to memorize Bible verses.

For the study of a text concept, the case of the English Bible is instructive because its complex textual history has given rise to a number of coexisting "versions," which are used by a large number of people who know that they differ but regard them as nonetheless alike. As a prelude to the conceptual analysis, the next section briefly reviews the causes and dimensions of variation in modern printed Bibles, so as to acquaint the reader with the environment in which those who use English Bibles find themselves. (The reader already familiar with the history of the Bible and the complexities of Bible translation may wish to skip ahead to the next section.)

---

[2] The name of the church and those of all attendees are pseudonyms.

Background

The plethora of English Bibles available today can overwhelm the novice.[3] About twenty major English Bible translations are readily available in Ann Arbor bookstores, and many more are available in libraries and over the internet. Although Bibles appear to be simple representations—"translations"—of ancient texts, they are not. A brief excursus into the kinds of complexities underlying the array of modern English Bibles will set the stage for consideration of the Bible concept as it appears among American evangelicals.

Most English Bibles are translations of texts in classical Hebrew, Aramaic, and Koine Greek. A first, obvious source of complication is translation: English Bibles are produced by committees with quite disparate translation philosophies. The King James Version (1611) and its revisions were all intended to be "literal" translations, to stay as close to word-for-word correspondence between the source and target languages as possible. The resulting texts are usually a bit stilted in English. But most recent translations—most notably the New International Version (1984)—attempt rather to render into

---

[3] The various versions of the Bible cited in this chapter are listed below. For full bibliographic information on all other material cited in this paper, see the bibliography at the end of this volume.

(1611). *The Bible: Translated according to the Ebrew and Greeke, and conferred with the best translations in diuers languages. With most profitable annotations vpon all the hard places, and other things of great importance, as may appeare in the epistle to the reader. And also a most profitable concordance for the ready finding out of any thing in the same conteined.* Imprinted at London, By Robert Barker printer to the Kings most Excellent Maiestie.

(1952). *The Holy Bible. Revised Standard Version Containing the Old and New Testaments.* New York: T. Nelson.

(1971). *The Holy Bible: New Living Translation.* Wheaton, IL: Tyndale House Publishers, Inc.

(1973). *New American Standard Bible.* La Habra, CA: Foundation Press Publications publisher for the Lockman Foundation.

(1984). *The Holy Bible: New International Version: Containing the Old Testament and the New Testament.* Colorado Springs, CO: International Bible Society.

(1987). *The Amplified Bible.* Grand Rapids, MI: The Zondervan Corporation; The Lockman Foundation.

(1989). *The Revised English Bible.* Oxford: Oxford University Press; Cambridge University Press.

(1990). *The Revised English Bible.* Oxford: Oxford University Press.

(1994). *Holy Bible: New King James Version.* Nashville, TN: Thomas Nelson Incorporated.

(1996). *The Holy Bible: New Living Translation.* Wheaton, IL: Tyndale House Publishers, Inc.

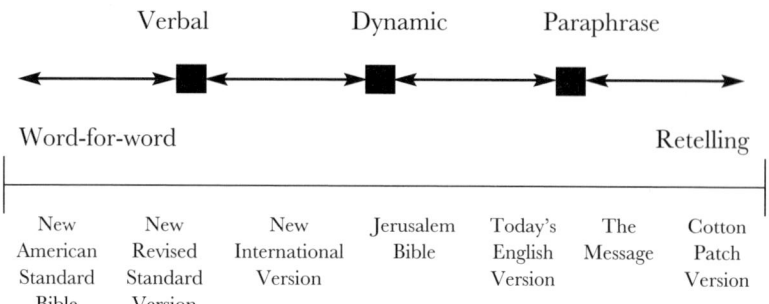

Figure 1: A Spectrum of Approaches to Translation

English the meaning and flavor of the source text without necessarily preserving any of its grammatical structures. The result of this "dynamic equivalence" philosophy is that the English text is highly readable—ideally, does not read like a translation at all—but often takes greater liberties with the text than do more literal translations. Still less literal than dynamic equivalence translations are retellings, or paraphrases. The different translation philosophies underlying some modern English versions are summarized in Figure 1, adapted from Steven Sheeley's and Robert Nash's short guide *Choosing a Bible* (Sheeley and Nash 1999: 17).

Bibles, therefore, may sound quite stilted or natural, formal or informal, literary or plain, depending on the philosophy of the translation committee and its target audience.

A second complication comes in establishing the translation's source text. Some translations take as the basis for their New Testament the *textus receptus*. The *textus receptus* is a variant of the Greek New Testament text standardized by the eighth century A.D. It is represented in the vast majority of late manuscripts, and is usually referred to simply as the Majority text.[4] Because late manuscripts were used for the printed Greek text, a variant of the Majority text has served, with slight modifications, as the most widely used Greek New Testament from Desiderius Erasmus' first printed edition of 1516 until the meticulous research of Brooke Fost Westcott and Fenton

---

[4] The *textus receptus* is not quite identical with the Majority text (Wallace 1994), but is quite close and the two are sometimes equated (e.g., Hodges 1968).

John Anthony Hort (1881) introduced modern textual criticism.[5] Most major translations of the New Testament, since the Authorized Version of 1881, have taken as their source text an eclectic New Testament text, usually based on one of the published critical editions.

Critical editions are syntheses of the best (i.e., most likely original) readings found in various manuscripts. The manuscripts themselves are very similar, but not identical. The critical editions pick and choose the readings most likely to be original from among the various manuscripts to come up with an eclectic text. The resultant text is not identical to that of *any* extant manuscript.[6] Bibles are based on slightly different texts depending on the manuscript evidence available to translators.

An example will illustrate this sort of textual variation. The rejection of the *comma Johannem* (1 John 5:7) as the result of textual criticism is clear in the comparison of the King James Version with the Revised Standard Version (1952):

King James Version	*Revised Standard Version*
[6]This is he that came by water and blood, *even* Jesus Christ; not by water only, but by water and blood. And it is the Spirit that beareth witness, because the Spirit is truth. [7]**For there are three that bear record in heaven, the Father, the Word, and the Holy Ghost: and these three are one**. [8]And there are three that bear witness **in earth**, the Spirit, and the water, and the blood: and these three agree in one.	[6] This is he who came by water and blood, Jesus Christ, not with the water only but with the water and the blood. [7] And the Spirit is the witness, because the Spirit is the truth. [8] There are three witnesses, the Spirit, the water, and the blood; and these three agree.

---

[5] While the dominance of the *textus receptus* from 1516 to 1881 is universally acknowledged, there were a number of attempts at critical editions of the Greek New Testament prior to Westcott and Hort. Bruce Metzger (1992: 119–21) thus traces the development of textual criticism to the work of Johann Jakob Griesbach (1745–1812), and Kurt Aland and Barbara Aland (1987: 11) attribute the program of overthrowing the *textus receptus* to the classicist Karl Lachmann (1793–1851).

[6] Reliance on eclectic ("pieced together," also called "theoretical") texts is the consequence of a long history in which various other ways of deciding on a text were tried. For a readable, if dated, history of this question, see Ernest Colwell, *What is the Best New Testament?* (1952).

This passage is markedly shorter in the Revised Standard Version (and most modern translations, including the American Standard Version (ASV), New American Standard Version (NAS 1973), New International Version (NIV), New Revised Standard Version (NRSV 1989), Contemporary English Version (CEV), and New Living Translation (NLT 1971)) because verse 7 of the King James Version has been eliminated on text-critical grounds. The longer variant appears only in late manuscripts, and its non-originality is accepted by nearly all textual critics. The versification has been maintained by dividing verse 6. While the NAS, NIV, NRSV, and NLT give the extended reading in the margin, the alternate reading is not even noted in the ASV, RSV, and CEV.

Different committees also sometimes weigh evidence differently: whereas the Septuagint (roughly, the ancient Greek translation of the Hebrew scriptures) was once considered unreliable, evidence from the Dead Sea scrolls suggests that it may in some cases be the *best* witness to the Hebrew scriptures at the time of Christ (Jobes and Silva 2000), and so recent committees have weighed the Septuagint more heavily when making text-critical judgments.

A third complication—though one on which the various translations largely agree—arises because the manuscripts themselves are often editions, in the sense that, at some point in their textual history, they added to the texts information about the author, date, and place of the original text's composition. For example, manuscripts of the Epistle to the Hebrews add to the epistle a variety of subscriptions:

Subscription	*Manuscript*[7]
To the Hebrews	04
To the Hebrews, he wrote from Rome	02
To the Hebrews, he wrote from Italy through Timothy	018
The epistle of the apostle Paul to the Hebrews, he wrote from Italy through Timothy	404

Many times, as here, the subscriptions themselves are copied and occasionally modified from earlier manuscripts. In this case, there is little question that the original subscription was simply "To the

---

[7] Manuscripts are referred to by their Gregory-Aland numbers, the main index of which is maintained by Kurt Aland (Aland, Welte et al. 1994).

Hebrews" and that later church traditions added information about its Pauline and Roman origin. But the earliest subscription was not part of the original text, probably being added when the letter was included in a collection of Pauline epistles circulating by the end of the first Christian century. All of these epistles were given simple titles referring to their destinations but not specifying the author— To the Romans, To the Corinthians, To the Galatians, . . ., To the Hebrews—and are grouped together in most manuscripts (Trobisch 2000). The subscription has a different textual history than the epistle itself.

Most English Bibles are translations of a critical text rather than any particular manuscript, but include in this critical textbook titles and authorship information that—even if accurate—was not original. The criterion of originality used for the text is replaced by criteria of accuracy and convenience for the titles. This makes sense, given that the book titles mainly serve as points of orientation, but it means that Bibles are really more than simple *translations*.

Finally, English Bibles vary in their canons. The early Christians adopted as their Scripture one of the then-current Jewish scriptures, the Septuagint. The Septuagint differed from the Hebrew scriptures in that it included both more books and longer versions of some books that existed also in the Hebrew collection. The church adopted the Septuagint as its "Old Testament." During the Reformation, under the influence of Renaissance sensibilities, the Protestants rejected all elements of the Septuagint that were not part of the Hebrew scriptures. The Roman Catholic Church, however, maintained these "apocryphal" books because they were part of its authorized version of the Bible, the Latin Vulgate. English Bibles, as a result, differ in the set of books they include depending on whether they are Catholic or Protestant in orientation. (The canon of the Ethiopian church is not represented in any English version of which I am aware.)

Those who would read, believe, and trust "the Bible," then, find themselves in an environment where multiple versions of "the Bible" are available. The question I consider here is what, given a bunch of texts described as "translations" or "versions" and a noun "the Bible," Bible believers think "the Bible" is. What sort of concept is "the Bible"? To what does it refer? What inferences does it generate?

Name

Consider first the obvious hypothesis that, for the people of Creekside Baptist, "the Bible" is a name, serving as the conventional way of referring to a particular text. On this hypothesis, they would regard "the Bible" as a proper noun, referring uniquely to some book.

As stated, this hypothesis is susceptible to two interpretations, owing to the ambiguity of the English "book":

(1) "The Bible" is the name of a particular text artifact, the physical artifact that is a particular copy of a text. This exemplar would then define the category "Bible": "Bibles" would then be "copies of" the Bible by virtue of some regular relation to this exemplar.
(2) "The Bible" is the name of an abstract text, but not any particular copy of that text. The text of the Bible would then define the category "Bible": "Bibles" would be those text-artifacts that stand in some regular relation to it.

I will consider these hypotheses in turn.

"The Bible" as Text Artifact

Let me start with facts, before moving to evangelical beliefs. Is there in fact some text-artifact to which all Bibles are related? There are several candidate answers worth considering here:

(1) The autographs. All biblical texts must have had some first copy, and all Bibles may therefore be said to be *genealogically related* to these originals. The genealogical relation, for texts, is not especially regular, but almost all of the Bibles in use at Creekside Baptist are closely related to the originals, as they are based on scholarly attempts to reconstruct the originals.
(2) Important manuscript witnesses. P^{46}, housed partly in the University of Michigan's papyrus collection, is the earliest copy of the Pauline letters, dating to c. 200. All attempts to reconstruct the autographs must at least reckon with this papyrus, and so they may be said to stand in some relation to it.

English Bibles do in fact stand in some relation to the autographs and to important textual witnesses like P^{46}, and it is a possibility worth considering that people use these as exemplars to define the category Bible. But this problem admits of another kind of answer as well.

(3) My first Bible. Another possibility is that at the core of every individual's Bible concept is the memory of the first Bible that individual encountered. For each individual, that first Bible is "the Bible," and serves as the measure of all subsequent "Bibles." Even though people would be basing their Bible concepts on different exemplars, the resemblance among these exemplars may suffice to generate similarity in their uses of the term "Bible."

I will consider the first two hypotheses together, inasmuch as the same kind of evidence is relevant to both, before turning to the third.

Manuscripts

One of the pastors of Creekside Baptist suggested to me in an interview that laypersons sometimes assume that behind Bible translations lay an actual *manuscript*:

> We did a Sunday school class ... about a year ago on what the Bible is and so I spent ... we just talked about that, I talked about the transmission of the biblical text. And the main reason I did that is because I just think that Christians should know, so that they can know how reliable it is, but they should also know that the New Testament in particular is a set of best readings. It's not like there's a manuscript out there that exists that *exactly* mirrors what the New Testament is. I find that that's more of a surprise to people. They've always thought it's a translation but they've never thought that it's a translation that's pieced together ... I just think there's a vast ignorance on the transmission of the [Bible].

This comment piqued my curiosity, and I began asking people, in interviews, *of what* did they think Bibles were translations? What did translators work with? The following is from an interview with Sidney, a 40 year old business owner who was heavily involved in church life.

Brian   If you think about a Bible, like this one right here [pointing to a Bible sitting next to us on an endtable in his living room], what is this Bible a translation of? When a committee goes to make this translation, what do they have in front of them?

Sidney   Well, at some point they had original manuscripts. Whether for this particular Bible they actually looked through original manuscripts or something that was taken from the original manuscripts, but the original documents would have been, original manuscripts. In the original languages.

Brian   But you think of them as looking at the manuscripts when they prepare this?

Sidney   That's a New International Version. Did they do that for the New International Version? Did they actually look at the papyrus, or did they look at, I'm sure some of them are very frail now and they probably don't have access to them. Are they looking at the actual papyrus? I don't know. Were they taking what someone else had done who had looked at the original papyrus? I don't know.

Brian   Can you tell me what you know about this original papyrus?

Sidney   There is a lot of different sources, and there are thousands of different manuscripts, most of which corroborate one another in great detail. Some are copies, and then there are copies made of the originals and so forth. There's the Q document in the New Testament and so forth is used, believed to have been used too. Is that what it is? Q?

Brian   In the Synoptic Gospels, yes.

Sidney   And, you know, they believe it is the basis of the Synoptic Gospels, but not John, type of thing, so . . . [his voice trails off]

Brian   What I'm trying to find out, is whether people think there is a particular manuscript lying behind translations? Whether somewhere there is an actual Hebrew and Greek manuscript that translations are made from?

Sidney   I don't think there's a *single* one. But there are hundreds and hundreds of early manuscripts that corroborate one another, that make up the whole New Testament. You know, there's bits and pieces here and there. At one point, did they all exist in one location? I don't know—I'd have to say probably not. Probably not in the original writings, they were by so many different people. I don't think they were ever put together until it was assembled in the 66 books that it is.

Brian   Do you know when that happened?

Sidney   The Middle Ages, wasn't it? That's pretty broad. [Laughter.] I was reading *The Case for Christ*, and it has a lot of that detail and it's, which I can't whip off the top of my head. [Laughter.] It's in the book. [Laughter.]

Sidney clearly had very vague ideas about what might lie behind modern translations like the NIV, and stated repeatedly that he did not know. Similar uncertainty was evident in an interview with a young woman who had attended the church for eight years.

Brian   What is the Bible a translation of? If I was to give you a regular English Bible and ask you what it is a translation of, could you tell me what you think it is a translation of?

Julie   It's a translation of the collection of works by the disciples of Jesus Christ, and some apostles, and prophets, I guess, of God, in the Old Testament.

Brian   Do you know what languages these are in?

Julie   Um, Greek, and I think there's some Latin?

Brian   Is there a Bible manuscript that underlies our Bible? What do the translators look at, when they sit down to do their translating, what do you think they're looking at?

Julie   Um, Dead Sea Scrolls.

Brian   Do you think they are sitting down with, just for an example, pictures of the Dead Sea Scrolls? When you envision it, what comes to mind?

Julie   Um, well since they're still assembling the Dead Sea Scrolls and fixing them, they must be looking at pictures of them because I assume there are pictures of them. Of course, it's already been done in English translations. And there are supposedly thousands of letters and . . . [her voice drifts off]

Julie had some idea of what manuscripts and processes lie behind English Bibles, but she knew few specifics. In her last answer, she resorts to inference rather than recall ("since . . . they must be . . . I assume . . ."), encounters a contradiction (they are still assembling the Dead Sea Scrolls, but English translations are already completed), before referring vaguely to "thousands of letters" without saying whose letters these are or whether these are many copies of the same letter or copies of many more letters than appear in the Bible.

Other interviewees gave similar responses. All recognized that English Bibles are translations, and most recognized that there were various manuscripts of the Bible, but none seemed to have more than vague ideas about how Bible versions are produced. The pastor's surmise, that people thought an actual manuscript lay behind English versions, was not particularly supported by the responses I received, not because people had some other well-defined view but because they had few ideas about it at all.

This is not to say that the relationship between modern Bibles and the autographs is unimportant to evangelicals. In evangelical doctrine, the authority of modern Bibles is derived from their status as the word of God revealed to ancient prophets and apostles, and so the authority of a Bible version is often linked to its accuracy. This evangelical doctrine contrasts with traditional Catholic doctrine from at least from the Council of Trent (1545–47, 1551–52, 1562–63 A.D.) to Vatican II (1952–1965 A.D.), according to which the official text of the church—the Vulgate ("the old Latin vulgate edition," Waterworth 1848: 17)—defined the Bible even over against earlier Hebrew and Greek manuscripts. This is connected with the longer-standing Roman Catholic doctrine that the authority of the scripture is derived from the authority of the church. Protestants, in elevating the authority of scripture over that of the church, linked the authority of the Bible to its status as God's word, i.e., the word of God revealed in a series of historical events. The reliability of modern Bibles as representations of the *texts* given in those events is therefore very important to evangelicals, and so modern English translations have eagerly taken advantage of advancements in textual criticism and philology (for an overview see Comfort 1990), and the most widely used critical edition of the Greek New Testament is a product of the International Bible Society designed to make the state of the art in New Testament textual scholarship available to translators (Aland, Aland et al. 1993). But their concern in these endeavors is to establish the *text* of the Bible, and not particularly to reconstruct the autographs as artifacts: they are not concerned particularly with the reconstruction of the autographs' number of columns and lines per column, size, hand, etc. (It might be objected that this information has been hopelessly lost to history, a point which must be conceded. Yet the fact that the text rather than all of these other features were copied suggests that the early copyists saw only the text of the autographs, rather than their other artifactual properties, as important.) I will consider the role of the autographs in establishing the biblical *text* below.

Overall, then, it is clear that the category "Bible" as used by the majority of people at Creekside Baptist is not anchored by reference to either autographs or important manuscript witnesses. Most of the people who use the term Bible do so without having any clear ideas about textual history or the translational processes.

My First Bible

The third version of the name-of-an-artifact hypothesis is that the concept Bible is defined by reference to the first copy of the Bible an individual uses.

There is evidence that the children of Creekside Baptist are intentionally exposed, early on, to most common artifactual features of Bibles. As part of the Sunday school curriculum, two-year-olds sing the *Pat the Bible* song. The children sit in a circle on carpet squares. The class size, during the time I observed, ranged from three to seven children, so the circles were always small. The lead teacher was a male in his forties. Sitting on a carpet square himself, he pulled out a plastic bin full of Gideon New Testaments. Gideon New Testaments are small, imitation-leather Bibles with gold lettering on the cover, a three-color picture of the American flag inside, and the King James Version text. Save for the ribbon marker, they fit the Bible stereotype exactly. They are nothing like the Bibles designed for children. The children came up and took a Bible each back to their carpet squares. Sometimes the teacher said, just before the *Pat the Bible* song: "God made my eyes to read his words. God made my hands to pat the Bible. Let's pat the Bible. We love the Bible."[8] The teacher and the students then sing a song together, all the while holding the little Bibles and patting their imitation leather covers. Four songs were used, each at a different time of the year:

Oh I Like to Pat the Bible (to the tune of *Did You Ever See a Lassie?*)
Oh I like to pat the Bible, the Bible, the Bible
Oh I like to pat the Bible with hands God gave me.
I'll pat-pat and pat-pat, I'll pat-pat and pat-pat,
Oh I like to pat the Bible with hands God gave me.

Pat the Bible (to the tune of *The Bus Song*)
The children in our class can pat pat pat
Pat pat pat, pat pat pat
The children in our class can pat pat pat
Pat the Holy Bible

Pat the Bible (to the tune of *Mulberry Bush*)
Oh it's fun to read the Bible
The Bible, the Bible
Oh it's fun to read the Bible
The Bible today
We read it, we learn it
We pat it, we love it
Oh it's fun to read the Bible
It is God's way.

---

[8] These are the words as prescribed in the lesson plan. Actual performances varied, of course, but were generally similar.

Pat the Bible (to the tune of *This Is The Way*)
This is the way we pat the Bible
Pat the Bible, pat the Bible
This is the way we pat the Bible
With our little hands

Sometimes the children held on to the Bibles through story time, other times they returned the Bibles to the plastic bin after the song. Once they had done this, the teacher prayed "Oh, Thank You God, for our hands to pat the Bible." *Pat the Bible* is a fun activity for two-year-olds, and those who are playing along do so (as is the way of two-year-olds) with relish.

The purpose of the *Pat the Bible* song is not necessarily to acquaint children with the stereotypical look and feel of Bibles. I interviewed the Director of Christian Education about the goals of the two-year-old curriculum.

Brian   What are some key things you try to teach kids about the Bible?
Mary   Well, let's see, for the very youngest child it's just to love that book, treat it very, very specially, up to the children who can go right to a particular book of the Bible, finding it. In other words, well if you can't use the book, what good is it? So there is that gamut of just the physical book itself, and then understanding how the books are divided into certain sections, and then knowing that there are different interpretations, and there's just all kinds of things, and I could probably go from the two's on up to fifth graders let's say, and each class would have some different goals, and of course carry along the other goals that they learned before. Do you want more specifics?
Brian   Sure, let's start with the two's. What are the goals for teaching the two's?
Mary   Well, like I say, respecting that book. And how do you respect it as a two year old? Well, they pat the Bible. You may remember that [from helping out in the class]: they pat the Bible. And that is showing love and respect and care for something. Otherwise what do you do with a book? Well, you throw it on the floor or you scribble in the pages. At two, that's the kind of thing that can be done. But no, you don't do that with *this* particular book. And of course we do that with small ones. We use actually New Testaments because they are small and the young child can hold them easily.
Brian   Do you select them at all because they look a lot like an adult Bible? Was that a factor in your selection of them?
Mary   Um, actually I don't, all the New Testaments that I know are going to look about the same. The New Testaments that I know all look pretty much the same, whether it's the Gideons or some other pub-

lisher. So, it's selected because of it's size.... Think about that little two year old hand. They really need something that they can hold and cradle in their hand. And that is on purpose in the curriculum.

Clearly, the diminutive size of the Gideon New Testaments is paramount in their selection for the *Pat the Bible* song. (The fact that they were probably free would not hurt either.) Yet the object of the lesson—to teach children to love and respect the Bible in particular, differently from other books—depends on the identifiability of Bibles. Whether or not this activity is designed to acquaint two-year-olds with the stereotypical characteristics of Bibles, it has this effect. Long before they can read the Bible, and well before they will have their own (very different) Bibles, these children were learning what adult Bibles look—and feel—like.

This sort of artifactual knowledge is instilled by early contacts with Bibles, and one might imagine that "the Bible" is taken by these children to be the name of the particular artifact held in hand, and that all other Bibles are identified as such by virtue of their resemblance to this one.

But if the stereotypical appearance of Bibles makes a lasting impression on these children, it does not amount to a *definition*. One of the curriculum goals for three-year-olds is to have them bring their own Bibles. Not all of them do, but, in the time I observed, *not a single child* brought a Gideon New Testament or any Bible that looked like one to the three-year-olds' Sunday school class. In fact, most of them brought children's Bibles, books that bear only a very abstract similarity either to the Gideon New Testament or to any other adult Bible. (They didn't even have the flag, the feature most studied by two-year-olds in the Gideon Bibles.) Moreover, when children enter first grade, they are given a NIV Adventure Bible, which is hardbound with a purple and gold cover. I found, in short, no evidence that children categorize Bibles by their similarity to Bibles encountered early on. While I do think that the stereotypical appearance of Bibles leaves a lasting impression on these children, it does not amount to a definition.

"The Bible" therefore does not seem to be the name of an artifact, whether autograph or manuscript or first Bible. The people of Creekside Baptist do not know enough about textual history or translation to identify Bibles on this basis, and they admit too many exemplars into the Bible category to be defining that category in terms of the first Bible they encounter. I turn now to the second interpretation of the Bible-as-name hypothesis, the claim that "the Bible" is a name not of a physical book but of a text.

"The Bible" as Text

The name-of-a-text hypothesis is subtly different from the name-of-an-artifact hypothesis. On the name-of-an-artifact hypothesis, "the Bible" is the name of an exemplar, a particular physical book, and the category Bible (as in "a Bible" and "Bibles") is defined by some regular relation to that exemplar. The category Bible, on this view, is organized around an exemplar, and other books' inclusion in the category Bible is derivative. The name-of-a-text hypothesis, in contrast, is an abstract category definition. A book is a Bible if it meets the criterion of having a particular text, and all copies of that text have the same sort of claim to category membership—no one copy defines the category. Thus the objection that there is no particular physical exemplar at the core of the Bible category—the stumbling block of the name-of-an-artifact hypothesis—is avoided by this view.

The notion of "text" used here is nicely captured by the Oxford English Dictionary's primary definition of the word: "The wording of anything written or printed; the structure formed by the words in their order; the very words, phrases, and sentences as written." This definition is biased toward highly literate societies in two ways. The first—the explicit restriction of the notion of text to written works—is normally recognized as a bias. But a second, more subtle, bias is not always identified: the very possibility of two text artifacts, equivalent in their wording, arises only with the advent of advanced print technology. (I say the possibility arises not because the exact replication of a lengthy text from one artifact to another is *absolutely* impossible in the absence of print, but because, even despite scrupulous precautions, it is *nearly* impossible, and does not describe the normal state of affairs except partially in one or two remarkable cases.) If, in the face of actual variation, text artifacts (e.g., manuscripts of the Iliad) are regarded as tokens of a type (e.g., the Iliad), people are doing something more than simply describing the environment.

Nonetheless, like the name-of-an-artifact hypothesis, the notion that "the Bible" is the name of a text must be examined with respect to several different texts.

(1) The text of the autographs. On this view, "the Bible" is the name of the original text, and this text then functions to define the category Bible.
(2) The text of a particular English version. On this view, "the Bible" is a particular translation, all copies of which are "Bibles."

I will consider each of these in turn.

Text of the Autographs

In the earlier consideration of the name-of-autographs hypothesis, I noted that evangelicals relate the authority of the Bible to ancient revelation-events, and that it is very important to them that English Bibles be faithful representations of the texts then revealed. The argument against the name-of-the-autographs hypothesis was that the people of Creekside Baptist have only vague and uncertain ideas about the autographs, and that these ideas are not rich enough to define the category "Bible" in relation to this exemplar.

Yet it is still possible that evangelicals define Bibles as copies of the autographs' text. Such a definition is compatible with very vague and uncertain ideas about the events of revelation, the autographs, the history of the Bible, or the process of translation. It would require no more than the definition of a text, perhaps only assumed to be the text of the autographs. (Indeed, given that the autographs are lost, it could *only* be an assumption that a particular text is the autographic text.)

I did find some evidence that the people of Creekside Baptist imagine that a particular original-language text lies behind English translations. During a 9:30 AM Sunday school class with 35–40 attendees, volunteers had just finished taking turns reading the text aloud for the class. A woman read John 1:19–27; a man, 1:29–34; and another man, 1:35–51. The discussion began with the Sunday school teacher noting that the woman had read "Bethabara" in 1:28, whereas the NIV has "Bethany." The name of the translation the woman was using was never mentioned, but I could see she was using the MacArthur Study Bible (MacArthur 1997), which is available in the New King James Version, and the NKJV does indeed read "Bethabara" there. The Sunday school teacher said, "This is a translation issue." I thought this odd, given that names are not usually translated, and quickly consulted the critical apparatus of my *Novum Testamentum Graece* (Nestle, Nestle et al. 1985), which showed that Bethabara was an old and well-attested reading. I spoke up, "The manuscripts vary here." The teacher then said to the class, "That's why it's good to have Brian in class—he has the original! So it's a translation issue..." and he proceeded to discuss the location of Bethany.

The difference between the NKJV text read aloud and the NIV text on which he had based his preparation had surprised the teacher, and he dismissed the difference as a "translation issue." When I suggested it was due to variation in the textual tradition, he seemed to take my comment as an *elaboration* of what he said rather than as an *alternative* explanation of the difference. This is suggested also by his reference to my Greek New Testament as "the original"—as if there was a single underlying text of which "Bethany" and "Bethabara" were alternate *translations*.

If churchgoers have gotten the impression that a particular text lies behind the different Bible versions, it is probably partly due to the way in which preachers' refer to the underlying Hebrew and Greek. The following is drawn from the sermon preached on January 11, 1998 at Creekside Baptist:

> [Mark 1:14–15] says that "after John was put in prison, Jesus went into Galilee and he proclaimed the good news of God."[9] Interesting phrase—"Good news of God"—that is just as ambivalent in English as it is in the original. What does that mean? It could mean "Good news originating in God"—"of God" in that way—or it could mean "Good news about God"—"Good news of God." And, in the Greek, it can be either way too. And I choose to think that perhaps here it is both. It is good news which originates in God from God and it's about God as well.

The foregoing comment implies two things of relevance to the hypothesis under consideration. First, reference to "the Greek" is a bit misleading. There are in fact two well attested Greek texts of the ending of Mark 1:14:

---

[9] The passage as quoted differs slightly from the actual text, which the pastor had just read aloud: "After John was put in prison, Jesus went into Galilee proclaiming the good news of God..."

- τὸ εὐαγγέλιον τοῦ θεοῦ ("the good news of God")
- τὸ εὐαγγέλιον **τῆς βασιλείας** τοῦ θεοῦ ("the good news **of the kingdom** of God")[10]

By "the Greek," the preacher probably had in mind the Greek text of his copy of the Greek New Testament, which he would recognize as an eclectic text, but which his audience would probably understand as the text of the autographs (as they understood my *Novum Testamentum Graece*). The preacher's passing reference was not quite deceptive, but between his understanding of "the Greek" and his audience's lay the entire history of the Bible.

Second, the preacher, when confronted with ambiguity in the English translation (NIV), implied that "the Greek" might resolve the ambiguity. Although in this case it did not, the reasoning in his comment suggests that it might have. "The Greek" was thus assigned a kind of primacy in determining the text's meaning. This was not purely a result of the English text's ambiguity: in other instances the same preacher appealed to "the Greek" over against the English translation, as in the following discussion on Romans 12:1–2, from October 18, 1998:

> And Paul [the author of Romans] even says that's "your logical response." There are some translations which say in that verse that it's "your spiritual worship," but really the basic underlying meaning there is it's your logical response to what God's done for you. And then, Paul, and here we get a little Greek lesson which I keep reminding you about, but this is in a tense which speaks about a once-for-all decisive sort of decision, an action. "I beg you, present—once and for all." "Get it settled, do it, present your bodies as living sacrifices."

Here the preacher, faced with slightly different semantics of the Greek and English, assigned to the original language texts a kind of primacy in relation to English-language Bibles. (This of course seems quite reasonable when dealing with translations, but only from within a certain epistemology of texts, which should not be taken for granted.)

It appears, therefore, that the people of Creekside Baptist assume that there is a single original-language text underlying the Bibles they

---

[10] Bruce Metzger, one of the committee members who developed the Greek text used by the preacher, comments on this passage in his *Textual Commentary on the Greek New Testament* (1994): "The insertion of τῆς βασιλείας was obviously made by copyists in order to bring the unusual Markan phrase into conformity with the much more frequently used expression "the kingdom of God" (cf. ver. 15)."

use, and that this text has a kind of primacy with respect to English Bibles. The next question is whether this underlying text functions cognitively to define the category "Bible."

I tried to test this with five informants. I held an English Bible in one hand and some other book—my notebook or any other book that was handy—in the other hand and asked if one of these two books was "the Bible." Informants invariably (1) looked at me as if I was a raving lunatic and (2) pointed to the Bible. I then took an English Bible in each hand and asked whether one of these two books was "the Bible," to which informants invariably replied that they were both Bibles. I said, "No, I mean *the* Bible." They invariably said, "They're *both* Bibles." I then held a Greek New Testament in one hand and an English Bible in the other and asked if the Greek New Testament was *the* Bible. (I asked them to imagine that the Greek New Testament was the very one used for the translation in the English Bible.) They always replied that it was "*a* Bible," but were unwilling to call it "*the* Bible." Their responses were the same when an English and an original language text were compared as when two English versions were compared. I only carried this out a few times, in an exploratory fashion, and the results might be variously interpreted, but my impression is that while the Greek text may be preferred in matters of semantics, it was no more "the Bible" than the English Bibles. Moreover, they thought the whole line of questioning quite strange, and had difficulty understanding what I was asking—not what one would expect if I was accessing a concept already in place. "The Bible" does not therefore seem to be the name of the autographic text.

An English Version

The next hypothesis is that "the Bible" is the name of some English text. The text might be selected in a couple of ways:

- It might be stipulated on doctrinal grounds. "The Bible," on this view, is the name of a particular translation.
- It might be the first Bible text read. Perhaps "the Bible" is taken to be the name of the first text a person hears called "the Bible" and reads. Once again, convergence among Bible categories would be the result of similarity between first Bibles.

Of these two means of selection, some readers will recognize the first as the condition that seems to obtain among "KJV-Only" advocates, those who believe that the King James Version of 1611 (also known as the Authorized Version) is the very word of God and reject all other English translations. First, however, I will consider the name-of-a-version hypothesis in the context of Creekside Baptist Church.

Creekside Baptist Church

Creekside Baptist is a community in which a number of different Bibles are in use. In a Sunday morning survey conducted on May 21, 2000, I asked attendees how many Bibles they owned, which versions they owned, and which they primarily used. The survey was conducted during Sunday school classes, which ran concurrently with church services. 84 responses were received, from nearly everyone age twelve and over who attended Sunday school classes that day. Missed in the survey were those adults who were involved in teaching young children's Sunday school classes, those involved in running the church service, and those who attended only the church service.

The people of Creekside Baptist own a lot of Bibles. Preliminary interviews suggested that, for the determination of effective access to Bibles, the most natural unit of Bible ownership was the household rather than the individual, inasmuch as members of a household readily made use of each others' Bibles. The survey question thus asked how many Bibles people had in their household, and respondents wrote in their answers. While most people gave specific numbers, a few wrote in verbal quantifiers. "A lot" was coded as 10; "several," as 4. The results are given in Figure 2.

The numbers given in Figure 2, while accurately representing survey answers, must be regarded as only approximate. It was difficult for people to count, from memory, the number of Bibles in their households. The number 10, either alone or as part of a range (e.g., "10 or more," "10–12") figures in 24 responses, strongly suggesting that people were rounding off their estimates of the numbers of Bibles in their households. On the other hand, it is clear that the average number of Bibles per household must be large. Those people who had between one and four Bibles in their households usually gave specific numbers, suggesting that they were counting rather than

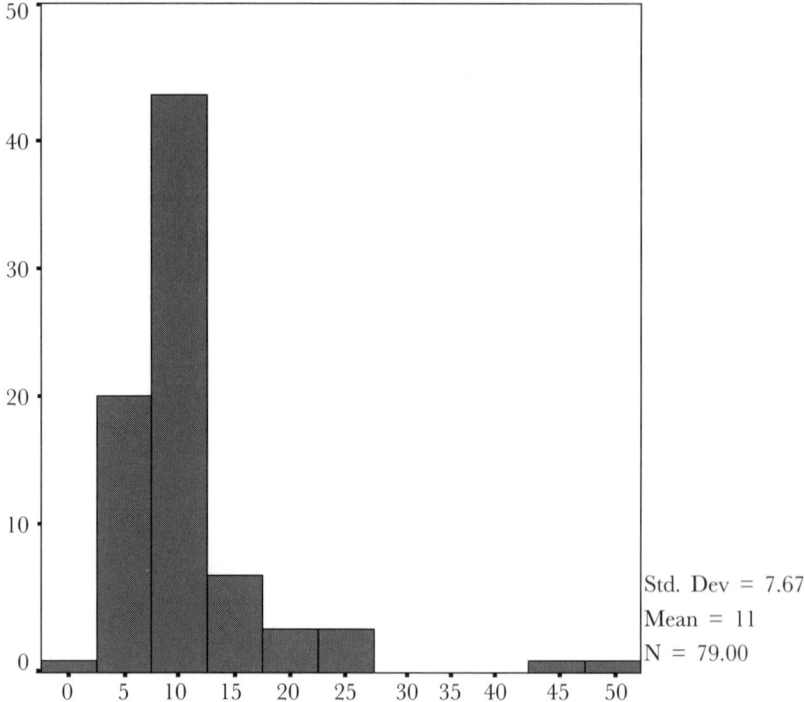

Figure 2: Number of Bibles per household

estimating. These numbers may therefore be regarded as more accurate than the larger ones. Conversely, however, there was a tendency—apparent from subsequent interviews—for people to overlook infrequently used Bibles: one man, who initially reported owning four Bibles, emailed me later that day saying that when he went home and counted, he had seventeen!

My initial impulse was to discard reports of 45 and 50 Bibles, on the assumption that such answers were forms of non-cooperation with the survey. Yet subsequent interviews suggested that such figures were not unreasonable for those who stockpile cheap Bibles for evangelistic distribution. One man told me that he and his wife would periodically purchase cases of Bibles from the International Bible Society to have on hand for the purpose of distributing to interested friends and acquaintances. It is therefore quite possible that these figures are accurate, if rounded. The central tendency of the responses therefore remains: the people of Creekside Baptist Church have a lot of Bibles.

More importantly, for consideration of the name-of-an-English-version hypothesis, they have a number of *different* Bibles. 79 people indicated which versions of the Bible they currently own or have owned.

Version	Number of Respondents
The New International Version	76
The King James Version	63
The Living Bible	45
The New American Standard	43
The Revised Standard Version	29
The New King James Version	27
The New Revised Standard Version	23
The New Living Translation	15
The Amplified Bible	14
The Contemporary English Version	14
The Message	13
The Good News Bible	7
J. B. Phillips' New Testament	4
The New English Version	3
The Discovery Bible	2
The Revised English Version	2
William Barclay's New Testament	2
The 20th Century Version	1
The Geneva Bible	1
The Revised New English Bible	1
The Revised Webster's Translation	1
The Word	1
Young's Literal Translation	1

Although the New International Version is far and away the most popular version at Creekside Baptist—in a separate item fully 75% of respondents reported that it was the primary version they used—most of the people had other versions that they occasionally read.

In interviews I inquired about how these different versions were used. Some people had different versions in different places in their home or workplace, and read indifferently from whichever was convenient. Others kept several versions together and, although primarily using one, occasionally consulted the others. They told me that they sometimes would consult several versions in order to "get a different perspective" or to "see it put another way." The following excerpt is from an interview with a man who occasionally used a variety of different versions and clearly enjoyed comparing them.

Scott   I have several Bibles and I have like a bookshelf, like a little section in that room [his reading room] where I keep the Bibles I'm reading. And usually I'll read a paraphrase like *The Message*. I like *The Message* because it makes me think in a new way about things. I don't always agree with his interpretations and his paraphrase, but... And then I probably use the NIV more than any [other] one [version], and I like the RSV too, not the new ones but the older ones.... I still have a Bible called the, I have a Jerusalem Bible, it's got kind of a Catholic slant to it, and then I've got, I bought a long time ago a quadrophonic New Testament, it's got four versions together...
Brian   A parallel Bible?
Scott   Yes, and that's fun to kind of see how the *Amplified*, the *New English*, the RSV, and I think the other one's a *Living Bible*, all right together.

Many of the adults with whom I talked had used several different versions over their life spans, such that they had memorized passages from the King James Version, read from the Revised Standard Version as young adults, and now used the New International Version.

A plurality of versions in use does not necessarily count against the name-of-a-version hypothesis, because one might imagine that while a particular version defines "the Bible," interested readers consult other versions as commentaries. On this view, the NIV, for instance, might really be "the Bible," but a person might have an NRSV to consult on difficult passages. The NRSV, in this case, would be considered a lesser Bible, not on a par with *the* Bible.

Yet this sort of ranking of versions is quite alien to normal practice at Creekside Baptist. Indeed, versional differences are practically celebrated, even in the most formal of all church contexts, the Sunday morning service.

Liturgical Bible reading at Creekside Baptist is usually carried out by regular attendees rather than church officials. Readers are typically contacted a week or so in advance of the service in which they are asked to read. The pastor asks them if they would be willing to read a particular passage. The reading is performed, in the order of service, shortly before the sermon. The reader walks from a pew to the front, and often begins with an introductory formula—most commonly, "Hear the word of the Lord"—and sometimes an identification of the passage to be read. The reader then reads the Bible passage, speaking into a microphone, as many in the audience follow along in their own Bibles, simultaneously listening and reading. The reading often concludes with "This has been the word of the Lord" or some similar phrase.

In interviews, I asked several people who had done the liturgical scripture reading about their preparation for reading. Their preparation ranged from merely reading over the passage ahead of time to a careful comparison of different versions and different intonations in reading the text. Some selected the NIV (used by the pastor) or a similar version, so as to provide listeners with the text to be preached upon. Others, focusing more on the impact of the reading itself, chose freer translations or even paraphrases. The purpose of choosing such translations was to enable the audience to hear the familiar text "in a new way," to be jarred into seeing it "from a different perspective."

To see how significant this impulse was for the practice of the church, I examined the liturgical Bible reading in 49 Sunday morning services from 1998. Of the 57 liturgical scripture reading events in these services, 42 were carried out by lay readers. In one instance, the same man read twice during the same service, and inasmuch as these two instances amount to a single choice of version, I have counted them together, reducing the total to 41. Given that the NIV is the preferred Bible of 75% of the congregation, I would expect this version to be selected at least 75% of the time. Yet the NIV was used only 65% of the time, suggesting that at least some of the time readers were indeed purposely selecting unusual versions.

This interpretation receives further support from several further considerations. First, some of the people who read from versions other than the NIV customarily used the NIV as their preferred version. Second, four of the readings were taken from Eugene Peterson's *The Message* (1995), a paraphrase that has become popular for its restatement of biblical ideas in modern terms—a particularly effective way of putting a passage in a new light. Third, both the NIV and other versions were sometimes introduced with formulas describing the text as "the word of the Lord" or "God's word." Finally, this conscious eclecticism is manifest also in Sunday school practices, where different translations of a difficult passage are sometimes explicitly compared. Taken together, these considerations strongly suggest that no particular English version defines the Bible at Creekside Baptist Church.

While use of multiple versions is common among American evangelicals, there are groups which use only a single English translation.

In some places this is simply a matter of preference, but in other churches the exclusive use of the King James Version is actually a matter of doctrine. In institutions where the King James Version is used exclusively, and other versions are actively rejected, the name-of-an-English-version hypothesis might fare better than it does at Creekside Baptist, and so the KJV-Only advocates merit special consideration in this regard.

KJV-Only

The KJV-Only debate traces its origin to the publication of the Revised Version of 1881 and its adoption of the Greek New Testament of Westcott and Hort. Westcott and Hort's new critical text marked the advent of modern textual criticism, and was perceived by some as a radical departure from the traditional New Testament reflected in the King James Version of 1611. Most of the differences were small, but they were enough to arouse the ire of the influential John Burgon, Dean of Chichester, who wrote a number of vitriolic tirades against the "new" Bible (collected in Burgon 1990). Burgon's central contentions were that the Majority text (the Greek text underlying the KJV New Testament) providentially preserved that of the autographs (the use of the Masoretic text for the Old Testament was then regarded as secure), and the King James Version was the best translation available of that text.

The debate has been renewed in recent years both in the form of a defense of the Majority text (for theoretical justification see Hodges 1968; for reviews and critiques see Fee 1978; Pickering 1981; for a critical edition see Hodges and Farstad 1985; Wallace 1994) and as an attack on the spate of new translations and revisions that have appeared in the last few decades, most notably the New International Version. Criticism of new Bibles has focused on allegedly heretical "changes to the Bible." Among the most vocal "defenders" of the King James Version have been David Fuller (1975), Edward Hills (1984 [1956]), Gail Riplinger (1993; 1994) and Peter Ruckman (1964; 1983; 1988; 1990).

One of the central rhetorical devices of KJV-Only advocates is to compare the text of the new Bibles with that of the King James Version. The central argument of these works is to suggest that the changes are concessions to various heresies, secularism, or New Age religion. The following is taken from Gail Riplinger's *New Age Bible Versions* (1993: 56–57), one of the more influential KJV-Only books:

Perhaps the most shocking discovery of my research was the admission by the New Age movement and esoteric community that there is, in fact, an occult version of the "Our Father" and it has found its way into Luke 11:2 in the new versions.

Riplinger then provides a comparison of Luke 11:2–4:

KJV	NIV, NASB, et al.
Our Father **which art in heaven**	Father
Hallowed be thy name	Hallowed be your name
Thy Kingdom come	Your kingdom come
Thy will be done, as in heaven, so on earth	
Give us this day our daily bread	Give us each day our daily bread
And forgive us our sins	Forgive us our sins
For we also forgive everyone that is indebted to us	For we also forgive everyone who sins against us.
And lead us not into temptation	And lead us not into temptation
But deliver us from evil	

After which she comments:

> The bold sections on the left indicate the words and sections which have been removed from the prayer in all modern versions, such as the NIV, NASB, *Living Bible*, NRSV, *Good News for Modern Man*, *New Century Version*, *The New American Bible*, and *The New Jerusalem Bible*. They are *the* very words which distinguish "Our" Father "in heaven" who "delivers us from evil" from "your father the devil" [John 8.44], who is "the god of . . . this present world."[11]

The structure of her critique is clear: the differences between the KJV and the modern versions are of a sinister sort.

Initially, this sort of argument seems to suggest that "the Bible" may be simply identified with the King James Version, especially since the KJV is being used as the standard for a true Bible. Yet on closer examination, Riplinger's argument does not support this identification. Note that she does not object to textual differences *per se*, such as are evident in virtually every line of the prayer above. Her objection is to textual differences where she thinks she can discern a Satanic agenda to misdirect prayers. The problem with new versions, according to Riplinger, is that they do not *mean the same thing* as the KJV. Even for Riplinger, "the Bible" is not *defined* by

---

[11] Although this last quotation sounds biblical, I have been unable to discover its source even with the aid of computer searches.

the KJV: she argues not against *textual* departure from the KJV, but against (putative) differences in *meaning*—a point to which I shall return below.

* * *

"The Bible" is not a name, or at least not the name *of anything*. It is worth noting that "the Bible" has all the linguistic characteristics of a generic noun: it can take the indefinite article—"a Bible"; and it can take adjectives between the definite article and the noun, as it does in the titles *The Holy Bible*, *The Amplified Bible*, and *The Good News Bible*. Among evangelicals, "the Bible" is not a proper noun, not a name.

But there is surely something name-like about "the Bible," and it is patent that most Bibles incorporate "the Bible" into their titles. "The Bible" seems rather like a meta-name, a naming template that is normally tailored in the course of application—e.g., *The New American Standard Bible*, *The Amplified Bible*—but which is not obligatory—e.g., *The Word*, *The Message*, *My Book—God*. This naming template aids readers in recognizing Bibles by their titles, and helps create the intuition that there really is something called "the Bible."

Category

If "the Bible" is not a name, then a second major hypothesis is that "the Bible" is a *category*, that is, a group of objects that are treated, in one respect or another, as an equivalence class. If the Bible is a category, then what objects are classified together, on what basis are they so classified, and in what sense are they treated as equivalent?

The set of objects classified as Bibles is, in most instances, quite clear. A list of Bibles would be sizable: I collected advertisements for English language Bibles from 1997–1999, and came up with advertisements for almost two hundred distinct editions. (This number does not include, however, special editions, those from some smaller publishers, those sold only in bulk, or those for institutional use.) Such a list, however, would seriously misrepresent American evangelicals' Bible concept, for they do not memorize a list of all the different books that count as Bibles. Rather, they have heuristics for determining whether a book is a Bible. Whether a book is a Bible is inferred from general principles and specific environmental cues. In an interview, I asked a man how, if I gave him a book and asked him whether it was a Bible, he would go about deciding. He shrugged and said, "Well, I would look at the title. But if it didn't say Bible, I would flip through it and look for things I recognize."

"Like what?" I asked.

"Well, like words at the top of the page . . . the names, or chapter breaks, you know, those headings that tell you what's in the passage" he said, referring to the fact that book and chapter references are placed at the top of the page in most printed Bibles, and that most Bibles also intersperse the text with section headings. (Section headings are usually more frequent than chapter divisions, but do often occur at chapter breaks.) The mere presence of headers and passage summaries would provide a clue that he was looking at a Bible, and would also give him a good idea of its contents.

"And then?" He stared at me for a moment, no doubt trying to comprehend what on earth I might be after in asking about such a bizarre situation. I added, "Suppose there was still reason to doubt it was a Bible."

"I guess if I still couldn't tell I would look up some verses I know, to see what it said. If it was close to what I expected—not exactly, you know—then I would assume it was a Bible."

"And after that, if there was still doubt?"

"I don't know."

Other informants described similar heuristics. In the contemporary U.S., it is normally quite clear, on even the most cursory inspection, whether a book is a Bible. Indeed, Bibles are usually highly marked volumes. I had hoped that, once the heuristics were exhausted, informants would finally give a definition of the Bible, such that, in the scenario I posed, they would know decisively whether the book was a Bible. In a sense, they did, but it took me a while to recognize their answer.

If heuristics and publishing conventions work together to delineate the Bible's extension, then what about the category's intension? How is this category conceptualized by American evangelicals?

The Bible as Text

In interviews, I inquired systematically whether a Bible might be rendered in various media. A Bible may be printed, read aloud, memorized, or recorded on CD-ROM, but it cannot be danced or shaped out of clay. Could it be a radio transmission traveling through outer space? It could. A video-recorded enactment of the Bible, however, would not be a Bible. Neither would a series of pictures, such as those found in church paintings or stained-glass windows. The Bible is a text: Bibles must be made out of words. These words may be inscribed in any medium or any encoding scheme whatsoever, but it must be *words* that are so encoded.

The specification of the Bible as a text has an important consequence for the way this category is organized. The most obvious way to specify a text is to reproduce it. The Bible might then be represented by its full text, from the first sentence to the last: "In the beginning God created... The grace of our Lord Jesus Christ be with you all. Amen." This way of conceptualizing the Bible is, of course, impractical: the Bible is far too lengthy to be memorized entire, though many people have memorized particular passages and I have heard tales of people committing large sections to memory. Still, it would, in principle, be possible to use sample passages to identify a book as a Bible.

But any definition that turned on the precise wording of a Bible would exclude all but one version, and I showed above that the people of Creekside Baptist Church practically celebrate versional variation.

A paradox therefore arises: American evangelicals conceive of the Bible as a text, but also know that the different Bible texts differ. "The Bible" is a text, but no specific text.

The Bible as Meaning

Texts not only *say* things, but very often also *mean* things, and usually it is the meaning of the Bible that interests evangelicals. ("Meaning" is here understood as a concept in (Western?) folk hermeneutic theory. Roughly, we use the term "meaning" to describe the set of inferences most regularly and reliably generated by a text. This set of inferences is reified and treated as a property of the text. Because this folk hermeneutic theory provides the terms in which American evangelicals think about the Bible, I will use it here. Below, where a more adequate theory is required, I will introduce some refinements.)

Textual critics are interested in the text *per se*. They will try to distinguish which of two semantically identical texts is more likely original. Their specialty, however, is arcane and, frankly, boring to most evangelicals. Most evangelicals can understand the need for textual criticism, but only insofar as the meaning of a text is in question. Few are interested in sorting out which of two semantically identical variants is likely to be original. Their interest in texts has to do primarily with their meaning.

It is with respect to their meaning that Bibles are considered alike. The people of Creekside Baptist take the semantic differences between versions to be minimal. The following excerpt is taken from an interview with Tom, a middle-aged business owner from the church. He distinguishes between versions and paraphrases, and while he thinks he can detect the biases in paraphrases, he feels less sure about those in versions.

Brian What do you think are the major differences between Bible versions?
Tom Well, you don't mean paraphrases do you, or do you?
Brian Let's include paraphrases.
Tom Paraphrases, I think. Well, take the *Living Bible*. It's a Baptist Bible, I think. It comes from a very Baptist slant. It emphasizes those things that are Baptist a little more than others. So I think that the paraphrases tend to interject . . . well, first of all they're usually done by a person, Peterson [author of *The Message*, a recent and popular paraphrase] or the guy who did the *Living Bible*. What's his name? I can't remember. He's a Baptist. No question about it. And Peterson has a certain slant. So I think the main differences—I think they take their theology into their interpretation. All of us do, I think, unless we have—what I hope I have—is a growing—a word people hate anymore—but a *tentative* theology that keeps . . . not changing in its central premises, but shifting a little bit as time goes on. I find myself doing that. I probably am frighteningly getting more liberal as I get older. Not liberal in the sense that just throw everything out, but being more graceful and less judging, and not so quick, snap to judgment. And sometimes that bothers me because I know that in evangelical circles that's not, for some people, a very acceptable way to be. You should toe the line. But your question about . . . now I don't know, now knowing that the more formal translations are agonized over by many people, I can't see a whole lot of, well word selection, when you get down to a word, you know, why did they do that here in the NIV and this in the RSV, that piques my curiosity, but I couldn't say I see a slant to the RSV that I don't see in the NIV. I'm not that good a scholar to know the difference. But I know how they do it, because I've had professors who've been on the NIV [translation committee]. I mean they just do one section of one book for *years*. They're on this committee evaluating, and I guess I take their word pretty quickly, you know?

Tom does not deny that versions have biases—he thinks that if he were more of a scholar he might be able to detect them—but that the biases are so minor that they do not substantially affect the meaning of the text. Given the denominational diversity of most recent translation committees (which he subsequently mentioned), his assessment is largely correct. He is much less sanguine about paraphrases, though he told me that he often finds Peterson's helpful. (Despite the fact that he attends a Baptist church, he does not particularly like the *Living Bible*, which he thinks has a Baptist slant. Such generic evangelical (non-denominationally-specific) feeling is common at Creekside Baptist.) The differences between versions are acknowledged, but felt to be relatively inconsequential with respect to the text's meaning.

Evangelicals are quite surprised in those few cases where Bible versions have different meanings. Consider James 4:5. The Greek text underlying this verse is very obscure, and honest translators differ as to what it might mean. Here are readings from two versions represented at Creekside Baptist:

New International Version	*New American Standard Version*
Or do you think Scripture says without reason that the spirit he caused to live in us envies intensely?	Or do you think that the Scripture speaks to no purpose: "He jealously desires the Spirit which He has made to dwell in us"?

These versions give two plausible interpretations of the underlying Greek text (ἢ δοκεῖτε ὅτι κενῶς ἡ γραφὴ λέγει· πρὸς φθόνον ἐπιποθεῖ τὸ πνεῦμα ὃ κατῴκισεν ἐν ἡμῖν); both versions note the other possibility in the margin.

I came across this passage when I had been asked to teach a Sunday school lesson on James 4:1–12. Although I personally enjoy thinking about textual problems of this sort, most evangelical lay people do not, and the responsible thing to do was to note the problem without drawing undue attention to it. The purpose of the class was to reflect on the meaning of scripture for people's lives, not to worry about unresolved translation problems. However, in talking informally with a friend who attends a different church, I brought it up. My friend is a Bible believer, a fundamentalist, and a very careful reader. He studied the different renditions for a moment, turned to me and exclaimed, "They contradict each other!" While I do not think he lost any sleep over it, he was surprised and momentarily disturbed. Like most Bible believers, he regards God's word as perfectly accessible through our English versions. The variance, evidence of their imperfection as translations, bothered him a bit.

Textual differences *per se* do not bother most evangelicals. As noted, the people of Creekside Baptist use them to open interpretive possibilities. Differences of meaning are more disturbing, because they threaten the equivalence of Bibles, the meaning with respect to which all Bibles are regarded as equal.

The category Bible, then, has a curious structure. Ontologically, Bibles are conceived as texts. But the sense in which they are considered equivalent has to do with their meaning, not with any specific feature of the texts *per se*.

It might be objected that evangelicals interpret the Bible in various ways, and know that they interpret the Bible in various ways. Differences between individuals' interpretations, however, are not at issue here. In fact, it does not matter in this regard *what* they think the text means. What matters is that each individual regards different Bibles as equivalent with respect to *whatever* that person thinks of as their contents—that no one thinks his interpretation is an interpretation only of a particular Bible. In fact, the meaning may not be defined at all: merely the presumption of common meaning would suffice. Meaning is the property in respect of which Bibles are grouped as an equivalence class, but the requisite meaning may be nothing more than a placeholder.

The NIVI Debate

The arguments that developed, among evangelical Christians, around the proposed American edition of the *New International Version: Inclusive Language Edition* (NIVI) illustrate the critical role of meaning for evangelical judgments about textual equivalence. An uproar erupted in 1997 when *World Magazine* reported, in a cover article entitled "Femme fatale" (Olasky 1997), that the International Bible Society, which produced the *New International Version*, and Zondervan Publishers were producing a revision of the NIV in which "man" was replaced by "people" or similar generic terms in those passages where the intent of the text in the original languages is not gender specific (see Carson 1998 for a history of the NIVI debate). The author of the article, Susan Olasky, attributed the not-yet-announced NIVI (she called it the "stealth Bible") to quiet inroads that feminism was making in conservative Christian circles by covering it together with other "feminist" developments such as churches not only allowing female elders and pastors but ostracizing those who held to more traditional views. By announcing the proposed NIVI before the translators and publisher and portraying itself as a decryer of moral compromise, *World Magazine* was able to excite fears far beyond what the proposed textual changes might seem to merit in themselves.

Two camps quickly developed as letters to the editor, articles, and press releases flew. In defense of the NIVI were the Committee for Bible Translation (CBT) of the International Bible Society, the group responsible for the NIV. On the attack was a group headed by Wayne Grudem, a professor of Biblical and Systematic Theology at Trinity Evangelical Divinity School and president of the Council on Biblical Manhood and Womanhood, and James Dobson, president of Focus on the Family, an influential Christian educational and political organization. The contention of the CBT was that the proposed NIVI was in fact a superior translation to the NIV, in that it rendered more faithfully the meaning of certain passages. The contention of their critics was that these changes were not justified and indicated moral compromise.

The central rhetorical strategy of critics was to compare the text of the NIVI to that of the NIV and to argue that the new text had a different *meaning* than the old. In a 1997 *World Magazine* article, Grudem offered the following comparisons of the current NIV with the Hodder and Stoughton edition of the NIVI, which was already available in England:

> TEXT: Genesis 1:26–27
> CURRENT NIV: Then God said, "Let us make man in our image...". So God created man in his own image ... male and female he created them.
> INCLUSIVE LANGUAGE NIV: Then God said, "Let us make human beings in our image...". So God created human beings in his own image ... male and female he created them.
> CHANGE IN MEANING: "Man" is the correct translation, because the Hebrew word '-ad-am is also used to refer to man in distinction from woman (Genesis 2:22, 25). An accurate translation should use the word man, which is the name both for males and for the human race. The unity of the race as "man" is also lost, and only diversity as "human beings" is affirmed. Parallel with God's unity and diversity is also lost.

Although Grudem's critique raises interesting issues of linguistic ideology (discussed in part by Carson 1998), Grudem's contention is that the textual changes have undesirable social and theological implications. His rationale is even clearer in his discussion of John 6:44:

> TEXT: John 6:44
> CURRENT NIV: No one can come to me unless the Father who sent me draws him, and I will raise him up at the last day.
> INCLUSIVE LANGUAGE NIV: No one can come to me unless the Father who sent me draws them, and I will raise them up at the last day.
> CHANGE IN MEANING: Might easily be understood to support the neo-orthodox and Arminian view that God chooses and calls groups of people, not individuals; this is done by mistranslating two singular Greek words. Individual assurance of resurrection is also obscured.

In this comparison, the NIVI's rendering is identified with a classic heresy—Arminianism—and one of the 20th century theological movements that fundamentalists and evangelicals reject—neoorthodoxy.

The NIVI debate is similar to the KJV-Only debate, and what the form of both debates illustrates is the focus on meaning rather than text. Textual changes *per se* were not at issue. More than one edition of the KJV is currently available, and even if a person set out to use the KJV only he might have any one of several texts (White 1995). The objection of KJV-Only advocates is not to textual differences but to differences in meaning. Similarly, the proposed NIVI would have incorporated other changes unrelated to gender, but these were not protested. (In fact the NIV was revised in 1984 without a similar uproar.) The protests over the NIVI focused on those cases where a textual difference could be (more or less plausibly) tied to feminism as a social trend.

But there is an objection here too: neither the KJV-Only advocates nor the NIVI critics denied that the translations they were protesting were Bibles. The critics said the Bibles were corrupt, but not that they weren't Bibles at all. This seems to constitute evidence against my contention that the Bible is defined by its meaning: if these new Bibles don't mean the same thing, how can they be Bibles?

Part of the issue here turns on the limitation of the folk hermeneutic notion of meaning I have used in my argument so far. Most of the Bible critics described above argued that new Bibles are corrupt in the nuances of meaning in certain passages, and suggested that these nuances can give rise (or are indicators of) doctrinal or moral compromise. But the Bibles they are criticizing look broadly similar to accepted Bibles: they have the same books, the same reference materials, and the overall text is unmistakably similar.

If, instead of "meaning," one thinks of sets of inferences, the problem is not so acute. When a reader is confronted with a text, a series of inferences are elicited, and these inferences are regarded by the reader as variously warranted by the text (Sperber and Wilson 1995, chapter 4). Some are fairly direct redescriptions of the text; these shade into other thoughts to which the text leads but which may or may not be considered "interpretations" of it in any strong sense. The reader's responsibility for the interpretation grows as its distance from the text increases.

When Bible critics object to nuances of a translation's meaning, they are attributing responsibility to the text and ultimately to the translators. They typically treat one or another existing version, however, as the word of God, and fail to recognize that the versions they accept are also—and in the same sense—the responsibility of translators (on this point see Carson 1979; White 1995; Carson 1998): hence their comparison is between a "true" version, taken to be the word of God, and one or more new versions, taken to be the word of translators. (For this reason too they are often very interested in the biographies and potential heretical leanings or moral shortcomings of the translators whose work they criticize.)

But the similarities between versions are obvious, and, since only the differences can be attributed to translators, the overwhelming majority of the interpretive inferences generated by new versions are the same as those generated by the old. Despite differences in specific texts, the majority of the generated inferences are the same, and so both are classified as Bibles, though not necessarily on a par. "Meaning" remains the key property.

* * *

"The Bible," it seems, is a bit like "Little Red Riding Hood," which does not refer to a particular text, but to a set of texts related by story line. Intuitively one feels that there really *is* a story of Little Red Riding Hood, and that one can pretty much tell whether a particular story is that story, but one cannot easily *define* the story. As Dan Sperber (1996a: 33–34) points out, even to *describe* the story one ends up *retelling* it. "The Bible" and "Little Red Riding Hood" then, seem to occupy a kind of middle ground between name (or title) and genre. Both *can* be names, though as names they are not as informative as titles normally are—they do not, by themselves, individuate a particular text. To specify a particular text, one has to say "Lisa Campbell Ernst's *Little Red Riding Hood*" or *The New International Version* of the Bible. "The Bible" and "Little Red Riding Hood" refer to groups of texts linked by shared storyline or meaning.

Synopsis

The various threads of this analysis may now be tied together. American evangelicals' Bible concept seems to involve several elements:

(1) A designation—"the Bible"—that can refer to various modern English Bibles. The presentation of these Bibles as "translations" and their common use of "the Bible" as a naming template suggests that they are all "versions" *of the same thing*. But the *same thing* of which they are all putative versions is little understood, in no case fully known, and may never have existed in the form evangelicals imagine.
(2) An artifactual stereotype—leather bound, ribbon marker, text layout, etc.—that provides recognition criteria for Bibles. Whether a particular book is a Bible is determined largely by its artifactual properties and the context in which it is encountered. Among these recognition criteria may be counted also the use of "the Bible" in the title and the use of reference points in the text itself.
(3) An assumption of textuality: the Bible is expected to be a text.
(4) A presumption of common meaning: the various texts called Bibles are expected to have (basically) the same contents and to say (basically) the same thing.

This conceptual structure has a number of very interesting consequences, to which I now turn.

Consequences

I have argued that the Bible concept, as it is found among American evangelicals, has four elements—a designation, an artifactual stereotype, an ontological assumption about textuality, and a presumption of common meaning among exemplars—and that these elements in combination hold the category Bible together and underwrite a variety of the inferences and judgments that evangelicals make about Bibles. Having begun by arguing that text concepts occur at the intersection of cognition and culture, I will conclude by exploring four consequences of this conceptual structure for the way in which evangelical culture is organized. The fourfold conceptual structure of "the Bible" has consequences for (1) its role as a conceptual placeholder, (2) the Bible's translatability, (3) the Bible category's "leakage" through paraphrases and children's Bibles, and (4) American evangelicals' fluid inference between treatment of actual Bibles and attitude toward the Bible's message.

The Bible as Placeholder

The dual presence of recognition criteria and a definitional criterion has an interesting consequence. The Bible is a text, but which texts count as Bibles, when push comes to shove, depends on their meaning. The recognition criteria that usually suffice to *identify* Bibles do not supply the *definition* of a Bible, and can be set aside in the appropriate circumstances. Thus, the radio transmission of a Bible has none of the artifactual properties of a Bible, but my informants indicated that it was a Bible nonetheless.

But in the contemporary U.S., push never comes to shove. Bibles are commercially produced and thus available in highly standardized versions, and it is usually to publishers' advantage to make their Bibles highly recognizable as such. Because of this economic relation, the recognition criteria normally suffice for the identification of Bibles, and "Bible" functions as if it were a well-defined category.

The *definition* of the Bible, then, can be curiously deferred. When my informants had exhausted their heuristics for identifying Bibles, they did not give me a definition of the Bible (as I had hoped they would) because they did not *have* a definition of the Bible. What they had was the notion that there was such a thing as the Bible, recognition criteria for identifying Bibles, and an environment that provided them with Bibles readily to hand and easily identifiable as Bibles.

If ever a situation arose in which they needed to decide whether a text was the Bible, these Bible believers would have ideas about how to go about doing so. They would know it had to be a text.

They would know it had to mean the same thing as the Bibles they already have. Given sufficient time and motivation, I think each individual would be able to make that decision to his or her own satisfaction. If it had to be a group decision, quarreling would doubtless ensue, but the quarreling would fall along predictable lines: does this new text *really* mean the same thing as our old ones? The debates would be about the meaning of the text, because, in the end, it is the meaning that counts.

The Bible concept thus functions as a cognitive placeholder. Without knowing precisely what defines a Bible, people are able to use them. Curiously, most of the recognition criteria mentioned—physical characteristics, a title, versification, section headings, running headers— were elements added, at some point in the Bible's history, to the biblical text proper. Bibles are thus open to a certain degree of redefinition by Bible publishers, so long as the recognition criteria are preserved, and the changes are not too obvious at any one time (or are marketed as improvements in Bible scholarship).

But the suspension of definition in terms of meaning has another consequence as well: it allows the text to serve as a perpetual source of meaning. If Bibles are (or would be, if necessary) defined by their meaning, then the meaning of the Bible would have to be fully known, and interpretation would cease. Yet ongoing interpretation is vital to Biblicism.

Translatability

Definition of the Bible in terms of its meaning offers a plausible account of its translatability. Not all texts are considered translatable. The Qur'an, for instance, is officially regarded by Muslims as an untranslatable text: the Qur'an is an essentially Arabic book. One explanation for this untranslatability is that the Qur'an is defined by its text, such that any text that differs from the Arabic Qur'an is, by definition, not a Qur'an. The Bible, in contrast, has been vigorously translated, and is available in more languages than any other book. In many languages it is available in more than one translation, the limiting case no doubt being English: by one count, over 2500 English-language editions of the Bible were published between 1777 and 1957 (Reid, Linder et al. 1990). Bible translations—by reputable translators (Thuesen 1999)—are considered Bibles because they are presumed to mean the same thing as the underlying Greek and

Hebrew texts. They are presumed to meet the semantic criterion for a book to be a Bible.

Leakage

Definition of the Bible in terms of its meaning may explain also the Bible category's leakage through paraphrases and children's Bibles. Paraphrases and children's Bibles constitute hazy edges of the Bible category. When evangelicals are speaking loosely (that is, normally), they consider paraphrases Bibles: a woman may refer to a paraphrase as her Bible, and paraphrases may even be read aloud in the service. Children's Bibles, too, are considered Bibles, but only for children. They *are* Bibles—when parents give *Bibles* to children, they almost always give them children's Bibles—but they are not on a par with regular Bible translations. Moreover, as Ruth Bottigheimer (1996) notes in her study of children's Bibles in European languages since the invention of the printing press, children's Bibles shade seamlessly into children's Bible story books and then into other genres of children's books: children's Bibles are not a distinctive category the way adult Bibles are. This leakage is possible because Bibles are defined in terms of their meaning, and both paraphrases and children's Bibles reproduce, in the main, evangelicals' understanding of the Bible's meaning.

Slippage Between Artifactual and Semantic Properties

In reading about Bible use, one often finds remarkable and sometimes bizarre stories about the way some particular individual or some small community handled Bibles. But such stories are scattered and seem not to reflect any coherent tradition. They seem to be individual expressions of an otherwise tacit sense of reverence for material copies of God's word. The Bible's sacredness seems to extend beyond its semantic properties to its artifactual ones.

Modern American evangelicals live in a highly literate, advanced print society, and, in general, view Bibles merely as particular copies of a text. As Protestants, they are deeply iconoclastic, and explicitly reject any notion that a Bible should be an object of worship. There is no room in Protestant theology for fetishism. Officially, Bibles are just copies of a book, albeit an especially important one.

In this respect evangelical Christianity seems to differ widely from other scriptural traditions, many of which have elaborate rules for the treatment of sacred texts. Indeed, the tendency to elaborate rules for scriptural handling is most developed in the two traditions genetically related to Christianity, Judaism and Islam. If such special handling really is part of a more general phenomenon of scripturalism, then at least the impulse to treat the Bible specially should be present among evangelicals.

I began investigating this in interviews. When asked, "Do you treat your Bible in a special way, different from other books?" evangelicals' answers were almost uniformly negative. The Protestant rejection of fetishism was alive and well. I then tried asking people to envision various scenarios and asked them how they would feel. The scenarios varied, being tailored to each individual. One young man, Fred, kept his Bible on the floor next to his bed, where he could read it before going to sleep. It was a new Bible, and he kept it in its box.

Brian   Would it be okay if you just set it on the floor, without putting it in its box?
Fred   Yes. I only keep it in its box because it's new. I used to put my old Bible on the floor.
Brian   Okay, let's imagine you're getting into bed and you accidentally step on your Bible. How would you feel about that?
Fred   Oh, I would feel really bad if that happened.
Brian   Would you feel guilty?
Fred   Yes, guilty, for sure.
Brian   Okay, now let's imagine that you're getting into bed and you accidentally step on one of your novels. (He liked to read science fiction novels.)
Fred   I've done that before. I don't really care about those.

A number of people expressed sentiments similar to this young man, but the results were mixed: one older man read his Bible in a very special way, always laying it flat on the table, preserving it such that his King James Version, though twenty years old and in regular use, looked nearly new. But then he reminded me that he had been a librarian, and treated all books carefully. And so it went. Some people knew someone who treated the Bible specially: one man told me his mother wouldn't set anything on top of a Bible, but he himself would—but not a TV remote control... A special etiquette surrounds the treatment of books in America, at least in the highly educated community of Creekside Baptist, and even when I could find special treatment of the Bible, it varied a great deal from person to person.

In subsequent survey research in a small fundamentalist church in Texas, I added an item on the special treatment of Bibles. The item, now phrased more specifically and positively than my earlier question, read "Should a copy of the Bible be handled more carefully than other books?" and subjects could check boxes labeled "Yes," "No," or "Undecided." The results were overwhelming: of 41 respondents, 35 said "Yes." This level of agreement was obtained despite the fact that they had not been explicitly taught that Bibles should be specially handled and despite the fact that, theologically, any veneration of objects is anathema. The impulse, then, to treat Bibles specially is there, but undeveloped and highly variable from one person to another.

The analysis offered here may explain this impulse. On the model given above, the dual nature of the Bible—as object on one hand and meaning on the other—turns out to be built into text concepts, such that inference from one sort of property to the other is very fluid. Any time people think of the Bible, they are automatically primed for two kinds of inferences: meaning inferences, such as "Who is the prophet criticizing here?" and object inferences such as "The print is too small." Slippage between these kinds of inferences is fluid for American evangelicals because the concept has both kinds of elements. The physical treatment of Bibles thus tends *automatically* to be interpreted as communication about the Bible's message.

A clarification: the claim here is not that physical treatment of a Bible has a particular meaning. Book burning, for instance, is, in addition to being a mechanism of censorship, a sign of abhorrence, disagreement, and disrespect. But one might imagine that it could mean something else: one might imagine that a tradition might develop whereby old, damaged Bibles, like old U.S. flags, would be ritually burned out of respect. The treatment of a text-artifact might be thus framed in different ways. The claim here is not that the physical treatment of Bibles has a particular meaning, but that such physical treatment will be taken as a metatextual message, a message about the text, performed on the text-artifact, the text's vehicle. There is nothing necessary about this transitivity. The dual nature of the concept—as a set of material objects defined by their common meaning—makes inferences between these aspects automatic.

I suggest that this automaticity gives rise to intuitive norms for treatment of the Bible. The young man who feels guilty for having accidentally stepped on his Bible does so automatically, without having to be taught that stepping on a Bible is a bad thing. Distinctiveness in Bibles' appearance, language, and presentation are felt to reflect on the distinctiveness of the message of the Bible. When individuals treat copies of the Bible specially, it is not usually because they have been taught to do so. The widespread impulse to treat Bibles specially arises in the absence of widespread Bible-handling traditions. The intuition to treat copies of the Bible specially is an intuitive inference facilitated by the dual nature of the Bible concept. The case of Protestant Christianity, then, far from undermining the comparative hypothesis that scriptures will be handled in a special way, provides a model of this impulse in the absence of an explicit tradition of special handling.

* * *

There are further, more subtle, implications worthy of exploration, particularly with respect to evangelical hermeneutic practices, but discussion of these is far beyond the scope of the present essay, and must be the stuff of future work.

So what is "the Bible"? I have argued that "the Bible" is a fourfold concept, consisting of a name, an artifactual stereotype, an expectation of textuality, and a presumption of common "meaning." This concept has both cognitive and cultural functions. Cognitively, it is a way of grouping diverse text-artifacts—Bibles—with respect to their role in American evangelical culture, a tool for mapping these artifacts' potentialities in a particular cultural meaning-system. Culturally, it is a point at which various patterns—traditions of Bible design, ownership, reading, interpretation, authority—are brought into articulation and become signifiers. All this and a good read, too.

17. LUCK BELIEFS:
A CASE OF THEOLOGICAL INCORRECTNESS*[1]

JASON SLONE

E. T. Lawson and R. N. McCauley's (1990) *Rethinking Religion: Connecting Cognition and Culture* offered scholars a comparative study of religion that made substantive, theoretical, and metatheoretical arguments about the cognitive foundations of cultural forms like religious systems (Lawson and McCauley 1990). At the heart of their work was the theoretical argument that agency is the central feature of religion. They write, "For the purposes of theorizing we construe a religious system as a symbolic-cultural system of ritual acts accompanied by an extensive and largely shared conceptual scheme that includes culturally postulated superhuman agents" (Lawson and McCauley 1990: 5).

Scholars who have since adopted the cognitive approach to comparative religion have assumed this definitional feature of religion as well. For instance, S. Guthrie states, "All religions do share a feature: ostensible communication with humanlike, yet nonhuman, beings through some form of symbolic action" (Guthrie 1993: 197). P. Boyer has observed, "That gods and spirits are construed very much like persons is probably one of the best known traits of religion" (Boyer 200: 142). And J. Barrett has characterized the approach as the "naturalness of religion thesis" because of the consensus that religious reasoning exploits important features of our ordinary cognition, such as the capacity to represent agents acting in the world (Barrett 2000).

The reasons for the consensus about agency are sound. For one, the ability to recognize agents from other objects that populate the world is a critical feature of our ordinary cognition (Hirschfeld and Gelman 1994). Two, research has demonstrated that the biases

---

* From *Theological Incorrectness: Why Religious People Believe What They Shouldn't* by Jason Slone, copyright 2003 by Oxford University Press, Inc. Used by permission of Oxford University Press, Inc.

[1] My thanks go to S. W. Johnson for his many insightful comments on this chapter.

imposed by the processing limitations of this naïve psychology favor the attribution of intentional agency (Premack and Premack 1995). Three, human beings in fact seem to possess what R.N. McCauley termed a "hyperactive agent-detection-device (H.A.D.D.)"[2] that leads to the promiscuous attribution of intentionality at work in world, even where none might exist (Keleman 1999a, 1999b, 1999c, 1999d; Guthrie 1993). It is precisely this "action representation system" that allows human beings to make sense of what occurs in the world and why, and provides the cognitive foundations for the recurrent conceptual schemes found in religious systems (McCauley and Lawson 2002; Lawson and McCauley 1990).

Historical, ethnographic and experimental data gathered from numerous cultures confirm these claims. Participants in religious systems across cultures and time reveal a central preoccupation with such superhuman agents as vengeful yet forgiving gods and goddesses, malicious ghost and ghouls, persnickety ancestors, and other sorts of beings that are presumed to possess the powers to affect our lives (Lawson 1994a). Yet, one fact that is also found in the historical, ethnographic and experimental record challenges this otherwise well-defined and well-documented feature of religious systems. Despite the fact that many theologies tend to be deterministic, in so far as they presuppose the existence of active and operative superhuman agents, human beings are also prone to representing certain types of occurrences as resulting from "luck." This fact should force the refinement of claims about the central role of agency in religious reasoning since the belief in luck (and similar representations such as chance, fate, fortune, etc.) suggests that human beings sometimes believe that life's occurrences are not caused by agents—at least not agents in any normal sense of this basic-level term (Rosch 1978). The widespread existence of luck beliefs suggests that the same cognitive constraints that predispose human beings to interpret occurrences in the world as events (occurrences caused by intentional agents) rather than happenings (occurrences that result from non-intentional [e.g. mechanical] causes) applies to unlikely occurrences, in which the agent of the "event" is ambiguous or unknown. In this sense, luck seems to function representationally as a type of intentional agent and is often treated as such ritualistically.

---

[2] Personal communication with J. L. Barrett and E. T. Lawson.

Luck Representations

Armando Benitez has been betting on horses for over 40 years. According to his own testimony he has tried every trick in the book to win. The best chances for winning, however, seem to challenge how one might expect a seasoned gambler to bet. Instead of basing bets on a horse's past performances, on track conditions, on the horse's health, or any other seemingly useful knowledge, he simply takes a novice to the track and asks that person to choose a horse. In a surprisingly high number of cases the novice picks correctly. What is the explanation? "Beginner's luck" seems to work at the track (Bechtel and Stains 1997).

Such anecdotal (ethnographic if you prefer) examples of luck beliefs are seemingly as numerous as those of religious beliefs. Here are just a few. It is good luck to find your initials in a spider web. If your birth date when added together can be divided by seven (e.g. 02/09/73 → 2 + 9 + 73 = 84), you'll be lucky all of your life. Telling entertainers to "break a leg" sends them good luck. Shooting stars are a sign of good luck. You'll be lucky if you accidentally wear clothing the wrong side out all day long; if a strange dog follows you; if a swallow builds a nest on your house; if a frog enters your home; if you see three butterflies together, or if you throw salt over your shoulder.

In contrast, it is bad luck to tell an entertainer "good luck." The number thirteen is unlucky, which is why it is uncommon to find a hotel that has a thirteenth floor. It is bad luck to walk under a ladder; to cross the path of a black cat; to not wear your lucky charm to an exam, or not to perform the usual action in preparation for a big game (Bechtel and Stains 1997; Shermer 1997; Vyse 1997; Singer and Singer 1995; Radford and Radford 1969).

The list of luck beliefs found throughout the world is indeed extensive. Bechtel and Stains' 1997 collection of luck beliefs is 374 pages long with nearly one luck belief presented per page. Radford and Radford's *Encyclopedia of Superstitions* is 264 pages long with at least two or three luck beliefs per page. And yet both books are based almost entirely on luck beliefs found in modern Western cultures alone. Examples from elsewhere also abound. In the first century A.D., Ovid is said to have proclaimed, "Luck affects everything. Let your hook always be cast in the stream. When you least expect it, there will be fish." The African church patriarch St. Augustine said,

"The force of chance is diffused throughout the whole order of things." In Japan, *daruma* dolls, which are stylized replicas of a sixth-century Buddhist monk, have been widely possessed as good-luck charms for years. Chinese calendars were created around lucky and unlucky days. In ancient Egypt, the hieroglyphic sign for the word *nefer* represented variants of good luck, like goodness, beauty, happiness, and youth. Elephants, among other things, have been long prized for good luck (and are signs of divine favor) throughout South Asia (Bechtel and Stains 1997; Radford and Radford 1969).

Furthermore, beliefs in luck are related to actions designed to improve one's luck. Buddhists throughout the world purchase amulets to wear around their necks or to hang in their cars, homes, and businesses in hopes of avoiding bad luck and attracting good luck (Swearer 1995; Earhart 1993; Tambiah 1984; Spiro 1982). Christians do the same. Lay Catholic disciples of St. Jude in the United States wear amulets to protect them from misfortune and to help them deal with "hopeless" causes (which must be, if amulets work, not hopeless after all) (Orsi 1996). In Africa, both the Zulu and the Yoruba have religious specialists who strive through ritual efforts to ward off misfortune and mishap for their groups (Lawson 1985a). Professional athletes are known to perform a host of seemingly arbitrary actions designed to bring about good luck. Michael Jordan wore his college basketball shorts under his professional uniform. Hank Aaron wore the same shower shoes for his entire career. Jimmy Connors tucked a note from his grandma in his socks during tennis matches. Wade Boggs ate chicken before every baseball game he played, as did Jackie Joyner-Kersee before track meets (Bechtel and Stains 1997; Vyse 1997).

I would be willing to bet (pun intended) that most people have experienced some unlikely event that they explained as resulting from luck. How else can we explain winning the lottery or randomly find a $100 bill lying in the street? How can we explain when a basketball player desperately throws the ball toward the basket from mid-court as the clock runs out and the ball goes in for the win? How about the fates of those people who stayed home from work in the World Trade Center on September 11th, versus those who didn't? How about those few people who, for some reason or another, missed their scheduled flights on the hijacked planes that same fateful morning? How can we explain even minor incidents like getting caught in traffic while late for an important meeting, or having your computer crash just before your report is due? All of these events, whatever the actual cause(s), are easily (i.e. naturally) attributable to luck, either good or bad.

Analysis

Why are humans so prone to representing life's occurrences as resulting from the "forces" of luck? Phrased differently, if religious people the world over presume that occurrences result from the activities of superhuman agents, then why do they believe in luck? Taking as a point of departure the work of psychologist J. Barrett, luck beliefs constitute a case of "theological incorrectness" (Barrett 1999). Using both ethnographic and experimental evidence (narrative recall tasks), Barrett has shown that religious people invoke theologically correct representations in "off-line" contexts in which required tasks allow them the time to reflect upon their concepts of God, but infer more anthropomorphic concepts of God in "on-line" contexts in which tasks require them to make rapid judgments. Barrett explained the existence of such "parallel representations" of God (which litter the historical and ethnographic record and have been called, though not explained, by scholars of comparative religion as the gap between the "ought" and the "is," the "Great" and "Little" traditions, "imagined" and "real" religion, "religious teachings" and "living religion," and so forth) in terms of cognitive constraints that impose processing limitations on task-specific mental activities (Barrett 1998). This phenomenon has been found in Indian Hindus' reasoning about Vishnu as well (Barrett 1998). Luck beliefs, as a case of theological incorrectness, seem susceptible to the same analysis as concepts of God. While not exclusively, luck beliefs tend to be produced in contexts that require on-line judgments. We often say without much reflection, "Best of luck today!" Sometimes we feel "lucky" to have avoided some "misfortune," or to have experienced something positive "just by chance." I have heard, interestingly, religious people say "I give thanks to God for being so lucky." I, myself, engage in such behavior as well. I wore the same socks to every game during my (amateur) baseball career for good luck. I sign certain pieces of correspondence, "Best of luck, Jason." And I always wish my students "good luck" at the outset of their exams, at semester's end, and when they graduate.

In some instances luck beliefs develop into systematic representations as is the case with the goddesses Fortuna of Western antiquity, and Lakshmi (pronounced "luck—shmee") in India. At the university where I teach, there is a long standing superstition among the student body to avoid walking through the campus arch, through which they ceremoniously enter as first-year students and exit as graduates, lest one not graduate. Scientists too occasionally appeal to the forces of luck, for instance as operating in evolution by natural selection, and philosophers of logic have for long been preoccupied with the foundations of chance (Ridley 1999; Pinker 1997; Dawkins 1989; Pierce 1955). However, most luck beliefs involve on-line, almost automatic, abductive inferences about the otherwise ambiguous causes of unlikely but personally important events. In fact, experimental studies in attribution-theory reveal that besides the attitudinal qualities of an individual, the unlikeliness of an event that is to be processed seems to be an important variable in the triggering of luck inferences (Lupfer, Tolliver, and Jackson 1996; Lupfer, DePaola, Brock, and Clement 1994; Lupfer, Brock, and DePaola 1992; Spilka, Shaver, and Kirkpatrick 1985; Gilovich, Vallone, and Tversky 1985; Spilka and Schmidt 1983).

In some sense luck is represented synonymously with chance. However, when individuals presume the workings of luck in their lives they interpret the outcomes as being good or bad. Furthermore, although the presumption of luck implies that events are beyond human control, much of the preoccupation with luck involves performing actions that are hoped to influence (mostly improve) luck. The latter suggests just the opposite of luck—that its forces are not beyond our control. So, which is it? Are the forces of luck beyond our control or do we have the capacity, at least do we *think* we have the capacity, to change our fates?

The answer is both because of the capacity for parallel representations. As noted, Barrett's research revealed that the types of representations that are produced on-line are inferentially efficient because they are closer to our everyday view of the world, like anthropomorphic concepts of God (Barrett 1998). On the other hand theologies grab our attention by violating theories built-in to our intuitive ontology (Boyer 1994, 2001b), but they are not easily accessed in on-line contexts. Luck beliefs are an interesting case of parallel representations because they simultaneously interpret occurrences as "just" happening, but humans are also prone to performing actions in which the cause(r?) of luck is meant to be influenced by an action or set of actions. Such representations imply that luck is being imbued with intentionality since it is presumed that the force(s) of luck can be influenced psychologically. The representation of luck involves the agentization of a non-agentive "cause."

The best possible explanation for this phenomenon is that, in addition to the processing demands of the context, the styles of reasoning one employs—abductive or deductive—will produce variant representations. For example, consider the representation of theologically correct representations. Systematic theologies tend to be constructed deductively. Theologians begin with the foundational premises of the faith, such as God exists, God is good, God is powerful, etc., and then deduce from those premises conclusions to questions that concern them. According to the standard social science model of religion, the followers of a religion supposedly learn the culturally-specific/ domain-general theological doctrines of a religion. Once learned, the theology "should" determine how one will think (Tooby and Cosmides 1992; Slone 2002). Since religion involves interacting with postulated (or presumed) agents, and agents control the events of the world, everything, it would seem deductively, is controlled. Hence, as we commonly hear people say, everything happens "for a reason." In this view, luck should be a *non sequitur*. Luck beliefs should not follow from accepted theological beliefs, regardless of tradition. Yet, this is not the case. Consider, for examples, causal theories from Buddhist theology and Christian theology.

Overall Buddhist theology, like all theologies, is quite complex (fortunately for our purposes, we can limit our attention to Buddhist views about causality, since luck beliefs turn on causal reasoning). A central feature of Buddhist theology regarding causality is the doctrine of *karma*. Karma means "action and the appropriate result of action" (Humphreys 1984). It is a basic theory of cause and effect that regulates the workings of the world, i.e. one reaps what one sows. According to the guidelines of this theology there is no problem of theodicy (i.e. "God's justice") because there is no innocent suffering. All events that one experiences in life are the result of one's actions.

In this conceptual scheme, any event that a person experiences is the consequence of previous action(s). If a person seems to have good luck, it is because s/he has accumulated great *karmic* "merit" (Sanskrit: *punna karma*), for example by thinking good thoughts and doing good deeds. In contrast, those people who have bad luck are believed to be reaping the effects of *papa karma*, or demerit. This notion is captured by the popular saying in Thailand, *thaam dii, dai dii; thaam chua, dai chua* ("Do good, get good; Do evil, get evil").

It takes little cognitive effort to grasp the Buddhist conception of *karma* because it resonates with our built-in conception of reciprocity (Ridley 1997; Tooby and Cosmides 1992; Dawkins 1989). However, Buddhist theology, upon further reflection, becomes much more complicated. Consider the fact that because humans live in groups all actions have effects on other people. This creates a complex web of *karmic* interaction in which the actions of each person potentially affect many different people. Thus, how do we know who or what has caused what? How do we locate, in this view, the agent that caused the event if all agents' actions are collectively interconnected? Furthermore, what about the complex notion that action follows from a person's intentions while a person's intentions result from previous actions? In other words, if all events are caused by previous actions, one's own or of others, where is the actual (i.e. "first") cause? Buddhist theology, as it turns out, is susceptible to the criticism of incoherence because it rejects causality altogether while simultaneously recognizing that events are the outcomes of actions (see Kalupahana 1975 for more on Buddhist theories of causality). It is no wonder that Buddhists simplify their causal inferences by appeals, however theologically incorrect, to luck (Keyes and Daniel 1983).

Similar reasoning occurs in individuals belonging to Christian groups. There is a popular notion in the United States[3] that is quite similar to the notion of *karma*: "what goes around comes around." As is the case with Buddhism, however, Christian theology does not provide upon reflection so simple an explanation of life's occurrences. Consider the long standing theological debates in (Protestant) Christianity over the tension between Calvinism and Arminianism, i.e. divine sovereignty and free-will. If God is an active, omnipotent God, then how can humans have free-will? In contrast, if humans don't have free-will, then how can they *choose* good/God? In fact,

---

[3] Though scholars like Diana Eck (2001) and Catherine Albanese (1999) have argued that "pluralism" is the defining feature of American religion, I agree with Peter Williams that America is, both culturally and demographically, primarily a "Christian" country. See Williams 2001 for an introduction to the history of religion(s) in America.

as it turns out, even though Christian thought turns on the notion of divine agents Christians do not always think that God controls every event in the world. In illuminating studies by Lupfer et al., and Spilka et al., luck was attributed as the cause of events in some cases more so than God... even by very conservative Christians (Lupfer et al. 1996, 1994, 1992; Spilka et al. 1985, 1983). It seems that Christians don't believe that God is in control because this theological postulation, like the theologically correct version of *karma*, is cognitively burdensome. Luck attributions are more efficient for Buddhists and Christians operating in real-world problem-solving contexts.

Cognitive Efficiency

Why are luck attributions so much more efficient than theologically correct postulations? There are at least two reasons. One, luck representations are generated abductively and abductive reasoning is much faster than deductive reasoning. Two, deductive reasoning is computationally restrictive; ideas generated abductively are cognitively more flexible (though admittedly at the cost of systematic coherence) (see Johnson-Laird and Byrne 2000 for more on the cognitive science of deduction).

Deductive reasoning involves deducing a conclusion from a set of premises according to rules of inference. The rules of inference constrain the ways in which conclusions can result; they are rules of thought. A typical example of a deductive argument is a syllogism, such as the following:

> All jocks are dumb.
> Jason Slone is a jock.
> Therefore, Jason Slone is dumb.

What's important about deductive arguments is that the truth of the conclusion is guaranteed if the premises are true and the logical deduction follows the established rules of inference. In other words, if the premise(s) is true, and the rules of inference are followed properly, then the conclusion will be true.

There are, unfortunately, significant problems with employing deductive thought that prevent this method of analysis from being widely employed. First, the need for the premise to be true weakens the possibilities of the conclusion being true. What if not all jocks are dumb? Might there be one smart jock somewhere in the world? If so, then the conclusion of this syllogism is false (even though by the rules of inference it is valid) (Solomon 1990).

Second, consider how long, in real problem solving time, it takes to deduce a conclusion that informs us about the mental prowess of Jason Slone. Readers had to deduce the conclusion via successive stages of thought. What if, after all that time-consuming effort it takes to deduce conclusions from premises, the premises are wrong? To construct a different answer would require a lengthy trek through another deductive process, and there would be no guarantee that that answer would be correct either. Here's a fanciful example of how deductive reasoning might be employed to explain why my wife cooked a bad meal.

> All women are bad cooks.
> My wife is a woman.
> Therefore, my wife is a bad cook.

What if it turns out that all women are not bad cooks? You might try this.

> All women from Minnesota are bad cooks.
> My wife is a woman from Minnesota.
> My wife is a bad cook.

What if my wife is not a bad cook, but rather simply cooked a bad meal? You might try this.

> All women from Minnesota, except my wife, are bad cooks.

Now readers have arrived at an incoherent premise. If but one woman from Minnesota is not a good cook, then the premise cannot include the pretense "all." If a premise cannot be inclusive it turns out to be very weak indeed.

The final problem is related to the last statement. Deductive reasoning involves starting from general, ideally universal, premises and deducing from those premises a conclusion to a specific problem. If the problem is that my wife is a good cook but cooked a bad meal, I would have a seemingly infinite number of premises from which to begin my deductive line of thought. "All married women cook poorly tasting salmon." "All college graduates cook poorly tasting salmon." "All fans of reality television shows cook poorly tasting salmon."

Cognitive tasks that require us to make on-line judgments are driven by the requirements of assessing what's going on in our world rapidly and in such a way that we can act advantageously. If we had to use theologically-constrained deductive reasoning our thinking might go something like this. "God is the creator of all life. Humans are part of life. All humans must eat. My wife is a human. My wife must eat. Cooked food is good to eat. My wife eats cooked food. Food is cooked by humans. . . ." This kind of thinking takes up too much time for our everyday traffic with the world, it is too restrictive, and it only deals with the event covered by the logical conclusion.

On-line cognitive tasks are often like little problems to be solved with explanations. If the problem to solve is explaining why my wife is a good cook, but cooked a bad meal, then I can do so very quickly by inferring an answer that, if true, would explain the puzzle. Abductive reasoning starts with such a conclusion and in so doing skips all the steps required by deductive logic. For example, maybe my wife is a good cook but never learned to cook salmon properly. This abductive answer to the problem is plausible and if true solves the problem. If it's not true, we can quickly discard the hypothesis and generate a new one. If she had in fact learned how to cook salmon well, maybe she didn't cook the salmon well because she is under a lot of stress at work and so is distracted at home. Or, maybe she is trying to make me loose weight and so is purposely cooking poorly tasting food. Or, maybe I have bought a bad piece of fish for her to cook with. This list also contains an infinite number of possibilities; but it is more efficiently perused for answers. In this way our mind takes a "short cut," by way of abductive reasoning, to a representation that is likely to be true because "likely to be true" is good enough for most humans most of the time (theologians, philosophers, and scientists are peculiar, in this sense, by comparison). It is fast and flexible because it is constrained by the limitations of cognitive processing, not by the limitations of deductive rules of inference and validation (Kahneman, Slovic, and Tversky 1982).

What is striking about this way of thinking is that so much of what is involved in the generation of abductive ideas is only *tacitly* known. Abductive reasoning takes for granted a host of assumptions that are necessary for the abductive generalization to be constructed at all (Nisbett and Ross 1980). Consider what is assumed in the above inferences. We know without having to think it consciously that my wife intends to produce a cooked meal that tastes good because we already know, based on intuitive presumptions, that she is a human; humans need to eat; that cooked food is good, etc. Furthermore, in the event that the food tastes bad, we assume that my wife is the primary cause (because of or in spite of her desire and effort) of the food tasting badly. Then, we perform a mental search for cause(s) of that cause. Intuitively we assume not only that there is a cause but also that we can detect it, whatever it may be. This type of causal reasoning is central to our basic cognition; humans need to know why things happen in order to survive. The belief in luck is a by-product of this cognitive capacity to identify events in the world and to infer, often quickly and from incomplete data, their cause(s) (Kahneman, Slovic, and Tversky 1982; Nisbett and Ross 1980).

Events

Happenings simply occur; events are caused. The former require only the representation of mechanical causation whereas the latter require the representation of intentional agency. Such causal inferences are constrained by domain specific tacit knowledge about what kinds of things are in the world and how those things work (Hirschfeld and Gelman 1994). At least this is true for older children, teenagers, and adults because the human conceptualization of causality actually changes as our cognitive capacities develop. Early in life, human beings are deterministic in their thinking. Young children have very clear ideas about how things in the world ought to work. This is revealed by experimental studies in which infants and young children are shown unusual causal events. For example, children are quite surprised to see a ball go through a wall. Given their intuitive physics, they know that this kind of event isn't supposed to happen (Spelke, Phillips, and Woodward 1995).

Sometime around the age of six or seven, however, children begin to switch from a deterministic to a probabilistic view of the world. For reasons having to do with the complex interaction of natural capacities and cultural experiences, children begin to infer outcomes of events from tacit knowledge of probability that is grounded in intuitive ontology. It is at this age, according to J. Piaget and B. Inhelder, when children begin to develop and hone an understanding of chance. At this stage of development children begin to think that outcomes are not a matter of either-or, but of more-or-less likely to occur. Prior to this stage of development, children believe that every event outcome has a cause, even if the cause is hidden. Older children, in contrast, develop the capacity to represent chance occurrences based on expectations about frequency. This cognitive capacity reveals that humans develop a probabilistic sense of expectation about how the world is generally supposed to work. The primary difference between children under and over the age of six is that children in the former group believe that event-outcomes must happen in a certain way, whereas children in the latter think that event outcomes will most likely, but not necessarily, happen in a certain way (Piaget and Inhelder 1976).

Such research suggests that cognitively developed humans regularly perform a kind of "informal calculus of probability" (Vyse 1997). We construct probabilistic theories about why things happen as well as what kinds of things will happen. In this sense, probabilistic inferences both explain and predict. Were the world not to operate in recognizable patterns (real or imagined) we would have great difficulty in making sense of why things happen and in turn great difficulty in making and acting on predictions about how things are reasonably going to happen (Pinker 1997). Yet, intuitive probability is not exactly like scientific probability, and so it is instructive to consider the difference.

Probability

Scientific probability turns on fairly precise mathematical formulae that can be tested for confirmation or disconfirmation. The goal is not perfect prediction *per se*, but rather to arrive at the odds, or probability, that a particular outcome will occur. One of the most famous experiments in statistics that reveals the phenomena of randomness and variability is the flipping of coins. In this experiment, researchers flip one or two fair, two-sided coins. There are four possible outcomes when two coins are flipped: HH (Heads/Heads), TT (Tails/Tails), HT (Heads/Tails), and TH (Tails/Heads). Since HH is only one of four possible outcomes, the probability that a flip of the coins will result in HH is 1:4 or 25%. This also goes for TT. However, since there are two variations of the same result for a non-same-side up, either TH or HT produces the same result, so that the possible outcomes are two of four. Therefore, the probability that a flip of the coins will render a non-same sided result is 2:4 or 50%. Thus, we can say that there is twice as much of a chance that two flips will result in a non-same sided result (TH or HT) than a same-sided result (TT or HH) because probability is the number of desired outcomes divided by the number of possible outcomes.

There are no guarantees of any particular outcome in this experiment. There are only probabilities that the results will show up in patterns. In the classical experiment that tests this theory, subjects flip two coins, but only once or twice. In just a few flips of the coins, there does not appear to be any recognizable pattern. The results are random. However, when these same people flip the coins 100 times, a visible pattern seems to emerge. Give or take a few variances, most results are around 25 TTs, 25 HHs, and 50 TH/HTs. For probability theorists, this suggests that if something is done once, anything can happen. However, if something is done many times, depending on its structural limitations a pattern will become visible. This is precisely why this method is an effective way to determine the beginnings of sporting matches and other games; since the results guarantee no outcomes for one side or the other it is considered to be fair. The results are a matter of chance ... or "luck."

Importantly, however, each flip of the coins in the above experiment is completely independent. What happens on one flip has no influence on what will result in the next flips. Despite this fact human beings not only predict a pattern of results but actually believe at some level that the consecutive flips of the coin are related in some way or another. For example, when presented with two possible sequences of flip results research subjects have shown a preference for a random sequence. If asked to infer which sequence is more likely to result from random flips of coins subjects prefer a sequence like TH, HT, TT, HT, TH, HH over something like HH, HH, HH, HH, HH, HH. Though the possibility of either sequence occurring is exactly the same, human beings seem to know, intuitively, that the latter is less likely to happen. Why? The latter sequence does not appear to be random at all, and so people infer that there must be hidden forces at work, like a slight of hand or some other trick, causing the unlikely sequence to occur. In a similar experiment involving inferences about likelihood, subjects were shown an outcome sequence that appeared to be systematically random and thus not really random at all. Subjects had difficulty accepting that random flips of a single coin could produce effects like H, T, H, T, H, T, H, T or H, H, T, T, H, H, T, T, because such results seem to violate our expectations about "how randomness ought to occur" (itself a complex, if not contradictory, representation) (Vyse 1997).

Having deeply rooted expectations about how the world ought to work leads to other interesting psychological effects that bear on the belief in luck. Two of the most common cognitive mistakes that humans make constitute the "gambler's fallacy," which combines the beliefs that (1) forces outside wholly mechanical processes can influence an outcome, and that (2) positive and negative results ought to average out over a period of time, a phenomenon known as the belief in the law of averages. In the first case, researchers find that human beings believe they can influence the outcome of an entirely mechanical and random process, for example by performing certain arbitrary actions (i.e. "superstitions"). This misconception is known as the gambler's fallacy for good reason. Gamblers are notoriously prone to performing rituals and other actions that they believe will influence the outcome of a game of chance. Those who play games like roulette or craps might chant an incantation before their turn (e.g. "Come on.... Daddy needs a new pair of shoes!!!"). While in some sense, humans know that the wheel is just a set of mechanical devices and thus that the results of such games are random, anyone who has ever gambled in a game of chance knows also how natural it feels to try to influence the outcome, often by talking to the game as if it had psychological agency (Hayano 1978; Langer and Roth 1975; Wallace, Singer, Wayner, and Cook 1979; Oldman 1974).

The second aspect of the gambler's fallacy, which is also widespread among people whose livelihoods (and lives in some cases) depend on variables outside of their control, like athletes, fishermen, and stock traders, is the belief in the law of averages. Informally, this is known as being "due." In this case, in games, sporting matches, and other activities in which forces significantly or entirely beyond one's control can determine outcomes, participants come to believe that a string of bad luck will be countered by a string of good luck. For example, athletes believe that when they go into "slumps," all they need is "one good break" to "open the floodgates" of good luck (Vyse 1997). Similarly, athletes are prone to the belief in having a "hot hand" and will perform arbitrary actions that they believe will make the string of good luck continue (Lopes and Oden 1987; Gilovich, Vallone, and Tversky 1985; Buhrmann, Brown, and Zaugg 1982; Buhrmann and Zaugg 1981; Becker 1975).

On the other hand gamblers believe that a string of losses at a game of chance increases the sense that a person is about to win despite the fact that, as shown in the coin-flipping examples, each successive try in the game occurs independently. Thus one could quite possibly lose every single time forever, even though one might be hard pressed to believe this statistical probability (R. Falk 1989, 1981; Lopes and Oden 1987; Timberlake and Lucas 1985; Blackmore 1985; Killeen 1977; Becker 1975; Langer and Roth 1975; Oldman 1974). Interestingly, the belief that things even out in the world is a presumption that recurs (cross-culturally) in religious conceptual schemes. Thus the ideas embedded in theological traditions don't cause people to think that things even out in life, but rather, because human beings intuitively presume that things even out, religious ideas, like other successful "memes," are "contagious" (i.e. transmittable) (Dawkins 1989). They exploit the sorts of presumptions already built-in to our mental repertoires (Boyer 2001b, 1994).

Fate

In addition to, with regard to luck beliefs, the varieties of cognitive inferences we make regarding randomness and variability humans also seem prone to spotting coincidences and to representing them as fateful events. Despite the randomness of many of life's events, humans tend to link events together in ways that make their relationship meaningful. Consider James Redfield's very popular book of the 1990s, *The Celestine Prophecy* (Redfield 1993). Its primary "thesis" (it was fiction) was that life moves in sequences of important events that link you with your destiny. Redfield's narrative led readers to reflect upon the most important events in their lives, namely those that have led them to where they are today. Why did you pick the college you attended? Why did you meet the person you ended up marrying? Why did you decide not to go to work on September 11th? According to Redfield's book, such events are not coincidences at all, but are in fact part of each person's "destiny." Thousands of readers, we can assume from the book's popularity, resonated with this idea. And Redfield is certainly not the first author to exploit this notion; it is a recurring theme throughout literature (from classics like Hemingway's *The Old Man and the Sea* to recent popular movies like *Serendipity*, starring John Cusack).

The popularity of this book (more accurately, its idea) supports anecdotal and experimental research that suggests that humans imbue things and events with "purpose." Psychologist Deb Kelemen has called the human tendency to use knowledge of functional design as a basis for inferring about behavioral properties, "promiscuous teleology." In her experiments, children not only assumed that cups had handles for people to drink from them, but also that rivers contain water for people to swim in them. Likewise, participants postulated that fanciful animals called "footles" used an elongated body part that protruded from their heads for the purposes of knocking fruit off of trees. Footles don't just happen to have such body parts; they are there for a reason (Kelemen 1999a, 1999b, 1999c, 1999d).

Making such inferential judgments is based on biased preconceptions about why events occur, and much of this bias is based in intuitions about the likelihood of events occurring. A famous example of this was produced by cognitive psychologists who asked a classroom of college students about the likelihood of two people in the same class having the same birthday (e.g., May 23). As predicted, most students were convinced that the likelihood was very low and therefore if two students did share the same birthday it would be a coincidence. As it turns out the probability is actually higher than 50% for classes with at least 23 students. This example when tested in classrooms has proven to shock students, and as such has become a favorite tool of professors of mathematics and statistics, because it violates expectations about the likelihood of the event occurring (Paulos 1988).

Furthermore, the element of surprise that underlies coincidence seems to lead people to infer that a hidden cause must be at play in such an event. This is because coincidences seem to challenge intuitions about how the world ought to work. It also reveals that human beings, when inferring causes of events (including the likelihood of their occurrence), employ selective remembering thus enhancing the feeling of the specialness of coincidental events (Vyse 1997; Falk 1989, 1981; Lopes and Oden 1987; Hintzman, Asher, and Stern 1978). Consider again the case of the coincidence of shared birth dates. What's also striking about this case is that in a class of 23 students or more subjects are shocked to learn that two people have the same birthday. What these same students overlook, however, is that at least 21 students do not share the same birth date. This suggests that humans tend to focus on singular events that are seemingly congruent and ignore the overwhelming majority of events that are not. This phenomenon is also found anecdotally in the notion that humans live in a "small world," a representation that is made whenever someone meets another person with whom they have some remote connection.

What most of this suggests is that a good portion of human thought is based not on what's learned from culture *per se*, but rather on what one infers given the available information (itself derived by employing cognitive strategies of perception and detection; Pinker 1997) and the concepts and theories that people can generate to account for that evidence (Medin 2000). Human thought requires postulations and presumptions that are based on tacit assumptions about the world and its workings as much as it does the recall of culturally learned "worldviews," as cultural determinists would maintain (e.g., Geertz 1973). Humans employ heuristics as a short cut to make sense of their world and the use of heuristics reveals that the mind biases reality in certain ways. Scholars might justifiably count the belief in luck and the tendency to believe one can influence luck as such cases.

Summary—The Persistence of Luck Beliefs

Why do luck beliefs persist, despite the efforts of folks like religious leaders, educators, scientists and others who prefer the coherence and accuracy typically produced in off-line thinking? One of the reasons is that because of task demands humans are still inclined to think abductively. Humans therefore simply misconceive of the reasons for why things happen in the ways they do. Human beings are products of natural selection and so are built to perceive and control their environment in ways that allow for survival. Obviously, in order to control what's around them, humans need to have a fairly solid grasp of what's happening. However, most ideas about what is going on in the world must be constructed from incomplete/ underspecified data. When one hears a rustling sound in the woods, she most likely doesn't have all of the data needed to know what's happening, but she knows enough to know that she ought to be on high alert. The presumption is that what is in the woods is a potentially dangerous psychological agent with the intention of having her as a meal. In turn, the subsequent presumption is that the likelihood of that something actually getting to have that meal decreases significantly if she leaves the area immediately. Notice that all of these presumptions are interrelated and inferred and that it is not necessary to calculate this information deductively. It is done instantly, abductively, and quite naturally.

The inferential process is important for our survival. Gaining control of a situation requires engaging in a very complicated mental process with a variety of cognitive tasks and doing so rapidly. This process turns out to be employed for most situations in the daily lives of *homo sapiens*. Thus when humans encounter circumstances in which they appear to have no control we ought not to be surprised that they will still tend to act if they do. Alternatively, they will try to figure out a way to gain control.

A good example of the illusion of control was already given in the gambler's fallacy. Much of the ritual behavior that is believed to improve luck is related to the presumption that actions we perform can influence the outcomes of otherwise mechanical processes (Malinowski 1972). Consider the activities people perform while on airplanes, where their fates are almost entirely out of their control and in the hands of pilots and the mechanical workings of the plane. Consider the rituals that athletes perform in preparation for and during competition. Consider the behavior of gamblers, stock traders, sailors, fishermen, and other folk whose livelihoods depend on processes that are largely beyond human control. Consider the thoughts and actions of individuals and their family members who are confronted with terminal illness. All of these people are prone to believe in the forces of luck and to perform rituals in hopes of receiving some good luck.

The persistence of this belief is supported by confirmation bias, which is based on the illusion of correlation (connecting an event with a postulated cause). For instance, athletes might believe that their pre-game ritual is the cause of positive outcomes of contests. Gamblers might believe that their incantations are the cause of their winning. In these cases correlations are confused with causes and correlation illusions fuel luck beliefs and luck rituals because they allow humans to identify some cause, most likely a controllable cause, to an event. Luck, in this sense, functions representationally as an agent. It therefore provides the person making the representation with a rich inference that explains the unlikely occurrence.

This leaves scholars of comparative religion with one intriguing question, are luck beliefs of the same category as religious beliefs? The answer is . . . not quite. While the same cognitive processes are involved, scholars should maintain a separation between luck beliefs and religious beliefs for at least two reasons. First, the category of "religion" itself, which despite its sordid scholarly history has been quite useful in demarcating an empirically tractable object of study. The scholarly category of religion would be stretched beyond its currently useful limits if phenomena like luck beliefs were considered religious. The same argument has been made about other religion-like phenomena (e.g., things that are attended to with religious-like devotion such as sports, nationalism, etc.). Second, and more importantly, while luck beliefs (like all symbolic-cultural forms) are produced by the same cognitive processes as religious ideas, luck beliefs differ significantly from religious beliefs in that they are typically not systematized, either conceptually or ritualistically. Therefore they rarely, if ever, develop balanced ritual systems with both special-patient and special-agent rituals. In fact luck "rituals" might not constitute rituals at all, at least according to Lawson and McCauley's stringent criteria (McCauley and Lawson 2002; Lawson and McCauley 1990).

However, even if not considered in the same category as religion, luck beliefs do merit scholarly attention. Their ubiquity challenges the assumption still taken for granted by scholars operating within the standard social science model that religions (and other environmental variables) determine what people think and do (Tooby and Cosmides 1992). If that view were correct, then religious people would not believe in luck at all. Obviously, this is not the case.

18. COGNITION AND CREDENCE[1]

Timothy Light

Introduction

In this paper I shall attempt to characterize how our general mental infrastructure is most likely designed so that it makes possible our religious conceptions and how we use them. I am concerned here only with *mental infrastructure*, that is, the standard architecture and processes that our minds must have for typical religious behavior to take place. I am not concerned with the content of religious concepts or their naturalness, with questions of evolutionary development, with the ubiquity of patterns of ritual behavior, or with the problems of storage and performance of stated religious acts. Boyer (1990, 1994, 2001b), McCauley (2000), Lawson and McCauley (1990, 2002), Sperber (1975, 1996a), and Whitehouse (1995, 2000) have dealt persuasively with these matters, and I have nothing here to add to what they have severally said. It is my hope that the notion of infrastructure that I present here will be found to support their basic proposals.

I begin with a story told by Tom Lawson at a departmental brown bag meeting several years ago.

---

[1] An earlier version of this paper was presented at the Mid-West Branch of the American Academy of Religion, Chicago, 6 April 2002. I wish to express my thanks to Dr. Jason Slone of Findlay University for reading the paper on my behalf, as I was unable to be there. In the preparation of the paper, I am especially indebted to two very generous people. Tom Lawson has been my teacher during my long transition from linguistics and language teaching to comparative religion and has been unstinting in willingness to discuss points both large and small over the decade-plus that we have worked together. He also supplied the story which is the central focus of the paper, though I piously hope that he might not have figured out just why I wanted it until he first opened this book. Eve Sweetser (Cognitive Science and Linguistics, U.C. Berkeley) was enormously generous with her time and instruction while I was on leave there in the spring of 2001; it was through her that I began to study Mental-Space theory. Naturally, all of the errors and infelicities in the paper are my fault and not theirs.

(1) One day while walking with a young Zulu man in Pietermaritzburg, Natal, I noticed him take something out of his pocket and swallow it. He grimaced so severely that I stopped and asked him what he had swallowed that had such an effect. He simply said: "I am making myself more beautiful." Rather than prying too deeply into his personal affairs, I said: "If I were to swallow that stuff would it make me more beautiful?" He answered: "That depends." "Well, what does it depend on?" "It depends on whether you have performed the *ukubuthwa* ritual." "Well, if I performed that ritual and then swallowed the stuff would it make me more beautiful?" "That depends." "On what?" "On whether you have performed the *thomba* ritual." "Now, if I have performed both rituals and then take that stuff, would it make me more beautiful?" "That depends." "On what?" "Whether you have performed the *qhumbaza* ritual." "If I had performed all three and then swallowed the stuff, would it make me more beautiful?" "That depends." "Depends on what?" "Whether you have gone through the *igamu* ritual." "O.K. If I have done all four, then?" "You would have to be born a Zulu."

Tom told this story as an illustration both of the riskiness in doing fieldwork[2] of relying solely on a participant's exegesis of any religious practice and as an illustration of how religious thinking may work. Both purposes are important for this paper. If a participant in any religious community provides explanations of ritual which seem tangential to that ritual, or which change on further questioning, or which differ significantly from those of other participants, then the concepts represented by those explanations cannot be taken as having the same permanence as that of a ritual itself which is performed numerous times by the explainer and by others. Minimally, this discrepancy suggests that religious knowledge may be compartmentalized between praxis and exegesis at least to the extent of there being no *necessary* link between them, though, of course, in other cases there *may* be a clear and direct link. Stated in common religious terms: belief and purportedly linked ritual *may* be quite unconnected, or they may be rather substantial reflections of each other,

---

[2] It is worth noting here that concern over informant explications has been a constant theme in linguistic fieldwork over the past century. That field, whose canons of fieldwork were developed earlier than those of religious studies, has moved over the past fifty years from a nearly absolute prohibition of the use of informants' comments to a recognition that those comments are always potentially a legitimate source of data and may be astute guides to analysis if independent data support those insights. That field's maturing into this distinction seems to me to suggest at least a parallel to the interpretation of compartmentalization given below.

or they may have a wide range of overlap, with there still being notable anomalies between them.

The exegesis in this story is explanation by explanation, or reiterated regress. In this case, the extension of causality dependence is halted only by the introduction of an element (a European-African becoming a Zulu) which is of questionable logical relevance to the chain of explanations and, equally important, utterly impossible, but which, nevertheless, pre-empts any reply. A great deal of religious explanation is of this sort, and so in addition to being compartmentalizable, religious reasoning must be acknowledged to be potentially reiterable pending the insertion of an external block. (The ubiquity of such reasoning outside of religions will become evident to academic readers by a few moments' reflection on the last faculty meeting they attended.)

The lesson of Tom Lawson's tale is of course not new. Robertson Smith pointed it out in 1889, and very recently, Robert A. Segal recalled Smith's comments in a retrospective essay concerning Smith's influence on Durkheim, who, of course was also greatly familiar with the problem (Segal 2002: 58–9).

The notion of infrastructure which I shall propose as basic to religious knowledge is particularly inspired both by a career spent in language teaching and linguistics and by recent work in those branches of cognitive science called "Mental-Space Theory" (following the work of Coulson [2001], Fauconnier [1997, 2001], Fauconnier and Turner [2002], and Sweetser and Fauconnier [1996]) and "Metaphor Theory" (following the work of Lakoff and Johnson 1980, 1999). In order to get to that point, I shall first take up the characteristics of credence statements in order to suggest that the apparent anomalies evident in the presentation of the young Zulu are *characteristic of religious discourse* rather than aberrations. Then I shall discuss the role of meaning, meaningfulness, and memory in the development of concepts and the associations which they form in our minds. The fourth section will provide a brief and highly simplified version of a Mental-Space analysis of the Zulu young man's response to Tom Lawson's queries, and the concluding section will offer reasons for believing that Mental-Space analyses are particularly appropriate to the description of religious behavior.

Beliefs and Believing

Together with others working in various cognitive science approaches to religious knowledge, I believe that our knowing in religion is fundamentally the same as our other ways of knowing. Furthermore, by examining the prominent features of credence, we are able to notice features of general concept development which have interest beyond the study of religion.

The participant in Tom Lawson's story seems successfully to segregate the practice of ritual from its exegesis and extends the exegesis in what might have become an endless chain whose relevance to the ritual acts becomes increasingly unclear. This sort of compartmentalization in human thought is not limited to a rather simple dichotomy between praxis and belief, with the latter sometimes turning out to be irrelevant to the former. Still less is it reducible to the most frequently discussed form of mental separation of incompatible concepts as when a verbal moralist commits unethical acts and is thereafter labeled a hypocrite.

Compartmentalization is a ubiquitous mental skill practiced by all of us to avoid the paralysis which results from actively recognized cognitive dissonance in situations where we need to adjust to incompatible or contradictory environmental circumstance. Ordinary politeness taking the form of not alluding to unpleasant truths in front of those who would be offended by them is perhaps the commonest culturally conditioned form of this capacity. Cognitive scientists (Boyer 2001b) draw attention to the ubiquity of educated people vigorously verbalizing modern scientific knowledge, yet acting as though the well established discoveries with which they are deeply acquainted had never been made. Continuing to refer to the sun *rising* and *setting* is the most frequent of such regular counter-scientific statements. In the development of religions, it is not unusual to find mutually anomalous convictions or directly contradictory convictions fervently held as doctrine and believed by adherents. In much of Chinese Buddhism there is strong belief in both reincarnation and the transformation of deceased ancestors into spirits who need to be ritually cared for. In Chinese popular religion, three divinities (Kuan Yin; Kuan Yu; T'ien Hou) occupy a separate category owing to their general efficacy and widespread worship. In this special role, these gods have risen above other deities in function and power in a way that makes them a closed set of three as opposed to the continuingly open set for all other gods, although little in formal accounts of practice would suggest why this is so. In much of Christianity, the Virgin Mary has risen to a special set consisting of only one member in that her powers not only exceed those of all the other saints (who, like the ordinary gods of China, form an open class) but even share part of the divine work of the second member of the Trinity to a degree that considerable theological effort is expended in distinguishing her from the divinity of the Trinity, despite practice and common exegeses thereof frequently blurring that line.

Compartmentalization, in other words, not only yields hypocrisy, but more importantly serves a critically positive role in keeping the parts of our system of conceptions in places wherein those parts do not conflict with each other. Our conceptual system as a whole is built upon sub-systems *within which* contradiction, anomaly, and redundancy are not allowed. However, since each of our conceptual sub-system is internally impermeable to the elements of other sub-systems, the contradictions between and among elements belonging to different sub-systems are not debilitating to us. Thus, The Virgin can be safely characterized as participating in the redemptive work of Christ ("Co-Mediatrix"), and a Buddhist nun at a Kuala Lumpur temple may readily say that the many figures in a glass case are indeed all gods but that she doesn't know their names, what they do, or pay attention to them, since her attention is on Kuan Yin.[3] Compartmentalization being common to all human beings and employed in all spheres of cognition, it does not seem too large a stretch to suppose that conceptualizing through systems and sub-systems which are closed to each other reflects a skill which has evolved in our species as an adaptive device to render conceptualization possible.

As important as it is to religious thought, compartmentalization is but a part of a much larger pattern of credence behavior. What the Zulu man tells Tom Lawson is a series of (potential) assertions about how things are and work which in English would be generally classified

---

[3] Further, as many others have pointed out, "strict" Buddhism does not acknowledge deity. Thus, even though the "Buddhist Philospy of Assimilation" (Matsunaga 1969) permits Buddhism to adjust to virtually any construal of reality, ultimate reality is attested to be a cleansing of mind from illusions such as deities. Any religious who has in fact been instructed in formal Buddhist "theology" and who affirms that belief system exhibits the same strength of compartmentalization as do Christians in veneration (worship?) of the Virgin and as the young Zulu man did.

as *beliefs*. Similar to his way of explaining his ritual, most of the statements that we make about our beliefs are not explicitly encoded with the ostensive cue *I believe*.... Nevertheless, a standard way of examining phenomena in order to analyze them is to examine first the formally archetypal case in order to determine its properties. Even though most religious exegeses are in fact not expressed in formal creeds, they may be reduced to explicit belief statements in order to examine their inherent implications. In order to keep this discussion simple and brief, I will now take up some properties of *belief* statements. The basic form of such statements is:

> (2) I/We believe(s) Y (where Y may represent "in God/spirits/ghosts, etc."; or may be followed by an object clause: "that [Verb Phrase]").

Now consider three sets of *believe* sentences: (3–5); (6–7); and (8–9).

> (3) I believe that John had already arrived before I left.
> (4) I believe that Aimee is the best pitcher on our softball team.
> (5) I don't really believe in God, but I do believe that there must be some sort of force or power in the world with which we always live, and it is that which keeps us alive.
> (6) I/We believe in one Lord, Jesus Christ, ... eternally begotten of the Father....
> (7) I/We believe in the Holy Spirit ... who proceeds from the Father and the Son.
> (8) I believe entirely in the Immaculate Conception of Mary Mother of God and in her bodily assumption into heaven.
> (9) I believe that Apostolic Succession is essential to the True Church.

The sentences in set (3–5) above suggest that the speaker has enough reason for expecting that the result of the clause which forms the object of believe is true, but insufficient evidence to assert positive knowledge about the matter. We who hear the speaker of such utterances justifiably assume the speaker's sincerity regarding the expectedness of that clausal object and its referent event. If it subsequently turns out that the speaker does not in fact expect this event, we are justified in thinking that he has dissembled. Note that a religious statement can be included in this category so long as some level of context makes it clear that the speaker is asserting a personal conviction. Of general importance to the study of religion in a post-Enlightenment framework, the first clause of (5) is just as much a belief statement as is the second clause. While a longer article would be needed to do justice to the matter, it is important to note that atheistic credence statements are not categorically different from deistic statements.

In contrast, the sentences in set (6–7) may or may not be amenable to a test of ordinary sincerity. Drawn from the Nicene Creed as recited in the Episcopal Church (my own religious affiliation), these sentences denote convictions which very few educated people of the 21st century actually hold as stated. They are recited and/or sung on a regular basis. They are a part of a cherished and regular ritual performed by people whose participation symbolizes their devotion to the worshiping body which has inherited these statements from its corporate predecessors and which continues their utterance within ritual as an affirmation of continuity of religious attachment. In this case, the affirmation is a sincere attestation of membership in that continuing community and its *faith*. No statement in such affirmations, however, is a clear assertion of the object of the verb *believe*. Or, where the verbal formulation differs (as in hymns and prayers, for example), no such assertion implicit in any descriptive sentence ("angels around a glassy sea," etc.) has a truth force greater than any other poetic imagery. Lest umbrage be taken at this intentional merging of creedal and other ritual statements, it is well to note the rather restricted semantic origins of the creeds which are today recited as general statements of faith-within-ritual. The Nicene Creed was fixed at the council held in 325 C.E., and the function of some of its wording was to settle disputes and to differentiate the convictions of one group of Christians over those of another group of Christians in a time of theological controversy when the terms of the first merger of early Christianity with late Hellenistic philosophy were still being settled. Not only do modern reciters of the Creed often only dimly understand what might be the metaphysical implications of such phrases as "of one being with the Father," few, if any, would realize that such statements may have been inserted polemically. To the authors of the Nicene Creed, being of one substance with the Father meant something that was of a piece with their construal of the nature of the universe as a whole. To me—even though as a longtime academic I can quickly spin out an apparently coherent exegesis—this phrase is largely without content that I can relate to anything else in my experience and therefore what is meant in ordinary terms by my recitation is at best moot, despite my deep faith in the main Christian message. Obviously, the Creeds also contain statements which continue to make sense despite radical alterations in connotation over the centuries. Thus, references to God as creator are for me as true as anything I would utter from group (3–5), even though my notions of what God's divine creation might mean are most likely rather different from what was intended by fourth- and fifth-century Christians. That the Creeds are a mixture of statements which can be affirmed denotatively and statements which can only be uttered as a statement of identification with the historical and continuing group rather clearly symbolizes the problem of verbal affirmations in religion.

Group (8–9) contains statements which may be affirmed both for their denotative value (i.e. like those in group (3–5), the object of the verb *believe* is precisely affirmed) and because for many adherents they actually assert identity with the worshiping body (like group (7–8), the affirmation of "I believe . . ." is an attestation of devotion with the group to its vision of God) for the simple reason that such statements may make precious little difference to the basic faith structure or to the lives of the participants in the religious communities to which they refer and therefore they can be acknowledged without examination as to whether one considers them "really true or not." Fundamental Christian notions of the deity and the relationship of creation to the deity are not necessarily perturbed by adhering to the doctrines of Immaculate Conception and Bodily Ascension of Mary. To grasp this, one need only recall the statistics regarding adherence among church-going Catholics in good standing to the Church's teachings on birth control. The overwhelming variance amongst the faithful on that issue is not paralleled in the case of the bodily assumption of Mary, even though an examination of the literal consequences of the latter belief has caused at least some educated people to have to rationalize extensively (cf. Schillibeex 1964). Similarly, while belief in a "Catholic and Apostolic church" technically means for Episcopalians that the sacraments are valid only when performed by individuals who have be been ordained through a chain of laying-on-of-hands which allegedly can be traced back to the original Apostles, very few these days actually fail in practice to recognize the full authority of other Christian clergy, and many would probably be astounded to learn that on the narrowest construction of ostensible Church doctrine their ecumenism might be heretical. Equally similarly, while inherited Buddhist doctrine is uniform in affirming reincarnation and the force of karma, in much in ordinary Chinese Buddhist practice, the pre-Buddhist practice of ancestor reverence is of greater actual force. That the two notions are directly contradictory (how can ancestors have a permanent spirit to which sacrifices can be made and which can somehow be contained in a spirit tablet if that ancestor is already reincarnated in a different form?) makes little difference to those Buddhist temples which display the appropriate Buddhist images on the altar and on the front side of the altar wall or screen while on the back of the same wall display ancestral tablets both for the departed spirits of members of the local congregation and even of deceased monks and nuns.

Given these examples and the great number (limitless?) of similar statements which could be adduced from experience and research, (10) below seems a reasonable statement:

(10) In a formal religious context, affirmations of belief (whether stated formally in the frame "I believe (in) X" or given in other sentential constructions) generally imply membership in a group which defines itself through making those statements and concurrence in the general faith of that group, and *may* imply direct denotative force between *believe* and its grammatical object on a case-by-case basis.

Among the implications of (10) is the standard caution of comparative religionists that the very types of belief statements represented by creedal statements are not central to all religions (in fact, not to the majority of religions), and (more importantly for the current paper) that verbal exegeses which are reduced to belief statements may or may not state what seems to be entailed by the grammatical construction of belief-type sentences. Thus, any description of religious knowledge and the capacities which underlie it must somehow capture the actual intent and implications of such statements. Further, if assertions of religious conviction, whether stated as belief statements or in other explanatory formats (e.g. (1) above), are not necessarily about what their verbal formulation seems to imply and yet may be a regular feature of religious behavior, then the common characteristic of such statements is their ritual feature rather than their denotative content. That is, although typically used by formal religious organizations as definitive enunciations of credence and official doctrine, statements of religious conviction operate as one of the available forms of religious *practice* (including, for example, both corporate transformational and reiterative maintenance rituals, and any activity which an individual adherent allies to her or his religion). Formal credence statements may be a necessary part of some religious practice, but only when it can be shown that the utterer holds to their denotative force are they doctrinal statements. And if that is true, then the infrastructure of religious knowledge must be the same for exegetical statements as it is for praxis. Given this, (10) must be reformulated:

> (11) Statements of religious credence are a standard part of the repertory of religious *practice*, from which religious groups and members thereof select for religious expression; when the denotative meaning of such statements can be shown consistently to align with other statements and the import of other practice, then such statements are also assertions of conviction in the same way as similar semantically and grammatically constructed statements would be in ordinary non-ritual language.

A consequence of this way of interpreting belief statements is that it raises a serious question regarding our seemingly natural tendency to dichotomize religious types according to doctrinal vs. ritual prominence. Certainly, it is legitimate to describe this division in discussing how it is that some religions analyze their own performance. As a general means of taxonomy, however, a doctrinal vs. ritual categorization is rendered shaky at best by examination of the actual implication of doctrinal statements. Doctrinal statements are one aspect of religious practice and are part of the overall exercise of exegesis, i.e. transposition of religious experience into verbal symbols. As with all verbal symbols, (in fact with all symbols, but particularly with verbal symbols, owing to the peculiarity of language that specifically allows human beings to *consciously* employ verbal symbols to define verbal symbols), the more ambiguous a particular symbol is (i.e. the less well defined), the more adherents it may draw and the more tightly defined it is, the more controversy it draws instead of adherence. To be treated fully, this matter would take a complete paper all by itself. For the purposes of this paper, the tenuousness of the doctrinal-praxis dichotomy will remain simply an observation.

Memory, Meaning and Meaningfulness

If the denotative content of belief statements does not always reflect the actual convictions of the believer, and yet if belief statements may be a part of practice, then how is it that formal statements of belief are part of the overall symbolic repertory from which religions "choose" their symbolic makeup? And how is it that on the one hand the Zulu young man relates convictions about desires and consequences to ritual efficacy on the one hand and group membership on the other, and adherents to creedal Christianity relate desires and consequences to the effects of the act of believing? I suggest that the underlying basis for such leaps of conviction lie in the fundamental infrastructure of our concept development. That infrastructure has two basic parts: the establishment of meaning through memory and the blending of concepts, through which humans transfer meaning and meaningfulness to those things which we value. In the remainder of this section, I shall discuss the development of meaning through memory, and in the next section briefly outline how meaning and meaningfulness are transferred through blending.

Generally speaking, the common infrastructure of meaning is the linkages between symbols or representations. That is, the meaning of X is that we define X through Y, or, in terms of very meaningful items, through X, Y, Z, and perhaps more. Relative meaningfulness is roughly a comparative measure of the associative links which we acknowledge between any two symbols, with the symbol which has the greater number of associations being the more meaningful to us.

This infrastructural and almost mechanical notion of meaningfulness operates completely irrespective of content. That some ideas and symbols may be inherently more meaningful to us (e.g., surprising, counter-intuitive, attention-grabbing) as argued by Boyer and Whitehouse among others is not in any sense disputed here. As I mentioned at the beginning, I assume that the *content* of our religious symbols and concepts arises pretty much along the lines which they and other cognitivists have suggested. At issue here is simply the mechanism through which those concepts which are inherently more likely to draw our attention become embedded. I suggest that mechanism is the associative linkage which underlies the operation of any such predilections with which we may be hard-wired or for which our lifetime learning may subsequently predispose us. Meaningfulness and memorability are developed simultaneously, with that which is more memorable being that which is also more meaningful because it is at the heart of a more intricate and dense network of links. Vocabulary learning in language provides the easiest example of how this works.

In language learning, new vocabulary is learned through a word's recurrence in multiple meaningful contexts. A new vocabulary item, in other words, becomes an embedded part of our repertoire to the degree that we perceive its meaning in a variety of contexts where the overall context itself is comprehensible to us and through which we grasp each further nuance of the word. Vocabulary is not learned just through repetition. Simple repetition carried very far produces a fatigue effect and disrupts potential learning. Language learning models which stress structure and are arranged with maximal logical clarity generally produce far lower results than those which are arranged according to graded levels of meaningfulness to the learner. This fundamental principle has been codified through Stephen Krashen's "Input Hypothesis" (Krashen 1985) and symbolized in the formula

(12) $i + 1$

In this formula i refers to input which the learner already knows and the additional 1 to a limited increment of new material which is learned through being perceived in the midst of i. Krashen's hypothesis was developed in response to significant evidence that it is *meaningful* material which is learned and that in any language learning it is vast amounts of meaningful inputs which must precede outputs for successful active participation in language ever to occur. The stress on inputs reflected in the work by Winitz and others (Winitz 1981a, 1981b, 1981c; Light 1985) is a deliberate replacement of an emphasis either on recursive performance as the key to learning or on an assumed high value for lengthy and complex explanation in learning. It turns out that reiterative performance of the cognitive tasks associated with language behavior results only in continuous reiterative performance, i.e., rote behavior. It also turns out that received explanations have, at best, a very imperfect influence on subsequent language performance. In contrast, the learner who continues to be exposed to massive amounts of meaningful language content derives from that content the meaning of the embedded items which the learner did not previously know and thereby integrates those new items into a meaningful and remembered repertoire.[4]

---

[4] It is necessary to note here that in this intentional detour into applied linguistics, I am deliberately relying on understandings gained through teaching and research in language and linguistics (Chinese and English), the field in which I spent

Readers familiar with cognitive work on general learning and religious development in particular will note a very strong parallel between the standard cognitive view of human conceptual development and the description of how vocabulary is acquired in language learning just given. In terms of the history of scholarship, this is far from surprising, since the initial impetus giving rise to what has become cognitive science began with the "Chomskian Revolution," and much of what has become generally accepted in general cognitive science is historically derivative from linguistic studies. This connection is immediately obvious in the work of Lawson and McCauley and equally evident to those who examine carefully the work of Boyer, Shore, Sperber, and others. What is reflected in those works is mainly the discoveries that have been made regarding how human beings possess a unique capacity for acquiring the systemic aspects of languages as manifested in syntactic and phonological structures. So far as I am aware, the implications for the learning of symbolic sets of systemically meaningful relativity that appear to be evident in the learning of vocabulary have not yet been elucidated.[5]

---

my academic career until a bit more than ten years ago. While fully aware that I could be justly charged with simply returning to a happy experience and unwarrantedly mating that to a discussion of religion, I believe that the relevance to religion of general principles of language acquisition is substantial. While I have suggested (Light 2000) that, unless specifically modified for religion, the tools of formal linguistic analysis inaccurately account for religious behavior, I do believe that the learning process of the vast array of representative symbols in both fields (vocabulary in language, verbal and other symbols in religion) is the same and that we in religious studies can learn a great deal from observing language-learning behavior.

[5] Among the important lessons from foreign language acquisition is that students develop through stages of learning, and those stages are correlated with (among other things) the length of utterance which any particular vocabulary and/or grammatical construction entails. Students may utter with perfect pronunciation and grammar utterances of 6–8 syllables in length, and then immediately thereafter render completely incomprehensible utterances composed entirely of language segments that they "know" (cf. Light 1987, chapter 2). The significance of this fact for religion and other major cultural spheres is that we may appear to a formal instructor in ritual and/or belief that we are mastering a particular piece of learning, but in fact be incapable of storing, retrieving, and replicating that learning as delivered and hence transpose it into what we are capable of, which turns out to be incomprehensible to other members of our religious community. For language study, the vast literature concerning "error analysis" deals (among other things) with this ubiquitous phenomenon. For the study of religion, the cognitive interest in cultural transmission deals (again among a host of other things) with this common phenomenon. However, students of religion have not been as precise as students of language regarding those cases where it is prior learning which causes the variance from what was initially delivered.

Not surprisingly, it is not only the process of learning itself which illustrates this process, but as well the operations of vocabulary once learned continue to reflect the process. Thus, in any count of the relative frequency of word occurrence in a given text, a pyramid emerges, with one or a very few words being the most frequent and the vast majority being relatively infrequent (cf. Wei and Light 1973 for a summary of results of frequency counts.) Further, it is the infrequent words whose denotative meaning is most easily defined, while the most frequently occurring terms are the most difficult to gloss. The so-called "function words" of a language (e.g. the prepositions in English) are among the most frequently occurring terms and also those which it is extremely difficult to provide for a non-English speaker a clear idea of the meaning. Structuralist linguists, indeed, defined such function words as empty of specific content. However, as Lakoff and Johnson (1980; 1999) have convincingly shown, these "little" words carry the greatest meaning and functional load because it is only they which give full contextual significance to the nouns, verbs, and adjectives whose definition is easily obtained. Words of a clear denotation cannot by themselves form utterances precisely because of their denotative limitations. Stated differently, the nouns, verbs, adjectives, and adverbs to which we devote the vast majority of our lexical, etymological and philological attention are definable both grammatically and semantically through very simple frames all of which are expressible in sentences. (13) is the basic frame for defining the content words of English.

(13) X _____ Y

Which is expandable as in (14)

(14) (a) John *hit* Mary with his fist.
(b) Peter got *hit* by a car and broke his leg.
(c) The hammer *hit* the window, but only cracked it.
(d) The flying glass *hit* his face with force, lacerating his cheek, but fortunately did not hit his eye.

In contrast, Lakoff and Johnson have shown, the prepositions which resist simple definition have clear and powerful meanings which can in fact be identified if we examine the larger concepts which they trigger. Arguing that our special concepts are all derived from our own bodies and the location of all other perceptions in relation to our bodies and their orientation, Lakoff and Johnson show, for example that the preposition *in* locates an object somewhere within defined physical boundaries and the preposition *at* locates an object at a particular point. Thus:

(15) Christina is lying *in* a field *in* Wyeth's famous painting, *Christina's World*.
(16) As usual, Dagwood Bumstead is standing *at* the bus stop still asleep.

More significantly, Lakoff and Johnson argue, the conceptualization of our concepts is itself developed through metaphorical extension of our own physical locatedness. Thus, time enclosure within boundaries is signaled by *in* and a point of time by *at* (*in* two hours, *at* three o'clock) and in abstract discussion (*in* his conception of things, *at* this juncture of the argument) the two prepositions have clearly analogous functions based on the prime of physical locatedness.

Whether one fully accepts Lakoff and Johnson's reduction of human thought to a metaphorical extension of human physical positioning, their more general point that our minds operate through metaphorical extension and that it is the most frequently occurring items (rather than the less frequently occurring terms which have clearer specific denotations) has considerable persuasiveness if for no other reason than that metaphorical extension gives a concreteness to the largely undefined notion of inference which is posited as the basic engine of human concept development beyond those conceptualization schemes with which we are hard-wired at birth.

If meaning is indeed regular associations amongst specific symbols and if meaningfulness is formed through a relatively high level of association and if the development of conceptualization operates through metaphorical extension to the degree that the metaphors which we spread become so deeply laid down in our minds that, like English prepositions, we are hardly conscious of their import until it is analytically explicated for us, then the basic infrastructure of the development of religious conceptions (along with all other conceptions) occurs with an automatic projection of learned and/or hard-wired conceptions onto new situations through the extension of the metaphors already at hand to us.

Conceptual Blending: Mental-Space Theory and Religion

The metaphorical extension that is at the heart of Lakoff and Johnson's version of cognitive processing has been analyzed more formally and abstractly by those cognitive scientists who work in "Mental-Space Theory." Included most prominently amongst this group are Coulson, Fauconnier, Sweetser, and Turner. Stated in its most elementary form, Mental-Space Theory envisions human thought as the creation of "mental spaces" or, if one prefers, conceptual representations, which schematize a perceiver's understanding of any particular concept at the moment of cognition. Mental Spaces are thought of as momentary conceptions in a continuously dynamic process of adaptation to the flow of new perceptions which continues in our minds even as we have perceived a situation to be a certain way. In the terms of cognitive theory, Mental Spaces are probably best thought of as a more explicit rendering of the generally inexplicit notion of the *inferences* which human minds make based upon what they know in the light of new information (cf. Boyer 1994, 2000, Lawson and McCauley 1990, 2002 for reference to inference as the fundamental mental procedure which takes us to new understanding in the light of new data).

In keeping with basic cognitive science theory, Mental-Space Theory presumes that we learn anew only on the basis of what we already know and that what we already know is a representation of perceptions governed both by the capacities with which we are hard-wired and the experiences which we have accumulated since birth. In Boyer's terms we are hard-wired to recognize, for example, agency and animacy as opposed to inanimacy and lifelessness, and we have expectations of what animate agents can do in a world where normal physical constraints obtain (e.g., time, space, gravity, etc.). When we perceive that these constraints are violated (for example by an entity going through solid objects), we develop concepts which most closely approximate what we already know—namely, that it is human agents which possesses the greatest amount of flexible agentive power—and merge that known understanding with the newly perceived phenomenon of the power to penetrate solid matter. That merger produces superhuman agents which are anthropomorphic in all but the particular feature (or few features) which make them superhuman.

Coulson (2001) argues that the blending of new perceptions with established ones invariably creates a new Mental Space which "recruits" the features of the new perception and the previously stored one which most suit the perception of the moment. Most important is that it is neither the old perception nor the newly perceived one which is the product of the blending of two Spaces, but a genuine merger of significant parts of the two. If one accepts that this is an accurate accounting of how human cognition seems to work (and, up to now, it seems to me to be the most accurate one), then it necessarily follows that human thought patterns are not naturally patterned after formal logic, but do have a logic of their own, one that can be grasped—like all other human behavior—only by deducing the principles which it is following from observing the mental leaps that are made in cognition. It is for this reason that Coulson and others must refer to each subsequent Mental Space in a chain as having "recruited" portions of preceding Mental Spaces. This is a critical point to grasp. Human cognition is sometimes described as though it were inherently governed by such formal rules as complete abhorrence to internal contradiction. As I have suggested above, one of the signs that religious knowledge is entirely natural is that it easily accommodates contradictory propositions within its overall system, which makes religious knowing no different from ordinary scientific knowing on the part of the astronomer who in daily speech refers to the sun rising and setting.

I would add to Coulson's and Fauconnier's analysis of Mental Spaces the observation that such systemic contradictions are maintained without difficulty through our segregating our different conceptual systems into Mental-Space groupings which are in effect mutually impermeable. Another way of saying the same thing is to say that much of our knowledge is so obviously context-sensitive that one of the basic primes with which we are hard-wired must be cognitive receptiveness to contextual stimuli. Obviously, as mentioned above, social context governs the level of honesty we will choose to employ in any given strategy of politeness, a range that can vary from brutal frankness through studied euphemism to utterly dissimulated avoidance; social context also governs which of the many different registers of speech we have at our disposal we will use on a given occasion. Context, of course, is what prompts how the scientist will describe the motion of other astronomical bodies relative to the earth. Contexts, however, do not have to be social, but may be triggered by the demands of competing conceptual systems. An instance of conceptually inspired compartmentalization is surely Barrett's (2000) wonderful study of "theological incorrectness" (as well as Slone's fine study of luck as an example of "theological incorrectness" in this volume), demonstrating that professing Christians may identify God as omniscient and omnipresent and then (without noticing the contradiction) narrate stories about God which puts God in a world governed by human sequentiality. I suggest that many theological issues in many religions are handled in a similar way. That some Christians' stories of God differ radically from their discursive descriptions is entirely natural and replicated in different ways in most religions.

Most studies of the development of human cognition presume that the reason process which moves from known concept A through new information B to blended new conception C involves analogy, and it has been widely held that analogy is the basic reasoning tool with which we are biologically endowed. While the majority of cases so far studied do indeed manifest analogical characteristics, recent work has suggested that there may be other reasoning processes which produce Mental Spaces. Examples (17) and (18) are offered as two versions of a well known case of religious behavior that readily lends itself to a blending analysis. Both refer to the establishment of the merger between the Spanish Catholic Virgin and Tonantzin, the Nahua goddess of compassion and mercy. If one accepts Eric Wolf's (1958) classic description of the process, then analogy is what is certainly taking place (followed by a rough syllogism):

(17) (a) The Spanish Catholic Virgin is the numinous figure of compassion and mercy and is very powerful.
(b) The Nahua Tonantzin is the numinous figure of compassion and mercy and is very powerful.
(c) Therefore, the two must be names for the same figure.

However, if one accepts Burkhardt's (1993) later revision in which there was no pre-Conquest Tonantzin in Nahua religion, then the chain of reasoning must be something like:

(18) (a) The Spanish Catholic Virgin is the numinous figure of compassion and mercy and is very powerful.
(b) There is no analogous figure in our system, but clearly one is needed.
(c) Therefore, the prominent characteristics of the Virgin are projected into our pantheon to fill the gap.

(17) and (18) are respectively given Mental-Space analyses in Charts (19) and (20). The format used is a simplified version of that employed in Coulson 2001. Coulson's tabular arrangement is eminently suitable for charting blends which involve specific conceptual features and shows the process of adaptation over time by reading left-to-right.

Input I	Input II	Selected	Blended Output
System of Saints	System of Gods	Both Saints and Gods	Saints/Gods
Mary	Tonantzin	Both names	Mary/Tonantzin
Virgin Saint	Goddess	Saint (Goddess?)	Virgin Saint (Goddess)
Image of Mercy	Image of Mercy	Same	Image of Mercy
Prayed to for Help & Forgiveness	Sacrificed to for Help	Approached for Help & Forgiveness	Prayed to/ Sacrificed to for Help & Forgiveness
Mother Figure	Mother Figure	Same	Mother Figure
Mother-of-God	N.A.	Mother of Jesus	Mother of Jesus
Co-Mediatrix in Salvation	N.A.	Image of Mercy	Efficacious in Salvation

Chart 19: Simplified Mental-Space diagram of Wolf's version of the Virgin of Guadalupe

Input I	Input II	Selected	Blended Output
System of Saints	General System of Gods	Both Saints and Gods	Saints/Gods
Mary		Mary/Tonantzin	Mary/Tonantzin
Virgin Saint		Virgin Saint (Goddess)	Virgin Saint (Goddess)
Image of Mercy		Image of Mercy	Image of Mercy
Prayed to for Help & Forgiveness		Prayed to/ Sacrificed to for Help & Forgiveness	Prayed to/ Sacrificed to for Help & Forgiveness
Mother Figure		Mother Figure	Mother Figure

(cont.)

Input I	Input II	Selected	Blended Output
Mother-of-God	N.A.	Mother of Jesus	Mother of Jesus
Co-Mediatrix in Salvation	N.A.	Efficacious in Salvation	Efficacious in Salvation

Chart 20: Mental-Space diagram of Burkhardt's version of the Virgin of Guadalupe

Explanation of charts 19 and 20: (1) As shown in (19), if there was actually a Tonantzin in the Nahua system, then the European missionaries apparently saw her as a close analogue to the Virgin. Presumably, they adapted the Nahua name in the same manner as did the Romans in matching their gods to the gods of conquered people. (2) Actual practice by the Nahuatl people, however, indicates that from their side the blend was interpreted an add-on to the existing goddess. Since religious practice regarding saints (especially popular Iberian practice) seems both then and now to look (at least to the outsider) strikingly like that of other people's behavior towards gods, the blend has to account for the likelihood of Mary/Tonantzin being termed a god in Nahua. (3) Finer points of Christian theology do not seem to have been selected. Thus, the singular Catholic image of "Mother-of-God" (with all of its implications and limitations in semantic field) becomes simply Mother of Jesus, and her salvific work is conflated with her general work of mercy. (4) Similarly, if there was a pre-Conquest Tonantzin, that goddess's other attributes do not become part of the blend. (5) Contrastingly, as in (20) if there was no such pre-Conquest goddess, then Mary/Tonantzin originated as a projection of the Iberian Catholic spirituality onto the system of Gods of the Nahuatl. The output is essentially the same in both cases because the receiving context is governed by the constraints of the indigenous system and because the peculiarities of Christian theology (the Trinity, the dual nature of Jesus/Christ, etc.) seem to have had as much difficulty in crossing cultural borders as was the case as early as the 2nd century.

Such conceptual mergers are easily evident in cases of obvious syncretism, and that is why this example used here. Another instance in this volume is given by Wilson in his perceptive analysis of the grotto at Amecameca. There, analogization is very clear. The ultimate numinous power of the cavern where Jesus was buried in Palestine is emulated according to Franciscans in that of St. Francis in Italy, and both are drawn on to contribute to the sacred space promoted by the rival Dominican order in New Spain. Even when obvious syncretism is not involved, examination of a tradition on its own terms will demonstrate basically the same conceptual development (which is, of course, why syncretism and not purity is the hallmark of religious thought).

Returning now to the example with which this essay began, the overall message which the Zulu young man gives to Tom Lawson after each of Lawson's queries is that Lawson simply does not have the capability of "making himself more beautiful" through well established Zulu rituals. All but the last reply to Lawson's inquiries regarding his own use of the rituals is the assertion of another ritual that must be performed as a condition of efficacy of the ritual with which the queries began. The last reply changes course and asserts that Lawson would have to become a Zulu to make any of the rituals work. Without a great deal more information than is given in the anecdote, no outsider can know whether the string of statements concerning further rituals was offered simply as an attempt to put Lawson off from further queries or whether the four rituals might indeed constitute a chain of acts which are recognized within the Zulu community to "make oneself more beautiful." Nevertheless, it is quite clear that the young man's chain of reasoning is not that of simple analogy, but adaptation to each new context provoked by Lawson's continued queries through "recruiting" from a repertoire of rituals several of which (at least for this interchange) are offered serially as plausibly relevant to the goal of ritual beautification. This form of "recruiting" is probably best considered simple projection of elements from one Mental Space to another in order to meet a changed circumstance to which the perceiver is attempting to adjust his conceptions. And when the iterative chain of required rituals does not end the iterative chain of queries, the Mental Space is changed again, this time to the obvious difference between Lawson and his informant, for the clinching riposte which ends the interchange: Lawson is not a Zulu and never will be.

The young man's probable Mental-Space adjustments are diagrammed in Figure (21), which is given in a form that has been simplified from that used by Fauconnier (1997, 2001). Fauconnier's format is particularly helpful in charting iteratively changing Mental Spaces resulting from a need to keep re-adapting to a situation which either is changing or the perceptions of which are changing.

(21) illustrates that analogy is not the issue with the young man's thought process. For there is simply no analogy present in the discussion. Lawson asks questions, and the young man provides as answers rituals that hitherto had not been mentioned. He draws those rituals from a repertoire of rituals. Cumulatively, they may be a formula for how one can make oneself beautiful. But as the final comment demonstrates, none of them is projected onto Lawson's situation (as

analogy or straight projection), but are in effect reasons why Lawson never can make himself beautiful through Zulu rituals. All are taken from the repertoire of sacred actions relating to sacred states, and they are told to a person who is inherently incapable of ever engaging in them or entering into the sacred world which they represent.

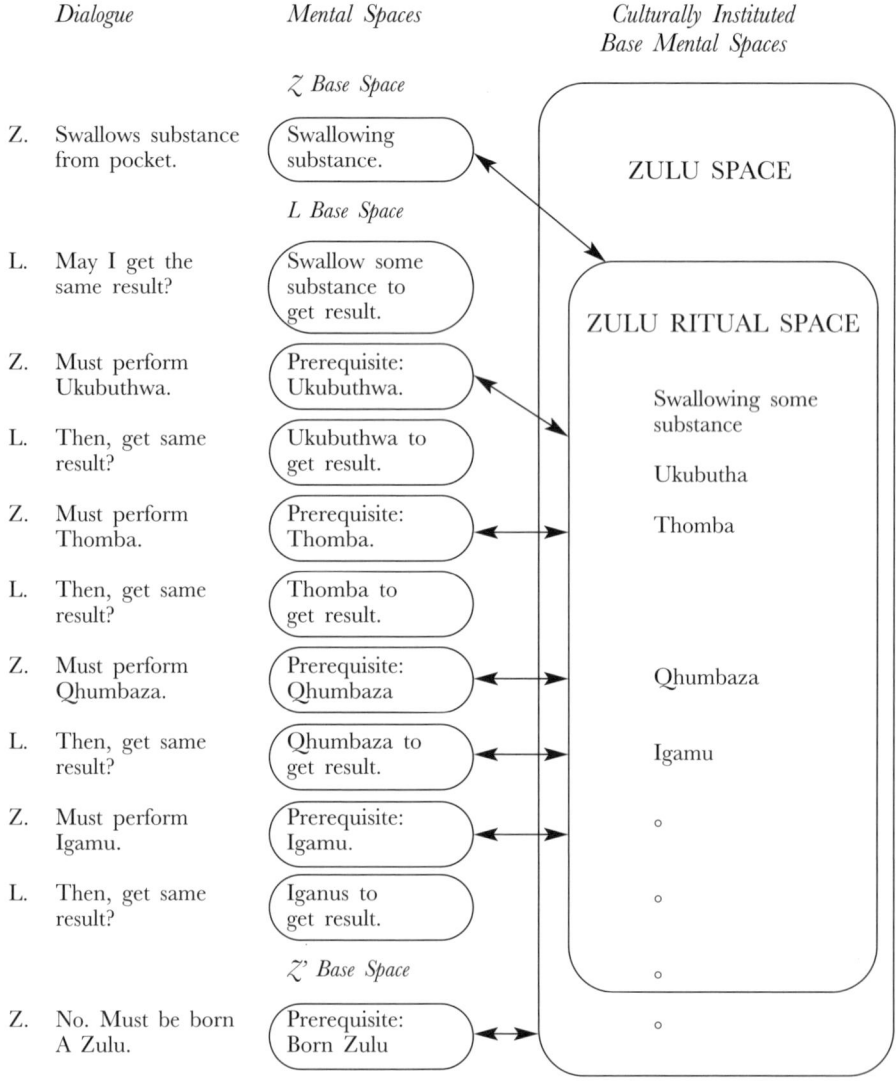

Chart 21: Cognition and Credence

Explanation of chart 21: What Chart 21 intends to show is: Z (Zulu man) and L (Lawson) have a shared element in their Base Mental Spaces for this encounter, but that shared element serves a distinctly different function for each and is respectively linked with dramatically different internal contexts. In the first exchange that element is the actual act of swallowing some substance. In the remaining exchanges that element is a named ritual which is not performed or visualized. For the Zulu, the ritual of swallowing is merely something that was seen, while each the remaining four named rituals is defined as a prerequisite to a result. For Lawson, all five of the rituals are received as leading to a result (which is why he asks only if he can get the same result, not if there is a result for the Zulu).

Finally, the Zulu man alters the base space by continuing to refer to prerequisites (which for him is the key aspect of the shared element), but now by naming not a member or function of the category of being Zulu, but the whole category itself. For Lawson, this is a very significant alteration of the Base Space, because it signals that which had been implied all along by the Zulu, but had not been part of Lawson's base understanding, namely, that the five rituals are in fact immediately efficacious, but are contingent of the real pre-requisite, birth membership in a group to which Lawson does not belong.

For Mental-Space theory, the importance of this way of analyzing the respective Mental Spaces of the Zulu man and Lawson is that the Zulu's dynamically altering Mental Spaces in the conversation with Lawson are defined by reiterative reversions to the established (or culturally instituted) major mental space of what it means to be Zulu and within that space specific Zulu rituals. Recognizing that our Mental Spaces in the natural dynamism of evolving encounters are themselves dynamic but are simultaneously dependent upon relatively more stable spaces which are marked by relatively closed sets of symbols which pertain to those sets, some of which may be inaccessible and/or opaque to an interlocutor is of critical significance in analyzing exchanges, particularly where those encounters result in misunderstanding or turn out to have been predicated on one participant's part on private, esoteric, or restricted knowledge.

For the theory of religion, the importance of this way of analyzing the respective Mental Spaces is that it helps account for the continued usefulness of an encompassing category such as [sacred], despite the recognition that no primary mental category or operation can be found to motivate such categories. I believe that it is in this sense that Anttonen uses the category and term *sacred* in writing from a cognitive standpoint in this volume.

Conclusions

I have suggested that borrowing the framework of Mental-Space and Metaphor Theories enhances cognitive accounts of religious behavior, and have used credence behavior as the major case in point. I have argued that the compartmentalization and the apparent "illogicality" of the Zulu man's statements to Lawson are nothing more than entirely normal human reasoning, and that credence assertions in other religious traditions reflect the same processes of ratiocination. I have attempted to analyze these processes through accounting for the development of meaning through normal memory acquisition and offering a description of how a given religious concept becomes blended with other concepts in response to altered circumstance. I believe that Mental-Space frameworks and diagram models offer a rich tool for the analyses of religious behavior for reasons which I shall summarize in brief "bullet" form in order to save space:

- As diagrams (19–21) demonstrate, Mental-Space analyses are able to restrict the field of inference to plausible limits through the notion of "recruitment" of fractional concepts already evident to the perceiver and thereby begin to add precision to this critical engine of cognitive processing.
- Understanding that Mental-Space and Metaphor Theories are offered as infrastructural possibilities allows us to recognize and allocate appropriate roles for the host of motivations which come to play in the development of religions. It seems incontestable that for various religious manifestations, social, economic, or biological motivations are at work. It is equally uncontestable (I believe) that attempts to explain religious behavior by purported theories based on the work of Durkheim, Weber, or Freud have their most helpful explanatory value mainly for a subset of religious behaviors at specific periods of time, but no general theoretical value regarding how humans universally develop our concepts, religious or otherwise. Mental-Space Theory is particularly suited to capture the highly contingent relevance of these and other such proposals regarding religion without either inflating their value or denying their importance altogether.
- The process outlined in (19–21) and verbally described in (10, 11, 17–18) reflects a fairly commonsense understanding of how our minds adjust to changing circumstance. Commonsense is not always to be preferred in scholarly analysis. After all, nothing in ordinary

common experience leads to modern physics. However, in the absence of compelling empirical evidence to the contrary, the shared evidence of our ordinary senses requires attentive respect. Ordinary people readily see that the Mexican, Chinese, and Roman Catholic cases noted above are mixtures of some kind, and ordinary people see that chained responses to reiterated queries are adjustment to the queries. If our analyses do not resemble such commonsense, we need to have a host of evidence to justify the dissimilarity.

- The notion of [sacred] as a potential mental category is debated in cognitive science. While Lawson and McCauley and Boyer dismiss the viability of sacred as a useful category, Antonnen accepts and uses [sacred] in his fine essay in this volume, and the cognitive linguist Eve Sweetser asserts, "The concept of the [sacred] is alive and well" (personal communication). Irrespective of whether one would assert that [sacred] is somehow a prime in human cognitive makeup or a projective derivation from the primes of agentivity and the ability to classify counterintuitive events as special sorts of agents, allowing for a superordinate Mental Space of [sacred] helps account for the precise sorts of compartmentalization and contradiction that we find specific to religion.

Finally, I suggest that this application of Mental-Space Theory to religion may contribute a useful concept to Mental-Space Theory itself. As given in the works by Fauconnier, Fauconnier and Sweetser, Turner, and Coulson cited in the bibliography, Mental-Space Theory offers only general assistance towards establishing such rules as there might be governing how inferences may develop and how they may not. The notion of superordinate Mental Spaces which embed sets of other Mental Spaces so that within such superordinate groupings contradictions may not occur (but they may occur between members of different such sets), could turn out to be a helpful guide to beginning to probe the constraints on inference. It seems to me that it is this sort of structural constraint that is not tied to the content of any specific conceptions which may hold good promise for a possible set of global conditions under which inference takes place.

If the arguments presented in this paper are in any way correct, then one of the coming tasks in Mental-Space Theory is to explore in more detail what possible constraints there are on the capacity for inference which cognitive scientists posit as the fundamental engine for human cognitive growth.

BIBLIOGRAPHY

Abbott, Walter (ed.). 1966. *The Documents of Vatican II*. New York: Guild Press.
Aberle, David F., Albert K. Cohen, Arthur K. Davis, Marion Levy and Francis Sutton. 1950. "The Functional Prerequisites of a Society." *Ethics* 60: 100–11.
Achtemeier, Paul J. (ed.) 1985. *Harper's Bible Dictionary*. San Francisco: Harper and Row.
Adorno, T. W. 1973. *Negative Dialectics*. New York: The Seabury Press.
——. 2000a. *Metaphysics: Concept and Problems*. Stanford: Stanford University Press.
——. 2000b. *Problems of Moral Philosophy*. Stanford: Stanford University Press.
——. 2001. *Kant's Critique of Pure Reason*. Stanford: Stanford University Press.
Aland, B., K. Aland, et al. (eds.). 1993. *The Greek New Testament*. London: United Bible Societies.
Aland, K. and B. Aland. 1987. *The Text of the New Testament: An Introduction to the Critical Editions and to the Theory and Practice of Modern Textual Criticisms*. Grand Rapids: W.B. Eerdmans Publishing Co.
Aland, K., M. Welte, et al. 1994. *Kurzgefasste Liste der griechischen Handschriften des Neuen Testaments*. Berlin: New York, W. de Gruyter.
Albanese, Catherine L. 1999. *America: Religions and Religion*. Belmont, CA: Wadworth.
Al-Karsani, Awad Al-Sid. 1993. "Beyond Sufism: The Case of Millennial Islam in the Sudan." In L. Brenner (ed.), *Muslim Identity and Social Change in Sub-Saharan Africa*. London: Hurst & Co., 135–53.
American Bible Society. 1976. *Good News Bible: The Bible in Today's English Version*. Nashville, TN: Broadman Press.
Anonymous. 1971. *Crónica de la Provincia Franciscana de Santiago, 1214–1614* (c. 1620), edited by Manuel de Castro. Madrid: Archivo Ibero Americano.
Anttonen, Veikko. 1996a. *Ihmisen ja maan rajat. 'Pyhä' kulttuurisena kategoriana. (The Making of Corporeal and Territorial Boundaries: 'Sacred' as a Cultural Category.)* (In Finnish.) Helsinki: Suomalaisen Kirjallisuuden Seura.
——. 1996b. "Rethinking the Sacred: The Notions of 'Human Body' and 'Territory' in Conceptualizing Religion." In Thomas A. Idinopulos and Edward A. Yonan (eds.), *The Sacred and its Scholars. Comparative Methodologies for the Study of Primary Religious Data*. Leiden: E. J. Brill, 36–64.
——. 1999. "Does the Sacred Make a Difference? Category Formation in Comparative Religion." In Tore Ahlbäck (ed.), *Approaching Religion*, part I (*Scripta Instituti Donneriani* 17:1). Åbo: The Donner Institute, 9–23.
——. 2000. "Sacred." In Willi Braun and Russell T. McCutcheon (eds.), *Guide to the Study of Religion*. London and New York: Cassell, 271–82.
——. 2002. "Identifying the Generative Mechanisms of Religion: The Issue of Origin Revisited." In Pyysiäinen and Anttonen (eds.) 2002, 14–37.
Appadurai, Arjun. 1998. "Dead Certainty: Ethnic Violence." *Public Culture* 10:2: 225–47.
Arnal, William. 2001a. "Black Holes, Theory, and the Study of Religion." *Studies in Religion/Sciences Religieuses* 30:2: 209–14.
——. 2001b. "The Segregation of Social Desire: 'Religion' and Disney World." *Journal of the American Academy of Religion* 69:1: 1–19.
Asad, Talal. 1992. *Genealogies of Religion: Discipline and Reasons of Power in Christianity and Islam*. Baltimore: John Hopkins University Press.
——. 1999. "Religion, Nation-State, Secularism." In Peter van der Veer and Hartmut

Lehmann (eds.), *Nation and Religion: Perspectives on Europe and Asia*. Princeton: Princeton University Press, 178–96.

Askew, Pamela. 1969. "The Angelic Consolation of St. Francis of Assisi in Post-Tridentine Italian Painting." *The Journal of the Warburg and Courtauld Institutes* 32: 280–306.

Astuti, Rita. 2001. "Are We All Natural Dualists? A Cognitive Development Approach." *The Journal of the Royal Anthropological Institute* 7: 429–48.

Atran, Scott. 2002. *In Gods We Trust: The Evolutionary Landscape of Religion*. Oxford: Oxford University Press.

Barkindo, Barwuro M. 1993. "Growing Islamism in Kano City Since 1970: Causes, Form and Implications." In L. Brenner (ed.), *Muslim Identity and Social Change in Sub-Saharan Africa*. London: Hurst & Company, 91–105.

Barkow, Jerome H., Leda Cosmides and John Tooby (eds.). 1992. *The Adapted Mind: Evolutionary Psychology and the Generation of Culture*. New York: Oxford University Press.

Barkun, Michael (ed.). 1996. *Millennialism and Violence*. London: Frank Cass.

Barrett, Justin L. 1998. "Cognitive Constraints on Hindu Concepts of the Divine." *Journal for the Scientific Study of Religion* 37:4: 608–19.

——. 1999. "Theological Correctness: Cognitive Constraints and the Study of Religion." *Method and Theory in the Study of Religion*. 11:4: 325–39.

——. 2000. "Exploring the Naturalness of Religious Ideas." *Trends in Cognitive Science* 4 (January 1): 29–34.

——. 2002. "Smart Gods, Dumb Gods, and the Role of Social Cognition in Structuring Ritual Intuitions." *Journal of Cognition and Culture*. 2: 183–93.

Barrett, Justin L. and F. C. Keil. 1996. "Anthropomorphism and God Concepts: Conceptualizing a Nonnatural Entity." *Cognitive Psychology* 3: 219–47.

Barrett, Justin L. and E. T. Lawson. 2001. "Ritual Intuitions: Cognitive Contributions to Judgments of Ritual Efficacy." *Journal of Cognition and Culture*. 1: 183–201.

Barrett, Justin L. and B. Malley. Forthcoming. "Who Needs Ordination? An Empirical Assessment of McCauley and Lawson's Theory of Religious Ritual."

Barth, Fredrik. 1964. *Nomads of South Persia*. London: Allen and Unwin.

——. 1975. *Ritual and Knowledge among the Baktaman of New Guinea*. New Haven: Yale University Press.

——. 1987. *Cosmologies in the Making: A Generative Approach to Cultural Variation in Inner Guinea*. Cambridge: Cambridge University Press.

Bartlett, John (ed.). *Bartlett's Familiar Quotations*, 125th Anniversary Edition. Boston: Little Brown, 1980.

Bateson, Gregory. 1936. *Naven*. Stanford: Stanford University Press.

——. 1972. *Steps to an Ecology of Mind*. New York: Ballantine Books.

Bechtel, S. and L. R. Stains. 1997. *The Good Luck Book*. New York: Workman Publishing.

Beck, Roger. 1996. "The Mysteries of Mithras." In J. S. Kloppenborg and S. G. Wilson (eds.), *Voluntary Associations in the Graeco-Roman World*. London: Routledge, 176–85.

——. 1998. "The Mysteries of Mithras: A New Account of Their Genesis." *The Journal of Roman Studies* 88: 115–28.

——. 2000. "Ritual, Myth, Doctrine, and Initiation in the Mysteries of Mithras: New Evidence from a Cult Vessel." *The Journal of Roman Studies* 90: 145–80.

Becker, J. 1975. "Superstition in Sport." *International Journal of Sport Psychology* 6: 148–52.

Bell, Catherine. 1992. *Ritual Theory, Ritual Practice*. New York: Oxford University Press.

Benevente (Motolinía), Fray Toribio de. 1971. *Memoriales o Libro de las cosas de la Nueva España y de los naturales de ella* (c. 1540), edited by Edmundo O'Gorman. México: Universidad Nacional Autónoma de México.

Benveniste, Emile. 1973. *Indo-European Language and Society*. London: Faber and Faber Ltd.
Berger, Peter L. and Thomas Luckmann. 1966. *The Social Construction of Reality: A Treatise in the Sociology of Knowledge*. Garden City: Doubleday.
Berger, Peter L. 1969. *The Sacred Canopy: Elements of a Sociological Theory of Religion*. New York: Anchor Doubleday.
Birai, Umar M. 1991. "Islamic Tajdid and the Political Process in Nigeria." In M. E. Marty and R. S. Appleby (eds.), *Fundamentalisms and the State*. Chicago: University of Chicago Press, 184–203.
Black Elk. 1979 [1932]. *Black Elk Speaks*, as told through John G. Neihardt. Lincoln: University of Nebraska Press.
Blackmore, S. 1985. "Belief in the Paranormal: Probability Judgments, Illusion of Control, and the Chance of Baseline Shift." *British Journal of Psychology* 76: 459–68.
Bloch, Maurice. 1988. *How We Think They Think: Anthropological Approaches to Cognition, Memory, and Literacy*. Boulder, CO: Westview Press.
Bonaventure. 1960. *The Works of Bonaventure*, Volume I, *Mystical Opuscula*, translated by José de Vinck. Paterson, NJ: St. Anthony Guild Press.
Bottigheimer, R. B. 1996. *The Bible for Children: From the Age of Gutenberg to the Present*. New Haven, CN: Yale University Press.
Boyer, Pascal. 1990. *Tradition as Truth and Communication: A Cognitive Description of Traditional Discourse*. Cambridge: Cambridge University Press.
——. 1994. *The Naturalness of Religious Ideas: A Cognitive Theory of Religion*. Berkeley: University of California Press.
——. 2001a. "Cultural Inheritance/Cognitive Predisposition: The Example of Religious Concepts," In Whitehouse (ed.), 57–89.
——. 2001b. *Religion Explained: The Evolutionary Origins of Religious Thought*. New York: Basic Books.
Boyer, Pascal and S. Walker. 2000. "Intuitive Ontology and Cultural Input in the Acquisition of Religious Concepts." In K. S. Rosengren, C. N. Johnson, and P. L. Harris (eds.), *Imagining the Impossible*. Cambridge: Cambridge University Press, 130–56.
Bradfield, Richard M. 1973, *A Natural History of Associations: A Study in the Meaning of Community*, Volume 2. London: Gerald Duckworth and Company Ltd.
Brandt, R. B. 1954. *Hopi Ethics: A Theoretical Analysis*. Chicago: University of Chicago Press.
Braun, Willi. 2000. "Religion." In Willi Braun and Russell T. McCutcheon (eds.), *Guide to the Study of Religion*. London: Cassell, 3–18.
Brooke, Rosalind B. (ed. and trans.). 1970. *Scripta Leonis, Rufini et Angeli Sociorum S. Francisci (The Writings of Leo, Rufino and Angelo, Companions of St. Francis)*. Oxford: Oxford University Press.
Brown, Delwin, Sheila Davaney, and Kathryn Tanner (eds.). 2001. *Converging on Culture: Theologians in Dialogue with Cultural Analysis and Criticism*. New York: Oxford University Press.
Brown, Donald E. 1991. *Human Universals*. Philadelphia: Temple University Press.
Brown, Peter. 1997. *Authority and the Sacred: Aspects of the Christianisation of the Roman World*. Cambridge: Cambridge University Press.
Brown, R. and J. Kulik. 1982. "Flashbulb Memory." In Ulrich Neisser (ed.), *Memory Observed: Remembering in Natural Contexts*. San Francisco: W. H. Freeman, 23–40.
Bruner, Jerome. 1986. *Actual Minds, Possible Worlds*. Cambridge, MA: Harvard University Press.
Bryan, Dominic. 2001. "In Search of the Imagistic Mode of Communication: Ritual, Violence and Identity in Northern Ireland." Paper presented at the British Academy Networks Project on "Modes of Religiosity," King's College, Cambridge, UK, 20–22 December 2001.

Buckley, Anthony D. 2000. "Royal Arch, Royal Arch Purple and Raiders of the Lost Ark: Secrecy in Orange and Masonic Ritual" In T. M. Owen (ed.), *From Corrib to Cultra: Folklife Essays in Honour of Alan Gailey*. Belfast: The Institute of Irish Studies, Queen's University Belfast, 161–81.

Buhrmann, H. and M. K. Zaugg. 1981. "Superstitions among Basketball Players: An Investigation of Various Forms of Superstitious Beliefs and Behavior among Competitive Basketballers at the Junior High School to University Level." *Journal of Sport Behavior* 4: 163–74.

Buhrmann, H., B. Brown, and M. Zaugg. 1982. "Superstitious Beliefs and Behavior: A Comparison of Male and Female Basketball Players." *Journal of Sport Behavior* 5: 175–85.

Burgon, J. W. 1990. *Unholy Hands on the Bible*. Lafayette, IN: Sovereign Grace Trust Fund.

Burkert, W. 1996. *Creation of the Sacred: Tracks of Biology in Early Religions*. Cambridge, MA: Harvard University Press.

Burkhardt, Louise M. 1989. *The Slippery Earth: Nahua-Christian Moral Dialogue in Sixteenth-Century Mexico*. Tucson: The University of Arizona Press.

——. 1993. "The Cult of the Virgin of Guadalupe in Mexico" In Gary H. Gossen (ed.), *South and Meso-American Native Spirituality: From the Cult of the Feathered Serpent to the Theology of Liberation*. New York: Crossroad, 198–227.

Campenhausen, Hans Von. 1969. *Ecclesiastical Authority and Spiritual Power in the Church of the First Three Centuries*, translated by J.A. Baker. London: Adam and Charles Black.

Capps, Walter H. 1979. "Commentary." In Lauri Honko (ed.), *Science of Religion. Studies in Methodology: Proceedings of the Study Conference of International Association for the History of Religions, held in Turku, Finland August 27–31, 1973. Religion and Reason 13*. The Hague: Mouton, 177–85.

Carmichael, David L., Jane Hubert, Brian Reeves, and Audhild Schanche (eds.). 1994. *Sacred Sites, Sacred Places (One World Archaeology 23)*. London and New York: Routledge.

Carrasco, David. 2000. "Member-at Large Interview." *Religious Studies News* 15:3/4: 16–18.

Carson, D. A. 1979. *The King James Version Debate: A Plea for Realism*. Grand Rapids, MI: Baker Book House.

——. 1998. *The Inclusive-Language Debate: A Plea for Realism*. Grand Rapids, MI: Baker Book House.

Chomsky, Noam. 1957. *Syntactic Structures*. The Hague: Mouton.

——. 1965. *Aspects of the Theory of Syntax*. Cambridge MA: M.I.T. Press.

——. 1980. *Rules and Representations*. New York: Columbia University Press.

——. 1986. *Knowledge of Language: Its Nature, Origin, and Use*. New York: Praeger.

Christelow, Allan. 1985. "Religious Protest and Dissent in Northern Nigeria: From Mahdism to Qura'anic Integralism." *Journal, Institute of Muslim Minority Affairs*. 6: 375–93.

Churchland, P. M. 1989. *A Neurocomputational Perspective: The Nature of Mind and the Structure of Science*. Cambridge, MA: M.I.T. Press.

Clark, Andy. 1999. "Embodied, Situated, and Distributed Cognition." In William Bechel and George Graham (eds.), *A Companion to Cognitive Science*. Malden, MA and Oxford: Blackwell Publishers, 506–17.

Clarke, Peter B. 1987. "The Maitatsine Movement in Northern Nigeria in Historical and Current Perspective." In R. I. J. Hackett (ed.), *New Religious Movements in Nigeria*. Lewiston, NY: Mellen, 93–155.

Clarke, Peter B. and Ian Linden. 1984. *Islam in Modern Nigeria: A Study of a Muslim Community in a Post-Independence State 1960–1983*. Mainz: Grunewald.

Clauss, Manfred. 2001. *The Roman Cult of Mithras: The God and his Mysteries*, translated by R. Gordon. New York: Routledge.

Clifford, James. 1997. *Routes: Travel and Translation in the Late Twentieth Century.* Cambridge, MA: Harvard University Press.
Clifford, James and George Marcus (eds.). 1986. *Writing Culture: The Poetics and Politics of Ethnography.* Berkeley: University of California Press.
Colpe, Carsten. 1987. "The Sacred and the Profane." *The Encyclopedia of Religion*, Volume 12. New York: Macmillan, 511–26.
Colwell, E. C. 1952. *What is the Best New Testament?* Chicago: University of Chicago Press.
Comfort, P. W. 1990. *Early Manuscripts and Modern Translations of the New Testament.* Wheaton, IL: Tyndale House Publishers.
Comstock, W. Richard. 1981. "A Behavioral Approach to the Sacred: Category Formation in Religious Studies." *The Journal of the American Academy of Religion* 49: 625–43.
Cosmides, Leda and John Tooby. 1992. "Cognitive Adaptations for Social Exchange." In Barkow, Cosmides and Tooby (eds.) 1992, 163–228.
Coulson, Seana. 2001. *Semantic Leaps: Frame-shifting and Conceptual Blending in Meaning Construction.* Cambridge: Cambridge University Press.
Crick, Francis. 1995. *The Astonishing Hypothesis: The Scientific Search for the Soul.* New York: Touchstone.
Crim, Keith (ed.). 1989. *The Perennial Dictionary of World Religions.* New York: Harper and Row.
Cross, F. L. (ed.). 1997. *The Oxford Dictionary of the Christian Church*, Third edition. New York: Oxford University Press.
Crossan, John Dominic. 1997. *Jesus: A Revolutionary Biography.* San Francisco: HarperSanFrancisco.
Cunningham, Graham. 1999. *Religion and Magic: Approaches and Theories.* New York: Washington Square.
D'Andrade, Roy G. 1995. *The Development of Cognitive Anthropology.* Cambridge: Cambridge University Press.
Davies, Paul. 2001. "A Cosmic Religious Feeling." In *Science and the Spiritual Quest Boston Conference: Held at the Memorial Church at Harvard University, October 21–23, 2001.* Berkeley: Center for Theology and the Natural Sciences, 1–12 (NB. chapters in document not continuously paginated).
Dawkins, R. 1989. *The Selfish Gene.* New York: Oxford University Press.
Dennett, Daniel C. 1991. *Consciousness Explained.* Boston: Little, Brown and Company.
Derham, William. 1713. *Physico-Theology: or, a Demonstration of Being and Attributes of God, from his Works of Creation.* London: W. Innys.
Diamond, J. 1998. *Guns, Germs, and Steel: The Fates of Human Societies.* New York: Norton.
Douglas, Mary. 1978. *Implicit Meanings: Essays in Anthropology.* London: Routledge and Kegan Paul.
——. 1989 [1966]. *Purity and Danger.* London: Ark Paperbacks.
Durkheim, Emile. 1933 [1893]. *The Division of Labour in Society.* London: Macmillan.
——. 1952 [1897]. *Suicide: A Study in Sociology.* London: Routledge and Kegan Paul.
——. 1964 [1915]. *The Elementary Forms of the Religious Life*, translated by Joseph Ward Swain. London: Allen and Unwin.
——. 1995 [1915]. *The Elementary Forms of Religious Life*, translated by K. E. Fields. New York: The Free Press.
Earhart, H. B. (ed.). 1993. *Religious Traditions of the World: A Journey Through Africa, Mesoamerica, North America, Judaism, Christianity, Islam, Hinduism, Buddhism, China, and Japan.* San Francisco: HarperSanFrancisco.
Eck, Diana L. 2000. "Dialogue and Method: Reconstructing the Study of Religion." In K. C. Patton and B. C. Ray (eds.), *A Magic Still Dwells: Comparative Religion in the Postmodern Age.* Los Angeles: University of California Press, 131–49.
——. 2001. *A New Religious America: How a "Christian Country" Has Become the World's Most Religiously Diverse Nation.* San Francisco: HarperSanFrancisco.

Edelman, Gerald M. and Giulio Tononi. 2001 [2000]. *Consciousness: How Matter Becomes Imagination*. Harmondsworth: Penguin.
Eggan, Dorothy. 1956. "Instruction and Affect in Hopi Cultural Continuity." *Southwestern Journal of Anthropology* 12:4: 347–70.
Eliade, Mircea. 1959. *The Sacred and the Profane: The Nature of Religion*. New York: A Harvest Book.
———. 1990 [1981]. *Autobiography Vol. I, 1907–1937, Journey East, Journey West*, translated by Mac Linscott Ricketts. Chicago: University of Chicago Press.
Elman, J. L., E. A. Bates, M. H. Johnson, A. Karmiloff-Smith, D. Parisi, and K. Plunkett. 1996. *Rethinking Innateness: A Connectionist Perspective on Development*. Cambridge, MA: M.I.T. Press.
Ennis, Arthur. 1971. "The Conflict Between the Regular and Secular Clergy." In Richard E. Greenleaf (ed.), *The Roman Catholic Church in Colonial Latin America*. New York: Knopf, 63–72.
Erasmus, D. and J. Froben (1516). *Novvm instrumentum omne, diligenter ab Erasmo Roterodamo recognitum & omendatum, no solum ad graecam ueritatem, uerumetiam ad multorum utriusq[ue]linguae codicum, eorumq[ue] ueterum simul & emendatorum fidem, postremo ad probatissimorum autorum citationem, emendationem & interpretationem, praecipue Origenis, Chrysostomi, Cyrilli, Vulgarij, Hieronymi, Cypriani, Ambrosij, Hilarij, Augustini, una cum annotationibus, quae lectorem doceant, quid qua ratione mutatum sit*. Colophon, Basiliae in aedibus Ioannis Frobenij Hammelburgensis mense februario.
Erikson, Erik. 1963 [1950]. *Childhood and Society*, Second edition. New York: Norton.
Esposito, John L. 2002. *Unholy War: Terror in the Name of God*. New York: Oxford University Press.
Evans-Pritchard, Edward E. 1937. *Witchcraft, Oracles, and Magic among the Azande*. Oxford: The Clarendon Press.
———. 1940. *The Nuer*. Oxford: Oxford University Press.
———. 1965. *Theories of Primitive Religion*. Oxford: Oxford University Press.
Falk, R. 1981. "On Coincidences." *Skeptical Inquirer* 6: 18–31.
———. 1989. "Judgment of Coincidences: Mine Versus Yours." *American Journal of Psychology* 102: 477–93.
Falola, Toyin. 1998. *Violence in Nigeria: The Crisis of Religious Politics and Secular Ideologies*. Rochester, NY: University of Rochester Press.
Fauconnier, Gillles. 1997. *Mappings in Thought and Language*. Cambridge: Cambridge University Press.
———. 2001. "Conceptual Blending and Analogy." In Gentner, et al. (eds.) 2001, 255–86.
Fauconnier, Gillles and Eve Sweetser (eds.). 1996. *Spaces, Worlds, and Grammar*. Chicago: University of Chicago Press.
Fauconnier, Gillles and Mark Turner. 2002. *The Way We Think: Conceptual Blending and the Minds and Hidden Complexities*. New York: Basic Books.
Fee, G. D. 1978. "Modern Textual Criticism and the Revival of the Textus Receptus." *Journal of the Evangelical Theological Society* 21: 19–33.
Firth, Raymond. 1964. *Essays in Social Organization and Values*. London: Athlone.
Fitzgerald, Timothy. 2000. *The Ideology of Religious Studies*. New York: Oxford University Press.
Flood, Gavin. 1999. *Beyond Phenomenology: Rethinking the Study of Religion*. London: Cassell.
Fortes, Meyer. 1945. *The Dynamics of Clanship among the Tallensi*. Oxford: Oxford University Press.
———. 1980. "Anthropology and the Psychological Disciplines" In Ernest Gellner (ed.), *Soviet and Western Anthropology*. London: Duckworth, 195–216.
Foucault, Michel. 1977. "Nietzsche, Genealogy, History." In Donald F. Bouchard and Sherry Simon (ed. and trans.), *Language, Counter-Memory, Practice: Selected Essays and Interviews*. Ithaca, NY: Cornell University Press, 139–64.

———. 1980. *Power/Knowledge: Selected Interviews and Other Writings, 1972–1977*, edited by Colin Gordon. New York: Pantheon.
———. 1988. *Technologies of the Self: A Seminar with Michel Foucault*, edited by Luther H. Martin, Huck Gutman, and Patrick H. Hutton. Amherst: University of Massachusetts Press.
———. 1990 [1976]. *The History of Sexuality, Vol. 1: An Introduction*, translated by Robert Hurley. New York: Vintage Books.
———. 1996 [1978]. "What is Critique?" In James Schmidt (ed.), *What is Enlightenment? Eighteenth-Century Answers and Twentieth-Century Questions*, translated by Kevin Paul Geiman. Berkeley: University of California Press, 382–98.
Fox, Matthew. 1983. *Original Blessing*. Santa Fe: Bear and Company.
Fox, Robin, 1989. *The Search for Society: Quest for a Biosocial Science and Morality*. New Brunswick, NJ: Rutgers University Press.
France, Anatole. 1975. *Penguin Island*, translated by A. W. Evans. Norwalk, CT: The Heritage Press.
Frazer, James. 1922. *The Golden Bough*. London: Macmillan.
Freud, Sigmund. 1938 [1913]. *Totem and Taboo*. Harmondsworth: Penguin Books.
———. 1957 [1910]. "The Antithetical Meaning of Primal Words." In James Strachey (ed.), *The Standard Edition of the Complete Psychological Works of Sigmund Freud*, Vol. XI. London: The Hogarth Press and the Institute of Psycho-Analysis, 219–52.
———. 1961. *The Future of an Illusion*, translated by James Strachey. New York: W. W. Norton.
Fuller, D. O. 1975. *Which Bible?* Grand Rapids, MI: Grand Rapids International Publications.
Geertz, Armin W. 1986. "A Typology of Hopi Indian Ritual." *Temenos* 22: 41–56.
———. 1987. *Hopi Indian Altar Iconography*. Leiden: E. J. Brill.
———. 1990. "Hopi Hermeneutics: Ritual Person among the Hopi Indians of Arizona." In Hans G. Kippenberg, Yme B. Kuiper and Andy F. Sanders (eds.), *Concepts of Person in Religion and Thought*. Berlin: Mouton de Gruyter, 309–35.
———. 1994 [1992]. *The Invention of Prophecy: Continuity and Meaning in Hopi Indian Religion*. Los Angeles: University of California Press.
———. 1999. "Definition as Analytical Strategy in the Study of Religion." *Historical Reflections/Réflexions Historiques*. 25:3: 445–75.
Geertz, Armin W. and Michael Lomatuway'ma. 1987. *Children of Cottonwood: Piety and Ceremonialism in Hopi Indian Puppetry*. Lincoln and London: University of Nebraska Press.
Geertz, Armin W. and Russell T. McCutcheon. 2000. "The Role of Method and Theory in the IAHR." In Armin W. Geertz and Russell T. McCutcheon (eds.), *Perspectives on Method and Theory in the Study of Religion. Adjunct Proceedings of the XVIIth Congress of the International Association for the History of Religions. Mexico City, 1995*. Leiden: E. J. Brill, 3–37.
Geertz, Clifford. 1973. *The Interpretation of Cultures*. New York: Basic Books.
Gellner, Ernest. 1985. *The Psychoanalytic Movement, or, the Coming of Unreason*. London: Paladin.
Gentner, Dedre, Keith J. Holyoak, and Boicho N. Kokinov (eds.). 2001. *The Analogical Mind: Perspectives from Cognitive Science*. Cambridge, MA: M.I.T. Press.
Giddens, Anthony. 1987. "Action, Subjectivity, and the Constitution of Meaning." In Murray Krieger (ed.), *The Aims of Representation: Subject/Text/History*. New York: Columbia University Press, 159–74.
Gilligan, Carol. 1982. *In a Different Voice*. Cambridge, MA: Harvard University Press.
Gilovich, T., R. Vallone, and A. Tversky. 1985. "On the Hot Hand in Basketball: On the Misperception of Random Sequences." *Cognitive Psychology* 17: 295–314.
Gil-White, Francisco. 2001 "Sorting is not Categorization: A Critique of the Claim that Brazilians Have Fuzzy Racial Categories." *Journal of Cognition and Culture* 1:3: 219–49.

Ginsburg, Herbert and Sylvia Opper. 1969. *Piaget's Theory of Intellectual Development: An Introduction*. Englewood Cliffs, NJ: Prentice-Hall.
Gluckman, Max. 1963. *Order and Rebellion in Tribal Africa*. London: Cohen and West.
Goldschmidt, Walter. 1990. *The Human Career: The Self in the Symbolic World*, Oxford: Basil Blackwell.
Graf, F. W. 1996. *Biographisch-bibliographisches Kirchenlexikon*. 11: 210–31.
Gross Jr., Francis L. with Toni Perior Gross. 1993. *The Making of a Mystic*. Albany: State University of New York Press.
Guthrie, Stewart. 1980. "A Cognitive Theory of Religion." *Current Anthropology* 21:2: 181–203.
———. 1993. *Faces in the Clouds: A New Theory of Religion*. New York: Oxford University Press.
———. 1996. "The Sacred: A Skeptical View." In Thomas A. Idinopulos and Edward A. Yonan (eds.), *The Sacred and Its Scholars: Comparative Methodologies for the Study of Primary Religious Data*. Leiden: E. J. Brill, 124–38.
———. 2002. "Animal Animism. Evolutionary Roots of Religious Cognition." In Pyysiäinen and Anttonen (eds.) 2002, 38–67.
Habermas, J. 1970. *Toward a Rational Society: Student Protests, Science and Politics*, Boston: Beacon Press.
———. 1971. *Knowledge and Human Interest*. Boston: Beacon Press.
———. 1975. *Legitimation Crisis*. Boston: Beacon Press.
———. 1982. "Reply to my Critics." In *Habermas: Critical Debates*, edited by John B. Thompson and David Held. Cambridge, MA: M.I.T. Press.
Hackett, Rosalind I. J. 2000. "Religious Freedom and Religious Conflict in Africa." In M. Silk (ed.), *Religion on the International News Agenda*. Hartford, CT: The Leonard E. Greenberg Center for the Study of Religion in Public Life, 102–19.
———. 2001. "Prophets, 'False Prophets' and the African State: Emergent Issues of Religious Freedom and Conflict." *Nova Religio* 4:2: 187–212.
———. 2003. "Managing or Manipulating Religious Conflict in the Nigerian Media." In J. Mitchell and S. Marriage (eds.), *Mediating Religion: Studies in Media, Religion and Culture*. Edinburgh: T & T Clark.
———. Forthcoming. *Nigeria: Religion in the Balance*. Washington, DC: United States Institute of Peace.
Hall, John R. 2002. "Religion and Violence: Social Processes in Comparative Perspective." In M. Dillon (ed.), *Handbook for the Sociology of Religion*. New York: Cambridge University Press.
Hall, John R., Philip D. Schuyler, and Sylvaine Trinh (eds.). 2000. *Apocalypse Observed: Religious Movements and Violence in North America, Europe, and Japan*. New York: Routledge.
Harrison, Peter. 1990. *"Religion" and the Religions in the English Enlightenment*. Cambridge: Cambridge University Press.
Hayano, D. 1978. "Strategies for the Management of Luck and Action in an Urban Poker Parlor." *Urban Life* 7: 475–88.
Hayes, Victor C. and Claude C. Welch. 1973. "Religious Studies in the United States: An Analysis of Religion in the Undergraduate Curriculum." *Journal of Christian Education* 16 (December 1973): 151–65.
Hillery, G. A. 1955. "Definitions of Community: Areas of Agreement," *Rural Sociology* 20: 119.
Hills, E. F. 1984 [1956]. *The King James Version Defended*. Des Moines, IW: Christian Research Press.
Hinde, R. 1999. *Why Gods Persist*. New York: Routledge.
Hintzman, D. L., S. J. Asher, and L. D. Stern. 1978. "Incidental Retrieval and Memory for Coincidences." In M. M. Gruneberg, P. E. Morris, and R. N. Sykes (eds.), *Practical Aspects of Memory*. London: Academic Press, 61–68.

Hirschfeld, L. and S. Gelman. (eds.). 1994. *Mapping the Mind: Domain Specificity in Cognition and Culture.* Cambridge: Cambridge University Press.

Hiskett, Mervyn. 1987. "The Maitatsine Riots in Kano 1980: An Assessment." *Journal of Religion in Africa* 17:3: 209–23.

Hodges, Z. and A. Farstad (eds). 1985. *The Greek New Testament According to the Majority Text.* Nashville, Thomas Nelson.

Hodges, Z. 1968. "The Greek Text of the King James Version." *Bibliotheca Sacra* 125: 334–45.

Holstein, James A. and Gale Miller (ed.). 1993. *Reconsidering Social Constructionism: Debates in Social Problems Theory.* New York: Aldine de Gruyter.

Horkheimer, M. 1972a. *Dialectic of Enlightenment.* New York: The Seabury Press.

——. 1972b. *Critical Theory.* New York: The Seabury Press.

——. 1974a. *Eclipse of Reason.* New York: The Seabury Press.

——. 1974b. *Critique of Instrumental Reason.* New York: The Seabury Press.

——. 1978. *Dawn and Decline*, Notes 1926–1931 and 1950–1969. New York: The Seabury Press.

Horn, H. G. 1994. "Das Mainzer Mithrasgefäß." *Mainzer Archäologische Zeitschrift*, 1: 21–66.

Humphreys, C. 1984. *A Popular Dictionary of Buddhism.* London: Curzon.

Ibrahim, Hassan Ahmed. 1980. "Imperialism and Neo-Mahdism in the Sudan: A Study of British Policy Towards Neo Mahdism, 1924–1927." *International Journal of African Historical Studies* 13:2: 214–39.

Idinopulos, Thomas A. 2002. "The Strengths and Weaknesses of Durkheim's Methodology for the Study and Teaching of Religion." In Idinopulos and Wilson (eds.) 2002, 1–14.

Idinopulos, Thomas A. and Brian C. Wilson (eds.). 2002. *Reappraising Durkheim for the Study and Teaching Religion Today.* Leiden: E. J. Brill.

Isichei, Elizabeth. 1987. "The Maitatsine Risings in Nigeria in 1980–85: A Revolt of the Disinherited." *Journal of Religion in Africa* 17:3: 194–208.

Jackendoff, Ray. 1994. *Consciousness and the Computational Mind.* Cambridge, MA: M.I.T. Press.

Jalpa Flores, Tomás. 1993. "La congregación de pueblos en la provincia de Chalco: reorganización del espacio administrativo, siglos XVI–XVII." In Alejandro Tortolero (ed.), *Entre lagos y volcanes: Chalco Amecameca: pasado y presente, volumen I.* México: El Colegio Mexiquense, A.C., 147–94.

Jensen, Tim and Mikael Rothstein (eds.). 2000. *Secular Theories on Religion: Current Perspectives.* Copenhagen: Museum Tuscalanum Press.

Jiménez, Fray Francisco. 1926. "Vida de Fray Martín de Valencia, escrita por su compañero Fr. Francisco Jiménez," edited by P. Atanasio López. *Archivo Ibero-Americano* 26: 48–83.

Jobes, K. H. and M. Silva. 2000. *Invitation to the Septuagint.* Grand Rapids, MI: Baker Academic.

Johnson-Laird, P.N. and R. M. J. Byrne. 2000. "The Cognitive Science of Deduction." In P. Thagard (ed.), *Mind Readings: Introductory Selections on Cognitive Science.* Cambridge, MA: M.I.T. Press, 29–58.

Johnston, Francis. 1981. *The Wonder of Guadalupe, The Origin and Cult of the Miraculous Image of the Blessed Virgin of Mexico.* Rockford, IL: Tan Books.

Kahneman, D., P. Slovic, and A. Tversky. 1982. *Judgment Under Uncertainty: Heuristics and Biases.* Cambridge: Cambridge University Press.

Kalupahana, D. 1975. *Causality—The Central Philosophy of Buddhism.* Honolulu: University Press of Hawaii.

Kane, J. P. 1975. "The Mithraic Cult Meal in its Greek and Roman Environment," In J. R. Hinnells (ed.), *Mithraic Studies: Proceedings of the First International Congress of Mithraic Studies.* Manchester: Manchester University Press, 313–51.

Kaplan, Jeffrey. 1997. "Interpreting the Interpretive Approach: A Friendly Reply to Thomas Robbins." *Nova Religio* 1:1: 30–49.
Kastefelt, Niels. 1989. "Rumours of Maitatsine: A Note on Political Culture in Northern Nigeria." *African Affairs* 88: 83–90.
Kegan, Robert. 1982. *The Evolving Self*, Cambridge, MA: Harvard University Press.
———. 1994. *In Over Our Heads*. Cambridge, MA: Harvard University Press.
Keil, Frank C. and Robert A. Wilson (eds.). 2000. *Explanation and Cognition*. Cambridge, MA: M.I.T. Press.
Kelemen, D. 1999a. "Beliefs about Purpose: On the Origins of Teleological Thought." In M. Corballis and S. Lea (eds.), *The Descent of Mind: Psychological Perspectives on Hominid Evolution*. Oxford: Oxford University Press, 278–94.
———. 1999b. "Function, Goals and Intention: Children's Teleological Reasoning about Objects." *Trends in Cognitive Sciences* 3:12: 461–68.
———. 1999c. "The Scope of Teleological Thinking in Preschool Children." *Cognition* 70: 241–72.
———. 1999d. "Why are Rocks Pointy?: Children's Preferences for Teleological Explanations of the Natural World." *Developmental Psychology* 35: 1440–52.
Keyes, C.F. and E. V. Daniel (eds.). 1983. *Karma: An Anthropological Inquiry*. Berkeley: University of California Press.
Killeen, P. R. 1977. "Superstition: A Matter of Bias, not Detectability." *Science* 199: 88–90.
Kingston, Paul. 2001. "Reflections on Religion, Modernization, and Violence in the Islamic Middle East." *Method and Theory in the Study of Religion* 13:3: 293–309.
Kipling, Rudyard. 1906. "A Song to Mithras (Hymn of the XXX Legion: Circa 350 A.D)." In Rudyard Kipling, *Puck of Pook's Hill*. New York: Doubleday, 193–94.
Kippenberg, Hans G. and E. Thomas Lawson (eds.). 1992. "Panel on Jonathan Z. Smith's *Drudgery Divine*." *Numen* 39 (November): 217–38.
Kippenberg, Hans G. 2002. *Discovering Religious History in the Modern Age*, translated by B. Harshav. Princeton: Princeton University Press.
Kloppenborg, John S. 1996. "Collegia and Thiasoi: Issues in Function, Taxonomy and Membership." In J. S. Kloppenborg and S. G. Wilson (eds.), *Voluntary Associations in the Graeco-Roman World*. London, New York: Routledge, 16–30.
Klor de Alva, Jorge. 1993. "Aztec Spirituality and Nahuatized Christianity." In Gary H. Gossen (ed.), *South and Meso-American Native Spirituality: From the Cult of the Feathered Serpent to the Theology of Liberation*. New York: Crossroad, 173–97.
Krashen, Stephen D. 1985. *The Input Hypothesis: Issues and Implications*. London and New York. Longman.
Kukah, Matthew Hassan. 1993. *Religion, Politics and Power in Northern Nigeria*. Ibadan: Spectrum.
Kung, Hans. 1967. *The Church*. New York: Sheed and Ward.
La Barre, Weston. 1970. *The Ghost Dance: Origins of Religion*. London: George Allen and Unwin.
Lacan, Jacques. 1982. "The Mirror-stage as Formative of the Function of the I." In *Ecrits: A Selection*, translated by Alan Sheridan. New York: W. W. Norton and Co., 1–7.
Lafaye, Jacques. 1987. *Quetzalcóatl and Guadalupe: The Formation of Mexican National Consciousness, 1531–1813*. Chicago: University of Chicago Press.
Lakoff, George and Mark Johnson. 1980. *Metaphors We Live By*. Chicago: University of Chicago Press.
———. 1999. *Philosophy in the Flesh: The Embodied Mind and its Challenge to Western Thought*. New York: Basic Books.
Langer, E. J. and J. Roth. 1975. "Heads I Win, Tails It's Chance: The Illusion of Control as a Function of the Sequence of Outcomes in a Purely Chance Task." *Journal of Personality and Social Psychology* 32: 951–55.

Lawrence, Bruce. 1995. *Defenders of God: The Fundamentalist Revolt Against the Modern Age*. Greenville, SC: University of South Carolina Press.
Lawson, E. Thomas. 1960. "Discourse on Dialogue." *Quest* 5:1 (Autumn): 20–24.
——. 1961. "God with Us." *Quest* 5:4 (May): 3–11.
——. 1963a. "On the Nature of the University." *Western Michigan University Magazine* 21:3 (Summer): 2–6.
——. 1963b. "Tillich and Hartshorne: An Essay on the Sovereignty of God." Ph.D. Dissertation, University of Chicago.
——. 1964. "Review of Charles H. Long, *Alpha: The Myths of Creation*." *Foundations* 7 (July): 294–96.
——. 1965. "Review of E. L. Mascall's *Christian Theology and Natural Science*." *Choice* 2:10 (December): 696.
——. 1966. "Review of Walter F. Otto's *Dionysus, Myth and Cult*." *Choice* 3:5–6 (July-August): 421.
——. 1967a. "Seminary, Department of Religion, and University." *Lutheran Quarterly* 9:1 (February): 87–90.
——. 1967b. "Implications for Theological Education in Seminaries of the Study of Religion in the University." *Theological Education* 3:3 (Spring): 396–402.
——. 1967c. "A Rationale for a Department of Religion in a Public University." In Milton McLean (ed.), *Religious Studies in Public Universities*. Carbondale, IL: Southern Illinois University Press, 38–44.
——. 1969. "Review of *The History of Religions*." *Journal of Ecumenical Studies* 6: 437–38.
——. 1973a. "The Case of Buddhism: The Problem of Definition in Religion." *Proceedings of the Heraclitan Society* 1:2 (September-December): 63–68.
——. 1973b. "Review of *The Study of Religion in Colleges and Universities*." *Journal of the American Academy of Religion* 41 (June): 298–302.
——. 1976a. "Religion and Rationality." *American Academy of Religion Philosophy of Religion and Theology Proceedings*: 201–09.
——. 1976b. "Review of Fritjof Capra's *The Tao of Physics*." *Religious Studies Review* 2:2 (April): 22.
——. 1976c. "Review of Robert D. Baird (ed.), *Methodological Issues in the Study of Religion*." *Religious Studies Review* 2:3 (July): 42.
——. 1976d. "Ritual as Language." *Religion* 6 (Autumn): 123–39.
——. 1977a. "Review of Dan Sperber's *Rethinking Symbolism*." *Religious Studies Review* 3:3: 162.
——. 1977b. "Review of Huston Smith's *Forgotten Truth*." *Religious Studies Review* 3:2 (April): 106.
——. 1978a. "Review of Keith H. Basso and Henry A. Selby's *Meaning in Anthropology*." *Religious Studies Review* 4:1 (January): 39.
——. 1978b. "The Explanation of Myth and Myth as Explanation." *Journal of the American Academy of Religion* 46 (December): 507–23.
——. 1983a. "Review of Joan M. Miller (ed.), *French Structuralism: A Multidisciplinary Bibliography*." *Religious Studies Review* (April): 168.
——. 1983b. "Review of Michael Izard (ed.), *Between Belief and Transgression: Structuralist Essays in Religion, History and Myth*." *Religious Studies Review* (September): 47.
——. 1983c. "Review of Sam Gill's *Beyond the Primitive: The Religion of Nonliterate Peoples*." *Journal of the American Academy of Religion* (September): 531.
——. 1985a. *Religions of Africa: Traditions in Transformation*. New York: Harper and Row.
——. 1985b. "Review of *Sacred Narrative: Readings in the Theory of Myth*." *Parabola* 10:1: 149–52.
——. 1987. "Review of Martin Prozesky's *Religion and Ultimate Well-being: An Explanatory Theory*." *Religion in Southern Africa* 8 (January): 47–52.
——. 1988. "Methodology, Africa." *Annals of Scholarship: Studies of the Humanities and Social Sciences* 5:2 (Winter): 242–46.

———. 1989a. "Fundamental Problems in the World-wide Pursuit of the Study of Religion." In Michael Pye (ed.), *Marburg Revisited: Institutions and Strategies in the Study of Religion*. Marburg: Verlag, 19–25.

———. 1989b. "Introduction to 'A Symposium on *Explaining Religion*.'" *Religion* 19 (October): 303–30.

———. 1989c. "The Illusions of Autonomy: Defining the History of Religions." *Annals of Scholarship: Studies of the Humanities and Social Sciences* 6:4: 485–92.

———. 1990a. "Report on the Religion and Teacher Education Program at Western Michigan University: Interview by J. H. Bolen." *Religion and Public Education* 17 (Spring-Summer): 235–39.

———. 1990b. "The Crisis in the Scientific Study of Religion and its Resolution." In Witold Tyloch (ed.), *Studies on Religion in the Context of the Social Sciences: Methodological and Theoretical Relations*. Warsaw: Polish Society for the Science of Religions, 93–97.

———. 1991a. "Dispatches from the Methodological Wars: A Review of *Tradition as Truth and Communication: A Cognitive Description of Traditional Discourse* by Pascal Boyer and *Impasse and Resolution: A Critique of the Study of Religion* by Hans Penner." *Numen* 38 (December): 261–65.

———. 1991b. "Review of Robert A. Segal's *Religion and the Social Sciences*." *Journal for the Study of Religion* 4 (Summer): 81–84.

———. 1992. "Review of Hans Penner's *Impasse and Resolution: A Critique of the Study of Religion*." *History of Religions* 32 (November): 189–90.

———. 1993a. "Cognitive Categories, Cultural Forms and Ritual Structures." In Pascal Boyer (ed.), *Cognitive Aspects of Religious Symbolism*. Cambridge: Cambridge University Press, 188–206.

———. 1993b. "Methodological Conceits and Theoretical Opportunities: Reflections on the Level of Analysis Appropriate for Explaining Socio-cultural Phenomena." In Luther H. Martin (ed.), *Religious Transformations and Socio-political Change: Eastern Europe and Latin America*. Berlin: Mouton de Gruyter, 441–51.

———. 1993c. "Review of Thomas Ryba's *The Essence of Phenomenology and Its Meaning for the Scientific Study of Religion*." *Journal of Religion* 73 (January): 127–28.

———. 1994a. "Counterintuitive Notions and the Problem of Transmission: The Relevance of Cognitive Science for the Study of History." *Historical Reflections* 20 (Fall): 481–95.

———. 1994b. Review of John S. Cumpsty's *Religion As Belonging*." *Journal of the American Academy of Religion* 62 (Spring): 184–86.

———. 1995. "Caring for the Details: A Humane Reply to Buckley and Buckley." *Journal of the American Academy of Religion* 63:2: 353–57.

———. 1996. "Theory and the Comparativism, Old and New: Reply to W. Paden." *Method and Theory in the Study of Religion* 8:1: 31–35.

———. 1998. "Defining Religion . . . Going the Theoretical Way." In Thomas A. Idinopulos and Brian C. Wilson (eds.), *What is Religion? Origins, Definitions, and Explanations*. Leiden: E. J. Brill, 43–49.

———. 1999. "Keeping Religion in Mind." In Tore Ahlbäck (ed.), *Approaching Religion: Based on Papers Read at the Symposium on Methodology in the Study of Religions Held at Abo, Finland, on the 4th–7th August, 1997, Part 1*. Stockholm: Donner Institute for Research in Religious and Cultural History, 139–49.

———. 2000a. "Cognition." In Willi Braun and Russell T. McCutcheon (eds.), *Guide to the Study of Religion*. New York: Cassell, 75–84.

———. 2000b. "Towards a Cognitive Science of Religion." *Numen* 47:3: 338–49.

———. 2001. "Psychological Perspectives on Agency." In Jensine Andersen (ed.), *Religion in Mind: Cognitive Perspectives on Religious Belief, Ritual, and Experience*. Cambridge: Cambridge University Press, 141–72.

———. 2002. "Interpreting the World Religiously." In Nancy Frankenberry (ed.), *Radical Interpretation*. Cambridge: Cambridge University Press, 117–28.

Lawson, E. Thomas, et al. 1967d. "The Study of Religion in Public Universities: A Panel Presentation." In Milton McLean (ed.), *Religious Studies in Public Universities*. Carbondale, IL: Southern Illinois University Press, 45–54.

Lawson, E. Thomas and Robert N. McCauley. 1990. *Rethinking Religion: Connecting Cognition and Culture*. Cambridge: Cambridge University Press.

——. 1993. "Crisis of Conscience, Riddle of Identity: Making Space for a Cognitive Approach to Religious Phenomena." *Journal of the American Academy of Religion* 61 (Summer): 201–23.

——. 2002. "The Cognitive Representation of Religious Ritual Form: A Theory of Participants' Competence with Religious Ritual Systems." In Pyysiäinen and Anttonen (eds.) 2002, 153–76.

Lawson, E. Thomas, Luther H. Martin and Donald Wiebe. 1990. "The Study of Religion in its Social-scientific Context: A Perspective on the 1989 Warsaw Conference on Methodology." *Method and Theory in the Study of Religion* 2:1 (Spring): 98–101.

Leach, Edmund R. 1957. "The Epistemological Background to Malinowski's Empiricism." In Raymond Firth (ed.), *Man and Culture*. London: Routledge and Kegan Paul.

——. 1958. "Magical Hair." *The Journal of the Royal Anthropological Institute* 88: 147–64.

Lease, Gary. 1994. "The History of 'Religious' Consciousness and the Diffusion of Culture: Strategies for Surviving Dissolution." *Historical Reflections/Réflexions Historiques* 20:3: 453–79.

——. 1999. "Response: Fighting over Religion (Notes from the Front)." *Historical Reflections/Réflexions Historiques* 25:3: 477–84.

Levine, M. P. 1998. "A Cognitive Approach to Ritual: New Method or No Method at All?" *Method and Theory in the Study of Religion* 10: 30–60.

Lévi-Strauss, C. 1966 [1949]. *The Savage Mind*. London: Weidenfeld and Nicholson.

Lienhardt, Godfrey. 1991 [1985]. "Self: Public, Private. Some African Representations." In Michael Carrithers, Steven Collins and Steven Lukes (eds.), *The Category of the Person: Anthropology, Philosophy, History*. Cambridge: Cambridge University Press, 141–55.

Light, Timothy. 1985. "Yi Tingdude Lingwe wei Jichude Waiyujiaoxuefa (The Comprehension Model of Foreign Language Teaching)." *Proceedings of the First International Conference on the Teaching of Chinese as a Second Language* (Taipei), 623–30.

——. 1987. *Xiandai Waiyu Jiaoxuefa: Lilun yu Shijian (Modern Foreign Language Teaching Methods: Theory and Practice)*. Beijing: Beijing Institute of Languages Press.

——. 2000. "Transcendent Identity." Paper read at the Quinquenniel meeting of the International Association for the History of Religions, Durban, South Africa, August 2000.

Lincoln, Bruce. 1997. "Conflict." In M. Taylor (ed.), *Critical Terms for Religious Studies*. Chicago: University of Chicago Press, 55–69.

——. 1999. *Theorizing Myth: Narrative, Ideology, and Scholarship*. Chicago: University of Chicago Press.

Loimeier, Roman. 1997. *Islamic Reform and Political Change in Northern Nigeria*. Evanston, IL: Northwestern University Press.

Lopes, L. L. and G. C. Oden. 1987. "Distinguishing Between Random and Non-random Events." *Journal of Experimental Psychology: Learning, Memory, and Cognition* 13: 392–400.

Lovejoy, Paul, and J.S. Hogendorn. 1990. "Revolutionary Mahdism and Resistance to Colonial Rule in the Sokoto Caliphate, 1905–1906." *Journal of African History* 31: 217–44.

Lubeck, Paul. 1985. "Islamic Protest under Semi-Industrial Capitalism: Yan Tatsine Explained." *Africa* 55:4: 369–89.

Lupfer, M. B., K. F. Brock, and S. J. DePaola. 1992. "The Use of Secular and

Religious Attributions to Explain Everyday Behavior." *Journal for the Scientific Study of Religion* 31:4: 486–503.
Lupfer, M. B., S. J. DePaola, K. F. Brock, and L. Clement. 1994. "Making Secular and Religious Attributions: The Availability Hypothesis Revisited." *Journal for the Scientific Study of Religion* 33:2: 162–71.
Lupfer, M. B., D. Tolliver, and M. Jackson. 1996. "Explaining Life-Altering Occurrences: A Test of the 'God-of-the-Gaps' Hypothesis." *Journal for the Scientific Study of Religion* 35:4: 379–91.
MacArthur, J. (ed). 1997. *The MacArthur Study Bible*. Nashville, TN: Word Publishing.
Malinowski, Bronislaw. 1935. *Coral Gardens and Their Magic*. London: Allen and Unwin.
———. 1944. *A Scientific Theory of Culture*. Chapel Hill: University of North Carolina Press.
———. 1972. *Magic, Science, and Religion*. New York: Doubleday.
Malley, Brian. 1995. "Explaining Order in Religious Systems." *Method and Theory in the Study of Religion* 7:1: 5–22.
Malley, Brian and J. L. Barrett. 2003. "Does Myth Inform Ritual? A Test of the Lawson and McCauley Hypotheses." *Journal of Ritual Studies* 17:2: 1–14.
Malotki, Eddehart (ed.). 1993. *Hopi Ruin Legends, Kiqötutuwutsi*, narrated by Michael Lomatuway'ma, Lorena Lomatuway'ma and Sidney Namingha, Jr. Lincoln, NB: University of Nebraska Press.
Malotki, Eddehart and Ken Gary. 2001. *Hopi Stories of Witchcraft, Shamanism, and Magic*. Lincoln, NB: University of Nebraska Press.
Martin, Luther H. 1987. *Hellenistic Religions: An Introduction*. New York: Oxford University Press.
———. 1994. "Reflections on the Mithraic Tauroctony as Cult Scene." In J. R. Hinnells (ed.), *Studies in Mithraism*. Rome: "L'Erma" di Bretschneider, 217–24.
———. 2001. "Comparison and Sociobiological Theory." *Numen* 48:3: 290–308.
———. 2002. "Rituals, Modes, Memory and Historiography: The Cognitive Promise of Harvey Whitehouse." *Journal of Ritual Studies* 16:2: 30–33.
———. Forthcoming. *Persuasion and Performance: Rhetoric and Reality in Early Christian Discourses*, edited by W. Braun. Waterloo, ON: Wilfrid Laurier University Press.
Martinéz Marin, Carlos. 1972. "Santuarios y Perigrinaciones en el México Pre-hispánico." In Jaime Litvak King and Noemi Castillo Tejero (eds.), *Religion en Mesoamerica: XII Mesa Redonda*. México: Sociedad Mexicana de Antropología, 161–78.
Matsunaga, Alicia. 1969. *The Buddhist Philosophy of Assimilation*. Tokyo: Sophia University & Tuttle.
Mayer, Jean-Francois. 2001. "Cults, Violence and Religious Terrorism: An International Perspective." *Conflict and Terrorism* 24: 361–76.
Mbembe, Achille. 1999. "At the Edge of the World: Boundaries, Territoriality, and Sovereignty in Africa." *CODESRIA Bulletin* 3/4: 4–16.
McCauley, Robert N. 1996. "Explanatory Pluralism and the Coevolution of Theories in Science." In R. N. McCauley (ed.), *The Churchlands and Their Critics*. Oxford: Blackwell Publishers, 17–47.
———. 1999. "Bringing Ritual to Mind." In E. Winograd, R. Fivush, and W. Hirst (eds.), *Ecological Approaches to Cognition: Essays in Honor of Ulric Neisser*. Hillsdale, NJ: Erlbaum, 285–312.
———. 2000. "The Naturalness of Religion and the Unnaturalness of Science." In Keil and Wilson (eds.) 2002, 61–85.
———. 2001. "Ritual, Memory, and Emotion: Comparing Two Cognitive Hypotheses." In Jensine Andresen (ed.), *Religion in Mind: Cognitive Perspectives on Religious Belief, Ritual, and Experience*. Cambridge: Cambridge University Press, 115–40.
McCauley, Robert N. and W. Bechtel. 2001. "Explanatory Pluralism and The Heuristic Identity Theory." *Theory and Psychology* 11: 738–61.

McCauley, Robert N. and E. Thomas Lawson. 1984. "Functionalism Reconsidered." *History of Religions* 23 (May): 372–81.
——. 1991. "Connecting the Cognitive and the Cultural: Artificial Minds as Methodological Devices in the Study of the Socio-Cultural." In Robert Burton (ed.), *Minds: Natural and Artificial*. Albany: State University of New York Press, 121–45.
——. 1996. "Who Owns 'Culture'?" *Method and Theory in the Study of Religion* 8: 171–90.
——. 1998. "Interactionism and the Non-Obviousness of Scientific Theories: A Response to Michael P. Levine." *Method and Theory in the Study of Religion* 10:1: 61–77.
——. 2002. *Bringing Ritual to Mind: Psychological Foundations of Cultural Forms*. Cambridge: Cambridge University Press.
McCutcheon, Russell. 1997. *Manufacturing Religion. The Discourse on Sui Generis Religion and the Politics of Nostalgia*. Oxford: Oxford University Press, 1997.
——. 2001. *Critics not Caretakers: Redescribing the Public Study of Religion*. New York: State University of New York Press.
——. 2003. *The Discipline of Religion: Structure, Meaning, and Rhetoric*. London: Routledge.
McMurtry, John. 1978. *The Structure of Marx's World-View*. Princeton: Princeton University Press.
Mead, George Herbert. 1962 [1943]. *Mind, Self, and Society: From the Standpoint of a Social Behaviorist*, edited with an introduction by Charles W. Morris. Chicago: University of Chicago Press.
Medin, D. L. 2000. "Concepts and Conceptual Structure." In P. Thagard (ed.), *Mind Readings: Introductory Selections on Cognitive Science*. Cambridge, MA: M.I.T. Press, 93–126.
Mendieta, Gerónimo de. 1870. *Historia eclesiástica indiana* (c. 1590), edited by Joaquin García Icazbalceta. México: Antigua Libreria.
Merkelbach, Reinhold. 1984. *Mithras*. Königstein/Ts.: Hain.
Metzger, B. M. and National Council of the Churches of Christ in the United States of America. Division of Christian Education. 1989. *The Holy Bible: Containing the Old and New Testaments*. Oxford: Oxford University Press.
Metzger, B. M. 1992. *The Text of the New Testament: Its Transmission, Corruption, and Restoration*. Oxford: Clarendon Press.
——. 1994. *Textual Commentary on the Greek New Testament*. New York: United Bible Societies.
Meyer, Birgit. 1999. *Translating the Devil: Religion and Modernity among the Ewe in Ghana*. Edinburgh: Edinburgh University Press.
Milhou, Alain. 1983. *Colón y su mentalidad mesiánica en el ambiente franciscanista español*. Valladolid: Casa-Museo Colón.
Miller, Gale and James A. Holstein (eds.). 1993. *Constructionist Controversies: Issues in Social Problems Theory*. New York: Aldine de Gruyter.
Mithen, Steven. 1996. *The Prehistory of the Mind: The Cognitive Origins of Art, Religion, and Science*. London: Thames and Hudson.
Molnár, Attila K. 2002. "The Construction of the Notion of Religion in Early Modern Europe." *Method and Theory in the Study of Religion* 14:1: 47–60.
Moore, Wilbert E. and Melvin Tumin. 1949. "Some Social Functions of Ignorance." *American Sociological Review* 14:6: 787–95.
Morris, Brian. 1987. *Anthropological Studies of Religion: An Introductory Text*. Cambridge: Cambridge University Press.
Muller, F. Max. 1889. *Natural Religion*. London: Longmans.
Munz, Peter. 1985. *Knowledge of Our Growth of Knowledge*. London: Routledge & Kegan Paul.
Nestle, E., E. Nestle, et al. 1985. *Novum testamentum Graece*. Stuttgart: Deutsche Bibelstiftung.

Nicolas, Guy. 1981. "Guerre Sainte à Kano." *Politique Africaine* 1: 47–70.
Nisbett, R., and L. Ross. 1980. *Human Inference: Strategies and Shortcomings of Social Judgment.* Englewood Cliffs, NJ: Prentice-Hall.
Noll, M. A. 2001. *American Evangelical Christianity: An Introduction.* London: Blackwell.
Obeyesekere, G. 1981. *Medusa's Hair.* Chicago: University of Chicago Press.
Odling-Smee, F. J. 1988. "Niche-Constructing Phenotypes." In H. C. Plotkin (ed.), *The Role of Behavior in Evolution.* Cambridge, MA: M.I.T. Press, 73–132.
Olasky, S. 1997. "Femme fatale." *World.* 12.
Oldman, D. 1974. "Chance and Skill: A Study of Roulette." *Sociology* 8: 407–26.
Oroz, Fray Pedro. 1972. *The Oroz Codex* (c. 1590), translated and edited by Angélico Chávez . Washington, DC: Academy of American Franciscan History.
Orsi, R. 1996. *Thank You St. Jude: Women's Devotion to the Patron Saint of Hopeless Causes.* New Haven: Yale University Press.
Otto, Rudolf. 1924. *Das Heilige.* Stuttgart: Verlag Friedrich Andreas Perthes A-G. Gotha.
Paden, William E. 1991. "Before 'The Sacred' Became Theological: Rereading The Durkheimian Legacy." *Method and Theory in the Study of Religion* 3: 10–23.
——. 1992. *Interpreting the Sacred: Ways of Viewing Religion.* Boston: Beacon Press.
——. 1994. *Religious Worlds: The Comparative Study of Religion.* Boston: Beacon Press.
——. 1996. "Sacrality as Integrity: 'Sacred Order' as a Model for Describing Religious Worlds." In Thomas A. Idinopulos and Edward A.Yonan (eds.), *The Sacred and its Scholars. Comparative Methodologies for the Study of Primary Religious Data.* Leiden: E. J. Brill, 3–18.
——. 1998. "Religion, World, Plurality." In Thomas A. Idinopulos and Brian C. Wilson (eds.), *What is Religion? Origins, Definitions, and Explanations.* Leiden: E. J. Brill, 91–106.
——. 1999. "Sacrality and the Worldmaking: New Categorial Perspective." In Tore Ahlbäck (ed.), *Approaching Religion*, part I (*Scripta Instituti Donneriani* 17:1). Åbo: The Donner Institute, 165–80.
——. 2000a. "World." In Willi Braun and Russell T. McCutcheon (eds.), *Guide to the Study of Religion.* London: Cassell, 334–47.
——. 2000b. "The Concept of World Habitation: Eliadean Linkages with a New Comparativism." In Bryan Rennie (ed.), *Changing Religious Worlds: The Meaning and End of Mircea Eliade.* Albany, NY: State University of New York Press, 249–59.
——. 2000c. "Elements of a New Comparativism." In Kimberley C. Patton and Benjamin C. Ray (eds.), *A Magic Still Dwells: Comparative Religion in the Postmodern Age.* Berkeley: University of California Press, 182–92.
——. 2000d. "Sacred Order." *Method and Theory in the Study of Religion* 12: 207–25.
——. 2001a. "The Creation of Human Behavior: Reconciling Durkheim and the Study of Religion." In Idinopulos and Wilson (eds.) 2001, 15–26.
——. 2001b. "Universals Revisited: Human Behaviors and Cultural Variations." *Numen* 48:3: 276–89.
Parsons, Talcott. 1951. *The Social System*, Glencoe: The Free Press.
Partington, Angela (ed.). 1981. *The Concise Oxford Book of Quotations*, Second edition. New York: Oxford University Press.
Paulos, J. A. 1988. *Innumeracy: Mathematical Illiteracy and its Consequences.* New York: Hill and Wang.
Penner, Hans. 1971. "The Poverty of Functionalism," *History of Religions* 11:1 (August): 91–97.
——. 1989. *Impasse and Resolution: A Critique of the Study of Religion.* New York: Peter Lang.
Peterson, E. H. (ed). 1995. *The Message: New Testament with Psalms and Proverbs.* Colorado Springs, CO: Navpress.
Pettazzoni, Raffaele. 1997 [1924]. *I Misteri: Saggio de una Theoria storico-religiosa.* Cosenza: Lionello Giordano Editore.

Piaget, J., and B. Inhelder. 1976. *The Origin of the Idea of Chance in Children*, translated by L. Leake, Jr., P. Burrell, and H. D. Fishbein. New York: W. W. Norton and Company.
Pick, John (ed.). 1953. *A Hopkins Reader* New York: Oxford.
Pickering, W. 1981. *The Identity of the New Testament Text*. Nashville, TN: Thomas Nelson.
Pierce, C. S. 1955. *Philosophical Writings of Pierce*, edited by J. Buchler. New York: Dover Publications, Inc.
Pinker, Steven. 1997. *How the Mind Works*. New York: W. W. Norton and Company.
Plotkin, Henry. 2001. "Some Elements of a Science of Culture." In Whitehouse (ed.) 2001, 91–109.
Poole, Stafford. 1968. "Opposition to the Third Mexican Council," *America* 25:2 (October): 111–59.
Popper, Karl. 1963. *Conjectures and Refutations: The Growth of Scientific Knowledge*. London: Routledge & Kegan Paul.
Porphyry. 1969. *The Cave of the Nymphs in the Odyssey*, a revised text with translation by "Seminar Classics 609," *Arethusa Monographs*, no. 1. Buffalo: State University of New York.
Pratchett, Terry. 1998. *Men at Arms*, London: Transworld Publishers Ltd.
Premack, D. and A. J. Premack. 1995. "Intention as Psychological Cause." In D. Premack, and A. J. Premack (eds.), *Causal Cognition: A Multidisciplinary Debate*. New York: Oxford University Press, 185–99.
Pyysiäinen, Ilkka. 2001. *How Religion Works: Towards a New Cognitive Science of Religion*. Leiden: E. J. Brill.
Pyysiäinen, Ilkka and Veikko Anttonen (eds.) 2002. *Current Approaches in the Cognitive Science of Religion*. London and New York: Continuum.
Radford, E. and M. A. Radford. 1969. *Encyclopedia of Superstitions*. Westport, CT: Greenwood Press, Publishers.
Ransom, John S. 1997. *Foucault's Discipline: The Politics of Subjectivity*. Durham, NC and London: Duke University Press.
Rappaport, Roy A. 1979a. "On Cognized Models." In Roy A. Rappaport, *Ecology, Meaning, and Religion*. Richmond, CA: North Atlantic Press, 97–144.
———. 1979b. "Adaptive Structure and Its Disorders." In Roy A. Rappaport, *Ecology, Meaning, and Religion*. Richmond, CA: North Atlantic Press, 145–72.
———. 1984 [1968]. *Pigs for the Ancestors: Ritual in the Ecology of a New Guinea People*. New Haven: Yale University Press.
———. 1999. *Ritual and Religion in the Making of Humanity*. Cambridge: Cambridge University Press.
Rashid, Ahmed. 2002. *Jihad: The Rise of Militant Islam in Central Asia*. New Haven: Yale University Press.
Redfield, J. 1993. *The Celestine Prophecy: An Adventure*. New York: Warner Books.
Reid, D. G., R. D. Linder, et al. 1990. *Dictionary of Christianity in America*. Downers Grove, IL: InterVarsity Press.
Ricoeur, P. 1971. "The Model of the Text: Meaningful Action Considered as a Text." *Social Research* 38: 529–62.
———. 1995. *Figuring the Sacred: Religion, Narrative, and Imagination*. Minneapolis: Fortress Press.
Ridley, M. 1997. *The Origins of Virtue: Human Instincts and the Evolution of Cooperation*. New York: Viking Press.
———. 1999. *Genome: The Autobiography of a Species in 23 Chapters*. New York: Perennial Books.
Riplinger, G. A. 1993. *New Age Bible Versions*. Munroe Falls, OH: A.V. Publications.
———. 1994. *Which Bible is God's Word?* Oklahoma City, OK: Hearthstone Publishing.
Robbins, Thomas. 1997. "Religious Movements and Violence: A Friendly Critique of the Interpretive Approach." *Nova Religio* 1: 17–33.

Robbins, Thomas and Susan J. Palmer (eds.). 1997. *Millennium, Messiahs, and Mayhem: Contemporary Apocalyptic Movements*. New York: Routledge.

Robertson, Roland. 1970. *The Sociological Interpretation of Religion*. New York: Schocken Books.

Rosch, E. 1978. "Principles of Categorization." In E. Rosch and B. B. Lloyd (eds.), *Cognition and Categorization*. Hillsdale, NJ: Erlbaum, 27–48.

Ross, Gillian. 1971. "Neo-Tylorianism: A Reassessment." *Man* n.s. 6: 1 (March): 105–16.

Ruckman, P. 1964. *The Bible "Babel."* Pensacola, FL: Bible Baptist Bookstore.

———. 1983. *About the "New" King James Bible*. Pensacola, FL: Bible Baptist Bookstore.

———. 1988. *Why I Believe the King James Version is the Word of God*. Pensacola, FL: Bible Baptist Bookstore.

———. 1990. *The Christian's Handbook of Manuscript Evidence*. Pensacola, FL: Pensacola Bible Press.

Rushdie, Salman. 2001. "Yes, This is About Islam: How Radical Politics Co-opts a Faith." *The New York Times* (Friday, November 2): A25, cols. 1–4.

Russell, Mary Doria. 1996. *The Sparrow: A Reader's Guide*. New York: Fawcett Columbine.

———. 1998. *Children of God*, New York: Fawcett Columbine.

Ryba, Thomas. 2000. "Manifestation." In Willi Braun and Russell T. McCutcheon (eds.), *Guide to the Study of Religion*. London: Cassell, 168–89.

Saler, Benson. 2000 [1993]. *Conceptualizing Religion: Immanent Anthropologists, Transcendent Natives, and Unbound Categories*. New York: Berghahn Books.

Sarbin, Theodore R. (ed.), 1986. *Narrative Psychology: The Storied Nature of Human Conduct*. New York: Praeger Publishers.

Schillebeecx, Edward. 1964. *Mary, Mother of the Redemption*, translated by N. D. Smith. New York: Sheed and Ward.

Schneider, D. M. 1980 [1968]. *American Kinship: A Cultural Account*. Chicago: University of Chicago Press.

Schroeder, Susan. 1989. "Chimalpahin's View of Spanish Ecclesiastics in Colonial Mexico." In Susan E. Ramirez (ed.), *Indian-Religious Relations in Colonial Latin America*. Syracuse: Maxwell School of Citizenship and Public Affairs, 21–38.

———. 1991. *Chimalpahin and the Kingdoms of Chalco*. Tucson: The University of Arizona Press.

Schutz, Alfred. 1971 [1932]. *Der Sinnhafte Aufbau der sozialen Welt*. The Hague: Martinus Nijhoff.

Searle, John R. 1995. *The Construction of Social Reality*. New York: Simon and Schuster.

———. 1997. *The Mystery of Consciousness*, New York: The New York Review of Books.

Segal, Robert A. 2002. "Robertson Smith's Influence on Durkheim's Theory of Myth and Ritual." In Idinopulos and Wilson (eds.) 2002, 59–72.

Sekaquaptewa, Emory. 1976. "Hopi Indian Ceremonies." In Walter Holden Capps (ed.), *Seeing with a Native Eye: Essays on Native American Religion*. New York: Harper and Row, 35–43.

Shankland, David. 2001. *The Alevis in Turkey: The Emergence of a Secular Islamic Tradition*. Richmond: Curson.

Sharf, Robert H. 1998. "Experience." In Mark C. Taylor (ed), *Critical Terms in Religious Studies*. Chicago: University of Chicago Press, 94–115.

Sharpe, Eric J. 1975. *Comparative Religion. A History*. London: Duckworth.

Sheeley, S. M. and R. N. Nash. 1999. *Choosing a Bible: A Guide to Modern English Translations and Editions*. Nashville, TN: Abingdon Press.

Shermer, M. 1997. *Why People Believe Weird Things: Pseudoscience, Superstition, and Other Confusions of Our Time*. New York: W. H. Freeman and Company.

Shore, Bradd. 1996. *Culture in Mind: Cognition, Culture, and the Problem of Meaning*. Oxford: Oxford University Press.

Siebert, R. J. 1987a. *Hegel's Philosophy of History: Theological, Humanistic and Scientific Elements*. Lewiston, NJ: Mellen.
———. 1987b. *Horkheimer's Critical Sociology of Religion: The Relative and the Transcendent*. Lewiston, NJ: Mellen.
———. 1987c. *From Critical Theory of Society to Theology of Communicative Praxis* Lewiston, NJ: Mellon.
———. 1994. *From Critical Theory to Critical Political Theology: Personal Autonomy and Universal Solidarity*. New York: Peter Lang Publisher.
———. 1999. "Life World: From Religion through Demythologization, Disenchantment, Deritualization and Deauraization to Secular Communicative Rationalization." *Synthesis Philosophica* 27/28: 1/2: 97–125.
———. 2001a. *The Critical Theory of Religion: The Frankfurt School*. Lanham, MD: The Scarecrow Press, Inc.
———. 2001b. "The Critical Theory of Religion." *Synthesis Philosophica*. 16:2: 295–330.
———. 2002a. "The Future of Religion: The Rescue of Religious Motives and Motivations through their Inversion into Secular Discourse." In R. Bachika (ed). *Traditional Religion and Culture in a New Era*. New Brunswick, NJ: Transaction Publishers, 69–114.
———. 2002b. "Las tres fáses de una teoría crítica de la religion." *BUS* 30 (Verano): 14–17.
Silverstein, M. and G. Urban 1996. *The Natural History of Discourse. Natural Histories of Discourse*. Chicago: University of Chicago Press.
Simmons, Leo W. (ed.). 1974 [1942]. *Sun Chief: The Autobiography of a Hopi Indian*. New Haven: Yale University Press.
Singer, A and L. Singer. 1995. *Divine Magic: The World of the Supernatural*. London: Boxtree Limited.
Sjobert, Gideon. 1959. "Community." In Julius Gould and William L. Kolb (eds.), *A Dictionary of the Social Sciences*. London: Tavistock Publications, 114–15.
Slone, D. J. 2002. "Why Religious People Believe What They Shouldn't: Explaining Theological Incorrectness in South Asia and America." Ph.D. dissertation, Western Michigan University.
Smith, C. and M. Emerson. 1998. *American Evangelicalism: Embattled and Thriving*. Chicago: University of Chicago Press.
Smith, Jonathan Z. 1982. *Imagining Religion: From Babylon to Jonestown*. Chicago: University of Chicago Press.
———. 1987. *To Take Place: Toward Theory in Ritual*. Chicago: Chicago University Press.
———. 1998. "Religion, Religions, Religious." In Mark Taylor (ed.). *Critical Terms for Religious Studies*. Chicago: University of Chicago Press, 269–84.
———. 2000. "Classification." In Willi Braun and Russell T. McCutcheon (eds.). *Guide to the Study of Religion*. London: Cassell, 35–44.
———. 2001. "A Twice-Told Tale: The History of the History of Religions' History." *Numen* 48:2: 131–46.
———. n.d. "The Necessary Lie: Duplicity in the Disciplines," <http://teaching.uchicago.edu/handbook/tac12.html>.
Smith, W. C., 1964. *The Meaning and End of Religion*. New York: Mentor Books.
Sontag, Susan. 2001 [1961]. *Against Interpretation and Other Essays*. New York: Picador.
Spelke, E. S., A. Phillips, and A. L. Woodward,. 1995. "Infants' Knowledge of Object Motion and Human Action." In D. Sperber, D. Premack, and A.J. Premack (eds.), *Causal Cognition: A Multidisciplinary Debate*. New York: Oxford University Press, 44–78.
Spencer, Herbert. 1876. *The Principles of Sociology*. London: Williams and Norgate.
Sperber, Dan. 1975. *Rethinking Symbolism*. Cambridge: Cambridge University Press.
———. 1985. "Anthropology and Psychology: Towards and Epidemiology of Representations." *Man* n.s. 20: 73–89.

———. 1996a. *Explaining Culture: A Naturalistic Approach.* Oxford: Blackwell Publishers.
———. 1996b. "Why are Perfect Animals, Hybrids, and Monsters Food for Symbolic Thought?" *Method and Theory in the Study of Religion* 8:2: 143–69.
Sperber, Dan, D. Premack, and A. J. Premack (eds.). 1995. *Causal Cognition: A Multidisciplinary Debate.* New York: Oxford University Press.
Sperber, Dan and Dierdre Wilson. 1986. *Relevance: Communication and Cognition.* Cambridge, MA: Harvard University.
Spilka, B., and G. Schmidt. 1983. "General Attribution Theory for the Psychology of Religion: The Influence of Event-Character on Attributions to God." *Journal for the Scientific Study of Religion* 22:4: 326–39.
Spilka, B., P. Shaver, and L. A. Kirkpatrick. 1985. "General Attribution Theory for the Psychology of Religion." *Journal for the Scientific Study of Religion* 24:1: 1–118.
Spiro, Melford. 1965. "Religious Systems as Culturally Constituted Defense Mechanisms." In Melford Spiro (ed.), *Context and Meaning in Cultural Anthropology.* New York: Free Press, 100–13.
———. 1966. "Religion: Problems of Definition and Explanation." In M. Bainton (ed.), *Anthropological Approaches to the Study of Religion.* London: Tavistock Press, 85–126.
———. 1982. *Buddhism and Society: A Great Tradition and Its Burmese Vicissitudes.* Berkeley: University of California Press.
Stewardson, Jerry and Ernest Saunders. 1967. "Reflections on the Mithraic Liturgy." In S. Laeuchil (ed.), *Mithraism in Ostia: Mystery Religion and Christianity in the Ancient Port of Rome.* Evanston, IL: Northwestern University Press, 67–84.
Strauss, Claudia and Naomi Quinn. 1997. *A Cognitive Theory of Cultural Meaning.* Cambridge: Cambridge University Press.
Strenski, Ivan. 2001. "Review of W. Braun and R. McCutcheon (eds.), *Guide to the Study of Religion*." *Journal of Religion* 81:4: 693–95.
———. 2002. "Review of R. McCutcheon, Critics Not Caretakers," *Journal of the American Academy of Religion* 70:2: 427–30.
Süssmilch, Johann Peter. 1741. *Die göttliche Ordnung in den Veränderungen des menschlichen Geschlechts aus der Geburt, dem Tode, und der Fortpflanzung desselben bewiesen.* Berlin: J. C. Spener.
Swearer, D. K. 1995. *The Buddhist World of Southeast Asia.* Albany: State University of New York Press.
Sweetser, Eve. 1996. "Mental Spaces and the Grammar of Conditional Constructions." In Fauconnier and Sweetser (eds.) 1996, 318–33.
Sweetser, Eve and Gilles Fauconnier. 1996. "Cognitive Links and Domains: Basic Aspects of Mental Space Theory." In Fauconnier and Sweetser (eds.) 1996, 1–28.
Szasz, Thomas. 1984 [1961]. *The Myth of Mental Illness.* London: Paladin Books.
Tambiah, S. 1984. *Buddhist Saints of the Forest and the Cult of Amulets: A Study in Charisma, Hagiography, Sectarianism, and Millennial Buddhism.* New York: Cambridge University Press.
Tarkka, Lotte. 1994. "Other Worlds—Symbolism, Dialogue and Gender in Karelian Oral Poetry." In Anna-Leena Siikala and Sinikka Vakimo (eds.), *Songs Beyond the Kalevala. Transformations of Oral Poetry. Studia Fennica. Folkloristica* 2. Helsinki: The Finnish Literature Society, 250–98.
Taylor, K. N. (ed). 1971. *The Living Bible.* Wheaton, IL: Tyndale House Publishers, Inc.
Taylor, Mark C. 1999. *About Religion. Economies of Faith in Virtual Culture.* Chicago: University of Chicago Press.
Teilhard de Chardin, Pierre. 1964. *The Future of Man,* translated by Norman Denny. New York: Harper and Row.
———. 1965. *The Divine Milieu.* New York: Harper and Row.

Thuesen, P. J. 1999. *In Discordance with the Scriptures: American Protestant Battles over Translating the Bible*. New York: Oxford University Press.

Timberlake, W. and G. A. Lucas. 1985. "The Basis of Superstitious Behavior: Chance Contingency, Stimulus Substitution, or Appetitive Behavior?" *Journal of the Experimental Analysis of Behavior* 46: 15–35.

Titiev, Mischa. 1943. "Notes on Hopi Witchcraft." *Papers of the Michigan Academy of Science, Arts, and Letters*. 28: 549–57.

Tooby, J., and L. Cosmides. 1992. "The Psychological Foundations of Culture." In Barkow, Cosmides, and Tooby (eds.) 1992, 19–136.

Torquemada, Fray Juan de. 1975–83. *Los veinte y un libros rituales y Monarquía indiana* (c. 1615), edited by Miguel León-Portilla. México: Porrúa.

Toulmin, Stephen Edelston. 1982. *The Return to Cosmology: Postmodern Science and the Theology of Nature*. Berkeley: University of California Press.

Tracy, James D. 1999. *Europe's Reformations, 1450–1650*. New York: Rowman and Littlefield Publishers, Inc.

Trobisch, D. 2000. *The First Edition of the New Testament*. Oxford: Oxford University Press.

Turcan, Robert-Alain. 1993. *Mithra et le mithriacisme*, Second edition. Paris: Presses Universitaires de France.

Turner, Victor. 1957. *Schism and Continuity in an African Society*. Manchester: Manchester University Press.

———. 1967. *The Forest of Symbols: Aspects of Ndembu Ritual*. Ithaca: Cornell University Press.

Turner, Victor and Edith Turner. 1978. *Image and Pilgrimage in Christian Culture: Anthropological Perspectives*. New York: Columbia University Press.

Tversky, A. 1977. "Features of Similarity." *Psychological Review*. 84: 327–52.

Tylor, Edward B. 1871. *Primitive Culture*. London: Murray.

Usman, Usufu Bala. 1987. *The Manipulation of Religion in Nigeria: 1977–1987*. Kaduna: Vanguard.

Varshney, Ashutosh. 2001. *Ethnic Conflict and Civic Life: Hindus and Muslims in India*. New Haven: Yale University Press.

Ventancurt, Fray Agustin de. 1961. *Teatro Mexicano* (c. 1698). Madrid: José Porrúa Turanzas.

Vera, Fortino Hipólito. 1881. *Santuario del Sacromonte, o lo que se ha escrito sobre él desde el siglo XVI hasta el presente*. Amecameca: Tipografia del "Colegio Católico."

Vermaseren, Maarten J. 1963. *Mithras, The Secret God*, translated by T. and V. Megaw. New York: Barnes and Noble.

———. 1971. *Mithriaca I: The Mithraeum at S. Maria Capua Vetere*. Leiden: E. J. Brill.

Vial, Theodore M. 1999. "Opposites Attract: The Body and Cognition in a Debate over Baptism." *Numen* 46: 121–45.

Vico, Giambattista. 1970 [1744]. *The New Science*, abridged, translated by T. G. Bergin and M. H. Misch. Ithaca: Cornell University Press.

Voegelin, C. F. and F. M. Voegelin. 1960. "Selection in Hopi Ethics, Linguistics and Translation." *Anthropological Linguistics* 2: 48–78.

von Neumann, J. 1958. *The Computer and the Brain*. New Haven, CN: Yale University Press.

Voth, Henry R. 1901. "The Oraibi Powamu Ceremony." *Field Columbian Museum Publication 83, Anthropological Series 3*, 2: 60–158.

Vries, Hent de. 2001. *Religion and Violence*. Stanford, CA: Stanford University Press.

Vyse, S. 1997. *Believing in Magic: The Psychology of Superstition*. New York: Oxford University Press.

Wach, Joachim. 1962 [1944]. *Sociology of Religion*, Chicago: University of Chicago Press.

Walker, Alice. 1982. *The Color Purple*. New York: Harcourt, Brace, Jovanovich.
Walker, S. J. 1992. "Supernatural Beliefs, Natural Kinds and Conceptual Structure." *Memory and Cognition* 20: 655–62.
Wallace, Anthony F. C. 1958. "Dreams and Wishes of the Soul: A Type of Psychoanalytic Theory among the Seventeenth Century Iroquois." *American Anthropologist* 60: 234–48.
———. 1961a. "The Psychic Unity of Human Groups." In Bert Kaplan (ed.), *Studying Personality Cross-Culturally*. Evanston, IL: Row, Peterson, 129–64.
———. 1961b. *Culture and Personality*. New York: Random House.
Wallace, D. 1994. "The Majority-Text Theory: History, Methods, and Critique." *Journal of the Evangelical Theological Society* (June).
Wallace, M., G. Singer, M. J. Wayner, and P. Cook. 1975. "Adjunctive Behavior in Humans During Game Playing." *Physiology and Behavior* 14: 651–54.
Waterworth, J. (ed). 1848. *The Canons and Decrees of the Sacred and Oecumenical Council of Trent*. London: Dolman.
Watts, Michael. 1996. "Islamic Modernities: Citizenship, Civil Society and Islamism in a Nigerian City." *Public Culture* 8: 251–89.
Weckman, George, 1987. "Community." In Mircea Eliade (ed.), *The Encyclopedia of Religion*, Volume 3. New York: Macmillan Publishing Company, 566–71.
Wei, Michael and Timothy Light. 1973. *A Newspaper's Vocabulary*. Hong Kong: Chinese University of Hong Kong Press.
Wellman, H., D. Cross, and J. Watson. 2001. "Meta-analysis of Theory of Mind Development: The Truth about False-belief." *Child Development* 72:3: 655–84.
Wessinger, Catherine. 2000. *How the Millennium Comes Violently: From Jonestown to Heaven's Gate*. New York: Seven Bridges Press.
Westcott, B. F., F. J. A. Hort, et al. 1881. *The New Testament in the Original Greek*. London: Macmillan and Co.
White, J. R. 1995. *The King James Only Controversy: Can You Trust the Modern Translations?* Minneapolis, MN: Bethany House.
Whitehouse, Harvey. 1992. "Memorable Religions: Transmission, Codification and Change in Divergent Melanesian Contexts." *Man* n.s. 27: 777–97.
———. 1995. *Inside the Cult: Religious Innovation and Transmission in Papua New Guinea*. Oxford: Oxford University Press.
———. 1996. "Apparitions, Orations, and Rings: Experience of Spirits in Dadul." In Jeannette Mageo and Alan Howard (eds.), *Spirits in Culture, History, and Mind*. New York: Routledge, 173–94.
———. 2000. *Arguments and Icons: Divergent Modes of Religiosity*. Oxford: Oxford University Press.
——— (ed.). 2001. *The Debated Mind: Evolutionary Psychology Versus Ethnography*. Oxford: Berg.
———. 2002. "Implicit and Explicit Knowledge in the Domain of Ritual." In Pyysiäinen and Anttonen (eds.) 2002, 133–52.
———. Forthcoming. "Modes of Religiosity: Towards a Cognitive Explanation of the Sociopolitical Dynamics of Religion." *Method and Theory in the Study of Religion*.
Wiebe, Donald. 1991. *The Irony of Theology and the Nature of Religious Thought*. Montreal: McGill-Queen's University Press.
———. 2000. *The Politics of Religious Studies: The Continuing Conflict with Theology in the Academy*. New York: Palgrave.
———. 2002. "Modern Western Science, the Study of Religion, and Orientalism and Religion." *Method & Theory in the Study of Religion* 14:2: 265–78.
Williams, Peter W. 2001. *America's Religions: Traditions and Cultures*. Chicago: Illinois University Press.
Williams, Raymond. 1990 [1977]. *Marxism and Literature*. New York: Oxford.
Wilson, S. G. 1996. "Voluntary Associations: An Overview." In J. S. Kloppenborg

and S. G. Wilson (eds.), *Voluntary Associations in the Graeco-Roman World*. London, New York: Routledge, 1–15.
Winitz, Harris (ed.). 1981a. *The Comprehension Approach to Foreign Language Instruction*. Rowley, MA: Newbury House.
——. 1981b. "The Comprehension Approach: An Introduction." In Winitz (ed.) 1981a, 1–13.
——. 1981c. "A Reconsideration of Comprehension and Production in Language Teaching." In Winitz (ed.) 1981a, 101–40.
Wolf, Eric. 1958. "The Virgin of Guadalupe: A Mexican National Symbol." *Journal of American Folklore* 71: 34–39.
Wolfe, Alan. 2002. "Faith and Diversity in American Religion." *The Chronicle of Higher Education* (February 8): B7
Wright, D. and G. D. Gaskell. 1992. "The Construction and Function of Vivid Memories." In M. A. Conway, D. C. Rubin, H. Spinnler and W. A. Wagenaar (eds.), *Theoretical Perspectives on Autobiographical Memory*. Netherlands: Kluwer Academic Publishers, 275–92.
Yinger, J. Milton. 1965 [1957]. *Religion, Society, and the Individual*. New York: Macmillan.
——. 1970. *The Scientific Study of Religion*. New York: Macmillan.
Zahradeen, Nasir B. 1988. *The Maitatsine Saga*. Zaria, Nigeria: Hudahuda Publishing Co.
Zaleski, Carol. 2002. "A Letter to William James." *The Christian Century* 119:2 (January 16–23): 32.
Ziegler, Charles A. n.d. "A Proposed Theoretical Framework for the Examination Of Witchcraft, Satanic Ritual Abuse, and Alien Abduction." Unpublished manuscript.

INDEX OF NAMES

Aaron, H., 378
Abbott, W., 226 n. 4
Aberle, D. F., 320, 321
Abraham, 229
Achtemeier, P. J., 225 n. 2
Adler, A., 75
Adorno, T. W., 135 n. 1, 140, 151, 155
Agabi, K. G., 193 n. 3
Akilu, H., 199
Aland, B., 335 n. 5, 342
Aland, K., 335 n. 5, 336 n. 7, 342
Albanese, C., 382 n. 3
Al-Karsani, A. A., 202, 202 n. 16
Al-Mahdi, 'A., 204
Allah, 200, 203
Aminu, J., 205 n. 21
Aniagolu, A., 205
Anthony of Padua, St., 210, 212
Anttonen, V., 18, 20, 112, 118, 417, 419
Apel, K.-O., 146
Appadurai, A., 198
Aquinas, T., 144
Arnal, W., 166 n. 2, 189
Asad, T., 189, 201 n. 15
Asher, S. J., 391
Askew, P., 215 n. 7
Astuti, R., 86
Atanasio Lopéz, P., 209 n. 4
Atran, S., 46, 86
Augustine, St., 144, 319, 377

Baker, J., 234
Baker, T. F., 234
Barkindo, B. M., 200, 202, 203 n. 17
Barkow, J. H., 125, 328
Barkun, M., 195
Barrett, J. L., 12, 21, 22, 269, 273–87, 375, 376 n. 2, 379–80, 412
Barth, F., 68, 72, 248 n. 2, 259, 259 n. 10
Barthes, R., 185
Bateson, G., 68, 99, 100, 331
Bechtel, S., 377–78
Bechtel, W., 63

Beck, R., 248, 248 n. 2, 249–51, 253, 255–59, 261 n. 12
Becker, J., 390
Beldi de Alcantara, M. L., 193
Bell, C., 167
Beneviste, E., 112
Benitez, A., 377
Benjamin, W., 140
Berger, P., 22, 128, 299–300
Bernstein, L., 16
Birai, U. M., 205 n. 21, 206, 206 n. 22
Black Elk, 231, 234
Blackmore, S., 390
Blair, T., 170, 171
Bloch, M., 86
Boggs, W., 378
Bonventure, 215 n. 7
Bottigheimer, R. B., 370
Boyer, P., 12, 17, 46, 49, 53, 54, 57 n. 9, 59–62, 86, 116, 121, 122, 125–29, 133, 161, 273, 319, 320, 327, 375, 380, 390, 395, 398, 405, 407, 410, 419
Bradfield, R. M., 301
Brandt, R. B., 306
Braun, W., 107, 177
Brock, K. F., 380
Brooke, R. B., 215 n. 7
Brooks, M., 185
Brown, B., 390
Brown, D., 168
Brown, D. E., 292
Brown, P., 178, 183
Brown, R., 305
Bruner, J., 298–99
Bryan, D., 256 n. 5
Buckley, A. D., 257 n. 9
Buhrmann, H., 390
Burgon, J., 356
Burkert, W., 50, 52 n. 5, 121
Burkhardt, L., 208 n. 3, 218, 412, 414
Burns, G., 222
Bush, G. W., 171
Bustamente, F., 208
Byrne, R. M. J., 383

Calvin, J., 144, 169
Campenhausen, H. V., 225
Capps, W. H., 105–106
Cardenal, E., 147
Carmichael, D. L., 117
Carrasco, D., 177–82
Carson, D. A., 363, 365, 366
Cassirer, E., 133
Cautes, 257, 257 n. 6
Cautpates, 257, 257 n. 6
Celsus, 250
Chapin, H., 233
Charles V. Hapsburg, 145
Chaucer, G., 237
Chesterton, G. K., 242
Chomsky, N., 10, 15–16, 58–59, 136, 143, 245, 331, 407
Christelow, A., 196, 197, 198 n. 9, 199, 202–203
Churchland, P. M., 50
Cihuacóatl, 207
Clark, A., 110
Clarke, P. B., 196, 201, 202
Clauss, M., 253, 254
Clement, L., 380
Clifford, J., 166, 176 n. 4, 331
Cohen, A. K., 320
Colpe, C., 112
Colwell, E., 335 n. 6
Comfort, P. W., 342
Comstock, R. W., 112
Comte, A., 150
Connors, J., 378
Cook, D., 199 n. 11
Cook, P., 389
Cortés, H., 207
Cosmides, L., 121, 124, 126, 130, 328, 381, 382, 394
Coulson, S., 397, 410–13, 419
Creuzer, F., 141–42
Crick, F., 312–13
Cross, F. L., 284
Crossan, J. D., 231
Cuauhtlehuanitzin, C., 210, 211
Cunningham, G., 11
Cusack, John, 391

dan Fodio, U., 203, 204
D'Andrade, R. G., 86
Daniel, E. V., 382
Darwin, C., 38
Davies, P., 222
Davila Padilla, A., 211 n. 6
Davis, A., 166

Davis, A. K., 320
Dawkins, R., 380, 382, 390
Dennett, D. C., 22, 295–96
DePaola, S. J., 380
Derham, W., 245 n. 1
Descartes, R., 100–101, 295
Diamond, J., 54
Díaz de Castillo, B., 207
Diego, J., 208
Dobson, J., 364
Donagan, Alan, 8
Douglas, M., 68, 113, 131
Durkheim, E., 67–68, 70, 91, 111–13, 128, 128 n. 1, 132, 133, 176, 181, 187, 290, 292, 299, 304, 397, 418

Earhart, H. B., 6, 378
Eck, D. L., 194, 382 n. 3
Edelman, G. M., 296–98
Eggan, D., 303–10
Eliade, M., 5, 8, 115, 133, 139, 143, 172–73, 177–82, 231
Elman, J. L., 49
Emerson, M., 332
Ennis, A., 215
Erasmus, D., 334
Erikson, E., 222
Ernst, L. C., 367
Esposito, J., 193 n. 2
Eubulus, 257 n. 7
Evans-Pritchard, E. E., 68, 71, 327

Falk, N. A., 6
Falk, R., 391
Falola, T., 197, 198, 203, 205
Farstad, A., 356
Fauconnier, G., 397, 410–11, 415, 419
Fee, G. D., 356
Fellini, F., 229
Firth, R., 68, 68 n. 2
Fitzgerald, T., 107
Fleck, L., 106 n. 1
Flood, G., 115
Fortes, M., 68, 72
Fortuna, 380
Foucault, M., 84 n. 7, 176, 181–84, 188
Fox, M., 226
Fox, R., 124
France, A., 261–62
Francis of Assisi, St., 20, 209–16, 414
Frazer, J., 70
Freud, S., 41, 71–75, 112, 133, 137, 140, 153–55, 174, 223, 418

INDEX OF NAMES

Fromm, E., 140
Fuller, D., 356

Ganesha, 229–30
Gary, K., 309
Gaskell, G. D., 305
Gautama Buddha, 141, 180, 224, 229
Geertz, A., 21, 296, 300, 301, 306, 307, 307 n. 4, 308 n. 5, 309, 309 n. 6, 310, 311
Geertz, C., 55 n. 6, 68–69, 81, 291, 299, 331, 392
Gellner, E., 73
Gelman, S., 375, 386
Giddens, A., 115
Giles, Brother, 215 n. 7
Gilligan, C., 241
Gilovich, T., 380, 390
Gil-White, F., 82
Ginsburg, H., 235
Gluckmann, M., 68
Goldberg, R., 17, 45, 48, 48 n. 3, 55, 62
Goldschmidt, W., 298
Goody, J., 9
Gould, S. J., 8
Graf, F. W., 245
Griesbach, J. J., 335 n. 5
Griffiths, P., 189
Gross, Jr., F. L., 21, 241
Gross, T. P., 241
Grudem, W., 364, 365
Guthrie, S., 12, 46, 50, 86, 110–12, 246, 320, 375, 376

Habermas, J., 135 n. 1, 140, 144, 147
Hackett, R. I. J., 20, 194, 195
Hall, J. R., 193, 195, 196, 198
Hamilton, W., 132
Harrison, P., 186–88
Hart, K., 89 n. 1, 90–91, 101
Hayano, D., 389
Hayes, V. C., 6 n. 3
Hegel, G. F. W., 139–141, 144, 147, 154, 156, 159
Helios, 254–55, 258
Hemingway, E., 391
Hempel, C. G., 8
Herclitus, 96 n. 10
Herodotus, 255
Hillery, G. A., 291
Hills, E. F., 356
Hilter, A., 137
Hin, B., 234

Hinde, R., 46, 86
Hintzman, D. L., 391
Hirschfeld, L., 375, 386
Hiskett, M., 196, 200
Hodder, 364
Hodges, Z., 334 n. 4, 356
Hogendorn, J. S., 203
Hölderlin, F., 147
Holstein, J. A., 300
Honko, L., 105
Hopkins, G. M., 226
Horkheimer, M., 135 n. 1, 140, 155
Horn, H. G., 250
Hort, F. J. A., 335, 335 n. 5, 356
Horton, R., 9, 133
Hume, D., 175
Humphreys, C., 381
Husserl, E., 115
Huxley, T. H., 100

Ibn Said, H., 203
Ibrahim, H. A., 204
Idinopulos, T., 187–88
Inhelder, B., 386, 387
Isichei, E., 196, 198, 199

Jackendoff, R., 118–19
Jackson, M., 380
Jacob, F., 100
Jalpa Flores, T., 210, 211
James, St., 224, 362
James, W., 170, 179, 297
Jaynes, J., 295
Jensen, T., 166 n. 2
Jesus, 141, 149, 215 n. 7, 216, 224, 225 230–32, 234, 261 n. 12, 282, 335, 336, 341, 348, 348 n. 9, 360, 399, 400, 413, 414
Jiménez, F., 209 n. 4, 216
Jobes, K. H., 336
John, St., 224, 347, 348, 348 n. 9, 357, 365
Johnson-Laird, P. N., 383
Johnson, M., 115, 397, 408–10
Johnston, F., 208 n. 2
Jonah, 231
Jordan, M. 378
Joyner-Kersee, J., 378
Jude, St. 378
Jung, C. G., 5, 133, 139
Justin Martyr, 255

Kahneman, D., 385, 386
Kalupahana, D., 382

Kane, J. P., 253, 255
Kant, I., 139, 147–48, 180
Kaplan, J., 197
Kastefelt, N., 194, 196, 196 n. 4
Kauffman, S., 8
Kaufmann, W., 174
Kegan, R., 233, 233 n. 7, 235, 238, 239
Keleman, D., 376, 391
Keyes, C. F., 382
Khomeini, Ayatollah, 202
Kileen, P. R., 390
Kingston, P., 193 n. 2
Kipling, R., 247
Kippenberg, H. G., 263
Kirkpatrick, L. A., 380
Kitagawa, J., 177
Kloppenburg, J. S., 253
Klor de Alva, J., 217
Koestler, A., 100
Kohlberg, L., 239
Krashen, S. D., 406
Kroeber, A. L., 72 n. 4
Kuan Yin, 398, 399
Kuan Yu, 398
Kukah, M. H., 200
Kulik, J., 305
Kung, H., 225

La Barre, W., 72
Lacan, J., 184
Lachmann, K., 335 n. 5
Lafaye, J., 207–209
Lakoff, G., 115, 397, 408–10
Lakshmi, 380
Landes, R., 199 n. 12
Lane, E., 199 n. 11
Langer, E. J., 389, 390
Lanum, J., 4
Lawrence, B., 195
Lawson, E. T., 3–13, 15, 16, 19, 21, 23, 40, 46–47, 56–60, 64, 65, 75–76, 86, 89 n. 1, 111, 121, 128 n. 1, 135–59, 161–77, 218 n. 8, 221, 244, 246–63, 265–90, 375, 376, 376 n. 2, 378, 394–99, 407, 410, 415–19
Lawson, J., 3 n. 1
Lawson (Jones), R., 3 n. 1, 4
Lawson, S., 4
Leach, E., 68 n. 2, 72
Lease, G., 162, 166, 174–75, 177
Leibnitz, G. W., 100, 157
Levine, M. P., 57 n. 10

Lévi-Straus, C., 10, 51, 113
Levy, M., 320
Lewontin, R., 8
Lienhardt, G., 290 n. 2
Light, T., 23, 130, 218 n. 8, 406, 407 n. 4
Lincoln, B., 167, 177, 193, 206
Linden, I., 201, 202
Linder, R. D., 369
Llewellyn, J., 177
Locke, J., 105
Loew, C., 4
Loimeier, R., 198 n. 8
Lomatuway'ma, M., 301, 306, 307 n. 4, 308 n. 5, 309, 309 n. 6
Long, C., 5, 8, 177
Lopes, L. L., 390, 391
Lord Acton, 242 n. 10
Lovejoy, P., 203
Lubeck, P., 194, 196, 200
Lucas, G. A., 390
Luckmann, T., 22, 299–300
Lucretius, 174
Luke, St., 357
Luhmann, N., 143
Lupfer, M. B., 380, 383
Luther, M., 144, 169, 171

MacArthur, J., 347
Macintyre, A., 8
Maël, Abbot, 261
Mahakasyapa, 180
Maitatsine, 20, 194–206
Malinowski, B., 67 n. 2, 70, 85, 393
Malley, B., 12, 22, 130, 279–87
Malotki, E., 309
Marcus, G., 331
Marcuse, H., 140
Mark, St., 348
Martín de Valencia, 20, 209–18, 251
Martin, L. H., 8 n. 5, 21, 132, 172, 184, 246, 247, 248 n. 2, 249, 252, 255, 256, 256 n. 5, 261
Martinéz Marin, C., 207
Marwa, M., 20, 196, 198
Marx, K., 73, 75, 100, 137, 140, 154
Mary Magdalene, 232
Matsunaga, A., 399 n. 3
Mayer, J.-F., 195
Mbembe, A., 201
McCauley, R. N., 3 n. 1, 8, 8 n. 4, 9 n. 5, 11, 12, 12 n. 6, 16–18, 21, 40, 46, 50, 51, 57 n. 10, 59, 61 n. 12, 63, 75–76, 86, 111, 121, 128

n. 1, 161, 218 n. 8, 246–63, 265–88, 375, 376, 394, 395, 407, 410, 419
McCutcheon, R., 19, 108–109, 111, 166, 176, 189, 189 n. 7
McMullin, N., 161
McMurty, J., 73 n. 5
Mead, G. H., 293–96, 303–304, 308, 311
Medin, D. L., 392
Melanchton, P., 169
Mendieta, G., 209 n. 5, 211, 214–16, 218
Merkelbach, R., 253, 255
Metzger, B., 335 n. 5, 349 n. 10
Meyer, B., 195
Miller, G., 300
Milhou, A., 215
Miriam, 229
Mithen, S., 86, 328
Mithras, 247–58
Molnár, A. K., 167
Monod, J., 100
Montúfar, A., 208, 209
Moore, W. E., 322
Morris, B., 70 n. 3
Moses, 227, 229
Motolinía, 209 n. 5, 210
Muhammad, 141, 202, 224, 229, 232
Müller, F. M., 70, 180
Munz, P., 103 n. 14
Münzer, T., 144, 145
Murray, J. C., 226 n. 4
Muy'ingwa, 301–302

Nash, R. N., 334
Neibuhr, R., 4
Nestle, E., 348
Nestle, E., 348
Nicolas, G., 196
Nietzche, F., 137, 140
Nisbett, R., 385, 386
Noah, 231
Noll, M., 332

Obeyesekere, G., 72
Oden, G. C., 390, 391
Odling-Smee, F. J., 130
Olasky, S., 363
Oldman, D., 389, 390
Opper, S., 235
Origen, 144, 250
Oroz, P., 209 n. 5
Orr, W. J., 3

Orsi, R., 378
Orwell, G., 145
Otto, R., 5, 115, 116, 180
Ovid, 377

Paden, W. E., 18, 20, 112, 122, 126, 131
Paez, J., 210, 213, 215
Pallas, 255
Palmer, S. J., 195
Pals, D., 180
Parsons, T., 291, 321
Partington, A., 242 n. 10
Paul, St., 336, 349
Paulos, J. A., 391
Penner, H., 8, 9, 112, 161
Peter, St., 224
Peterson, E. H., 355, 361, 362
Pettazzoni, R., 262 n. 13
Phillips, A., 386
Piaget, J., 235, 386–87
Pick, J., 226
Pickering, W., 356
Pierce, C. S., 380
Pinker, S., 380, 387, 392
Plato, 139
Plotkin, H., 127
Plutarch, 253, 255
Poole, S., 215
Popper, K., 8, 74–75, 164
Porphyry, 255, 257, 257 n. 6, 257 n. 7
Pratchett, T., 289
Premack, D., 376
Premack, A. J., 376
Pyysiäinen, I., 12, 46, 53, 55 n. 6, 56 n. 8, 57 n. 9, 59, 62, 64 n. 13, 64 n. 14, 86, 110, 319

Qaddafi, M., 20, 199
Quinn, N., 68–69, 86

Radford, E., 377–78
Radford, M. A., 377–78
Ransom, J., 174
Rappaport, R., 18, 89–103, 113, 121, 131
Rashid, A., 193 n. 2
Redfield, J., 390–91
Reid, D. G., 369
Ricouer, P., 115, 167, 331
Ridley, M., 380, 382
Rimi, A., 197, 199, 200
Riplinger, G., 356–57

Robbins, T., 195, 197
Roberts, O., 234
Robertson, P., 234
Robertson, R., 291
Rosch, E., 376
Ross, G., 9,
Ross, L., 385, 386
Roth, J., 389, 390
Rothstein, M., 166 n. 2
Rousseau, J. J., 323
Ruckman, P., 356
Rushdie, S., 171
Russell, M. D., 223, 229
Ruth, 229
Ryba, T., 115

Sagan, C., 100
Sahagún, B., 207, 208, 210
Saler, B., 22, 53, 108, 115
Sambo, A. I., 204
Sandoval, G., 207
Sarbin, T. R., 298
Saunders, E., 253–55
Saussure, F. de, 58 n. 11
Schelling, F., 144, 147, 159
Schillibeex, E., 402
Schmidt, G., 380
Schneider, D. M., 331
Scholem, G., 143
Schopenhauer, A., 140
Schroeder, S., 216, 217
Schutz, A., 22, 299
Schuyler, P. D., 195, 198
Searle, J., 296, 299
Segal, R. A., 180, 397
Sekaquaptewa, E., 304
Shagari, A., 204, 205
Shankland, D., 76–77, 85
Sharf, R. H., 167
Sharpe, E. J., 106
Shaver, P., 380
Sheely, S. M., 334
Shermer, M., 377
Shore, B., 407
Siebert, R. J., 19, 135 n. 1
Silva, M., 336
Silverstein, M., 331
Simmons, L. W., 302
Singer, A., 377
Singer, G., 389
Singer, L., 377
Sjoberg, G., 291
Slone, D. J., 13 n. 7, 22, 381, 412
Slovic, P., 385, 386

Smith, C., 332
Smith, H., 172
Smith, J. Z., 108–13, 126, 167, 169, 176, 177, 181, 185–86, 188 n. 6, 189, 195
Smith, R., 397
Smith, W. C., 56, 172, 177, 186, 188 n. 6
Solomon, 384
Sontag, S., 174–75
Spelke, E. S., 386
Spencer, H., 70
Sperber, D., 10, 46 n. 2, 48 n. 4, 51, 67 n. 1, 86, 115–16, 128 n. 1, 246–47, 366, 395, 407
Spilka, B., 380, 383
Spiro, M., 9, 60, 72, 378
Stains, L. R., 377, 378
Staupitz, J. von, 144
Stern, L. D., 391
Stewardson, J., 253–55
Stoughton, 364
Strabo, 255
Strauss, C., 68–69, 86
Strenski, I., 175, 189
Sulaiman, I., 198 n. 7
Suppe, F., 8
Süssmilch, J. P., 245, 245 n. 1
Sutton, F., 320
Swearer, D. K., 378
Sweetser, E., 397, 410, 419
Szasz, T., 112

Talayesva, D., 302
Tambiah, S., 378
Tarkka, L., 116
Taylor, M. C., 107, 108
Teilhard de Chardin, P., 100, 226, 229
Teresa of Avila, St., 241
Tertullian, 255
Theodosius, 247
Thomas, St., 224
Thuesen, P. J., 369
T'ien Hou, 398
Tillich, P., 4, 56
Timberlake, W., 390
Timothy, 336
Titiev, M., 309
Tolliver, D., 380
Tonantzin, 207–208, 412–14
Tononi, G., 296–98
Tooby, J., 121, 124, 126, 130, 328, 381, 382, 394
Torquemada, J. de, 209 n. 5

INDEX OF NAMES

Toulmin, S. E., 99–101
Tracy, J. D., 169
Trinh, S., 195, 198
Trobisch, D., 337
Tumin, M., 322
Turcan, R., 256
Turner, E., 208 n. 2
Turner, V., 68, 208 n. 2, 397, 410, 419
Tversky, A., 380, 385, 386, 390
Tylor, E. B., 9, 50, 70, 133

Umar Abdullah, M. S., 199, 201
Urban, G., 331
Usman, U. B., 200 n. 13

Vallone, R., 380, 390
Varsheney, A., 202
Ventancurt, A de, 209 n. 5
Vera, F. H., 209 n. 4, 211 n. 6
Vermaseren, M. J., 251, 255, 262 n. 13
Vial, T. M., 247
Vico, G., 245–46
Virgin Mary, 207, 208, 208 n. 3, 230, 232, 399, 399 n. 3, 400, 402, 412–14
Vishnu, 379
Voegelin, C. F., 306
Voegelin, F. M., 306
Voltaire, 157, 174
von Neumann, J., 331
Voth, H., 301, 302
Vries, H. de, 193
Vyse, S., 377, 378, 387, 389, 391

Wach, J., 5, 8, 291
Waggoner, M., 166
Walker, A., 222
Walker, S. J., 61
Wallace, A. F. C., 22, 321–23, 327
Wallace, D., 334 n. 4, 356, 389
Wallace, M. G., 389
Waterworth, J., 342
Watson, J., 284

Watts, M., 195–96, 200–203
Wayner, M. J., 389
Weber, A. L., 233
Weber, M., 151, 156, 418
Weckman, G., 292
Wei, M., 408
Welch, C. C., 6 n. 3
Wellman, H., 284
Welte, M., 336 n. 7
Wessinger, C., 195, 198
Westcott, B. F., 334, 335 n. 5, 356
Wheatley, P., 177
White, J. R., 365, 366
Whitehead, A. L., 144
Whitehouse, H., 12, 17, 46, 117–18, 248 n. 2, 251, 260 n. 11, 261, 273, 284, 305, 395, 405
Wiebe, D., 8 n. 5, 18, 89 n. 3, 95 n. 9, 161, 164, 171, 180, 185, 189
Wiley, T. T., 4
Williams, P., 382 n. 3
Williams, R., 175
Wilson, B. C., 15, 20–21, 414
Wilson, B. R., 8
Wilson, D., 86, 366
Wilson, D. S., 121, 126–27, 132
Wilson, E. O., 8
Wilson, S. G., 253
Winitz, H., 406
Wolf, E., 412–13
Wolfart, J., 178
Wolfe, A., 165
Woodward, A. L., 386
Wright, D., 305
Wyeth, A., 409

Yahweh, 146
Yinger, M., 291

Zahradeen, N. B., 199, 203
Zaleski, C., 179
Zaugg, M. K., 390
Ziegler, C. A., 318, 325–26
Zoroaster, 257 n. 7
Zwingli, H., 144, 169

INDEX OF SUBJECTS

"A Rationale for a Department of Religion in a Public University" (Lawson), 5
Aarthi, 279–81
Abductive Reasoning, 23, 380, 381, 383, 385, 392, 393
Abhishekam, 279–81
Academic Study of Religion, 89, 89 n. 1, 89 n. 3, 109, 115, 167
Action Representation System (Lawson and McCauley), 11, 31, 41, 43, 60, 112, 138, 267–68, 270–72, 376
African Religions, 6, 15, 166
Agency, Agent, 30–33, 37 n. 3, 38–39, 47, 50, 54, 60–61, 64 n. 13, 66, 111, 113, 263, 267–76, 279, 287, 375–76, 381–82, 386, 389, 393–94, 410
Albigensians, 154
Alienation, 156
Alpha: The Myths of Creation (Long), 5
Alterity, 79
Alternative Future I, 140, 146, 152, 153
Alternative Future III, 138, 139, 149, 151, 160
Amarcord (Fellini), 229
American Academy of Religion (AAR), 163, 165, 167, 184
American Exceptionalism, 176
American Society for the Study of Religion (ASSR), 13
American Standard Version Bible, 336
Amplified Bible, The, 353, 354, 358
An Arabic-English Lexicon (Lane), 199 n. 11
Anabaptists, 154
Analogy, 412, 415–16
Ancestors, 31, 33, 37, 40, 41, 49, 50, 57, 61, 123, 131, 284, 311, 376, 398, 403
Anglicanism, 53
Aniagolu Commision of Inquiry, 196 n. 4, 196 n. 5, 197 n. 5, 199, 205
Anima (Jung), 139
Animus (Jung), 139
Anthropological Psychology, 298

Anthropology, 5, 9 n. 5, 34, 50, 65–88, 90, 90 n. 4, 91, 98 n. 12, 105–19, 130, 137, 172, 229, 246, 247, 265, 305, 313
Anthropomorphism, 380, 410
Apocalypticism, 100, 195, 197
Apochrypha, 337
Apostolic Succession, 144, 272, 402
Archaeology, 65, 79, 82–83, 85–87, 102 n. 2
Archetypes (Jung), 139
Arguments and Icons (Whitehouse), 12
Arminianism, 365, 382
Artificial Intelligence, 87
Astonishing Hypothesis, The (Crick), 312
Astrology, 249, 327
Astronomy, 65, 249, 411
Atheism, 401
Attribution Theory, 380
Aum Shinrikyo, 198
Australian Religion, 262 n. 13
Authorized Version of the Bible, 335, 351
Autographs, Biblical, 338, 341–42, 347, 349, 350
Autonomy, Disciplinary, 5, 7, 62
Axial Age, 136

Baha'i, 199
Balanced Ritual Systems, 260, 394
Baptism, 261 n. 12, 266, 270, 271, 282, 283, 285
Baptists, 361–62
Bar/Bat Mitzvah, 279–81
Base Christian Communities, 145, 147
Base Mental Space (Light), 416–17
Behaviorism, 312
Bible, The, 20, 22, 227, 231, 234, 331–73
Bible Translation, 332–70
Bible, Concept of, 337–73
Biography, 231
Biological Materialism, 17
Biology, 15, 79, 86, 98 n. 12, 102, 129, 163, 412
Blazing Saddles (Brooks), 185
Bodily Ascension of Mary, 402
Body Theory, 109
Branch Davidians, 198

Bringing Ritual to Mind (McCauley and Lawson), 12, 41, 260 n. 11, 265
Bris, 279–81, 285
British Association for the Study of Religion (BASR), 290 n. 1
Brodmann's Area 24, 313
Brothers of the Free Spirit, 154
Buddhism, 28, 136, 141, 224, 225, 228, 234, 238, 339 n. 3, 378, 381–83, 398–99, 402, 493
Buddhist Philosophy of Assimilation (Matsunga), 399 n. 3

Calvinism, 282–83, 287, 382
Capitalism, 139, 140, 142, 145, 150, 151, 154, 156, 196
Carmelite Order, 241
Cartesianism, 100–101, 295
Categorization Judgement (Jackendoff), 119
Category-Theoretical Approach to the Study of Religion (Anttonen), 118
Cathari, 154
Celestine Prophecy, The (Redfield), 390
Centrality Hypothesis (Barrett), 21, 273, 282–83, 286–87
Chametz, 279, 280
Charisma, 37, 123
Chemistry, 102, 137
Chicago School of History of Religions, 177–79, 182
Children of God (Russell), 229
Children's Bibles, 370
Chinese Buddhism, 398, 402
Chinese Popular Religion, 398
Choosing a Bible (Sheely and Nash), 334
Christian Reformed Church, 282
Christianity, 5, 6, 29, 99, 100, 105, 107, 114, 136, 141, 142, 146, 147, 151, 153, 164, 160, 183, 193, 194, 200, 203 n. 17, 204, 205, 207–20, 224–28, 230–34, 242, 261, 261 n. 12, 319, 331–74
Christmas, 227
Classification Systems, 114, 116, 118–19, 123, 126, 163, 170–71, 176–77, 187, 292, 299
Cloning, 140
Cofradía del Descendimiento y Sepulchro de Cristo Nuesto Señor, 210
Cognitive Anthropology, 137
Cognitive Dissonance, 398
Cognitive Ethics, 146
Cognitive Linguistics, 118
Cognitive Psychology, 11, 58, 86, 87, 117, 119, 136, 141, 150, 153, 154, 245, 265, 294, 391
Cognitive Sociology, 141, 159
Cognitive Theory of Ritual (Lawson and McCauley), 21, 65–88, 136, 138, 143, 149, 245–64
Cognized Models (Rappaport), 95 n. 9, 97 n. 11, 98, 98 n. 12
Coincidence, 390–91
Collective Unconscious (Jung), 139
Colonialism, 79, 82
Color Purple, The (Walker), 222
Comma Johannem, 335
Communicative Ethics, 148
Communicative Rationality, 150, 154
Community, Concept of, 291
Comparative Religion, 86, 105–12, 118, 121–22, 125, 133, 141, 167 n. 2, 225, 231, 265, 375, 379, 394, 395 n. 1, 403
Comparative Religion: A History (Sharpe), 106
Comparativism, 5, 21, 121, 126, 127, 177
Compartmentalization, 23, 396, 396 n. 2, 397–99, 399 n. 3, 412, 418, 419
Competence, Linguistic (Chomsky), 10–11, 58, 136, 245
Competence, Ritual (Lawson and McCauley), 245–47, 262–63
Complexity Theory, 130
Conceptual Blending (Light), 405, 410–18
Conciousness Explained (Dennett), 295
Confession, 310
Confirmation, 282, 283
Confirmation Bias, 393
Consilience, 61, 63
Contemporary English Version Bible, 336, 353
Converging on Culture (Brown, et al.), 168
Conversion Ritual, 279, 280
Correspondence Theory of Truth, 95, 97, 102
Cosmology, 33, 38, 100, 101, 218, 257
Cotton Patch Gospel (Chapin), 233
Council of Trent, 342
Counter-intuitiveness (Boyer), 17, 18, 31, 38, 48–52, 54–55, 57, 57 n. 9, 60–64, 64 n. 13, 116, 118, 319–20, 405, 419
Credence (Light), 23, 395–418
Credulity (Saler), 22, 315–29
Creeds, 400–403

Critical Theory (Frankfort School), 19, 135–60
Critical Theory of Religion (Siebert), 138–64
Critics not Caretakers (McCutcheon), 109
"Critique of Hegel's Philosophy of Right" (Marx), 154
Critique of Practical Reason (Kant), 146
Cultural Anthropology, 55
Cultural Determinism, 392
Cultural Studies, 83, 107, 331
Culturally Postulated Sacralities, 130
Culturally Postulated Sacred Objects, 131
Culturally Postulated Superhuman Agents (CPS Agents), 11, 18, 60, 111, 112, 123, 138, 144–47, 155, 158, 248, 250, 254–56, 258, 261 n. 12, 266, 267, 270–75, 277, 279, 287, 288, 375, 381
Culture, Concept of (Malley), 331

Darwanism, 38
De Antr. Nymph. (Porphyry), 257, 257 n. 6, 257 n. 7
Dead Sea Scrolls, 336, 341
Deception, Adaptive Advantages of, 325
"Declaration of Religious Freedom" (Murray), 226 n. 4
Deconstructionism, 136
Deductive Reasoning, 381–85
Deism, 226
Denkkolletiv (Fleck), 106 n. 1
Developmental Psychology, 222, 233, 235, 265, 294, 298
Dialectical Theory of Religion, 138, 140, 148, 154, 155, 158
Die Enstehung und Entwicklung einer wissenschaftliche Tatsche (Fleck), 106 n. 1
Dietary Rules, 114
"Dispatches from the Methodological Wars" (Lawson), 161–62
Distributed Cognition, 70
Divorce, 240, 279, 281
Doctrinal Religion (Whitehouse), 117–18, 260, 260 n. 11, 261, 261 n. 12, 305
Dominican Order, 20, 210–15, 414
"Dr. Faust" (Goethe), 27
Dujal, 203

Dumb God Condition (Barrett), 277–78, 284
Dynamic Core (Edelman and Tononi), 297–98
Dynamic Equivalence Translation Philosophy, 334

Easter, 144, 211, 232
Ecological Anthropology, 93 n. 7
Ecology, 99–102
Economics, 150, 236
Edomites, 154
Egyptian Religion, 96, 157
8 1/2 (Fellini), 229
El Santo Entierro, 211, 214, 215
Elementary Forms of the Religious Life, The (Durkheim), 127
Embeddedness (Kegan), 233 n. 7
Emotion, 115–18, 128, 129, 133, 143, 251, 272, 273, 279, 281, 287–88, 303, 305–306, 316, 320
Enabling Rituals, 250, 256, 273
Enculturation, 265
Encyclopedia of Superstitions, The (Radford and Radford), 377
Enlightenment, The, 96, 107 n. 3, 108, 155, 400
Entextualization, 331
"Epilogue, 1984" (Rappaport), 92 n. 7, 95 n. 9, 96 n. 10
Episcopal Church, 10, 401
Epistemology, 98, 102–103, 172, 349
Epistle of James, 362
Epistle to the Hebrews, 336
Epistle to the Romans, 349
Error Analysis (Linguistics), 407 n. 4
Eschatology, 156, 199 n. 12, 202–203
Essence vs. Manifestation, 170
Ethiopian Orthodox Church, 337
Ethnocentrism, 78, 87
Ethnography, 65, 83, 85–86, 112, 114, 116, 246, 260 n. 11, 262, 284, 287, 327, 331, 332, 376, 377, 379
Ethnology, 5, 106
Ethos (Geertz), 299
Eucharist, 72, 255, 261 n. 12, 266, 272, 282, 283, 285, 287
Eugenics, 152
European Association for the Study of Religion (EASR), 290 n. 1
Evangelicalism, 22, 331–73
Evolution, 15, 17, 22, 27, 39–40, 48, 52 n. 5, 66, 92, 93 n. 7, 95 n. 9,

99, 100, 102, 110, 113, 121–31, 137, 140, 141, 143, 145, 149, 152, 157, 226, 315–16, 324–25, 328–29, 380, 392, 395, 399
Evolutionary Biology, 39
Evolutionary Psychology, 78, 125
Excommunication, 285
Exodus, 224
Exorcism, 310
Explanation, Theoretical, 7–8, 15, 31, 41–43, 46–47, 53–59, 63, 64, 64 n. 14, 65–88, 90, 90 n. 4, 98 n. 12, 99, 101, 106, 110, 111, 118, 121, 125–26, 129, 132, 136, 137, 141–43, 151, 158, 161, 163–65, 174, 176, 181, 246, 286
Explanatory Pluralism, 59
Externalized Language (Chomsky), 58

Faces in the Clouds (Guthrie), 12
Facial Expressions, 326
Faith, Concept of (Saler), 317, 319
Faith, Concept of (W. C. Smith), 186
Family Resemblance Definitions of Religion, 17, 53, 64 n. 14, 108, 327
Feminism, 363–64
"Femme fatale" (Olasky), 363
Fetishism, 157, 158, 206, 371
"55 Minutes of Maitatsine" (Television Documentary), 197 n. 5
"Fighting Over Religion" (Lease), 162
First Vatican Council, 242 n. 10
Fitna, 199, 199 n. 11
Flashbulb Memory (Brown and Kulik), 305
Folk Hermeneutic Theory, 360, 365
Folk Tales, 52, 54, 55
Folklore, 31, 107 n. 2, 114, 118
"Footles," 391
Franciscan Order, 20, 21, 207–19, 414
Free Methodism, 64
Free Will, 312–13, 382
Function Words, 408
"Functional Prerequisites of a Society" (Aberle, et al.), 320
Functionalism, 8–9, 68–69, 71–73, 123–24, 127, 128 n. 1, 132, 294
Fundamentalism, 195, 199, 205 n. 19, 234, 362, 365, 372
Funerals, 292

Gambler's Fallacy, 389, 393
Gardawa, 200
Gender, 79, 133, 292, 365
Genealogy (Foucault), 176
Generative Linguistics, 16
Genesis, 72, 234
Geneva Bible, 353
Genuflection, 144, 270, 271
Gideon New Testament, 343–45
Globalization, 79
"God-is-Dead" Theology, 147
Godspell (Weber), 233
Good Friday, 144
Good News Bible, 353, 358
Good News for Modern Man (Bible), 357
Gospel of John, 347, 357, 365,
Gospel of Luke, 357
Gospel of Mark, 348, 349 n. 10
Gospel of Matthew, 228
Gospels, The, 147, 223, 224, 231–33
Gossip, 308–309
Graeco-Roman Philosophy, 249, 401
Great vs. Little Traditions, 379
Greek Mystery Religions, 262 n. 13
Greek New Testament, 334, 342, 348–50, 356
Greek Religion, 139, 157, 249
Gregory-Aland Numbers, 336 n. 7
Group and Grid Markers (Douglas), 131
Gypsies, 107 n. 3

Hadith, 202
Hajj, 279–81
Hasidic Judaism, 238
Hausa, 200
Havadalah, 279, 280
Hebrew Scriptures, 223, 336, 337
Hegelianism, 139, 154, 156, 159
Heliodromus (Mithraic Grade of Initiation), 254, 254 n. 3, 257, 258, 260
Hermeneutics, 65, 68, 75–76, 83, 85, 87, 90, 161, 165, 167 n. 2, 173, 291
High Holy Days, 56
Hinduism, 53, 229–30, 270, 279–81, 380
Historia de la Fundacion, etc. (Davila Padilla), 211 n. 6
Historia eclesiástica indiana (Mendieta), 211
Historia General (Sahagún), 208
Historical Anthropology, 217, 218

Historical Materialism, 74, 154
Historiography, 85, 100, 246, 247
History, 65, 86, 231–32, 236, 246, 247, 261 n. 12, 262, 263, 284, 287
History of Religions, 5–8, 121–22, 126, 176, 248, 263
Holocaust (Shoah), 157, 223
Holy Sepulcher, 211, 215
Holy Spirit, 400
Holy Water, 144, 266, 270
Holy, The, 60, 90, 95, 96
Homo Religiosus, 47
Homo Symbolicus, 148
Hopi Cosmology, 303
Hopi Initiation Rituals, 21, 289, 301–306
Hopi Prophecy, 301
Hopi Religion, 301, 303, 305, 312
How Religion Works (Pyysiäinen), 12, 64 n. 14
Human Ethnosystems (Fox), 124
Human Ethology, 124
Human Nature, 79, 152, 319
Human Sciences, 107, 163, 164, 167, 172, 181, 313, 331
Humanism, 75
Humanities, 98 n. 12, 108, 109, 142
Husserlian Phenomenology, 115
Hyperactive Agent Detection Device (HADD), 376

Iconoclasm, 370
Ideology (Marx), 74
Ideology of Religious Studies (Fitzgerald), 107
Igamu Ritual, 396, 416
Illiad, The, 346
Illusion of Correlation, 393
Imagistic Religion (Whitehouse), 117, 260, 260 n. 11, 261, 395
Immaculate Conception, 402
Impasse and Resolution (Penner), 161
Imperialism, 75, 76, 79, 178
Incest Taboo, 71
Infant Baptism, 282
Infant Initiation Rituals, 285
Input Hypothesis (Krashen), 406
Instrumental Rationality, 150, 154
Intellectualism, 9–11, 50, 70–72, 137
Intelligence (Mead), 293–94
Internalized Language (Chomsky), 58
International Association for the History of Religions (IAHR), 58 n. 11, 89 n. 1, 105, 168 n. 3

International Bible Society, 342, 352, 363
Interpretation, 55, 58–60, 68, 75, 90, 98 n. 12, 137, 141–43, 151, 158, 173, 331
Interpretative Anthropology, 56, 68
Intersubjectivity, 115
Intifada, 149
Intuitive Ontologies (Boyer), 121, 319–20, 380, 386
Intuitive Physics, 386
Irony of Theology and the Nature of Religious Thought (Wiebe), 94 n. 8
Iroquois, 327
Islam, 28, 53, 105, 107 n. 3, 114, 141, 146, 149, 151, 160, 170, 171, 193–206, 224, 225, 228, 232, 234, 238, 279, 368, 371
Islamism, 171, 194, 196, 203 n. 17

J. B. Phillips' New Testament, 353
Japanese Religions, 166
Jerusalem, 199, 199 n. 12, 207, 215, 215 n. 7, 216, 224
Jerusalem Bible, 354
Jerusalem Temple, 149, 157
Jesuit Order, 221, 240
Jesus Christ Superstar (Weber), 233
Jesus of Montreal (Arcand), 233
Jihad, 203
Journal of Cognition and Culture, 12
Journey of the Mind to God (Bonaventure), 215 n. 7
Judaism, 6, 28, 105, 107 n. 3, 114, 146, 151, 157, 160, 174, 223–25, 228, 238–39, 279, 280, 285, 371

Ka'bah, 181
Kalakato, 204
Kantianism, 139, 180
Karma, 381–83, 402
Katsinas, 21, 301–305, 309–11
King James Bible, 333, 335, 336, 343, 353, 354, 356–58, 371
King-James-Only Churches, 351, 356, 365
Kinship, 130, 132, 292
Kiva, 303, 308
Kivung, 64
Knowledge of Our Growth of Knowledge (Munz), 103 n. 14
Koyaanisqatsi, 310
Kwaio, 29

La Dolce Vida (Fellini), 229
Language, 59, 115, 122, 138, 245, 292, 298, 320, 329, 407
Law of Averages, 23, 389
Law of Universalization, 148
Lent, 212
"Letter to William James" (Zaleski), 179
"Letters to a Provincial" (Eliade), 182
Liberal Humanism, 162, 181, 195
Liberalism, 234
Liberation Theology, 145, 147, 154
Linguistic Formal Pragmatic (Apel), 146
Linguistics, 10, 15, 57–58, 87, 98 n. 12, 112, 114, 136–37, 143, 232, 245, 265, 395 n. 1, 396 n. 2, 397, 406 n. 4, 407, 407 n. 4,
Literary Criticism, 82
Liturgy, 93, 95 n. 9, 96, 112, 169
Living Bible, 353, 354, 357, 361, 362
Logos, The, 97, 96 n. 10
Lord's Prayer, The, 228, 357
Luck, 22, 376–94, 412
Lutheranism, 270–71

MacArthur Study Bible, 347
Magic, 52, 97, 127, 128, 157, 158, 266, 309, 310
Mahdism, 20, 195, 202–204
Mainz Mithraic Cup, 250, 257–59
Maitatsine Movement, 193–205
Majority Text, 334, 334 n. 4, 356
Manufacturing Religion (McCutcheon), 109
Maring Religion, 97
Marriage, 144, 240, 271
Marxism, 73–75, 100, 164, 175, 200, 201
Masoretic Text, 356
Mass, 145, 147, 211, 213, 214, 224, 266, 271
Materialism, Western, 195
Mathematics, 65
Meaning and End of Religion (Smith), 188 n. 6
Meaning and Meaningfulness (Light), 23, 404–409, 418
Mecca, 199, 199 n. 12
Memes (Dawkins), 390
Memory, 42, 51, 61, 65, 66, 69, 86, 117, 118, 137, 140, 143, 251, 259, 272, 295, 299, 305, 329, 391, 395, 397, 404–406, 418
Men at Arms (Prachett), 289

Mental Infrastructure (Light), 395, 397, 404, 405, 409, 418
Mental-Space Theory, 23, 395–19
Message, The (Bible), 353–55, 358, 361
Messianism, 151, 202
Messuzzah, 279, 280
Metaphor, 298
Metaphor Theory (Lakoff and Johnson), 397, 409–410, 418
Method and Theory in the Study of Religion, 163
Migration of Semantic Content of Myths (Siebert), 146, 158–60
Mikvah, 279, 280
Miles (Mithraic Grade of Initiation), 257–59
Millennialism, 20, 194–95, 202, 202 n. 16
Mind, 293–94, 311
Mind/Brain, 19, 110, 140, 144, 145, 329
"Mirror-State as Formative of the Function of the I" (Lacan), 184
Mithraeum, 249–58
Mithraic Imagery, 253, 254 n. 3, 255, 257 n. 6, 258, 259 n. 10
Mithraic Initiation Rituals, 245–63
Mithraic Meal, 253–56, 256 n. 5, 258, 262
Mithraic Procession, 257–62
Modernity, 101, 148–49, 188, 195–96
Modes of Religiosity (Whitehouse), 117, 305
Monotheism, 160
Morality, 29, 32–33, 39, 93, 96 n. 10, 100, 127, 129, 131, 132, 145–47, 150, 155, 159, 160, 224, 237, 239, 241, 292, 299, 307–309
Multiple Drafts Model (Dennett), 22, 295
Mutually Facilitating Equivalence Structures (Wallace), 22, 312, 323
My Book-God (Bible), 358
Myth, 9–10, 21, 35, 55, 97 n. 11, 98 n. 12, 126, 128, 130, 132, 133, 137, 138, 141, 145, 146, 148–52, 155, 157–60, 165, 167, 174, 179, 217, 231, 244, 248 n. 2, 261, 303
Myth, Concept of, 167

Nahua (Aztec) Religion, 412, 414
Nahua (Aztecs), 207–19, 412–14

Naïve Psychology, 267–68, 376
Naïve Realism, 166 n. 2
Nanotechnology, 152
Narrative Selves, 298
Narrative Theory, 298
National Romanticism, Finnish, 107 n. 3
Nationalism, 56 n. 7, 79, 188, 394
Natural History of Religion (Hume), 175
Natural Language, 137, 245
Natural Religion, 137, 155
Natural Science, 99, 110, 137, 142, 164
Natural Theology, 100–101
Naturalism, Scientific, 90–91, 142, 150, 161, 174, 312
Naturalness of Religious Ideas (Boyer), 12
Nature-Nuture Debate, 79, 312
Neo-Orthodxy, 365
Neo-Paganism, 160
Neo-Platonism, 141–42
Neurally Organized Mobile Adaptive Device (NOMAD), 296
Neuroscience, 87, 296
New Age Bible Versions (Riplinger), 356
New Age Religion, 56, 356–57
New American Standard Version Bible, 336, 353, 357, 358, 362
New Century Version Bible, 357
New English Version Bible, 353, 354
New International Version Adventure Bible, 345
New International Version Bible, 333, 336, 340, 348, 349, 353–57, 361–65, 367
New International Version: Inclusive Language Edition Bible, 363–64
New Jerusalem Bible, 357
New King James Version Bible, 347, 348, 353
New Living Translation Bible, 336, 353
New Revised Standard Version Bible, 336, 353, 357
New Testament, 223–26, 228, 231, 334–35, 335 n. 5, 339–40, 342, 344, 354, 356
Nicene Creed, 401
Niche-Constructing Prototypes (Odling-Smee), 130
Nights of Calabria (Fellini), 229
North American Association for the Study of Religion (NAASR), 9 n. 5, 163, 171
Novum Testamentum Graece, 348–49

Nuer, 53
Numen, 13, 161
Numinous, The, 21, 23, 90, 94, 95, 102, 115, 116, 412, 414
Nymphus (Mithraic Grade of Initiation), 258–59

Objective Ideas (Plato), 139
Oedipus Complex (Freud), 71–72
Off-Line Reasoning, 379, 392
Oglala Sioux, 231
Oh, God! (Reiner), 222
Old Man and the Sea, The (Hemingway), 391
Old Testament, 226, 228, 337, 356
On-Line Reasoning, 23, 379, 380, 385
Ontological Subjectivity (Searle), 296
Ontology, 142, 266, 363, 367
Ontology, Faulty, 65, 67–69, 78
Operational Models (Rappaport), 95 n. 9, 98 n. 12
Ordination, 144, 271, 272, 282, 283, 285, 402
Orthodox Christianity, 141, 147, 148

P46 (Pauline Letters Papyrus), 338
Paganism, 158, 208
Paleolithic Societies, 329–30
Panhuman Universals, 121–25, 137–38, 246, 292, 327, 418
Papa Karma, 382
Papal Infallibility, 242 n. 10
Parallel Representations, 379–80
Passion of Jesus, 210, 211, 214, 215
Pat the Bible Song, 343–44
Pater (Mithraic Grade of Initiation), 250–56
Participant Observation, 79–80, 85
Patterns in Comparative Religion (Eliade), 181
Pauline Epistles, 337
Pedophilia, 239 n. 8, 240
Penguin Island (France), 261
Pentecost, 224
Pentecostalism, 195
People's Temple, 198
Performance, Linguistic, 10, 245
Phenomenological Sociology, 299
Phenomenology, 7, 65, 107, 108, 110, 114, 115, 161, 166 n. 2, 170, 298
Philology, 175, 342
Philosophy, 5, 15, 65, 82, 86, 98 n. 12, 106, 145, 150, 167 n. 2, 168,

168 n. 3, 241, 246, 296, 313, 380, 385
Philosophy of Science, 8, 64 n. 14, 135
Physico-Theology (Derham), 245 n. 1
Physics, 102, 137, 419
"Piety without Content" (Sontag), 174
Pilgrimage, 20, 21, 207–19, 281
Platonism, 139
Pleistocene Era, 329
Pluralism, 239, 244, 382 n. 3
Political Science, 106, 150
Polymethodism, 105
Polytheism, 153, 158, 160
Pomio Kivung, 284
Pope, The, 144, 240
Positivism, 19, 137, 138, 142, 143, 145, 146, 150, 151, 153, 156, 157, 159
Post-Colonialism, 83
Postmodernism, 56, 58, 59, 81, 99, 100, 102, 107, 121, 122, 147
Potential Reversability Hypothesis (Barrett), 271, 273, 278, 280, 285, 286
Powamuya, 301
Prayer, 32, 157, 212, 214, 224, 227, 266, 306, 311, 413
Premodernity, 142
Presbyterianism, 174
Primacy of Agency Hypothesis (Barrett), 268–69, 273–75, 277, 284
Primary Functions (Malinowski), 67 n. 2, 68 n. 2
Principi di una Scienza Nuova (Vico), 245 n. 1
Principle of Superhuman Agency (Lawson and McCauley), 11, 248, 270–71
Principle of Superhuman Immediacy (Lawson and McCauley), 11, 250
Probability Theory, 386–91
Professional Guilds, 78, 80
Promiscuous Teleology (Keleman), 391
Protestantism, 6, 170, 226, 238, 274, 276, 282, 283, 286, 337, 342, 370, 371, 373, 382
Prototype Definitions of Religion, 105
Providence, 149
Psuedo-Natural Kinds, 33
Psychic Unity of Humanity, 88
Psychoanalytic Movement (Gellner), 73
Psychoanalytic Psychology, 71–75, 155, 184

Psychology, 5, 15, 53, 70, 78, 79, 83, 86, 87, 106, 121, 126, 128, 128 n. 1, 132, 137, 140, 143, 158, 163, 172, 246, 265, 267, 292, 293, 295, 298, 307, 313, 389
Psychopathology, 133
Puja, 270, 271
Punna Karma, 382

Q Document, 340
Qhumbaza Ritual, 396, 416
Quakers, 53
Qualia (Searle), 296–97
Qualitative Methods, 85–86, 106
Quantitative Methods, 79–80, 106
Qur'an, 56, 200, 203, 205, 223, 232, 368

Raksha Bandhan, 279–81
Raven (Mithraic Grade of Initiation), 258–59
Real Presence, Doctrine of, 261 n. 12
Reciprocity, 382
Reductionism, 5, 8, 17, 18, 27, 40, 43, 59, 63, 78, 81, 123, 163
Reformation, Protestant, 107 n. 3, 136, 141, 169, 337
Reformed Church of America, 282
Reincarnation, 398, 402–403
Relativism, 75, 78, 87
Reliability Assessments, 325–29
Relics, Saints', 131, 144, 211, 213–18
Religion and Rationality Debate, 9
Religion and the Religions in the English Enlightenment (Harrison), 186
Religion and Violence (Lincoln), 193
"Religion der Loyalität" (Merkelbach), 253
Religion Explained (Boyer), 31
Religion from Tolstoy to Camus (Kaufmann), 174
Religion, Concept of, 8–9, 11, 19, 27, 28, 35, 42, 45, 53–60, 63, 64, 64 n. 14, 105–108, 118, 161–89, 375, 394
Religions of Africa (Lawson), 6
Religious Experience, 7, 96, 102, 164, 167, 172, 178
Religious Guilds, 28, 33, 33 n. 2, 35–37, 37 n. 8, 38, 183
Religious Ontologies, 61
Religious Specialists, 29, 33, 35–38, 378
Religious Studies, 6, 23, 91, 101,

107–108, 165, 171, 196 n. 2, 313, 407 n. 4
Religious Studies News, 167 n. 2, 177
Religious Violence, 193–96
Renaissance, 337
Repeatability Hypothesis (Barrett), 270, 272, 273, 278, 279, 281, 285, 286
Repression, Psychological, 73, 153, 156, 159
Research Assessment Exercise (REA), 77
Research Methods, Anthropology, 80, 81, 84 n. 7, 85, 86, 125
Research Methods, Religious Studies, 90, 91, 105, 106, 109, 110, 115, 142, 162, 165–67, 167 n. 2, 177
Rethinking Religion (Lawson and McCauley), 11, 12, 27, 31, 40, 42, 163, 218 n. 8, 265, 375
Rethinking Symbolism (Sperber), 10
Return to Cosmology (Toulmin), 100
Revised New English Bible, 353
Revised Standard Version Bible, 335, 336, 353, 354, 361
Revised Webster's Translation Bible, 353
Right Intentions Hypothesis (Barrett), 269, 273, 276–78, 284, 285
Right Reason (Wiebe), 95 n. 9, 96 n. 10, 99
Ritual and Religion in the Making of Humanity (Rappaport), 18, 89–92, 96 n. 10, 101
Ritual Naïvete, 268, 269, 273, 274, 278
Ritual Pollution, 39
Ritual, Competence, 268
Ritual, Concept of, 93, 167, 266, 279
Roman Catholicism, 6, 20, 64, 136, 141, 143, 144, 147–49, 169, 174, 207–19, 221, 226 n. 6, 238, 239, 239 n. 9, 240, 242 n. 10, 261 n. 12, 266, 270, 272, 285, 337, 341, 342, 354, 402, 413, 414, 419
Roman Religion, 157, 249, 255
Rosary, 56
Rules of Inference, 383–85
Rules of Purity, 131

Sabbath, 223
Sacred Space, 18, 20, 55, 116–18, 149, 207–19, 414

Sacred, The, 7, 11, 18, 39, 60, 90, 94, 96, 97, 111–19, 129, 131, 132, 138, 140, 147, 164, 177–81, 187, 217, 417, 419
Sacrifice, 32, 40, 112, 255, 349, 403, 413
Saints, 144, 216, 217, 241, 261, 299, 413, 414
Scientism, 158
Scripturalism, 371
Scripture, 21, 131, 225, 229–34, 337, 342, 362, 371, 373
Second Vatican Council, 149, 239, 342
Secondary Functions (Malinowski), 68 n. 2
Secret Societies, 256 n. 5, 257 n. 9
Secular Theories of Religion (Jensen), 166 n. 2
Sedimentation (Berger and Luckmann), 22, 299
Self, The, 293–98, 309, 312
"Self: Public, Private" (Lienhardt), 290 n. 2
Semantic Holism, 59
Semiotics, 291
Sensory Pageantry, 251, 256, 260, 261 n. 12, 272, 273, 279, 281, 287–88
Sensory Pageantry Hypothesis, 21, 272, 278, 281, 286, 287
September 11th, 2001, 149, 170, 193, 378, 390
Septuagint, 336, 337
Seraphic Christ of La Verna, 210, 215
Serendipity (Chelsom), 391
Sermon on the Mount, 145
Shabbat Candle, 279, 280
Shakers, 53
Shamanism, 33, 36, 37, 117, 217, 309
Shari'a, 193, 193 n. 3
Shema, 95
Shinto, 174
Sioux Ghost Dance, 53
Skeptical Epistemology, 317–20
Smart God Condition (Barrett), 277–78, 284
Social Constructivism, 299–300
Social Contract (Rousseau), 323
Social Facts (Durkheim), 67–68
Social Formations, 162, 174, 182
Social Intelligence (Mead), 293–94
Social Psychology, 127, 293, 300, 303, 308, 312

Social Realism, 300
Social Sciences, 11, 106, 108, 109, 129, 138, 142, 159, 323
Socialism, 139
Socialization, 295, 299, 303, 304, 312, 325
Society for Biblical Literature (SBL), 165, 184
Society, Concept of, 126–29, 291
Sociobiology, 132
Sociology, 15, 65, 67, 106, 107, 109, 114, 172, 236, 290, 291, 312, 313
Sociology of Knowledge, 128, 299
"Some Social Functions of Ignorance" (Moore and Tumin), 322
Soteriology, 28, 29, 37, 38, 147, 155, 250, 257, 258, 261, 413, 414
Sparrow, The (Russell), 229
Special Agent Rituals (Lawson and McCauley), 21, 250–51, 256, 259–62, 270–73, 279–87, 394
Special Instrument Rituals (Lawson and McCauley), 270–88
Special Patient Rituals (Lawson and McCauley), 21, 254–62, 270–88, 394
Standard Social Science Model, 124, 126, 128, 381, 394
Statistics, 79, 245, 387, 390, 391
Stem Cell Research, 140
Structural Anthropology, 10
Structural Functionalism, 67–69, 72–73, 143
Structural Linguistics, 408
Structuralism, 10, 100, 133, 137, 161
Subjective Idealism (Kant), 139
Subscriptions, Biblical, 336–37
Sui Generis Religion, 35, 62, 172, 178, 179, 187
Suicide, 240
Sunna, 199, 202
Super Permanence (Lawson and McCauley), 41, 251, 254, 256, 262, 271, 272
Super-Ego, 306, 312
Suyanisqatsi, 310
Symbolic Universe, 300–301
Symbolism, 137, 149, 179, 180, 183, 214, 218, 255, 375, 394, 404, 405, 407, 407 n. 4, 409, 417
Syncretism, 21, 130, 209, 218 n. 8, 219, 414
Synoptic Gospels, 340

Syrian Religion, 157
System Centrality Hypothesis (Barrett), 272

Taboo, 39, 114, 127
Tacit Knowledge, 385, 386, 392
Talion Rituals, 149, 157
Tallensi, 174
Tauroctony, 248–49, 253, 255
Text, Concept of, 331–32, 346, 359–60, 367, 372–73
Text-Artifact, 332, 338, 346, 372, 373
Textual Commentary on the Greek New Testament (Metzger), 349 n. 10
Textual Criticism, 335, 335 n. 5, 336, 342, 360,
Textus Receptus, 334, 334 n. 4, 335 n. 5
Theism, 175
Theodicy, 28–29, 33, 37–38, 147, 148, 156–59, 381
Theological Incorrectness (Barrett), 22, 375, 378, 382, 412
Theology, 4–5, 65, 89, 89 n. 1, 89 n. 2, 91, 100, 107–109, 116, 126, 138, 144–45, 151, 164, 167 n. 2, 168, 221, 232, 246, 267, 278, 313, 319, 361, 365, 371–72, 376, 380–81, 383, 390, 410, 412, 414
Theory, 5 n. 2, 7, 46, 135, 140, 166–68, 171, 178, 201
Theory of Mind, 31, 39, 267
Theory/Praxis Dialectic, 150–51
Therevada Buddhism, 53
Thick Descriptions (Geertz), 69
Thomba Ritual, 396, 416
Thread Ceremony, 279–81
Tibetan Buddhism, 225
Tijaniyya Sufi Order (Hamaliyya), 202
"Tillich and Hartshorne" (Lawson), 4
Tlaquimilolli, 217–18
Torah, 146
Totem and Taboo (Freud), 71, 72 n. 4
Totemism, 128 n. 1
Tradition as Truth and Communication (Boyer), 161
"Traditional" Religions, 28–2
Transactional Selves, 298
Transcendence, 19, 160
Transcendentalism (Kant), 139, 148
Translation, 75, 336, 337, 339
Transmission, Cultural, 31, 35–37, 41, 51–52, 74, 86, 110, 112, 118, 123, 125, 128–30, 132, 143, 246–47, 256,

259 n. 10, 260, 260 n. 11, 261 n. 12, 295, 300, 316–17, 327, 331, 339, 407 n. 4
Transubstantiation, 282
Trinity, 144, 399, 414
Trust, Concept of (Saler), 317
20th Century Version Bible, 353

Ukubuthwa Ritual, 396, 416
Ultimate Concern (Tillich), 56
Ultimate Sacred Postulate (Rappaport), 94–95, 102, 113
Understanding (*Verstehen*), 106

Varieties of Religious Experience (James), 179
"Vida de Fray Martín de Valencia" (Jiménez), 209 n. 4
Viet Nam War, 236, 241
Virgin of Guadalupe, 21, 207–19, 413–14
Virtual Selves, 295, 312
"Vita Beati Fratris Efidii" (Brooke), 215 n. 7
Vulgate, 337, 342

Wedding, 279, 280, 282, 283, 285

What is the Best New Testament? (Colwell), 335
William Barclay's New Testament, 353
Witchcraft, 33, 154, 308–10, 319
Word, The (Bible), 353, 358
World Religions, 28–29, 85, 136, 148, 158, 165
Worldmaking (Paden), 126–31
Worldview (Geertz), 299, 392
Wuduu, 279, 280

Yan Izala, 198 n. 8, 197, 198, 198 n. 8, 202, 204
Yoruba, 378
Young's Literal Translation Bible, 353

Zande, 53, 327
Zen Buddhism, 180, 225
Zionism, 199
Zodiac, 249
Zondervan Publishers, 363
"Zoo Approach" to the Study of Religion, 6
Zoroastrianism, 96, 157
Zulu Creation Myth, 15
Zulus, 23, 53, 136, 142, 396, 397, 399, 399 n. 3, 405, 415–18

STUDIES IN THE HISTORY OF RELIGIONS
NUMEN BOOK SERIES

8 K.W. Bolle. *The Persistence of Religion*. An Essay on Tantrism and Sri Aurobindo's Philosophy. Repr. 1971. ISBN 90 04 03307 6

17 *Liber Amicorum*. Studies in honour of Professor Dr. C.J. Bleeker. Published on the occasion of his retirement from the Chair of the History of Religions and the Phenomenology of Religion at the University of Amsterdam. 1969. ISBN 90 04 03092 1

19 U. Bianchi, C.J. Bleeker & A. Bausani (eds.). *Problems and Methods of the History of Religions*. Proceedings of the Study Conference organized by the Italian Society for the History of Religions on the Occasion of the Tenth Anniversary of the Death of Raffaele Pettazzoni, Rome 6th to 8th December 1969. Papers and discussions. 1972. ISBN 90 04 02640 1

31 C.J. Bleeker, G. Widengren & E.J. Sharpe (eds.). *Proceedings of the 12th International Congress, Stockholm 1970*. 1975. ISBN 90 04 04318 7

34 V.L. Oliver, *Caodai Spiritism*. A Study of Religion in Vietnamese Society. With a preface by P. Rondot. 1976. ISBN 90 04 04547 3

41 B. Layton (ed.). *The Rediscovery of Gnosticism*. Proceedings of the International Conference on Gnosticism at Yale, New Haven, Conn., March 28-31, 1978. Two vols.
  1. *The School of Valentinus*. 1980. ISBN 90 04 06177 0   Out of print
  2. *Sethian Gnosticism*. 1981. ISBN 90 04 06178 9

43 M. Heerma van Voss, D.J. Hoens, G. Mussies, D. van der Plas & H. te Velde (eds.). *Studies in Egyptian Religion, dedicated to Professor Jan Zandee. 1982.* ISBN 90 04 06728 0

44 P.J. Awn. *Satan's Tragedy and Redemption*. Iblīs in Sufi Psychology. With a foreword by A. Schimmel. 1983. ISBN 90 04 06906 2

45 R. Kloppenborg (ed.). *Selected Studies on Ritual in the Indian Religions*. Essays to D.J. Hoens. 1983. ISBN 90 04 07129 6

50 S. Shaked, D. Shulman & G.G. Stroumsa (eds.). *Gilgul*. Essays on Transformation, Revolution and Permanence in the History of Religions, dedicated to R.J. Zwi Werblowsky. 1987. ISBN 90 04 08509 2

52 J.G. Griffiths. *The Divine Verdict*. A Study of Divine Judgement in the Ancient Religions. 1991. ISBN 90 04 09231 5

53 K. Rudolph. *Geschichte und Probleme der Religionswissenschaft*. 1992. ISBN 90 04 09503 9

54 A.N. Balslev & J.N. Mohanty (eds.). Religion and Time. 1993. ISBN 90 04 09583 7

55 E. Jacobson. *The Deer Goddess of Ancient Siberia*. A Study in the Ecology of Belief. 1993. ISBN 90 04 09628 0

56 B. Saler. *Conceptualizing Religion*. Immanent Anthropologists, Transcendent Natives, and Unbounded Categories. 1993. ISBN 90 04 09585 3

57 C. Knox. *Changing Christian Paradigms*. And their Implications for Modern Thought. 1993. ISBN 90 04 09670 1

58 J. Cohen. *The Origins and Evolution of the Moses Nativity Story*. 1993. ISBN 90 04 09652 3

59 S. Benko. *The Virgin Goddess*. Studies in the Pagan and Christian Roots of Mariology. 1993. ISBN 90 04 09747 3
60 Z.P. Thundy. *Buddha and Christ*. Nativity Stories and Indian Traditions. 1993. ISBN 90 04 09741 4
61 S. Hjelde. *Die Religionswissenschaft und das Christentum*. Eine historische Untersuchung über das Verhältnis von Religionswissenschaft und Theologie. 1994. ISBN 90 04 09922 0
62 Th.A. Idinopulos & E.A. Yonan (eds.). *Religion and Reductionism*. Essays on Eliade, Segal, and the Challenge of the Social Sciences for the Study of Religion. 1994. ISBN 90 04 09870 4
63 S. Khalil Samir & J.S. Nielsen (eds.). *Christian Arabic Apologetics during the Abbasid Period (750-1258)*. 1994. ISBN 90 04 09568 3
64 S.N. Balagangadhara. *'The Heathen in His Blindness...'* Asia, the West and the Dynamic of Religion. 1994. ISBN 90 04 09943 3
65 H.G. Kippenberg & G.G. Stroumsa (eds.). *Secrecy and Concealment*. Studies in the History of Mediterranean and Near Eastern Religions. 1995. ISBN 90 04 10235 3
66 R. Kloppenborg & W.J. Hanegraaff (eds.). *Female Stereotypes in Religious Traditions*. 1995. ISBN 90 04 10290 6
67 J. Platvoet & K. van der Toorn (eds.). *Pluralism and Identity*. Studies on Ritual Behaviour. 1995. ISBN 90 04 10373 2
68 G. Jonker. *The Topography of Remembrance*. The Dead, Tradition and Collective Memory in Mesopotamia. 1995. ISBN 90 04 10162 4
69 S. Biderman. *Scripture and Knowledge*. An Essay on Religious Epistemology. 1995. ISBN 90 04 10154 3
70 G.G. Stroumsa. *Hidden Wisdom*. Esoteric Traditions and the Roots of Christian Mysticism. 1996. ISBN 90 04 10504 2
71 J.G. Katz. *Dreams, Sufism and Sainthood*. The Visionary Career of Muhammad al-Zawâwî. 1996. ISBN 90 04 10599 9
72 W.J. Hanegraaff. *New Age Religion and Western Culture*. Esotericism in the Mirror of Secular Thought. 1996. ISBN 90 04 10695 2
73 T.A. Idinopulos & E.A. Yonan (eds.). *The Sacred and its Scholars*. Comparative Methodologies for the Study of Primary Religious Data. 1996. ISBN 90 04 10623 5
74 K. Evans. *Epic Narratives in the Hoysaḷa Temples*. The Rāmāyaṇa, Mahābhārata and Bhāgavata Purāṇa in Haḷebīd, Belūr and Amṛtapura. 1997. ISBN 90 04 10575 1
75 P. Schäfer & H.G. Kippenberg (eds.). *Envisioning Magic*. A Princeton Seminar and Symposium. 1997. ISBN 90 04 10777 0
77 P. Schäfer & M.R. Cohen (eds.). *Toward the Millennium*. Messianic Expectations from the Bible to Waco. 1998. ISBN 90 04 11037 2
78 A.I. Baumgarten, with J. Assmann & G.G. Stroumsa (eds.). *Self, Soul and Body in Religious Experience*. 1998. ISBN 90 04 10943 9
79 M. Houseman & C. Severi. *Naven or the Other Self*. A Relational Approach to Ritual Action. 1998. ISBN 90 04 11220 0
80 A.L. Molendijk & P. Pels (eds.). *Religion in the Making*. The Emergence of the Sciences of Religion. 1998. ISBN 90 04 11239 1

81 Th.A. Idinopulos & B.C. Wilson (eds.). *What is Religion?* Origins, Definitions, & Explanations. 1998. ISBN 90 04 11022 4
82 A. van der Kooij & K. van der Toorn (eds.). *Canonization & Decanonization.* Papers presented to the International Conference of the Leiden Institute for the Study of Religions (LISOR) held at Leiden 9-10 January 1997. 1999. ISBN 90 04 11246 4
83 J. Assmann & G.G. Stroumsa (eds.). *Transformations of the Inner Self in Ancient Religions.* 1999. ISBN 90 04 11356 8
84 J.G. Platvoet & A.L. Molendijk (eds.). *The Pragmatics of Defining Religion.* Contexts, Concepts & Contests. 1999. ISBN 90 04 11544 7
85 B.J. Malkovsky (ed.). *New Perspectives on Advaita Vedānta.* Essays in Commemoration of Professor Richard De Smet, sj. 2000. ISBN 90 04 11666 4
86 A.I. Baumgarten (ed.). *Apocalyptic Time.* 2000. ISBN 90 04 11879 9
87 S. Hjelde (ed.). *Man, Meaning, and Mystery.* Hundred Years of History of Religions in Norway. The Heritage of W. Brede Kristensen. 2000. ISBN 90 04 11497 1
88 A. Korte (ed.). *Women and Miracle Stories.* A Multidisciplinary Exploration. 2000. ISBN 90 04 11681 8
89 J. Assmann & A.I. Baumgarten (eds.). *Representation in Religion.* Studies in Honor of Moshe Barasch. 2001. ISBN 90 04 11939 6
90 O. Hammer. *Claiming Knowledge.* Strategies of Epistemology from Theosophy to the New Age. 2001. ISBN 90 04 12016 5
91 B.J. Malkovsky. *The Role of Divine Grace in the Soteriology of Śaṃkarācārya.* 2001. ISBN 90 04 12044 0
92 T.A. Idinopulos & B.C. Wilson (eds.). *Reappraising Durkheim for the Study and Teaching of Religion Today.* 2002. ISBN 90 04 12339 3.
93 A.I. Baumgarten (eds.). *Sacrifice in Religious Experience.* 2002. ISBN 90 04 12483 7
94 L.P. van den Bosch. *F.M. Müller. A Life Devoted to the Humanities.* 2002. ISBN 90 04 12505 1
95 G. Wiegers. *Modern Societies & the Science of Religions.* Studies in Honour of Lammert Leertouwer. 2002. ISBN 90 04 11665 6
96 D. Zeidan. *The Resurgence of Religion.* A Comparative Study of Selected Themes in Christian and Islamic Fundamentalist Discourses. 2003. ISBN 90 04 12877 8
97 S. Meyer (ed.). *Egypt — Temple of the Whole World / Ägypten — Tempel der Gesamten Welt.* Studies in Honour of Jan Assmann. 2003. ISBN 90 04 13240 6
98 I. Strenski. *Theology and the First Theory of Sacrifice.* 2003. ISBN 90 04 13559 6
99 T. Light & B.C. Wilson (eds.). *Religion as a Human Capacity.* A Festschrift in Honor of E. Thomas Lawson. 2003. ISBN 90 04 12676 7
100 A.E. Buss. *The Russian-Orthodox Tradition and Modernity.* 2003. ISBN 90 04 13324 0
101 K.A. Jacobsen & P.P. Kumar (eds.). *South Asians in the Diaspora.* Histories and Religious Traditions. 2004. ISBN 90 04 12488 8
102 M. Stausberg. *Zoroastrian Rituals in Context.* 2003. ISBN 90 04 13131 0